Lecture Notes in Computer Science 11063

Commenced Publication in 1973
Founding and Former Series Editors:
Gerhard Goos, Juris Hartmanis, and Jan van Leeuwen

Editorial Board

David Hutchison
Lancaster University, Lancaster, UK
Takeo Kanade
Carnegie Mellon University, Pittsburgh, PA, USA
Josef Kittler
University of Surrey, Guildford, UK
Jon M. Kleinberg
Cornell University, Ithaca, NY, USA
Friedemann Mattern
ETH Zurich, Zurich, Switzerland
John C. Mitchell
Stanford University, Stanford, CA, USA
Moni Naor
Weizmann Institute of Science, Rehovot, Israel
C. Pandu Rangan
Indian Institute of Technology Madras, Chennai, India
Bernhard Steffen
TU Dortmund University, Dortmund, Germany
Demetri Terzopoulos
University of California, Los Angeles, CA, USA
Doug Tygar
University of California, Berkeley, CA, USA
Gerhard Weikum
Max Planck Institute for Informatics, Saarbrücken, Germany

More information about this series at http://www.springer.com/series/7409

Xingming Sun · Zhaoqing Pan
Elisa Bertino (Eds.)

Cloud Computing and Security

4th International Conference, ICCCS 2018
Haikou, China, June 8–10, 2018
Revised Selected Papers, Part I

 Springer

Editors
Xingming Sun (iD)
Nanjing University of Information Science
and Technology
Nanjing
China

Zhaoqing Pan (iD)
Nanjing University of Information Science
and Technology
Nanjing
China

Elisa Bertino (iD)
Department of Computer Science
Purdue University
West Lafayette, IN
USA

ISSN 0302-9743   ISSN 1611-3349 (electronic)
Lecture Notes in Computer Science
ISBN 978-3-030-00005-9   ISBN 978-3-030-00006-6 (eBook)
https://doi.org/10.1007/978-3-030-00006-6

Library of Congress Control Number: 2018952646

LNCS Sublibrary: SL3 – Information Systems and Applications, incl. Internet/Web, and HCI

This Springer imprint is published by the registered company Springer Nature Switzerland AG
The registered company address is: Gewerbestrasse 11, 6330 Cham, Switzerland

Preface

The 4th International Conference on Cloud Computing and Security (ICCCS 2018) was held in Haikou, China, during June 8–10, 2018, and hosted by the School of Computer and Software at the Nanjing University of Information Science and Technology. ICCCS is a leading conference for researchers and engineers to share their latest results of research, development, and applications in the field of cloud computing and information security.

We made use of the excellent Tech Science Press (TSP) submission and reviewing software. ICCCS 2018 received 1743 submissions from 20 countries and regions, including USA, Canada, UK, Italy, Ireland, Japan, Russia, France, Australia, South Korea, South Africa, India, Iraq, Kazakhstan, Indonesia, Vietnam, Ghana, China, Taiwan, and Macao. The submissions covered the areas of cloud computing, cloud security, information hiding, IOT security, multimedia forensics, and encryption, etc. We thank our Technical Program Committee members and external reviewers for their efforts in reviewing papers and providing valuable comments to the authors. From the total of 1743 submissions, and based on at least two reviews per submission, the Program Chairs decided to accept 386 papers, yielding an acceptance rate of 22.15%. The volume of the conference proceedings contains all the regular, poster, and workshop papers.

The conference program was enriched by six keynote presentations, and the keynote speakers were Mauro Barni, University of Siena, Italy; Charles Ling, University of Western Ontario, Canada; Yunbiao Guo, Beijing Institute of Electronics Technology and Application, China; Yunhao Liu, Michigan State University, USA; Nei Kato, Tokyo University, Japan; and Jianfeng Ma, Xidian University, China. We thank them very much for their wonderful talks.

There were 42 workshops organized in conjunction with ICCCS 2018, covering all the hot topics in cloud computing and security. We would like to take this moment to express our sincere appreciation for the contribution of all the workshop chairs and their participants. In addition, we would like to extend our sincere thanks to all authors who submitted papers to ICCCS 2018 and to all PC members. It was a truly great experience to work with such talented and hard-working researchers. We also appreciate the work of the external reviewers, who assisted the PC members in their particular areas of expertise. Moreover, we would like to thank our sponsors: Nanjing University of Information Science and Technology, Springer, Hainan University, IEEE Nanjing Chapter, ACM China, Michigan State University, Taiwan Cheng Kung University, Taiwan Dong Hwa University, Providence University, Nanjing University of Aeronautics and Astronautics, State Key Laboratory of Integrated Services Networks, Tech Science Press, and the National Nature Science Foundation of China. Finally, we would like to thank all attendees for their active participation and the organizing team, who nicely managed this conference. Next year, ICCCS will be renamed as the International Conference on Artificial Intelligence and Security (ICAIS). We look forward to seeing you again at the ICAIS.

July 2018

Xingming Sun
Zhaoqing Pan
Elisa Bertino

Organization

General Chairs

Xingming Sun   Nanjing University of Information Science
                        and Technology, China
Han-Chieh Chao   Taiwan Dong Hwa University, Taiwan, China
Xingang You   China Information Technology Security Evaluation
                        Center, China
Elisa Bertino   Purdue University, USA

Technical Program Committee Chairs

Aniello Castiglione   University of Salerno, Italy
Yunbiao Guo   China Information Technology Security Evaluation
                        Center, China
Zhangjie Fu   Nanjing University of Information Science
                        and Technology, China
Xinpeng Zhang   Fudan University, China
Jian Weng   Jinan University, China
Mengxing Huang   Hainan University, China
Alex Liu   Michigan State University, USA

Workshop Chair

Baowei Wang   Nanjing University of Information Science
                        and Technology, China

Publication Chair

Zhaoqing Pan   Nanjing University of Information Science
                        and Technology, China

Publicity Chair

Chuanyou Ju   Nanjing University of Information Science
                        and Technology, China

Local Arrangement Chair

Jieren Cheng   Hainan University, China

Website Chair

Wei Gu   Nanjing University of Information Science
and Technology, China

Technical Program Committee Members

Saeed Arif	University of Algeria, Algeria
Zhifeng Bao	Royal Melbourne Institute of Technology University, Australia
Lianhua Chi	IBM Research Center, Australia
Bing Chen	Nanjing University of Aeronautics and Astronautics, China
Hanhua Chen	Huazhong University of Science and Technology, China
Jie Chen	East China Normal University, China
Xiaofeng Chen	Xidian University, China
Ilyong Chung	Chosun University, South Korea
Jieren Cheng	Hainan University, China
Kim-Kwang Raymond Choo	University of Texas at San Antonio, USA
Chin-chen Chang	Feng Chia University, Taiwan, China
Robert H. Deng	Singapore Management University, Singapore
Jintai Ding	University of Cincinnati, USA
Shaojing Fu	National University of Defense Technology, China
Xinwen Fu	University of Central Florida, USA
Song Guo	Hong Kong Polytechnic University, Hong Kong, China
Ruili Geng	Spectral MD, USA
Russell Higgs	University College Dublin, Ireland
Dinh Thai Hoang	University of Technology Sydney, Australia
Robert Hsu	Chung Hua University, Taiwan, China
Chih-Hsien Hsia	Chinese Culture University, Taiwan, China
Jinguang Han	Nanjing University of Finance & Economics, China
Debiao He	Wuhan University, China
Wien Hong	Nanfang College of Sun Yat-Sen University, China
Qiong Huang	South China Agricultural University, China
Xinyi Huang	Fujian Normal University, China
Yongfeng Huang	Tsinghua University, China
Zhiqiu Huang	Nanjing University of Aeronautics and Astronautics, China
Mohammad Mehedi Hassan	King Saud University, Saudi Arabia
Farookh Hussain	University of Technology Sydney, Australia
Hai Jin	Huazhong University of Science and Technology, China
Sam Tak Wu Kwong	City University of Hong Kong, China
Patrick C. K. Hung	University of Ontario Institute of Technology, Canada

Jin Li	Guangzhou University, China
Chin-Feng Lai	Taiwan Cheng Kung University, Taiwan
Peng Li	University of Aizu, Japan
Chengcheng Li	University of Cincinnati, USA
Daniel Xiapu Luo	Hong Kong Polytechnic University, Hong Kong, China
Guangchi Liu	Stratifyd Inc., USA
Mingzhe Liu	Chengdu University of Technology, China
Kuan-Ching Li	Providence University, Taiwan, China
Jiguo Li	Hohai University, China
Zhe Liu	University of Waterloo, Canada
Sungyoung Lee	Kyung Hee University, South Korea
Haixiang Lin	Leiden University, The Netherlands
Xiaodong Lin	University of Ontario Institute of Technology, Canada
Joseph Liu	Monash University, Australia
Xiangyang Li	Illinois Institute of Technology, USA
Yangming Li	University of Washington, USA
Quansheng Liu	University of South Brittany, France
Junzhou Luo	Southeast University, China
Yonglong Luo	Anhui Normal University, China
Guohua Liu	Donghua University, China
Feifei Li	Utah State University, USA
Xiaodong Liu	Edinburgh Napier University, UK
Loukas Lazos	University of Arizona, USA
Jing Li	Rutgers University, USA
Suzanne McIntosh	New York University, USA
Sangman Moh	Chosun University, South Korea
Yi Mu	University of Wollongong, Australia
Rafal Niemiec	University of Information Technology and Management, Poland
Zemin Ning	Wellcome Trust Sanger Institute, UK
Shaozhang Niu	Beijing University of Posts and Telecommunications, China
Srikant Ojha	Sharda University, India
Jeff Z. Pan	University of Aberdeen, UK
Wei Pang	University of Aberdeen, UK
Rong Peng	Wuhan University, China
Chen Qian	University of California Santa Cruz, USA
Jiaohua Qin	Central South University of Forestry and Technology, China
Yanzhen Qu	Colorado Technical University, USA
Kui Ren	State University of New York, USA
Zheng-guo Sheng	University of Sussex, UK
Shengli Sheng	University of Central Arkansas, USA
Robert Simon Sherratt	University of Reading, UK
Jianyong Sun	Xi'an Jiaotong University, China
Yun Q. Shi	New Jersey Institute of Technology, USA

Krzysztof Szczypiorski	Warsaw University of Technology, Poland
Frank Y. Shih	New Jersey Institute of Technology, USA
Arun Kumar Sangaiah	VIT University, India
Jing Tian	National University of Singapore, Singapore
Cezhong Tong	Washington University in St. Louis, USA
Shanyu Tang	University of West London, UK
Tsuyoshi Takagi	Kyushu University, Japan
Xianping Tao	Nanjing University, China
Yoshito Tobe	Aoyang University, Japan
Cai-Zhuang Wang	Ames Laboratory, USA
Xiaokang Wang	St. Francis Xavier University, Canada
Jie Wang	University of Massachusetts Lowell, USA
Guiling Wang	New Jersey Institute of Technology, USA
Ruili Wang	Massey University, New Zealand
Sheng Wen	Swinburne University of Technology, Australia
Jinwei Wang	Nanjing University of Information Science and Technology, China
Ding Wang	Peking University, China
Eric Wong	University of Texas at Dallas, USA
Pengjun Wan	Illinois Institute of Technology, USA
Jian Wang	Nanjing University of Aeronautics and Astronautics, China
Honggang Wang	University of Massachusetts-Dartmouth, USA
Liangmin Wang	Jiangsu University, China
Xiaojun Wang	Dublin City University, Ireland
Q. M. Jonathan Wu	University of Windsor, Canada
Shaoen Wu	Ball State University, USA
Yang Xiao	The University of Alabama, USA
Haoran Xie	The Education University of Hong Kong, China
Zhihua Xia	Nanjing University of Information Science and Technology, China
Yang Xiang	Deakin University, Australia
Naixue Xiong	Northeastern State University, USA
Shuangkui Xia	Beijing Institute of Electronics Technology and Application, China
Fan Yang	University of Maryland, USA
Kun-Ming Yu	Chung Hua University, Taiwan, China
Xiaoli Yue	Donghua University, China
Ming Yin	Harvard University, USA
Aimin Yang	Guangdong University of Foreign Studies, China
Qing Yang	University of North Texas, USA
Ching-Nung Yang	Taiwan Dong Hwa University, Taiwan, China
Ming Yang	Southeast University, China
Qing Yang	Montana State University, USA
Xinchun Yin	Yangzhou University, China

Yong Yu	University of Electronic Science and Technology of China, China
Guomin Yang	University of Wollongong, Australia
Wei Qi Yan	Auckland University of Technology, New Zealand
Shaodi You	Australian National University, Australia
Yanchun Zhang	Victoria University, Australia
Mingwu Zhang	Hubei University of Technology, China
Wei Zhang	Nanjing University of Posts and Telecommunications, China
Weiming Zhang	University of Science and Technology of China, China
Yan Zhang	Simula Research Laboratory, Norway
Yao Zhao	Beijing Jiaotong University, China
Linna Zhou	University of International Relations, China

Organization Committee Members

Xianyi Chen	Nanjing University of Information Science and Technology, China
Yadang Chen	Nanjing University of Information Science and Technology, China
Beijing Chen	Nanjing University of Information Science and Technology, China
Chunjie Cao	Hainan University, China
Xianyi Chen	Hainan University, China
Xianmei Chen	Hainan University, China
Fa Fu	Hainan University, China
Xiangdang Huang	Hainan University, China
Zhuhua Hu	Hainan University, China
Jielin Jiang	Nanjing University of Information Science and Technology, China
Zilong Jin	Nanjing University of Information Science and Technology, China
Yan Kong	Nanjing University of Information Science and Technology, China
Jingbing Li	Hainan University, China
Jinlian Peng	Hainan University, China
Zhiguo Qu	Nanjing University of Information Science and Technology, China
Le Sun	Nanjing University of Information Science and Technology, China
Jian Su	Nanjing University of Information Science and Technology, China
Qing Tian	Nanjing University of Information Science and Technology, China
Tao Wen	Hainan University, China
Xianpeng Wang	Hainan University, China

Lizhi Xiong   Nanjing University of Information Science
                             and Technology, China
Chunyang Ye   Hainan University, China
Jiangyuan Yao   Hainan University, China
Leiming Yan   Nanjing University of Information Science
                             and Technology, China
Yu Zhang   Hainan University, China
Zhili Zhou   Nanjing University of Information Science
                             and Technology, China

Contents – Part I

Cloud Computing

Cloud Computing

3D Airway Tree Centerline Extraction Algorithm for Virtual Bronchoscope

Xiang Yu[1(✉)], Yanbo Li[1], Hui Lu[2(✉)], and Le Wang[2]

[1] College of Computer Science and Technology, Heilongjiang Institute of
Technology, Harbin 150050, China
1267013@qq.com, liyanbo210@126.com
[2] Cyberspace Institute of Advanced Technology, Guangzhou University,
Guangzhou 510006, China
{luhui,wangle}@gzhu.edu.cn

Abstract. Centerline extraction is the basis to understand three dimensional structure of the lung. Since the bronchus has a complex tree structure, bronchoscopists easily tend to get disoriented path to a target location. In this paper, an automatic centerline extraction algorithm for 3D virtual bronchoscopy is presented. This algorithm has three main components. Firstly, a new airway tree segmentation method based on region growing is applied to extract major airway branches and sub-branches. Secondly, the original center is adjusted according to the geometry features of Jacobian matrix, and modified Dijkstra shortest path algorithm is applied in the centerline algorithm to yield the centerline of the bronchus. Then, the airway tree structure and feature calculation are represented from many features. Our algorithm is tested with various CT image data and its performance is efficient.

Keywords: Airway tree segmentation · Evaluation function · Centerline Jacobian matrix · Topological structure analysis · Virtual bronchoscopy

1 Introduction

Virtual bronchoscopy system becomes very common tool to guide a bronchoscopist. In the pneumology, a bronchoscope is a very useful tool for diagnosis of inside the bronchus. Since the bronchus has a complex tree structure, a bronchoscopist easily gets disoriented and lost the way to a target location. In addition, image reconstruction artifacts, patient motion, and the partial volume effect introduce degradations that make it difficult to automatically segment small peripheral airways and extract the centerline.

To construct the centerlines, some approaches operate on the airway tree segmentation while others use airway tree surfaces. As such, the correctness of the airway tree segmentation and surfaces affects the quality of the airway tree centerline. The results of existing segmentation and centerline analysis methods may not completely represent the airway trees. For instance, segmentation methods often fail to identify peripheral airways. The missed peripheral airways could provide an appropriate route to the region of interest.

© Springer Nature Switzerland AG 2018
X. Sun et al. (Eds.): ICCCS 2018, LNCS 11063, pp. 3–12, 2018.
https://doi.org/10.1007/978-3-030-00006-6_1

Previously, may automatic airway tree segmentation methods rely on region growing method [1–8] because of its simplicity, speed and flexibility, whereby the final segmented result is a set of airway voxels connected to a seed voxel [9–12]. While region growing is fast and assumes no prior knowledge of the shape or size of the airways, it does require the choice of a global threshold that separates air and soft tissue voxels. This choice is difficult, however, as the lungs are filled with air, and mis-classifying a single airway wall voxel can allow the segmentation to leak into the lung parenchyma. To overcome the leakage problem, many improved the region growing method [7, 8] are proposed. They used the region growing method to segment the airway tree, then according to the graph theory to trim the pseudo branches and optimize the tree structure.

Centerline is a curve that traverses the center of a hollow organ, which should be satisfy the following requirements: connectivity, robustness, efficiency, centricity, singularity, automaticity [13]. Many methods for 3D skeletonization or centerline extraction of objects have been introduced in recent years, which were mainly based on distance transform, morphological operators, model flitting, medialness filter, fuzzy connectedness and so on. The distance transform method [14–16] is widely applied because of its connectivity and singularity. But the results are undesirability especially for multi-branches organ. He [17] proposed a reliable path extraction method, which mainly contain four steps: distance transform, find local maximum, visibility test and shortest path generation. Furthermore, Li [18] proposed a new method based on TaoSong He. These methods have more significance for centerline extraction, but still have some shortcomings need to improvement.

Therefore, the aim of our work was to develop an automatic method for centerline extraction based on CT images. Firstly, we describe an automatic 3D airway tree segmentation method that provides many more peripheral airways than previously proposed methods. Secondly, describes the centerline extraction method based on the geometric features of Jacobian matrix. Finally, represents the airway tree structure and feature calculation.

Section 2 details the proposed centerline extraction method. Section 3 presents results demonstrating the efficacy of the method. Finally, Sect. 4 offers concluding remarks.

2 Method

Definition 1 Boundary voxel: locall all 2-D cross sections A_i and their boundaries ∂A_i, where
$A_i = \{(x, y, z_i)|$ set of four-connected voxel (x, y, z_i), satisfying $I(x, y, z_i) \geq t$, $t \in [-1000, -600]\}$;
$\partial A_i = \{(x, y, z_i)|$ voxels $\notin \partial A_i$ that are 4-neighbors of a voxel $\in \partial A_i\}$;

Definition 2 Reliable path: reliable path in virtual organ is defined as a set of connected points inside the model. It must be satisfy the following requirements: (1) entire interior surface can be seen; (2) the path as short as possible; (3) do not through the surface; (4) ensure it has a wide perspective for navigation, and as far as possible away from the surface of model.

The airway tree centerline extraction method consists of the following main steps and as show in Fig. 1:

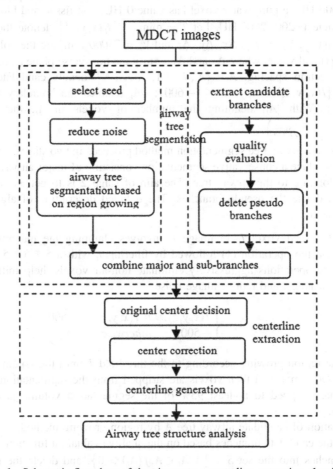

Fig. 1. Schematic flowchart of the airway tree centerline extraction algorithm

(1) Airway segmentation: A modified 3D region growing algorithm extracts major branches from the input CT image. For some sub-branches, we need to delete the pseudo branches according to the quality evaluation.

(2) Centerline extraction and generation: Adjust the original center of cross section according to the geometry features of Jacobian matrix. The shortest path generation method of Dijstra is used to generate centerline.

(3) Airway tree structure analysis: Represent the main center information including the length, running direction, relative position from the parent branch and average direction of the child branches.

2.1   Airway Tree Segmentation

Let I denote an input CT image, (x, y, z) represent a constituent voxel, and $I(x, y, z)$ denote the intensity value of voxel (x, y, z). Voxel intensity values are given in Hounsfiedld units (HU), whereby an CT scanner is calibrated so that a pure air voxel has value 1000 HU, a pure water voxel has value 0 HU, soft tissue and blood voxels are in the range $[-200, 200]$ HU. Let $T = \min_{(x,y,z)}\{I_f(x, y, z)\}$ denote the smallest voxel for image I_f, $V_T = |I_S| \cdot \Delta x \cdot \Delta y \cdot \Delta z$ and $V_e = 75000$ mm^3 are the volume of I_S and volume critical value, where Δx and Δy signify the transverse plane resolution and Δz denotes section spacing. $A = \{A_i, i = 1, 2, \ldots, N\}$ denote candidate section, where $A_i = \{I(x, y, z_i), I(x, y, z_i) \leq -600\}$; ∂A_i denotes the boundary voxels of cross section. With $|A_i|$ denoting the number of voxels in A_i, the center is $c_i = \left(\frac{1}{|A_i|}\sum x, \frac{1}{|A_i|}\sum y, z_i\right)$.

Our proposed airway tree segmentation method proceeds in two stages. The goal of stage 1 is to produce a conservative segmentation consisting of major airway branches definitely belonging to the airway tree. The aim of stage 2 is to get all sub airway branches and delete the pseudo branches. The detailed description of algorithm as summarized next:

1. We select a seed voxel I_S in image I, involves clamping the maximum voxel intensity via the operation (1) followed by filtering I_f with a 5 * 5 * 5 Gaussian filter. These operations aggressively eliminate non-air voxels, help mitigate segmentation leakage, and reduce image noise.

$$I_f(x, y, z) = \begin{cases} I(x, y, z), & \text{if } I(x, y, z) < -500 \\ -500, & \text{otherwise} \end{cases} \tag{1}$$

2. Repeat the region growing according to the threshold T until the volume $V_T > V_e$ ($V_e = 75000$ mm^3), and then voxels are stripped from the segmentation until the volume has dropped to at least 95% of the segmentation volume just prior to explosion.
3. Determination of candidate airway tree A by region growing method.
4. Analysis the candidate branches based on the quality evaluation function, retain the good branches into the set $S = \{A_i | A_i \in A, f(A_i) > 0\}$, and delete the bad ones. Quality evaluation function $f(A_i)$ equals to the intensity difference between the weakest airway-wall voxel $\in \partial A_i$ and the average airway-lumen voxel $\in A_i$, as equal (2).

$$f(A_i) = \min_{(x,y,z_i)\in\partial A_i}\{I(x, y, z_i)\} - \frac{1}{|A_i|}\sum_{(x,y,z_i)\in A_i} I(x, y, z_i) \tag{2}$$

5. For each section $A_i \in A$ of set S, select a pair of cross sections $\{A_{i-1}, A_{i+1}\} \in A$ directly adjacent to A_i, A_i is considered a real branch when the three adjacent cross sections satisfy the condition 0.5 mm $\leq |c_{i-1} - c_i| \leq 3$ mm, repeat this step until there has not the eligible cross section in set A.

2.2   Centerline Extraction and Generation

For the regular shape bronchus, its geometry center can satisfy the requirement of centerline. But for irregular bronchus, the center is bad. The important feature of the Jacobian matrix is that it reflects a differentiable equation with given point optimal linear approximation. Therefore, Jacobian matrix is used to modify the initial center.

For 3D image data, suppose $I : (x, y, z) \rightarrow (u, v, w)$, where $u = u(x, y, z)$, $v = v(x, y, z)$, $w = w(x, y, z)$, the Jacobian matrix of I is

$$JI(p) = \begin{vmatrix} \frac{\partial u}{\partial x} & \frac{\partial u}{\partial y} & \frac{\partial u}{\partial z} \\ \frac{\partial v}{\partial x} & \frac{\partial v}{\partial y} & \frac{\partial v}{\partial z} \\ \frac{\partial w}{\partial x} & \frac{\partial w}{\partial y} & \frac{\partial w}{\partial z} \end{vmatrix}$$

The Jacobian of a given point P represents important information about I close to this point. For example, if Jacobian determinant of a continuously differentiable function I at point p is not zero, so it has an inverse function near this point, called inverse function theorem. Furthermore, if the jacobian of point p is positive, the orientation of function I at the point p is constant. Otherwise, the orientation is reversed. The absolute value of jacobian determinant is the scaling factor of function I at point p. $I(p)$ is the optimal linear approximation of x close to point p, $p : I(x) \approx I(p) + JI(p) \cdot (x - p)$.

For boundary voxel of each cross section, we adjust the coordinate of center C_i according to the relationship with position of p_m and p_n, where p_m and p_n are intersection between boundary voxel with transverse axis or longitudinal axis which pass center point C_i. Denote $JI(p_m)$ and $JI(p_n)$ are the value of the Jacobian of p_m and p_n, C_i close to p_m, therefore, $I(c_i) \approx I(p_m) + JI(p_m) \cdot (x - p_m)$, the determine criterion of the relationship between C_i with p_m and p_n as follow:

1. (1) if $JI(p_m) = JI(p_n) = 0$, the center C_i is the point of centerline.
2. (2) if $JI(p_m) \cdot JI(p_n) < 0$, the value of Jacobian of p_m and p_n with the different symbol. It represents that the original center at the inside of boundary voxles, so
   $C_i = C_i + \frac{(|JI(p_m)| - |JI(p_n)|)}{2}$
3. (3) if $JI(p_m) \cdot JI(p_n) > 0$, the value of Jacobian of p_m and p_n with the same symbol. It represents that the original center at the outside of boundary voxels, so
   $C_i = C_i + \frac{(|JI(p_m)| + |JI(p_n)|)}{2}$

The shortest path generation algorithm of Dijstra is a more mature algorithm. But for complex model, this method will connect the two nonadjacent models together. Therefore, in the process of centers connection, we need to judged whether or not the centerline through the boundary of model. If the centerline through the boundary, we need break the two point, and insert new one until the line does not through the boundary.

2.3   Airway Tree Structure Analysis

In order to save the space, this method mainly from two aspects to represent the airway tree structure and measure information: main key point and branch features.

The main key point includes start point, end point and branch point of bronchus as Fig. 2 shows. The date structure information of bronchus includes node (NodeNo), parent node (ParentNo), child node number (NoDaughters), node type (Type), root node R, branch node B or leaf node E, node coordinate (Location), distance between node with its parent (Distances), and so on.

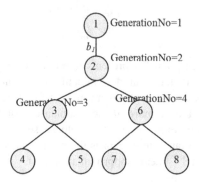

Fig. 2. Airway tree topology structure and data structure information

In Fig. 2, a tree structure is represented as a set of connected lines corresponding to the bronchial branches b_i (i = 1, ... M, M is the number of branches). In particular, b_1 denotes the root of the tree structure. Also, the coordinates of the start point and the end points of b_i are represented as $S(b_i)$ and $E(b_i)$. $N(b_i)$ is the name of b_i. $C(b_i)$ represents child branches b_i, and $D(b_i)$ represents descendant branches of b_i, is defined recursively as Eqs. (3) and (4)

$$C(b_i) = \{b_l; N(b_i) = N(P(b_i))\} \tag{3}$$

$$D(b_i) = C(b_i) \cup \{b_l; b_l \in D(b_k), b_k \in C(b_i)\} \tag{4}$$

Feature calculation of bronchial branches b_i are calculated: length l_i, running direction d_i, relative position e_i from the parent branch, and average direction of the child branches m_i. These features are computed as (5)–(8):

$$l_i = \|E(b_i) - S(b_i)\| \tag{5}$$

$$d_i = \frac{E(b_i) - S(b_i)}{\|E(b_i) - S(b_i)\|} \tag{6}$$

$$e_i = E(b_i) - S(P(b_i)) \tag{7}$$

$$m_i = \frac{\sum\limits_{b_k \in D(b_i)} (E(b_k) - E(b_i))}{\left\| \sum\limits_{b_k \in D(b_i)} (E(b_k) - E(b_i)) \right\|} \tag{8}$$

3 Experiments

The visible human male CT data set was used as the basis for the lung lobes and the initial airway tree structure. The CT data consists of transaxial CT scans of the entire body taken at 1 mm intervals at a resolution of 512 pixels by 512 pixels. The pixel size of the images was 0.898 mm.

The improved airway tree segmentation method can extract 60% of airways at a depth up to the 5 generation subsegmental level. It is reconstructed using the Marching Cube method as Fig. 3 shows.

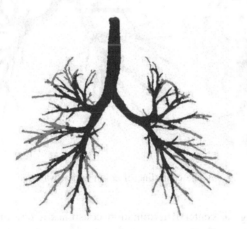

Fig. 3. Airway tree model

Table 1 summarizes the airway tree segmentation results. The number of branches using the proposed method is 1.6 as much as the region growing method, and the accuracy can reach 76%. In the time, conservation segmentation is very fast, but the segmentation and filtering for sub branches need 147 s. Overall calculation time is no more than 3 min. The hybrid method need roughly 13 to 20 min. Therefore, the proposed method can improve the calculation speed.

For centerline extraction analysis, using the lung slice and colon slice images of CT. As Fig. 4 shows that this method can effectively extract the centerline, and ensure the uniqueness.

Table 2 summarizes the number of inner voxels, branches, centers and running time, includes the center extraction time, center correction time and centerline

Table 1. Number of branches, accuracy and time analysis

	No. branches	Branch number/accuracy		Time (s)
		Proposed	Hybrid	
Main branch	112	112/100%	112/100%	4.3
Sub-branch	1010	738/73%	500/43%	147
All	1112	850/76%	612/55%	151.3

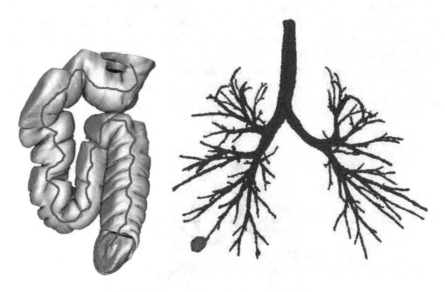

Fig. 4. The centerline of colon and airway tree

generation time. Original center determination consumes a few times, because it is determined in the process of organ segmentation. But center correction involves matrix and center calculation, so this step will consume a lot of times. All of these closely relate to the inner voxel, boundary voxel, and complexity of the models.

Table 3 summarizes the accuracy of the feature calculation of branches: including length l_i, running direction d_i, relative position e_i from the parent branch, and average

Table 2. Centerline information and running time

	No. inner voxels	No. branches	No. center	Running time (s)			All
				Original center	Center correction	Path generation	
Bronchial	510152	168	384	20	256	151	427
Colon	561521	1	172	17	126	21	164

direction of the child branches m_i 。 The accuracy increased 9.5% compare with the Mori's method [9].

Table 3. The feature calculation accuracy of bronchial branches

Features	Accuracy (%)
Length l_i	55.8
Running direction d_i	89.5
Relative position from the parent branch e_i	88.0
Average direction of the child branches m_i	86.5

4 Conclusion

Image based planning and guidance of peripheral bronchoscopy requires the reliable path. Our proposed method is computationally efficient, not only segmented the complete the airway tree and solved the leakage problem, but also generated the uniqueness centerline for navigation. In addition, we have successfully applied the method to represent the airway tree structure. Future work includes: (1) to solve the problem that how to guide the doctors to observe the organ inner structure, (2) research for route planning.

Acknowledgment. This work was supported by National Natural Science Foundation of China under Grant No 61572153, and the National Key research and Development Plan (Grant No. 2018YFB0803504). key research topics of economic and social development in Heilongjiang province under Grant No WY2017048-B.

References

1. Graham, M.W., Gibbs, J.D., Higgins, W.E.: Computer-based route-definition system for peripheral bronchoscopy. J. Digit. Imaging **25**(2), 307–317 (2012)
2. Kiraly, A.P., Higgins, W.E., Hoffman, E.A., et al.: 3D human airway segmentation method for virtual bronchoscopy. Acad. Radiol. **19**(10), 1153–1168 (2002)
3. Suter, M., Schirren, J.T., Reinhardt, J.: Evaluation of the human airway with multidetector X-ray-computed tomography and optical imaging. Inst. Phys. Publ. Physioligical Meas. **25**(4), 837–847 (2004)
4. Tan, W., Yang, J., Zhao, D., et al.: A novel method for automated segmentation of airway tree. In: 24th Chinese Control and Decision Conference, pp. 976–979 (2012)
5. Fabijanska, A.: Two pass region growing algorithm for segmenting airway trees for MDCT chest scans. Comput. Med. Image Graph. **11**(23), 1353–1364 (2009)
6. Law, T.Y., Heng, P.: Automated extraction of bronchus from 3D CT images of lung based on genetic algorithm and 3D region growing. Proceeding SPIE Med. Imaging **3979**, 906–916 (2000)
7. Schlathalter, T., Lorenz, C., Carlsen, I., et al.: Simultaneous segmentation and tree reconstruction of the airways for virtual bronchoscopy. In: Proceeding of SPIE Medical Imaging, vol. 4684, pp. 103–113 (2002)

8. van Ginneken, B., Baggerman, W., van Rikxoort, E.M.: Robust segmentation and anatomical labeling of the airway tree from thoracic CT scans. In: Metaxas, D., Axel, L., Fichtinger, G., Székely, G. (eds.) MICCAI 2008. LNCS, vol. 5241, pp. 219–226. Springer, Heidelberg (2008). https://doi.org/10.1007/978-3-540-85988-8_27
9. Mori, K., Hasegawa, J., Toriwaki, J., et al.: Recognition of bronchus in three dimensional X-Ray CT images with application to virtualized bronchoscopy system. In: Proceeding 13th International Conference on Pattern Recognition, vol. 8, pp. 528–532 (1996)
10. Kiraly, A.P., Higgins, W.E., Hoffman, E.A., et al.: 3D human airway segmentation methods for virtual bronchoscopy. Acad. Radiol. 9(10), 1153–1168 (2002)
11. Summers, R.M., Feng, D.H., Holland, S.M., et al.: Virtual bronchoscopy: segmentation method for real-time display. Radiology 200(3), 857–862 (1996)
12. Suter, M., Tschirren, J., Reinhardt, J., et al.: Evaluation of the human airway with multidetector X-ray-computed tomography and optical imaging. Physiol. Meas. 25, 837–847 (2004)
13. Wang, Y., Zhou, M., Geng, G.: A study on extracting centerline in virtual endoscopy. J. Northwest Univ. (Nat. Sci. Ed.) 35(6), 695–698 (2005)
14. Saito, T., Toriwaki, J.I.: New algorithm for Euclidean distance transformation of an n-dimensional digitized picture with applications. Pattern Recogn. 27(11), 1551–1565 (1994)
15. Hu, Y., Hou, Y., Xu, X.: A 3D center path finding algorithm base on two distance fields. J. Image Graph. 8(11), 1272–1276 (2003)
16. Hai, Z., Hongbing, J., Xinbo, G.: An automatic centerline extraction algorithm based on distance from boundary. J. Comput. Aided Des. Comput. Graph. 18(6), 860–864 (2006)
17. He, T.S., Hong, L.C., Chen, D.Q., Liang, Z.R.: Reliable path for virtual endoscopy: ensuring complete examination of human organs. IEEE Trans. Vis. Comput. Graph. 7(4), 333–342 (2001)
18. Li, G., Jie, T., Mingchang, Z., Huiguang, H.: Centerline extraction based on Hessian Matrix. J. Softw. 14(12), 2074–2081 (2003)

A Collective Computing Architecture Supporting Heterogeneous Tasks and Computing Devices

Yang Li[1], Yunlong Zhao[2]([✉]), Zhenhua Zhang[2], Qian Geng[2], and Ran Wang[2]

[1] Harbin Engineering University, Harbin 150001, China
[2] Nanjing University of Aeronautics and Astronautics, Nanjing 211106, China
zhaoyunlong@nuaa.edu.cn

Abstract. Abowd shows a new vision of computer framework - collective computing. In this case, kinds of remote computing devices including people who is regarded as a kind of computing devices connect with each other in a group for completing a complexed work. Therefore, the computing capacity of the various computing devices is fully exploited in different tasks. However, most of the current researches focus on the dedicated system, the heterogeneous tasks and computing devices performance in the infrastructure is not paid enough attentions. This paper presents a collective computing architecture that supports heterogeneous tasks and computing devices, which uses a series of centralized managers for analysing and distributing tasks and controlling heterogeneous computing devices. The whole architecture is layered in order to obtain loads balance, centralized dispatch and low delay communication. This architecture provides a common infrastructure for processing heterogeneous tasks by heterogeneous devices but not for some specialized systems or functions. At last, we implement a prototype system by virtual computers and android phones for proving that the architecture can use heterogeneous devices to perform heterogeneous tasks well.

Keywords: Collective computing · Architecture
Heterogeneous tasks · Heterogeneous devices · Multiple managers

1 Introduction

The collective computing is a new computing framework [1] that is composed of a large number of computing devices self-organizing and cooperating to complete various types of computing tasks. In collective computing, the types of computing devices are varied, even including "people" as a variety of special intelligent computing devices. The types of tasks are also varied, for instances: arithmetic logic tasks, storage tasks, sensing tasks, and service tasks.

Y. Li and Y. Zhao—This research was supported by Defense Industrial Technology Development Program under Grant No. JCKY2016605B006, Six talent peaks project in Jiangsu Province under Grant No. XYDXXJS-031.

© Springer Nature Switzerland AG 2018
X. Sun et al. (Eds.): ICCCS 2018, LNCS 11063, pp. 13–25, 2018.
https://doi.org/10.1007/978-3-030-00006-6_2

However, the requirements of collective computing also brings some new challenges. The main challenge is brought by the heterogeneity of the tasks, such as the solution of human subjective results and the mathematical logic operations are completely different. It is worthy of study to design an architecture for supporting a unified system to manage these heterogeneous tasks and publish to a suited computing device. But now, the relevant researches are very few, this paper is the only one which researches on the collective computing architecture (according to the authors' knowledge). Most of researches are focused on solving some certain goals or just using some certain devices. For instances, "PEIR" collects data for calculating the environmental impact which is organized based on the location [2], Sun [3] propose the appropriate supports in the architecture for data monitoring. This kind of researches is commonplace which cannot be used for different scenarios and aims.

The aim of this paper is to propose a paradigm of a large-scale integrated architecture, which is compatible for current system designs and feasible extension. Ours contributions is as follows: (a) a common architecture is presented which is used to preform the heterogeneous tasks by remote heterogeneous computing devices. The components and the relationship among them are designed by indispensable functions and realistic requirements. And it could be used for deploying common specified system and extends components and functions. (b) In order to solve uncertain tasks and devices, the specified tasks distribution manager are proposed in this paper, which are used to manage the tasks, analyse the kinds and features of tasks. And the specified computing devices managers correlate the computing devices, select the device by the characteristics of the computing devices and tasks. (c) this architecture is multi-layer for providing loads balance and dynamic extension. The different layers have the similar structures and functions which the coupling is unbending that makes the architecture unified and easy to transform. Finally, it achieves the unified management of heterogeneous tasks and computing devices under the same architecture.

The rest of this article is arranged as follows. The work is discussed in Sect. 2. The Sect. 3 describes the design, the features and theoretical analysis of the architecture. Section 4 illustrates system implementation and evaluation. Finally, we summarize the full text.

2   Related Work

The collective computing is an emerging research area with open questions and challenges. Before the collective computing was formally named, some researchers began a series of prospective studies. Firstly, the preprocessing for analysing the features of heterogeneous tasks is important for performing. Jabberwocky [4] allows users to deploy their own programs on the server and perform by people that is a common method for heterogeneous tasks. In the similar way, a hybrid cloud framework is proposed for analysing tasks by people, then performs them by corresponding devices [5]. Smirnov and Ponomarev explore a framework to solve different tasks by an analysis module [6]. And it considers about the geo-information. The other main problem is to use heterogeneous devices to perform the tasks. Ganti puts forward a series of important key points, such as data integration, coincident API interface, extensibility, etc [7]. Guo et al. proposed an architecture paradigm that is compatible with heterogeneous data and provides analysis [8] which is a practical method for heterogeneous data from different types of devices. Estrin illustrates the importance of the individuality of data, and gives the corresponding architecture [9]. Sun [3] propose the importance of data monitoring, and give the appropriate supports in the architecture respectively.

In addition, there are some issues that are worth noting, such as data and devices selection, communication, security, and extension. The location of the sensing data and the topology of the sensors are very important in the framework like participant sensing. "PEIR" uses a divisional structure based on the location to collect data for calculating the environmental impact and exposure of the personalized estimate [2]. In work [10], the minimization power communication method is proposed for that devices simultaneously communicate through multiple independent channels. Pipes et al. implements a multi-layer architecture that uses the inference management firewall to analyze the context to reduce the risk of sensor data [11]. Multi-layer middleware structure can simplify the logic of processing, improve the interaction, and reduce the interference between the various logical units [3]. Hill et al. proposed the use of middleware to analyze heterogeneous results [12]. Messaoud et al. proposed a model for selecting sensors through data quality and energy consumption [13].

3   Architecture Design

In view of the characteristics of the collective computing, the architecture will be described and analysed in this section.

3.1   Devices and Tasks Analyses

We defines the common tasks and computing devices in collective computing for designing the topology and interaction of devices by the requirements of the tasks, and provide the interfaces and special platforms of the architecture by the characteristics of the computing devices for adapting devices and selecting devices rapidly.

Characteristics of Task. The common heterogeneous tasks are divided into the following five types according to their own characteristics: (a) The real-time operation tasks are mostly interacting directly with the user. But the computation is not complicated, and the required persistence storage is small. (b) The computationally intensive tasks often have the high computational complexity, which requiring high computational and buffer abilities, and some of them may require high parallel computing capacity. (c) The I/O intensive tasks are used to store large amounts of data, the implementation requires a lot of persistent storage space. Compared to others, the computationally and I/O intensive tasks mean that cannot perform by personal devices. (d) The sensing tasks are often used to sense environmental data. Its computing performance, storage performance requirements are not high. (e) The artificial subjectivity tasks mostly aims to solve the fuzzy operations, evaluation, high semantic operations.

Characteristics of Devices. The devices are defined 4 types corresponding to the types of tasks: computationally intensive, I/O intensive, sensing, and artificial subjectivity (human) devices. Most of the real-time tasks do not need a special device because that could be executed in users' access devices.

3.2   Architecture Description

We propose the heterogeneous tasks and computing devices supported collective computing architecture (called HS-architecture for short) as Fig. 1 shows. The HS-architecture is logical layered architecture. Each layer is set on the basis of its own location for reducing the delay by network and some tasks' requirements based on locations. The management layer receives and analyses the task, then distributes the task to devices and waits for the results through access layer when some devices suit to perform the task. if there is no appropriate device, the management layer will request assistances through extension or root layer.

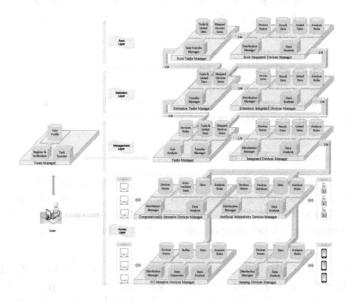

Fig. 1. Architecture supported heterogeneous tasks and devices.

Access Layer. The access layer is in charge of accessing devices straightly, which selects devices for performing the task, delivers the task, recycles the result and communicates with device during task executing. Each manager communicates with the devices which is the special type suited to the manager, in order to interact by the homogeneous data. The sensing devices manager is abstract in the figure for intuitional expression. Obviously, there are many types of sensing devices with their own datum, so the sensing devices manager should be a serial managers for different types of devices. And some of the devices are multifunction which might be accessed to multiple managers. There are some different requirements for different managers. The computationally intensive devices may produce lots of useful intermediate data which should be stored. The I/O intensive devices managers often transfer huge data without analysis, so it needs a data dispatcher and buffers. And the artificial subjectivity devices use a devices attribute database records their own attributes like professions and habits which influences selection and calculation dramatically.

Management Layer. The management layer includes task manager and integrated devices manager. It analyses the task and sends it to the most suitable platforms in access layer. The integrated devices manager accesses to one or more access devices managers in adjacent areas by the actual conditions for tasks load and devices diversity, etc. In selecting device stage, it should pay more attention on the types, the locations and the abilities of "devices" unlike access layer focus on performances or costs, which is derived from recording the integral states of managers periodically. Furthermore, the integrated devices manager has an important function for coordinating some heterogeneous devices if some tasks need different types of devices to work together. In this case, the interpretation, analysis and storage of the data should be put in integrated devices manager. Most of special data need designated rules for interpretation and analysis by the user, which can be regarded as a rules for analysis. The tasks manager is the core transfer station including task analysis and transfer manager. The main functions of the tasks manager is to preprocess the tasks and transfer them which is understandable to provide services. And it communicates with the user who submits tasks through the user management platform. These tasks submitted by the users are confined to the services provided by system. Therefore, the different methods and arms of services and the services themselves are confined in an expandable services rules database which could provide extension. The task analysis is in charge of selecting the service and detailed methods of the task. The transfer manager selects "devices" (managers) and waits for getting the results. There are some functions need to be supported in HS-architecture. It should analyse the task for select service and the detailed processing scheme in the task analysis platform. Then, the devices are selected for executing unless the similar tasks are detected in the transfer manager. Furthermore, it should map the task to higher layer for reducing the repetitive executions. The coordinating services have distinct procedures by different devices. The procedures should be dispatched by steps through tasks manager but not devices managers.

Extension Layer. The extension layer supervises the managers in the lower layer which is a logical middleware in this architecture for centralizing managers in a larger area than the management layer does. It is an abstract performance in Fig. 1 which may be many managers in extension layer. Some lower extension managers access their own higher individual which manage themselves, in order to balance the tasks load. The extension layer has the similar structures as management layer keeping consistency of the architecture. The devices manager controls the lower tasks manager as a "device" because it distributes the tasks received from the tasks manager in the same layer. And the extension tasks manager is the simple task transfer station comparing with the individual in management layer. Its main functions are transferring the task requested from lower layer and mapping the completed tasks. Due to the task has been analysed in management layer, there is no task analysis platform.

Root Layer. The root layer is the final decider in this architecture, which maps all tasks and managers incapable distribute in extension layer. The functions are only a little different from those of the extension integrated devices manager, as no device states mapping, no task assistance to higher layer. Similarly, the root task manager is the final services provider for managing all the task scheduling in the whole system. The tasks database in root tasks manager is only used to store the tasks' results. Therefore, the only function of root tasks manager is to transfer tasks.

Users Manager and Users. The users manager is the interacting platform between the user and the collective computing system which does not influence the task performing, so it does not belongs to the collective computing architecture straightly but an intermediary agent. It charges of managing users' identities and transferring the tasks. Therefore, the function of register and verification links with the user profile database. As for the user, a user with a communication device may be also a computing device in collective computing system. Therefore, all devices are found through users apply for.

3.3   Architecture Analysis

This architecture divides the covered area to a lot of subdomains for organizing the devices zonally based on the location of the devices, and finally, centralized managing their managers in lower layer. In this condition, the system loads are shared by each managers platforms. In the other hand, the organization based on location and task execution locally avoid the high delay which affects the user experience and the performance of the system dramatically. Furthermore, there are a lot of tasks which are restricted by the location, especially the sensing task.

The interpretation and analysis of the datum through assignable rules is the main method for processing the heterogeneous datum. The interpretations of the datum give the computers a way to "understand" the meaning of the datum. The assignable analysis rules allow the user to use a special method for integrating and analysing the datum, which makes the specified system could be embedded in this collective computing system.

The potential attacks on the system by an adversary operating within the network must be considered during the design of the integrated architecture [2]. The sensitive information is also hardly exposed to external attackers. There are some strategies for keeping anonymity of the data [14,15]. If the strategy needs a credit authority, this system could select one or some trusted devices, which is due to the collective computing system has to be a public welfare system hardly to organize personally. All the strategies could be set in this architecture.

4   Prototype Evaluation

In order to prove the usability and the efficiency by a rational system, we implement a system prototype based on the design thinking in HS-architecture. This section describes the implementation overview and the evaluation results.

4.1   Implementation Overview

The system prototype is implemented by JAVA. The equipment includes a PC (Xeon E3-1230, 16 GB RAM), a Sony laptop (Intel i5-2450M, 4 GB RAM), and 2 phones (Google Nexus3 and Samsung Note3). There are 4 virtual computers with Ubuntu 17 regarded as computing devices running in the PC by VMware, the configurations are as following: device 0 (dual-cores, 2 GB RAM, SSD), device 1 (4 cores, 2 GB RAM, HDD), device 2 (single-cores, 1 GB RAM, SSD), and device 3 (dual-cores, 2 GB RAM, HDD). And each phone simulates 100 devices. The integrated devices manager and all accessing manager is in PC, and the laptop is regards as a tasks manager and a user. We set 5 types of tasks to perform in this prototype, which includes: $task1$ is an arithmetical operation task, a high frequency I/O task ($task2$), the $task3$ having 2 parts consisting of arithmetical operation task and high frequency I/O (for simulating collaboration task), a sensing task requiring 30 devices ($task4$), and an artificial task requiring 20 devices ($task5$). The artificial task is an automatic reacting programmer in phones. All devices require the costs if a task performs in this device. And the similar task detection is ignored for showing the system operation better.

Then, we introduce the main functions. Before that, the operation system of collective computing itself is a very valuable study which is out of the research scope of this paper. Therefore, we implement functions of the system prototype in a series of simple methods for proving the usability of HS-architecture.

Task Preprocessing. In this paper, the task analysis consist of 3 points: task features detection, task decomposition and combination, and task execution time estimation. The system recognizes the task that could use tags brought by the task [16]. We ask the task to bring some tags to indicate its own features, which includes the task type, devices requirements and procedures. The task decomposition and combination is easy when the task has tags showing its procedure. We use the tags to build the task tree for decomposition and combination [16]. In order to keep the experiments objectives, each part of the same task could be decomposed and combined is constant which will not change by task resubmitting. And the system use nonparametric regression technique based on tags to estimate the execution time [17]. There are some initial execution times for every task which will change with the system iterates.

Device Section. The devices selection is the importance in collective computing, which is different from previous system due to combining calculation of heterogeneous devices. We propose a basic strategy devices selection. In addition, the task scheduling is FIFO for this system.

Early Completion First (ECF): For computationally and I/O intensive devices, the completion time only includes execution time and delay obviously. The devices' reliabilities take into consideration of the complete tasks probability and the result accuracy at least. The system selects the devices which use the shortest execution times and high reliabilities. For sensing and people (artificial subjectivity devices) devices, the execution time is very fast, so that is not necessary to consider about it. But some devices cannot finish the task due to offline or profession and enthusiastic. Therefore, the system selects the devices based on the coincidence probability of devices' reliabilities. It needs to choose as few devices as possible and keep the probability and the number of devices are higher than requirements. Therefore, the complexity is $O(n^2)$.

For the devices in the coordination task, which includes some the multifunction devices are regarded as more than one devices in access devices manager. This type of devices are managed by integrated devices managers at that moment, so the manager can record their reliability probabilities based on functions used simultaneously. The calculation process is like the other selection methods. The coincidence reliability probabilities could be calculated according to their type which each of them needs to be higher than requirements.

Early Completion First with Costs (ECF-C): The devices need the more costs is unloved by the user, so the costs is inverse to selection possibility that all the ECF equations divided by costs is the final ECF-C equation.

4.2   Performance Evaluation

First, we set up a series of costs for all computing devices. In order to simplify the experiments, the cost is charged for each task performed by a device. The costs of 4 virtual computers are as following: cost 0 (4.4, 3.7, 4.2, 3.9), cost 1 (4.8, 3.5, 4.5, 3.7), cost 2 (5.6, 3.5, 4.7, 3.7), and cost 3 (6.0, 2.2, 4.8, 3.1). All the costs increase with the own performances of devices grow but not absolutely or symmetrically. The distribution of cost 2 is most close to the performances of 4 devices. We generate cost 3 through increasing the dispersion of the costs symmetrically as possible as we can. In the same way, the cost 1 is the product by decreasing dispersion. The cost 0 has the minimum variance, but the costs of device 3 is adjusted upwards and that of device 1 is set downwards. In addition, all the reliability probabilities are 1 so that does not need to selects multiple devices to prevent from device disable.

We evaluate the execution time of the whole processing by different devices selection algorithms and costs. The user manager generates a series of tasks and sends them to the task manager for executing. Those tasks queue includes the equal number of 5 types but the sequence is random. In this experiment, we also tested that the system selects the device sequentially without considering about the execution time and cost. The results are shown in Fig. 2(a) and (b). Obviously, the execution time by ECF is usually the shortest. The sequence method can be regards as a common method in traditional architecture. The worst is the theoretical longest execution time for sequence method. Furthermore, the ECF-C is in complicated situation. The ECF-C is getting closer to the sequence method when the costs approximate the performances of devices.

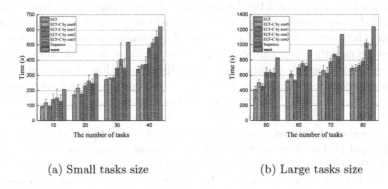

(a) Small tasks size   (b) Large tasks size

Fig. 2. The execution time for different tasks size.

The total incentives by 4 different costs for virtual computer as Fig. 3(a)–(d) shows. Due to the costs from the task 4 and 5 influence the result dramatically their own costs will analyse later separately. As expected, the intensity of the difference is basically proportional to the efficiency of performance. Figure 3(a) and (d) show the results when the better devices request extreme incentives. In this case, ECF spends more incentives than the others do. The other figures illustrate the difference is less due to the symmetrical costs setting. Nevertheless, the costs of ECF and ECF-C are near, which are not like sequence method does in Fig. 3(b). The differences in Fig. 3(c) are very distinct, and their execution times are also distinct dramatically.

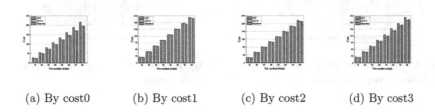

(a) By cost0   (b) By cost1   (c) By cost2   (d) By cost3

Fig. 3. The incentives of sensing tasks by different costs.

Next, we evaluate the selection of sensing devices and people. The artificial tasks test gets the same result due to the processing is the same as sensing task.

In this experiments, we simulates 200 devices in the system with the reliability possibilities obeying to $N(0.70, 0.017)$, and the cost obeying to $N(0.68, 0.015)$, which the device with a higher reliability possibilities will require a higher cost. The total reliability possibilities of selected devices for keeping the number of task completion successfully satisfying requirement exceed 0.9544 before the task executes. Figure 4 shows the number of selected devices increase with the requirement rises. With more good devices are occupied, the system selects more devices with lower reliability possibilities for keeping the task completion. Comparing to ECF, ECF-C uses more devices because it considers about the cost that makes more worse but low-cost device be selected. The number of selected devices will not decrease rapidly when the requirements is far away from the total number of devices or the average of reliability possibilities is so low. The total costs of previous experiments is shown in Fig. 5. The difference in costs is very obvious between ECF and ECF-C due to many devices calculation together. It shows that the differences of cost between two methods will increasing dramatically with the number of devices requirement. Next, we evaluate the time of computationally and I/O devices selection. Figure 6 shows to simulate less than 5000 devices in the system for selecting without devices grouping. Due to the whole process needs to traverse all devices, the time for devices selection increases linearly with the total number of devices. Figure 7 shows the time of sensing devices selection (or people selection) among 200 devices. The selection method is different from the corresponding individual for computationally and I/O devices. Except to traverse all equipment, this method also requires progressively iterative calculations to calculate all reliability possibilities to meet the requirements. Therefore, the time of select devices shows a non-linear growth as requirements grow which is $O(n^2)$ as expected.

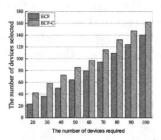

Fig. 4. The number of device selected for different requirements.

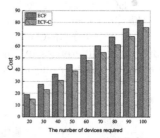

Fig. 5. The total costs for different requirements.

We evaluate the time of the task analysis in tasks manager. Because the processing is classification based on tags, which is simple in this system. Figure 8 the execution time is very low (about 6.1 ms for 1000 tasks). And its increasing follows the number of tasks growing linearly due to traverse all the tasks. At last, we put work [15] into this system for evaluating the compatibility. In work [15], there are 3 entities if it does not use the trusted third party, including: DC, SP, and participants. We regards DC as user, SP as a service in task manager, and participants as devices. Comparing to the architecture in work [15], HS-architecture has extra two middleware: the integrated and access device manager, which bring extra double data transfers. The data size is 8 kb which is so little makes the transfer latencies in different group size are similar (about 3 s). Figure 9 shows the execution time for a whole processing. The difference in two architecture are almost the extra transfer latencies, except that, there is no difference. And the time of transfer latency is much lesser than that of calculation, so the differences decrease with group size rises.

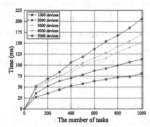

Fig. 6. The time of computationally and I/O devices selection.

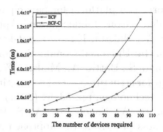

Fig. 7. The time of sensing and people devices selection.

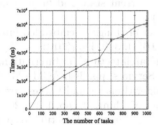

Fig. 8. The execution time of task analysis.

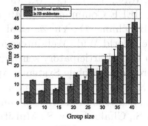

Fig. 9. The execution time of anonymous reporting.

5 Conclusion

The objective of this paper is to propose a common collective computing architecture that supports heterogeneous tasks and computing devices. On the basis of architecture's required functions, designing each model for different functions and the relationship among them. Describing the data communication and common workflow of system supported. Therefore, we do not illustrate most of functions in detailed instead basic paradigms, in order to aim to the architecture itself. This paper provides the compatibility of heterogeneous tasks and computing devices through extensible analysis and services models. The layered structure based on location balances the loads. The expandability is guaranteed through identical logical structure. And the corresponding access platforms are designed for different connect rapidly.

References

1. Abowd, G.D.: Beyond Weiser: from ubiquitous to collective computing. Computer **49**(1), 17–23 (2016)
2. Min, M., Reddy, S., Shilton, K., et al.: PEIR, the personal environmental impact report, as a platform for participatory sensing systems research. In: International Conference on Mobile Systems, Applications, and Services. DBLP, pp. 55–68 (2009)
3. Sun, Y., Nakata, K.: An agent-based architecture for participatory sensing platform. In: Universal Communication Symposium, pp. 392–400. IEEE (2010)
4. Ahmad, S., Battle, A., Malkani, Z., et al.: The jabberwocky programming environment for structured social computing. ACM Symposium on User Interface Software and Technology, pp. 53–64 (2011)
5. Smirnov, A., Ponomarev, A., Shilov, N.: Hybrid crowd-based decision support in business processes: the approach and reference model. Approach Ref. Model **16**, 376–385 (2014)
6. Smirnov, A., Ponomarev, A.: Crowd computing framework for geoinformation tasks. In: Popovich, V., Claramunt, C., Schrenk, M., Korolenko, K., Gensel, J. (eds.) Information Fusion and Geographic Information Systems. LNGC, pp. 109–123. Springer, Cham (2015). https://doi.org/10.1007/978-3-319-16667-4_7
7. Ganti, R.K., Ye, F., Lei, H.: Mobile crowdsensing: current state and future challenges. IEEE Commun. Mag. **49**(11), 32–39 (2011)
8. Guo, B., Zhang, D., Yu, Z., et al.: From the internet of things to embedded intelligence. World Wide Web-internet Web Inf. Syst. **16**(4), 399–420 (2013)
9. Estrin D.L.: Participatory sensing: applications and architecture. In: International Conference on Mobile Systems, Applications, and Services, pp. 3–4. ACM (2010)
10. Zhai, X., Guan, X., Zhu, C., et al.: Optimization algorithms for multi-access green communications in internet of things. IEEE Internet of Things J., pp. 1–10 (2018)
11. Pipes, S., Chakraborty, S.: Multitiered inference management architecture for participatory sensing. IEEE International Conference on Pervasive Computing and Communication Workshops, pp. 74–79. IEEE (2014)
12. Hill, R., Al-Muhtadi, J., et al.: A middleware architecture for securing ubiquitous computing cyber infrastructures. IEEE Distrib. Syst. Online **5**(9), 1 (2004)
13. Messaoud, R.B., Ghamri-Doudane, Y.: QEMSS: a selection scheme for participatory sensing tasks. International Conference on Protocol Engineering, pp. 1–6 (2016)
14. Zhang, F., He, L., He, W., et al.: Data perturbation with state-dependent noise for participatory sensing. In: IEEE INFOCOM, pp. 2246–2254. IEEE (2012)

15. Li, Y., Zhao, Y., Ishak, S., et al.: An anonymous data reporting strategy with ensuring incentives for mobile crowd-sensing. J. Ambient Intell. Humanized Comput. **2017**(B), 1–15 (2017)
16. Qing-shan, L., Hua, C., Man, Z., et al.: Collaboration strategy for software dynamic evolution of multi-agent system. J. Cent. South Univ. **22**(7), 2629–2637 (2015)
17. Iverson, M.A., Ozguner, F., Follen, G.J.: Run-time statistical estimation of task execution times for heterogeneous distributed computing. In: IEEE International Symposium on High Performance Distributed Computing, p. 263 (1996)

A Control Approach Using Network Latency Interval to Preserve Real-Time Causality

Hangjun Zhou[1,2(✉)], Guang Sun[1], Shuyang Du[3], Feng Liu[4],
Bo Yang[1], and Yaqian Zhuo[1]

[1] Hunan University of Finance and Economy, Changsha, China
zhjnudt@gmail.com
[2] Nanjing University of Science and Technology, Nanjing, China
[3] School of Software Engineering, Tongji University, Shanghai, China
[4] National University of Defense Technology, Changsha, China

Abstract. A Distributed Virtual Environment (DVE) is to simulate the real world and offer the fidelity with real-time constraint. However, existing causal order control methods could not function well due to the large and dynamic network transmission latency in big data scale environments. In this paper, a novel control approach using network latency interval to preserve real-time causality is proposed to effectively select the causal control information dynamically adapted to the network latency and irrelevant to the computing node scale. The results of groups of experiments indicate that the proposed approach is more efficient in preserving causal order delivery of events in large-scale networks, and in the meanwhile, meets the real-time constraint of causality preservation in a DVE.

Keywords: Distributed virtual environment · Network latency interval
Causality preservation

1 Introduction

A DVE system is a computer-generated 3D virtual world where multiple participants could exchange data simultaneously and interact immersively with each other [1, 2]. The sites in a DVE don't share any memory and communicate merely by message transmitting [3]. Furthermore, when a DVE is applied in wide area network or big data scale environments, it is usually hard for all the nodes to communicate normally [4]. In order to make a DVE system resembling our living world, not only the causality of events should be preserved correctly, but also the causality should be maintained with real-time constraint due to the real-time property of events happened in real world.

2 Related Works

In related works, Vector Times [5] and Immediate Dependence Relation (IDR) [6] are the two classical categories of the traditional asynchronous causal order control approaches. However, as these approaches usually ignore the time validity of event and

© Springer Nature Switzerland AG 2018
X. Sun et al. (Eds.): ICCCS 2018, LNCS 11063, pp. 26–35, 2018.
https://doi.org/10.1007/978-3-030-00006-6_3

assume the events can always arrive in time, it is hard for them to reduce the causality violations with real-time property. A Δ-causal order method is proposed [7], which has taken the time validity of event into consideration. Nevertheless, this method requires that the simulation time of each node is accurately synchronized and each event must have the identical valid time "Δ", which is not suitable for the asynchronous DVEs.

The rest of the paper is organized as follows. The Causality Preservation with Real-time Constraint is defined in Sect. 3. The approach using network latency interval to preserve causality is described in Sect. 4. Experiments are implemented in Sect. 5. Conclusions are stated in Sect. 6.

3   Causality Preservation with Real-Time Constraint

Assuming that a peer-to-peer distributed virtual environment system is a finite set P of n sequential sites $\{p_1, p_2, ..., p_n\}$, each message transmitted in this system mainly consists of two parts: an event and its control information. An event is the occurrence of an action performed at a process, such as a participant's action, collision, explosion, etc., which is assumed to be atomic and modeled as having a zero delivery duration. Furthermore, an event in a DVE system can be classified as either a local event, which is generated at a process but is not sent to other processes, or a global event, which is generated at a process and is sent to other processes. The control information is utilized to ensure to deliver the event in the message and its causally dependent events in causal order at the destination processes. Therefore, the causal order delivery of messages can be also equally considered as the causal order delivery of events. And then it is easy to know that all local events are properly ordered, thus we only need to consider the ordering of global events. For the rest of this paper, all the discussions on causality are focused on the causal relations among global events.

Generally, an event generated at the process p_i is denoted as e which can be identified with $r(e)$ where $r(e) = (i, a)$ and a is the logical time when e is generated at p_i. E_i denotes all the events that have been generated at p_i, V_i denotes all the events that have been received at p_i, and H_i denotes all the events that have been delivered at p_i. $E = \cup_{i=1}^{n} E_i$ denotes all the events generated at P. As a DVE is a real-time system, a global clock value with respect to physical time is bounded. Usually, it is called wallclock time. Many clock synchronization algorithms exist that can synchronize clocks in the large-scale. We use t to denote the current wallclock time of the DVE system and t_x to denote the time when event e_x is generated.

Nevertheless, such causal order delivery has been defined solely for distributed systems in which events in the application messages have unlimited time validity, which is not concerned with real-time issues. However, a DVE system is essentially a multimedia real-time application that demands to have a good and fast interactivity, thus the events of messages should be delivered in causal order and within a well-defined validity time.

The validity time, we denote it as ΔT, of the event in a message is the physical time duration, after its sending time, during which the data of the event in the message is meaningful and consequently can be used by its destination sites.

In DVE systems, because distinct types of messages usually have different validity time values, they need to be differentiated, such as the validity time of e_y can be denote as ΔT_y.

With real-time property constraint, some events that may not arrive the destination in time can be identified. For example, in Fig. 1, e_1, e_2, e_3 and e_y are causally dependent events with the cause-effect relation as: $e_1 \rightarrow e_2 \rightarrow e_3 \rightarrow e_y$. p_{des} denotes any one of the common destination of these events. Each event has its own validity time so that the delivery deadline is not identical, such as deadline $e_y = t_y + \Delta T_y$. From Fig. 1, we can see that when wallclock time $t = deadline\_e_y$, e_y, e_3 and e_2 have been already received by p_{des}, but e_1 is still on the transmission in the network.

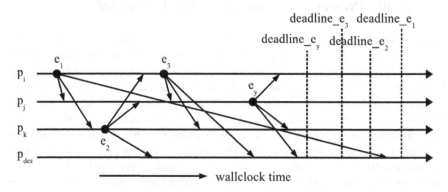

Fig. 1. A delayed event e1 missing deadlines

To prevent causal order violation, (1) e_y, e_3 and e_2 may be forced to wait until e_1 arrives, or (2) the late message containing e_1 may have to be discarded. The first approach is not suitable for real-time settings because when e_1 misses e_y's deadline, forced waiting may also force e_y, e_3 and e_2 to miss their deadlines. In real-time environments, it makes more sense to allow delayed e1 to be dropped than to force all of e_y, e_3 and e_2 to be expired. For this case, causality preservation of events with real-time constraint is given.

Definition 1 (Causality Preservation with Real-time Constraint).

$\forall p_{des} \in P$, the real-time causal order delivery of events at p_{des} is preserved iff

(1) $\forall e_y \in V_{des} - H_{des}$, at the time when the lifetime of e_y is terminated or e_y is required to be delivered, $\forall e_x \in V_{des} - H_{des}$, if $e_x \rightarrow e_y$, e_x must be delivered before e_y at p_{des};

(2) $\forall e_y \in V_{des} - H_{des}$, let $F_y = \{e_x | \forall e_x \in E \land e_x \rightarrow e_y\}$, if the lifetime of e_y is still valid and $F_y \subseteq H_{des}$, e_y must be delivered immediately at p_{des}.

Where V_{des} denotes all the events that have been received at p_{des}, and H_{des} denotes all the events that have been delivered at p_{des}, and E denotes all the events generated at P.

4 Using Network Latency Interval to Preserve Causality

From Definition 1, we know the delivery order of concurrent events is not considered in causal order control approaches. For example, as $e_2\|e_4$ and $e_3\|e_4$ in Fig. 2(a), the graph can be equivalently separated into the two paths: $w_1(e_1, e_y) = e_1d(_{1,\,2})e_2d(_{2,\,3})e_3d$ $(_{3,\,y})e_y$ and $w_2(e_1, e_y) = e_1d(_{1,\,4})e_4d(_{4,\,y})e_y$, as shown in Fig. 2(b). Thea aim to preserve the real-time causality is to preserve causality of $w_1(e_1, e_y)$ and $w_2(e_1, e_y)$ with real-time constraint respectively.

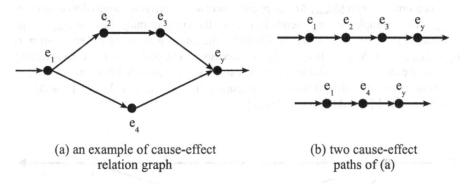

(a) an example of cause-effect   (b) two cause-effect
   relation graph   paths of (a)

Fig. 2. Cause-effect relation graph and its paths

We take the path $w_1(e_1, e_y)$ in Fig. 2(b) into consideration. It is quite possible, especially on WAN, that When $t = t_y + \Delta T_y$ or e_y is required to be delivered, item (2) is not satisfied yet such as $e_1, e_2 \in V_{des}$ but $e3$ is not in V_{des} due to large transmission delay. Then, the original cause-effect relations among them would be broken, as shown in Fig. 3(a), which may result in cause-effect relation of received events changing into concurrent relation and produce causal order violations if without effective causality control. For this circumstance, p_{des} needs to reconstruct causal relation between e_2 and e_y (denoted as $e_2 \downarrow e_y$), as shown in Fig. 3(b), and uses $CI(e_2)$ to identify e_1 from V_{des} recursively. And then p_{des} deliveries them in the order e_1, e_2, e_y to preserve causality between e_x and e_y of $w_1(e_1, e_y)$ in real-time.

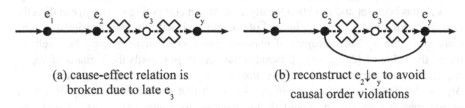

(a) cause-effect relation is   (b) reconstruct $e_2 \downarrow e_y$ to avoid
   broken due to late e_3 causal order violations

Fig. 3. The broken cause-effect relation and the reconstruction of it

In order to dynamically select effective control information $CI(e_y)$ to preserve the real-time causality, we can predict the round trip time between p_i and p_j at first with the distributed predicting mechanism [8]. In the application level of a distributed system, it may regard the half value of the round trip time as the message transmission delay time from p_i to p_j, which is denoted as Δt_{ij}. However, Δt_{ij} merely means the transmission time from p_i to p_j, based on which we can solely calculate the causal control information suitable for p_j. As shown in Fig. 4, event e_y is generated at p_j, and sent to p_i and p_k at the moment t_y in a message. Respectively, experiencing different transmission time Δt_{ji} and Δt_{jk}, e_y arrives at p_i and p_k. Therefore, p_j can record and update a message transmission time interval: $[\Delta t_{min}, \Delta t_{max}]$, where Δt_{min} indicates the minimal transmission time at current moment and Δt_{max} indicates the maximal transmission time at current moment. With $[\Delta t_{min}, \Delta t_{max}]$, p_j can calculate the arriving range of an event sent to p_{des}. For example, when p_j sends e_y is at t_y, the arriving range of e_y at p_{des} can be denoted as $[t_y + \Delta t_{min}, t_y + \Delta t_{max}]$. Similarly, the arriving range of e_x sent from p_i is $[t_x + \Delta t_{xmin}, t_x + \Delta t_{xmax}]$. If e_x is the predecessor event and e_y is the corresponding successor event, $CI(e_y)$ suitable for all p_{des} to preserve causality between e_x and e_y in real time could be selected through comparing $[t_y + \Delta t_{min}, t_y + \Delta t_{max}]$, $[t_x + \Delta t_{xmin}, t_x + \Delta t_{xmax}]$ and $[t_x + \Delta t_{xmin}, t_x + \Delta t_{xmax}]$.

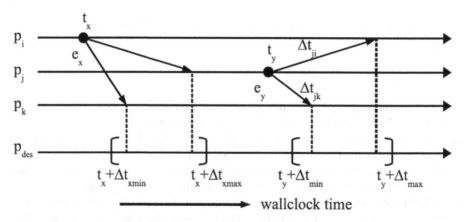

Fig. 4. The arriving time range of e_x and e_y

To maintain $[\Delta t_{min}, \Delta t_{max}]$, a n-dimensional vector of network coordinates, $\{X_1, X_2, ..., X_n\}$, has been set and modified locally at p_j. When computing $CI(e_y)$, p_j can directly read the value of $[\Delta t_{min}, \Delta t_{max}]$ instead of computing it with the n-dimensional vector. Only when the update messages of network coordinates arrive, p_j may be likely to renew the value of $[\Delta t_{min}, \Delta t_{max}]$. Besides the vector, p_j records the variants of Δt_{min}, Δt_{max}, mn and mx. mn and mx are the site logic number recording variants. If $\Delta t_{min} = \Delta t_{ji}$ and $\Delta t_{max} = \Delta t_{jq}$, it can get the result that $mn = i$ and $mx = q$. When an update message arrives, p_j would decide whether to renew $[\Delta t_{min}, \Delta t_{max}]$ with the procedure showed in Fig. 5. If this network coordinate update isn't about X_j, X_{mn} or X_{mx} and doesn't lead to the variation of $[\Delta t_{min}, \Delta t_{max}]$, there is unnecessary to update $[\Delta t_{min}, \Delta t_{max}]$; if it isn't about X_j, X_{mn} or X_{mx} but leads to the change of $[\Delta t_{min}, \Delta t_{max}]$, p_j

could directly replace Δt_{min} or Δt_{max} with the new value; if it is the update about X_j, X_{mn} or X_{mx}, there is possible for p_j to update $[\Delta t_{min}, \Delta t_{max}]$ with n-dimensional vector.

```
Procedure ProcNCMsg(Message)   % processing an update message about X_k of p_k, k=1 , 2 ,..., n.
{
      % if X_j or X_mn or X_mx updates and leads to that Δt_min or Δt_max has to be renewed, p_j would
      % compute variants Δt_min, Δt_max, mn, mx again.

      if( (k==mn)&&(new Δt_jk > Δt_min) || (k==mx)&&(new Δt_jk < Δt_max) || (k==j) )
          for( s=1; s<=n; s++ )
          {
                if( s==1 ) { Δt_min=Δt_max=Δt_js; mn=mx=s; continue; }   % initialize Δt_min,Δt_max,mn,mx
                if( s==j ) continue;                                       % ignore Δt_jj
                if( Δt_js<Δt_min ) { Δt_min=Δt_js; mn=s; }              % new Δt_min and mn
                if( Δt_js>Δt_max ) { Δt_max=Δt_js; mx=s; }              % new Δt_max and mx
          }

      % if X_j or X_mn or X_mx doesn't update but new Δt_jk results in that Δt_min or Δt_max has to be
      % renewed, p_j would directly update Δt_min, Δt_max, mn, mx.

      else
      {
            if( Δt_jk<Δt_min ) { Δt_min=Δt_jk; mn=k; }                 % new Δt_min and mn
            if( Δt_jk>Δt_max ) { Δt_max=Δt_jk; mx=k; }                 % new Δt_max and mx
      }
}
```

Fig. 5. $[\Delta t_{min}, \Delta t_{max}]$ update procedure

Message sending algorithm

For event e_y generated at p_j, $CI(e_y)$ is selected through comparing and calculating $[t_y + \Delta t_{min}, t_y + \Delta t_{max}]$, $[t_x + \Delta t_{xmin}, t_x + \Delta t_{xmax}]$ and $[t_x + \Delta t_{xmin}, t_x + \Delta t_{xmax}]$ so as to acquire control information dynamically adapted to network latency and maintain causality of events at p_{des}. Before describing the algorithm of sending the message, several structures of local variants are given as follows.

$VT(p_j)$—the vector of logical times to track the numbers of messages diffused by processes. The size of i is equal to n. $VT(p_j)$ records the logical time of p_j.

$CG(pj)$—the multi-linked list storing the current effective cause-effect relation graph of p_j. To represent an event and its relation, each node of $CG(p_j)$ contains four variants: $(r(e_x); t_x; [\Delta t x_{min}, \Delta t x_{max}]; ptr[num])$, where $ptr[num]$ is a set of multiple pointers of which each one is pointed to the node that represents the predecessor which has immediate dependency relation with the event represented by this node. To avoid the unlimited increment of $CG(p_j)$, p_j would periodically delete redundant nodes in it. Assume the current time is t, then $t < t + \Delta t_{min}$. If a node $(r(e_x); t_x; [\Delta t x_{min}, \Delta t x_{max}]; ptr$ $[num])$ meets that $t_x + \Delta t_{xmax} < t$, it can obtain that $tx + \Delta t_{xmax} \leq t + \Delta t_{min}$. Thus the other causal nodes of it could be deleted if they are not in multiple paths.

CI(ey)—the vector storing causal information which would be sent to p_{des} to with e_y in a message. Each element also contains four parts: $(r(e_x); t_x; [\Delta tx_{min}, \Delta tx_{max}]; lc [num])$. $r(e_x)$, t_x, $[\Delta tx_{min}, \Delta tx_{max}]$ could be obtained from $CG(p_j)$ and the function of $lc [num]$ is similar to $ptr[num]$ in $CG(p_j)$ by storing the indexes of its immediate dependent elements in $CI(e_y)$.

CD_M—the vector storing the indexes of the immediate dependent elements containing $r(e_x)$ such that $e_x \downarrow e_y$ in $CI(e_y)$. An element in CD_M contains two variants: $(r (e_x); ltr)$, where l_{tr} denotes the index of one immediate dependent element containing $r (e_x)$. With the CD_M, p_{des} could begin to traverse $CI(e_y)$ using Depth-First Search algorithm.

$CN(p_j)$—the vector storing the pointers to the immediate dependent nodes containing $r(e_x)$ such that $e_x \downarrow e_y$ in $CG(p_j)$. An element in $CN(p_j)$ has two parts: $(r(e_x); ptr)$, where ptr denotes the pointer to one immediate dependent node containing $r(e_x)$. With the $CN(p_j)$, p_j could traverse $CG(p_j)$ using Depth-First Search algorithm.

The sending algorithm calling the procedure of causal order control information selection is demonstrated in Fig. 6.

The algorithm of sending message M

1. VT(p$_j$)[j]=VT(p$_j$)[j] + 1 ;   % *update the logical time of p$_j$*
2. t$_y$ = timeGetTime() ;   % *obtain wallclock time t$_y$*
3. for(a=0; a<CN(p$_j$).size(); a++)   % *traverse CG(p$_j$) from each pointer in CN(p$_j$)*
4.   SelectCI(null, null, CN(p$_j$)[a].ptr);   % *recursively compute CI(e$_y$) and its CD$_M$*
5. M ← (e$_y$, j, VT(p$_j$)[j], t$_y$, [Δt$_{min}$, Δt$_{max}$], ΔT$_y$, CD$_M$, CI(e$_y$));   % *message M*
6. SendMessage(M);
7. p = CG(p$_j$).add(r(e$_y$), t$_y$, [Δt$_{min}$, Δt$_{max}$], ptr[CN(p$_j$).size()]);   % *add the new node representing*
                                                             % *e$_y$ into CG(p$_j$) and return the pointer to it*
8. for(a=0; a<CN(p$_j$).size(); a++)   % *each pointer in ptr[num] of the new node points to the*
9.   p→ ptr[a]=CN(p$_j$)[a].ptr;   % *node representing the immediate dependent event of e$_y$*
10. CN(p$_j$).clear;   % *clear the original elements in CN(p$_j$)*
11. CN(p$_j$).add(r(e$_y$), p);   % *add new element (r(e$_y$), p) into CN(p$_j$)*
12. CI(e$_y$).clear();   % *clear content of CI(e$_y$)*
13. CD$_M$.clear();   % *clear content of CD$_M$*
14. exit();

Fig. 6. Message sending algorithm

Message receiving algorithm

When p_{des} receives the message M containing e_y and $CI(e_y)$, it is necessary for it to determine whether M should be delivered, discarded or buffered in $MQ(p_{des})$, which is achieved by the message receiving algorithm described in Fig. 7.

The algorithm of receiving message M

1. t = timeGetTime() ;   % *obtain current wallclock time t*
2. if($(t>t_y+\Delta T_y)$ || $(VT(p_j)[j] \leq VT(p_{des})[j])$)   % *M is expired or has been discarded*
   {
3.   AbandonMessage(M) ;   % *abandon M*
4.   exit() ;
   }
5. else   % *M is valid*
   {
6.   for($b=0$; $b<CD_M$.size(); $b++$)   % check *whether item (2) in Definition 4 is satisfied*
7.   if($CD_M[b].r(e_x).a > VT(p_{des})[CD_M[b].r(e_x).i]$)   % *if there exists e_x such that $e_x \downarrow e_y$*
           {   % *and e_x is not delivered at p_{des}*
8.   BufferMessage(M) ;   % *buffer M to $MQ(p_{des})$*
9.   exit() ;
           }
10.   ProcessMessage(M) ;   % *if item (2) in Definition 4 is satisfied, process M immediately*
11.   exit() ;   }

Fig. 7. Message receiving algorithm

In the receiving algorithm, $MQ(p_{des})$ is the message buffer queue at p_{des}. If the received messages cannot satisfy the condition of causal order delivery, and they are respectively within their own lifetimes and not requested to delivery by their successor message, p_{des} would buffer these messages.

5 Experiments

In the groups of experiments implemented to evaluate the performance of the proposed approach, the framework of the distributed causality verification environment is running on run time infrastructure is BH-RTI [9] developed by Beijing University of Aeronautics and Astronautics following the High Level Architecture (HLA) standards [10–13]. The middleware between BH-RTI and federates is designed to consists of the network coordinate computation module and the real-time causal order delivery module. A distributed real-time simulation is developed to run at federates to display the effects of causal order control algorithms. The ordering mechanism in BH-RTI is set to be Receive Order (RO) in the experiments. Figure 8 demonstrates the average message delivery time costs of the three approaches in different scales. The cost of our approach is low and could meet the real-time constraint with the small overhead of transmission and computation even in big data scale environments.

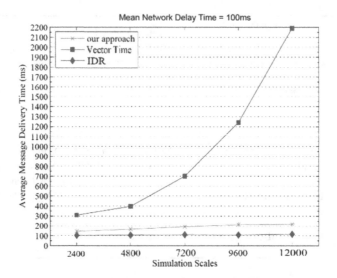

Fig. 8. Average message delivery time

6 Conclusions

With the rapid development of Internet and mobile technologies, more and more large-scale distributed virtual environments (DVEs) are implemented on the asynchronous WAN, where the real-time causal order preservation becomes a new and important issue. In this article, we present a novel real-time causality preservation approach using network latency interval to dynamically and recursively select the causal control information adapted to the network latency and deliver received messages with real-time constraint. Experiments demonstrate that our approach could effectively reduce the numbers of causal order violations in real time and decrease the average amount of control information overhead.

Acknowledgement. This research work is supported by Hunan Provincial Education Science 13th Five-Year Plan (Grant No. XJK016BXX001), Hunan Provincial Natural Science Foundation of China (Grant No. 2017JJ2016), Social Science Foundation of Hunan Province (Grant No. 17YBA049), 2017 Hunan Provincial Higher Education Teaching Reform Research Project (Grant No. 564) and Scientific Research Fund of Hunan Provincial Education Department (GrantNo. 16C0269 and No. 17B046). The work is also supported by Open foundation for University Innovation Platform from Hunan Province, China (Grand No. 16K013) and the 2011 Collaborative Innovation Center of Big Data for Financial and Economical Asset Development and Utility in Universities of Hunan Province. We also thank the anonymous reviewers for their valuable comments and insightful suggestions.

References

1. Fujimoto, M.: Parallel and Distributed Simulation Systems. Wiley Interscience Press, New York (2000)
2. Balci, O., Fujimoto, R.M., Goldsman, D., Nance, R.E., Zeigler, B.P.: The state of innovation in modeling and simulation: the last 50 years. In: Simulation Conference (WSC), pp. 821–836. IEEE, Las Vegas Country (2017)
3. Raynal, M.: Distributed Algorithms For Message-Passing Systems. Springer, Berlin (2013)
4. Lamport, L.: Time, clocks, and the ordering of events in a distributed system. Commun. ACM 21(7), 558–565 (1978)
5. Schwarz, R., Mattern, F.: Detecting causal relationships in distributed computations. in search of the holy grail. Distrib. Comput. 7(3), 149–174 (1994)
6. Hernndez, S.P., Fanchon, J.: The immediate dependency relation: an optimal way to ensure causal group communication. Ann. Rev. Scalable Comput. 6(3), 61–79 (2004)
7. Baldoni, R., Raynal, M.: Efficient Δ-causal broadcasting. Int. J. Comput. Syst. Sci. Eng. 13, 263–271 (1998)
8. Dabek, F., Cox, R.: Vivaldi: a decentralized network coordinate system. In: Proceedings of SIGCOMM Conference, pp. 426–437 (2004)
9. Zhang, Y., Zhou, Z., Wu, W.: A hierarchical time management mechanism for HLA-based distributed virtual environment. J. Comput. Inf. Syst. 1(2), 7–15 (2006)
10. IEEE Standard for Modeling and Simulation (M&S) High Level Architecture (HLA)—Framework and Rules (IEEE Std 1516-2000). The Institute of Electrical and Electronics Engineers, Inc., USA (2000)
11. IEEE Standard for Modeling and Simulation (M&S) High Level Architecture (HLA)—Federate Interface Specification (IEEE Std 516.1-2000). The Institute of Electrical and Electronics Engineers, Inc., USA (2001)
12. IEEE Standard for Modeling and Simulation (M&S) High Level Architecture (HLA)—Object Model Template (OMT) Specification (IEEE Std 1516.2-2000). The Institute of Electrical and Electronics Engineers, Inc., USA (2001)
13. IEEE Recommended Practice for High Level Architecture (HLA) Federation Development and Execution Process (FEDEP) (IEEE Std 1516.3-2003). USA: The Institute of Electrical and Electronics Engineers, Inc. (2003)

A Co-occurrence Matrix Based Multi-keyword Ranked Search Scheme over Encrypted Cloud Data

Nan Jia[1], Shaojing Fu[1], Dongsheng Wang[2], and Ming Xu[1(✉)]

[1] National University of Defense Technology, Changsha, Hunan, China
xuming@nudt.edu.cn
[2] Academy of Military Science, Beijing, China

Abstract. Searchable encryption has become a very important technique for secure data search in cloud systems. It can conduct search functions over encrypted cloud data and protect the data privacy meanwhile. There are many searchable encryption schemes that support basic search functions like single keyword search, multi-keyword search, similiarity search and so on. To enrich the search functionality, several searchable encryption schemes that support semantic search have been proposed recently. However, these schemes only focus on the existence of keywords during the search process. They have not considered the semantic relation between keywords, which have significant influence on the search results.

To solve this problem, in this paper, we propose a new co-occurrence matrix based Semantic Multi-keyword Ranked Search scheme (SMRS) which considers both the semantic relation of keywords and keyword weight for more accurate search results over encrypted cloud data. We design a term co-occurrence matrix to quantize the semantic correlation of keywords and adopt the widely-used TF-IDF rule to measure the keyword weight. In particular, our scheme can effectively retrieve data items that match the users' intention better. The indexes and queries are encrypted by the secure kNN algorithm. We also add some randomness in the encryption process for stronger protection. Security analysis prove that SMRS is secure under the known background model. The performance evaluation shows that our scheme achieves high search accuracy and practical search efficiency.

Keywords: Searchable encryption · Semantic search
Co-occurrence matrix

1 Introduction

With the cloud computing becoming prevalent, more and more enterprizes and individuals choose to outsource their data to the cloud. It brings great convenience to users because of its flexibility and accessibility. However, outsourcing

© Springer Nature Switzerland AG 2018
X. Sun et al. (Eds.): ICCCS 2018, LNCS 11063, pp. 36–49, 2018.
https://doi.org/10.1007/978-3-030-00006-6_4

data to the cloud directly can bring some privacy risk because the data stored in the untrusted cloud may contain lots of sensitive information. To protect the privacy, users usually choose to encrypt the data before transmission. However, encryption makes it a challenging problem to search on the encrypted data. Searchable encryption (SE) is wildly considered to be an efficacious way to settle this matter. So far, there have been many searchable encryption schemes which focus on various search functionalities such as single keyword search (e.g., [3,12]), similarity search (e.g., [8–10]), multi-keyword ranked search (e.g., [2,13,17]), etc.

Among these schemes, multi-keyword ranked search is considered to be the most significant because of its high practicability. Multi-keyword ranked search schemes allow users to search by one or more keywords and they can retrieve the top-k most relevant results instead of all the results containing the keywords. Wang et al. [15] first investigated the issue of ranked search over encrypted data. However, their scheme can only support single keyword. Cao et al. [2] first proposed a multi-keyword ranked search scheme. It uses vectors to represent indexes and queries and adopts the principle of "coordinate matching" to capture the similarity of the search query and documents. The search results are ranked by the number of matched keywords. Recently, to extend the search functionality, Fu et al. proposed a semantic search scheme over encrypted data that maps the semantically close words to the same stem in [7]. Later, they presented a more advanced scheme which realizes semantic search based on conceptual graphs in [6]. However, these schemes only consider the existence of the keywords during the search process, they have not taken the semantic correlation between keywords into account, which can make contribution to select more accurate results.

The multi-keywords that users input always have semantic correlation to a certain extent. For example, suppose that a user chooses "cloud computing" as keywords to search over the dataset. It is obvious that the result he wants to retrieve is more possible about the knowledge of Internet such as "cloud computing general situation" rather than the irrelevant "the computing of cloud atmosphere". It is a vital ability for the searchable encryption scheme to select and return the items that match the users' intention.

Term co-occurrence is generally utilized in plaintext information retrieval [1,4,11]. It means the co-occurrence of terms in a document. If two terms often occurs in similar linguistic contexts, they are considered to have some semantic correlation with each other [5]. Term co-occurrence can indicate the relation of keywords and help retrieve items that are close to the user's intention when the users' queries contain multi-keywords. Among numerous term co-occurrence measures, the co-occurrence matrix is wildly used because it is the simplest measure for computation. However, it is a very difficult task to conduct the computation of term co-occurrence matrix on encrypted data. To the best of our knowledge, the utilization of term co-occurrence matrix as relevance metric to search on encrypted data has not been well investigated in the literature.

In this paper, we propose a new privacy-preserving searchable encryption scheme that realizes co-occurrence matrix based Semantic Multi-keyword

Ranked Search (SMRS). For the first time, we consider the term co-occurrence factors for multi-keyword semantic search in ciphertext form. SMRS measures the semantic correlation of keywords utilizing a newly-designed term co-occurrence matrix. It uses the widely-used statistical measurement term frequency (TF) and inverse document frequency (IDF) to express the keyword weight meanwhile. To protect the privacy, our scheme adopts the secure kNN algorithm to encrypt the indexes and queries, which can preserve the inner product of two vectors. We adopt the threat model introduced by Cao et al. [2], i.e., the known background model and analysis the security under the threat model. The performance evaluation shows that our scheme achieves high search accuracy and efficiency. The contributions of this paper are summarized as follows:

(1) We propose a new multi-keyword ranked search scheme that can realize co-occurrence matrix based semantic search over encrypted data and retrieve items which satisfy the users' intention better.
(2) For the first time, we adopt the term co-occurrence measurement to construct the index set of searchable encryption scheme. We design a term co-occurrence matrix which can quantize the semantic correlation of keywords and transform the semantic relation into matrix computation.
(3) Our scheme protects the data privacy under the known background model and achieves high security level. We evaluate our scheme using real data sets and the results prove that our scheme is efficient.

The rest of the paper is organized as follows: Sect. 2 describes the formulation of the problems and some preliminaries. Section 3 describes the framework of our scheme and analyze the security. Section 4 gives the performance evaluation of our scheme. Finally, we conclude the paper in Sect. 5.

2   Problem Formulation

We formulate the problem of our proposed scheme in this section. We first introduce the system model and threat model of our scheme. Then we present our design goals. Finally, we give the preliminaries of our scheme.

2.1   System Model

In this paper, as shown in Fig. 1, we consider a cloud system which consists of three entities: data owner, data user and cloud server. The data owner has a data set D and extracts keywords from D to generate the keyword set W. Then the owner generates a set of indexes I based on the keyword set. To protect the privacy, the data owner encrypts the data set D as well as the index set I. Finally, the owner outsources them to the cloud and distributes the keys to authorized users.

To retrieve items from the encrypted data set, the user generates a query with several keywords. In most searchable encryption schemes, the data users are assumed to have the mutual authentication capability with the data owner.

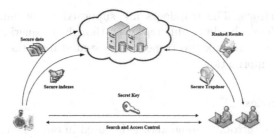

Fig. 1. System model.

Therefore, the search control mechanisms such as broadcast encryption [3] can be applied in the scheme. The users can obtain the query through the mechanisms. Then the user generates a secure trapdoor T and sends it to the cloud. After receiving the trapdoor T, the cloud server searches over the encrypted index set and selects the relevant items in a ranked order. Finally, the cloud server sends back the top-k most relevant results to the user.

2.2 Threat Model

The cloud server in our proposed scheme is considered to be *"honest but curious"*, which is the same as most previous searchable schemes. It means that the cloud server would execute the designed instructions honestly, but it is always curious about sensitive information of the dataset, indexes and queries so that it will collect and analyze the sensitive data to get some available information. We adopt the threat model proposed by Cao et al. [2]: the known background model, which is stronger than the commonly-used known ciphertext model. In the known background model, the cloud server may have more background knowledge. It may obtain some statistic information, such as the frequency of keywords in a certain document, which can reveal the importance of keywords. The cloud server can utilize such information to implement the statistic attack. Therefore, our proposed scheme is required to protect data privacy under the known background model. Specifically, the information that should be preserved mainly involves aspects as follows:

(1) *Data Set and Indexes Privacy.* The cloud server should not know other information except for the encrypted data set and indexes. Although the data set and indexes are encrypted before outsourcing, the encryption scheme should be robust enough to resist the attack from cloud server and malicious users. Moreover, it cannot deduce any available details from the trapdoors.
(2) *Keyword Privacy.* The trapdoor generated from user's query ought not to leak any information about the query keywords. The cloud server and vicious users should not identify any keyword even though they can analyze the statistic information (such as term frequency) of the query keywords.

(3) *Trapdoor Privacy.* The trapdoors are supposed to be unlinkable, which means trapdoors should be different even though the queries are same. The cloud server cannot link two trapdoors generated from the same queries to obtain more information.

2.3 Preliminaries

In this section, we introduce some knowledge used in our scheme:

TF-IDF. TF-IDF measurement is the most wildly-used statistic approach in keyword extraction and information retrieval. It reflects how significance a keyword is to a data set. TF is term frequency, which is the number of times that a term appears in a document. It can reveal the importance of a keyword for a document. IDF is inverse document frequency, which is the result of diving the total number of the documents in a data set by the number of documents that containing a certain term. It can quantize the specificity of a term in a data set. The notions in the calculation are as follows:

- $TF_{i,t} \rightarrow$ The standardized TF value of keyword w_i in document d_t.
- $IDF_i \rightarrow$ The standardized IDF value of keyword w_i in data set D.
- $f_{i,t} \rightarrow$ The frequency of keyword w_i that occurs in document d_t.
- $N \rightarrow$ The total number of documents in data set D.
- $n_i \rightarrow$ The number of documents in dataset D that contains w_i.

Suppose that there is a data set D that contains a series of document $d_t (1 \leq t \leq N)$, the keyword set that are extracted from D is $W = \{w_i\}_{1 \leq i \leq m}$. The TF value of a keyword w_i in document d_t is:

$$TF_{i,t} = \frac{\ln(1 + f_{i,t})}{\sqrt{\sum_{w_i \in d_t} \ln(1 + f_{i,t})^2}}, \tag{1}$$

The IDF value of w_i in the data set D is calculated as:

$$IDF_i = \frac{\ln(1 + N/n_i)}{\sqrt{\sum_{w_i \in D} \ln(1 + N/n_i)}}, \tag{2}$$

Then the TF-IDF score of a keyword is calculated as $S_i = TF_{i,t} \times IDF_i$.

Secure kNN Computation. Secure kNN (k-nearest neighbor) computation can find the k nearest neighbors from an encrypted data set by calculating the Euclidean distance between the data record p and a query q [16]. It can preserve the inner product of two vectors. The key set of secure kNN algorithm includes a binary vector s for splitting and two invertible random matrices M_1 and M_2 for encryption. Given a data vector p and a query vector q, the algorithm kNN($\cdot$) splits p into p' and p'', then the algorithm kNN($\cdot$) splits q into q' and q'' in a related but different way. Then the algorithm encrypts the index vector using M_1 and M_2 as: $\hat{p} = \{\hat{p}', \hat{p}''\} = \{M_1^T \boldsymbol{p}', M_2^T \boldsymbol{p}''\}$. The query vector is encrypted as: $\hat{q} = \{\hat{q}', \hat{q}''\} = \{M_1^{-1} \boldsymbol{q}', M_2^{-1} \boldsymbol{q}''\}$.

kNN($\cdot$) can preserve the inner product of two vectors as $\hat{p} \cdot \hat{q} = \hat{p}' \cdot \hat{q}' + \hat{p}'' \cdot \hat{q}'' = \boldsymbol{p} \cdot \boldsymbol{q}$. After such a series of splitting and encryption, the cloud server and vicious users cannot obtain neither the data vector or the query vector by analyzing the ciphertext without the secret key.

3 The Framework of SMRS

In this section, we present the framework of our proposed scheme. We first introduce the main idea of our scheme and then present the scheme construction. Finally, we analyze the security of the scheme.

3.1 Main Idea

Our main idea is to realize a secure and semantic multi-keyword ranked search scheme over encrypted data (SMRS). We aim at designing a relevance ranking scheme that considers both the term co-occurrence and the keyword weight. In particular, we design a term co-occurrence matrix based on the distance of keywords which is used to quantize the semantic relation of keywords in a document. The dimension of the square co-occurrence matrix is the same as the number of keywords in the dataset. Each element in the term co-occurrence matrix represents the predefined distance of every two keywords in a document. Specifically, the keywords are more correlative to each other if they are closer in a document. In addition, we adopt the wildly-used TF-IDF measurement to represent the keyword weight. The keywords with high TF-IDF values have larger weight when calculating the relevance score. Meanwhile, our scheme can resist attacks from the untrusted third parties and protect the data privacy by adopting the secure kNN algorithm to protect the indexes and query. Moreover, we introduce some randomness in the encryption process to disturb the frequency distribution. As for the term co-occurrence matrix, we add some dummy elements into it to hide the co-occurrence distribution of keywords. In addition, we conduction a pseudo-random permutation function to further protect the privacy.

In this subsection, we list the main steps of our scheme. We will introduce the key idea of index generation, query vector generation and the search algorithm.

(1) Index Generation. The index generation process includes the generation of TF vector, IDF vector and term co-occurrence matrix.

Let $D = \{d_t\}_{(1 \leq t \leq N)}$ be the data set. $W = \{w_i\}_{1 \leq i \leq m}$ is the keyword set extracted from D. For each d_t in D, the scheme generates a TF vector $\boldsymbol{F}_t$ as $\boldsymbol{F}_t = (TF_{1,t}, TF_{2,t}, ...TF_{m,t})$. Each element $TF_{i,t}$ in $\boldsymbol{F}_t$ represents the formalized frequency of keyword w_i in document d_t. If the keywords w_i exists in d_t, the value of $TF_{i,t}$ is calculated as Eq. (1). On the contrary, if w_i does not exist in d_t, $TF_{i,t}$ is set as 0.

For the dataset D, the scheme also generates a IDF vector $\boldsymbol{R} = (IDF_1, IDF_2, \ldots IDF_m)$. The elements in $\boldsymbol{R}$ represent the formalized inverse document frequency of the keywords in the dataset, which is calculated as Eq. (2). After that, the algorithm extends $\boldsymbol{R}$ into a diagonal IDF matrix C, i.e., $C = diag(c_{11}, c_{22}, \ldots, c_{mm})$, in which $C(i, i) = \boldsymbol{R}[i]$.

The distance of two keywords in a document can reflect their correlation to a large extent. Therefore, we construct the co-occurrence matrix based on the distance between keywords. Let w_i and w_j be two keywords in document d_t. Note that they are likely to appear more than once in d_t, we only take the shortest distance between them into account since it can mainly represent the relation of keywords. In our scheme, the distance between w_i and w_j, which is denotes as $h_{(i-j),d_t}$, refers to the number of words between them. In particular, if w_i and w_j do not exist in d_t simultaneously, $h_{(i-j),d_t} = \infty$. In the actual calculation, $h_{(i-j),d_t}$ is set as the total number of the keywords in d_t on this occasion.

Note that smaller distance between two keywords means closer correlation, to achieve a directly proportional relationship between the co-occurrence relevance score and ranking order, we calculate the standardized distance $H_{(i-j),d_t}$ of w_a and w_j as

$$H_{(i-j),d_t} = \frac{\eta}{\eta + h_{(i-j),d_t}},$$

where $h_{(i-j),d_t}$ is the distance between w_i and w_j, η is a regulation parameter. For each document d_t, the scheme generates a matrix $S_t \in R^{m \times m}$ as:

$$S_t = \begin{bmatrix} S_t(1,1) & S_t(1,2) & \ldots & S_t(1,m) \\ S_t(2,1) & S_t(2,2) & \ldots & S_t(2,m) \\ \vdots & \vdots & & \vdots \\ S_t(m,1) & S_t(m,2) & \ldots & S_t(m,m) \end{bmatrix}$$

where $S_t(i, j)$ represents the co-occurrence degree of w_i and w_j. $S_t(i, j)$ is generated as:

$$S_t(i,j) = \begin{cases} H_{(i-j),d_t}, & if\, i \neq j \\ 0, & otherwise. \end{cases}$$

Finally, we obtain the index set I of keyword set W which consists of the TF vector $\boldsymbol{F}_t (1 \leq t \leq N)$, the co-occurrence matrix $S_t (1 \leq t \leq N)$ for each document d_t in D and an IDF vector $\boldsymbol{R}$ for the whole dataset D.

(2) Query Generation. Suppose that the query keyword set the user inputs is W_q. The query vector $\boldsymbol{Q}$ which is generated with the query keywords W_q is a m-dimension binary vector. Each element in $\boldsymbol{Q}$ represents whether the corresponding keyword exists in the query keyword set. If the keyword $w_q \in W_q$, then, the correspondent position of $\boldsymbol{Q}$ (i.e., $\boldsymbol{Q}(q)$) is set to be 1, otherwise (i.e., $w_q \notin W_q$), $\boldsymbol{Q}(q) = 0$.

(3) Search Algorithm. As mentioned above, the final index set includes vector $\boldsymbol{F}_t$, $\boldsymbol{R}$ and matrix S_t, in which each element corresponds to a keywords in the data set. The query $\boldsymbol{Q}$ is a binary vector that the corresponding positions of query keywords are set as 1. The algorithm scans the dataset and calculate the relevance score for each d_t. Let $Rvc(d_t, q)$ be the relevance score between the query q and document d_t. $Rvc(d_t, q)$ can be calculated as $Rvc(d_t, q) = \boldsymbol{F}_t \cdot C \cdot (\boldsymbol{Q})^T + (\boldsymbol{Q})^T \cdot S_t \cdot \boldsymbol{Q}$.

3.2   Scheme Construction

In this section, we introduce the construction of our scheme. We will present details of the scheme with privacy protection mechanisms. Our basic scheme contains four main algorithms. The details are as follows:

- **KeyGen($\cdot$).** Given a secure parameter κ, the algorithm outputs the secure key set $SK = \{M_1, M_2, G_1, G_2, Z, spk, ssk\}$, where M_1, M_2, G_1, G_2, Z are $(m + m') \times (m + m')$ random invertible matrices, spk is a $(m + m')$ random binary vector and ssk is a symmetric encryption key.
- **IndexBuild($\cdot$).** The algorithm extracts the keywords set $W = \{w_1, w_2, \ldots, w_m\}$ from the data set D. For each document d_t in D, the algorithm generates a TF vector $\boldsymbol{F}_t$, an extended diagonal IDF matrix C and a co-occurrence matrix $S_t(C, S_t \in R^{m \times m})$. Then the algorithm extends the vectors $\boldsymbol{F}_t$ into $(m + m')$-dimensional vectors, where the extended elements are set as random numbers. The algorithm also extends matrix C and S_t into $(m + m') \times (m + m')$ matrices, the additional elements in which are also set as random numbers. The algorithm then uses a pseudo-random permutation (SPRP) function $\pi(\cdot)$ with the secret key pk to permute the elements in the vector and matrices.

  After that, the algorithm splits $\boldsymbol{F}_t$ into two vectors in the following way: for each element $\boldsymbol{F}_t(i)$ in $\boldsymbol{F}_t$, if $spk(i) = 1$, $\boldsymbol{F}_t(i)'$ and $\boldsymbol{F}_t(i)''$ are set randomly under the premise that $\boldsymbol{F}_t(i)' + \boldsymbol{F}_t(i)'' = \boldsymbol{F}_t(i)$; If $spk(i) = 0$, $\boldsymbol{F}_t(i)' = \boldsymbol{F}_t(i)'' = \boldsymbol{F}_t(i)$. Then the algorithm encrypts $\{\boldsymbol{F}_t', \boldsymbol{F}_t''\}$ into $\{\hat{F}_t', \hat{F}_t''\} = \{\boldsymbol{F}_t' M_1, \boldsymbol{F}_t'' M_2\}$.

  The secure kNN algorithm is used to preserve the inner product of two vectors. Here we extend the algorithm to support vector-matrix multiplication. Note that C is a diagonal matrix, let $C(j)$ be the j-th column of C. As for each $C(j)$, the algorithm splits it into $\{C(j)', C(j)''\}$ under spk just following the same rule as $\boldsymbol{F}$. Thus the algorithm generates two matrices $\{C', C''\}$. After that, the algorithm encrypts it as $\{\hat{C}', \hat{C}''\} = \{M_1^{-1}C'Z, M_2^{-1}C''Z\}$. In the same way, the algorithm splits the co-occurrence matrix S_t to generate $\{S_t', S_t''\}$ and then encrypts it into $\{\hat{S}_t', \hat{S}_t''\} = \{M_1^{-1}S_t'G_1, M_2^{-1}S_t''G_2\}$. Finally, we get the secure index as $\hat{I} = \{\{\hat{F}_t', \hat{F}_t''\}, \{\hat{C}', \hat{C}''\}, \{\hat{S}_t', \hat{S}_t''\}\}$.
- **TrapdoorGen($\cdot$).** With the query keywords W_q, the algorithm generates the query vector $\boldsymbol{Q}$, where each dimension of $\boldsymbol{Q}$ represents whether the keyword exists in the query keyword set W_q. Then the algorithm extends $\boldsymbol{Q}$ into a $(m + m')$-dimensional vector, in which some of the extended elements are set as 1 and others are set as 0. The vector is then permuted by $\pi(pk)$.

Subsequently, Q is split into two vectors $\{Q', Q''\}$ in such a way: for each element $Q(i)$ in Q, if $spk(i) = 1$, $Q(i)' = Q(i)'' = Q(i)$; If $spk(i) = 0$, $Q(i)'$ and $Q(i)''$ are set randomly under the premise that $Q(i)' + Q(i)'' = Q(i)$. After that, the query Q is encrypted into $\hat{Q} = \{Z^{-1}Q, G_1^{-1}Q, G_2^{-1}Q, M_1 Q', M_2 Q''\}$.

- **Search**($\cdot$). With the secure index $\hat{I}$ and trapdoor $\hat{Q}$, the algorithm scans each index $\hat{I}_t \in \hat{I}$ and calculates the relevance score between them in ciphertext form. The algorithm calculates the TF-IDF relevance score first as:

$$
\begin{aligned}
\phi(\hat{I}_t, &\hat{Q}) \\
&= F_t{}' M_1 \cdot M_1^{-1} C' Z \cdot Z^{-1} Q + \\
&\qquad F_t{}'' M_2 \cdot M_2^{-1} C'' Z \cdot Z^{-1} Q \\
&= F_t{}' C' Q + F_t{}'' C'' Q \\
&= F_t \cdot C \cdot Q.
\end{aligned}
$$

After that, the algorithm calculates the term co-occurrence relevance score similarly as:

$$
\begin{aligned}
\varphi(\hat{I}_t, &\hat{Q}) \\
&= (M_1{}^T Q')^T \cdot M_1^{-1} S_t' G_1 \cdot G_1^{-1} Q + \\
&\qquad (M_2{}^T Q'')^T \cdot M_2^{-1} S_t'' G_2 \cdot G_2^{-1} Q \\
&= (Q')^T \cdot S_t' \cdot Q + (Q'')^T \cdot S_t'' \cdot Q \\
&= Q^T \cdot S_t \cdot Q.
\end{aligned}
$$

The final relevance score over encrypted index and query is calculated as:

$$
\hat{R}vc(\hat{I}_t, \hat{Q}) = \alpha \phi(\hat{I}_t, \hat{Q}) + \beta \varphi(\hat{I}_t, \hat{Q}) \propto Rvc(d_t, q) + \sum \sigma_i,
$$

where α and β are regulation parameters which is used to balance the keyword weight factor and term co-occurrence factor. $\sum \sigma_i$ is the sum of the dummy components and i represent the position where $Q(m + i) = 1$.

3.3   Security Analysis

In this section, we investigate the security analysis of our scheme from three aspects proposed in the threat model.

(1) *Data Set and Indexes Privacy.* In our scheme, the original data set D is encrypted by a standard symmetric encryption algorithm which can properly protect the privacy of the original dataset. The indexes and query in our scheme are split and encrypted by the secure kNN algorithm. The cloud server is unable to infer the original indexes and query without the key set *SK*. According to [16], the attackers cannot calculate the matrices in *SK* which are Gaussian random matrices with the statistic background information. Moreover, the random numbers added in the vectors and matrices further protect the indexes. Thus, the data set and indexes can be properly protected in the known background model.

(2) *Trapdoor Privacy.* The query is encrypted by kNN algorithm which is proved to be secure. The query is split randomly with the key *spk* in *SK*. Note that if $spk(i) = 0$, $\boldsymbol{Q}(i)'$ and $\boldsymbol{Q}(i)''$ are set randomly as long as $\boldsymbol{Q}(i)' + \boldsymbol{Q}(i)'' = \boldsymbol{Q}(i)$, the split operation is random so that even queries with the same keywords can be encrypted into different trapdoors. In addition, the trapdoor is protected better by adding the random numbers, which can ensure that the query vectors and the relevance scores are different even with the same queries. Thus, the trapdoor unlinkability can be well protected.

(3) *Keywords Privacy.* In our scheme, the indexes and query are protected effectively and the search process leaks no information about the keywords. In the known background model, the cloud server have more background knowledge about the keywords, such as the frequency of keywords. In SMRS, the randomness $\sum \sigma_i$ can disturb the distribution of term frequency, which is proved in Ref. [17]. It means that both the values and the frequency distribution of keywords can be well protected in the known background model.

In summary, SMRS can protect the privacy of indexes, trapdoors and the keywords during the interactive process between the user and untrusted cloud server. The scheme is secure under the known background model since it can properly resist the attacks from the untrusted third parties with certain background information.

Table 1. Comparison of the schemes

	Wang's	Cao's	Fu's	Our scheme
Multi-keyword	No	Yes	Yes	Yes
Ranked	Yes	Yes	Yes	Yes
keyword weight	No	No	Yes	Yes
term co-occurrence	No	No	No	Yes

4   Performance Evaluation

In this section, we evaluate the performance of our proposed scheme using C language. The implementation platform is a Windows10 machine with two Intel CPU cores both running at 3.30 GHz. We conduct the evaluation over real data set. The data set is an ACM publication database. We use approximately 2000 documents in the dataset and extract about 20000 keywords from these documents. We evaluate our proposed scheme from three aspect: the functionality comparison with other schemes, the search precision and the search efficiency of our proposed scheme.

4.1 Functionality Comparison

We compare the performance of functionality strength of our proposed scheme with Wang's scheme [14], Cao's scheme [2] and Fu's scheme [6] from several aspects. The comparison among the schemes is shown in Table 1.

As mentioned above, our scheme can support multi-keyword ranked search and considers both the keyword weight and semantic correlation of the keywords. Comparing to the previously proposed typical schemes, our scheme can realize greater flexibility than other schemes in practical application.

4.2 Precision

We mainly analysis the precision of our scheme in this section. The precision we refer to here indicates whether the users obtain the search results that meet with their desire. In theory, it is most likely to retrieval all the results that are satisfy users' desire on account of the construction of the term co-occurrence matrix. The index set of our scheme includes the keyword weight and term co-occurrence factor, which is commendable to represent the semantic relationship among keywords. Compared with the schemes that only consider the keyword weight, our scheme can rank the items in a more proper way. The items containing the query keywords and have similar semantic meaning with users' intention will be ranked ahead. on the contrary, the files which contain the query keywords but unmatch the users' desire will be ranked backward. In addition, the variable regulation parameters are used in our scheme to adjust the weight of two factors in practical application. It is reasonable that our search scheme can realize high precision.

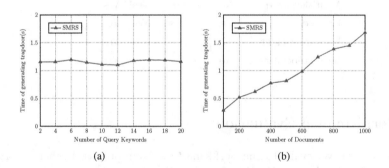

Fig. 2. Time of generating trapdoor: (a) For different number of query keywords with the same number of documents in the dataset (500); (b) For different number of documents with the same number of query keywords (10).

4.3 Efficiency

We investigate the efficiency of our scheme through evaluating the trapdoor generating time cost of data user and the search time in the cloud server side.

Trapdoor Generation. The generation of trapdoor includes generating the query vector and encrypting the vector. We evaluate the efficiency of the trapdoor generation from two aspects. In general, the number of keywords utilized by users for a search process is usually no more than 20. We can see from Fig. 2(a) that the time cost of generating trapdoor is hardly influenced by the number of query keywords. However, Fig. 2(b) shows that the trapdoor generating time increases linearly with the increasing number of documents in the dataset. It is because that the dimension of query vector is related to the size of dataset.

Search Efficiency. The search process is calculating the inner product of the query and each documents in the dataset, which is executed by the cloud server. Figure 3(a) shows the time cost of searching increases linearly with the number of documents in the dataset. This is because the cloud server should scan the documents in the dataset, calculate the relevance score between the query and each document and finally select the results. Therefore, the search time is proportional to the quantity of documents. Moreover, the search time is scarcely affected by the query keywords, as shown in Fig. 3(b). We can see that the search time is practically efficient.

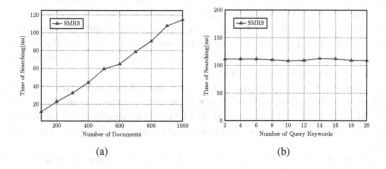

(a)   (b)

Fig. 3. Time of searching: (a) For different number of documents with the same size of query keywords (10); (b) For different number of query keywords with the same number of documents in the dataset (500).

5   Conclusion

In this paper, we propose a searchable encryption scheme that realizes term-occurrence matrix based semantic multi-keyword ranked search over encrypted data. We consider both the semantic correlation of keywords and the keyword weight. We design a distance-based term co-occurrence matrix to measure the semantic relation of keywords and adopt the TF-IDF rule to represent the keyword weight. Compared with the existing semantic searchable encryption schemes, our scheme can return items that are closer to the users' intention. To protect the privacy, we adopt the secure kNN algorithm to encrypt the indexes and queries. The performance evaluation shows that our scheme achieves high search accuracy and practical search efficiency.

Acknowledgment. This work is supported by the National Natural Science Foundation of China (No. 61672195, 61379144, 61572026), Foundation of Science and Technology on Information Assurance Laboratory (No. KJ-15-001).

References

1. Bullinaria, J.A., Levy, J.P.: Extracting semantic representations from word co-occurrence statistics: a computational study. Behav. Res. Methods **39**(3), 510–526 (2007)
2. Cao, N., Wang, C., Li, M., Ren, K., Lou, W.: Privacy-preserving multi-keyword ranked search over encrypted cloud data. IEEE Trans. Parallel Distrib. Syst. **25**(1), 222–233 (2011)
3. Curtmola, R., Garay, J., Kamara, S., Ostrovsky, R.: Searchable symmetric encryption: improved definitions and efficient constructions. In: Proceedings of CCS 2006, pp. 79–88. ACM (2006)
4. Figueiredo, F., et al.: Word co-occurrence features for text classification. Inf. Syst. **36**(5), 843–858 (2011)
5. Firth, J., Halliday, M., Allen, W., Robins, R., Palmer, F., Mitchell, T.: Studies in Linguistic Analysis. Blackwell, Oxford (1962)
6. Fu, Z., Huang, F., Sun, X., Vasilakos, A., Yang, C.N.: Enabling semantic search based on conceptual graphs over encrypted outsourced data **PP**(99), 1 (1939)
7. Fu, Z., Shu, J., Sun, X., Zhang, D.: Semantic keyword search based on trie over encrypted cloud data. ACM (2014)
8. Fu, Z., Wu, X., Guan, C., Sun, X., Ren, K.: Toward efficient multi-keyword fuzzy search over encrypted outsourced data with accuracy improvement **11**(12), 1 (2016)
9. Kuzu, M., Islam, M.S., Kantarcioglu, M.: Efficient similarity search over encrypted data. In: IEEE International Conference on Data Engineering, pp. 1156–1167 (2012)
10. Li, J., Wang, Q., Wang, C., Cao, N., Ren, K., Lou, W.: Fuzzy keyword search over encrypted data in cloud computing. In: Conference on Information Communications, pp. 441–445 (2010)
11. Matsuo, Y., Ishizuka, M.: Keyword extraction from a single document using word co-occurrence statistical information. Int. J. Artif. Intell. Tools **13**(01), 157–169 (2004)
12. Song, D., Wagner, D., Perrig, A.: Practical techniques for searches on encrypted data. In: Proceedings of Symposium on Security and Privacy, pp. 44–55. IEEE (2000)
13. Sun, W., et al.: Privacy-preserving multi-keyword text search in the cloud supporting similarity-based ranking. In: ACM SIGSAC Symposium on Information, Computer and Communications Security, pp. 71–82 (2013)
14. Wang, C., Cao, N., Li, J., Ren, K., Lou, W.: Secure ranked keyword search over encrypted cloud data. In: International Conference on Distributed Computing Systems, ICDCS, pp. 253–262 (2010)
15. Wang, C., Ren, K., Yu, S., Urs, K.M.R.: Achieving usable and privacy-assured similarity search over outsourced cloud data. In: Proceedings of INFOCOM 2012, pp. 451–459. IEEE (2012)

16. Wong, W.K., Cheung, D.W., Kao, B., Mamoulis, N.: Secure kNN computation on encrypted databases. In: Proceedings of SIGMOD 2009, pp. 139–152 (2009)
17. Xia, Z., Wang, X., Sun, X., Wang, Q.: A secure and dynamic multi-keyword ranked search scheme over encrypted cloud data. IEEE Trans. Parallel Distrib. Syst. **27**(2), 340–352 (2016)

A Cooperative Spectrum Sensing Method Based on Clustering Algorithm and Signal Feature

Shunchao Zhang[1], Yonghua Wang[1,2(✉)], Pin Wan[1],
Yongwei Zhang[1], and Xingcheng Li[1]

[1] School of Automation, Guangdong University of Technology,
Guangzhou 510006, China
gdut_zsc630@163.com, sjzwyh@163.com, wanpin2@163.com,
gdut_zyw@163.com, 770829826@qq.com
[2] Key Laboratory of Machine Intelligence and Advanced Computing,
Ministry of Education, Sun Yat-Sen University, Guangzhou 510006, China

Abstract. To solve the problem that the threshold is difficult to calculate in the spectrum sensing method of random matrix, this paper proposes a spectrum sensing method based on the combination of clustering algorithm and signal features. At the same time, in order to improve the performance of feature estimation and the detection performance under the condition of small number of cooperative users, a concept based on stochastic matrix splitting and reorganization is introduced to logically increase the number of cooperative users. In order to further obtain the information from the signal matrix and improve the feature accuracy, the signal perceived by each secondary user (SU) is decomposed into I and Q (IQ) components. Firstly, the signal matrix is split and reassembled and IQ decomposed. Then the covariance matrices of split matrix and matrix after IQ decomposition are calculated respectively and the corresponding eigenvalues are obtained. Then, the features are formed into a feature vector. Finally, the algorithm classifies these feature vector. The simulation experiments under different signal characteristics and different clustering algorithms show that the proposed method can effectively improve the performance of spectrum sensing.

Keywords: Spectrum sensing · Splitting and reorganization
Clustering algorithm · IQ decomposition · Feature extraction

1 Introduction

In recent years, the application of stochastic matrix theory to spectrum sensing has aroused many interest of researchers. The spectrum sensing method based on stochastic matrix obtains the matrix of sampled signals by obtaining the perceived data of multiple SUs, and then calculates the covariance matrix to obtain the corresponding eigenvalues as the decision statistic [1, 2]. Many cooperative sensing algorithms based on random matrices have been proposed, including the difference between the maximum eigenvalue and the average energy value (MSE) algorithm, the maximum and

© Springer Nature Switzerland AG 2018
X. Sun et al. (Eds.): ICCCS 2018, LNCS 11063, pp. 50–62, 2018.
https://doi.org/10.1007/978-3-030-00006-6_5

minimum eigenvalue ratio (MME) algorithm, the difference between the maximum eigenvalue and the minimum eigenvalue (DMM) algorithm and the maximum eigenvalue and trace ratio (RMET) algorithm [3–6]. However, these algorithms do not perform well under the condition of fewer cooperating users. Hu et al. in order to solve the problem of less cooperative users and low channel ratio spectrum sensing performance, the matrix split and recombination process is introduced, which can be divided into sequential split reassembly and interval split reassembly according to the split mode, so as to logically increase The number of collaborative SUs [7]. The spectrum sensing methods based on stochastic matrix all have the problem of threshold derivation complexity and the problem of storing threshold precision.

Due to the development and progress of machine learning, the research on the application of machine learning to the direction of spectrum sensing has become a hot topic. Spectrum sensing can be considered as a dichotomous problem, that is, the existence and non-existence of the primary user. Kumar, Kandpal et al. studied the spectrum sensing using K-means clustering algorithm in machine learning. The method takes the signal energy value as the feature, and then classifies the features into available class and unavailable class to Achieve Spectrum Sensing [8]. Thilina et al. studied the spectrum sensing using unsupervised K-means, Gaussian mixture models (GMM) and neural networks, and support vector machines in supervised learning [9]. Xue et al. used the spectrum sensing method combining the support vector machine with the maximum and minimum eigenvalues of the signal covariance matrix [10]. Sobabe et al. proposed a cooperative spectrum sensing algorithm based on unsupervised learning. K-means clustering and GMM were selected as the unsupervised learning framework respectively. The leading eigenvalues and the maximum and minimum eigenvalue combinations are the eigenvectors for training the classifier [11]. Zhang et al. proposed a spectrum sensing method based on clustering algorithm combined with eigenvalues, which decomposed the sampled signal matrix in feature extraction to obtain the signal feature information of the sampled signal matrix more likely [12].

In this paper, we propose a spectrum sensing method combining clustering algorithm with eigenvalues in a random matrix. K-means and K-mediods algorithm will be used as the learning framework of the clustering algorithm in this paper. In the eigenvector extraction process, three new matrices are obtained by introducing sequential disassembly and reassembly, interval reassembly and reassembly, and IQ decomposition. Then the covariance matrices of matrices are calculated and then the corresponding eigenvalues are calculated respectively to form a three-dimensional Feature vector. Finally, the feature vectors are used to train the classifiers. Compared with the energy feature vector, the feature vector extracted by this method can more accurately represent the signal characteristics. The proposed spectrum sensing technique does not require any prior information about the communication system, and unlabeled training data is more readily available. In the experiment, we further analyze the spectrum sensing performance of MSE, MME, DMM and RMET under the same clustering algorithm and the spectrum sensing performance of the same eigenvalue under different clustering algorithms. Simulation results show that this method has good spectrum sensing performance.

2 System Model

In a cognitive radio network (CRN), a SU spectrum sensing technology is relatively mature and easy to implement. However, in view of the impact on the PU in the process of the fading, shadow, and noise instability of the surrounding path, the perceived performance of the SU will be degraded, and it is difficult to satisfy the demand. In order to improve the perceived performance of the system, using cooperative spectrum sensing (CSS) technology, each SU in the CRN needs to transmit the sensed data to the fusion center (FC) and finally make the judgment by the FC.

Suppose there is a PU and a number M of SUs in the CRN and that the number of sampling points per SU is N. In the case of centralized CSS, a FC receives the sensing data of this SUs and then determines whether the PU exists. Suppose H_0 indicates that the PU does not exist and that H_1 indicates that the PU exists. Therefore, under the two assumptions, the model of the received signal can be expressed by Eq. 1.

$$x_i(n) = \begin{cases} w_i(n), & H_0 \\ s_i(n) + w_i(n), & H_1 \end{cases} \tag{1}$$

where $s_i(n)$ denotes the PU signal and $w_i(n)$ denotes the Gaussian white noise with mean of 0 and variance of σ^2. The channel availability A can be defined as:

$$A = \begin{cases} 0, & H_1 \\ 1, & H_0 \end{cases} \tag{2}$$

where $A = 0$ means the channel cannot be used and $A = 1$ means the channel can be used. The system's false alarm probability (P_f) and detection (P_d) probability can be defined as:

$$\begin{aligned} P_f &= P[A = 0 | A = 1] \\ P_d &= P[A = 0 | A = 0] \end{aligned} \tag{3}$$

3 Feature Extraction

Assuming $x_i = [x_i(1) x_i(2), \ldots, x_i(N)]$ represents the sampling vector of the i-th SU user, the perceptual matrix in a perceptual time period can be expressed as:

$$X = \begin{bmatrix} x_1(1) & x_1(2) & \cdots & x_1(N) \\ x_2(1) & x_2(2) & \cdots & x_2(N) \\ \vdots & \vdots & \ddots & \vdots \\ x_M(1) & x_M(2) & \cdots & x_M(N) \end{bmatrix} \tag{4}$$

Denote with N the number of samples. Therefore, the signal covariance matrix can be expressed as $R_X(N) = \frac{1}{N} XX^T$. To obtain the signal characteristics more accurately, we introduced the decomposition methods of signal matrix O-DAR and IQ decomposition, and simultaneously performed Order-DAR (O-DAR), Interval-DAR (I-DAR) [7] and IQ decomposition on the signal matrix [13]. This algorithm not only logically increases the number of collaborative users, and the feature information of the sampled signal can be further accurately acquired. The specific algorithm is as follows [7]:

In the O-DAR process, $x_{i(i=1,2,3,...,M)}$ is divided into $q(q > 0)$ segments in order of $s = N/q$ long sub-signal vectors, then $x_i(i = 1, 2, 3, ..., M)$ is split into the following form:

$$x_i \begin{cases} x_{i1} = [x_i(1) \, x_i(2) \, \cdots \, x_i(s)] \\ x_{i2} = [x_i(s+1) \, x_i(s+2) \, \cdots \, (2s)] \\ \vdots \\ x_{iq} = [x_i((q-1)s+1) \, x_i((q-1)s+2) \, \cdots \, x_i(qs)] \end{cases} \quad (5)$$

The signal vector obtained by sampling each SU is split according to the above formula. After the entire signal matrix is divided, a signal matrix Y_1 of $(qM) \times s$ dimensional can be obtained.

$$Y_1 = \begin{bmatrix} x_{11} \\ \vdots \\ x_{1q} \\ \vdots \\ x_{im} \\ \vdots \\ x_{Mq} \end{bmatrix} = \begin{bmatrix} x_1(1) & x_1(2) & \cdots & x_1(s) \\ \vdots & & & \\ x_1((q-1)s+1) & x_1((q-1)s+1) & \cdots & x_1(qs) \\ \vdots & & & \\ x_i((m-1)s+1) & x_i((m-1)s+2) & \cdots & x_i(ms) \\ \vdots & & & \\ x_M((q-1)s+1) & x_M((q-1)s+2) & \cdots & x_M(qs) \end{bmatrix} \quad (6)$$

Different from the disassembly method of the O-DAR process, the I-DAR process uses interval sampling and splitting, resamples the sampling signal every $q-1$ units, and then the signal matrix is reorganized.

According to the splitting method, the sampled data can be split into sub-signal vectors of $(q > 0)s = N/q$ long, then $x_{i(i=1,2,3,...,M)}$ can be split into the following form:

$$x_i \begin{cases} x_{i1} = [x_i(1) \quad x_i(q+1) \quad \cdots \quad x_i((s-1)q+1)] \\ x_{12} = [x_i(2) \quad x_i(q+2) \quad \cdots \quad x_i((s-1)q+2)] \\ \vdots \\ x_{iq} = [x_i(q) \quad x_i(q+q) \quad \cdots \quad x_i((s-1)q+q)] \end{cases} \quad (7)$$

After reconstructing each signal vector after I-DAR, a $(qM) \times s$ dimensional signal matrix Y_2 can be obtained.

$$Y_2 = \begin{bmatrix} x_{11} \\ \vdots \\ x_{1q} \\ \vdots \\ x_{im} \\ \vdots \\ x_{Mq} \end{bmatrix} = \begin{bmatrix} x_1(1) & x_1(q+1) & \cdots & x_1((s-1)q+1) \\ \vdots & & & \\ x_1(q) & x_1(q+q) & \cdots & x_1((s-1)q+q) \\ \vdots & & & \\ x_i(m) & x_i(q+m) & \cdots & x_i((s-1)q+m) \\ \vdots & & & \\ x_M(q) & x_M(q+q) & \cdots & x_M((s-1)q+q) \end{bmatrix} \qquad (8)$$

In the IQ decomposition process, $x_{i(i=1,2,3,\ldots,M)}$ is decomposed into x_i^I and x_i^Q vectors. The specific algorithm is as follows [13]:

$$\begin{aligned} x_i^I &= x_i \sin\left(\frac{2\pi f_c n}{f_s}\right) & n = 1,2,\ldots,N \\ x_i^Q &= x_i \cos\left(\frac{2\pi f_c n}{f_s}\right) & n = 1,2,\ldots,N \end{aligned} \qquad (9)$$

Where f_c is the carrier frequency and f_s is the sampling frequency. After IQ decomposition, get a $2M \times N$ matrix, the matrix is as follows:

$$Y_3^{IQ} = \begin{bmatrix} x_1^I \\ x_1^Q \\ \vdots \\ \vdots \\ x_M^I \\ x_M^Q \end{bmatrix} = \begin{bmatrix} x_1^I(1) & x_1^I(2) & \cdots & x_1^I(N) \\ x_1^Q(1) & x_1^Q(2) & \cdots & x_1^Q(N) \\ \vdots & \vdots & & \vdots \\ \vdots & \vdots & & \vdots \\ x_M^I(1) & x_M^I(2) & \cdots & x_M^I(N) \\ x_M^Q(1) & x_M^Q(2) & \cdots & x_M^Q(N) \end{bmatrix} \qquad (10)$$

After O-DAR, I-DAR and IQ decomposition, three new matrices Y_1, Y_2 and Y_3^{IQ} will be obtained. Then calculate the corresponding covariance matrix $R_{Y_2} = \frac{1}{s}Y_2Y_2^T$ $R_{Y_2} = \frac{1}{s}Y_2Y_2^T$ and $R_{Y_3^{IQ}} = \frac{1}{N}Y_3^{IQ}(Y_3^{IQ})^T$. The trace of the covariance matrix $R_g, g \in \{Y_1, Y_2, Y_3^{IQ}\}$ is $tr(R_g)$, the maximum eigenvalue is λ_{max}, and the minimum eigenvalue is λ_{min}. Therefore T_{MSE} is characterized by:

$$T_{MSE} = \lambda_{max} - \frac{1}{bM}\sum_{u=1}^{bM} \lambda_u \quad b \in \{q,2\} \qquad (11)$$

T_{MME} is characterized by:

$$T_{MME} = \lambda_{max}/\lambda_{min} \qquad (12)$$

T_{DMM} is characterized by:

$$T_{DMM} = \lambda_{max} - \lambda_{min} \tag{13}$$

T_{RMET} is characterized by:

$$T_{RMET} = \lambda_{max}/tr(R_g) \tag{14}$$

In the conventional spectrum sensing method based on a stochastic matrix, the T_{MSE}, T_{MME}, T_{DMM} or T_{RMET} is used as characteristic of the signal. A suitable feature is selected in the derivation of the corresponding threshold for judgment. These methods all have the problem of threshold accuracy. To solve this problem, we introduce a clustering algorithm in machine learning, which can effectively solve the threshold precision and the threshold derivation problems. The eigenvalues $T_{1,z}$, $T_{2,z}$ and $T_{3,z}$, $z \in \{MSE, MME, DMM, RMET\}$ corresponding to each covariance matrix are calculated, and finally a three-dimensional eigenvector $T_z = [T_{1,z}, T_{2,z}, T_{3,z}]^T$ is obtained for representing the signal feature.

4   Cooperative Spectrum Sensing Based on Feature and Clustering Algorithm

In this section, we will use two clustering algorithm to produce the classification of feature vectors. First, we need to prepare a sufficient number of training feature vectors $\overline{T}$:

$$\overline{T} = \{T_z^1, T_z^2, \ldots, T_z^L\} \tag{15}$$

where T_z^l is a three-dimensional vector and L is the number of training feature vectors. The clustering algorithm separates the unlabeled training feature vectors into K non-overlapping clusters. Let C_k denote the set of training feature vectors belonging to cluster k, with $k = 1, 2, \ldots, K$.

$$C_k = \{T_z^l | T_z^l \in \text{Cluster } k \, \forall l\} \tag{16}$$

Cluster C_k has a centroid ψ_k.

4.1   Cooperative Spectrum Sensing Based on Feature and K-means Clustering Algorithm

Unlike the traditional K-means clustering algorithm, the centroid for C_1 is fixed to the mean of T_z conditioned on H_0, because the actual cluster will contain only the noise samples, and the centroid can be fixed offline. Hence, ψ_1 is defined as [9–11]:

$$\psi_1 = E[T_z^l | H_0] \tag{17}$$

Where $E[\cdot]$ denotes the expectation operator. The centroids for all other clusters $k = 2, 3, \ldots, K$ are defined as the arithmetic mean of all the training features in ψ_k as:

$$\psi_k = \frac{1}{n(C_k)} \sum_{T_z^l \in \psi_k} T^l \tag{18}$$

Where $n(.)$ denotes the cardinality. The distortion Φ of the K-means clustering algorithm is defined as the sum of the squared distances between all the points and their corresponding centroids summed over all the clusters K.

$$\Phi(C_1, \ldots, C_k, \psi_1 \ldots, \psi_k) = \sum_{k=1}^{K} \sum_{T_z^l \in \psi_k} \left\| T_z^l - \psi_k \right\|^2 \tag{19}$$

Where $\|\cdot\|^2$ is the ℓ^2-norm. The clustering algorithm tries to minimize Φ. Hence, the optimization objective can be formulated as [9–11]:

$$\min_{\substack{C_1, \ldots, C_k \\ \psi_1 \ldots, \psi_k}} \Phi(C_1, \ldots, C_k, \psi_1 \ldots, \psi_k) \tag{20}$$

After successful training, we can use Eq. 21 to test whether the channel is available.

$$\frac{\left\| \widehat{T} - \psi_1 \right\|}{\min_{k=2,3,\ldots,K} \left\| \widehat{T} - \psi_k \right\|} > \xi \tag{21}$$

Where $\widehat{T}$ stands for data to be classified. If Eq. 10 is satisfied, it indicates that the channel is not available (A = 0), otherwise the channel is available (A = 1). The parameter ξ is used to control the missed detection probability and the false alarm probability when calculating the detection probability in the experiment. The entire training and testing flow chart is as follows Table 1:

Table 1. K-means clustering algorithm for CSS

Algorithm 1. K-means clustering algorithm for CSS	
Input:	Train data: $\overline{T} = \{T_z^1, T_z^1, \ldots, T_z^L\}$, The number of categories: K
Step 1:	Initialize the centroid $(\psi_1, \psi_2, \ldots, \psi_K)$ where ψ_1 is given by Eq. 17
Step 2:	Calculate the distance between each feature T_z^l and each centroid Ψ and return the feature to the nearest class
Step 3:	For the features in class $C_{k=2,3,\ldots,K}$, the mean of all the points in the class is calculated by Eq. 18 and the mean is taken as the centroid $\psi_{k=2,3,\ldots,K}$
Step 4:	If converges then algorithm will stops, otherwise it return the **step 2**
Step 5:	Import the test date $\widehat{T} = \{T_z^1, T_z^1, \ldots, T_z^L\}$
Step 6:	If $\dfrac{\left\| \widehat{T} - \psi_1 \right\|}{\min_{k=2,3,\ldots,K} \left\| \widehat{T} - \psi_k \right\|} > \xi$ **Output:** A = 1, Else **Output:** A = 0

4.2 Cooperative Spectrum Sensing Based on Feature and K-medoids Clustering Algorithm

In this section, the K-medoids clustering algorithm is used to classify the eigenvalues. CSS based on K-medoids clustering algorithm is similar to that of CSS based on K-means clustering algorithm. The difference is that the K-medoids clustering algorithm uses the real feature vector as the center and computes the center with Eqs. 22 and 23.

$$\Psi_1 = \arg\min \sum\nolimits_{T^j|H_0} \left\| T^j - \Psi_1 \right\|^2 \tag{22}$$

$$\Psi_k = \arg\min_{\Psi_k \in C_k} \sum\nolimits_{T^j \in C_k} \left\| T^j - \Psi_k \right\|^2, k = 2, 3, \ldots, K \tag{23}$$

Cooperative spectrum sensing process based on K-medoids clustering algorithm is shown in Table 2:

Table 2. K-medoids clustering algorithm for CSS

Algorithm 1. K-medoids clustering algorithm for CSS	
Input:	Train data: $\overline{T} = \left\{ T_z^1, T_z^1, \ldots, T_z^L \right\}$, The number of categories: K
Step 1:	Initialize the centroid $(\Psi_1, \Psi_2, \ldots, \Psi_K)$, the centroid is really a point in the training data, where Ψ_1 is given by Eq. 22
Step 2:	Calculate the distance between each eigenvector T_z^l and each centroid Ψ, and return the eigenvectors to the nearest classes to form K classes. Among them, the centroid $\Psi_k \in C_k$
Step 3:	For eigenvectors in cluster $C_{k=2,3,\ldots,K}$, $\psi_{k=2,3,\ldots K}$ is updated by Eq. 23
Step 4:	If converges then algorithm will stops, otherwise it return the **step 2**.
Step 5:	Import the test date $\widehat{T} = \left\{ T_z^1, T_z^1, \ldots, T_z^L \right\}$
Step 6:	If $\dfrac{\left\| \widehat{T} - \psi_1 \right\|}{\min_{k=2,3,\ldots,K} \left\| \widehat{T} - \psi_k \right\|} > \xi$ **Output:** A = 1, Else **Output:** A = 0

5 Experiments

We choose the covariance matrix MSE, MME, DMM or RMET as the signal features. The signal used in this experiment is an AM signal, with a carrier frequency of 702 kHz, and a sampling ratio of 4 MHz. The parameter for decomposition and reorganization was $q = 2$. To ensure the accuracy of the experiment, we extracted 2000 signal feature vectors, of which 1000 are training sets, and another 1000 signal feature vectors as a test sets. The number of cooperative SU in Figs. 2, 3 and 4 are $M = 2$. The sampling point for each SU is $N = 1000$.

5.1   Cooperative Spectrum Sensing Based on Feature and K-means Clustering Algorithm

Figure 1 shows the unclassified 1000 feature vectors, of which 500 are noise feature vectors and the rest are signal plus noise feature vectors. Next, we will classify these feature vectors using K-means and K-mediods clustering algorithms.

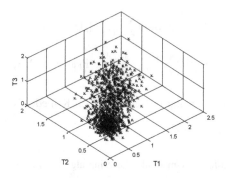

Fig. 1. Unclassified training feature vectors.

Figures 2 and 3 shows the classification of noise feature vectors (blue points) and the signal with noise feature vectors (red points) of MSE feature with SNR = −11 dB from the K-means clustering algorithm and the K-medoids clustering algorithm. The circle is a centroid of noise cluster, the triangle is a centroid of signal and noise cluster.

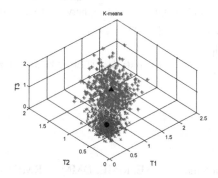

Fig. 2. Classification effect of K-means (Color figure online)

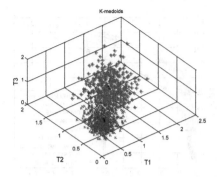

Fig. 3. Classification effect of K-medoids (Color figure online)

5.2 Detection Performance Under Different Clustering Algorithms

Figure 4 shows the performance of K-means clustering algorithm and K-medoids clustering algorithm under different characteristics under SNR = −13 dB. The experimental results show that when the two algorithms do spectrum sensing based on eigenvalues, K-means algorithm in general has a good effect. In the following experiment, the K-means algorithm is chosen as the clustering algorithm in combination with the eigenvalues.

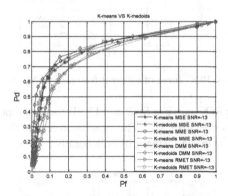

Fig. 4. Classification effect of K-means and K-medoids.

5.3 K-means Clustering Algorithm Under the Detection Performance

Figures 5 and 6 show ROC curves for MSE, MME, DMM, and RMET when SNR = −11 dB and SNR = −13 dB for DAR and IQ, respectively, using a K-means clustering algorithm. Experimental results show that the proposed method has good performance of perception.

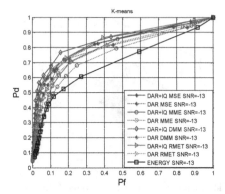

Fig. 5. The ROC curve of different features in SNR = −13 dB.

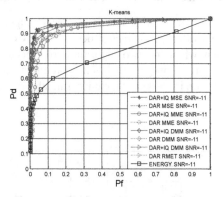

Fig. 6. The ROC curve of different features in SNR = −11 dB.

Figure 7 shows the ROC curve at SNR = −13 dB for the proposed algorithm under a different number of cooperative SUs. The simulation results show that the perceived performance increases with the increase of collaborative users.

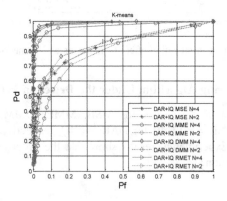

Fig. 7. The ROC curves for different numbers of SUs.

6   Conclusions

In this paper, we propose a spectrum sensing method based on clustering algorithms and features. A feature extraction method based on DAR is proposed to obtain a two-dimensional matrix of features. Then, the K-means clustering algorithm is used to classify the features. In the experimental section, the spectrum sensing performance of the four eigenvalues of MME, MSE, DDM and RMET are analyzed. Experimental results show that the proposed method has a better spectral sensing performance than other methods.

Acknowledgments. This work was supported in part by special funds from the central finance to support the development of local universities under No. 400170044, the project supported by the State Key Laboratory of Management and Control for Complex Systems, Institute of Automation, Chinese Academy of Sciences under grant No. 20180106, the science and technology program of Guangdong Province under grant No. 2016B090918031, the degree and graduate education reform project of Guangdong Province under grant No. 2016JGXM_MS_26, the foundation of key laboratory of machine intelligence and advanced computing of the Ministry of Education under grant No. MSC-201706A and the higher education quality projects of Guangdong Province and Guangdong University of Technology.

References

1. Tulino, A.M.: Random matrix theory and wireless communications. Found. Trends® Commun. Inf. Theory **1**(1), 1–182 (2004)
2. Xiao, L.: Cloud-based malware detection game for mobile devices with offloading. IEEE Trans. Mob. Comput. **16**(10), 2742–2750 (2017)
3. Cao, K.T.: A novel cooperative spectrum sensing algorithm based on the maximum eigenvalue. J. Electron. Inf. Technol. **2**(5), 1367–1372 (2011)
4. Zeng, Y.: Eigenvalue based spectrum sensing algorithms for cognitive radio. IEEE Trans. Commun. **57**(6), 1784–1793 (2008)
5. Wang, Y.X.: DMM based spectrum sensing method for cognitive radio systems. J. Electron. Inf. Technol. **32**(11), 2571–2575 (2010)
6. Ahmed, A., Ahmed, A.S.: Random matrix theory based spectrum sensing for cognitive radio networks. In: Internet Technologies and Applications (ITA), Wrexham, pp. 479–483. IEEE (2015)
7. Hu, W., Zhao, Z.: Cooperative spectrum sensing algorithm based on bistable stochastic resonance. In: 10th International Conference on Wireless Communications, Networking and Mobile Computing, Hangzhou, pp. 126–130. IET (2014)
8. Kumar, V., Kandpal, D.C.: K-mean clustering based cooperative spectrum sensing in generalized κ-μ fading channels. In: 22nd National Conference on Communication (NCC), Guwahati, pp. 1–15. IEEE (2016)
9. Thilina, K.M.: Machine learning techniques for cooperative spectrum sensing in cognitive radio networks. IEEE J. Sel. Areas Commun. **31**(11), 2209–2221 (2013)
10. Xue, H., Gao, F.: A machine learning based spectrum-sensing algorithm using sample covariance matrix. In: 10th International Conference on Communications and Networking in China (ChinaCom), Shanghai, pp. 476–480. IEEE (2015)

11. Sobabe, G.C., Song, Y.: A cooperative spectrum sensing algorithm based on unsupervised learning. In: 10th International Congress on Image and Signal Processing, BioMedical Engineering and Informatics (CISP-BMEI), Shanghai, pp. 1–6. IEEE (2017)
12. Zhang, Y.: A spectrum sensing method based on signal feature and clustering algorithm in cognitive wireless multimedia sensor networks. Adv. Multimed. **2017**(4), 1–10 (2017)
13. Song, Y., Zhou, Y.: An improved spectrum sensing algorithm based on random matrix theory. In: 19th International Conference on Advanced Communication Technology (ICACT), Bongpyeong, pp. 715–720. IEEE (2017)

A Dynamic Network Change Detection Method Using Network Embedding

Tong Sun and Yan Liu[⊠]

China State Key Laboratory of Mathematical Engineering
and Advanced Computing, Zhengzhou, China
ms_liuyan@aliyun.com

Abstract. Dynamic networks are ubiquitous. Detecting dynamic network changes is helpful to understand the network development trend and discover network anomalies in time. It is a research hotspot at present. The structure of the network in the real world is very complex, the current feature learning method is difficult to capture a variety of network connectivity patterns, and the definition of efficient network features requires a large number of neighborhood knowledge and computational costs. In order to overcome this limitation, this paper presents a method of dynamic network change detection using network embedding, which automates the whole process by using feature extraction as a embedding problem, and carries out dynamic network change detection by analyzing the distribution of nodes in space after network embedding processing. We use this method to simulate dynamic network and real dynamic network datasets to prove the validity of this method.

Keywords: Dynamic network · Change detection · Network embedding

1 Introduction

Dynamic network change detection is a hot topic in dynamic network research [1]. In recent years, various industries related to computers and internet have developed rapidly, and the amount of network data has increased exponentially. At present, social networking site Facebook's monthly active user volume of about 2 billion people, shopping sites such as Amazon, Alibaba's monthly order number reached 400 million and 800 million respectively. With the increasing of network scale and the complexity of network structure, the traditional dynamic network change detection method faces many challenges. Traditional dynamic network change detection method is mainly based on the characteristics of network structure, but it is difficult to extract the exact characteristics of network structure in the face of large-scale and complex network data.

Network embedding [2] has caused the widespread research upsurge in recent years, the basic idea is to represent network nodes as low dimension vectors, the network after embedding process no longer exists "edge", which is expressed as isolated points in the space, the distance between nodes in European space reflects the proximity or similarity of nodes. On this basis, many network analysis tasks such as multi-label classification, link prediction, community detection, etc. can be solved more easily [3]. Dynamic networks are often accompanied by the increase and decrease of

© Springer Nature Switzerland AG 2018
X. Sun et al. (Eds.): ICCCS 2018, LNCS 11063, pp. 63–74, 2018.
https://doi.org/10.1007/978-3-030-00006-6_6

nodes and edges in the process of evolution. Our research does not aim at specific nodes and edges, but analyzes the change of the whole network structure. We find that the variation of the distribution of nodes in space after network embedding can correspond to the structural change of the original network to a certain extent. According to this, we propose a dynamic network change detection method based on network embedding.

The contributions of this paper are listed as follows:

- A dynamic network change detection method based on network embedding is designed, which takes network feature extraction as a network embedding problem and detects dynamic network changes by using the degree of separation of nodes in space after network embedding. In this case, we do not need any manually designed features.
- Experiments are carried out on two dynamic network datasets: simulated Small World network and Enron email dataset to verify the effectiveness of the proposed dynamic network change detection method.

The rest of the paper is arranged as follows: Sect. 2 introduces the related work of dynamic network change detection. Section 3 is the related definition and problem analysis of dynamic network change detection. Section 4 introduces the dynamic network change detection model based on network embedding. Section 5 is the experimental part and the 6th section is the summary of the full text.

2 Related Work

Dynamic network change detection can be applied to network anomaly detection, user behavior analysis, link prediction and many other aspects. At present, researchers have put forward many methods to solve this problem. McCulloh et al. [4] proposed to use the method of cumulative sum control chart (CUSUM) to detect the structure parameters of the network in real time, and it could alarm the anomaly when the cumulative sum exceeds the set threshold. The method has been applied in the dynamic network analysis software ORA [5] developed by Carnegie Mellon University. ORA detects the network anomaly from the network parameters such as network density, intermediation and tightness. Wang et al. [6] represent the network structure in the form of adjacency matrix, decompose the matrix into time-dependent matrices and do regression analysis to detect network changes by comparing the difference between the predicted and true values of the elements in the matrix. Neill et al. [7] used the method of scan statistics to detect the difference between the current node attribute value and the historical value and to find the subgraph of abnormal change during the network evolution. But these methods all need to set the network characteristics artificially. When the network scale is large and the structure is complex, it is often difficult to get the ideal result.

In the study of network embedding, Deepwalk generates node sequences by random walk, and then uses Skipgram model to learn the vector representation of nodes [2]. Line method considers the first-order and second-order proximity of nodes while doing network embedding [8]. Node2vec method takes into account both the homophily and the structural equivalence of the network [9]. Recently, some network embedding methods based on deep learning have been proposed [10]. Network embedding uses low dimensional vectors to represent network nodes, describes network characteristics in a completely new way, overcomes the dependence between nodes in the original network, and implements dimensionality reduction for the network, which makes some machine learning methods easier to apply. Network embedding performs well in a number of network analysis tasks such as multi-label classification, link prediction, community detection, etc.

3 Correlation Definitions and Problem Analysis

In this section we first give some definitions of the problem, and then analyze the key problems in the dynamic network change detection and the purpose of introducing the network embedding.

3.1 Problem Definitions

Definition 1 (Dynamic Network). Unlike static networks, dynamic networks change over time. A dynamic network containing n time slices is represented as $G = \{G_1, G_2, \ldots, G_t, G_{t+1}, \ldots, G_n\}$, where the t th time slice network is $G_t = (V_t, E_t)$. V_t is the set of vertices in the network, and E_t is the edge set representing the relationship between the vertices. $G_t = (V_t, E_t, W_t)$ when the network is a weighted network and W_t is the weights set.

Definition 2 (Network Embedding). Given a network $G = (V, E)$, the purpose of network embedding is to learn a mapping function F to map each node in the network to a low-dimensional vector: $v_i \rightarrow y_i \in R^d$, $d \ll |V|$. The algorithm finally gets the low-dimensional dense vector representations of network nodes, which is very effective when dealing with large scale complex networks.

3.2 Problem Analysis

Doing dynamic network change detection needs to solve three problems: dynamic network model construction, network feature selection and design detection strategy.

1. Dynamic network modeling: At present, the method widely used in dynamic network modeling is time slice partitioning, which needs to choose the appropriate time slice size to divide the network. Too short time slice may lead to little information contained in a time slice network, and too long time slice setting may make the important change information of the network hidden in the time slice window.
2. Network feature selection: Traditional network structure parameters can only embody the characteristics of a certain aspect of the network, and it is incomplete to express the network structure with them. For example, several networks with the same number of nodes may have very different connections within them. If we examine the network with only one parameter, the number of nodes, we will not be able to find the difference in their connection patterns. In addition, it is difficult to

extract network characteristics in large scale complex networks. Network embedding defines the network from a completely new perspective, which can greatly reduce the complexity of the original network and preserve its structural features. The features of the nodes in the original network are preserved in the mapped vectors. We need to construct statistical parameters suitable for representing the whole structure of the network from these vectors.

3. Detection strategy: To detect changes in dynamic networks, from the statistical point of view we can set the threshold range of the statistics to be detected in the steady state of the network. Only a very small probability of the statistics in the stable state will exceed the threshold. When the statistics exceed the threshold, we can determine that the network has changed.

Using the network embedding method can extract the network structure characteristic more effectively, however, it is necessary to point out that there is a loss of any kind of network embedding method. Networks after embedding may miss some network structure features, but this does not affect it as a very effective supplement to the traditional network change detection method.

4 Dynamic Network Change Detection Model Based on Network Embedding

In this section, we introduce the dynamic network change detection model based on network embedding, which is mainly divided into two parts, one is the dynamic network embedding, the other is the dynamic network change detection method based on network embedding.

4.1 Dynamic Network Embedding

Applying dynamic network embedding needs to divide the dynamic network into time slices first, and the size of the time slice depends on the specific problem. In this paper, we use the Deepwalk method to embed each time slice network. This method draws lessons from natural language processing by using words in the text to predict its context, that is, solving the following optimization problems:

$$\max_{\Phi} \log \Pr(\{v_{i-w}, \cdots, v_{i-1}, v_{i+1}, \cdots, v_{i+w}\} | \Phi(v_i)) \tag{1}$$

Φ is a mapping function: $\Phi : v \to R^{|V| \times d}$, It represents each node v as a d-dimensional vector, w is the window size. Node v corresponds to the word in the language model, and window w is the scope of the word context. The purpose of this optimization is to find a node expression $\Phi : v \to R^{|V| \times d}$ that maximizes the co-occurrence probability of the node v_i and all nodes on the path within w from the node.

The Deepwalk method process, shown in Algorithm 1, contains two main parts: a random walk generator and an update process (SkipGram). The random walk generator randomly and evenly selects the network nodes and generates a random walk sequence with fixed length, it generates γ random walk sequences of length t for each node.

SkipGram is a language model that maximizes the probability of cooccurrence between words appearing in a window [11]. When the previous path is generated, it is used as input to the Skipgram model, and every time the Skipgram is executed, the mapping function Φ is updated, and finally the vector representation of each node is obtained. It is worth noting that we need to set all time slice networks to be the same embedding size and dimension.

Algorithm 1 Deepwalk(G, w, d, γ, t)

Input: Graph $G(V, E)$

window size w

embedding size d

walks per vertex γ

walk length t

Output: matrix of vertex representations $\Phi : v \to \mathrm{R}^{|V| \times d}$

1: Initialization: Sample Φ from $U^{|V| \times d}$

2: for i=0 to γ do

3:    for each $v_i \in V$ do

4:        $W_{v_i} = RandomWalk(G, v_i, t)$

5:        SkipGram(Φ, W_{v_i}, w)

6:    end for

7:end for

4.2 Dynamic Network Change Detection Method Based on Network Embedding

Definition 3 (Network Dispersion). We use variance to measure the degree of dispersion of graph G_X' (the degree of discretization of nodes in graph) after network embedding. The network dispersion $D(G_X')$ is defined as the sum of the variance of the values of all nodes in the graph on each dimension. So we have:

$$D(G_X') = \sum_{k=1}^{d} \sum_{i=1}^{m} (v_{ik}' - \mu_k)^2 \tag{2}$$

where d is the dimension of the node vector, m is the number of nodes in graph G_X', and μ_k is the mean value of all nodes in the graph on the k dimension.

The dynamic network obtained from the embedding of the original network G is recorded as $G' = \{G_1', G_2', \cdots, G_t', G_{t+1}', \cdots, G_n'\}$. We use $D(G_X')$ to detect changes in the network. Using the data in the steady state of the network as the training set $\{D(G_1'), D(G_2'), \cdots, D(G_m')\}$, here we assume that the first m time slice is the steady state of the network. The distribution of $D(G_X')$ in the steady state of the network is recorded as f, and the mean and variance of all sample data in the training set are calculated as the estimate of the mean and variance of f.

$$\mu = \frac{1}{m}\sum_{i=1}^{m} D(G_i'), \ \sigma^2 = \frac{1}{m}\sum_{i=1}^{m} (D(G_i') - \overline{D(G_X')})^2 \qquad (3)$$

Given a threshold α, when the new i th time slice network G_i' arrives, if the value of $D(G_i')$ falls outside of $[\mu - \alpha, \mu + \alpha]$, the network is judged to have changed at this time. When f is a normal distribution, we usually set $\alpha = 3\sigma$, because the probability of a value falling outside the region is only 0.3%, which is a small probability event. Of course, we can also determine the value of α according to the actual situation.

The dynamic network change detection model designed by using the network embedding method takes the discrete degree $D(G_X')$ of G_X' as the "characteristic" of the network after the network embedding, which can be regarded as a high generalization of the original network structure. When the traditional network structure parameters can not describe the dynamic network structure change well, the method in this paper can be used as a very effective supplement to the traditional dynamic network change detection method. In the later experiments, we discussed the effect of this method on the simulated Small World network [12] and an actual network: "Enron email network" [13].

Dynamic network change detection algorithm pseudo code as shown in Algorithm 2.

Algorithm 2 Dynamic network change detection

Input: Network $G = \{G_1, G_2, \cdots, G_t, G_{t+1}, \cdots, G_n\}, (w, d, \gamma, t)$ of Deepwalk

Output: earliest alarm time point

Network embedding stage

Execute Deepwalk on G

we get $G' = \{G_1', G_2', \cdots, G_t', G_{t+1}', \cdots, G_n'\}$ after embedding process

Detection stage

For each G_i' in G' :

    Computing $D(G_i')$

Using training set $\{D(G_1'), D(G_2'), \cdots, D(G_m')\}$ to calculate μ and σ

Set threshold $\alpha = k\sigma$

If the value $D(G_i')$ of the new i th time slice network G_i' falls outside of $[\mu - \alpha, \mu + \alpha]$:

    Mark the alarm time point at time i

Complexity Analysis: The time cost of this method mainly includes the computation of network embedding and the computation of node discretization in the graph after network embedding. The complexity can be expressed as $O(nmdlT)$. n is the number of network nodes, m is the number of edges, d is the dimension of the node vector after embedding, l is the number of iterations, T is the number of time slices. The values of n and m are different in each time slice network, which can be understood as the average of n and m for all the time slice networks.

5 Experiments

In this section, we evaluate our method on simulated Small World networks and real datasets, and the experimental results prove the feasibility of our proposed method.

5.1 Simulating Small World Network Experiments

We randomly generate a Small World network with n nodes, k neighbors per node, and reconnect edges by probability p using parameter (n, k, p). We fix the parameter $n = 5000, k = 10$, adjust the value of p from $0.1, 0.2, 0.3, \cdots, 1$. We think that different p values correspond to different network structures, the network changed 10 times during this period, corresponding to 10 time slice networks. In this case, because the number of nodes and edges in the network remain constant during this period, so the network changes cannot be detected with these two parameters as network features. This makes us have to continue to look for other network characteristics.

In the dynamic network change detection method proposed in this paper, we set the dimension d of Deepwalk for network embedding to 128. Repeat the experiment 1000 times for each probability p and calculate the value of $D(G'_X)$. The experimental results are shown in Table 1, where $\bar{\mu}$ is the mean of 1000 experiments and σ is the standard deviation.

Table 1. Experiment results of simulating Small World network

p	$\bar{\mu}$	σ	p	$\bar{\mu}$	σ
0.1	12.73	0.011	0.6	9.98	0.012
0.2	12.25	0.010	0.7	9.79	0.008
0.3	11.40	0.006	0.8	9.68	0.007
0.4	10.76	0.007	0.9	9.64	0.006
0.5	10.31	0.012	1.0	9.63	0.006

We take p as the horizontal axis and $\bar{\mu}$ as the ordinate to draw a line chart, as shown in Fig. 1. In the figure we can see that the value of $\bar{\mu}$ decreases with the increase of p. Also, the value of standard deviation σ at the same p value is very small, indicating that the value of $D(G'_X)$ is stable in the same connection mode. $D(G'_X)$ distinguishes poorly only in the last three cases where $p = 0.8, 0.9, 1.0$, and the distance of $\bar{\mu}$

corresponding to the rest of p is above 5σ. $D(G_X')$ can distinguish different network structures well, so it is feasible to use $D(G_X')$ as the network characteristic for change detection. However, this method has some limitations. There may be some cases where the difference between the values of $D(G_X')$ is small but the real network structure is very different. This is rarely the case in practice, first, because the probability of such a coincidence is low, and second, because most of the network evolution process has a short-term smoothness, the adjacent time period of network changes will not be too obvious.

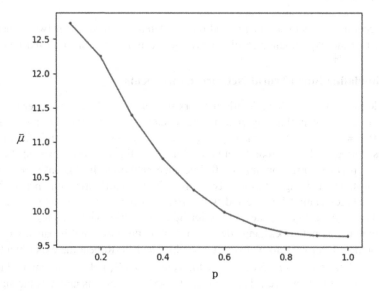

Fig. 1. $D(G_X')$-Change line chart for Small World networks.

As comparative experiments, we select 5 common network parameters as network structure characteristics to detect network changes. (1) nodes count, (2) edges count, (3) average clustering coefficient, (4) network dimer, (5) network centralization. The change line chart for these parameters are shown in Fig. 2. It can be seen that the average clustering coefficient has similar results with our method. The nodes count and the edges count can not identify this network change. The network dimer equals 6 when p is taken as $0.4, 0.5, 0.6, 0.7, 0.8, 1.0$, so it is not possible to distinguish between different network connection modes. The change of the network centralization is not monotonic when the value of p is in $[0.3–0.5]$ and $[0.6–0.9]$, so different connection modes in these two intervals will have the same network centralization. Therefore, these two parameters are not sensitive to identifying such network changes.

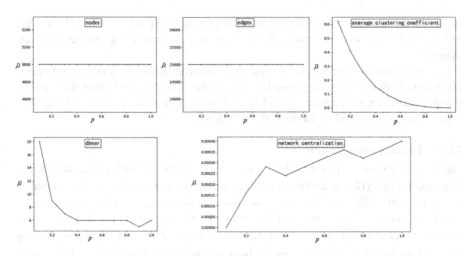

Fig. 2. The line chart of five network parameters.

5.2   Real Dynamic Network Experiments

5.2.1   Experimental Dataset

This paper uses the Enron email data set to build a mail network for dynamic network change detection. Enron's email data set is Enron's (formerly one of the world's largest integrated gas and power companies, and is the number one natural gas and power wholesaler in North America) 150 senior executives of the email. It has been publicly available by the US Federal Energy Regulatory Commission and is currently available online [13].

Data preprocessing: We extract the email address and the sending time of the sender and receiver in the email record to build the mail network. A node in the network represents a communicating member, and if member a sends a message to member b, an edge is added between a and b. The time slice size is set to one week, (7 days) and the messaging records for 364 days from 2001/1/1 to 2001/12/30 are divided into 52 time slices. Since there is less communication data in 7 days, in order to ensure the smoothness of the data, we have combined the data in 7 days with the data in the previous 60 days. Each time slice network now contains 67 days of email communication.

5.2.2   Experimental Design

The first half of 2001 was a steady period for Enron, we used the first 26 time slice networks as training set and the second 26 time slice networks as testing set. First, the network embedding of all 52 time slice networks is carried out, and the $D(G_i')$ of each time slice network after network embedding is calculated. Using the training data $\{D(G_1'), D(G_2'), \cdots, D(G_{26}')\}$ to compute the parameters μ and σ of the distribution f of

$D(G_X')$ of the mail network under the stability of Enron. We set the threshold $\alpha = 5\sigma$, and when the test data falls outside the interval $\mu \pm \alpha$ we think the network has changed.

As comparative experiments, we use the 5 network parameters in the simulation experiment in Sect. 5.1 as the network structure characteristics, and judge the network changes according to the training and testing process mentioned above. (These five experiments do not need to do network embedding).

5.2.3 Experimental Results

Figure 3 shows the variation of $D(G_i')$ over time. The calculated parameters of the distribution f of $D(G_X')$ under Enron stability are $\mu = 8.79$, $\sigma = 0.16$, and the interval of $\mu \pm \alpha$ is [7.99–9.59]. The time when the first statistic that falls outside the interval is called the earliest change point of the network. Starting from the 31st time slice network, $D(G_{31}') = 7.86$ is less than the lower bound 7.99, and the corresponding $D(G_i')$ of the later time slice network is also less than the set lower bound. Test results for the remaining five parameters are shown in Table 2.

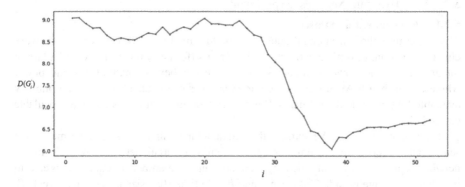

Fig. 3. $D(G_i')$-Change line chart for Enron mail network.

The reality is that Enron entered the August 2001, a series of important events occurred in the company, which led to the bankruptcy of Enron (see Table 3) [14]. The time that our method detected the changes in the network coincided with the time when Enron began to decline. Network changes were also detected at the same time point using the network centralization. The network changes detected by nodes count, edges count, and average clustering coefficients are later. Network diameter does not detect network changes. In addition, we find that $D(G_X')$ has the largest μ/σ in 6 groups of experiments, indicating that this parameter has the least fluctuation during the stable period of Enron company.

Table 2. Summary of test results.

	μ	σ	μ/σ	$\mu \pm \alpha$	Earliest change point
$D(G'_X)$	8.79	0.16	54.9	[7.99–9.59]	31
Nodes	5318	649	8.2	[2073–8563]	36
Edges	27266	3048	8.9	[12026–42506]	35
Dimer	11.69	1.93	6.1	[2.04–21.34]	–
Average clustering coefficient	0.112	0.004	28	[0.092–0.132]	37
Network centralization	0.061	0.011	5.5	[0.006–0.116]	31

Table 3. Enron's important events.

Time	Event
2001/8/14	Skilling announced his resignation as CEO after half a year. Skilling served as president and chief operating officer for a long time and then promoted to chief executive officer
2001/10/16	Enron announced that they had restated their financial statements for the years 1997 to 2000 to correct accounting irregularities
2001/10/22	The Securities and Exchange Commission conducted a survey of potential conflicts of interest between Enron and its directors and their special partnerships
2001/11/8	Enron restated its financial for the prior four years to consolidate partnership arrangements retroactively. Earnings from 1997 to 2000 declined by $591 million, and debt for 2000 increased by $658 million
2001/11/9	Enron entered merger agreement with Dynegy
2001/11/28	Dynegy pulled out of the proposed merger
2001/12/2	Enron filed for bankruptcy in New York and simultaneously sued Dynegy for breach of contract

6   Conclusion

Detecting dynamic network changes is an important problem in dynamic network analysis. With the increasing of the network scale and the complexity of the structure, the traditional network change detection method encounters a series of bottlenecks. In this paper, we propose a dynamic network change detection method based on network embedding, and judge the network change by the degree of discretization of nodes after network embedding. In the simulated Small World network experiment department, we prove the validity of this method, and has achieved better results than existing methods in the actual dynamic network.

Acknowledgments. This research was supported by the National Natural Science Foundation of China (Grant No. 61309007, U1636219) and the National Key R&D Program of China (Grant No. 2016YFB0801303, 2016QY01W0105).

References

1. Carley, K.M.: Dynamic Network Analysis. Alphascript Publishing (2003)
2. Perozzi, B., Al-Rfou, R., Skiena, S. (eds.): DeepWalk: online learning of social representations. In: ACM SIGKDD International Conference on Knowledge Discovery and Data Mining (2014)
3. Goyal, P., Ferrara, E.: Graph embedding techniques, applications, and performance: a survey (2017)
4. McCulloh, I.A., Carley, K.M.: Social network change detection (2008)
5. Carley, K.M.: ORA: a toolkit for dynamic network analysis and visualization. In: Alhajj, R., Rokne, J. (eds.) Encyclopedia of Social Network Analysis and Mining, pp. 1219–1228. Springer, New York (2014). https://doi.org/10.1007/978-1-4614-6170-8
6. Yu, W., Aggarwal, C.C., Wang, W. (eds.): Temporally factorized network modeling for evolutionary network analysis. In: Tenth ACM International Conference on Web Search and Data Mining (2017)
7. Chen, F., Neill, D.B.: Non-parametric scan statistics for event detection and forecasting in heterogeneous social media graphs. J. Biol. Chem. **268**, 1166–1175 (2014)
8. Tang, J., Qu, M., Wang, M., Zhang, M., Yan, J., Mei, Q. (eds.): LINE: large-scale information network embedding. In: International Conference on World Wide Web (2015)
9. Grover, A., Leskovec, J.: node2vec: scalable feature learning for networks. In: KDD 2016, pp. 855–864 (2016)
10. Tu, K., Cui, P., Wang, X., Wang, F., Zhu, W.: Structural deep embedding for hyper-networks (2017)
11. Goldberg, Y., Levy, O.: Word2vec explained: deriving Mikolov et al.'s negative-sampling word-embedding method. Eprint Arxiv (2014)
12. Watts, D.J., Strogatz, S.H.: Collectivedynamics of 'small-world' networks. Nature **393**, 440 (1998)
13. Priebe, C.E., Conroy, J.M., Marchette, D.J., Park, Y.: Scan statistics on Enron graphs. Comput. Math. Organ. Theory **11**(3), 229–247 (2005)
14. Healy, P.M., Palepu, K.G.: The fall of Enron. J. Econ. Perspect. **17**(2), 3–26 (2003)

A Genetic Algorithm Based Method of Early Warning Rule Mining for Student Performance Prediction

Chunqiao Mi[1,2]($\boxtimes$), Xiaoning Peng[1,2], Zhiping Cai[3], Qingyou Deng[1], and Changhua Zhao[1,2]

[1] Huaihua University, Huaihua 418000, Hunan,
People's Republic of China
michunqiao@163.com
[2] Key Laboratory of Intelligent Control Technology for Wuling-Mountain
Ecological Agriculture in Hunan Province,
Huaihua 418000, Hunan, People's Republic of China
[3] National University of Defense Technology,
Changsha 410073, Hunan, People's Republic of China

Abstract. Prediction of student failure in course learning has become a very difficult issue due to the large number of factors that can affect student's low performance, and it is difficult to use classical statistical methods because the results are usually very difficult to being understood by end-user. In this study, a genetic algorithm approach is proposed to deal with these problems using a data set of 576 higher education students' course learning information. Firstly, a mechanism of chromosome encoding is designed to represent associated individual namely classification rule. Secondly, a flexible fitness function is proposed in order to evaluate the quality of each individual, which can make a trade-off between sensitivity and specificity. Thirdly, a set of genetic operators including selection, crossover and mutation are constructed to generate offspring from the fittest individuals so as to select out the best solution to our problem, which can be easily used as an early warning rule to predict student failure in course learning. Finally, by testing the model, consistency was shown between the predicted results and the observed data, indicating that the employed method is promising for identifying at-risk students. The interpretable result is a significant advantage over other classical methods as it can obtain a both accurate and comprehensible classifier for student performance prediction.

Keywords: Classification rule mining · Genetic algorithm
Student performance prediction

1 Introduction

The failure in course learning is a comprehensive result of various factors and is characterized by uncertainty. In order to early predict it, machine learning and data mining methods [1–4] can be used, which are powerful to deal with complex problem and uncertain issues. Predicting student study risk or academic performance with data

© Springer Nature Switzerland AG 2018
X. Sun et al. (Eds.): ICCCS 2018, LNCS 11063, pp. 75–85, 2018.
https://doi.org/10.1007/978-3-030-00006-6_7

mining methods can be traced back to the very early of 2000s. In recent years there have been some related researches. Chen et al. [5] and Ma et al. [6] used decision trees and association rules in identifying students who are potential weak in learning. Minaei-Bidgoli et al. [7] and Morris et al. [8] used discriminant analysis for predicting online course completion success and student final outcome grades. Campbell [9], Bravo et al. [10] and Macfadyen et al. [11] detected underperforming students using a method combining factor analysis and logistic regression. Barber and Sharkey [12], and Sandeep et al. [13] reported predictive models to identify academically at-risk students. Baker et al. [14] and Jay et al. [15] studied early indicators of student success and failure. Detoni et al. [16] and Geraldine et al. [17] predicted student failing risk based on interaction data. Capao et al. [18] used naive bayes algorithm to predict academic performance based on intelligence, motivation and study habits factors. Tripathi et al. [19], Mollica et al. [20], and Hamoud et al. [21] used bayes classification to determine student study performance. Martin et al. [22] and Kevin et al. [23] used a classification system to identify poor performers during current course studying. Yang et al. [24] and Mi et al. [25] applied artificial neural network approach to student grade prediction and learning failure risk early warning. Yang et al. [26] used principal component analysis and multiple linear regression for predicting student academic performance. All these researches cover many machine learning methods, but there is little report about genetic algorithm application in this field. These above attempts provide valuable inspirations for this study, while most of the current researches mainly focus on the mathematic modeling process rather than giving an easily comprehensible result. So it is usually very difficult for educators, who are not data mining experts, to apply the results obtained from the classical methods. In addition, most current researches only use few factors with static historical educational data which can't well reflect the complexity of student failure risk.

The aim of this study is to predict student study failure using a genetic algorithm based method, which can deal with more related influence factors and can also easily make concept become into implementation and apply to educational practice of predicting student study performance. It is of very good significance in helping them improve their studies.

2 Method

Genetic algorithm is a paradigm coming from the Darwin's evolution theory, in which each individual represents a solution and evolves into a better individual by means of genetic operators including selection, crossover and mutation [27]. It is essentially a search algorithm based on the mechanics of natural selection and natural genetics, which has been widely used in applications where the size of the search space is very large. It is inspired on the principle of survival of the fittest, where the fittest individuals are selected to produce offspring for the next generation. In the context of search, individuals are candidate solutions to a given search problem. Hence, reproduction of the fittest individuals means reproduction of the best current candidate solutions. Genetic operators such as selection, crossover and mutation generate offspring from the fittest individuals. One of the advantages of genetic algorithm over traditional search methods is that the former performs a kind of global search using a population of individuals, rather than performing a local, hill-climbing search. Global search methods are less likely to get trapped into local maxima, in comparison with local search methods [28].

In the context of classification rule mining, the population in genetic algorithm represents the solution search space, where a solution is an IF-THEN rule. A chromosome is an IF-THEN rule and a gene represents a sub-condition in the IF-THEN rule. Based on the notion of survival of the fittest, a new population is formed to consist of the fittest rules in the current population, as well as offspring of these rules. Typically, the fitness of a rule is assessed by its classification accuracy on a set of training samples [29]. The algorithm iterates to find the best rules for the different classes. The rules are constructed to find the conjunction of conditions on the relevant attributes that best discriminates a class from the other classes. To do so, there is a genetic operator that employs the not-yet covered attributes of the rule to find the best condition on any other attribute that, when appended to the rule, improves its accuracy. The iterative process continues until the stop criteria are met.

2.1 Individual Encoding

The genetic algorithm's main task was to create populations and to recombine them such that after the evaluation of each individual (chromosome), an optimal individual to be found. The chromosomes were ranked, recombined and evaluated. A chromosome is divided into n genes, where each gene corresponds to a condition involving one attribute, and n is the number of predicting attributes in the data being mined. The genes are positional, i.e. the first gene represents the first attribute, and the second gene represents the second attribute, and so on. Each gene corresponds to one condition in the IF part of a rule, and the entire chromosome corresponds to the entire IF part of the rule. The THEN part is corresponded to class label. In this study, each chromosome was encoded into a binary string. If a discrete characteristic attribute has k possible values, k bits were assigned to it, and each bit corresponds to a specific attribute category value, where for this problem digit 1 means that the following category value is taken and 0 means that it is dropped.

2.2 Fitness Function Definition

The fitness function evaluates the quality of each individual (rule in this study). In order to construct fitness function for evaluating the performance of classification algorithms, normally the confusion matrix is used. This matrix contains information about actual and predicted classifications shown in Table 1 for a two-class problem. The true positives (TP) and true negatives (TN) are correct classifications. A false positive (FP) occurs when the outcome is incorrectly predicted as 1 (or positive) when it is actually 0 (negative). A false negative (FN) occurs when the outcome is incorrectly predicted as negative when it is actually positive.

In order to access how well the model can classify the instances, we used two measures, fitness and accuracy. The fitness function evaluates the quality of the represented solutions. We used a combination of two measures that are commonplace in

Table 1. Confusion matrix for classification performance evaluation.

Actual class\Predicted class	Positive (Class = 1)	Negative (Class = 0)
Positive (Class = 1)	True Positive (TP)	False Negative (FN)
Negative (Class = 0)	False Positive (FP)	True Negative (TN)

classification, namely the sensitivity and the specificity. Sensitivity, also called recall or true positive rate, is the proportion of actual positives which are predicted to be positive and is calculated as Eq. (1). Specificity, also called true negative rate, is the proportion of actual negatives which are predicted to be negative and is calculated as Eq. (2). Then, the fitness value, determined by Eq. (3), is a measure of the central tendency and indicates the balance between classification performances in the positive and negative classes, so as to maximize the accuracy of a classifier. The accuracy measure is determined by Eq. (4), representing the ratio between correctly classified instances and the sum of all instances classified, both correct and incorrect ones.

$$sensitivity = \frac{TP}{TP + FN} \tag{1}$$

$$specificity = \frac{TN}{TN + FP} \tag{2}$$

$$fitness = \sqrt{sensitivity * specificity} \tag{3}$$

$$accuracy = \frac{TP + TN}{TP + TN + FP + FN} \tag{4}$$

2.3 Genetic Selection Operator

In genetic evolution, a general thought is that the fitter chromosomes should have more opportunities to produce off-springs. So in this study, we used a fitness proportionate selection operator which is realized by Eq. (5), where T_i is the number of times that the ith individual is expected to reproduce, f_i is the fitness value of the individual, and $\bar{f}$ is the average fitness value of the population. It means that the number of times an individual is expected to reproduce is equal to the ratio of its fitness to the average fitness of the population. Therefore, in our genetic algorithm, the pair of parent chromosomes could be selected from current population according to their fitness, reflecting the principle of "the fittest ones survive".

$$T_i = \frac{f_i}{\bar{f}} \tag{5}$$

2.4 Genetic Crossover Operator

After parent chromosomes were selected in the previous step, a crossover operator is needed to produce new off-springs. Crossover, in biological terms, is nothing but reproduction. It can result in two new offspring by exchanging subparts of the two parent chromosomes. In this study, we used the most basic form of crossover, known as one point crossover, where at first a random crossover point was selected and then the tails of both the chromosomes are swapped to produce new off-springs (note that the class label bit does not crossover). In our practice, we also used crossover rate for the population, denoted as crossover probability p_c. It means, for each pair of selected parent chromosomes, if its corresponding probability (a randomly value between 0 and 1) is smaller than p_c then crossover, otherwise do not crossover. So at first, we use a generator, producing random numbers in the range between 0 and 1, to get a random number (denoted as r_c) for each pair of parental chromosomes. Then, if the random number r_c produced by the generator for the pair of parental chromosomes is less than the crossover probability p_c, then apply crossover to the parental chromosomes at a randomly chosen locus, otherwise do not apply crossover. If a pair of parents do not undergo crossover, their offspring are their identical copies.

2.5 Genetic Mutation Operator

In the biological sense, there is always some change in the genes of children which makes them different from their parents, which also promotes the idea of diversity in the population. This process is known as mutation. In genetic algorithm, in order to avoid the trend that would lead to chromosomes that are more close to one another in a few next generations, and therefore less diversity, mutation operator is usually used, which may be defined as a random tweak in the chromosome. The most used mutation operator is binary operator, where the mutation modifies the content in a randomly locus of chromosome, by replacing the value 0 with 1, or the value 1 with 0. In our practice, we also used mutation rate for the population, denoted as mutation probability p_m. So at first, we use a generator, producing random numbers in the range between 0 and 1, to get a random number (denoted as r_m) for each chromosome. Then, if the random number r_m produced by the generator for the chromosome is less than the mutation probability p_m, then apply mutation to the chromosome, namely flip a bit at a randomly chosen locus, otherwise do not apply mutation.

2.6 Stop Criteria

The off-springs thus produced are again validated using our fitness function, and if considered fit then will replace the less fit chromosomes from the population. So the population evolves better and better, but in practice we should get to know that we have reached our best possible solution. Therefore, we set three different termination conditions, which are: when there is no improvement in the population, or when our fitness function has reached a predefined value, or when the max number of generation has reached.

3 Experiment and Result

3.1 Data Description and Preprocessing

In this study, we used course learning information about first-year higher education students in our university who were mostly between the ages of 19 and 20, as this was the year with the highest failure rate. The accuracy of study failure risk assessment depends on the significance of the chosen factors, with respect to their effects on course final outcome grade. There are many factors related to student study outcome performance in a course, of which student personal background is the basic one that reflects student potential of success or failure, online participation is the important one that reflects the students' attention and time spent to the course, and offline performance is the most important one that reflects student mastery of course knowledge points. Therefore, those three categories of attribute information and students' final course scores have been gathered during the period of semester 2016 to 2017. All data came from four sources. Firstly, a general survey on personal background is completed by students when they register in a course, which purpose was to obtain personal and family information to identify some important factors that could affect school performance. Secondly, for each student, the daily study process data during the course were collected from an online study system named BDedu developed by ourselves. These data were used to measure student online participation which affects study outcome performance. Thirdly, student offline performance records are come from the teacher or tutor, combined with some online test records. Fourthly, in order to validate our obtained calculation results, for each student the course final outcome grade point data was also collected from the educational administration management system, which uses the hundred percentage point system with 60 points as the passing grade. At last, there were totally 576 students included in our sample. Among them, 1/4 of the students were randomly selected as test sample. So the sizes of train sample and test sample were 432 and 144 respectively. For each student, nine related data which could influence their final performance in course study were collected, including X1: attendance record; X2: assignment earned score; X3: leadership earned score, reflected by whether a student was a class leader in college study, if yes then 'A' otherwise 'B'; X4: online study earned score; X5: offline study earned score; X6: gender, if male then 'A' and if female then 'B'; X7: high school rank, reflected by whether a student attended a key high school before college study, if yes then 'A' otherwise 'B'; X8: college entrance examination score; X9: major discipline, if engineering then 'A' and if liberal arts then 'B'; Y: study result, if a student's final score of the course $\geq$ 60 points then 'success' otherwise 'fail'.

It must be pointed out that a very important task in this work was data preprocessing, due to the quality and reliability of available information, which directly affects the results obtained. In fact, some specific pre-processing tasks were applied to prepare all the previously described data so that the classification task could be carried out correctly. Firstly, all available data were integrated into a single dataset. During this process those students without 100% complete information were eliminated. All students who did not answer our survey were excluded. Secondly, due to the different score point system used by different variables, the raw data should be unified before fed into our model. So in our study, all numerical origin data, including X1, X2, X4, X5 and X8, were normalized at first by Eq. (6), where i is the index of X, X_i' is the normalized value; X_i is the original value; $X_{i,max}$ and $X_{i,min}$ are the original max and min values. Furthermore, some modifications were also made to the values of these numerical attributes, that the continuous variables were transformed into discrete variables, which provide a much more comprehensible view of the data. So the numerical values at last were changed into categorical values in the following way shown in Eq. (7), where XC_i is the final processed value for X1, X2, X4, X5 and X8. The value of Y is determined by Eq. (8).

$$X_i' = \frac{X_i - V_{i,min}}{V_{i,max} - V_{i,min}} \tag{6}$$

$$XC_i = \begin{cases} A, & \text{if } 1 \geq X_i' \geq 0.8 \\ B, & \text{if } 0.8 > X_i' \geq 0.6 \\ C, & \text{if } 0.6 > X_i' \geq 0.4 \\ D, & \text{if } 0.4 > X_i' \geq 0 \end{cases} \quad \text{with } i = 1, 2, 4, 5, 8 \tag{7}$$

$$Y = \begin{cases} 1, & \text{if } 1 \geq \text{final score} \geq 60 \\ 0, & \text{if } 60 > \text{final score} \geq 0 \end{cases} \tag{8}$$

3.2 Computational Results

We carried out several experiments to improve the accuracy of our genetic algorithm based classification model for predicting student failure in course learning. The sample data set was randomly partitioned into two parts, with 75% of the records used for training and the remaining 25% of the record used for testing the quality of the discovered rule. This partition was done in such a way that the proportion of examples belonging to each class (the relative frequency of the class) was kept the same in both the training and the testing set. The evolutionary classification system requires that further control parameters be specified. In order to determine the optimal parameters, including population size s_p, maximum number of evolution generations g_m, crossover probability p_c, and mutation probability p_m, at first their initial values were set as $s_p = 50$, $g_m = 500$, $p_c = 0.6$, and $p_m = 0.06$ according to experts' experiences. Then the method of trial and error was used to test and optimize them.

For each experiment, the initial population was initialized with a different random seed. At first, we kept $g_m = 50$, $p_c = 0.6$ and $p_m = 0.06$, and for different values of s_p the tested average fitness and its standard deviation were shown in Fig. 1, from which we can see that in the beginning the slop of the average fitness curve is very steep, after the point $s_p = 200$ the slop variation becomes slow, and in the point $s_p = 376$ the fitness reaches its maximum value with the least standard deviation. After that the slop does not vary too much and becomes stable. Therefore, in this study it can be stated that the optimized population size is $s_p = 376$. Secondly, we used $s_p = 376$, $p_c = 0.6$ and $p_m = 0.06$ to investigate the best value of g_m, which is shown in Fig. 2. It is noticed that the accuracy average on train data is generally higher than that on test data, and the optimal $g_m = 60$ with the highest accuracy and after which the accuracy do not vary too much with a slightly decrease. Then, using similar approaches we also obtained the optimal crossover probability value as $p_c = 0.7$ and the optimal mutation probability value as $p_m = 0.1$. The details were shown in Table 2.

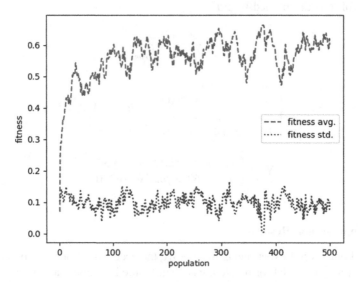

Fig. 1. The tested average fitness and its standard deviation with variation of population size.

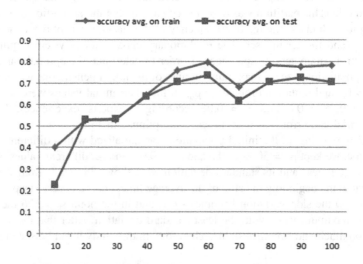

Fig. 2. The optimization of the max number of generations.

Table 2. The details of parameters optimization.

Parameter	Initial value	Testing value	Optimal value
s_p	500	[1, 500] step = 1	376
g_m	50	[10, 100] step = 10	60
p_c	0.6	[0.1, 1] step = 0.1	0.7
p_m	0.06	[0.02, 0.2] step = 0.02	0.1

Each run of our genetic algorithm model solves a two-class classification problem, where the goal is to predict whether or not the student fails in course learning. Then the best rule among all the outputs from the evolutionary processes is selected to predict the students in testing data set, which is very easy to be used and understood by educators. At last, with the optimized parameters shown in Table 2, we finally obtained the predicted results on train and test data. In general, the model used in this study placed students into right classes at accuracy of 72% and 68% in train and test data sets respectively, with a slightly better train accuracy than test. Besides, in terms of predicting student learning failure, we can also grasp the information that the model used in our study resulted in a smaller 'Type II' errors (classifying a fail student as a success student) than 'Type I' errors. Considering the importance of identifying students at risk of failure early in their course study process, the Type I error is of relatively less concern. In other words, it is relatively better to mistakenly identify a student as at risk of failure than to neglect a student who is in needing of additional help and learning support. So in general our model is promising in student failure prediction.

4 Discussion and Conclusion

A major difference between our model and the traditional approaches like regression analysis, artificial neural network, SVM in educational data mining domain is that we proposed a white box classification algorithms obtain models that can explain their predictions at a higher level of abstraction by IF-THEN rules. In our case, induction rule algorithms produce IF-THEN rules directly, which are one of the most popular forms of knowledge representation due to their simplicity and comprehensibility. In this way a non-expert user of data mining such as a teacher or instructor can directly use the output obtained by these algorithms to detect students with problems and to make decisions about how to help them and prevent their possible failure.

Although this time, the accuracy rates are 72% and 68% in the training set and in the test set, respectively. It seems that the rule discovered from the training set did not generalize so well for examples of the test set. This is due to the fact that this is a considerably more difficult classification problem, as student failure is actually affected by a lot of factors and the data we used also have some noise. Besides, in order to keep the simplicity for users we only used the best one rule in measuring accuracy. It is meaningful to evaluate the outcome as a whole, therefore the model is accurate and comprehensible classification model for predicting student failure with an appropriate trade-off regarding accuracy versus interpretability.

The preliminary results reported in this paper allow us to conclude that the chromosome encoding and its associated rule set representation are a good alternative for extracting comprehensible classification rule, which is important in the educational data mining especially for non-expert users. Future work will include the application of the model proposed to some other real-world datasets in order to further validate the promising results.

Acknowledgement. We are very thankful that our study is supported by the Hunan Provincial Educational Science 13th Five-Year Planning Program (No. XJK016QXX003), the Hunan Provincial Philosophy and Social Sciences Foundation (No. 17YBQ087), the Program of Hunan Provincial Social Science Achievements Evaluation Committee (No. XSP18YBC182), the Hunan Provincial Natural Science Foundation (No. 2017JJ3252), and the teaching reform project "Research on the individualized teaching reform of software engineering major under the background of new engineering". The authors are also very grateful to the reviewers and editors who give constructive comments and inspiring suggestions for the paper work.

References

1. Kamal, P., Ahuja, S.: A review on prediction of academic performance of students at-risk using data mining techniques. J. Today's Ideas Tomorrow's Technol. **5**(1), 30–39 (2017)
2. Long, J., Yin, J., Zhu, E., Cai, Z.: An active learning algorithm by selecting the most possibly wrong-predicted instances. J. Comput. Res. Dev. **45**(3), 472–478 (2008)
3. Lin, J., Yin, J., Zhang, C., Cai, Z.: A secure and practical mechanism of outsourcing extreme learning machine in cloud computing. IEEE Intell. Syst. **28**(6), 35–38 (2013)
4. Shahiri, A.M., Husain, W., Rashid, N.A.: A review on predicting student's performance using data mining techniques. Procedia Comput. Sci. **72**, 414–422 (2015)
5. Chen, G.D., Liu, C.C., Ou, K.L., Liu, B.J.: Discovering decision knowledge from web log portfolio for managing classroom processes by applying decision tree and data cube technology. J. Educ. Comput. Res. **23**(3), 305–332 (2000)
6. Ma, Y., Liu, B., Wong, C.K., Yu, P.S., Lee, S.M.: Targeting the right students using data mining. In: Proceedings of the 6th International Conference on Knowledge Discovery and Data Mining, Boston, pp. 457–464 (2000)
7. Minaei-Bidgoli, B., Punch, W.F.: Using genetic algorithms for data mining optimization in an educational web-based system. In: Cantú-Paz, E., et al. (eds.) GECCO 2003. LNCS, vol. 2724, pp. 2252–2263. Springer, Heidelberg (2003). https://doi.org/10.1007/3-540-45110-2_119
8. Morris, L.V., Wu, S., Finnegan, C.: Predicting retention in online general education courses. Am. J. Distance Educ. **19**(1), 23–36 (2005)
9. Campbell, J.P.: Utilizing student data within the course management system to determine undergraduate student academic success: an exploratory study. Doctoral dissertation, Purdue University, USA (2007)
10. Bravo, J., Sosnovsky, S., Ortigosa, A.: Detecting symptoms of low performance using prediction rules. In: Proceedings of the 2nd Educational Data Mining Conference, pp. 31–40. Universidad de Cordoba, Cordoba (2009)
11. Macfadyen, L.P., Dawson, S.: Mining LMS data to develop an early warning system for educators: a proof of concept. Comput. Educ. **54**(2), 588–599 (2010)
12. Barber, R., Sharkey, M.: Course correction: using analytics to predict course success. In: Proceedings of the 2nd International Conference on Learning Analytics and Knowledge, Vancouver, pp. 259–262 (2012)

13. Sandeep, M.J., Erik, W.M., Eitel, J.M.L., James, R.R., Joshua, D.B.: Early alert of academically at-risk students: an open source analytics initiative. J. Learn. Anal. 1(1), 6–47 (2014)
14. Baker, R.S., Lindrum, D., Lindrum, M.J., Perkowski, D.: Analyzing early at-risk factors in higher education e-learning courses. In: Proceedings of the 8th International Conference on Educational Data Mining, Madrid, pp. 150–155 (2015)
15. Bainbridge, J., Melitski, J., Zahradnik, A., Lauría, E., Jayaprakash, S., Baron, J.: Using learning analytics to predict at-risk students in online graduate public affairs and administration education. J. Public Affairs Educ. 21(2), 247–262 (2015)
16. Detoni, D., Cechinel, C., Matsumura, R.A., Brauner, D.F.: Learning to identify at-risk students in distance education using interaction counts. Revista de Informática Teóricae Aplicada 23(2), 124–140 (2016)
17. Geraldine, G., Colm, M., Philip, O., Markus, H.: Learning factor models of students at risk of failing in the early stage of tertiary education. J. Learn. Anal. 3(2), 330–372 (2016)
18. Capao, K.A., Cantara, A.D., Ceniza, A.M., Eduardo, P.M.J., Polinar, S.B., Tero, J.M.: Predicting academic performance with intelligence, study habits and motivation factors using Naive Bayes algorithm. Int. J. Eng. Res. Technol. 5(3), 182–185 (2016)
19. Tripathi, M., Agarwal, A.K.: Probabilistic determination of student performance using Naive Bayes classification algorithm. Int. J. Eng. Sci. Comput. 7(8), 14749–14752 (2017)
20. Mollica, C., Petrella, L.: Bayesian binary quantile regression for the analysis of bachelor-to-master transition. J. Appl. Stat. 44(15), 2791–2812 (2017)
21. Hamoud, A.K., Humadi, A.M., Awadh, W.A., Hashim, A.S.: Students' success prediction based on Bayes algorithms. Int. J. Comput. Appl. 178(7), 6–12 (2017)
22. Martin, H., Zdenek Z., Jaroslav, Z.: Ouroboros: early identification of at-risk students without models based on legacy data. In: Proceedings of the Seventh International Learning Analytics & Knowledge Conference, Vancouver, pp. 6–15 (2017)
23. Kevin, C., David, A.: Utilizing student activity patterns to predict performance. Int. J. Educ. Technol. High. Educ. 14(1), 1–15 (2017)
24. Yang, T.Y., Brinton, C.G., Joe, W.C., Chiang, M.: Behavior-based grade prediction for MOOCs via time series neural networks. IEEE J. Sel. Top. Signal Process. 11(5), 716–728 (2017)
25. Mi, C., Peng, X., Deng, Q.: An artificial neural network approach to student study failure risk early warning prediction based on TensorFlow. In: Sun, G., Liu, S. (eds.) ADHIP 2017. LNICST, vol. 219, pp. 326–333. Springer, Cham (2018). https://doi.org/10.1007/978-3-319-73317-3_38
26. Yang, S.J.H., Lu, O.H.T., Huang, A.Y.Q., Huang, J.C.H., Ogata, H., Lin, A.J.Q.: Predicting students' academic performance using multiple linear regression and principal component analysis. J. Inf. Process. 26, 170–176 (2018)
27. Vera, C.M., Cano, A., Romero, C., Ventura, S.: Predicting student failure at school using genetic programming and different data mining approaches with high dimensional and imbalanced data. Appl. Intell. 38(3), 315–330 (2013)
28. Fidelis, M.V., Lopes, H.S., Freitas, A.A.: Discovering comprehensible classification rules with a genetic algorithm. In: Proceedings of the 2000 Congress on Evolutionary Computation, La Jolla, pp. 805–810 (2000)
29. Muntean, M., Rotar, C., Ileană, I., Vălean, H.: Learning classification rules with genetic algorithm. In: Proceedings of the 2010 International Conference on Communications, pp. 213–216. IEEE, USA (2010)

A Hybrid Resource Scheduling Strategy in Speculative Execution Based on Non-cooperative Game Theory

Williams Dannah[1], Qi Liu[1(✉)], and Dandan Jin[2]

[1] Jiangsu Collaborative Innovation Center of Atmospheric Environment and Equipment Technology (CICAEET), Nanjing University of Information Science & Technology, Nanjing 210044, China
1005949332@qq.com, qi.liu@nuist.edu.cn
[2] School of Computer & Software, Nanjing University of Information Science & Technology, Nanjing, China

Abstract. Hadoop is a well-known parallel computing framework for processing large-scale data, but there is such a task in the Hadoop framework called the "Straggling task" and has a serious impact on Hadoop. Speculative execution is an efficient method of processing "Straggling Tasks" by monitoring the real-time rate of running tasks and backing up "Straggler" on another node to increase the chance of an early completion of a backup task. The proposed speculative execution strategy has many problems, such as misjudgement of "Straggling task" and improper selection of backup nodes, which leads to inefficient implementation of speculative execution. This paper proposes a hybrid resource scheduling strategy in speculative execution based on non-cooperative game theory (HRSE), which transforms the resource scheduling of backup task in speculative execution into a multi-party non-cooperative game problem. The backup task group is the game participant and the game strategy is the computing node, the utility function is the overall task execution time of the cluster. When the game reaches the Nash equilibrium state, the final resource scheduling scheme is obtained. Finally, we implemented the strategy in Hadoop-2.6.0, experimental results show that the scheduling scheme can guarantee the efficiency of speculative execution and improve the fault-tolerant performance of the computation under the condition of high cluster load.

Keywords: Hadoop · Speculative execution · Resource scheduling
Non-cooperative game theory

1 Introduction

In recent years, from the pace of Internet information technology to the booming trend of e-commerce, Internet data information has been rapidly expanding, the big data storage and processing platform emerged as the times require [1, 2]. It was hailed as yet another technological revolution in the computer industry following the Internet of Things and cloud computing, and it also made the storage and analysis programs based on big data a research hotspot in academic circles both at home and abroad [3, 4].

© Springer Nature Switzerland AG 2018
X. Sun et al. (Eds.): ICCCS 2018, LNCS 11063, pp. 86–96, 2018.
https://doi.org/10.1007/978-3-030-00006-6_8

As the mainstream open source processing framework for big data, the Hadoop platform has been widely used due to its ease of use. At present, it has become a top project of Apache and has been used by some large Internet companies for customization [5]. Hadoop was originally part of the open source project "Nutch", which is implemented by Doug Cutting with reference to Google's distributed big data storage model "GFS" and distributed parallel computing model "MapReduce" [6, 7]. With the continuous improvement and development of the Hadoop platform, many applications based on HDFS and MapReduce are becoming more and more abundant, such as HBase [8] and Hive [9] etc., which aim at improving the performance of the cluster and allow people to store and process data more easily. However, these applications are based on the Hadoop distributed storage framework "HDFS" [10] and the computing framework "MapReduce" [7]. Therefore, many famous IT companies like Microsoft, Yahoo!, Google, Amazon, have launched their own big data storage and computing platforms such as Storm [11], Spark [12], Dryad [13], and let the development of big data platform optimization technology as the core development trend in the future [14].

Just as the storage and CPU constitute the bottom of the computer, the distributed storage system "HDFS" and the distributed computing framework "MapReduce" also constitute the bottom layer of the Hadoop distributed platform. Therefore, the performance of HDFS and MapReduce directly affects the overall performance of the Hadoop cluster, such as job execution time, cluster throughput, etc. [15]. MapReduce 2.0 is the core component of the Hadoop ecosystem, although its performance has been greatly improved compared to MapReduce 1.0, the gradual increase in the amount of data has also caused its performance bottleneck. Especially dealing with PB-level data when the data is skewed and the node processing efficiency is low, there will be a certain type of task running at a significantly slower speed than other tasks or even more than five times the average task time, which will slow down the overall running time of the cluster and greatly reduce resource utilization [16]. Hadoop speculative execution mechanism is an efficient way to reduce the impact of this kind of "straggler" on cluster performance. It judges and discovers slow tasks through certain conditions, once a task is confirmed as a "straggler", Hadoop will start a backup task for it, when the backup task is completed before the original task, the original task is killed, which can reduce the cluster running time and improve the fault-tolerant performance of Hadoop.

The original speculative execution mechanism in Hadoop was called "Hadoop-Naive", but its performance is poor in heterogeneous environments due to it uses task progress to determine whether the task is a "Straggler", so many researchers began to optimize the SE from any other aspects and several optimized strategies are proposed [17], Such as LATE, MCP, ERUL and so on. These determination of the "straggler" tasks in the proposed strategy are based on the estimation of the remaining time of the real-time task, but the inaccurate estimation will lead to improper node allocation. At the same time, if there exist multiple "Straggler" in the cluster, speculative execution performance will greatly affect the overall performance of the cluster, so the scheduling strategy of the backup task is very important. Based on the whole study of speculative execution, we proposed a hybrid resource scheduling model in speculative execution based on non-cooperative game theory called "HRSE" that introduced the idea of game theory. In the HRSE algorithm, the resource scheduling model of the backup task in execution is transformed into a classic multi-party non-cooperative game problem, the game participants are the backup task group and the game strategies are the node in the cluster, the game's utility function is the cluster's overall task execution time, and finally when the game reaches the Nash equilibrium, the task scheduling scheme will be obtained.

2 Related Work

The Ref. [17] lists the three core components in the speculative execution strategy:

- Finding out the "straggler" task during the task is running.
- The selection of a suitable backup node.
- Make sure that the benefit of starting the backup task to the cluster is greater than not enabling it.

Hadoop considered the three components at the beginning of the design, it implied the original speculative execution strategy in Hadoop, which is called "Hadoop-Naive". Since Hadoop-Naïve shows many deficiencies in the heterogeneous cloud environments, Zaharia et al. first proposed the heuristic speculative execution strategy called LATE, this strategy uses the remaining execution time of the task as the priority for the determination of the "straggler" tasks, and also considers the proper backup node [18]. The LATE strategy has been optimized to a certain extent relative to the Naïve strategy, but many problems have been found in the application process, such as the estimation error of the task's remaining time and not considering the impact of real-time workload on task execution. Therefore, the literature [19] further proposes a heuristic strategy "ERUL" by finding the linear relationship between system load and task remaining time. The MCP strategy is proposed [20], which maximizes the benefits of the cluster by establishing the maximum cluster performance model and guarantee that the backup task gains more benefit to the cluster than the original task, but the model does not consider the value of the node itself when calculating the benefits. The Ex-MCP strategy is the optimization of the MCP strategy, which takes the node value into the benefit model [21].

In addition to these strategies such as LATE, MCP and ex-MCP, domestic and foreign researchers have also conducted research and exploration of speculative execution strategies from different aspects and proposed their own optimization plans. SSE (Smart Speculative Execution) is an optimization strategy based on the node classification which depends on the hardware performance of the node and the amount of computational data in the node [22]. Wang et al. also proposed a Partial Speculative Execution (PSE), which uses the detection point of the original task to start the speculative execution without restarting the entire process, which enhanced the Hadoop performance [23]. Since speculative execution is a classical space-for-time thinking, most optimization strategies ignore the storage space occupied by backup tasks. Therefore, Liu et al. propose a speculative execution strategy based on space-time optimization for multi-objection, the strategy optimized the load balancing problem during speculative execution based on extreme learning machine and multi-objective space-time optimization algorithm [24]. SECDT is a new speculative execution algorithm based on the C4.5 decision tree, which estimates the completion time of the scheduled task based on the C4.5 decision tree [25]. The ATAS strategy improves the success rate of backup tasks by reducing the reaction time and quickly starting backup tasks [26]. The data skew of the data itself has always been one of the factors which result in "straggler" tasks, the Flexslot's strategy can adaptively change the number of slots on each compute node to further mitigate the problem of data skew [27].

3   Model and Algorithm

The model of resource scheduling for the backup task in the speculative implementation is a hybrid strategy and can be represented by this binary group (T, N), where T is the backup task set in the cluster, and N is the compute node set in the cluster. For each backup task t, the data volume is σ_t, and for each compute node n, the processing rate is v_n. Therefore, when the RM allocates the backup task t to the node k, the running time of the node k is also the sum of the execution time of the backup task plus the execution time of the original task group waiting on the node, which is shown in formula (1).

$$time\_cost_t^k = tc_t^k = \frac{\left(\sum_{i \neq t} \sigma_i p_i^k + \sigma_t\right)}{v_k} \tag{1}$$

Among them, v_k is the processing rate of the computing node k, p_i^k is the probability that the original task i is assigned to the node k, σ_i is the data quantity of each task in the task set to be completed on the node, and σ_t is the work amount of the backup task t allocated by the RM.

After the scheduler determines all the backup task allocation strategies, a single backup task cannot achieve higher benefits by changing its own computing node. At this point, the Nash equilibrium status of the non-cooperative game-based Hadoop speculative execution resource scheduling model is reached.

For this resource scheduling model, to make it reach the Nash equilibrium point of the game, that is RM cannot improve the revenue of the whole cluster by changing the scheduling strategy of any current task, then it must satisfy the following conditions, such as formula (2) shows.

$$p_t^k \Rightarrow tc_t^k = \min_{j \in N} tc_t^j \tag{2}$$

Where p_t^k is the probability that task t is assigned to node k, and tc_t^k is the cost function that task t is scheduled by RM to the node k, which is shown in formula (1), N is the set of compute nodes in the cluster.

Therefore, the resource scheduling model for the speculative backup task can be transformed into a classic non-cooperative game problem. The participants of the game are the set of backup tasks, the game strategy is the different computing nodes in the cluster, the utility function of the game is the final completion time of the task. In the distributed cloud environment, the task scheduling optimization goal is that the task can be completed as soon as possible, so the game's utility function is the task's completion time, that is, when a task t is scheduled to a computing node k, then the cluster has a gain, the income becomes the profit of task t on the node k. The individual task revenue function is shown in Formula (3), and the overall system's revenue function brought by the overall scheduling scheme is shown in Formula (4).

$$Task\_Profit_{tk} = f(a_{tk}) \tag{3}$$

$$Cluster\_Profit_i = f(d_i) \tag{4}$$

Where a_{tk} is game strategy, which is the plan that task t dispatches to node k, d_i is the scheduling scheme i.

According to the above, after the RM schedules the backup task every time, the metric of the task is the task completion time, and the metric of the scheduling strategy is the overall running time of the tasks on the cluster, which are shown in the following formulas (5) and (6).

$$Task\_Profit_{tk} = f\left(\frac{\left(\sum_{i\in N_t^k} \sigma_i\right) + \sigma_t}{v_k}\right) \tag{5}$$

$$Schedule\_Profit_i = f\left(\max_{k\in N}\left(\frac{\left(\sum_{i\in N_k} \sigma_i\right)}{v_k}\right)\right) \tag{6}$$

In formula (5), σ_i is the workload of task i, N_t^k represents the original task set that are uncompleted on node k when backup task t is scheduled to node k, and v_k is the execution rate of node k, σ_t is the workload of the backup task t that is scheduled to be on the node k during execution. In Eq. (6), σ_i is the workload of task i, v_k is the execution rate of node k, N is the set of compute nodes in the cluster, and N_k are the task sets assigned by the RM to node k in the entire cluster.

In the actual cloud environment, the cluster load is high (the number of nodes is smaller than the current task to be processed) or the cluster load is low. In this strategy, the RM generates a possibility execution node sets for the backup task generated during speculative execution, which are the highest-revenue computing nodes q for the backup task t, where q is the minimum value between the number of tasks and nodes, that is called the set of possible running nodes of the backup task, as shown in the formula (7).

$$Possible\_node_t = \begin{cases} \underset{i=1}{\arg\max} \, P_q, & T > N \\ P^T_{i=1}, & T \le N \end{cases} \tag{7}$$

Where $\underset{i=1}{\overset{N}{\arg\max}} \, P_q$ are the computing nodes N that make backup task t the most profitable, $P^T_{i=1}$ is M nodes in the cluster, and M is the number of nodes, T is the number of backup tasks that need to be scheduled. At this time, due to the limited number of tasks and the number of nodes, the scheduling strategy for this backup task is a classical limited non-cooperative game problem. Therefore, according to the definition of non-cooperative games, there must be a Nash equilibrium solution, that is the Nash equilibrium scheme. When encountering a situation where there are intersections in the set of possible processing nodes for two or more backup tasks, these two become conflicting task sets *Conflict_Tasks*.

4   Results and Evaluation

In order to fully analyze the performance of the HRSE, we conducted a series of comparative experiments in the heterogeneous environment, including job execution time, cluster throughput, and speculative execution accuracy. The experimental heterogeneous environment is mainly built on the servers in the lab, there are eight nodes in the cluster, which is shown in Table 1, and the Hadoop-2.6.0 system is deployed on it. At the same time, LATE and MCP strategies have been deployed in the cluster to meet the contrasting experimental requirements. Each group of experiments is run five times in order to ensure the accuracy of the results, and finally the performance comparison results are obtained. Next, the experimental results are compared and analyzed in detail.

Table 1. The detailed information of each node

NodeID	Memory (GB)	Core processors
Node 1	10	8
Node 2	8	4
Node 3	8	1
Node 4	8	8
Node 5	4	8
Node 6	4	4
Node 7	18	4
Node 8	12	8

The data sets used in this experiment are all provided by Purdue University's performance testing benchmark suite including WordCount and Sort. Among them, WordCount's input data volume is 50G, of which the Map task volume is 200, and the

Reduce task volume is 16; the input data volume of Sort It is 30G, of which the Map task volume is 200 and the Reduce task volume is 15.

4.1   Performance Evaluation Metrics

In this paper, three metrics are chosen for performance evaluation, including job execution time, cluster throughput and speculative execution efficiency.

- Job Execution Time
  Job Execution Time is the completion time of a task, as an important indicator to indicate the performance of an optimized Algorithm in the Hadoop system.
- Cluster Throughput
  Cluster Throughput is defined as the number of jobs that the cluster runs per unit of time.
- speculative execution efficiency
  Speculative Execution efficiency is the ratio of the number of effective backup tasks (the rate of backup tasks is higher than the original task) to the number of overall "Straggler" tasks.

4.2   Performance of the HRSE Strategy in a High-Load Heterogeneous Environment

As mentioned earlier, the introduction of game theory is mainly to solve the problem of how to dynamically schedule the cluster resources to maximize the cluster resource utilization when the cluster is under high load. Therefore, in the design of the experiment in this chapter, we select three nodes among the eight nodes in the cluster to perform I/O operations such as file reading tasks to compete for resources in order to simulate the cluster high load scenario. At this time, the accuracy of the monitoring performed and the accuracy of backup node selection become particularly important. The experimental results are shown in Figs. 1 and 2.

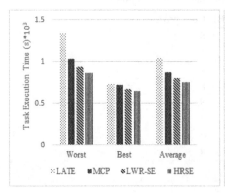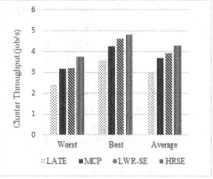

Fig. 1. Performance of different SE strategies on Wordcount jobs in a high load scenario

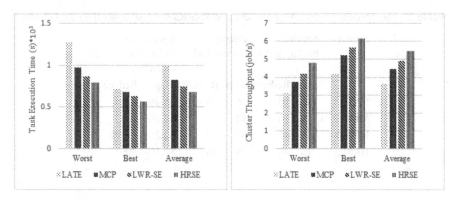

Fig. 2. Performance of different SE strategies on sort jobs in a high load scenario

As can be seen from Fig. 1, For Wordcount, on average, HRSE consumes job execution time 27.3% less than LATE and 13.4% less than MCP and 6.1% less than LWR-SE, moreover, HRSE improves cluster throughput by 43.2% over LATE and 15.6% over MCP and 9.5% over LWR-SE.

Similarly, we can see from Fig. 2, HRSE gains a corresponding degree of optimization in Sort comparing with MCP, LATE and LWR-SE. On average, LWR-SE executes jobs 31.9% faster than LATE and 18.3% faster than MCP and 9.4% faster than LWR-SE, moreover, HRSE improves cluster throughput by 49.1% over LATE and 21.9% over MCP and 11.1% over LWR-SE.

When the cluster resources are in shortage, "Stragglers" may be misjudged and performed on the slow node by LATE, MCP optimizes the performance through the cluster benefit guarantee strategy, but in Hadoop 2.6.0, the Slot concept is canceled, all the resources in the cluster are Container resources, and Maps and Reduce types are not divided, therefore, the accuracy of the MCP cannot be satisfied. The LWR-SE avoids partial misjudgment on the basis of the MCP, however, the efficiency of the selection will be partially insufficient. HRSE dynamically schedules the node computing resources of the backup task based on the LWR-SE determination and calculates the execution time and revenue of the backup task, then, it finds the set of possible nodes for each task to reach the Nash balance, so as to ensure that the cluster's free computing resources are maximized when the cluster appears a set of backup tasks.

Tables 2 and 3 show the speculative execution efficiency of various strategies during task execution. It can be seen that in the case of clusters with high load, tasks in the cluster may have more Straggler due to resource constraints. However, the misjudgment of LWR-SE in the Reduce stage caused the inefficient execution of speculative execution, but the HRSE improves the efficiency in determining the "Straggler" and the allocation of backup tasks. The main reason is that the backup task evaluation in the Reduce stage of LWR-SE has errors, and HRSE dynamically dispatches cluster resources through game theory. The execution node of the backup task reaches an equilibrium state to ensure the effectiveness of the backup task execution. Experimental results show that it performs better under high-load clusters.

Table 2. The speculative execution efficiency of WordCount task under high load cluster

Strategy	Sum of backup tasks		Effective backup task		Speculative execution efficiency	
	Map	Reduce	Map	Reduce	Map	Reduce
LATE	137	0	76	0	55.4%	–
MCP	130	0	84	0	64.6%	–
LWR-SE	81	46	67	19	82.7%	41.3%
HRSE	76	45	68	36	89.4%	80%

Table 3. The speculative execution efficiency of Sort task under high load cluster

Strategy	Sum of backup tasks		Effective backup task		Speculative execution efficiency	
	Map	Reduce	Map	Reduce	Map	Reduce
LATE	141	0	71	0	50.3%	–
MCP	128	0	83	0	64.8%	–
LWR-SE	89	57	72	27	80.9%	47.3%
HRSE	83	51	75	42	90.3%	82.3%

5 Conclusion

In order to solve the problem that the efficiency of the backup node allocation strategy of classical speculative execution algorithm is not high, this paper proposes a speculatively executed hybrid resource scheduling strategy HRSE based on non-cooperative game, which transforms the resource scheduling problem of backup task into a classic non-cooperative game problem. The participants of the game are the set of backup tasks. The game strategy is the computing node in the cluster. The utility function of the game is the final completion time of the task. The experimental results show that HRSE has better performance than LATE, MCP, and LWR-SE strategies, and can make greater use of the cluster's computing resources, improve cluster throughput, and estimate the efficiency of execution.

Acknowledgements. This work has received funding from the European Union's Horizon 2020 research and innovation programme under the Marie Sklodowska-Curie grant agreement No. 701697, Major Program of the National Social Science Fund of China (Grant No. 17ZDA092) and the PAPD fund.

References

1. Armbrust, M., et al.: A view of cloud computing. Commun. ACM **53**(4), 50–58 (2010)
2. Mell, P., Grance, T.: The NIST definition of cloud computing. Natl. Inst. Stand. Technol. **53** (6), 50 (2011)
3. Kong, Y., Zhang, M., Ye, D., et al.: An intelligent agent-based method for task allocation in competitive cloud environments. Concurr. Comput. Pract. Exp. **6**, e4178 (2017)
4. Kong, Y., Zhang, M., Ye, D.: An auction-based approach for group task allocation in an open network environment. Comput. J. **59**(3), 403–422 (2016)
5. Apache Hadoop. http://Hadoop.Apache.Org/. Accessed 11 Feb 2018
6. Ghemawat, S., Gobioff, H., Leung, S.T.: The Google file system. ACM SIGOPS Oper. Syst. Rev. **37**(5), 29–43 (2003)
7. Dean, J., Ghemawa, S.: MapReduce: simplified data processing on large clusters. Proc. Oper. Syst. Des. Implentation **51**(1), 107–113 (2004)
8. Apache Hive. https://hive.apache.org/. Accessed 11 Mar 2018
9. Vijayalakshmi, B., Ravi, P.R.: The down of big Data-Hbase. In: IT in Business, Industry and Government, pp. 1–4. IEEE (2015)
10. Chang, F., Dean, J., Ghemawa, S.: A distributed storage system for structured data. ACM Trans. Comput. Syst. **26**(2), 1–26 (2008)
11. Toshniwal, A., Taneja, S., Shukla, A., et al.: Storm@ Twitter. In: Proceedings of the 2014 ACM SIGMOD International Conference on Management of Data, pp. 147–156. ACM (2014)
12. Zaharia, M., Chowdhury, M., Franklin, M.J., Shenker, S., Stoica, I.: Spark: cluster computing with working sets. the USENIX Conference on Hot Topics in Cloud Computing, USENIX Association, pp. 1765–1773 (2010)
13. Isard, M., Budiu, M., Yu, Y., Birrel, A., Fetterly, D.: Dryad: distributed data-parallel programs from sequential building blocks. In: Proceedings of the 2nd ACM SIGOPS/EuroSys European Conference on Computer Systems, pp. 59–72. ACM (2007)
14. Yoo, D.G., Sim, K.M.: A comparative review of job scheduling for MapReduce. In: IEEE International Conference on Cloud Computing and Intelligence Systems (CCIS), pp. 353–358. IEEE (2011)
15. Dinu, F., Ng, T.S.E.: Understanding the effects and implications of compute node related failures in Hadoop. In: International Symposium on High-Performance Parallel and Distributed Computing, pp. 187–198. ACM (2012)
16. Nenavath, S.N., Atul, N.: A review of adaptive approaches to MapReduce scheduling in heterogeneous environments. In: International Conference on Advances in Computing, Communications and Informatics, pp. 677–683. IEEE (2014)
17. Liu, Q., Jin, D., Liu, X., Linge, N.: A survey of speculative execution strategy in MapReduce. In: Sun, X., Liu, A., Chao, H.-C., Bertino, E. (eds.) ICCCS 2016. LNCS, vol. 10039, pp. 296–307. Springer, Cham (2016). https://doi.org/10.1007/978-3-319-48671-0_27
18. Zaharia, M., Konwinski, A., Joseph, A., Katz, R., Stoica, I.: Improving MapReduce performance in heterogeneous environments. In: Proceedings of the 8th USENIX Conference on Operating Systems Design and Implementation (OSDI), pp. 29–42 (2008)
19. Huang, X., Zhang, L.X., Li, R.F., Wan, L.J., Li, K.Q.: Novel Heuristic speculative execution strategies in heterogeneous distributed environments. In: Computers and Electrical Engineering (2015)
20. Chen, Q., Liu, C., Xiao, Z.: Improving MapReduce performance using smart speculative execution strategy. IEEE Trans. Comput. **63**(4), 954–967 (2014)

21. Wu, H.C., Li, K., Tang, Z., Zhang, L.: A heuristic speculative execution strategy in heterogeneous distributed environments. In: Sixth International symposium on Parallel Architectures, Algorithms and Programming (PAAP), pp. 268–273 (2014)

22. Liu, Q., Cai, W., Shen, J., Fu, Z., Linge, N.: A smart strategy for speculative execution based on hardware resource in a heterogeneous distributed environment. Int. J. Grid Distrib. Comput. **9**, 203–214 (2015)

23. Wang, Y., Lu, W., Lou, R., Wei, B.: Improving MapReduce performance with partial speculative execution. J. Grid Comput. **13**(4), 587–604 (2015)

24. Liu, Q., Cai, W., Shen, J., Fu, Z., Linge, N.: A speculative approach to spatial-temporal efficiency with multi-objective optimization in a heterogeneous cloud environment. Secur. Commun. Netw. **9**(17), 4002–4012 (2016)

25. Li, Y., Yang, Q., Lai, S., Li, B.: A new speculative execution algorithm based on C4.5 decision tree for Hadoop. In: Wang, H., et al. (eds.) ICYCSEE 2015. CCIS, vol. 503, pp. 284–291. Springer, Heidelberg (2015). https://doi.org/10.1007/978-3-662-46248-5_35

26. Yang, S., Chen, Y.: Design adaptive task allocation scheduler to improve MapReduce performance in heterogeneous clouds. J. Netw. Comput. Appl. **57**, 61–70 (2015)

27. Guo, Y., Rao, J., Jiang, C., Zhou, X.: Moving Hadoop into the cloud with flexible slot management and speculative execution. IEEE Trans. Parallel Distrib. Syst. **28**(3), 798–812 (2017)

A Joint Approach to Data Clustering and Robo-Advisor

Jingming Xue[1,2], En Zhu[1](✉), Qiang Liu[1], Chuanli Wang[1], and Jianping Yin[3]

[1] College of Computer, National University of Defense Technology, Changsha
410076, China
enzhu@nudt.edu.cn
[2] Bank of Changsha Co., Ltd., Changsha 410076, China
[3] Dongguan University of Technology, Dongguan 400044, China

Abstract. Robo-advisor is a type of financial recommendation that can provide investors with financial advice or investment management online. Data clustering and item recommendation are both important and challenging in Robo-advisor. These two tasks are often considered independently and most efforts have been made to tackle them separately. However, users in data clustering and group relationship in item recommendation are inherently related. For example, a large number of financial transactions include not only the user's asset information, but also the user's social information. The existence of relations between users and groups motivates us to jointly perform clustering and item recommendation for Robo-advisor in this paper. In particular, we provide a principle way to capture the relations between users and groups, and propose a novel framework CLURE, which fuses data CLUstering and item REcommendation into a coherent model. With experiments on benchmark and real-world datasets, we demonstrate that the proposed framework CLURE achieves superior performance on both tasks compared to the state-of-the-art methods.

Keywords: Robo-advisor · Data clustering · Item recommendation
Data privacy

1 Introduction

With the rapid development of internet finance, robo-advisor is the hot spot of recent fintech innovation, and has attracted the attention of consulting companies, banks and financial startups (e.g., Betterment, Charles Schwab, VisualVest) [1,2]. Robo-advisor is an automated investment solution which engages individuals with digital tools to guide them through a self-assessment process and shape their investment behavior towards rudimentary goal-based decision-making [4,5].

For traditional robo-advisors or portfolio management in financial field, some researchers treated these tasks as recommendation problems. Recommendation systems have become increasingly popular in recent years and have been used in various fields including e-commerce, movies, music, news, books, search queries,

© Springer Nature Switzerland AG 2018
X. Sun et al. (Eds.): ICCCS 2018, LNCS 11063, pp. 97–109, 2018.
https://doi.org/10.1007/978-3-030-00006-6_9

social networking and general products. There are also experts, restaurants, clothing, financial services, life insurance and more [8–15].

For each task of user cluster and recommender system, we have witness a large body of literature in recent years [16–20, 22–24]. Recommender systems apply several data mining algorithms and artificial neural networks (NN) such as popularity-based methods, collaborative filtering [26, 27], content-based filtering [28, 29], hybrid techniques [30], knowledge-based or case-based reasoning depending on the characteristics of the financial domain, the quality of available data and the business goals [31].

More and more recommended algorithms are applied to the financial field. In our previous research, we propose an Incremental Multiple Kernel Extreme Learning Machine (IMK-ELM) model, which initializes on a generic training database and then tunes itself to the classification task. Experimental results demonstrate that the proposed method appropriately solves a wide range of classification problems and is able to efficiently deal with large-scale tasks like robo-advisor [2, 3]. Zibriczky et al. [31] overview the application of recommender systems in various financial domains and provide a basis for further scientific research and product development in financial field.

Collaborative filtering is one of the successful technologies in the recommendation system. It recommends items to users by analyzing user's transaction data, and obtains data by tracking browsing history records, investment records, and sharing records [32, 33]. Although collaborative filtering has many successful application, it cannot solve problems such as cold start and sparsity [34]. Recent work shows that if the user's social information (such as the user's friend group and page preferences) is rich enough, it can alleviate the cold start problem to some extent [35]. In order to resolve the user interest ambiguity and avoid the redundancy in the recommendation itemset, a number of diversification techniques have been designed which optimize the top-k items collectively, in terms of both relevance and diversity [36]. Although the works of [37–41] proposed improvements to the clustering algorithm and can be integrated into the recommendation system to solve the cold start problem [42], data clustering and item recommendation are often considered independently and most efforts have been made to tackle them separately.

In this paper, we propose an effective robo-advisor framework based on user preference clustering, which is different from the above. On the one hand, user groups are introduced to select more accurate and reliable neighbors for active users. As we know, users with different risk preferences have different investment habits, and the frequency of user transactions directly affects their loyalty. Therefore, users can be grouped into different user groups. (1) Optimistic investor groups, in which users clearly prefer high-risk investments (such as equity funds); (2) Pessimistic investor groups, users obviously hate venture capital (only concerned with savings deposits or money funds); (3) Neutral investor groups, where users have no clear investment preferences. On the other hand, we note that most of the previous similarity measure methods are not suitable for capturing user preferences. We propose a new similarity measure method to calculate the user's similarity in the clustering process. In addition, a large number of experiments show that our proposed algorithm can significantly improve the performance of sparse rating data. Finally, the main contributions of this work can be summarized as follows:

1. An CLURE algorithm is first developed, the main idea is to capture the relations between users and groups, and propose a novel framework CLURE, which fuses data CLUstering and item REcommendation into a coherent model.
2. Robo-Advisors are mainly used to allocate customer assets in many investment products such as stocks, bonds, futures, commodities, real estate, which cannot avoid the existence of a large number of heterogeneous data. In order to resolve this problem, the above method is firstly proposed to handle information fusion in Robo-Advisors.
3. To verify the effectiveness of the algorithm, detailed comparisons of the CLURE algorithm with other recommendation algorithms are achieved by simulation on benchmark problems and real-world data sets. Extensive experiments demonstrate that our proposed approach outperforms other state-of-the-art methods.

The remainder of this paper is organized as follows. Section 2 discusses the related work of robo-advisor and collaborative filtering. Section 3 describes the proposed CLURE recommendation system. Section 4 covers the experiments, which include data preparation, evaluation metrics and experiment results. The conclusion and the future research are presented in Sect. 5.

2   Related Work

2.1   Collaborative Filtering in Recommender Systems

Collaborative filtering is one of the more mature technologies in the recommendation system. It has been successfully applied to many fields. With the development of the recommendation system for many years, it has been recognized that this recommendation technology can be mainly divided into two categories: model-based methods and memory-based methods. As an example, The memory-based approach uses user rating data to compute the similarity between users or items. This is used for making recommendations. This was an early approach used in many commercial systems. It's effective and easy to implement. Typical examples of this approach are neighborhood-based CF and item-based/user-based top-N recommendations. For example, in user based approaches, the value of ratings user u gives to item i is calculated as an aggregation of some similar users' rating of the item:

$$r_{u,i} = aggr_{u' \in U} r_{u',i} \tag{1}$$

where U denotes the set of top N users that are most similar to use u who rated item i. Some examples of the aggregation function includes: $r_{u,i} = \frac{1}{N} \sum_{u' \in U} r_{u',i}$, $r_{u,i} = k \sum_{u' \in U} simil(u, u') r_{u',i}$ and so on.

The Pearson correlation similarity of two users x, y is defined as:

$$simil(x,y) = \frac{\sum_{i \in I_{xy}} (r_{x,i} - \bar{r}_x)(r_{y,i} - \bar{r}_y)}{\sqrt{\sum_{i \in I_{xy}} (r_{x,i} - \bar{r}_x)^2} \sqrt{\sum_{i \in I_{xy}} (r_{y,i} - \bar{r}_y)^2}} \tag{2}$$

where I_{xy} is the set of items rated by both user x and user y.

2.2 Basic Concept in Asset Allocation

After all, the focus of the robo-advisor is asset allocation. Asset allocation is an investment strategy that needs to be strictly implemented. It tries to adjust the relationship between risk and return by adjusting the percentage of each asset in the portfolio according to the investor's risk tolerance, goals, and investment time frame.

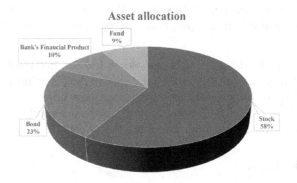

Fig. 1. Illustration of a diversified investment portfolio

As shown in Fig. 1, a portfolio is a collection of investments held by an investment company, hedge fund, financial institution or individual. The term portfolio refers to any combination of financial risk such as stocks, bonds and cash. Portfolios may be held by individual investors and/or managed by financial professionals, hedge funds, banks and other financial institutions. It is a generally accepted principle that a portfolio is designed according to the investor's risk tolerance, time frame and investment objectives. The monetary value of each asset may influence the risk/reward ratio of the portfolio and is referred to as the asset allocation of the portfolio.

3 Methodology

In this section, we first briefly discuss the framework of CLURE. Then, we introduce our clustering algorithm based on user preference and finally describe the recommendation algorithm.

3.1   The Framework of CLURE

In the process of collaborative filtering algorithms, the traditional way of searching for neighbors for active investors depends on the rating information of the two investors jointly scoring items (or the number of times that investors repeatedly invest in a financial product). However, after practice and theoretical proof, traditional collaborative filtering methods have some deficiencies, namely, factors that do not consider user preferences, and use a small part of the collected user data. Most importantly, unlike other e-commerce platforms, financial services rarely lead investors to score services. To overcome these deficiencies, a new and effective robot advisor framework based on user preference clustering and transaction networks was proposed. The algorithm's framework is shown in Fig. 2.

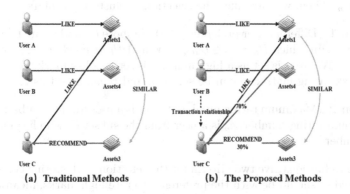

(a) Traditional Methods   (b) The Proposed Methods

Fig. 2. Differences between existing methods and the proposed method

Asset allocation is the implementation of an investment strategy that balances returns and risks by adjusting the percentage of each asset within a given investment time frame based on investor risk tolerance. It is difficult to predict or to control the return of a portfolio, however, it is easy to control the risk. For example, if you invest only half of your capital, the investment risk will be reduced to half accordingly. Simply put, the less you bet on, the less risk you are taking. You could have good control to the level of investment you are comfortable with. In general, investment level adjustment could be considered as risk management tools for wealth management. However, adjusting the investment level of a portfolio could do more than risk management. Doing this right, adjusting investment level dynamically could be a tactical investment strategy. One example is Kelly Strategy [25]. In inter-temporal portfolio choice, Kelly Strategy is the formula used to determine the best size for a series of bets. In most investment scenarios, the Kelly strategy will do better than other strategy in the long run. This strategy is appropriately to investors who rebalance their portfolio a lot more frequent than those who do long-term asset allocation.

3.2   Clustering Based on User Preference

If we match the investment risk rating with the rating system of the recommendation system, high risk represents high scores and low risk represents low scores. In actual recommended applications, users may have very different opinions on the same asset. For example, some investors are radical and they may prefer high-risk financial products (or more frequent financial transactions). On the contrary, some users have a conservative attitude towards investment, and they may be inclined to low-risk financial products (or rarely trade). Finally, based on the user's investment behavior and asset allocation, the user's rating of financial products can be analyzed. As mentioned above, users can be assigned to several different user groups. Suppose C_o, C_p, and C_n represent optimistic user group, pessimistic user group, and neutral user groups respectively. Meanwhile, c_o is the clustering center of C_o, c_p is the clustering center of C_p, and c_n is the clustering center of C_n. Then, we introduce the selection of clustering centers.

Definition 1 (Different user preferences [6]). Suppose U_h and U_l are two subsets of user set U. In which $U_h = u \in U | \bar{r_u} \geq \alpha$, and $U_l = u \in U | \bar{r_u} < \beta$. $c_o \in U_h$, and $c_p \in U_l$. Where α is set as a high mark, β is set as a low mark. For example, in a 1–5 risk rating matrix, α can be set as 4, and β can be set as 2.

Definition 2 (Maximum rating number [6]). c_o is a user from the subset U_h who has maximum rating number; c_p is a user from the subset U_l who has maximum rating number.

The above Definitions give two criteria for the selection of clustering centers, i.e., the expected c_o should be with the preference to rate high marks, meanwhile, c_o should have as many ratings as possible on items.

3.3   User Similarity

In the process of clustering, the rating information of clustering centers is with special characteristics, i.e., c_o prefers to rate high marks, and the determination of a user's preference depends on the similarity between the user and these clustering centers. Therefore, an effective similarity measure method is helpful for assigning the remaining users into different user groups. In order to highlight the importance of user preference, we propose a new similarity measure method to calculate the similarity between users, as follow:

$$sim(a,b)^{UPS} = exp(-\frac{\sum_{i \in I_{ab}} |r_{ai} - r_{bi}| \times |\bar{r}_a - \bar{r}_b|}{|I_{ab}|}) \times \frac{|I_a| \cap |I_b|}{|I_a| \cup |I_b|} \qquad (3)$$

From (3), we know that two important factors are involved. In the global perspective, user preference is reflected by calculating the average rating on all items, and the higher he difference of average ratings between users, the more different preferences of them are shown.

3.4 Recommendation Algorithm

As we all know, the recommendation problem can be considered as a binary classification task. Algorithm 1 describes in detail the CLURE system proposed using the user clustering theory. Feature extraction space includes investor set, asset set and transaction set. We recommend that part of the model enter the risk appetite including the reverser. Output is the recommended result set.

Algorithm 1. Robo-advisor based on user preference clustering

Input:
    the rating matrix R, threshold values: α and β.

Output:
    the prediction p_{ti} of active user t

1: Calculate the similarity between users, and the similarity matrix generated is denoted by sim^{UPS}
2: Determine c_o, c_p, and c_n as clustering centers
3: Generate optimistic user group U_o, pessimistic user group U_p, and neutral user group U_n
4: Obtain the neighbor selection range of active user t, and then generate neighbor set U_{nei} based on the similarity between users.
5: Predict rating p_{ti}
6: Generate asset allocation.

---

4 Experiments and Results

In this section, a series of experiments are conducted to evaluate the CLURE algorithm in MovieLens and BCSs datasets. In the following sections, the evaluation metrics is described first. Then, the experiment setting is introduced. Finally, the experimental results and analysis are presented.

4.1 Data Selection

In general, the performances of Robo-Advisors are closely bound up with micro-economy like Shanghai Composite Index (SCI), during the SCI rise, the accuracy of the recommendation algorithm is higher, but during the SCI fall, the accuracy of recommendation algorithm is very low or even completely incorrect [2]. In order to examine whether the proposed model has made improvement in prediction accuracy, we select time series at four different periods of the real stock market in China as the experiment data. As the user's data are related to the user's personal privacy, we use the data which are removed from the user's privacy as the experimental data (Fig. 3).

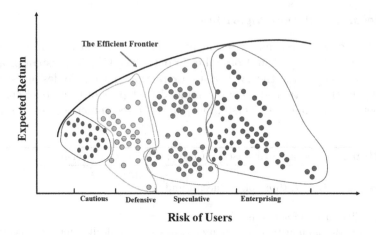

Fig. 3. The investor's risk preference

4.2   Evaluation Metrics

To date, researchers have presented many metrics to evaluate the performance of recommender systems [6,45]. Generally, evaluation metrics are classified into two categories: (1) evaluation metrics of the prediction quality, such as mean reciprocal rank (MRR), mean absolute error (MAE), coverage, and accuracy; (2) evaluation metrics of the recommendation quality, such as precision, recall, and novelty. In order to estimate the performance of our proposed method, we utilize the MAE and coverage to measure the prediction quality, and the precision and recall to measure the quality of the recommendation set. The MRR is the average of the reciprocal ranks of results for a sample of queries Q:

$$MRR = \frac{1}{|Q|} \sum_{i=1}^{|Q|} \frac{1}{rank_i} \tag{4}$$

where $rank_i$ refers to the rank position of the first relevant document for the i-th query.

The two metrics are first calculated separately on each investor's recommendation list and then taken an average among all test investors. The higher values of the two metrics are favored in comparisons.

4.3   Experimental Results and Analysis

This work has aimed to demonstrate the applicability of the novel recommendation system using CLURE. As a case study, benchmark and real-world datasets have been chosen for applying the proposed method.

A Case Study on MovieLens. The MovieLens [46] datasets are widely used in education, research, and industry.

For further validating our proposed algorithm, we compare our proposed algorithm with some state-of-the-art recommendation algorithms, i.e., UPUC-CF [6], CLARE [7], ARM-RS [11], and ART-RS [18]. Results of the different algorithm comparisons are shown in Fig. 4.

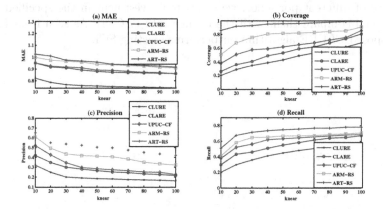

Fig. 4. Algorithms comparison based on MovieLens

As can be seen from Fig. 4, our proposed algorithm can obtain better prediction quality and recommendation performance than other methods. As in the previous method mentioned in Sect. 1, we use user clustering to improve the traditional collaborative filtering algorithm and make full use of the user's preferences and social relationships to improve the performance of the recommendation system.

A Case Study on BCSs. In order to examine the effectiveness of the proposed algorithm on improving the prediction accuracy, we select data at many different periods of the BCS's real trading market as the experiment data. According to [13], we randomly select 512,000 users from the investor user database to fuzzy clustering and divide those users into several categories according to the threshold of clustering. By the nature of the clustering, the value of the threshold can control the number of the user categories. The value of the threshold and the number of the user categories are inversely related. The threshold can be in the range from 0 to 1. If the threshold is set too high, we will get very few user categories. Contrarily, if the threshold is set too small, we will get much more user categories. For example, if the threshold is set to 1, we will get 512,000 user categories. Clearly, if the threshold is set to 0, we will get one user categories. The complexity of clustering the users increases exponentially with the number of the user categories.

According to the risk endurance and investment preference, investors can choose different investment instrument. Under normal circumstances, according to investment preferences, investors are divided into the following four categories:

cautious, defensive, speculative, enterprising. After making several experiments, we divide 512,000 users into four categories.

The purpose of this work is to demonstrate the applicability of the CLURE algorithm in the Robo-Advisors. As a case study, the real-world datasets have been chosen for applying the proposed method. To study the investment performance of different portfolios, we simulated investment in the specified time periods and compare them with the change rate (%Chg). As seen from Fig. 5, the proposed CLURE algorithm outperforms existing SCI.

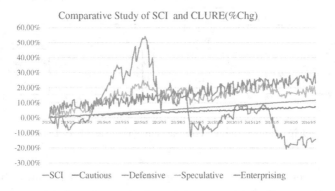

Fig. 5. Investment performance of CLURE with different risk levels. (Note that the Y axis denotes the investment return and X axis is the value of time period)

5   Conclusion and Future Work

In this paper, we have studied the difficulties and challenges of building a recommendation system in the financial sector. On the one hand, investors have very little information on the rating of investment behavior. On the other hand, in order to pursue investment returns, many investors' risk assessments do not clearly match actual risk tolerance. In order to overcome this challenge, we propose a new recommendation system using the CLURE model. This system not only includes the coupling relationship between users and financial products, but also includes the transaction behavior between users and users. Although our work aims have certain similarities with the traditional recommendation system, we propose a collaborative filtering algorithm based on user preference clustering that is applied to the field of robo-advisor. This approach takes full account of users with different investment habits, also incorporates transaction behavior between users, and defines different typical users to generate user groups with different preferences. In addition, we have also proposed a new similarity measure method for the field of smart investing. This method not only considers the user's ratings information for common financial products, but also considers global information of user preferences. In short, the experimental results on benchmark and real-world datasets show that the algorithm is effective for improving the prediction quality and recommendation performance.

Acknowledgments. This work was supported by the National Key R&D Program of China 2018YFB1003203 and the Natural Science Foundation of China (Grant No. 61672528, 61773392, 61702539).

References

1. Goeke M.: Kompetenz und Trends im Private Banking. Banking and Innovation 2016. Springer Fachmedien Wiesbaden, 3–9(2016)
2. Xue, J., Liu, Q., Li, M., et al.: Incremental multiple kernel extreme learning machine and its application in Robo-advisors. Soft Computing **4**, 1–11 (2018)
3. Xue J, Huang L, Liu Q.: A Bi-directional Evolution Algorithm for Financial Recommendation Model. Theoretical Computer Science. 341–354(2017)
4. Jung, D., Dorner, V., Weinhardt, C., et al.: Designing a robo-advisor for risk-averse, low-budget consumers. Electron Markets, 2017
5. Jung, D., Dorner, V., Glaser, F., et al.: Robo-Advisory: Digitalization and Automation of Financial Advisory. Business and Information Systems Engineering **60**(1), 81–86 (2018)
6. Zhang, J., Lin, Y., Lin, M., et al.: An effective collaborative filtering algorithm based on user preference clustering. Applied Intelligence **45**(2), 230–240 (2016)
7. Wang Y, Wang S, Tang J, et al.: CLARE: A Joint Approach to Label Classification and Tag Recommendation. AAAI. 2017
8. Huang, Z., Chung, W., Chen, H.: A graph model for E-commerce recommender systems. Journal of the American Society for Information Science & Technology **55**(3), 259–274 (2014)
9. Felfernig A, Zachar P, Zachar P, et al.: The VITA financial services sales support environment. National Conference on Innovative Applications of Artificial Intelligence. AAAI Press, 1692–1699 (2007)
10. Fr Sayyed, Rv Argiddi, Ss Apte.: GENERATING RECOMMENDATIONS FOR STOCK MARKET USING COLLABORATIVE FILTERING. International Journal of Computer Engineering & Science, 46–49 (2013)
11. Parikh V, Shah P.: E-commerce Recommendation System using Association Rule Mining and Clustering. International Journal of Innovations and Advancement in Computer Science. 2015
12. Paranjape-Voditel P, Deshpande U.: An Association Rule Mining Based Stock Market Recommender System. International Conference on Emerging Applications of Information Technology. IEEE, 21–24 (2011)
13. Yang, Yujun and Li, Jianping and Yang, Yimei.: An Efficient Stock Recommendation Model Based on Big Order Net Inflow. Mathematical Problems in Engineering. (9):1–15 (2016)
14. Lili Zhao, Zhongqi Lu, Sinno Jialin Pan, Qiang Yang.: Matrix Factorization+ for Movie Recommendation. Proceedings of the Twenty-Fifth International Joint Conference on Artificial Intelligence, 3945–3951 (2016)
15. Cheng, H., Lu, Y.C., Sheu, C.: An ontology-based business intelligence application in a financial knowledge management system. Expert Systems with Applications **36**(2), 3614–3622 (2009)

16. Su, X., Khoshgoftaar, T.M.: A survey of collaborative filtering techniques. Advances in Artificial Intelligence **2009**(12), 4 (2009)
17. Hofmann, T.: Latent semantic models for collaborative filtering. ACM Transactions on Information Systems **22**(1), 89–115 (2017)
18. Huang, Z., Chen, H., Zeng, D.: Applying associative retrieval techniques to alleviate the sparsity problem in collaborative filtering. ACM Transactions on Information Systems **22**(1), 116–142 (2015)
19. Gomez-Uribe, C.A., Hunt, N.: The Netflix Recommender System. ACM Transactions on Management Information Systems **6**(4), 1–19 (2015)
20. Wang, S., Huang, S., Liu, T.Y., et al.: Ranking-Oriented Collaborative Filtering: A List wise Approach. ACM Transactions on Information Systems **35**(2), 10 (2016)
21. Yang, L., Hsieh, C.K., Yang, H., et al.: Yum-Me: A Personalized Nutrient-Based Meal Recommender System. ACM Transactions on Information Systems **36**(1), 7 (2017)
22. Liu X, Zhou S, Wang Y, et al.: Optimal Neighborhood Kernel Clustering with Multiple Kernels. AAAI. 2017
23. H Zhao, Z Ding, Y Fu, et al.: Multi-View Clustering via Deep Matrix Factorization. AAAI. 2017
24. Yang, D., Yang, D., Yang, D., et al.: Learning Informative Priors from Heterogeneous Domains to Improve Recommendation in Cold-Start User Domains. ACM Transactions on Information Systems **35**(2), 13 (2016)
25. Kelly, J.L.: A New Interpretation of Information Rate. Ire Transactions on Information Theory **2**(3), 185–189 (2003)
26. Hu, W., Yang, F., Feng, Z.: Item-based collaborative filtering recommendation algorithm based on MapReduce[M]. Multimedia, Communication and Computing Application (2015)
27. Zhang J, Lin Z, Xiao B, et al.: An optimized item-based collaborative filtering recommendation algorithm. IEEE International Conference on Network Infrastructure and Digital Content, Ic-Nidc. IEEE, 414–418 (2009)
28. Pazzani M J, Billsus D.: Content-Based Recommendation Systems. Adaptive Web. Springer-Verlag, 325–341 (2007)
29. Liu Y, Tong Q, Du Z, et al.: Content-Boosted Restricted Boltzmann Machine for Recommendation. In: Wermter S. et al. (eds) Artificial Neural Networks and Machine Learning, 8681:773–780 (2014)
30. Burke, Robin.: Hybrid Recommender Systems: Survey and Experiments. User Modeling and User-Adapted Interaction, 12(4):331–370 (2002)
31. Zibriczky D.: Recommender Systems meet Finance: A literature review. International Workshop on Personalization and Recommender Systems in Financial Services. 2016
32. Goldberg, D., Nichols, D., Oki, B.M., et al.: Using collaborative filtering to weave an information tapestry. Communications of the Acm **35**(12), 61–70 (1992)
33. Bobadilla, J., Hernando, A., Ortega, F., et al.: Collaborative filtering based on significances. Information Sciences An International Journal **185**(1), 1–17 (2012)
34. Leavitt, N.: A Technology that Comes Highly Recommended. Computer **46**(3), 14–17 (2013)
35. S Sedhain, AK Menon, S Sanner, et al.: Low-Rank Linear Cold-Start Recommendation from Social Data. Proceedings of the Thirty-First AAAI Conference on Artificial Intelligence(AAAI2017), 2017
36. C Sha, X Wu, J Niu.: A Framework for Recommending Relevant and Diverse Items. Proceedings of the Twenty-International Joint Conference on Artificial Intelligence (IJCAI-16), 2016

37. Son J W, Jeon J, Lee A, et al.: spectral clustering with brainstorming process for multi-view data. Proceedings of the Thirty-First AAAI Conference on Artificial Intelligence (AAAI2017), 2017
38. Liu X, Zhou S, Wang Y, et al.: Optimal Neighborhood Kernel Clustering with Multiple Kernels. Proceedings of the Thirty-First AAAI Conference on Artificial Intelligence (AAAI2017), 2017
39. Kalintha W, Ono S, Numao M, et al.: Kernelized Evolutionary Distance Metric Learning for Semi-supervised Clustering. Proceedings of the Thirty-First AAAI Conference on Artificial Intelligence(AAAI2017), 2017
40. Roweis, S.T., Saul, L.K.: Nonlinear Dimensionality Reduction by Locally Linear Embedding. Science **290**(5500), 2323–6 (2000)
41. Gong, S.: A Collaborative Filtering Recommendation Algorithm Based on User Clustering and Item Clustering. Journal of Software **5**(7), 745–752 (2010)
42. Sobhanam H, Mariappan A K.: Addressing cold start problem in recommender systems using association rules and clustering technique. International Conference on Computer Communication and Informatics. IEEE, 1–5 (2013)
43. Chen, K., Peng, Z., Ke, W.: Study on collaborative filtering recommendation algorithm based on web user clustering. International Journal of Wireless and Mobile Computing **5**(4), 401–408 (2012)
44. Chen, K.H.: User Clustering Based Social Network Recommendation. Chinese Journal of Computers **36**(2), 349–359 (2013)
45. Bobadilla, J., Hernando, A., Ortega, F., et al.: A framework for collaborative filtering recommender systems. Expert Systems with Applications An International Journal **38**(12), 14609–14623 (2011)
46. Harper F M, Konstan J A.: The MovieLens Datasets: History and Context. ACM, 2016

A Measurement Allocation for Block Image Compressive Sensing

Xiaomeng Duan, Xu Li, and Ran Li[✉]

School of Computer and Information Technology, Xinyang Normal University,
Xinyang 464000, China
liran@xynu.edu.cn

Abstract. In this paper, we propose a measurement allocation to reduce the blocking artifacts existing in the Block Compressive Sensing (BCS) system of image. We compute the error between each image block and its adjacent ones, and evaluate the structure complexity of each block. According to the error energy, each block is adaptively measured and reconstructed. Experimental results show that the proposed method improves the qualities of reconstructed images from both subjective and objective points of view when compared with BCS of image.

Keywords: Compressive Sensing · Measurement allocation
Feature extraction · Spatial correlation

1 Introduction

Compressive Sensing (CS) [1–3] is a new theory of data acquisition, which realizes the simultaneity of sampling and compressing signal. Based on some achievements on statistics, optimization and sparse representation, CS can accurately recover signal at sub-Nyquist rate. By combing CS into image coding, the high-dimensional image can be compressed with a low storage cost and computational complexity. Therefore, many researchers pay the more attentions on the combination of CS and image coding [4–6], in which the Block CS (BCS) framework [7, 8] is a popular scheme because of its simplicity. However, BCS introduces some blocking artifacts, so we require a new scheme to overcome this problem.

In order to overcome the above-mentioned defect, many researchers have been attempting to develop some reconstruction algorithms to reduce blocking artifacts. For BCS framework, the sensed object is divided into non-overlapped blocks, and each image block is measured independently using the same measurement matrix. BCS requires a small storage capacity in the measurement process, so the high-dimensional image can be acquired with a low cost. However, due to different structural details of image blocks, if using the same measurement rate to measure each image block, each block would be reconstructed at a low level, especially that many blocking artifacts occurs on the reconstructed image. Based on BCS framework, Adaptive BCS (ABCS) is proposed by Ref. [9–11] to reduce the blocking artifacts. ABCS adaptively sets the block measurement rate according to different structural details, e.g., Ref. [9] proposed to adaptively allocate CS measurements based on the block standard deviations, and

© Springer Nature Switzerland AG 2018
X. Sun et al. (Eds.): ICCCS 2018, LNCS 11063, pp. 110–119, 2018.
https://doi.org/10.1007/978-3-030-00006-6_10

Ref. [10] used the nonlocal structures of natural image to allocate CS measurements. ABCS is a successful scheme to suppress the reconstructing noise. However, due to the requirement of computing structural details, ABCS has to increase some time and space complexities at encoder. Therefore, it is necessary to design a simple indicator to measure the block structural details.

In this paper, we propose a novel measurement allocation, which uses the error between blocks to allocate measuring resources under the ABCS framework. The error between blocks is a simple feature, which measure the correlation between a block and its adjacent blocks. According to the characteristic of local statistics in image, the error between blocks can reveal the variations of smooth, edge and texture details in a block, so this indicator can assist CS-based encoder to improve its efficiency. Experimental results show that the proposed measurement allocation effectively improves the visual quality of the reconstructed image, and it cannot introduce excessive computations.

The rest of this paper is organized as follows. Section 2 describes the background on CS theory and ABCS framework. Section 3 presents the proposed measurement allocation based on error between blocks. Experimental results are provided in Sect. 4, and we conclude this paper in Sect. 5.

2 Background

2.1 CS Theory

CS theory indicates that a sparse or compressible signal can be reconstructed without distortion from a small number of random measurements. Suppose $x \in R^{N \times 1}$, the random measurement is performed as:

$$y_i = \varphi_i^T \cdot x, \tag{1}$$

in which $\varphi_i \in R^{N \times 1}$ is the measurement vector, and y_i is the CS measured value. Generally, φ_i is generated by a pseudorandom sequence, in which each element obeys to Gaussian distribution with 0 mean. By performing M random measurements, the CS measured vector $y \in R^{M \times 1}$ is acquired as:

$$y = \left[\varphi_1^T; \varphi_2^T; \cdots; \varphi_M^T \right] \cdot x = \Phi \cdot x, \tag{2}$$

in which Φ is the measurement matrix. Due to the fact that M is far less than N, it is difficult to solve x with the known y and Φ. However, if x is sparse or compressive, it can be found from the infinite solutions of linear system (2). x is called be sparse or compressive once satisfying

$$x = \Psi \cdot \alpha, \tag{3}$$

in which α is a sparse or compressive vector, i.e., a few of elements in α have the large values, and others are the small values, Ψ is a sparse representation matrix, e.g., DCT, wavelet, etc. By plugging Eq. (3) into Eq. (2), and using the sparse prior, the CS recovery model can be constructed as follows,

$$\alpha_{opt} = \arg\min\|\alpha\|_1 \text{ s.t. } y = \boldsymbol{\Phi\Psi} \cdot \alpha, \qquad (4)$$

in which $\|\cdot\|_1$ is l_1 norm, which is a criterion to measure the sparsity of signal. The model (4) can be solved by some numerical iterative algorithms, e.g., Orthogonal Matching Pursuit (OMP) [12, 13], Iterative Shrinkage Thresholding (IST) [14, 15].

2.2 ABCS Framework

ABCS framework is constructed based on the CS theory, and its core is to determine the number of random measurements according to the structural details of each image block. Details are as follows:

A natural scene is captured by a CMOS sensor, and CMOS sensor outputs a full-sampling image X of $I_r \times I_c$ in size. X is divided into n blocks of $B \times B$ in size, and image blocks are extracted from top to bottom and from left to right. Let x_i represent the i-th block, $i = 1, 2, 3, \ldots, n$, $n = N/B^2$. By some criterions, the structural feature of x_i is computed, e.g., block variance [8], edge [10], etc. According to the structural feature, we allocate a proper measurement number M_i to x_i, and construct M_i random measurement vectors to observe x_i:

$$y_i = \boldsymbol{\Phi}_{Bi} x_i. \qquad (5)$$

Each block has the different measurement number, and we use the block measurement rate to express the differences among blocks as:

$$S_i = M_i/B^2. \qquad (6)$$

By using y_i and $\boldsymbol{\Phi}_{Bi}$, x_i can be recovered by the following formulas:

$$\hat{\alpha}_i = \arg\min\|\alpha_i\|_1 \text{ s.t. } y_i = \boldsymbol{\Phi}_{Bi}\boldsymbol{\Psi}_{Bi} \cdot \alpha_i, \qquad (7)$$

$$\hat{x}_i = \boldsymbol{\Psi}_{Bi} \cdot \hat{\alpha}_i, \qquad (8)$$

in which $\boldsymbol{\Psi}_{Bi}$ is a fixed representation matrix. Many optimization algorithms including OMP and IST can solve the model (7). However, due to the inaccuracy of existing features measuring structural details, by model (7), many blocking artifacts occurs on the reconstructed image. Therefore, we needs some features to accurately express the varying block structures.

3 Proposed Measurement Allocation

Figure 1 presents the framework of the proposed ABCS system. First, the original image x is divided the non-overlapped blocks x_i, $i = 1, 2, 3, \ldots, n$. Then, we extract the feature from each block. To accurately measure the structural details of blocks, we compute the error E_i between x_i and its adjacent blocks to reveal the structure variations. Afterward, according to E_i, we allocate M_i measurements for x_i, and construct the measurement matrix $\boldsymbol{\Phi}_{Bi}$. Last, we use Eq. (5) to measure x_i, and reconstruct it by solving the model (7).

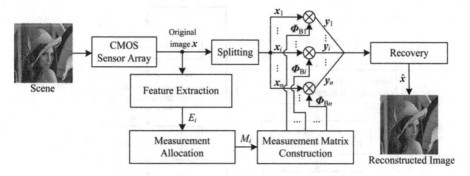

Fig. 1. Proposed ABCS framework

3.1 Feature Extraction

We compute the error between blocks as the feature of each block. First, for x_i, we select its four neighboring blocks $x_{iОj}$ ($j = 1, 2, 3, 4$), and calculate respectively the error between x_i and its single neighbors as follows,

$$e_{i,j} = \frac{1}{B^2} \left\| x_i - x_{ioj} \right\|_2,$$ (9)

in which $B \times B$ is the size of x_i. We take the above errors as the feature w_i of x_i, i.e.,

$$w_i = \max\{e_{i1}, e_{i2}, e_{i3}, e_{i4}\}.$$ (10)

We calculate the features for all blocks and normalize them by

$$E_i = w_i / \sum_{i=1}^{n} w_i,$$ (11)

in which E_i is the normalized feature of x_i. According to the distribution of block features, we set the measurement number of each block. A large E_i means a weak spatial correlation, so the structural feature is complex. Otherwise, a small E_i means a strong spatial correlation, so the structural feature is simple. According to this experience, the CS measurements should be allocated more in blocks whose error between blocks is larger and less in blocks which are otherwise.

3.2 Measurement Allocation

After obtaining the features of blocks, we set the measurement number which be adaptive to the feature distribution. The core of measurement allocation is to assign more CS measurements for blocks with large values. The flow is shown as Fig. 2, and described as follows:

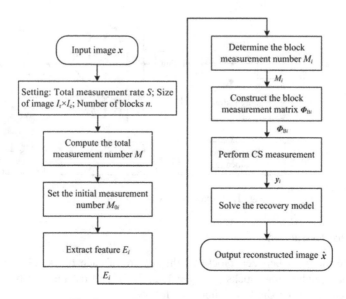

Fig. 2. The flow of measurement allocation

Step 1: Set the total measurement rate S for the original image x, and determinate the total measurement number M as:

$$M = S \times I_r \times I_c, \tag{12}$$

in which $I_r \times I_c$ is the size of x.

Step 2: To provide a basic reconstruction quality, we first assign the initial measurement number M_{0i} to x_i. M_{0i} is set to be

$$M_{0i} = C \cdot M/n, \tag{13}$$

in which n is the total number of blocks, and C is a constant. It is not necessary to set a big M_{0i}, so we invest 30% of CS measurements to uniformly provide each block.

Step 3: We use Eqs. (9)–(11) to computer E_i of x_i, and set the final measurement number M_i of x_i as:

$$M_i = M_{0i} + \text{round}[(1 - C) \cdot E_i \cdot M], \tag{14}$$

in which round[·] is a rounding operator.

Step 4: To ensure that the measurement number is less than the pixel number for any block, we set the upper bound of block measurement number to be $0.9B^2$.

Step 5: According to M_i, we construct the measurement matrix Φ_{Bi}, and perform Eq. (5) to generate the measured vector y_i.

By the above-mentioned measurement allocation, all CS measured vectors can be transmitted to the recovery node. At the recovery node, we construct the model (7) to solve the estimation of all blocks, and combine them into the final reconstructed image.

4   Experimental Results

We evaluate the performance of our ABCS system on the 5 grayscale images of 512 × 512 in size including *Lenna, Barbara, Peppers, Goldhill* and *Mandrill*. For our ABCS system, the block size B is set to 16, Ψ_{Bi} is constructed by DCT matrix. We select the BCS system as benchmark, and the OMP algorithm is used to recover image blocks in the BCS and our ABCS system when the total measurement rate S is set to be between 0.1 and 0.5, respectively. First, we provide the visual results of test images to subjectively evaluate our ABCS system. Second, the Peak Signal- Noise Ratio (PSNR) is used to objectively evaluate our ABCS system. The experimental hardware platform is a dual-core CPU computer with a frequency of 2.80 GHz, and the software platform is 32-bit Windows 7 operating system and MATLAB 7.6.

4.1   Subjective Evaluation

Figure 3 shows the visual qualities of reconstructed *Lenna* by BCS and the proposed ABCS systems when S is set to be 0.1, 0.3 and 0.5, respectively. From the first column of Fig. 3, we can see that there are many blocking artifacts on both the reconstructed images by BCS and ABCS systems. Due to the limited CS measurements when S is 0.1, our system cannot also effectively reduce blocking artifacts. When we increase S to 0.3, for our system, there is almost no blocking artifact, but the obvious blocking

Fig. 3. Visual comparison of reconstructed *Lenna* by BCS and the proposed ABCS systems when S is set to be 0.1, 0.3 and 0.5, respectively. Left from right on the top row are reconstructed images by BCS system when S is set to be 0.1, 0.3 and 0.5, respectively. Left from right on the bottom row are reconstructed images by the proposed ABCS system when S is set to be 0.1, 0.3 and 0.5, respectively.

artifacts still occurs for BCS system. When S is 0.5, the CS measurements is sufficient, so BCS and our ABCS systems provide the good visual results.

Figure 4 shows the visual qualities by reconstructed *Goldhill* by BCS and the proposed ABCS systems when S is set to be 0.1, 0.3 and 0.5, respectively. Similar to the results of *Lenna*, our ABCS system has the less blocking artifacts than BCS system when S is 0.3. When the CS measurements are limited, BCS and ABCS systems cannot both remove the blocking artifacts, but there is no blocking artifact for the BCS and ABCS systems when the CS measurements are sufficient.

Fig. 4. Visual comparison of reconstructed *Goldhill* by BCS and the proposed ABCS systems when S is set to be 0.1, 0.3 and 0.5, respectively. Left from right on the top row are reconstructed images by BCS system when S is set to be 0.1, 0.3 and 0.5, respectively. Left from right on the bottom row are reconstructed images by the proposed ABCS system when S is set to be 0.1, 0.3 and 0.5, respectively.

Figure 5 shows the visual qualities by reconstructed *Mandrill* by BCS and the proposed ABCS systems when S is set to be 0.1, 0.3 and 0.5, respectively. From the first column of Fig. 5, we can see that there is no obvious blocking artifacts for BCS and our ABCS systems when $S = 0.1$, but these reconstructed images contain severe blurs on the fur region due to the limited CS measurements. When $S = 0.3$, our ABCS system suppresses the blurs, and preserves a rich texture details than BCS. When we increase S to 0.5, because CS measurements are sufficient, BCS and our ABCS system both provide the satisfying results. In above, our measurement allocation provides the advantage of ABCS system when CS measurements are moderate.

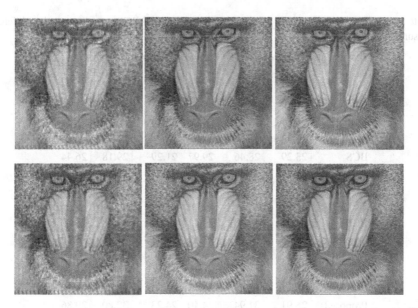

Fig. 5. Visual comparison of reconstructed *Mandrill* by BCS and the proposed ABCS systems when S is set to be 0.1, 0.3 and 0.5, respectively. Left from right on the top row are reconstructed images by BCS system when S is set to be 0.1, 0.3 and 0.5, respectively. Left from right on the bottom row are reconstructed images by the proposed ABCS system when S is set to be 0.1, 0.3 and 0.5, respectively.

4.2 Objective Evaluation

Table 1 lists the PSNR values of reconstructed images by BCS and the proposed ABCS systems at the different measurement rates. Compared with the BCS system, the proposed ABCS system achieves the higher PSNR values at any measurement rate, e.g., our system obtains the average PSNR gains of 0.47 dB, 0.33 dB and 0.53 dB when $S = 0.1$, 0.3, 0.5, respectively, which indicates that our scheme assists ABCS system to get the better objective quality. From Table 1, we also see that the PSNR gains of our ABCS system increase as the measurement rate increases, especially for *Mandrill*, e.g., when $S = 0.1$, the PSNR gain of our system is 0.19 dB, and when $S = 0.5$, the PSNR gain improves 0.42 dB. From these results, we can see that the measurement allocation presents its utilization efficiency of CS measurements for the high-texture image. However, for *Lenna*, the PSNR gain has a little change when the measurement rate varies, so the measurement allocation has the limited ability to explore the information in CS measurements.

Table 1. PSNR comparison of BCS and the proposed ABCS systems at the different measurement rates.

Test Image	Barnara	Goldhill	Lenna	Mandrill	Pepper	Avg.
$S = 0.1$						
BCS	21.56	25.97	26.72	19.57	26.18	24.00
Proposed	21.78	26.30	27.41	19.76	26.79	24.47
ΔPSNR	0.22	0.33	0.69	0.19	0.61	0.47
$S = 0.2$						
BCS	23.29	28.46	29.97	21.29	29.18	26.44
Proposed	23.46	28.69	30.53	21.51	29.57	26.75
ΔPSNR	0.17	0.23	0.56	0.22	0.39	0.31
$S = 0.3$						
BCS	24.45	30.10	32.11	22.61	31.08	28.07
Proposed	24.68	30.40	32.67	22.91	31.36	28.40
ΔPSNR	0.23	0.30	0.56	0.30	0.26	0.33
$S = 0.4$						
BCS	25.61	31.45	33.71	23.75	32.42	29.39
Proposed	25.91	31.94	34.40	24.23	32.80	29.86
ΔPSNR	0.30	0.49	0.69	0.48	0.38	0.47
$S = 0.5$						
BCS	26.82	32.84	35.35	25.01	33.73	30.75
Proposed	27.24	33.40	36.04	25.62	34.11	31.28
ΔPSNR	0.42	0.56	0.69	0.61	0.38	0.53

Note: ΔPSNR is the PSNR gain of the proposed ABCS system over BCS system.

5 Conclusions

In this paper, we propose a measurement allocation for the ABCS system. By this measurement allocation, the ABCS system adaptively measures each block according to error between blocks. We set adaptively the measurement rate of each block by the distribution of errors between blocks. Because this criterion reveals the spatial correlation between blocks, the block structure can be expressed effectively. Experimental results show that the proposed measurement allocation improves the objective and subjective reconstruction qualities of test images when compared with BCS system.

Acknowledgement. This work was supported in part by the National Natural Science Foundation of China, under Grants nos. 61501393.

References

1. Donoho, D.L.: Compressed sensing. IEEE Trans. Inf. Theor. **52**(4), 1289–1306 (2006)
2. Becker, S., Bobin, J., Candès, E.J.: Nesta: a fast and accurate first-order method for sparse recovery. SIAM J. Imaging Sci. **4**(1), 1–39 (2009)
3. Chen, J., Zhang, Y., Zhang, L.Y.: On the security of optical ciphers under the architecture of compressed sensing combining with double random phase encoding. IEEE Photonics J. **9**(4), 1–11 (2017)
4. Mun, S., Fowler, J.E.: DPCM for quantized block-based compressed sensing of images. In: Proceedings of the 20th European Signal Processing Conference, pp. 1424–1428. IEEE, Bucharest (2012)
5. Zhang, J., Zhao, D., Jiang, F.: Spatially directional predictive coding for block-based compressive sensing of natural images. In: IEEE International Conference on Image Processing, pp. 1021–1025. IEEE, Melbourne (2013)
6. Mun, S., Fowler, J.E.: Block compressed sensing of images using directional transforms. In: IEEE International Conference on Image Processing, pp. 2985–2988. IEEE Press, Snowbird (2009)
7. Zhang, B., Liu, Y., Zhuang, J., et al.: A novel block compressed sensing based on matrix permutation. In: Visual Communications and Image Processing, pp. 1–4. IEEE, Chengdu (2017)
8. Gan, L.: Block compressed sensing of natural images. In: International Conference on Digital Signal Processing, pp. 403–406. IEEE, Cardiff (2007)
9. Zhang, J., Yin, Y., Yin, Y., Chen, C., Luo, X.: Adaptive compressed sensing for wireless image sensor networks. Multimed. Tools Appl. **76**(3), 1–16 (2017)
10. Canh, T.N., Dinh, K.Q., Jeon, B.: Edge-preserving nonlocal weighting scheme for total variation based compressive sensing recovery. In: IEEE International Conference on Multimedia and Expo, pp. 1–5. IEEE, Chengdu (2014)
11. Xin, L., Zhang, J., Chen, C., et al.: Adaptive sampling rate assignment for block compressed sensing of images using wavelet transform. Open Cybern. Syst. J. **9**(1), 683–689 (2018)
12. Tropp, J.A., Gilbert, A.C.: Signal recovery from random measurements via orthogonal matching pursuit. IEEE Trans. Inf. Theor. **53**(12), 4655–4666 (2007)
13. Jellali, Z., Atallah, L.N., Cherif, S.: Linear prediction for data compression and recovery enhancement in wireless sensors networks. In: Wireless Communications and Mobile Computing Conference, pp. 779–783. IEEE, Paphos (2016)
14. Beck, A., Teboulle, M.: A fast iterative shrinkage-thresholding algorithm for linear inverse problems. SIAM J. Imaging Sci. **2**(1), 183–202 (2009)
15. Eslahi, N., Aghagolzadeh, A., Andargoli, S.M.H.: Block compressed sensing images using accelerated iterative shrinkage thresholding. In: Iranian Conference on Electrical Engineering, pp. 1569–1574. IEEE, Tehran (2015)

A Method of Small Sample Reliability Assessment Based on Bayesian Theory

Hongbin Wang[1], Nianbin Wang[1](✉), Lianke Zhou[1],
Zhenbei Gu[1], and Ruowen Dang[2]

[1] College of Computer Science and Technology, Harbin Engineering University,
Harbin 150001, China
wangnianbin@hrbeu.edu.cn
[2] Beijing General Institute of Electronic Engineering, Beijing 100854, China

Abstract. In this paper, for the problem of how to improve the accuracy of Bayesian small sample reliability evaluation, we improve the pre-test information preprocessing and Bayesian reliability evaluation. In the preprocessing stage of pre-test information, the conversion of pre-test information is mainly studied. Aiming at the problem of information conversion in similar systems, this paper presents a novel method, which based on the correlation coefficient to determine the relationship between similar systems, and the use of D-S evidence theory to integrate the conversion method; At the same time, In this paper, an improved method based on improved HS algorithm is proposed to improve the accuracy of information partitioning and matching, and then improve the conversion efficiency. In the Bayesian reliability evaluation stage, the distribution of pre-test information is determined by using the method of conjugate pre-distribution distribution, and a mixed pre-test model is proposed to solve the problem of pre-test information "submerged" small sample field test information and the problem of multi-source pre-test distribution of the weight; and the evaluation results of the reliability parameters are obtained effectively.

Keywords: Small sample · Reliability assessment · Bayesian theory
Information conversion

1 General Method

With the rapid development of science and technology, reliability experiments of high-tech products can hardly be carried out in large samples due to high cost and complex production process and the like, which results in test data under small sample conditions. Consequently, it has become a major topic that how to use the field test data of small samples scientifically and rationally to provide a basis for the decision making of reliability assessment of products. In recent years, Bayesian theory [1, 2] has received extensive attention in the field of reliability evaluation of small samples because it promises an objective evaluation of system reliability by effectively integrating pre-test and field test information.

© Springer Nature Switzerland AG 2018
X. Sun et al. (Eds.): ICCCS 2018, LNCS 11063, pp. 120–131, 2018.
https://doi.org/10.1007/978-3-030-00006-6_11

(1) Acquisition and Pre-processing of Pre-test Information

The main sources of pre-test information are historical information of test products, test information of similar systems and test data in different environments. Since pre-test information comes from different sources, it can only be applied after information conversion, information fusion and other methods of processing [3, 4].

(2) Determination of Pre-test Distribution

It is necessary to determine the distribution type and the statistical parameters of the distribution type after acquire the pre-test information.

(3) Acquisition of Field Test Data of Small Samples

Before the reliability assessment takes place, the Bayesian method requires the integration of pre-test and field test information. Hence this step is of great importance.

(4) Bayesian Reliability Assessment

Pre-test and field test information are integrated with the Bayesian formula to obtain the post-test distribution function of parameters [5–7]. Then the assessment is based on various types of reliability parameters of the post-test distribution function in the statistical model (Fig. 1).

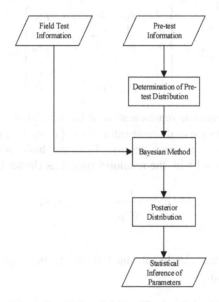

Fig. 1. General steps of small sample reliability assessment based on Bayesian theory

2 Pre-test Information Conversion

The pre-processing procedure of pre-test information mainly includes information collection, information sorting, compatibility testing, information conversion and other steps [8–10]. The most important step is the conversion of pre-test information. In this paper, the prerequisite for information conversion is a certain degree of uniformity within the products in terms of their failure mechanism or failure mode in different states.

2.1 Conversion Algorithm of Similar Systems

Assume that there are n kinds of similar systems in A system, expressed as X_i whose test information is expressed as $X_i = (x_{i1}, x_{i2}, x_{i3}, \ldots, x_{in})$; A system is expressed as Y whose test information is expressed as $Y = (y_1, y_2, \ldots, y_n)$. The relationship between systems are defined with correlation coefficients in this paper. Therefore, system X and system Y can be expressed as Eq. 1.

$$\rho_{XY} = \frac{n\sum_{i=1}^{n} x_i y_i - \sum_{i=1}^{n} x_i \sum_{i=1}^{n} y_i}{\sqrt{n\sum_{i=1}^{n} x_i^2 - \left(\sum_{i=1}^{n} x_i\right)^2} \sqrt{n\sum_{i=1}^{n} y_i^2 - \left(\sum_{i=1}^{n} y_i\right)^2}} \tag{1}$$

The relationship between different similar systems can be determined by using the above equation to express the interaction between similar systems. This can basically ensure the determination of conversion factor and further obtain the correlation matrix between different similar systems, whose expression is shown in Eq. 2.

$$\rho_M = \begin{bmatrix} 1 & \rho_{01} & \rho_{02} & \cdots & \rho_{0n} \\ \rho_{10} & 1 & \rho_{12} & \cdots & \rho_{1n} \\ \rho_{20} & \rho_{21} & 1 & \cdots & \rho_{2n} \\ \vdots & \vdots & \vdots & \vdots & \vdots \\ \rho_{n0} & \rho_{n1} & \rho_{n2} & \cdots & 1 \end{bmatrix} \tag{2}$$

The matrix is a reasonable representation of the relationship between similar systems. Now express the frame of discernment as $\Theta = \{x_1, x_2, \cdots, x_n\}$ and consider each group of similar systems as one category. Then the basic probability distribution function can be established with the relational model as shown in Eq. 3.

$$M_i(x_j) = \frac{\rho_{ij}}{\sum_{j=1}^{n} \rho_{ij}} (i = 1, \cdots, n) \tag{3}$$

The combination rule can be obtained from the basic probability distribution function as shown in Eq. 4.

$$M(x) = \begin{cases} K^{-1} \sum_{\cap x_i = \Theta} M_1 M_2 \cdots M_n & (x \neq \varnothing) \\ 0 & (x = \varnothing) \end{cases} \tag{4}$$

Where K can be expressed as $K = \sum_{\cap \theta \neq \varnothing} M_1 M_2 \ldots M_n$, then the conversion factor of similar system No. i can be calculated with Eq. 5.

$$C_i = \rho_{0i} \times M(x_i)(i = 1, 2, \cdots, n) \tag{5}$$

2.2   Conversion Algorithm of Test Information in Different Environments

In the reliability assessment of small samples, the test information in different environments serves as a major source of the pre-test information. The specific flow chart is shown in Fig. 2.

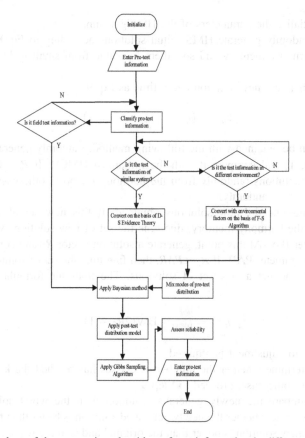

Fig. 2. Flow chart of the conversion algorithm of test information in different environments

Step 1: Arrange the sample data from small to large to form a new order.

Step 2: According to Eqs. 6 and 7, calculate the median of the test data in different environments respectively.

$$\left| x_{(c)} - \overline{X} \right| = \min_{1 \le i \le n} \left| x_{(i)} - \overline{X} \right| (1 \le c \le n) \tag{6}$$

$$\left| y_{(s)} - \overline{Y} \right| = \min_{1 \le j \le m} \left| y_{(j)} - \overline{Y} \right| (1 \le s \le m) \tag{7}$$

Step 3: Find the minimum number of test data k_l, k_r, on both sides of the test data median and use them as the value of k, the number of the data split point, in Eq. 8.

$$\min f(k, i_1, i_2, \cdots, i_k) = \sum_{j=1}^{k-1} \sum_{s=i}^{j} (x_s - \overline{x_{ij}})' (x_s - \overline{x_{ij}}) \qquad (8)$$

Step 4: Initialize the parameters of the HS algorithm.

Step 5: Randomly generate HMS initial solutions according to Eq. 8, then place them in the harmony memory and sort them by value from small to large to ensure orderliness.

Step 6: Generate a new solution every time as Eq. 9.

$$\mathbf{I}_{new} = (i_{new1}, i_{new2}, \cdots, i_{newk}) \qquad (9)$$

Where i_{newj} can be obtained with the following method: randomly generate a variable R_1 between [0, 1] and compare it with the initialized HMCR. If $R_1 <$ HMCR, then obtain a set of solutions randomly from the harmony memory; otherwise, generate a new set of solutions randomly.

Step 7: Fine-tune the new solutions obtained. If this new set of solutions are obtained from the harmony memory, fine-tune the set of new solutions with the fine-tuning parameter BW. At this point, generate a solution vector R_2 and compare it with the initialized parameter PAR. If $R_2 < PAR$, then fine-tune the set of solutions with the parameter BW and get a new set of solutions. The fine-tune formula is shown in Eq. 10.

$$i_{newj} = i_{newj} + \mathrm{BW}(2R_2 - 1) \qquad (10)$$

Otherwise, no adjustment is required.

Step 8: Determine whether the number of classes has reached the k class. If not, return to Step 6; otherwise, proceed to Step 9.

Step 9: Compare the newly generated solution with the worst solution in the memory to determine whether the newly generated solution is better than the worst and solution. If the new solution is better than the original and also the worst solution, then replace the worst solution with the new solution and update the memory; otherwise, change nothing and proceed to step 10.

Step 10: Repeat steps from 6 to 9 in above, until the termination condition or the maximum number of iterations is reached. Then terminate the loop at this point to obtain the optimal split point sequence.

Step 11: Segment the two sets of test data effectively according to the optimal split point sequence and obtain the average value of each group and the new data sequence after segmentation.

Step 12: Pair the test data according to the pairing principle, and then calculate the environmental factor by substituting Eq. 11.

$$K = \sqrt[m]{\frac{y_1^* \, y_2^*}{y_1 \, y_2}, \ldots, \frac{y_m^*}{y_m}} \qquad (11)$$

Step 13: Convert the reliability of the test information.

3   Method of Small Sample Reliability Assessment Based on Bayesian Theory

Assuming that there are n kinds of pre-test information, the distribution function of each information is expressed as $\pi_i(\theta)$, respectively, the credibility of each information as C_i and the importance of each information as V_i. Then define the confidence blend weight of the pre-test distribution as ε_{C_i} whose calculation method is shown in Eq. 12.

$$\varepsilon_{Ci} = \frac{C_i}{\sum\limits_{i=1}^{n} C_i} \qquad (12)$$

Define the importance blend weight of the pre-test distribution as ε_{V_i} whose calculation method is shown in Eq. 13.

$$\varepsilon_{Vi} = \frac{V_i}{\sum\limits_{i=1}^{n} V_i} \qquad (13)$$

Determine the blend weight ε_i for each pre-test information distribution and the calculation method of new blend weight is shown in Eq. 14.

$$\varepsilon_i = \frac{\varepsilon_{Ci}\varepsilon_{Vi}}{\sum\limits_{i=1}^{n} \varepsilon_{Ci}\varepsilon_{Vi}} \qquad (14)$$

Multi-source pre-test information is effectively integrated according to Eq. 15 after the blend weight is calculated. And then obtain the mixed pre-test distribution model after the integration of pre-test information.

$$\pi(\theta) = \sum\limits_{i=1}^{n} \varepsilon_i \pi_i(\theta) \qquad (15)$$

The mixed pre-test distribution model takes into account the confidence and importance of the pre-test information respectively and preserves useful information effectively by eliminating invalid information.

1. Determination of Credibility C. In this paper, the method of Outlier Test is used to calculate the credibility. The specific steps of the calculation method are as follows:

Step 1: Set the initial conditions: the initial value of control variable $i = 1$, the simulation accuracy ω, the field test data, the number of cycles N, the record variable of the number of simulation $R = 0$.

Step 2: Start the simulation. If $i < N$, generate the parameter θ_i of $\pi(\theta)$ randomly and obtain its corresponding distribution function $f(X|\theta_i)$. Continue with Step 3; If $i > N$, then proceed to Step 4.

Step 3: Select different methods of outlier test according to different distribution functions. If an outlier appears in the inspection process, only let $i = i + 1$. If there is zero outlier, then let $i = i + 1$ and proceed to Step 4.

Step 4: Obtain the value of C_N with the following equation: $C_N = R/N$ and proceed to Step 5.

Step 5: Determine whether C_N meets the requirements or not. If C_N satisfies $|C_N - C_{N-1}| \le \omega$, then stop the simulation and let $C = C_N$; If not, then let $N = N + 1$ and proceed to Step 2.

Step 6: The cycle ends and obtain the value of confidence C.

According to the above steps, the confidence degree of different pre-test information, C can be obtained and the blend weight ε_{C_i} can also be calculated with Eq. 12.

2. Determination of Importance V. Assuming that the field test information is described by the distribution function $v(\theta)$ and the pre-test information is described by the distribution function $\pi(\theta)$, the graphical relationship between the two is shown in Fig. 3. There is overlapping area between the graphs of the two distribution functions as shown in Fig. 3. In this paper, it is believed that the overlapping area of the graphs actually reflects the importance that $\pi(\theta)$ is $v(\theta)$. The larger the area of the overlap is, the greater the importance is. Therefore, the overlapping degree of the graphs can be used to define the importance of pre-test information, v. The calculation method is shown in Eq. 16.

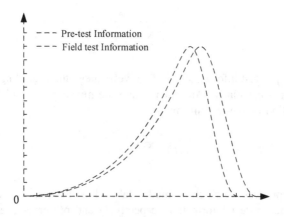

Fig. 3. Calculation graph of the importance of pre-test information

$$v = \int_0^1 (\min(\pi(\theta), v(\theta)))d\theta \qquad (16)$$

Assuming that there are n kinds of pre-test information, the importance degree between two is calculated in order to obtain the metric matrix of importance degree between each two distribution functions of pre-test information. The matrix is expressed as below.

$$v_{n,n} = \begin{bmatrix} 1 & v_{12} & v_{13} & \cdots & v_{1n} \\ v_{21} & 1 & v_{12} & \cdots & v_{2n} \\ v_{31} & v_{32} & 1 & \cdots & v_{3n} \\ \vdots & \vdots & \vdots & \vdots & \vdots \\ v_{n1} & v_{n2} & v_{n3} & \cdots & 1 \end{bmatrix} \qquad (17)$$

When the above-mentioned metric matrix of importance degree is obtained, the importance degrees that one distribution function of information is of to any others can be obtained by adding up metric matrixes of importance degree by column provided that the rows and columns differ in sequence numbers. Importance degree V can be calculated with Eq. 18.

$$V_j = \sum_{i=1}^n v_{ij}, \quad j = 1, 2, \cdots, n \qquad (18)$$

The importance degrees of different pre-test information can be obtained with the above-mentioned method and the blend weight ε_{V_i} can be calculated with Eq. 13. Then, integrate field test information and pre-test information with Bayesian formula to obtain the conditional distribution function of the unknown distribution parameter θ, $\pi(\theta|x)$ with given field test information. The method of calculating post-test distribution model $\pi(\theta|x)$ is shown as below:

$$\pi(\theta|x) = \frac{f(x|\theta)\pi(\theta)}{\int_\Theta f(x|\theta)\pi(\theta)d\theta} \qquad (19)$$

Then simulation sample data can be obtained by iterative sampling. That is to apply Gibbs sampling algorithm on post-test distribution $\pi(\theta|x)$. Then the parameter can be estimated with simulation sample data.

4 Test Results and Analysis

4.1 Selection of Data Sets

The test data used in this paper is provided by the Minitab Data Set Library which provides a considerable number of sample data sets collected from real cases in many different industries and research fields. So far, the test data provided by Minitab is widely used in over 10000 countries in the world and over 4800 higher educational institutions. In this test, various data of emergency diesel-electric generators (EDG) from 2013 to 2016 was screened from the reliability data sets in the Minitab data set library. From the perspective of statistics, relevant data of EDG multiple similar systems and test data in different environments were also obtained to provide data support for relevant tests.

4.2   Results and Analysis

In order to fully verify the information conversion method and the mixed pre-test distribution model proposed in this paper, the following three sets of contrast experiments are designed:

(1) Contrast tests between two conversion methods based on D-S evidence theory and Failure Rate Estimation;
(2) Contrast tests between two conversion methods based on the improved HS algorithm and Fisher segmentation;
(3) Contrast tests among mixed pre-test distribution model in this paper, traditional Bayesian method and weighted pre-test distribution model based only on confidence.

First, contrast tests between conversion methods of similar systems: in order to verify the conversion effect of the conversion method provided in the paper and that of the conversion method based on the failure rate in converting information of similar systems, relevant tests are conducted this paper according to the evaluation criteria of conversion method. This test applies Wilcoxon test method to determine whether the converted data and the original data belong to the same dist. In this test, the pre-test information is converted with the conversion method based on Failure Rate Estimation and the conversion method based on D-S evidence theory under the condition that the number of similar systems is controlled. Each situation receives 100 times of test and the probability of two types of data consistent with the same distribution is calculated according to the result of each test. Test results are shown in Fig. 4.

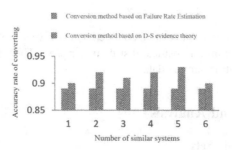

Fig. 4. Accuracy comparison of conversion methods applied on similar systems under different number of similar systems

It can be detected from the test results in Fig. 5 that the probability of the converted data with D-S evidence theory and the original data falling into the same distribution is above 90% without exception, which meets the requirements of the evaluation criteria. This indicates that the method can effectively convert the information of similar systems; Compared with the original method, the new method increases the probability of test data being in the same distribution, which indicates that the new method greatly improves the conversion effect of similar system information after fully considering the relationship between similar systems and thus meets actual requirements.

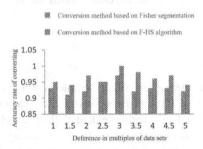

Fig. 5. Accuracy comparison of conversion methods under different multiple deference of data sets

Next, the contrast test on conversion methods of environmental factors: control the number of data, m, in environment A and the number of data, n, in complicated environment B to determine whether they belong to the same distribution. Test results are shown in Fig. 5.

It can be detected from the test results in Fig. 4 that the probability of the converted data with F-HS algorithm in this paper and the original data falling into the same distribution is above 0.90 without exception, which meets the requirements of the evaluation criteria. This indicates that the method can effectively convert the information in different environments;

Last, the contrast test of mixed pre-test distribution model: this test data forms a binomial distribution model. In this paper, the Beta distribution is used as the conjugate pre-test distribution of success probability α. The main purpose of this test is to verify the estimated lower limit of confidence of the reliability parameter. The test results are shown in Fig. 6.

It can be concluded from the contrast test that the parameters' lower limit of confidence obtained with the improved version of mixed pre-test distribution method is smaller than that of the traditional Bayesian method and that of the pre-test distribution method based only on confidence. The test results show that the method proposed in this paper can avoid the abuse of pre-test information, which could lead to the exaggeration of reliability assessment results and thus weakens the dependency of reliability assessment results on multi-source pre-test information.

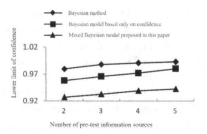

Fig. 6. Influence from different mixed Bayesian models on the estimated upper limit of confidence

5   Conclusion

The effectiveness of the method of small sample reliability assessment based on Bayesian theory is validated through three sets of contrast tests and the assessment results can also be improved to a certain extent with this method. In the method of small sample reliability assessment based on Bayesian theory, the application of pre-test information is a crucial link of the assessment process. The relevant conversion method and mixed pre-test distribution model proposed in this paper are of considerable innovation and value in use. Due to the limited research ability, the relevant methods proposed in this paper do improve the accuracy of the reliability assessment but at the same time increase the consumption of time. It is hoped that with continuous efforts in future study and research, the algorithm can be further improved.

Acknowledgments. This work was funded by the National Natural Science Foundation of China under Grant (No. 61772152 and No. 61502037), the Basic Research Project (No. JCKY2016206B001, JCKY2014206C002 and JCKY2017604C010), and the Technical Foundation Project (No. JSQB2017206C002).

References

1. Bernardo, J.M., Smith, A.F.M.: Bayesian Theory (2008)
2. Dietrich, F.: A Theory of Bayesian Groups. Noûs (2017)
3. Shipman, J.P., Cunningham, D.J., Holst, R., Watson, L.A.: The informationist conference: report. J. Med. Libr. Assoc. **90**, 458 (2002)
4. Dubois, D., Prade, H.: Dealing with multi-source information in possibilistic logic. In: European Conference on Artificial Intelligence, pp. 38–42 (1992)
5. Frigola, R., Rasmussen, C.E.: Integrated pre-processing for Bayesian nonlinear system identification with Gaussian processes. In: Decision and Control, pp. 5371–5376 (2013)
6. Guo, J., Riebler, A.: meta4diag: Bayesian bivariate meta-analysis of diagnostic test studies for routine practice. Statistics (2015)
7. Dutta, R., Bogdan, M., Ghosh, J.K.: Model selection and multiple testing - a Bayesian and empirical Bayes overview and some new results. Statistics (2015)

8. Mangia, M., Rovatti, R., Setti, G.: Rakeness in the design of analog-to-information conversion of sparse and localized signals. IEEE Trans. Circuits Syst. I Regul. Pap. **59**, 1001–1014 (2012)
9. Liu, C.Z., Gal-Or, E., Kemerer, C.F., Smith, M.D.: Compatibility and proprietary standards: the impact of conversion technologies in IT markets with network effects. Inf. Syst. Res. **22**, 188–207 (2011)
10. Braun, A.G., Lettnin, D.V., Gerlach, J., Rosenstiel, W.: Automated conversion of SystemC fixed-point data types. IFIP Int. Fed. Inf. Process. **200**, 55–72 (1969)

A Modified Dai-Yuan Conjugate Gradient Algorithm for Large-Scale Optimization Problems

Gonglin Yuan and Tingting Li[✉]

College of Mathematics and Information Science, Guangxi University,
Nanning 530004, Guangxi, People's Republic of China
ltt@st.gxu.edu.cn

Abstract. It is well know that DY conjugate gradient is one of the most efficient optimization algorithms, which sufficiently utilizes the current information of the search direction and gradient function. It is regrettable that DY conjugate gradient algorithm fails to address large scale optimization model and few scholars and writers paid much attention to modifying it. Thus, to solve large scale unconstrained optimization problems, a modified DY conjugate gradient algorithm under Yuan-Wei-Lu line search was proposed. The proposed algorithm not only has a descent character but also a trust region property. At the same time, the objective algorithm meets the demand of global convergence and the corresponding numeral test proves it is more outstanding compare with similar optimization algorithms.

Keywords: Conjugate gradient · Global convergence · Trust region

1 Introduction

Generally speaking, quasi-Newton method [3,12,17] is a very effective method to solve unconstrained optimization problems when the dimension of objective function is not very large. And this kind of method has been quite mature in theoretical analysis and algorithm. But the conjugate gradient method has a strong application background. Besides, unconstrained optimization problems in many application fields, such as power distribution [29], oil exploration [22], economic management [21] and weather forecasting [1], are often complex since the variable's dimension is large. Quasi-Newton method [23] can not solve large-scale optimization problems because of the need to store large matrices. But conjugate gradient method is particularly effective for solving large-scale optimization problems because it just needs to store a few n-dimensional vectors. To design perfect optimization algorithms, scholars from all over the world have been studying in depth and have made many gratifying achievements. HS algorithm was first proposed by Hestenes and Stiefel [20] to solve linear equations in 1952, which has good numerical performance. In 1964, Fletcher and Reeves

X. Sun et al. (Eds.): ICCCS 2018, LNCS 11063, pp. 132–142, 2018.
https://doi.org/10.1007/978-3-030-00006-6_12

(FR) [24] firstly proposed conjugate gradient method for solving nonlinear optimization on the basis of HS algorithm. Dai and Yuan (DY) analyzed FR method more thoroughly [27] and firstly proposed DY optimization algorithm in 1995. In addition, PRP conjugate gradient method is proposed by Polak, Ribiere and Polyak [6] and is one of conjugate gradient methods, which is considered as the best numerical performance at present. It is regrettable that PRP conjugate gradient algorithm does not satisfy the convergence property under general conditions. The conjugate descent method (CD) was introduced by Fletcher [16] in 1987 and its convergence property is extremely serious. Later, Dai and Yuan proved strictly one of the important properties of DY method by introducing a descent direction of each steps under Wolfe line search technique [14]. And Dai and Yuan [25, 26] discussed the global convergence of CD method under the generalized Wolfe line search technique. Recently, Lian and Wang [18] studied the global convergence of CD method under Armijo line search [19]. Yuan and Wei raised the two-point gradient method. In addition to the above several famous conjugate gradient method, the hybrid conjugate gradient method [4,11], conjugate gradient method cluster [2] and three-term conjugate gradient method [15,19] have been greatly developed in recent years. Touti-Ahmed [5], Gilbert [13] and Nocedal and Storey firstly introduced the hybrid conjugate gradient method, which combined the FR method with PRP method, and obtained ideal results. In this paper, the DY method is modified under Yuan-Wei-Lu linear search technique [7]. Some of the necessary information is given below.

In general, the unconstrained optimization model is considered:

$$\min\{f(x) \mid x \in \Re^n\}, \tag{1}$$

where $f : \Re^n \to R$ is the continuous and differentiable function. For (1), the iterative formula of the conjugate gradient algorithm is defined by

$$x_{k+1} = x_k + \alpha_k d_k, k = 0, 1, 2, ..., \tag{2}$$

where x_k is a kth iteration point, $\alpha_k > 0$ is the steplength, d_k is a conjugate gradient search direction. And d_k is defined as follows:

$$d_{k+1} = \begin{cases} -g(x_{k+1}) + \beta_k d_k, & \text{if } k \geq 1, \\ -g(x_{k+1}), & \text{if } k = 0. \end{cases} \tag{3}$$

where parameter β_k is a scalar. In 1999, Dai and Yuan proposed a conjugate gradient algorithm which can guarantee the global convergence under the Wolfe line search technique [25, 26], where the parameter β_k is given by the following formula

$$\beta_k^{DY} = \frac{\|g_k\|^2}{d_k^T Y_k}, \tag{4}$$

where $g(x_{k+1}) = \nabla f(x_{k+1}), g(x_k) = \nabla f(x_k)$ are the gradient at x_k and x_{k+1}, $Y_k = g(x_{k+1}) - g(x_k)$. And $\|.\|$ denotes the Euclidean norm of vectors. This equivalent formula will play a very important role in the convergence of the DY method for (1). It has a good convergence under Yuan-Wei-Lu (YWL) line search technique [9] for (1). However, the numerical performance is not as effective as the PRP [28] method. For steplength α_k under YWL line search technique, it is expressed by following

$$f(x_k + \alpha_k d_k) \leq f(x_k) + \eta \alpha_k g_k^T d_k + \alpha_k \min[-\eta_1 g_k^T d_k, \frac{\eta \alpha_k \|d_k\|^2}{2}] \tag{5}$$

and

$$g(x_k + \alpha_k d_k)^T d_k \geq \varphi g_k^T d_k + \min[-\eta_1 g_k^T d_k, \eta \alpha_k \|d_k\|^2], \tag{6}$$

where $\eta \in (0, 1/2), \eta_1 \in (0, \eta), \varphi \in (\eta, 1)$. Under inexact line search technique, YWL has partly resolved the global convergence of normal BFGS method, which is regarded as one of major problems in the twentieth century [10]. It is observed more comparison of the normal weak Wolfe-Powell technique between YWL technique from the paper [8]. On the basis of the above conclusions, a new algorithm can be proposed for (1). The new DY algorithm has the following features:

 (i) The new algorithm has the sufficient descent property and the trust region feature to the search direction.
 (ii) The global convergence of the DY algorithm under YWL linear search technique is proved.
(iii) Its numerical results are more effective than those of the normal HS method.

The whole structure of this paper is as follows. The conjugate gradient formula and algorithm steps of the modified DY methods are given in Sect. 2. In Sect. 3, the sufficient descent property, the trust region feature and the global convergence is testified. The numerical experiments are given to verify the effectiveness of the new algorithm in Sect. 4. Make a summary of the whole article in Sect. 5.

2   Modified DY Algorithm

The conjugate gradient algorithm has simple and obvious features, which are often used to solve large-scale optimization problems. And the DY method is one of the most effective methods. Dai analyzes the intrinsic properties of the DY method without using any line search and proves that the method is far from the optimal point, the sufficient descent must be true for most iterations point. DY method has good theoretical properties, but the numerical performance is not ideal. The starting point of this paper is how to design a new conjugate gradient method on the basis of DY method, which has good theoretical properties and good numerical performance. A modified DY formula is presented under YWL line search technique for (1), which is devised by

$$d_{k+1} = \begin{cases} -g_{k+1} + \frac{\|g_{k+1}\|^2 d_k - d_k^T g_{k+1} g_{k+1}}{\max\{2\gamma\|d_k\|\|g_{k+1}\|, |d_k^T Y_k|\}}, & \text{if } k \geq 1, \\ -g_{k+1}, & \text{if } k = 0. \end{cases} \tag{7}$$

where $g_k = g(x_{k+1})$, and γ is a positive constant. The above is inspired by the literature [19]. The specific steps of the new algorithm are follows:

Algorithm 1: Modified three-term DY conjugate gradient algorithm(M-TT-DY)

Step 1: $x_0 \in \Re^n, \epsilon \in (0,1), \eta \in (0,1/2), \eta_1 \in (0,\eta), \varphi \in (\eta,1), \gamma^* = 1 + \frac{1}{\gamma}$ is a positive constant. Let $k = 0$ and $d_0 = g(x_0)$.

Step 2: If $\|g_k\| \leq \epsilon$ holds, the algorithm will stop.

Step 3: Using YWL line search (5) and (6) to find α_k.

Step 4: Set $x_{k+1} = x_k + \alpha_k d_k$.

Step 5: The algorithm will stop if $\|g_{k+1}\| \leq \epsilon$.

Step 6: Find d_k by (7).

Step 7: Set $k = k + 1$ and continue Step 3.

3   Some Basis Properties and Globally Convergence

This section mainly proves the global convergence of the DY method by Algorithm 1, and it is first necessary to indicate that the sufficient descent property and the trust region feature are established for (7). The general assumption is necessary as follows:

Assumption A(a) The level set $\Gamma = \{x \in \Re^n \mid f(x) \leq f(x_o)\}$ is bounded.
(b) The function $f(x)$ is differentiable and bounded from below, and its gradient g is Lipschitz continuous, namely,

$$\|g(x) - g(y)\| \leq \chi \|x - y\|, \forall x, y \in \Gamma \tag{8}$$

holds, where $\chi > 0$ is called as Lipschitz constant.

Lemma 1. *The search direction d_k is designed by (7), the following two relations*

$$\|d_k\| \leq \gamma^* \|g_k\| \tag{9}$$

and

$$g_k^T d_k = -\|g_k\|^2 \tag{10}$$

hold, where $\gamma^* = 1 + \frac{1}{\gamma}(\gamma > 0)$ is a positive constant.

Proof: If k = 1, (9) and (10) are clearly established. If $k \geq 1$, by (7), we have

$$\|d_{k+1}\| = \|g_{k+1} + \frac{\|g_{k+1}\|^2 d_k - d_k^T g_{k+1} g_{k+1}}{\max\{2\gamma \|d_k\| \|g_{k+1}\|, |d_k^T Y_k|\}}\|$$
$$\leq \|g_{k+1}\| + \frac{\|g_{k+1}\|^2 \|d_k\| + \|d_k\| \|g_{k+1}\|^2}{\max\{2\gamma \|d_k\| \|g_{k+1}\|, |d_k^T Y_k|\}}$$

$$\leq \|g_{k+1}\| + \frac{2\|g_{k+1}\|^2\|d_k\|}{2\gamma\|d_k\|\|g_{k+1}\|}$$

$$\leq (1 + \frac{1}{\gamma})\|g_{k+1}\|$$

$$= \gamma^*\|g_{k+1}\|,$$

where

$$\max\{2\gamma\|d_k\|\|g_{k+1}\|\} \geq 2\gamma\|d_k\|\|g_{k+1}\|.$$

By (7), we obtain

$$g_{k+1}^T d_{k+1} = g_{k+1}^T[-g_{k+1} + \frac{\|g_{k+1}\|^2 d_k - d_k^T g_{k+1} g_{k+1}}{\max\{2\gamma\|d_k\|\|g_{k+1}\|, |d_k^T Y_k|\}}]$$

$$= -\|g_{k+1}\|^2 + \frac{\|g_{k+1}\|^2 g_{k+1}^T d_k - d_k^T g_{k+1} g_{k+1}^T g_{k+1}}{\max\{2\gamma\|d_k\|\|g_{k+1}\|, |d_k^T Y - k|\}}$$

$$= -\|g_{k+1}\|^2.$$

The proof is completed. The region trust feature (9) of new algorithm is proved, and the inequality (10) has demonstrated the modified DY method possesses the sufficient descent property under the YWL line search technique. Through observing (7) and Assumption A, similar to [7], is difficult to show the YWL line search technology is reasonable and Algorithm 1 is more clear. The following theorem will prove the global convergence of Algorithm 1.

Theorem 1. *Let Assumption A holds, and M-TT-DY exists the iterate sequence $\{x_k, \alpha_k, d_k, g_k\}$. According to Lemma 1, the following formula*

$$\lim_{k \to \infty} \|g_k\| = 0 \tag{11}$$

holds.

Proof: By (5), we get

$$f(x_k + \alpha_k d_k) \leq f(x_k) + \eta\alpha_k g_k^T d_k + \alpha_k \min[-\eta_1 g_k^T d_k, \frac{\eta\alpha_k\|d_k\|^2}{2}]$$

$$\leq f(x_k) + \eta\alpha_k g_k^T d_k - \alpha_k\eta_1 g_k^T d_k$$

$$\leq f(x_k) + \alpha_k(\eta - \eta_1)g_k^T d_k$$

$$\leq f(x_k) - \alpha_k(\eta - \eta_1)\|g_k\|^2,$$

where

$$\min[-\eta_1 g_k^T d_k, \frac{\eta\alpha_k\|d_k\|^2}{2}] \leq -\eta_1 g_k^T d_k,$$

so the second inequality holds. And the last inequality can be derived from (10). Summing the above inequalities from k from 0 to ∞, we have

$$\sum_{k=0}^{\infty} \alpha_k(\eta - \eta_1)\|g_k\|^2 \leq f_0 - f_\infty < +\infty.$$

The above inequality indicates

$$\lim_{k \to \infty} \alpha_k \|g_k\|^2 = 0 \tag{12}$$

holds. By (6) and (10), we have

$$
\begin{aligned}
g(x_k + \alpha_k d_k)^T d_k &\geq \varphi g_k^T d_k + \min[-\eta_1 g_k^T d_k, \eta \alpha_k \|d_k\|^2] \\
&> \varphi g_k^T d_k \\
&= \varphi \|g_k\|^2.
\end{aligned}
$$

The two sides of the last equality are subtracted $g_k^T d_k$, i.e.,

$$
\begin{aligned}
-(\varphi - 1)\|g_k\|^2 &= (\varphi - 1)g_k^T d_k \\
&\leq [g(x_k + \alpha_k d_k) - g(x_k)]^T d_k \\
&\leq \|g(x_k + \alpha_k d_k) - g(x_k)\| \|d_k\| \\
&\leq \alpha_k \chi \|d_k\|^2
\end{aligned}
$$

is true, and the last inequality is from Assumption A(b). Combine (9), we obtain

$$\alpha_k \geq \frac{(1 - \varphi)\|g_k\|^2}{\chi(\gamma^*)^2 \|g_k\|^2} = (1 - \varphi)/(\chi(\gamma^*)^2).$$

Again combining with (12) the following formula

$$\lim_{k \to \infty} \|g_k\|^2 = 0 \tag{13}$$

holds. Thus the proof is complete.

4 Numerical Results

In order to further observe the effectiveness of the Algorithm 1, the Algorithm1 is compared with HS algorithms, which is named as Algorithm 2. And this section consists of test questions and experimental results. In the paper mainly compares the NI, NF, CPU of Algorithm 1 and Algorithm 2, whose results have been shown in tables and figures. Where NI: the total number of iterations, NF: the number of the function and gradient evaluations, CPU: the CPU time in second.

Calculation: The calculation environment of the experiment is a computer with 2GB of memory, and operating system of a Pentium(R) Dual-Core CPU E5800 @ 3.20 GHz and the 64-bit Windows 7 operating system.

Parameters: The parameters were chosen to be $\eta = 0.05, \eta_1 = 0.01, \varphi = 0.01$.

Stopping ruler: If $|f(x_k)| \leq 10^{-5}$, let qq1 $= |f(x_{k+1}) - f(x_k)|$; Otherwise, let qq1 $= \frac{|f(x_{k+1}) - f(x_k)|}{|f(x_k)|}$. If $\|g(x_k)\| \leq 10^{-6}$ or qq1 $\leq 10^{-5}$ hold, the program stops.

Dimension: 1200, 3000, 6000, 9000.

In the experiment, 73 problems are tested. And its experimental results are given in Table 1 in 6000 and 9000 dimensions. Where the NI, NF and CPU data of Algorithm 1 and Algorithm 2 are given in the tables. Observation of the tables shows that in solving most problems, NI, NF, CPU of Algorithm 1 is smaller than that of Algorithm 2. Next, to analyze the figures, the Fig. 1 and Fig. 2 are the NI and NF curves of Algorithm 1 and Algorithm 2 respectively. From the figures, we can see that the red curve of eventually all exceed the black curve, which means that Algorithm 1 has fewer number of iterations in dealing with the same problem. For Fig. 3, the two curve shows that algorithm1 is lower than Algorithm 2 in the CPU time in second. From the above analysis, it can be concluded that the modified DY method is more effective than the HS method.

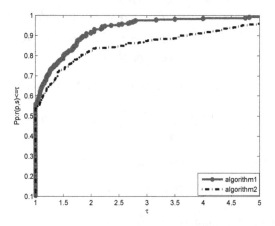

Fig. 1. Performance profiles of these methods (NI)

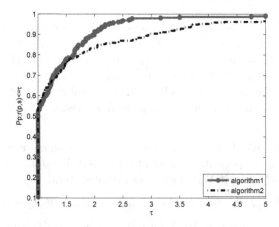

Fig. 2. Performance profiles of these methods (NF)

Table 1. The results of the algorithm 1 and algorithm 2.

NO	Dim	algorithm 1			algorithm 2			NO	Dim	algorithm 1			algorithm 2		
		NI	NFG	CPU	NI	NFG	CPU			NI	NFG	CPU	NI	NFG	CPU
1	6000	3	26	0.0624	37	76	0.468003	38	6000	11	36	0.0312	10	26	0.0312
1	9000	3	26	0.156001	37	76	0.702004	38	9000	17	57	0.0624	12	30	0.0624
2	6000	11	110	0.234002	52	119	0.436803	39	6000	5	14	0.001	10	27	0.001
2	9000	9	105	0.312002	58	130	0.733205	39	9000	5	14	0.0312	10	27	0.0312
3	6000	202	916	0.530403	96	250	0.156001	40	6000	37	393	1.669211	2000	4015	42.213871
3	9000	34	202	0.202801	66	186	0.171601	40	9000	91	655	5.210433	2000	4017	62.759202
4	6000	100	499	1.450809	229	493	1.840812	41	6000	16	62	0.124801	32	70	0.0312
4	9000	46	265	0.982806	117	257	1.49761	41	9000	42	153	0.249602	31	68	0.0624
5	6000	72	280	0.530403	38	82	0.187201	42	6000	4	33	0.0312	4	33	0.0312
5	9000	72	280	0.733205	44	97	0.343202	42	9000	4	33	0.0624	4	33	0.0312
6	6000	22	160	0.109201	110	240	0.218401	43	6000	5	50	0.187201	51	104	1.060807
6	9000	15	137	0.124801	104	230	0.249602	43	9000	5	50	0.280802	52	106	1.51321
7	6000	2000	4011	3.806424	463	928	0.764405	44	6000	7	46	0.218401	60	122	1.216808
7	9000	2000	4011	5.491235	569	1140	1.450809	44	9000	7	46	0.374402	61	124	1.809612
8	6000	44	100	0.156001	27	56	0.093601	45	6000	5	52	0.218401	83	168	1.450809
8	9000	44	100	0.343202	27	56	0.109201	45	9000	5	52	0.296402	85	172	2.386815
9	6000	3	26	0.0312	8	18	0.001	46	6000	7	63	0.249602	607	1216	10.810869
9	9000	3	26	0.0312	8	18	0.0312	46	9000	7	63	0.358802	659	1320	17.17571
10	6000	2	13	0.093601	2	13	0.0624	47	6000	154	544	165.875863	19	56	18.236517
10	9000	2	13	0.093601	2	13	0.124801	47	9000	347	1224	728.852272	33	82	58.437975
11	6000	46	365	0.436803	158	327	0.655204	48	6000	47	165	14.118091	858	1721	189.525615
11	9000	4	38	0.156001	241	494	1.435209	48	9000	71	256	42.260671	354	713	154.50339
12	6000	35	72	0.171601	15	32	0.124801	49	6000	2000	4011	3.291621	465	932	0.982806
12	9000	35	72	0.280802	15	32	0.124801	49	9000	2000	4011	4.570829	571	1144	1.466409
13	6000	6	41	0.093601	25	55	0.156001	50	6000	2000	4011	493.883566	461	924	108.951098
13	9000	3	24	0.202801	3	24	0.124801	50	9000	2000	4011	947.846476	565	1132	254.656032
14	6000	4	19	2.808018	5	13	2.106013	51	6000	3	27	0.0624	12	26	0.156001
14	9000	4	19	4.804831	5	13	3.993626	51	9000	3	27	0.124801	12	26	0.234001
15	6000	9	87	3.369622	64	140	9.562861	52	6000	15	183	0.218401	143	316	0.936006
15	9000	5	41	3.213621	61	133	17.940115	52	9000	16	196	0.312002	150	332	1.466409
16	6000	7	45	0.0624	9	21	0.0312	53	6000	3	18	0.093601	2000	4002	3.510023
16	9000	7	45	0.0624	8	19	0.0624	53	9000	3	18	0.093601	2000	4002	6.364841
17	6000	214	447	3.276021	21	45	0.312002	54	6000	135	475	0.436803	102	232	0.421203
17	9000	214	447	4.804831	24	51	0.499203	54	9000	47	176	0.218401	49	131	0.249602
18	6000	18	69	0.093601	3	10	0.0312	55	6000	3	26	1.185608	13	28	1.56001
18	9000	18	69	0.0624	3	10	0.001	55	9000	3	26	2.496016	13	28	3.728424
19	6000	3	9	0.0312	3	9	0.0312	56	6000	7	30	0.0312	2000	4000	3.291621
19	9000	3	9	0.0312	3	9	0.0312	56	9000	7	30	0.0312	2000	4000	5.413235
20	6000	13	71	0.0312	10	28	0.0312	57	6000	5	51	0.218401	154	312	3.697224
20	9000	27	124	0.093601	12	32	0.0312	57	9000	5	51	0.280802	160	324	5.023232
21	6000	8	90	0.124801	35	76	0.124801	58	6000	7	64	0.249602	118	242	2.496016
21	9000	8	92	0.156001	35	76	0.218401	58	9000	7	64	0.421203	126	258	3.697224
22	6000	5	48	0.0624	7	41	0.0468	59	6000	350	741	6.349241	73	152	1.419609
22	9000	5	48	0.0624	6	31	0.0624	59	9000	397	835	10.701669	79	164	2.293215
23	6000	23	129	0.312002	203	454	1.825212	60	6000	8	67	0.249602	609	1220	12.199278
23	9000	40	287	0.889206	182	401	2.496016	60	9000	8	67	0.468003	659	1320	17.830914
24	6000	5	55	0.093601	21	111	0.093601	61	6000	5	51	0.218401	148	300	3.10442
24	9000	5	55	0.140401	21	111	0.124801	61	9000	5	51	0.312002	156	316	4.196427
25	6000	4	21	0.001	8	16	0.001	62	6000	7	75	0.265202	133	272	2.371215
25	9000	4	21	0.0156	2000	4038	4.274427	62	9000	7	75	0.421203	143	292	3.759624
26	6000	9	108	0.093601	61	140	0.202801	63	6000	9	87	0.421203	213	432	4.290028
26	9000	8	97	0.156001	61	140	0.343202	63	9000	9	87	0.624004	234	474	7.051245
27	6000	269	958	0.733205	63	158	0.0624	64	6000	10	62	0.312002	25	56	0.436803
27	9000	358	1258	1.63801	71	187	0.218401	64	9000	11	64	0.436803	25	56	0.655204
28	6000	25	156	0.124801	464	958	0.811205	65	6000	4	39	4.149627	20	42	6.645643
28	9000	25	149	0.124801	103	226	0.265202	65	9000	4	39	7.628449	20	42	12.183678
29	6000	2	14	0.001	4	22	0.001	66	6000	7	16	1.653611	21	46	5.054432
29	9000	2	14	0.0312	4	21	0.0312	66	9000	7	16	3.10442	12	26	5.085633
30	6000	2000	4011	7.425648	433	868	0.686404	67	6000	8	73	0.0312	7	63	0.0624
30	9000	2000	4011	5.772037	541	1084	1.123207	67	9000	92	472	1.981213	5	35	0.0312
31	6000	5	53	0.0312	35	76	0.078001	68	6000	25	79	0.0624	18	38	0.0312
31	9000	5	53	0.0624	37	80	0.109201	68	9000	25	79	0.093601	18	38	0.0624
32	6000	6	56	0.0624	81	164	0.343202	69	6000	8	60	0.0312	40	238	0.187201
32	9000	5	44	0.0624	34	74	0.171601	69	9000	8	60	0.0624	41	249	0.327602
33	6000	2	7	0.001	3	7	0.001	70	6000	8	62	4.118426	40	101	10.826469
33	9000	2	7	0.001	2	5	0.001	70	9000	6	38	5.038832	147	340	71.604459
34	6000	3	24	0.0156	4	8	0.001	71	6000	5	22	0.0624	2000	4000	3.447622
34	9000	3	17	0.0156	4	8	0.0312	71	9000	5	22	0.093601	2000	4000	5.023232
35	6000	3	26	0.001	6	12	0.001	72	6000	383	1372	418.815885	2000	4084	1689.724831
35	9000	3	26	0.001	6	12	0.0156	72	9000	347	1237	731.410689	2000	4148	3311.745229
36	6000	8	41	2.979619	12	32	3.13562	73	6000	2000	4011	3.276021	602	1206	0.842405
36	9000	8	42	6.27124	26	61	12.604881	73	9000	2000	4011	4.64883	740	1482	1.49761
37	6000	1768	6186	4.914032	981	1966	1.778411								
37	9000	2000	6998	7.76885	831	1666	2.152814								

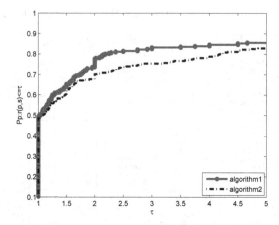

Fig. 3. Performance profiles of these methods (CPU)

5   Conclusion

In this paper, a modified DY three-term conjugate gradient algorithm under YWL line search technique is proposed for large-scale optimization problems and the related properties are proved. Firstly, the sufficient descent property and trust region feature of the modified DY algorithm are proved. According to these two properties, the global convergence of DY is obtained. Because the numerical performance of HS is superior, the next step is to compare the numerical results of HS and new DY. The maximum dimension of the test problem is 9000 dimensions. The results show that the new algorithm is superior to HS method. It can also be found that more and more effective algorithms will be proposed in the future.

Acknowledgements. We would like to thank reviewers and editors for their meaningful suggestions. This work is supported by the National Natural Science Foundation of China (Grant No. 11661009), the Guangxi Science Fund for Distinguished Young Scholars (No. 2015GXNSFGA139001), and the Guangxi Natural Science Key Fund (No. 2017GXNSFDA198046).

References

1. Akkraoui, A., Trmolet, Y., Todling, R.: Preconditioning of variational data assimilation and the use of a bi-conjugate gradient method. Q. J. R. Meteorol. Soc. **139**, 731–741 (2013)
2. Jordan, A., Bycul, R.P.: The parallel algorithm of conjugate gradient method. In: Grigoras, D., Nicolau, A., Toursel, B., Folliot, B. (eds.) IWCC 2001. LNCS, vol. 2326, pp. 156–165. Springer, Heidelberg (2002). https://doi.org/10.1007/3-540-47840-X_15
3. Shanno, D.: Conditioning of quasi-Newton methods for function minimization. Math. Comput. **24**, 647–656 (1970)

4. Touati-Ahmed, D., Storey, C.: Efficient hybrid conjugate gradient techniques. J. Optim. Theor. Appl. **64**, 379–397 (1990)
5. Touati-Ahmed, D., Storey, C.: Globally convergent hybrid conjugate gradient methods. J. Optim. Theor. Appl. **64**, 379–397 (1990)
6. Polak, E., Ribire, G.: Note sur la convergence de mthodes de directions conjugues. Rev. Franaise Informat. Recherche Oprationnelle **16**, 35–43 (2009)
7. Yuan, G., Hu, W., Sheng, Z.: A conjugate gradient algorithm with Yuan-Wei-Lu line search. In: Sun, X., Chao, H.-C., You, X., Bertino, E. (eds.) ICCCS 2017. LNCS, vol. 10603, pp. 738–746. Springer, Cham (2017). https://doi.org/10.1007/978-3-319-68542-7_64
8. Yuan, G., Sheng, Z., Wang, B.: The global convergence of a modified BFGS method for nonconvex functions. J. Comput. Appl. Math. **327**, 274–294 (2017)
9. Yuan, G., Wei, Z., Lu, X.: Global convergence of BFGS and PRP methods under a modified weak Wolfe-Powell line search. Appl. Math. Model. **47**, 811–825 (2017)
10. Darzentas, J.: Problem complexity and method efficiency in optimization. J. Oper. Res. Soc. **35**, 455 (1984)
11. Dong, J., Jiao, B., Chen, L.: A new hybrid HS-DY conjugate gradient method. In: International Joint Conference on Computational Sciences and Optimization, vol. 4, pp. 94–98 (2011)
12. Gilbert, J., Lemarchal, C.: Some numerical experiments with variable-storage quasi-Newton algorithms. Math. Program. **45**, 407–435 (1989)
13. Gilbert, J., Nocedal, J.: Global convergence properties of conjugate gradient methods for optimization. SIAM J. Optim. **2**, 21–42 (1990)
14. Tang, J., Dong, L., Zhang, X.: A new class of memory gradient methods with Wolfe line search. J. Shandong Univ. **44**, 33–37 (2005)
15. Dixon, L., Ducksbury, P., Singh, P.: A new three-term conjugate gradient method. J. Optim. Theor. Appl. **47**, 285–300 (1985)
16. Fletcher, R.: Practical Methods of Optimization, vol. 1, pp. 71–94. Wiley (1980)
17. Surhone, L.M., Timpledon, M.T., Marseken, S.F.: Quasi-Newton method. Betascript Publ. **14**, 115–150 (2010)
18. Lian, S., Wang, C.: Global convergence properties of the conjugate descent method. OR Trans. **7**, 1–9 (2003)
19. Zhang, L., Zhou, W., Li, D.: Global convergence of a modified Fletcher-Reeves conjugate gradient method with Armijo-type line search. Numerische Mathematik **104**, 561–572 (2006)
20. Hestenes, M., Stiefel, E.: Methods of conjugate gradients for solving linear systems. J. Res. Natl. Bur. Stand. **49**, 409–436 (1952)
21. Islam, M., Robert, A., James, W.: Integrated economic-hydrologic modelling for groundwater basin management. Int. J. Water Resour. Dev. **13**, 21–34 (1997)
22. Qin, P., Huang, D., Yuan, Y.: Integrated gravity and gravity gradient 3D inversion using the non-linear conjugate gradient. J. Appl. Geophys. **126**, 52–73 (2016)
23. Byrd, R., Nocedal, J.: A Tool for the analysis of quasi-Newton methods with application to unconstrained minimization. Soc. Ind. Appl. Math. **26**, 727–739 (1989)
24. Fletcher, R., Reeves, C.: Function minimization by conjugate gradients. Comput. J. **7**, 149–154 (1964)
25. Dai, Y., Han, J., Liu, G.: Convergence properties of nonlinear conjugate gradient methods. SIAM J. Optim. **10**, 345–358 (1998)
26. Dai, Y., Yuan, Y.: Convergence properties of the conjugate descent method. Adv. Math. **26**, 552–562 (1996)

27. Dai, Y., Yuan, Y.: Convergence properties of the Fletcher-Reeves method. IMA J. Numer. Anal. **16**, 155–164 (1996)
28. Dai, Z., Tian, B.: Global convergence of some modified PRP nonlinear conjugate gradient methods. Optim. Lett. **5**, 615–630 (2011)
29. Pan, Z., Cai, Y., Tan, S.: Transient analysis of on-chip power distribution networks using equivalent circuit modeling. In: International Symposium on Quality Electronic Design Proceedings, pp. 63–68 (2004)

A Modified Wei-Yao-Liu Conjugate Gradient Algorithm for Two Type Minimization Optimization Models

Xiaoliang Wang[2], Wujie Hu[1], and Gonglin Yuan[1(✉)]

[1] College of Mathematics and Information Science,
Guangxi University, Nanning, Guangxi, People's Republic of China
yuangl0417@126.com
[2] College of Mathematics and Science, Dalian University of Technology,
Dalian, Liaoning 116024, People's Republic of China

Abstract. This paper presents a modified Wei-Yao-Liu conjugate gradient method, which automatically not only has sufficient descent property but also owns trust region property without carrying out any line search technique. The global convergence property for unconstrained optimization problems is satisfied with weak Wolfe-Powell (WWP) line search. Meanwhile, the present method can be extended to solve nonlinear equations problems. Under some mild condition, line search method and project technique, the global convergence is established. Some preliminary numerical tests are presented. The numerical results show its effectiveness.

Keywords: Conjugate gradient · Unconstrained optimization
Nonlinear equations · Sufficient descent property · Trust region
Project strategy · Global convergence

AMS 2010 subject classifications. 90C26.

1 Introduction

Consider the following optimization models

$$\min_{x \in \Re^n} \psi(x), \tag{1.1}$$

where $\psi(x) : \Re^n \to \Re$ is a continuously differentiable function. There are many methods for unconstrained optimization (1.1) such as Newton methods [1,2],

This work is supported by the National Natural Science Foundation of China (Grant No. 11661009), the Guangxi Science Fund for Distinguished Young Scholars (No. 2015GXNSFGA139001), and the Guangxi Natural Science Key Fund (No. 2017GXNSFDA198046).

© Springer Nature Switzerland AG 2018
X. Sun et al. (Eds.): ICCCS 2018, LNCS 11063, pp. 143–159, 2018.
https://doi.org/10.1007/978-3-030-00006-6_13

quasi-Newton methods [3–7], conjugate gradient methods [8–23] and so on. However, the conjugate gradient (CG) methods are one of the most effective methods for (1.1) due to its simplicity and much low memory. The iterative formula is usually defined by

$$x_{k+1} = x_k + \alpha_k d_k, \ k = 0, \ 1, \ 2, \cdots, \tag{1.2}$$

where x_k is the k-th iteration, x_{k+1} is the next iterative point; $\alpha_k > 0$ is the step-length which is determined by some line search methods; and d_k is the search direction usually defined by

$$d_k = \begin{cases} -g_k, & \text{if } k = 0, \\ -g_k + \beta_k d_{k-1}, & \text{if } k \geq 1, \end{cases} \tag{1.3}$$

where g_k is the abbreviation of $g(x_k)$, which is the gradient $\nabla \psi(x_k)$ of $\psi(x)$ at the point x_k; and β_k is a scalar. Different scalars β_k mean different CG methods. Some well-known CG methods include the Fletcher-Reeves (FR) method [16], the Polak-Ribiére-Polyak (PRP) method [17,18], the Dai-Yuan (DY) method [8], and the Wei-Yao-Liu (WYL) method [19] and so on. The parameters β_k of these methods are stated as follows:

$$\beta_k^{FR} = \frac{\|g_k\|^2}{\|g_{k-1}\|^2}, \quad \beta_k^{PRP} = \frac{g_k^T y_{k-1}}{\|g_{k-1}\|^2}, \quad \beta_k^{DY} = \frac{\|g_k\|^2}{d_{k-1}^T y_{k-1}}, \quad \beta_k^{WYL} = \frac{g_k^T (g_k - \frac{\|g_k\|}{\|g_{k-1}\|} g_{k-1})}{\|g_{k-1}\|^2}.$$

where $y_{k-1} = g_k - g_{k-1}$, $k \geq 1$ and $\| \ \|$ is the Euclidean norm.

In the implementations and convergence analysis of CG methods, one of the most usefull line search methods is the weak Wolfe-Powell line search method (WWP), that is:

$$\psi(x_k + \alpha_k d_k) \leq \psi_k + \lambda \alpha_k g_k^T d_k \tag{1.4}$$

and

$$g(x_k + \alpha_k d_k)^T d_k \geq \mu g_k^T d_k \tag{1.5}$$

where $\lambda \in (0, \frac{1}{2})$, and $\mu \in (\lambda, 1)$.

Over the past few years, The following sufficient descent condition:

$$g_k^T d_k \leq -\tau \|g_k\|^2, \quad \forall k \geq 1. \tag{1.6}$$

is often used to analyze the CG methods'global convergence by the inexact line search techniques with some positive constant τ (see [11–15]).

In this paper, we design a modified CG algorithm which has the following attributes: The method has the sufficient descent property without any line search method; The global convergence of the method is established for large-scale unconstrained optimization problems under mild conditions; the proposed modified algorithm with norm descent inexact line search technology is suitable for solving large-scale nonlinear equations.

This paper is organized as follows. In the next section, the new formula and the corresponding algorithm are discussed. In Sect. 3, the global convergence is established for the unconstrained optimization. The proposed method is applied to another type optimization model in Sect. 4. The convergence analysis and the numerical results are reported in Sects. 5 and 6, respectively.

2   The New Formula and the Corresponding Algorithm

It is well-known that the global convergence of the most numerical effective PRP method can not hold with weak Wolfe-Powell line search; However, some algorithms which posses global convergence, such as FR method, do not perform better than the PRP method in numerical behavior. Does there exist a method which not only posses better computational results as the PRP method but also nice convergence properties as the FR method? In the recent years, many efforts have been done to find new CG methods which not only possess both global convergence property for general functions but also good numerical performance (see [20, 21]).

In this paper, we present a new scalar as follow

$$\beta_k^N = \frac{\|g_k\|^2 - \max\{0, \frac{\|g_k\|}{\|g_{k-1}\|} g_k^T g_{k-1}\}}{\mu_2 \|g_k\| \|d_{k-1}\| + \|g_{k-1}\|^2 + \eta_2 |g_{k-1}^T d_{k-1}|} \tag{2.1}$$

Note that if $\mu_2 = 0$, $\eta_2 = 0$, and $g_k^T g_{k-1} \geq 0$, then $\beta_k^N = \beta_k^{WYL}$. In this paper, we set $\mu_2 > 1$ and $\eta_2 > 0$. Then the search direction d_k is calculated by

$$d_k = \begin{cases} -g_k, & \text{if } k = 0, \\ -g_k + \beta_k^N d_{k-1}, & \text{if } k \geq 1, \end{cases} \tag{2.2}$$

In the next, we will present the algorithm:

Algorithm 1
Step 0: Given $x_0 \in \Re^n$, $0 < \delta < \sigma < 1$, $\mu_2 > 1, \eta_2 > 0$, let $k := 0$.
Step 1: If $\|g_k\| \leq \epsilon$, then, stop; otherwise, proceed to next step.
Step 2: Compute step size α_k by line search rules (1.4) and (1.5).
Step 3: Calculate the search direction by (2.2).
Step 4: Let $x_{k+1} = x_k + \alpha_k d_k$.
Step 5: If $\|g_{k+1}\| \leq \epsilon$, stop; otherwise, let $k := k + 1$, go to step 2.

3   The Sufficient Descent Property and Global Convergence

The following assumption is usually used in the analysis of the global convergence of the CG methods.

Assumption A

(i) The level set $C = \{x \in \Re^n | \psi(x) \le \psi(x_0)\}$ is bounded, where x_0 is the initial point.

(ii) In an open convex set C_0 that contains C, $\psi(x)$ owns the following properties: it is differentiable and its gradient $g(x)$ is Lipschitz continuous, that is, there exists a constant $L > 0$ satisfying:

$$\|g(x) - g(y)\| \le L\|x - y\|, \quad \forall x, y \in C_0. \tag{3.1}$$

The following lemmas state some interesting properties of the new CG method.

Lemma 3.1. *The search direction d_k produced by (2.2) satisfies*

$$g_k^T d_k \le -(1 - \frac{1}{\mu_2})\|g_k\|^2 \tag{3.2}$$

Proof. If $k = 0$, by the definition of d_k, we have $d_0 = -g_0$, then $g_0^T d_0 = -\|g_0\|^2 \le -(1 - \frac{1}{\mu_2})\|g_0\|^2$. If $k \ge 1$, by the definition of d_k, we have

$$g_k^T d_k = -\|g_k\|^2 + \beta_k^N g_k^T d_{k-1}$$

$$\le -\|g_k\|^2 + \frac{\|g_k\|^2}{\mu_2\|g_k\|\|d_{k-1}\| + \|g_{k-1}\|^2 + \eta_2|g_{k-1}^T d_{k-1}|} g_k^T d_{k-1}$$

$$\le -\|g_k\|^2 + \frac{\|g_k\|^2}{\mu_2\|g_k\|\|d_{k-1}\|} g_k^T d_{k-1}$$

$$\le -\|g_k\|^2 + \frac{\|g_k\|^2}{\mu_2} = -(1 - \frac{1}{\mu_2})\|g_k\|^2$$

then the lemma is completed.

Lemma 3.2. *The parameter β_k^N satisfies $0 \le \beta_k^N \le \beta_k^{FR}$, and the search direction d_k satisfies*

$$(1 - \frac{1}{\mu_2})\|g_k\| \le \|d_k\| \le (1 + \frac{1}{\mu_2})\|g_k\| \tag{3.3}$$

Proof. From the definition of β_k^N, we have

$$\beta_k^N = \frac{\|g_k\|^2 - \max\{0, \frac{\|g_k\|}{\|g_{k-1}\|} g_k^T g_{k-1}\}}{\mu_2\|g_k\|\|d_{k-1}\| + \|g_{k-1}\|^2 + \eta_2|g_{k-1}^T d_{k-1}|}$$

$$\ge \frac{\|g_k\|^2 - \frac{\|g_k\|}{\|g_{k-1}\|}\|g_k\|\|g_{k-1}\|}{\mu_2\|g_k\|\|d_{k-1}\| + \|g_{k-1}\|^2 + \eta_2|g_{k-1}^T d_{k-1}|} = 0$$

$$\beta_k^N = \frac{\|g_k\|^2 - \max\{0, \frac{\|g_k\|}{\|g_{k-1}\|} g_k^T g_{k-1}\}}{\mu_2\|g_k\|\|d_{k-1}\| + \|g_{k-1}\|^2 + \eta_2|g_{k-1}^T d_{k-1}|} \le \frac{\|g_k\|^2}{\|g_{k-1}\|^2} = \beta_k^{FR}$$

then we have $0 \le \beta_k^N \le \beta_k^{FR}$.

From the sufficient descent property (3.2), we can get

$$\|g_k\|\|d_k\| \geq -g_k^T d_k \geq (1 - \frac{1}{\mu_2})\|g_k\|^2 \tag{3.4}$$

If $\|g_k\| = 0$, then $\|d_k\| = 0$, the conclusion is obviously. If $\|g_k\| \neq 0$, then it is easy to have $\|d_k\| \geq (1 - \frac{1}{\mu_2})\|g_k\|$. By the definition of d_k, we have

$$
\begin{aligned}
\|d_k\| &= \| - g_k + \beta_k^N d_{k-1}\| \\
&\leq \|g_k\| + |\beta_k^N|\|d_{k-1}\| \\
&\leq \|g_k\| + \frac{\|g_k\|^2}{\mu_2\|g_k\|\|d_{k-1}\|}\|d_{k-1}\| \\
&= (1 + \frac{1}{\mu_2})\|g_k\|
\end{aligned}
$$

Then the proof is completed.

Lemma 3.3. *Let Assumption A hold and the step-size α_k is obtained by the Wolf line search (1.4), (1.5), then we have*

$$\sum_{k=1}^{\infty} \frac{(g_k^T d_k)^2}{\|d_k\|^2} < \infty \tag{3.5}$$

Proof. By the condition of the Wolf line search (1.5), we have

$$g_{k+1}^T d_k - g_k^T d_k \geq (\mu - 1)g_k^T d_k \tag{3.6}$$

While by the Assumption A, we get

$$g_{k+1}^T d_k - g_k^T d_k = (g_{k+1} - g_k)^T d_k \leq L(x_{k+1} - x_k)^T d_k = \alpha_k L\|d_k\|^2 \tag{3.7}$$

by (3.6) and (3.7), it is easy to have

$$\alpha_k \geq \frac{\mu - 1}{L} \frac{g_k^T d_k}{\|d_k\|^2} \tag{3.8}$$

The Wolf line search condition (1.4) and (3.8) indicate that

$$\psi_k - \psi_{k+1} \geq \frac{\lambda(1 - \mu)}{L} \frac{(g_k^T d_k)^2}{\|d_k\|^2}$$

Utilizing the above inequality recursively and noting that $\psi(x)$ is bounded, we have (3.5) hold.

Theorem 3.1. *Suppose that the Assumption A holds, The step-size α_k is obtained by the Wolf line search (1.4), (1.5) and consider the definition β_k^N, then we have*

$$\liminf_{k \to \infty} \|g_k\| = 0 \tag{3.9}$$

Proof. We will prove (3.9) by contradiction. Suppose that (3.9) does not hold and Let ϵ be a positive constant such that $\|g_k\| \geq \epsilon$ holds for all $k \geq 0$.

By the definition of d_k, we have

$$\|d_k\|^2 = \| - g_k + \beta_k^N d_{k-1}\|^2 = \|g_k\|^2 - 2\beta_k^N g_k^T d_{k-1} + (\beta_k^N)^2 \|d_{k-1}\|^2 \quad (3.10)$$

From (2.1) and the Lemma 3.2, we can obtain

$$- \beta_k^N g_k^T d_{k-1} \leq |\beta_k^N| \|g_k\| \|d_{k-1}\| \leq \frac{\|g_k\|^2}{\mu_2} \quad (3.11)$$

From (3.10), (3.11) and the Lemma 3.2, we can induce

$$\|d_k\|^2 \leq \|g_k\|^2 + \frac{2\|g_k\|^2}{\mu_2} + (\beta_k^{FR})^2 \|d_{k-1}\|^2 \quad (3.12)$$

$$= (1 + \tfrac{2}{\mu_2})\|g_k\|^2 + \frac{\|g_k\|^4}{\|g_{k-1}\|^4}\|d_{k-1}\|^2 \quad (3.13)$$

Diving both sides of (3.12) by $\|g_k\|^4$, then we have

$$\frac{\|d_k\|^2}{\|g_k\|^4} \leq (1 + \frac{2}{\mu_2})\frac{1}{\|g_k\|^2} + \frac{\|d_{k-1}\|^2}{\|g_{k-1}\|^4} \quad (3.14)$$

Utilizing (3.14) recursively and noting that $\|d_0\|^2 = -g_0^T d_0 = \|g_0\|^2$, then it can deduce

$$\frac{\|d_k\|^2}{\|g_k\|^4} \leq (1 + \frac{2}{\mu_2})\sum_{j=0}^{k}\frac{1}{\|g_j\|^2} \quad (3.15)$$

Since $\|g_k\| \geq \epsilon$, then we have

$$\frac{\|g_k\|^4}{\|d_k\|^2} \geq \frac{\mu_2}{\mu_2 + 2}\frac{\epsilon^2}{k+1}$$

which indicates

$$\sum_{k=0}^{\infty}\frac{\|g_k\|^4}{\|d_k\|^2} = \infty \quad (3.16)$$

From the Lemma 3.3, we have

$$\infty > \sum_{k=1}^{\infty}\frac{(g_k^T d_k)^2}{\|d_k\|^2} \geq (1 - \frac{1}{\mu_2})^2 \sum_{k=0}^{\infty}\frac{\|g_k\|^4}{\|d_k\|^2} = \infty \quad (3.17)$$

which is a contraction, then the proof is completed.

In recent years, many authors applied CG methods with mild line search techniques to solve nonlinear equations problems and got attractive numerical results (see [24–26,30]). Motivated by that, we apply our method to nonlinear equations problems.

4   The New Method for Nonlinear Equations

Consider the following equations

$$\varphi(x) = 0, \ x \in \Re^n \qquad (4.1)$$

where $\varphi : \Re^n \to \Re^n$ is monotone continuously differentiable and the Jacobian $\nabla\varphi(x)$ of φ is symmetric for all $x \in \Re^n$. Let ϕ be the norm function defined by $\phi(x) = \frac{1}{2}\|\varphi(x)\|^2$, where $\|\cdot\|$ is the Euclidean norm. Then, (4.1) is equivalent to the following global optimisation model:

$$\min \phi(x), \ x \in \Re^n. \qquad (4.2)$$

There exist many algorithms for the above models (see [24–30] etc.). One of the most attractive factors of the numerical algorithms for solving the above model is how to deal with large-scale problems. It is normally believed two factors which are the step-length α_k and the search direction d_k should be considered. For α_k, some derivative free line search methods have been presented. Here we only state some formula for simplify.

Li and Fukashima [33] presented an approximately monotone line search method:

$$\phi(x_k + \alpha_k d_k) - \phi(x_k) \leq -\delta_1\|\alpha_k d_k\|^2 - \delta_2\|\alpha_k \varphi_k\|^2 + \varepsilon_k\|\varphi_k\|^2$$

where $\delta_1, \delta_2 > 0$, $\varphi_k = \varphi(x_k)$, $\alpha_k = r^{i_k}, r \in (0,1)$, and i_k is the smallest nonnegative integer i such that the inequality holds and meanwhile ε_k satisfies $\sum_{k=0}^{\infty} \varepsilon_k < \infty$. For the nonlinear symmetric equations, They established the global and superlinear convergence properties. However the method is not norm descent.

In order to obtain a norm descent method, Yuan and Lu [34] gave a new line search methods:

$$\phi(x_k + \alpha_k d_k) - \phi(x_k) \leq \beta\alpha_k^2 \phi_k^T d_k \quad \beta \in (0,1)$$

The new method avoided computing the Jacobian matrix $\nabla\phi(x)$ of $\phi(x)$, meanwhile the global and superlinear convergence properties were established under mild conditions. Numerical results showed the method was much effective especially for large-scale problems.

Li and Li [35] presented another new line search method (LLM for abbreviation) to determine $\alpha_k = \max\{s, \rho s, \rho^2 s \cdots\}$ such that

$$-\varphi(x_k + \alpha_k d_k)^T d_k \geq \sigma \alpha_k \|\varphi(x_k + \alpha_k d_k)\| \cdot \|d_k\|^2 \qquad (4.3)$$

where $\sigma, s > 0$ and $\rho \in (0,1)$. The method comes from an extension of the spectral gradient method and some modified conjugate gradient methods, and its global convergence is established under the equations are Lipschitz continuous even if the equations are not differentiable.

The search direction d_k is given by the new proposed parameter β_k:

$$d_k = \begin{cases} -\varphi_k, & \text{if } k = 0, \\ -\varphi_k + \beta_k^{NN} d_{k-1}, & \text{if } k \geq 1, \end{cases} \qquad (4.4)$$

where

$$\beta_k^{NN} = \frac{\|\varphi_k\|^2 - \max\{0, \frac{\|\varphi_k\|}{\|\varphi_{k-1}\|} \varphi_k^T \varphi_{k-1}\}}{\mu_2 \|\varphi_k\| \|d_{k-1}\| + \|\varphi_{k-1}\|^2 + \eta_2 |\varphi_{k-1}^T d_{k-1}|}.$$

For the monotone equations, we have

$$(\varphi(x) - \varphi(y))^T (x - y) \geq 0, \, for \quad all \quad x, y \in \Re^n \qquad (4.5)$$

Let $z_k = x_k + \alpha_k d_k$, by the monotonicity, we have the hyperplane

$$H_k = \{x \in \Re^n \mid \langle \varphi(z_k), (x - z_k) \rangle = 0\} \qquad (4.6)$$

which strictly separates x_k from the set of the Eq. (4.1). Solodov and Svaiter [2] advised the next iterate x_{k+1} should be determined by projecting the current x_k onto the hyperplane, that is:

$$x_{k+1} = x_k - \frac{\varphi(z_k)^T (x_k - z_k)}{\|\varphi(z_k)\|^2} \varphi(z_k) \qquad (4.7)$$

Motivated by line search direction (4.4) where β_k^N comes from (2.1), the search technique (4.3) and the iterative method (4.7), we propose our algorithm.

Algorithm 2
Step 0: Given $x_0 \in \Re^n$, as the initial point, $\sigma, s > 0$ and constants $\rho, \varepsilon \in (0, 1)$, let k:=0
Step 1: If $\|\varphi_k\| \leq \varepsilon$, then stop; Otherwise, go to next step.
Step 2: Compute step size α_k by line search rules (4.3).
Step 3: Compute d_k by (4.4).
Step 4: Let the next iterative be $z_k = x_k + \alpha_k d_k$.
Step 5: If $\|\varphi(z_k)\| \leq \varepsilon$, stop and let $x_{k+1} = z_k$. Otherwise compute x_{k+1} by (4.7)
Step 6: If $\|\varphi_{k+1}\| \leq \varepsilon$, then stop; Otherwise, Let $k := k + 1$. Go to step 2.

5   Convergence analysis

The following assumptions are needed to establish the global convergence of Algorithm 2.

Assumption B
(i) The solution set of (4.1) is not empty.
(ii) The functions $\varphi : \Re^n \to \Re^n$ are monotone and Lipschitz continuous, that is, there exists a positive constant L such that

$$\|\varphi(x) - \varphi(y)\| \leq L\|x - y\|, \forall x, y \in \Re^n.$$

The condition (ii) implies that there exists a positive constant ζ such that

$$\|\varphi_k\| \leq \zeta. \tag{5.1}$$

From the Lemma 3.1 and the Lemma 3.2, we have

$$\varphi_k^T d_k \leq -(1 - \frac{1}{\mu_2})\|\varphi_k\|^2 \tag{5.2}$$

$$(1 - \frac{1}{\mu_2})\|\varphi_k\| \leq \|d_k\| \leq (1 + \frac{1}{\mu_2})\|\varphi_k\| \tag{5.3}$$

where $\mu_2 > 1$. Similar to the Lemma 2.4 of [35], we can get the following lemma.

Lemma 5.1. *Let $\{x_k\}$ and $\{z_k\}$ be generated by Algorithm 2. Then we get*

$$\alpha_k \geq \min\{s, \frac{c_0\rho}{L + \sigma\|\varphi(z_k')\|} \frac{\|\varphi(x_k)\|^2}{\|d_k\|^2}\} \tag{5.4}$$

where $c_0 = (1 - \frac{1}{\mu_2})$, $z_k' = x_k + \alpha_k' d_k$ and $\alpha_k' = \alpha_k \rho^{-1}$.

Proof. By the line search rule (4.3), if $\alpha_k \neq s$, then $\alpha_k' = \alpha_k \rho^{-1}$ does not satisfied the (4.3), which means:

$$-\varphi(x_k + \alpha_k d_k)^T d_k < \sigma\alpha_k\|\varphi(x_k + \alpha_k d_k)\| \cdot \|d_k\|^2 \tag{5.5}$$

By the Lipschitz continuity and (5.2), we get

$$c_0\|\varphi_k\|^2 \leq -\varphi_k^T d_k \leq (\varphi(z_k') - \varphi(x_k))^T d_k + \sigma\alpha_k'\|\varphi(z_k')\| \cdot \|d_k\|^2 \tag{5.6}$$

$$\leq \alpha_k'(L + \sigma\|\varphi(z_k')\|)\|d_k\|^2 \tag{5.7}$$

This yields the conclusion.

The following lemma comes from the Lemma 3.1 in Yuan and Zhang [30] and the Lemma 2.1 in Solodov and Svaiter [2].

Lemma 5.2. *Let Assumption B hold and the sequence $\{x_k\}$ be generated by Algorithm 2. For any $\bar{x}$ satisfying $\varphi(\bar{x}) = 0$, then we have*

$$\|x_{k+1} - \bar{x}\|^2 \leq \|x_k - \bar{x}\|^2 - \|x_{k+1} - x_k\|^2 \tag{5.8}$$

and

$$\sum_{k=0}^{\infty} \|x_{k+1} - x_k\|^2 < \infty \tag{5.9}$$

hold.

Proof. By the definition of $\overline{x}$, the hypothesis of the hyperplane H_k and the monotonicity of the function φ, we have

$$< \varphi(z_k) - \varphi(\overline{x}), \overline{x} - z_k > = < \varphi(z_k), \overline{x} - z_k > \leq 0 \tag{5.10}$$

It is also easy to verify that x_{k+1} is the projection of x_k onto the halfspace $M_k = \{x \in \Re^n | < \varphi(z_k), x - z_k > \leq 0\}$. Since $\overline{x}$ belongs to the halfspace M_k, then we have $< x_k - x_{k+1}, x_{k+1} - \overline{x} > \geq 0$ by the basis properties of the projection operator. Then

$$\|x_k - \overline{x}\|^2 = \|x_k - x_{k+1}\|^2 + \|x_{k+1} - \overline{x}\|^2 + 2 < x_k - x_{k+1}, x_{k+1} - \overline{x} >$$
$$\geq \|x_k - x_{k+1}\|^2 + \|x_{k+1} - \overline{x}\|^2$$

Then, it is easy to have (5.8) hold. By (5.8), we have

$$\|x_{k+1} - x_k\|^2 \leq \|x_k - \overline{x}\|^2 - \|x_{k+1} - \overline{x}\|^2$$

Utilizing the above formula recursively and taking k limit to ∞, then (5.9) holds.

From the linear search (4.3) and the projection (4.7), we have

$$\|x_{k+1} - x_k\| = \frac{|\varphi(z_k)^T(x_k - z_k)|}{\|\varphi(z_k)\|} = \frac{-\alpha_k \varphi(z_k)^T d_k}{\|\varphi(z_k)\|} \geq \sigma \alpha_k^2 \|d_k\|^2 \tag{5.11}$$

From (5.9), we conclude

$$\|x_{k+1} - x_k\| \to 0 \quad as \quad k \to \infty$$

which means

$$\lim_{k \to \infty} \alpha_k d_k = 0 \tag{5.12}$$

Now we establish the global convergence theorem of Algorithm 2.

Theorem 5.1. *Let Assumption B hold and $\{\alpha_k, d_k, x_{k+1}, \varphi_{k+1}\}$ be generated by Algorithm 2. Then we have*

$$\liminf_{k \to \infty} \|\varphi_k\| = 0 \tag{5.13}$$

Proof. We will prove (5.13) by contradiction. Suppose that (5.13) does not hold and Let γ be a positive constant such that $\|\varphi_k\| \geq \gamma$ holds for all $k \geq 0$. From (5.3), we have

$$\gamma c_0 \leq c_0 \|\varphi_k\| \leq \|d_k\| \leq c_1 \|\varphi_k\| \leq c_1 \zeta \tag{5.14}$$

where $c_1 = (1 + \frac{1}{\mu_2})$. From the Lemma 6.1, we have

$$\alpha_k \|d_k\| \geq \min\{\beta, \frac{c_0 \rho}{L + \sigma \|\varphi(z_k')\|} \frac{\|\varphi(x_k)\|^2}{\|d_k\|^2}\} \|d_k\|$$
$$\geq \min\{\gamma c_0 \beta, \frac{c_0 \rho \gamma}{c_1 \zeta (L + \sigma \zeta)}\} > 0$$

which contracts (5.12). Consequently, (5.13) holds.

6   Numerical Results

In this section, we will test the numerical behavior of the Algorithm 2 with the normal PRP algorithm for large-scale nonlinear equations. The test problems with the associated initial guess x_0 are listed with

$$\varphi(x) = (f_1(x), f_2(x), \cdots, f_n(x))^T. \tag{6.1}$$

Function 1. Trigonometric function:

$$f_i(x) = 2(n + i(1 - \cos x_i) - \sin x_i - \sum_{j=1}^{n} \cos x_j)(2 \sin x_i - \cos x_i), i = 1, 2, \cdots, n.$$

Initial guess:$x_0 = (\frac{101}{100n}, \frac{101}{100n}, \cdots, \frac{101}{100n})$.
Function 2. Logarithmic function:

$$f_i(x) = \ln(x_i + 1) - \frac{x_i}{n}, i = 1, 2, \cdots, n.$$

Initial guess:$x_0 = (1, 1, \cdots, 1)^T$.
Function 3. Broyden Tridiagonal function:

$$f_1(x) = (3 - 0.5x_1)x_1 - 2x_2 + 1,$$

$$f_i(x) = (3 - 0.5x_i)x_i - x_{i-1} + 2x_{i+1} + 1, i = 2, 3, \cdots, n - 1,$$

$$f_n(x) = (3 - 0.5x_n)x_n - x_{n-1} + 1.$$

Initial guess:$x_0 = (-1, -1, \cdots, -1)^T$.
Function 4. Trigexp function:

$$f_1(x) = 3x_1^3 + 2x_2 - 5 + \sin(x_1 - x_2) \sin(x_1 + x_2),$$

$$f_i(x) = - x_{i-1}e^{x_{i-1}-x_i} + x_i(4 + 3x_i^2) + 2x_{i+1}$$
$$+ \sin(x_i - x_{i+1}) \sin(x_i + x_{i+1}) - 8, i = 2, 3, \cdots, n - 1,$$

$$f_n(x) = -x_{n-1}e^{x_{n-1}-x_n} + 4x_n - 3.$$

Initial guess:$x_0 = (0, 0, \cdots, 0)^T$.
Function 5. Exponential function:

$$f_1(x) = e^{x_1-1} - 1,$$

$$f_i(x) = \frac{i}{10}(e^{x_i} + x_{i-1} - i), i = 2, 3, \cdots, n.$$

Initial guess:$x_0 = (\frac{1}{n^2}, \frac{1}{n^2}, \cdots, \frac{1}{n^2})^T$.
Function 6. Troesch problem:

$$f_1(x) = 2x_1 + \varrho h^2 \sin h(\varrho x_1) - x_2,$$

$$f_i(x) = 2x_i + \varrho h^2 \sin h(\varrho x_i) - x_{i-1} - x_{i+1}, i = 2, 3, \cdots, n-1,$$

$$f_n(x) = 2x_n + \varrho h^2 \sin h(\varrho x_n) - x_{n-1}, h = \frac{1}{n+1}, \varrho = 10.$$

Initial guess:$x_0 = (0, 0, \cdots, 0)^T$.
Function 7. Variable dimensioned function:

$$f_i(x) = x_i - 1, \quad i = 1, 2, \cdots, n-2,$$

$$f_{n-1}(x) = \sum_{j=1}^{n-2} j(x_j - 1),$$

$$f_n(x) = \left(\sum_{j=1}^{n-2} j(x_j - 1) \right)^2.$$

Initial guess:$x_0 = (1 - \frac{1}{n}, 1 - \frac{2}{n}, \cdots, 0)^T$.
Function 8. Discrete boundary value problem:

$$f_1(x) = 2x_1 + 0.5t^2(x_1 + t)^3 - x_2,$$

$$f_i = 2x_i + 0.5t^2(x_i + ti)^3 - x_{i-1} + x_{i+1}, i = 2, 3, \cdots, n-1.$$

$$f_n(x) = 2x_n + 0.5t^2(x_n + tn)^3 - x_{n-1}, t = \frac{1}{n+1},$$

Initial guess: $x_0 = (t(t-1), t(2t-1), \cdots, t(nt-1))^T$.

In the experiments, all procedures are run on a PC with Intel Pentium (R) Dual-Core E5800 3.20 GHZ, 2.00G bytes of SDRAM memory, and Windows 7 operating system. Meanwhile, all codes are written in MATLAB R2010b and the parameters are chosen as

$$\mu_2 = 1.1, \eta_2 = 0.01, s = 1, \rho = 0.1, \sigma = 0.01, \varepsilon = 10^{-5}$$

we stopped the problems when the conditions $\|\varphi(x)\| \leq 10^{-5}$ or $NI \geq 500$ were satisfied. The test results are listed in Table 1 and the columns in Table 1 have the following meanings:

Dim: the dimension of the test problems;

NI: the number of iterations;

NF: the number of the function evaluations;

$\psi(x)$: the function value at final iteration;

CPU-Time: the run time for solving problems in second.

From the above numerical results, we have Algorithm 2 performs more effective than PRP algorithm for test functions 1, 2, 3, 8. For test functions 6, 7, Algorithm 2 and PRP algorithm have almost the same performance. For test function 5, Algorithm 2 is more effective in dimensions 500 and 5000 while PRP algorithm is better for dimensions 1000 and 10000. PRP algorithm is more situable for solving test function 4. For the all, Algorithm 2 is more effective to solve the test problems.

Table 1. Test results of Algorithm 2 and the normal PRP method.

Problem	Dim	Algorithm 2			PRP		
		NI/NF	Cpu-time	$\psi(x)$	NI/NF	Cpu-time	$\psi(x)$
	500	47/94	0.109201	8.531508e−006	52/103	0.093601	9.995417e−006
	1000	45/90	0.171601	9.433480e−006	51/101	0.187201	8.534401e−006
1	5000	42/84	5.226034	8.234199e−006	46/91	5.803237	9.736889e−006
	10000	40/80	13.915289	9.072317e−006	44/87	14.757695	9.984195e−006
	500	5/6	0.031200	9.488069e−008	11/12	0.031200	3.337834e−008
	1000	5/6	0.031200	3.598949e−008	11/12	0.062400	1.864381e−008
2	5000	5/6	0.358802	6.263903e−009	11/12	0.982806	8.539532e−009
	10000	5/6	1.138807	3.618055e−009	11/12	2.636417	7.621585e−009
	500	89/178	0.156001	9.546197e−006	97/194	0.124801	9.562961e−006
	1000	92/184	0.249602	8.615071e−006	100/200	0.280802	9.093736e−006
3	5000	97/194	10.842069	9.048770e−006	106/212	11.294472	9.130520e−006
	10000	99/198	33.477815	9.441561e−006	108/216	35.802230	9.878046e−006
	500	297/762	0.624004	9.522342e−006	249/641	0.405603	9.984508e−006
	1000	296/761	1.060807	9.348946e−006	250/645	0.920406	9.195939e−006
4	5000	292/755	42.635073	9.757295e−006	249/647	34.881824	9.184726e−006
	10000	291/754	119.293965	9.924638e−006	249/649	102.851459	9.217773e−006
	500	11/34	0.078001	9.368134e−006	60/177	0.140401	9.971921e−006
	1000	270/952	1.092007	9.916586e−006	207/731	0.858006	9.923217e−006
5	5000	7/29	1.653611	9.334349e−006	24/97	4.134027	9.754454e−006
	10000	128/583	81.073720	9.890139e−006	105/479	64.475213	9.816376e−006
	500	0/1	0.000000	0.000000e+000	0/1	0.000000	0.000000e+000
	1000	0/1	0.000000	0.000000e+000	0/1	0.000000	0.000000e+000
6	5000	0/1	0.062400	0.000000e+000	0/1	0.062400	0.000000e+000
	10000	0/1	0.234001	0.000000e+000	0/1	0.140401	0.000000e+000
	500	1/2	0.000000	0.000000e+000	1/2	0.031200	0.000000e+000
	1000	1/2	0.000000	0.000000e+000	1/2	0.000000	0.000000e+000
7	5000	1/2	0.078001	0.000000e+000	1/2	0.078001	0.000000e+000
	10000	1/2	0.358802	0.000000e+000	1/2	0.327602	0.000000e+000
	500	41/82	0.093601	8.370906e−006	46/92	0.109201	8.646168e−006
	1000	39/78	0.218401	8.337909e−006	44/88	0.140401	8.458416e−006
8	5000	34/69	4.243227	8.657414e−006	39/78	3.915625	9.198351e−006
	10000	32/65	10.701669	9.305922e−006	37/74	12.729682	9.416687e−006

In order to perform numerical results simply, Dolan and Moré [36] gave a new tool to analyze the efficiency of different algorithms. They introduced the notion of a performance profile as a way to evaluate and compare the performance of a set of solvers S on a test set P. According to the rules, we conclude that one solver whose performance profile plot is on the top right will win over the rest solvers.

By the similar way, we can have Figs. 1, 2 and 3 of the performance profile
for the total number of iterations, the total number of the function evaluations
and the total time for solving the test problems, respectively.

From the three figures, it is not difficult to have that Algorithm 2 performs
more effective for these test problems.

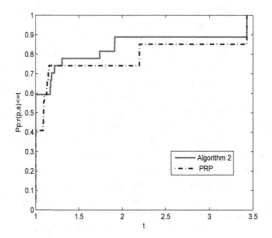

Fig. 1. Performance profiles of these methods (NI)

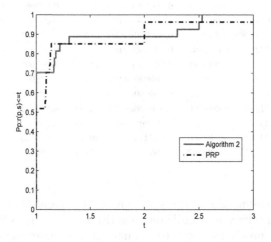

Fig. 2. Performance profiles of these methods (NF)

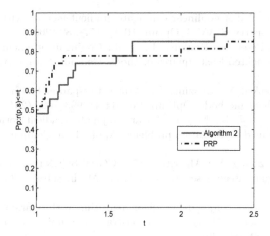

Fig. 3. Performance profiles of these methods (CPU-Time)

7 Conclusion

(i) In this paper, we presented a modified WYL conjugate gradient algorithm for minimization optimization models. The global convergence is established.

(ii) The presented method possesses the sufficient descent property and the trust region property without carrying out any line search techniques. Numerical results show that the proposed method is more effective for large-scale optimization problems.

References

1. Brown, P.N., Saad, Y.: Convergence theory of nonlinear Newton-Krylov algorithms. SIAM J. Optim. **4**(2), 297–330 (1994)
2. Solodov, M.V., Svaiter, B.F.: A globally convergent inexact Newton method for systems of monotone equations. In: Reformulation: Nonsmooth, Piecewise Smooth, Semismooth and Smoothing Methods, pp. 355–369. Springer, US (1999)
3. Andrei, N.: An adaptive scaled BFGS method for unconstrained optimization. Numer. Algorithms **77**(2), 413–432 (2018)
4. Huang, W., Absil, P.A., Gallivan, K.A.: A Riemannian BFGS method without differentiated retraction for nonconvex optimization problems. SIAM J. Optim. **28**(1), 470–495 (2018)
5. Yuan, G., Sheng, Z., Wang, B., Hu, W., Li, C.: The global convergence of a modified BFGS method for nonconvex functions. J. Comput. Appl. Math. **327**, 274–294 (2018)
6. Yuan, G., Wei, Z., Lu, X.: Global convergence of the BFGS method and the PRP method for general functions under a modified weak Wolfe-Powell line search. Appl. Math. Model. **47**, 811–825 (2017)
7. Yuan, G., Wei, Z.: Convergence analysis of a modified BFGS method on convex minimizations. Comp. Optim. Appl. **47**, 237–255 (2010)

8. Dai, Y.H., Yuan, Y.: A nonlinear conjugate gradient method with a strong global convergence property. SIAM J. Optim. **10**(1), 177–182 (2000)
9. Fornasier, M., Peter, S., Rauhut, H., et al.: Conjugate gradient acceleration of iteratively re-weighted least squares methods. Comput. Optim. Appl. **65**(1), 205–259 (2016)
10. Sellami, B., Laskri, Y., Benzine, R.: A new two-parameter family of nonlinear conjugate gradient methods. Optimization **64**(4), 993–1009 (2015)
11. Wei, Z., Li, G., Qi, L.: New nonlinear conjugate gradient formulas for large-scale unconstrained optimization problems. Appl. Math. Comput. **179**(2), 407–430 (2006)
12. Hager, W.W., Zhang, H.: Algorithm 851: CG-DESCENT, a conjugate gradient method with guaranteed descent. ACM Trans. Math. Softw. (TOMS) **32**(1), 113–137 (2006)
13. Andrei, N.: Another conjugate gradient algorithm with guaranteed descent and conjugacy conditions for large-scale unconstrained optimization. J. Optim. Theory Appl. **159**(1), 159–182 (2013)
14. Hager, W.W., Zhang, H.: A new conjugate gradient method with guaranteed descent and an efficient line search. SIAM J. Optim. **16**(1), 170–192 (2005)
15. Dai, Z., Tian, B.S.: Global convergence of some modified PRP nonlinear conjugate gradient methods. Optim. Lett. **5**(4), 615–630 (2011)
16. Fletcher, R., Reeves, C.M.: Function minimization by conjugate gradients. Comput. J. **7**(2), 149–154 (1964)
17. Polyak, B.T.: The conjugate gradient method in extremal problems. USSR Comput. Math. Math. Phys. **9**(4), 94–112 (1969)
18. Polak, E., Ribière, G.: Note sur la convergence de directions conjuges, Rev. Franaise Informat. Recherche Opertionelle, 3e année **16**, 35–43 (1969)
19. Wei, Z., Yao, S., Liu, L.: The convergence properties of some new conjugate gradient methods. Appl. Math. Comput. **183**(2), 1341–1350 (2006)
20. Zhang, L.: An improved Wei-Yao-Liu nonlinear conjugate gradient method for optimization computation. Appl. Math. Comput. **215**(6), 2269–2274 (2009)
21. Dai, Z., Wen, F.: Another improved Wei-Yao-Liu nonlinear conjugate gradient method with sufficient descent property. Appl. Math. Comput. **218**(14), 7421–7430 (2012)
22. Yuan, G., Lu, X.: A modified PRP conjugate gradient method. Anna. Operat. Res. **166**, 73–90 (2009)
23. Yuan, G., Lu, X., Wei, Z.: A conjugate gradient method with descent direction for unconstrained optimization. J. Comput. Appl. Math. **233**, 519–530 (2009)
24. Li, X., Wang, X., Sheng, Z., et al.: A modified conjugate gradient algorithm with backtracking line search technique for large-scale nonlinear equations. Int. J. Comput. Math. **95**(2), 382–395 (2018)
25. Yuan, G., Meng, Z., Li, Y.: A modified Hestenes and Stiefel conjugate gradient algorithm for large-scale nonsmooth minimizations and nonlinear equations. J. Optim. Theory. Appl. **168**, 129–152 (2016)
26. Li, D.H., Wang, X.L.: A modified Fletcher-Reeves-type derivative-free method for symmetric nonlinear equations. Numer. Algebra Control Optim. **1**(1), 71–82 (2011)
27. Yuan, G., Wei, Z., Lu, X.: A BFGS trust-region method for nonlinear equations. Computing **92**, 317–333 (2011)
28. Yuan, G., Wei, Z., Lu, S.: Limited memory BFGS method with backtracking for symmetric nonlinear equations. Math. Comput. Model. **54**, 367–377 (2011)

29. Yu, Z., Lin, J., Sun, J., et al.: Spectral gradient projection method for monotone nonlinear equations with convex constraints. Appl. Numer. Math. **59**(10), 2416–2423 (2009)
30. Yuan, G., Zhang, M.: A three-terms Polak-Ribière-Polyak conjugate gradient algorithm for large-scale nonlinear equations. J. Comput. Appl. Math. **286**, 186–195 (2015)
31. Dai, Z., Chen, X., Wen, F.: A modified Perrys conjugate gradient method-based derivative-free method for solving large-scale nonlinear monotone equations. Appl. Math. Comput. **270**, 378–386 (2015)
32. Dai, Z., Li, D.W.: Worse-case conditional value-at-risk for asymmetrically distributed asset scenarios returns. J. Comput. Anal. Appl. **20**, 237–251 (2016)
33. Li, D., Fukushima, M.: A global and superlinear convergent Gauss-Newton-based BFGS method for symmetric nonlinear equations. SIAM J. Numer. Anal. **37**, 152–172 (1999)
34. Yuan, G., Lu, X.: A new backtracking inexact BFGS method for symmetric nonlinear equations. Comput. Math. Appl. **55**(1), 116–129 (2008)
35. Li, Q., Li, D.H.: A class of derivative-free methods for large-scale nonlinear monotone equations. IMA J. Numer. Anal. **31**(4), 1625–1635 (2011)
36. Dolan, E.D., Moré, J.J.: Benchmarking optimization software with performance profiles. Math. Program. **91**(2), 201–213 (2002)

A New Fully Homomorphic Encryption Scheme on Batch Technique

Mengtian Li$^{(\boxtimes)}$ and Bin Hu

Information Engineering University,
Zhengzhou 450001, People's Republic of China
`skylil993@163.com`

Abstract. In 2011, Naehrig et al. proposed a RLWE-based Homomorphic Encryption scheme. In this paper, we designed a new scheme which combined with the batch technique. Concretely, the technique packed multiple "plaintext slots" into a ciphertext by using the Chinese Remainder Theorem, and then performed homomorphic operations on it. Considering the exponential growth of the noise in each multiplication operation, we used the key switching and modulus switching technique to reduce the noise size in ciphertext, ensuring the correct decryption and the next homomorphic computation. In particular, We can encrypt $O(n\lambda)$ plaintexts in the encryption process, improving the efficiency of λ times compared to the original scheme. Finally, we analyzed the security and parameters of the scheme. It was proven that our scheme is CPA security.

Keywords: Fully homomorphic encryption · Batch technique
Key switching · Modulus switching

1 Introduction

In cloud computing, the client's data is stored in the cloud server [1], hence cannot ensure the security of their private data. Therefore, the best way to deal with the problem is to encrpt the data. The cloud server must be able to perform various complex operations on encrypted data. Obviously, the traditional cryptographic system cannot meet this demand. Fully Homomorphic Encryption (FHE) is a powerful encryption system which can do arbitrary operations on encrypted data, despite not having the secret decryption key. It has a very wide range of applications in the cloud security, cloud computing and ciphertext retrieval et al.

In 1978, the idea of "Homomorphic encryption" was first proposed by Rivest, Shamir and Adleman [2]. In 2009, Gentry described the first plausible construction of a fully homomorphic encryption scheme based on ideal lattices [3]. Gentry's construction supports both addition and multiplication operations of encrypted data. In 2010, Gentry and Halevi [4] described a working implementation of a variant of Gentry's fully homomorphic encryption scheme. Next year, Smart and Vercauteren [5] presented how to select parameters to enable SIMD operations, whilst still maintaining practicality of the key generation technique of Gentry and Halevi. They combined the Chinese Remainder Theorem and cyclotomic polynomial to construct "plaintext slots". In 2012, Gentry, Halevi and Smart [6] showed that homomorphic evaluation of

X. Sun et al. (Eds.): ICCCS 2018, LNCS 11063, pp. 160–171, 2018.
https://doi.org/10.1007/978-3-030-00006-6_14

arithmetic circuits can be accomplished with only polylogarithmic overhead. Morever, they introduced permuting techniques to move plaintext elements across "packed" ciphertexts efficiently without "unpack" the plaintext vectors. The same year, Brakerski, Gentry and Vaikuntanathan [7] constructed the leveled homomorhpic encryption scheme with Key switching and Modulus switching technique.

In [8], Lauter, Naehrig and Vaikuntanathan presented the somewhat homomorphic encryption scheme of [BV11b] based on Ring LWE, and provided an optimization to reduce ciphertext size. The main point of this paper is to show how to combined [8] with the batch technique to construct a leveled homomorphic encryption scheme with the key switching and modulus switching technique. In particular, We can encrypt $O(n\lambda)$ plaintexts in the encryption process, improving the efficiency of n times compared to the original scheme.

1.1   Organizations

The rest of the paper is organized as follows. In Sect. 2, we describe some preliminaries about basic definitions. In Sect. 3, we review the somewhat homomorphic encryption scheme of [8] based on Ring LWE. We give our batch encryption scheme based on Ring LWE, and describe key switching and modulus switching techniques to decrease the size of error in Sect. 4. In Sect. 5, we prove that our sheme is CPA-secure, and we also give the way of parameters setting. We give conclusions in Sect. 6.

2   Preliminaries

2.1   Notations

Assignment to variables will be denoted by $x \leftarrow y$. If A is an algorithm then $x \leftarrow A$ implies that x is obtained from running A, with the resulting probability distribution being induced by the random coins of A. If A is a set then $x \leftarrow A$ implies that x is selected from A using the uniform distribution. For an integer q, we identify the quotient group $\mathbb{Z}_q$ with its representatives in the symmetric interval $[-q/2, q/2)$ (except $\mathbb{Z}_2$ which is identified with $\{0,1\}$). For integer x, we denote $[x]_q$ when the operation maps integers to the interval $[-q/2, q/2)$. If y is a vector then we let y_i denote the i'th element of y. We write the dot product of $a, b \in R^m$ as $\langle a, b \rangle = (\sum a_i \cdot b_i)_{i \in [1,...,m]}$, and denote $a \odot b = (a_i \cdot b_i)_{i \in [1,...,m]}$.

Below let m, q be arbitrary positive integers. Elements of finite fields and number fields defined by a polynomial $f(x)$, i.e. elements of $\mathbb{Z}[x]/f(x)$, $\mathbb{Q}[x]/f(x)$, can also be represented as polynomials in some fixed root of $f(x)$ in the algebraic closure of the base field. Let $\Phi_m(x)$ denote the m'th cyclotomic polynomial, and denote ring $R = \mathbb{Z}[x]/\Phi_m(x)$. For $r \in R$, $\|r\|$ refers to the Euclidean norm of i's coefficient vector. We say $\gamma_R = \max\{\|a \cdot b\|/(\|a\| \cdot \|b\|) : a, b \in R\}$ is the expansion factor of R. For $R = \mathbb{Z}[x]/(x^d + 1)$, the value of γ_R is at most $\sqrt{d}$ by Cauchy-Schwarz.

2.2 Cyclotomic Polynomial and Chinese Remainder Theorem

Definition 1 (Cyclotomic polynomial [9]). We say $\Phi_m(x) = \prod_{i \in (\mathbb{Z}/m\mathbb{Z})^*}^m (x - \zeta_m^i)$ is the m'th cyclotomic polynomial, where ζ_m is the complex primitive m'th root of unity, $\zeta_m = e^{2\pi i/m}$. The degree of $\Phi_m(x)$ is $\phi(m)$, where $\phi(\cdot)$ is Euler's phi-function. There is a theorem for cyclotomic polynomial in finite fields:

Lemma 1 ([9]). Let F_p be a finite field, where the prime p is the characteristic of F_p. We have that the polynomial $\Phi_m(x)$ splits mod p into l distinct factors $f_i(x)$, each of degree d, where $l \cdot d = \phi(m)$ and $p^d \equiv 1 (\mod m)$.

Definition 2 (Chinese remainder theorem). If $f_0(x), \ldots, f_{l-1}(x)$ are pairwise coprime polynomial, let $f(x) = f_0(x) \cdot f_1(x) \cdots f_{l-1}(x)$. And if $r_0(x), \ldots, r_{l-1}(x)$ are any polynomial, then there exists a polynomial $g(x)$ such that

$$
\begin{cases}
g(x) \equiv r_0(x) \mod f_0(x) \\
g(x) \equiv r_1(x) \mod f_1(x) \\
\qquad\qquad \vdots \\
g(x) \equiv r_{l-1}(x) \mod f_{l-1}(x)
\end{cases}
$$

The unique solution of the equations is $g(x) = \sum_{i=0}^{l-1} r_i(x)h_i(x)m_i(x)(\mod f(x))$, where $m_i(x) = f(x)/f_i(x)$, $h_i(x) = 1/m_i(x)(\mod f_i(x))$.

We define $R_p = \mathbb{Z}_p[x]/\Phi_m(x)$ to be the ring of polynomials over $\mathbb{Z}_p$, where multiplication and addition are defined modulus $\Phi_m(x)$ and p. By Lemma 1, we have that

$$
\begin{aligned}
R_p &= \mathbb{Z}_p[x]/f_0(x) \cdot f_1(x) \cdots f_{l-1}(x) \\
&\cong \mathbb{Z}_p[x]/f_0(x) \times \cdots \times \mathbb{Z}_p[x]/f_{l-1}(x) \\
&\cong \mathbb{F}_{p^d} \times \cdots \times \mathbb{F}_{p^d} = \mathbb{L}_0 \times \cdots \times \mathbb{L}_{l-1}
\end{aligned}
$$

i.e. R_p is isomorphic to l copies $\mathbb{L}_i = \mathbb{Z}_p[x]/f_0(x)$ of $\mathbb{F}_{p^d}$. Each message in R_p corresponds to l messages in $\mathbb{F}_{p^d} \cong \mathbb{Z}_p[x]/f_0(x)$. We call them a "slot". By Definition 2, additive and multiplicative operations in R_p correspond to SIMD operations on the slots. These isomorphisms are explicitly given by

$$
\psi : \begin{cases}
\mathbb{F}_{p^d}^l \to \mathbb{Z}_p[x]/f_0(x) \times \cdots \times \mathbb{Z}_p[x]/f_{l-1}(x) \\
(m_0, \ldots, m_{l-1}) \mapsto (\psi_0(m_0), \ldots, \psi_{l-1}(m_{l-1}))
\end{cases}
$$

$$
\varphi : \begin{cases}
\mathbb{Z}_p[x]/f_0(x) \times \cdots \times \mathbb{Z}_p[x]/f_{l-1}(x) \to R_p \\
(h_0, \ldots, h_{l-1}) \mapsto \sum_{i=0}^{l-1} h_i H_i(x) M_i(x)
\end{cases}
$$

Where $M_i(x) = \Phi_m(x)/f_i(x)$, $H_i(x) = 1/M_i(x)(\mod f_i(x))$.

Obviously, the mapping of $CRT_p = \psi \circ \varphi$ is isomorphic from $\mathbb{F}_{p^d}^l$ to R_p.

2.3   The Ring Learning with Errors Problem

In 2010, the ring learning with errors (RLWE) problem was introduced by Lyu-baskevsky, Peikert and Regev [10]. The security of our construction relies on the RLWE problem, the definition as follows.

Definition 3 (RLWE [10]). For security parameter λ, let $f(x) = x^n + 1$ where $n = n(\lambda)$ is a power of 2. Let $q = q(\lambda)$ be an integer. Let $R = \mathbb{Z}[x]/f(x)$ and let $R_q = R/qR$. Let $\chi = \chi(\lambda)$ be a distribution over R. The $RLWE_{d,q,\chi}$ problem is to distinguish the following two distributions: In the first distribution, one samples (a_i, b_i) uniformly from R_q^2. In the second distribution, one first draws $s \leftarrow R_q$ uniformly and then samples $(a_i, b_i = a_i \cdot s + e_i) \in R_q^2$, where $e_i \leftarrow \chi$. The $RLWE_{d,q,\chi}$ assumption is that the $RLWE_{d,q,\chi}$ problem is infeasible.

The RLWE problem is very important and useful, because the shortest vector problem (SVP) over ideal lattices can be reduced to it.

Theorem 1 ([10]). For any n that is a power of 2, ring $R = \mathbb{Z}[x]/(x^d + 1)$, prime integer $q = q(n) = 1 (\mod d)$, and $B = \omega(\sqrt{d \log d})$, there is an efficiently samplable distribution χ that outputs elements of R of length at most B with overwhelming probability, such that if there exists an efficient algorithm that solves $RLWE_{d,q,\chi}$, then there is an efficient quantum algorithm for solving $d^{\omega(1)} \cdot (q/B)$ approximate worst-case SVP for ideal lattices over R.

2.4   Homomorphic Encryption

Definition 4 (Homomorphic Encryption scheme). A homomorphic encryption scheme ε consists of four procedures, $\varepsilon = $ (KeyGen, Encrypt, Decrypt, Evaluate):

- KeyGen(1^λ): Takes the security parameter λ and outputs a secret/public key-pair.
- Encrypt(pk, m): Given the public key pk and a plaintext bit m, outputs a ciphertext c.
- Decrypt(sk, c): Given the secret key sk and a ciphertext c, outputs a plaintext bit m.
- Evaluate(pk, C, c): Takes a public key pk, a circuit C, a vector of ciphertexts $c = (c_0, \ldots, c_{l-1})$, one for every input bit of C, and outputs another vector of ciphertexts c^*.

Definition 5 (Correctness). The scheme ε is correct for a given l inputs circuit C, if for any key-pair (sk, pk) output by KeyGen(1^λ), any l plaintext bits $m_0, \ldots, m_{l-1}$, and any ciphertexts $c = (c_0, \ldots, c_{l-1})$ with $c_i \leftarrow$ Encrypt(pk, m_i), it is the case that:

$$\text{Decrypt}(sk, \text{Evaluate}(pk, C, c)) = C(m_0, \ldots, m_{l-1})$$

Definition 6 (Compactness). The scheme ε is compact if there exists a fixed polynomial bound $B(\lambda)$, the size of the ciphertext c^* is not more than $B(\lambda)$ bits (independently of the size of C).

Definition 7 (Homomorphic Encryption). The scheme ε is homomorphic for circuits in C_ε if ε is correct and Decrypt can be expressed as a circuit D_ε of size $B(\lambda)$.

Definition 8 (Fully Homomorphic Encryption). The scheme ε is fully homomorphic if it is homomorphic for all circuits.

Definition 9 (Leveled homomorphic encryption). The scheme ε is a leveled homomorphic encryption scheme if it is correct for a family C such that, for all τ, C_τ contains all Boolean circuits of depth up to τ.

3 Encryption Scheme

In this section, we first describe the somewhat homomorphic encryption scheme of [8] based on Ring LWE.

3.1 Somewhat Homomorphic Encryption

The somewhat homomorphic encryption scheme is associated with a numbers of parameters:

- The dimension n, and is a power of 2,
- The cyclotomic polynomial $f(x) = x^n + 1$,
- The modulus q, which is a prime such that $q \equiv 1 \pmod{2n}$,
- The ciphertext space of the scheme as $R_q := R/qR = \mathbb{Z}_q[x]/f(x)$,
- A prime $t < q$, which define the message space of the scheme as $R_t = \mathbb{Z}_t[x]/f(x)$,
- The error parameter σ, which defines a discrete Gaussian error distribution $\chi = D_{\mathbb{Z}^n, \sigma}$ with standard deviation σ.

SH.Keygen($params$): Sample a ring element $s \leftarrow \chi$ and define $sk := s$. Sample a uniformly random ring element $a_1 \leftarrow R_q$ and an error $e \leftarrow \chi$ and define public key is $pk := (a_0 = -(a_1 s + te), a_1)$.

SH.Enc(pk, m): Given the $pk = (a_0, a_1)$ and a message $m \in R_t$, the encryption algorithm samples $u \leftarrow \chi$, and $f, g \leftarrow \chi$, and computes the ciphertext $ct = (c_0, c_1) = (a_0 u + tg + m, a_1 u + tf)$.

SH.Dec(sk, ct $= (c_0, c_1)$): To decrypt, we first compute $\tilde{m} = c_0 + c_1 \cdot s$, and output the message as $m = \tilde{m} \pmod{t}$.

SH.Eval(ct $= (c_0, c_1)$, ct$' = (c_0', c_1')$):

SH.Add(pk, ct, ct$'$): Given the ciphertexts ct $= (c_0, c_1)$ and ct$' = (c_0', c_1')$. Homomorphic addition is done by simple component-wise addition of the ciphertexts. Namely, compute and output $ct_{add} = (c_0 + c_0', c_1 + c_1') \in R_q^2$.

SH.Mult(pk, ct,ct$'$): Given the ciphertexts ct $= (c_0, c_1)$ and ct$' = (c_0', c_1')$. Let v be a symbolic variable and compute $(c_0 + c_1 \cdot v) \cdot (c_0' + c_1' \cdot v)$. We can get $c_0 c_0' + (c_0 c_1' + c_0' c_1)v + c_1 c_1' v^2$, the output ciphertext is $ct_{mlt} = (c_0 c_0', c_0 c_1' + c_0' c_1, c_1 c_1')$.

3.2   Correctness

Below we show how to make an analysis of its correctness.

Let ct be a fresh ciphertext under the secret key s, it follows from encryption algorithm that

$$SH.Dec(sk, ct = (c_0, c_1)) = (c_0 + c_1 s)(\bmod p \bmod t)$$
$$= a_0 u + tg + m + a_1 us + tfs$$
$$= (-a_1 s + te)u + tg + m + a_1 us + tfs$$
$$= m + t(eu + g + fs)$$
$$= m + t\tilde{e}(\bmod t)$$
$$= m$$

Therefore, we can get the original plaintext $m \in R_t$ accurately when $\|m + t\tilde{e}\| < p/2$.

4   Batch FHE Scheme

In this section, we present a batch homomorphic encryption scheme based on Sect. 3, which packed many plaintext bits in a ciphertext by using the CRT technique. We also describe key switching and modulus switching techniques to decrease the ciphertext expansion rate and improve the efficiency of encrypting.

4.1   Our Construction

Our batch FHE scheme consists of five algorithms as follows.

Batch.FHE.Setup($1^\lambda, 1^L$): For the security parameter λ and a number of levels L, let $R = \mathbb{Z}[x]/\Phi_m(x)$, where $\Phi_m(x) = \prod_{i=0}^{l-1} f_i(x)$ is Cyclotomic polynomial, and $\phi(m) = n = dl = n(\lambda, L)$. Choose a prime integer p independent of χ, such that $p \ll q, \gcd(p, m) = 1$, and $p^d \equiv 1(\bmod m)$. Set $L + 1$ prime modulus $q_0 < q_1 < \cdots < q_L$, and the circuit of i'th level is $R_{q_i} = \mathbb{Z}[x]_{q_i} / \Phi_m(x)$. Let χ, with the bound $B(\lambda)$, be a discrete Gaussian distribution over R. The mapping CRT_p is isomorphic between $\mathbb{F}_{p^d}^l$ and R_p.

Batch.FHE.Keygen(*params*): Sample $a_i \leftarrow R_{q_i}$ randomly, and $s_i, e \leftarrow \chi$, let $b_i = -a_i \cdot s_i + te$, where $i = 0, 1, \ldots, L$. Set vectors $\mathbf{a} = (a_0, a_1, \ldots, a_L)$, $\mathbf{b} = (b_0, b_1, \ldots, b_L)$, and let $pk = (\mathbf{b}, \mathbf{a})$, $sk = \mathbf{s} = (s_0, s_1, \ldots, s_L)$.

Batch.FHE.Enc($pk, \{(m_{i,0}, \ldots, m_{i,l-1})\}_{i=0}^L$): Given public key pk and a plaintext vector $(m_{i,0}, \ldots, m_{i,l-1}) \in \mathbb{F}_{p^d}^l, i = 0, 1, \ldots, L$. To encrypt the plaintext vectors, one performs the following steps.

- Compute each aggregate plaintext $m_i \leftarrow CRT_p(m_{i,0}, \ldots, m_{i,l-1}) \in R_p$, $i = 0, 1, \ldots, L$,
- Let $\boldsymbol{m} = (m_0, \ldots, m_L)$,
- Sample $u \leftarrow \chi, f \leftarrow \chi$ and $g \leftarrow \chi$ randomly. Let $\boldsymbol{f} = (f, f, \ldots, f)$, $\boldsymbol{g} = (g, g, \ldots, g)$, whose number of elements are $L + 1$.
- Output the ciphertext $\mathbf{ct} = (\boldsymbol{c}_0, \boldsymbol{c}_1) = ((\boldsymbol{bu} + t\boldsymbol{g} + \boldsymbol{m}), (\boldsymbol{au} + t\boldsymbol{f})) \in R_q^{(L+1) \times 2}$.

$Batch.\text{FHE.Dec}(sk, \mathbf{ct})$: Do the steps below.

- Let $\boldsymbol{m} = (m_0, \ldots, m_L) = (\boldsymbol{c}_0 + \boldsymbol{c}_1 \odot \boldsymbol{s})(\bmod p \bmod t) \in R_p^{L+1}$.
- Output $(m_{i,0}, \ldots, m_{i,l-1}) \leftarrow CRT_p^{-1}(m_i) \in \mathbb{F}_{p^d}^l$.

$Batch.\text{FHE.Eval}(\mathbf{ct} = (\boldsymbol{c}_0, \boldsymbol{c}_1), \mathbf{ct}' = (\boldsymbol{c}'_0, \boldsymbol{c}'_1))$:

$Batch.\text{FHE.Add}(evk, \mathbf{ct}, \mathbf{ct}')$:

Let $\mathbf{ct} = (\boldsymbol{c}_0, \boldsymbol{c}_1)$, $\mathbf{ct}' = (\boldsymbol{c}'_0, \boldsymbol{c}'_1)$ as input. If they are in the same circuit level, homomorphic addition is done by simple component-wise addition of the ciphertexts, namely, compute and output $\mathbf{ct_{add}} = (\boldsymbol{c}_0 + \boldsymbol{c}'_0, \boldsymbol{c}_1 + \boldsymbol{c}'_1) \in R_q^{(L+1) \times 2}$. If not, one shoule call the algorithm $\text{Scale}(\mathbf{ct}', q_i, q_{i-1}, t)$ to ensure that they are in the same circuit level.

$Batch.\text{FHE.Mult}(evk, \mathbf{ct}, \mathbf{ct}')$:

- Let $\boldsymbol{v} = (v_0, v_1, \ldots, v_L)$ be a symbolic variable vector, compute $(\boldsymbol{c}_0 + \boldsymbol{c}_1 \odot \boldsymbol{v}) \odot (\boldsymbol{c}'_0 + \boldsymbol{c}'_1 \odot \boldsymbol{v})$, and the coefficient of the result regard as the ciphertext after one multiplication operation.
- Compute $\text{KeySwitch}(sk', sk'', (c_0, c_1, c_2))$, and output $\mathbf{ct}' = (c_0, c_1)$.
- Compute $\text{Scale}(\mathbf{ct}', q_i, q_{i-1}, t)$.

Below we describe a detailed explanation of the above multiplication operation. We set $\boldsymbol{c}_0 = (\boldsymbol{bu} + t\boldsymbol{g} + \boldsymbol{m}) = (c_{0,0}, c_{0,1}, \ldots, c_{0,L})$, $\boldsymbol{c}_1 = (\boldsymbol{au} + t\boldsymbol{f}) = (c_{1,0}, c_{1,1}, \ldots, c_{1,L})$, similarly, we have $\boldsymbol{c}'_0 = (c'_{0,0}, c'_{0,1}, \ldots, c'_{0,L})$, $\boldsymbol{c}'_1 = (c'_{1,0}, c'_{1,1}, \ldots, c'_{1,L})$, and compute

$$
\begin{aligned}
&(\boldsymbol{c}_0 + \boldsymbol{c}_1 \odot \boldsymbol{v}) \odot (\boldsymbol{c}'_0 + \boldsymbol{c}'_1 \odot \boldsymbol{v}) \\
&= \boldsymbol{c}_0 \odot \boldsymbol{c}'_0 + (\boldsymbol{c}_0 \odot \boldsymbol{c}'_1 + \boldsymbol{c}_1 \odot \boldsymbol{c}'_0) \odot \boldsymbol{v} + \boldsymbol{c}_1 \odot \boldsymbol{c}'_1 \odot \boldsymbol{v} \odot \boldsymbol{v} \\
&= (c_{0,0} \cdot c'_{0,0}, \ldots, c_{0,L} \cdot c'_{0,L}) + ((c_{0,0} \cdot c'_{1,0} + c_{1,0} \cdot c'_{0,0}) \cdot v_0, \ldots, \\
&\quad (c_{0,L} \cdot c'_{1,L} + c_{1,0} \cdot c'_{0,0}) \cdot v_L) + (c_{1,0} \cdot c'_{1,0} \cdot v_0^2, \ldots, c_{1,L} \cdot c'_{1,L} \cdot v_L^2) \\
&= ((c_{0,0} \cdot c'_{0,0} + (c_{0,0} \cdot c'_{1,0} + c_{1,0} \cdot c'_{0,0}) \cdot v_0 + c_{1,0} \cdot c'_{1,0} \cdot v_0^2), \ldots, \\
&\quad (c_{0,L} \cdot c'_{0,L} + (c_{0,L} \cdot c'_{1,L} + c_{1,0} \cdot c'_{0,0}) \cdot v_L + c_{1,L} \cdot c'_{1,L} \cdot v_L^2))
\end{aligned}
$$

Therefore, the ciphertext after one multiplication operation is $\mathbf{ct_{mlt}} = \{(c_{0,i} \cdot c'_{0,i}, c_{0,i} \cdot c'_{1,i} + c_{1,i} \cdot c'_{0,i}, c_{1,i} \cdot c'_{1,i})_{i \in [0,L]}\}$.

In [6], Gentry et al. introduced permuting techniques to move plaintext elements across "packed" ciphertexts efficiently. They were able to implement general arithmetic circuit in a batched fashion without ever needing to "unpack" the plaintext vectors. We use this technique, namely permute π_{CRT}, to allow us to evaluate arbitrary circuits while keeping the ciphertexts packed.

4.2   Correctness

Below we verify the correctness of the above scheme.

Let **ct** be a fresh packed ciphertext, it follows from encryption algorithm that

$$\mathbf{ct} = (c_0, c_1) = ((bu + tg + m), (au + tf))$$
$$= ((b_0 u + tg + m_0, \ldots, b_L u + tg + m_L), (a_0 u + tf, \ldots, a_L u + tf))$$

From $Batch.\text{FHE.Dec}(sk, \mathbf{ct})$, we have that

$$\boldsymbol{m} = (m_0, \ldots, m_L) = (c_0 + c_1 \odot s)(\bmod\, p \bmod t)$$
$$= (b_0 u + tg + m_0, \ldots, b_L u + tg + m_L) + (a_0 u + tf, \ldots, a_L u + tf) \odot \boldsymbol{s}$$
$$= (b_0 u + tg + m_0, \ldots, b_L u + tg + m_L) + (a_0 u s_0 + tf s_0, \ldots, a_L u s_L + tf s_L)$$
$$= (b_0 u + tg + m_0 + a_0 u s_0 + tf s_0, \ldots, b_L u + tg + m_L + a_L u s_L + tf s_L)$$
$$= (m_0 + t(eu + g + f s_0), \ldots, m_L + t(eu + g + f s_L))(\bmod\, p \bmod t)$$
$$= (m_0, m_1, \ldots, m_L) = \boldsymbol{m}$$

If $\max(\|t(eu + g + f s_i)\|_{i \in [0,L]}) < p/2$, we can get the original plaintext, namely $(m_{i,0}, \ldots, m_{i,l-1}) \leftarrow CRT_p^{-1}(m_i) \in \mathbb{F}_{p^d}^l$.

The correctness of the homomorphic addition operation and homomorphic multiplication operation is easy to verify, so we omit it.

4.3   Key Switching

Recall that $\mathbf{ct}_{mlt} = \{(c_{0,i} \cdot c'_{0,i}, c_{0,i} \cdot c'_{1,i} + c_{1,i} \cdot c'_{0,i}, c_{1,i} \cdot c'_{1,i})_{i \in [0,L]}\}$, the corresponding secret key is $sk' = (1, \boldsymbol{s}, \boldsymbol{s} \odot \boldsymbol{s})$. To make the expression clearer, we set $(c_{0,i} \cdot c'_{0,i}, c_{0,i} \cdot c'_{1,i} + c_{1,i} \cdot c'_{0,i}, c_{1,i} \cdot c'_{1,i}) \stackrel{\triangle}{\longleftarrow} (c_{0,i}, c_{1,i}, c_{2,i})$ and $(\boldsymbol{c}_0, \boldsymbol{c}_1, \boldsymbol{c}_2) \leftarrow \{(c_{0,i}, c_{1,i}, c_{2,i})\}_{i=0}^{L}$. To decrease the dimension of $\mathbf{ct}_{mlt}$ and sk', we present the Key switching algorithm, details as below.

Algorithm 1: KeySwitch(sk',sk'',(c_0,c_1,c_2))

Input: sk',sk'',$\mathbf{ct}_{mlt}=(c_0,c_1,c_2)$

Output: $\mathbf{ct}'=(c_0,c_1)$

Compute: i From 0 to L

$$b_{\kappa_i,i}=-(a_{\kappa_i,i}s'_i+te)+t^{\kappa_i}s_i^2\,,$$

$$b'_{\kappa_i,i}=-(a'_{\kappa_i,i}s'_i+te')+t^{\kappa_i}s_i\,,$$

where $\kappa_i=0,\ldots,\lceil\log_t^{q_i}\rceil-1$.

Let $h_{\kappa_i,i}=(a_{\kappa_i,i},b_{\kappa_i,i}=-(a_{\kappa_i,i}s'_i+te)+t^{\kappa_i}s_i^2)$, $l_i=(a'_{\kappa_i,i},b'_{\kappa_i,i}=-(a'_{\kappa_i,i}s'_i+te')+t^{\kappa_i}s_i)$, and

set the auxiliary information is $\tau_{sk'\to sk''}=\{h_{\kappa_i,i},l_{\kappa_i,i}\}_{\kappa_i=0}^{\lceil\log_t^{q_i}\rceil-1}$.

Let $c_1\leftarrow(\sum_{\kappa_i=0}^{\lceil\log_t^{q_i}\rceil-1}c_{1,0,\kappa_i}t^{\kappa_i},\ldots,\sum_{\kappa_i=0}^{\lceil\log_t^{q_i}\rceil-1}c_{1,L,\kappa_i}t^{\kappa_i})$, $c_2\leftarrow(\sum_{\kappa_i=0}^{\lceil\log_t^{q_i}\rceil-1}c_{2,0,\kappa_i}t^i,\ldots,\sum_{i=0}^{\lceil\log_t^{q_i}\rceil-1}c_{2,L,\kappa_i}t^{\kappa_i})$, where

$c_{1,i,\kappa_i},c_{2,i,\kappa_i}\in R_t$, and compute:

$$c_0^{relin}\leftarrow c_0+(\sum_{\kappa_i=0}^{\lceil\log_t^{q_i}\rceil-1}c_{2,0,\kappa_i}b_{\kappa_i,i},\ldots,\sum_{j=0}^{\lceil\log_t^{q_i}\rceil-1}c_{2,L,\kappa_i}b_{\kappa_i,i})\,,$$

$$c_1^{relin}\leftarrow(\sum_{\kappa_i=0}^{\lceil\log_t^{q_i}\rceil-1}c_{2,0,\kappa_i}a_{\kappa_i,i},\ldots,\sum_{\kappa_i=0}^{\lceil\log_t^{q_i}\rceil-1}c_{2,L,\kappa_i}a_{\kappa_i})\,,$$

$$c_0'\leftarrow c_0^{relin}+(\sum_{\kappa_i=0}^{\lceil\log_t^{q_i}\rceil-1}c_{1,0,\kappa_i}b'_{\kappa_i,i},\ldots,\sum_{\kappa_i=0}^{\lceil\log_t^{q_i}\rceil-1}c_{1,L,\kappa_i}b'_{\kappa_i})\,,$$

$$c_1'\leftarrow c_1^{relin}+(\sum_{\kappa_i=0}^{\lceil\log_t^{q_i}\rceil-1}c_{1,0,\kappa_i}a'_{\kappa_i,i},\ldots,\sum_{\kappa_i=0}^{\lceil\log_t^{q_i}\rceil-1}c_{1,L,\kappa_i}a'_{\kappa_i})\,.$$

The new ciphertext is (c_0',c_1') , and the secret is $(1,s')$ 。

4.4 Modulus Switching

In [11], who suggested to scale down the ciphertext vector after every multiplication (they call this "modulus switching"). That is, to go from a vector c over $\mathbb{Z}_q$, into the vector c/w over $\mathbb{Z}_{q/w}$. Scaling "switches" the modulus q to a smaller q/w, and reduces the noise by the same factor. The algorithm is as follows.

Algorithm 2: Scale($\mathbf{ct}$,q_i,q_{i-1},t)

Input: $\mathbf{ct}$,q_i,q_{i-1},t

Output: $\mathbf{ct}'$

Compute：

$$\mathbf{ct}'=[(q_{i-1}/q_i)\cdot\mathbf{ct}]\,,$$

$$\mathbf{ct}'\equiv\mathbf{ct}(\mathrm{mod}\,t)\,.$$

5 Security and Parameters

The security of this scheme is based on the RLWE assumption, which is security and high efficiency, so it is widely used in the design of FHE. Under the circular security assumption, we prove that the scheme is CPA-secure. For space reasons, the proofs are omitted.

Lemma 2. [12] Let $pk \leftarrow Batch.\text{FHE}.\text{Keygen}(params)$. Then under the assumption $\text{RLWE}_{n,q_i,\chi}$, public key pk is computationally indistinguishable from uniform over $R_p^{(L+1)\times 2}$.

Theorem 2 (Security). The scheme in this paper is CPA-secure under the assumptions of $\text{RLWE}_{n,q_i,\chi}$ and circular security.

Discrete Gaussian distribution $\chi = D_{\mathbb{Z}^n,\sigma}$, and the standard deviation σ has the following Lemma 3.

Lemma 3   [9].   Let $n \in \mathbb{N}, \forall \sigma > \omega(\sqrt{\log n})$,   for $\mathbf{x} \leftarrow D_{\mathbb{Z}^n,\sigma}$,   have   that $\Pr[\|\mathbf{x}\|_\infty > \sigma\sqrt{n}] \leq 2^{-n+1}$.

Therefore, the bounds of the elements in the Gaussian distribution is $\sigma\sqrt{n}$.

Definition 10 [13] (Hermite factor). Let Λ be a lattice with m dimensions, one of lattice bases is $\mathbf{B}$, $\exists \delta^m$, $\ni \|b_1\| = \delta^m \det(\Lambda)^{1/m}$, where b_1 is the shortest vector in $\mathbf{B}$. we call δ^m is the Hermite factor, and δ is the root Hermite factor.

Given δ, the time it takes to make a lattice bases with Hermite factor δ^m mainly depends on δ.

Theorem 3 [14]. Given the root Hermite factor δ, the shortest vector is $\alpha \cdot q/\sigma \leq 2^{2\sqrt{n \log q/\log \sigma}}$, where $\alpha = \sqrt{\ln(1/\varepsilon)/\pi}$, and the total computing time is $\log T = 1.8/\lg \delta - 110$.

Therefore, the parameters of the scheme can be determined by $\alpha \cdot q/\sigma \leq 2^{2\sqrt{n \log q/\log \sigma}}$. Set distinguish advantage $\varepsilon = 2^{-64}$, take security parameter $\lambda = 128$ and the attack time $T = 2^{128}$. Thus we can get $\alpha \approx 3.758$, $\sigma \approx 1.005$, plug into $\alpha \cdot q/\sigma \leq 2^{2\sqrt{n \log q/\log \sigma}}$, the result is $1.910 + \log q - \log \sigma \leq 0.173\sqrt{n \log q}$. We fixed a value for n to determin the value of q, σ. See Table 1 for the specific parameter setting. And we compare the batch homomorphic encryption scheme with the scheme in Sect. 3, and the results are shown in Table 2.

Table 1. Parameter setting.

n	$\log q$	σ
256	19	6.58
512	20	13.41
1024	38	55.06
2048	64	9.69

Table 2. Efficiency comparison.

Scheme	Size of ciphertext	Size of public key	Size of secret key
Batch FHE	$O(\lambda \log_t^{qB})$	$O(\lambda \delta_R)$	$O(\lambda B)$
Original	$O(\log_t^{qB})$	$O(\delta_R)$	$O(B)$

6 Conclusions

Under the background of big data and cloud computing, the application prospect of FHE is very broad. We present a leveled batch FHE based on [8]. In this paper, we use the Chinese Remainder theorem to pack the plaintexts to support SIMD-type operations which can reduce the ciphertext expansion ratio, and the efficiency of the scheme is improved obviously: The size of public key and secret key is λ times of the original scheme, and the number of encrypted plaintexts is $n\lambda$ times of the original scheme. Finally, we also describe the parameter setting with highly practical.

Acknowledgments. This work is supported by the National Nature Science Foundation of China under Grand No. 61601515, and Nature Science Foundation of Henan Province under Grand No. 162300410332.

References

1. Feng, D.G., Zhang, M., Zhang Y., et al.: Study on cloud computing security. J. Softw. **22**(1), 71–83 (2011)
2. Rivest, R.L., Adlman, L., Dertouzos, M.L.: On data banks and privacy homomorphisms. Found. Secure Comput. **4**(11), 169–180 (1978)
3. Gentry, C.: Fully homomorphic encryption using ideal lattices. In: Proceedings of the 41st Annual ACM Symposium on Theory of Computing, pp. 169–178. ACM Press, New York (2009)
4. Gentry, C., Halevi, S.: Implementing gentry's fully-homomorphic encryption scheme. In: Paterson, K.G. (ed.) EUROCRYPT 2011. LNCS, vol. 6632, pp. 129–148. Springer, Heidelberg (2011). https://doi.org/10.1007/978-3-642-20465-4_9
5. Smart, N.P., Vercauteren, F.: Fully homomorphic SIMD operations. Des. Codes Crypt., **71**(1), 57–81 (2014)
6. Gentry, C., Halevi, S., Smart, N.P.: Fully homomorphic encryption with polylog overhead. In: Pointcheval, D., Johansson, T. (eds.) EUROCRYPT 2012. LNCS, vol. 7237, pp. 465–482. Springer, Heidelberg (2012). https://doi.org/10.1007/978-3-642-29011-4_28
7. Brakerski, Z., Vaikuntanathan, V.: Efficient fully homomorphic encryption from (standard) LWE. In: Proceedings of the 52nd Annual Symposium on Foundations of Computer Science, pp. 97–106. IEEE Computer Society, Washington DC (2011)
8. Naehrig, M., Lauter, K., Vaikuntanathan, V.: Can homomorphic encryption be practical? In: Proceedings of the 3rd ACM Workshop on Cloud Computing Security Workshop, pp. 113–124. ACM (2011)
9. Lidl, R., Niederreiter, H.: Finite Fields. Cambridge University Press (1997)

10. Lyubashevsky, V., Peikert, C., Regev, O.: On ideal lattices and learning with errors over rings. In: Gilbert, H. (ed.) EUROCRYPT 2010. LNCS, vol. 6110, pp. 1–23. Springer, Heidelberg (2010). https://doi.org/10.1007/978-3-642-13190-5_1
11. Micciancio, D.: The shortest vector in a lattice is hard to approximate to within some constant. SIAM J. Comput. **30**(6), 2008–2035 (2001)
12. Gama, N., Nguyen, P.Q.: Predicting lattice reduction. In: Smart, N. (ed.) EUROCRYPT 2008. LNCS, vol. 4965, pp. 31–51. Springer, Heidelberg (2008). https://doi.org/10.1007/978-3-540-78967-3_3
13. Lindner, R., Peikert, C.: Better key sizes (and attacks) for LWE-based encryption. In: Kiayias, A. (ed.) CT-RSA 2011. LNCS, vol. 6558, pp. 319–339. Springer, Heidelberg (2011). https://doi.org/10.1007/978-3-642-19074-2_21
14. Gentry, C.: A fully homomorphic encryption scheme. Doctoral thesis. Stanford University (2009)

A Novel Convolution Neural Network for Background Segmentation Recognition

Wei Fang[1,2], Yewen Ding[1(✉)], and Feihong Zhang[1]

[1] School of Computer and Software, Jiangsu Engineering
Center of Network Monitoring, Nanjing University
of Information Science and Technology, Nanjing, China
20171211475@nuist.edu.cn, ml5695218160@163.com
[2] State Key Laboratory for Novel Software Technology,
Nanjing University, Nanjing, China

Abstract. The convolution neural network for image classification is an application of deep learning on image processing. Convolutional neural networks have the advantage of being able to convolve directly with image pixels and extract image features from image pixels. This approach is closer to the treatment of the human brain's visual system. However, up to now, it is impossible to achieve 100% classification accuracy regardless of any kind of convolutional neural network models. At the same time, we also found that sometimes the picture background will also affect the recognition effect of the neural network on the picture, and after removing the picture background, it can correctly recognize the same picture. Therefore, we design a model based on the convolutional neural network to remove the image background for some specific images (such as selfies, animals, flowers, etc.) here, and then the image after processing will be identified and classified. Experiments show that the proposed method can maintain a high level of integrity of the target to be detected in the image after removing the background (here the indicator is Intersection Over Union, IOU); moreover, through multiple classification models verify that the classification accuracy of some background-removed pictures is significantly higher than that of pictures without any treatment.

Keywords: CNN · Segmentation · Classification

1 Introduction

First of all, we need to consider the background removal of the image, the background removal is a task that can be easily accomplished manually or semi-manually. There is also an online background removal, such as Clipping Magic, which requires the user to select the parts they need to remove and need to keep. As far as we know, automatic background removal is a challenging task, but there are still no products that can achieve satisfactory results.

When we started our work, we thought a lot about the problem: the universal background remover to automatically distinguish the foreground and background of various types of pictures. However, when the preliminary model is trained, we recognized that it is more reasonable to focus on a particular set of images. Therefore, we

X. Sun et al. (Eds.): ICCCS 2018, LNCS 11063, pp. 172–182, 2018.
https://doi.org/10.1007/978-3-030-00006-6_15

only used specific images for analyzing and processing. Central to Computer Vision is the process of Segmentation, which divides whole images into pixel groupings which can then be labelled and classified. Moreover, Semantic Segmentation goes further by trying to semantically understand the role of each pixel in the image e.g. is it a cat, dog or some other type of class?

It is believed that some of the most important contributions in the field of image segmentation should be attributed to the FAIR laboratory. Since 2015, they have launched a research project called DeepMask [1]. DeepMask can roughly generate a primary version of the partition on the object (that is a mask). In 2016, Fair Laboratories developed the SharpMask [2] system, which corrects the segmentation area provided by DeepMask, corrects missed details and improves semantic segmentation. Based on this, MultiPathNet [3] recognized the objects described by each of the divided regions.

Then, we need to consider which classification model to validate these processed images. In recent years, as deep learning has been popular, the development of convolutional neural networks has also been rapid, a large number of convolutional neural network models have emerged. In the 1990s, LeCun [4, 5] and others published papers that established the modern structure of CNN and later refined it. They designed a multi-layered artificial neural network called LeNet-5, which can classify handwritten numbers. LeNet-5 can also be trained by using backpropagation [6]. In order to overcome the difficulty of training CNN deeply, Krizhevsky et al. proposed a classic CNN structure and made a major breakthrough in image recognition tasks. The overall framework for this approach is called AlexNet [7], similar to LeNet-5, but with a more hierarchical structure. At the same time, ReLu [8] and Dropout [9], which are nonlinear activation functions, have been used to achieve remarkable results. Since then, researchers have proposed other improvements, the most famous networks were ZFNet [10], VGGNet [11], GoogleNet [12] and ResNet [13]. In terms of structure, one of the directions of CNN development is that the number of layers has increased. The ILSVRC 2015 champion ResNet is 20 times deeper than AlexNet and 8 times deeper than VGGNet. By increasing the depth, the network can use the added non-linearities to derive the approximate structure of the objective function, leading to better characterization of the features. However, it also increases the overall complexity of the network, making it difficult to optimize the network and it is easy to overfitting. Here we also consider the economic issues, so we use a shallower convolutional neural network for image classification tasks.

The major contributions of this paper are as follows:

We design a novel convolutional neural network model for background segmentation recognition. And, we evaluate our novel model in some real datasets. First of all, for certain types of images, by using the background removal model, it can effectively remove the background of the images, and the novel model can achieve fully automated effects; Moreover, after removing the background of certain types of images, we take them into the classification model for recognition, which can effectively improves the recognition and classification effects of convolutional neural network models.

2 Related Work

2.1 Semantic Segmentation

The earliest idea is to use early classification networks, such as SVM [14, 15], VGG and Alexnet. VGG is an image classification model that emerged in 2014 and commonly used due to its simple and straightforward network structure. Analyzing the shallow network layer of VGG, it can be found that there is a high degree of activation near the object that needs to be classified. The deeper network, the higher activation. However, due to the influence of pooling layer, the activation result is rather rough. Based on this understanding, it is assumed that the classification network can find/segment objects with some adjustments.

This idea was further improved in the FCN [16], in which some layers are connected to obtain richer expression information. According to different up-sampling rate, it is noted as FCN-32, FCN-16 and FCN-8, as shown in Fig. 1.

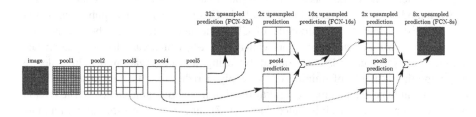

Fig. 1. Different types of FCN network structure

By adding some skip connections between network layers, the prediction results can be used to encode better detail information of the original image, and further training can improve the prediction. This technique illustrates that deep learning-based techniques can indeed be effective for semantic segmentation. The segmentation effect of FCN is indeed very significant, as shown in Fig. 2.

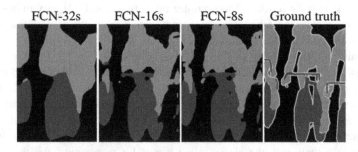

Fig. 2. FCN segmentation results

FCN opens the chapter in segmentation, and researchers continue to study semantic segmentation based on different networks. The main idea is the same: based on the existing network, upsampled, and skip connection.

2.2 Convolution Neural Network

Convolutional Neural Network (CNN) is a common deep learning architecture inspired by biological natural visual recognition mechanism. In 1959, Hubel and Wiesel [17] found that animal visual cortex cells are responsible for detecting optical signals. Inspired by this, in 1980 Kunihiko Fukushima proposed the predecessor of CNN, neocognitron [18].

In the 1990s, LeCun et al. published papers that established the CNNs modern structure and later refined it. They devised a multi-layered artificial neural network named LeNet-5.

CNN is able to derive an efficient representation of the original image, which allows the CNN to recognize the images directly from the original pixel with minimal preprocessing. However, due to the lack of large-scale training data at that time and the inability of computers to keep up with computational power, LeNet-5 did not handle the complicated problems satisfactorily.

Since 2006, many methods have been devised to overcome the difficulty of training CNN deeply. Among them, the most famous one is Krizhevsky et al. proposed a classic CNN structure and made a major breakthrough in image recognition tasks. The whole framework of its approach, called AlexNet, is similar to LeNet-5, but more deeply. After the success of AlexNet, the researchers put forward other improved methods, of which the four most famous are ZFNet, VGGNet, GoogleNet and ResNet.

3 BGRM-CNNs

After analyzing and researching, we chose three models: FCN, Unet [19] and Tiramisu [20]. We also considered Mask-RCNN [21], but its implementation was beyond the scope of the project.

The FCN seems to have nothing to do with the project because its effect does not work as expected, but the remaining two models are satisfactory. Unet is relatively easy to implement (based on keras), Tiramisu is also achievable.

Based on these two models, we started training on the data set. Unet did not seem to be suitable and the result was unsatisfactory. As shown in Fig. 3.

3.1 Data

After determining the model, we started selecting the appropriate data set. The most extensive segmentation dataset is the COCO dataset [22], which includes 80 K images in 90 categories; VOC Pascal dataset with 11 K images in total, 20 categories; and ADE20 K dataset. Since COCO dataset has more people, animal annotation images, it is more relevant to our background removal task, which is selected here.

Fig. 3. Tiramisu, Unet contrast

COCO dataset provides a direct API, so we can accurately know each object in a picture. After experiments, we decided to sort out the COCO dataset: First, only kept the pictures which contains people or animals, got a total of 50 K; then, deleted the picture which have many objects in the picture, to ensure that each picture only 1–2 characters or objects, this is what we need to deal with. Lastly, only 20%–80% of the area of the marked object in the picture was preserved, removing very small people or objects in the background, as well as some weird annotations. The final dataset contained 10 K images, it should be enough for training. As shown in Fig. 4.

Fig. 4. (Left) Picture that meets the requirements; (Medium) Object is too small; (Right) Contains too many objects

3.2 Tiramisu Model

Although its full name is "The One Hundred Layers Tiramisu", it sounds like a big model, but it's actually very concise with just 9 million parameters. In contrast, the parameters of VGG16 are as much as 130 million. Tiramisu is based on DenseNet [23] and DenseNet is a recent image classification model in which all layers are interconnected. And, similar to Unet, Tiramisu adds some skip connections to up-sampling layers.

In DenseNet, let x_l be the output of the lth layer. In the standard CNN, x_l is calculated by applying the nonlinear transformation H_l to the output of the previous layer x_{l-1}.

$$x_l = H_l(x_{l-1}) \tag{1}$$

Where H is commonly defined as a convolution followed by a rectifier non-linearity (ReLU) and often dropout.

In order to train the deep network, ResNets introduce the equivalent map, and the output x becomes:

$$x_l = H_l(x_{l-1}) + x_{l-1} \tag{2}$$

DenseNets design a more sophisticated connectivity pattern that iteratively concatenates all feature outputs in a feedforward fashion. Thus, the output of the lth layer is defined as:

$$x_l = H_l([x_{l-1}, x_{l-2}, \ldots, x_0]) \tag{3}$$

Where [...] represents the concatenation operation. In this case, H is defined as BN, followed by ReLU, a convolution and dropout. Such connectivity pattern strongly encourages the reuse of features and allows all layers in the architecture to receive direct supervision signal.

Because the upsampling path increases the spatial resolution of the feature map, and the linear increase in the number of features will be very memory-intensive, especially the full-resolution feature in front of the softmax layer. In order to solve this limitation, in the upsampling layer, the input of the dense block is not associated with its output. Therefore, transposed convolution applies only to the feature map that generated by the nearest dense block, not all feature maps. The nearest dense block adds the information obtained from all preceding dense blocks of the same resolution. It should be noted that some of the information generated by the previous dense block was lost due to the pool operation in the transition down. However, this information can be obtained in the down-sampling path of the network and can be passed via a skip connection. Therefore, the dense block in the upsampling path is calculated by using all available feature maps of a given resolution. The model is shown in Fig. 5.

3.3 Training

The training network uses: standard cross-entropy loss, 1e-3 learning rate, and smaller attenuation RMSProp optimizer. 80% of the 10 K data set is for training and 20% for verification. We set the epoch size to 100 pictures. This allows us to save the training model periodically.

3.4 Results

Here, we use Intersection over Union to evaluate the removal effect, as shown in Fig. 6.

Although our results are satisfactory, it is not perfect enough: we use the data set to test the model, and we get the IOU value of about 70. The numbers are hard to count because they fluctuate as long as they encounter different datasets and categories. Some categories are easier to segment, such as aircraft, horses, etc., and the model can handle

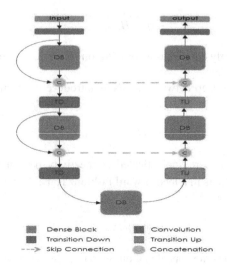

Fig. 5. Tiramisu Network

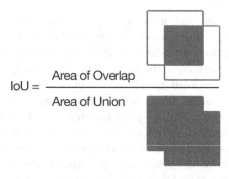

Fig. 6. Computing the IoU is as simple as dividing the area of overlap between the bounding boxes by the area of union.

IOU values up to 90 for these categories. The intractable categories include flowers and humans, and the model's IOU value fluctuates upwards at 60 when these categories are processed. In order to limit the degree of difficulty, our model only focuses on some certain types of images.

4   Classification Model

We need to complete the classification task, here we also use the convolutional neural network to achieve. We use the more economical models of convolution neural networks, such as LeNet-5, AlexNet. Although models such as VGG have more powerful classification performance, but requirements are too high for ordinary users.

Since we only implement classification for certain types of images here, there is no need to use convolutional neural network models such as VGG, DRL, which are applied to the classification of thousands of images. We use the VGG-RM to evaluate our image classification effect. Here, we make the following changes:

The model contains a total of 11 layers, the front 8 layers are a convolutional layer plus a pooling layer, and the last 3 layers are fully connection layers.

The first layer of convolution input is the original image, the original image size is $224 \times 224 \times 3$. The convolution filter has a size of 5×5 and a depth of 32, using a full 0 complement with the step size of 1. The filter used in the second convolution layer is 5×5 in size and 64 in depth. It uses a full 0 complement with the step size of 1. The filter used in the third convolution layer is 3×3 in size and 128 in depth. It uses a full 0 complement with the step size of 1. The filter used in the fourth convolution layer is 3×3 in size and 128 in depth. It uses a full 0 complement with the step size of 1.

All pooling layers use a filter size of 2×2, step size is 2.

The number of output nodes in first full connection layer is 1024. The number of input nodes in second full connection layer is 1024, and the number of output nodes is 512. The number of input nodes in third full connection layer is 512, and the number of output nodes is 10. Network structure is shown in Fig. 7.

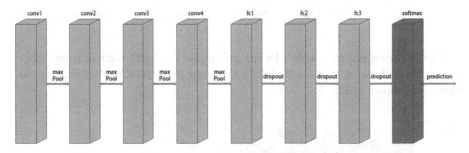

Fig. 7. Classification model structure diagram

5 Experiments Evaluation

We selected 10 types of pictures (flowers, portraits, horses, dogs, cats, elephants, cars, cows, sheep, bells) from the COCO dataset and put them into a trained classification model to verify them (each category contains 1000 images). The requirement of the image is that the number of characters and objects contained in each image is 1–2, and it needs to occupy more than 20% of the entire image.

Here, we used AlexNet, VGGNet variants (used in this article as VGG-RM), model A in VGGNet to test our images; first, tested the unprocessed image, and then tested the background removed images, it can be found that its classification accuracy rate remains at the same level, as shown in Table 1.

Next, we stored the unprocessed images in a folder with the wrong classification, performed background removal on all these images, and put them into the trained classification model to verify again. The accuracy is shown in Table 2.

Table 1. Classification Accuracy

	Model	Total number	Identification number	Classification accuracy
Untreated image	AlexNet	10k	5693	56.93%
	VGGNet-A	10k	7817	78.17%
	VGG-RM	10k	7532	75.32%
Background removed image	AlexNet	10k	4922	49.22%
	VGGNet-A	10k	7971	79.71%
	VGG-RM	10k	7721	77.21%

Table 2. Classification Accuracy (only misclassified images)

	Model	Total number	Identification number	Classification accuracy
Untreated image	AlexNet	4307	0	0%
	VGGNet-A	2183	0	0%
	VGG-RM	2468	0	0%
Background removed image	AlexNet	4307	1507	34.98%
	VGGNet-A	2183	1495	68.48%
	VGG-RM	2468	1604	64.99%

The following picture couldn't be recognized by VGG-RM without using background removal, but it was successfully recognized by VGG-RM after background removal, as shown in Fig. 8.

Fig. 8. (Left) Not Recognized; (Right) Successfully Recognized

This shows that the misclassified images can be effectively classified as a real type after the background is removed. It also shows that the background will affect the accuracy of image classification, and our model can improve the classification accuracy.

6 Discussion and Conclusion

The experimental results show that the recognition effect on some specific images is obviously better than that of the image without any processing after removing the background of the image. Especially when the image only contains one person or an object. Next, we will further improve it and test it in real world in future.

Our model was obtained after training about 300 epochs on the training data set. After this, the model began to overfit. We have reached a segmentation result that is close to the issue. Therefore, no further application data has been expanded.

Model training used a 224 * 224 size input image. If further training, based on more data, a larger image size (original COCO dataset image size of 600 * 1000) may enhance the segmentation effect.

Acknowledgements. This work was supported in part by the Priority Academic Program Development of Jiangsu Higher Education Institutions.

References

1. Pinheiro, P., Collobert, R., Dollár, P.: Learning to segment object candidates. In: Neural Information Processing Systems Conference, pp. 1990–1998 (2015)
2. Pinheiro, Pedro O., Lin, T.-Y., Collobert, R., Dollár, P.: Learning to refine object segments. In: Leibe, B., Matas, J., Sebe, N., Welling, M. (eds.) ECCV 2016. LNCS, vol. 9905, pp. 75–91. Springer, Cham (2016). https://doi.org/10.1007/978-3-319-46448-0_5
3. Zagoruyko, S., et al.: A MultiPath network for object detection. In: British Machine Vision Conference (2016)
4. LeCun, Y., Bottou, L., Bengio, Y., Haffner, P.: Gradient-based learning applied to document recognition. Proc. IEEE **86**(11), 2278–2324 (1998)
5. Le Cun, Y., Denker, J., Henderson, D., Howard, R., Hubbard, W., Jackel, L.: Handwritten digit recognition with a back-propagation network. In: Advances in Neural Information Processing Systems, pp. 396–404 (1990)
6. Hecht-Nielsen, R.: Theory of the backpropagation neural network. In: International Joint Conference on Neural Networks, pp. 445–448 (1988)
7. Krizhevsky, A., Sutskever, I., Hinton, G.: Imagenet classification with deep convolutional neural networks. In: Advances in Neural Information Processing Systems, pp. 1106–1114 (2012)
8. Nair, V., Hinton, G.: Rectified linear units improve restricted boltzmann machines. In: International Conference on Machine Learning, pp. 807–814 (2010)
9. Hinton, G., Srivastava, N., Krizhevsky, A., Sutskever, I., Salakhutdinov, R.: Improving neural networks by preventing co-adaptation of feature detectors. arXiv. abs/1207.0580 (2012)
10. Zeiler, M.D., Fergus, R.: Visualizing and understanding convolutional networks. In: Fleet, D., Pajdla, T., Schiele, B., Tuytelaars, T. (eds.) ECCV 2014. LNCS, vol. 8689, pp. 818–833. Springer, Cham (2014). https://doi.org/10.1007/978-3-319-10590-1_53
11. Simonyan, K., Zisserman, A.: Very deep convolutional networks for large-scale image recognition. arXiv. abs/1409.1556 (2014)
12. Szegedy, C., et al.: Going deeper with convolutions. In: Computer Vision and Pattern Recognition, pp. 1–9. IEEE (2015)

13. Wang, T., Wu, D., Coates, A., Ng, A.: End-to-end text recognition with convolutional neural networks. In: Pattern Recognition, pp. 3304–3308. IEEE (2012)
14. Gu, B.: A regularization path algorithm for support vector ordinal regression. Neural Networks **98**, 114–121 (2018)
15. Gu, B., Sheng, V.S.: A solution path algorithm for general parametric quadratic programming problem. IEEE Trans. Neural Netw. Learn. Syst. **99**, 1–11 (2017)
16. Long, J., Shelhamer, E., Darrell, T.: Fully convolutional networks for semantic segmentation. In: Computer Vision and Pattern Recognition, pp. 3431–3440. IEEE (2015)
17. Hubel, D.H., Wiesel, T.N.: Receptive fields and functional architecture of monkey striate cortex. J. Physiol. **195**(1), 15–43 (1968)
18. Fukushima, K., Miyake, S.: Neocognitron: a self-organizing neural network model for a mechanism of visual pattern recognition. Biol. Cybern. **36**(4), 193–202 (1980)
19. Ronneberger, O., Fischer, P., Brox, T.: U-net: convolutional networks for biomedical image segmentation. In: Medical Image Computing and Computer-Assisted Intervention, pp. 234–241 (2015)
20. Jégou, S., Drozdzal, M., Vazquez, D., Romero, A., Bengio. Y.: The One Hundred Layers Tiramisu: Fully Convolutional DenseNets for Semantic Segmentation. arXiv. abs/1611.09326 (2016)
21. He, K., Gkioxari, G., Dollar, P., Girshick, R.: Mask R-CNN. In: International Conference on Computer Vision, pp. 2980–2988. IEEE (2017)
22. Lin, T.-Y., et al.: Microsoft COCO: Common Objects in Context. In: Fleet, D., Pajdla, T., Schiele, B., Tuytelaars, T. (eds.) ECCV 2014. LNCS, vol. 8693, pp. 740–755. Springer, Cham (2014). https://doi.org/10.1007/978-3-319-10602-1_48
23. Huang, G., Liu, Z., Weinberger, K.Q., Maaten, L.: Densely connected convolutional networks. arXiv. abs/1608.06993 (2016)

A Parallel Pre-schedule Max-Min Ant System

Ying Zheng[1,2], Qianlong Yang[1], Longhai Jin[2], and Lili He[1(✉)]

[1] College of Computer Science and Technology, Jilin University,
Changchun 130012, China
helili@jlu.edu.cn
[2] Center for Computer Fundamental Education, Jilin University,
Changchun 130012, China

Abstract. The parameter sensitivity of MMAS algorithm is analyzed in this paper. And then, we propose a multi-ant colony parallel optimization algorithm based on dynamic parameter adaptation strategy, aiming at the performance lack of traditional ACO algorithm. This algorithm makes use of cloud computing parallelism to design and analyze the MMAS system. The convergence solution comparison results show that this method has certain advantages.

Keywords: Max-Min Ant System · Parameter sensitivity · Parallel computing
Pre-schedule · Cloud computing

1 Introduction

Ant colony optimization (ACO) is a meta-heuristic algorithm designed to simulate the behavior of real world ants. It was first proposed by Marco Dorigo, Mauro Birattari, and Thomas Stützle [1]. In nature, the path finding process of a single ant presents a kind of randomness, but when the ant forms a population, the ant colony's path finding process will have a clear orientation. The ant colony optimization strategy focuses on the improvement of the basic ant system (Ant System, AS) algorithm itself. This type of study can effectively improve the performance of the algorithm by restricting and constraining the algorithm. Among them, there are two ACO's improved algorithms that are most widely known, namely: max-min ant system (MMAS) [2] and ant colony system (ACS) [3]. The two algorithms have very little overhead for computing resources, and the stability is greatly improved compared with the original AS algorithm. Since ACO put forward, over the years, there has been a lot of work to improve the performance of ACO. In the early stage, the optimization of ant colony algorithm is devoted to the transformation of the AS algorithm to reduce the path exploration time of the algorithm and further increase the stability of the algorithm [4]. In recent years, due to the large development of parallel technology, the introduction of parallel technology into ACO algorithm has become the main research direction of ant colony optimization [5, 6]. This paper will analyze the parameters of MMAS algorithm based on the characteristics of ACO, and will propose the parameter modification strategy of MMAS, and introduce the parallel technology on this basis, so that the real-time performance of ACO algorithm is significantly improved. On the basis of the above,

© Springer Nature Switzerland AG 2018
X. Sun et al. (Eds.): ICCCS 2018, LNCS 11063, pp. 183–193, 2018.
https://doi.org/10.1007/978-3-030-00006-6_16

the parallel technology is introduced, and the real-time performance of ACO algorithm is improved obviously.

2 Max-Min Ant System

MMAS is an improved algorithm of AS algorithm. The main improvement of the MMAS algorithm lies in the further control of pheromone updates. First, after each iteration, there is only one solution path, and the pheromones on each side will increase. This solution path may be an iterative optimal solution, or it may be the best solution so far. Then, the value of pheromone will be limited to the range. The pheromone release rules are as follows:

$$\tau_{ij} \leftarrow max\left\{\tau_{ij}, \quad min\left\{\tau_{max}, \quad (1-\rho) \cdot \tau_{ij} + \Delta\tau_{ij}^{best}\right\}\right\}$$

In this formula, $\Delta\tau_{ij}^{best}$ is defined as:

$$\Delta\tau_{ij}^{best} = \begin{cases} 1/C^{best}, & \text{If } (i,j) \text{ is on the optimal solution path } T^{best} \\ 0, & \text{Others} \end{cases}$$

In addition, the improvement of the MMAS algorithm includes: Before the algorithm is executed, each side will set a pheromone initial value. The initial value is the upper bound in the range of values, and the pheromone evaporation rate is small. If the algorithm is stuck or after a certain number of iterations, a higher quality solution cannot be obtained, the pheromone on each side will be reset to the initial value.

3 Pre-analysis

3.1 Parametric Impact Analysis

We mainly studied the influence of parameter —heuristic factor β, number of ants m, and pheromone evaporation rate ρ—in MMAS on the real-time performance of the algorithm.

For the heuristic factor β, it can be seen from Fig. 1(a) that if a local search strategy is not introduced under the MMAS, the β needs to be set a relatively large value. At this time, the real-time performance of the algorithm is significantly better than the default setting ($\beta = 2$), and this advantage is more obvious in the initial stage of the algorithm path construction. Under the default setting, MMAS can obtain high quality iteration final solution after long path searching. If the β is less than 2, the real-time performance of the algorithm and the quality of the final solution will be greatly reduced. As can be seen in Fig. 1(b), after introducing a local search strategy, the impact of different values of β on the algorithm is greatly reduced, and the gap between the algorithms in various operating phases is not significant. This conclusion shows that for MMAS, setting a large value of β during the initial execution of the algorithm will effectively improve the initial performance of the algorithm; and after the algorithm is executed for a period of time, properly reducing the value of β will help improve the real-time performance of the algorithm.

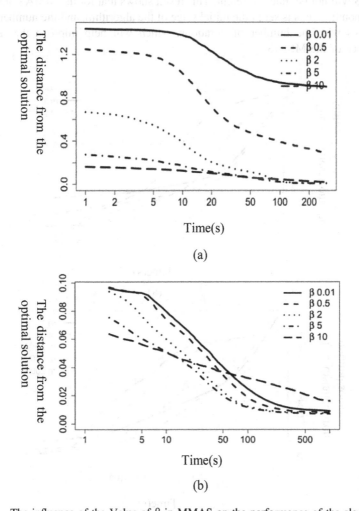

Fig. 1. The influence of the Value of β in MMAS on the performance of the algorithm

Figure 2(a) and (b) show that regardless of whether a local search strategy is introduced in the MMAS, the number of ants m has a clear orientation to the MMAS algorithm both at the beginning and end of the operation. When the number of ants takes a small value, MMAS can get the best solution so far until now in the early stage of operation. Although the initial performance of the algorithm is low, an MMAS with more ants ($m > 100$) can obtain a better quality solution at the later stage of the algorithm. Without introducing a local search strategy, MMAS with a small number of ants will quickly stabilize and enter the local path development phase. With the introduction of local search strategies, MMAS with fewer ants also cannot improve the quality of iterative optimal solutions. In fact, under a certain number of ants ($m > 25$), if the algorithm can be executed long enough, the quality of the final solution obtained by MMAS will not be much different. This result shows that for the MMAS algorithm, a small amount of ants is set in the initial stage of the algorithm, and the number of ants m increases with the number of iterations, which will help improve the real-time performance of the MMAS.

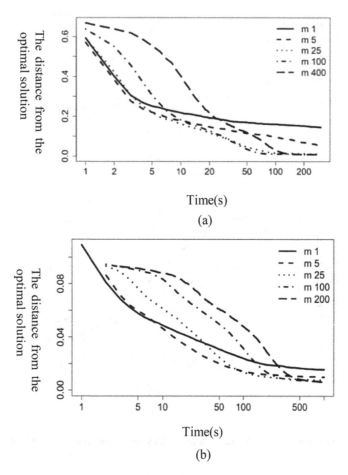

Fig. 2. The influence of the Value of m in MMAS on the performance of the algorithm

Figure 3(a) and (b) show that the algorithm converges faster when ρ is chosen for a larger value for the pheromone evaporation rate ρ. For example, the algorithm that ρ takes 0.6 is faster to converge than the algorithm that ρ takes 0.02. However, if the algorithm runs long enough, the MMAS with lower ρ will get the same high-quality iterative final solution. Even in individual cases, the MMAS algorithm with a lower value of ρ can get a better iterative final solution. This conclusion is more obvious under MMAS without introducing a local search strategy. Therefore, setting a higher pheromone evaporation rate at the beginning of the algorithm and dropping it back to the default value as the number of iterations increases will probably improve the performance of the algorithm.

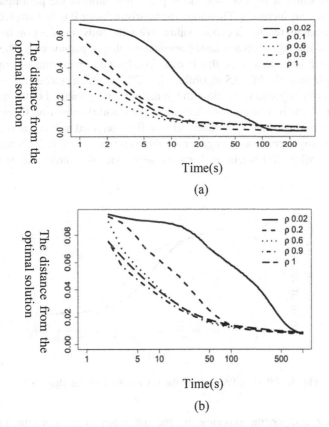

Fig. 3. The influence of the Value of ρ in MMAS on the performance of the algorithm

The above research shows that for the MMAS algorithm, the parameters in the MMAS have a very significant influence on the real-time performance of the algorithm under the condition that the algorithm runtime can be controlled. In particular, it is necessary to point out that if the heuristic factor β and the number of ants m in the MMAS algorithm are introduced into an appropriate parameter correction strategy, the real-time performance of the algorithm will be effectively improved.

3.2 Pre-set Parameter Strategy of MMAS

In this section, we will study the correction of various parameters of MMAS. In this regard, the presetting strategy of each parameter of the MMAS will be provided. Such research will help us to get a strategy that can really improve the real-time performance of the MMAS algorithm. After the parameter ρ is set to a large value, there is no subsequent correction scheme. Therefore, the pheromone evaporation rate ρ will not be considered in this section.

For the parameter β, the characteristics of the MMAS determine that linearly decreasing the value of the heuristic factor β can not improve the performance as the number of iterations increases. Therefore, the heuristic factor β is first studied when the number of iterations reaches a certain value. We will study an effect on the real-time performance of the algorithm at a larger or smaller value of parameter β. Therefore, the initial value of β is set to a value that is more conducive to performance improvement in the initial phase of the MMAS algorithm ($\beta = 20$), and then at a certain iteration, the β value is directly adjusted to be close to the default setting value. For the three curves shown in Fig. 4, the rest of the parameters are fixed, and the heuristic factor β is fixed at 20 at the beginning of the algorithm, and then β is corrected to $\beta = 2$ at one iteration. The corresponding correction timings for the three curves are: $\alpha\beta$ 1, 50 iterations; $\alpha\beta$ 2, 100 iterations; $\alpha\beta$ 3, 200 iterations. It can be seen that $\alpha\beta$ 1 shows the best real-time performance.

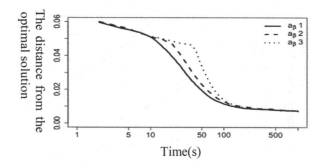

Fig. 4. Effect of Preset β on the performance of the algorithm

For further comparison experiments, the parameter correction strategy $\alpha\beta$ 1 is compared with the fixed heuristic factor β. Figure 5(a) and (b) respectively provide the performance comparison between the parameter modification strategy $\alpha\beta$ 1 and the fixed parameter values $\beta = 2$ and $\beta = 20$ when the MMAS without and with the local search strategy. It can be seen that $\alpha\beta$ 1 is always superior to the strategy that fixes the heuristic factor β regardless of whether the local search strategy is combined. The real-time performance of the parameter correction strategy $\alpha\beta$ 1 has been significantly improved.

For the number of ants m, we first investigate the case where the initial number of ants m is set to 1 and then the algorithm runs slowly. The five parameter correction strategies shown in Fig. 6 have their initial ant counts set to one. The strategy a_m 1 is to add one ant every 10 iterations; the strategy a_m 2 to add one ant per second; the strategy a_m 3 to add one ant for each iteration; the strategy a_m 4 to add 2 ants per iteration; The a_m 5 add 5 ants per iteration. The results show that as the rate of increase in the number of ants increases, the performance of the algorithm not only fails to improve but even

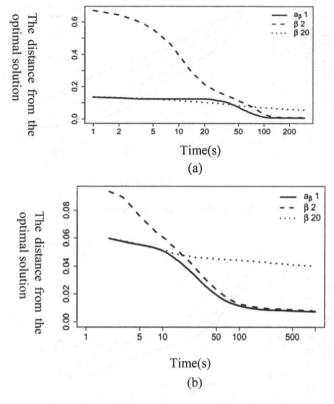

Fig. 5. Preset β change versus fixed β performance

decreases. Among them, the best performance strategy is a_m 1. Figure 7(a) and (b) respectively show the comparison of the pre-set parameter modification strategy a_m 1 with the fixed parameter strategy under MMAS with and without local search strategy. Experiments show that the strategy a_m 1 always obtains the best performance regardless of whether the local search strategy is used or not.

3.3   Parallel Multi-ant Colony with Preset Parameters

As mentioned above, the parameter preset strategy is a good way to improve the performance of the ACO algorithm. However, an inappropriate parameter preset strategy not only fails to improve the performance of the algorithm, but also stagnates at very poor results in the early iterations of the algorithm. The suitability of this parameter to a preset strategy depends on two aspects: the scale of the TSP problem, and the path that the ant initially built when the algorithm was run. Therefore, it is not feasible to adopt the same parameter preset strategy for multiple TSP issues. We propose a simple multi-ant colony parallel optimization strategy. According to the scale of the problem, multiple initial β values are set. Each thread performs a search process

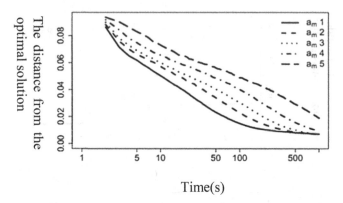

Fig. 6. Performance on Preset m

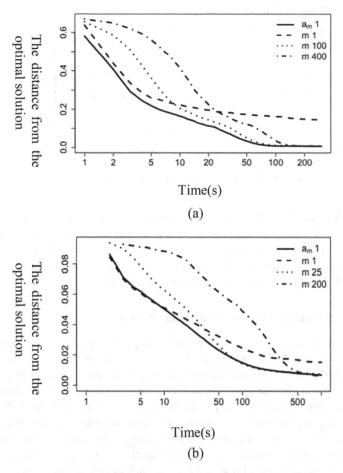

Fig. 7. Preset m vs. fixed m

for a single ant colony. These ant colonies are assigned to different β values and β preset strategies. The flow of this strategy under MMAS is as follows:

Step 1: System initialization. The main thread reads in the TSP data and creates a child thread. The sub-threads establish separate TSP problem related data structures (intercity distance/nearest neighbor list/pheromone matrix, etc.), initialize ants, and randomly assign algorithm parameters.

Step 2: Build the solution path. Each thread contains an ant colony. Each ant colony performs a complete path patrol in parallel based on the MMAS mechanism and current parameter settings.

Step 3: Select the iterative optimal solution. Each child thread selects its own iterative optimal path in a protocol.

Step 4: Pheromones evaporate. Evaporation of global pheromones is performed based on a certain pheromone evaporation rate.

Step 5: Pheromone update. The pheromone matrix updates the pheromone within a given interval.

Step 6: Determine whether ACO converges. If yes, the child thread returns the result to the main thread; otherwise, each thread determines whether the current number of iterations satisfies the parameter correction condition and skips back to step 2.

Step 7: After each sub-thread returns the ant colony iteration optimal solution to the main thread, the main thread compares the above optimal solution and returns a global optimal solution.

According to the characteristics of the strategy, the strategy is named parallel pre-schedule MMAS (P-PSMMAS). Among them, according to the summary of Sect. 3.1, let the initial value be $\beta \in [5, 20]$, and the value of β will be halved after every 50 iterations. In this multi-ant colony parallel strategy, there is no information interaction among different populations. Its significance lies in that: for the TSP problem, when the problem is large in scale and there is no so-called "known optimal solution", most adaptive strategies based on the number of nodes in the TSP problem and the distance between nodes, the optimal solution between the current iterative solution and the best known solution are not effective.

The P-PSMMAS strategy is essentially a trial and error process. For the ant colonies on each thread, there are always one or more strategies for the preset parameters of the assigned parameters, and the performance of the ant colonies will be obviously better than other preset parameters. Multiple ant colony parallel executions with parameter preset strategies increase the chances of the ant colony obtaining a more adaptive parameter setting, and thus improve the performance of the algorithm.

4 The Experimental Results

We experimented with TSP issues to illustrate. The TSP problem is selected from the TSP standard library TSPLIB. The following control experiments are the adaptive adjustment information exchange cycle strategies proposed by Chen ling et al. This strategy aims to selectively share certain information of the pheromone matrix through adaptive means to increase the diversity of the algorithm. The parallelism of this strategy is relatively high. The computational overhead and communication overhead are basically the same as the strategies proposed in this paper. The computer hardware used in the experiment was configured as Intel Xeon E3-1230 v2 (8 Threads) and 8G ram. The operating system was Win7 64bit ultimate. Parallel mechanism shared memory parallel programming OpenMP combined with VS 2010 to achieve multiple ant colony parallel execution and information exchange.

The average stagnation optimal solution is always the primary indicator of ACO algorithm performance evaluation. We run 50 times under each TSP instance, and then choose the optimal solution obtained by its lag and average it. The experimental results are shown in the following table:

Table 1 shows the average optimal solution of P-PSMMAS and the control algorithm in each TSP instance. As you can see, P-PSMMAS is better than a control algorithm in some instances.

Table 1. The performance comparison

	Known optimal solution	P-PSMMAS	Controlled experiment
Eil51	426	428.98	428.15
KroA100	21282	21336.72	21301.08
Lin318	42029	42335.37	42066.41
Att532	27686	27813.92	27719.34
pr76	108159	109026.46	108974.45
ts225	126643	128716.84	128946.23
pcb442	50778	51291.01	51169.47
rat783	8806	9204.34	9173.94
Lin105	14379	14834.03	14964.86
Pr226	80369	82846.77	83462.93

5   Conclusion

Therefore, this paper proposes a parallel multi-ant colony parameter modification mechanism: a dynamic parametric adaptive multi-ant colony parallel optimization algorithm. Experiments have shown that, without significantly increasing the computational burden and communication burden, the parameter correction mechanism improves the average convergence and stability of the ACO algorithm. This improvement reaches the level of the current mainstream ACO parallel strategy. And the real-time performance of the algorithm has been significantly improved.

Acknowledgments. This work was supported in part by the National Natural Science Foundation of China (51409117, 51679105, 61672261), Jilin Province Department of Education Thirteen Five science and technology research projects [2016] No. 432, [2017] No. JJKH20170804KJ.

References

1. Dorigo, M., Maniezzo, V., Colorni, A.: Ant system: optimization by a colony of cooperating agents. IEEE Trans. Syst. Man Cybern. B Cybern. **26**(1), 29–41 (1996)
2. Stützle, T., Hoos, H.H.: MAX–MIN ant system. Future Gener. Comput. Syst. **16**(8), 889–914 (2000)
3. Dorigo, M., Gambardella, L.M.: Ant colony system: a cooperative learning approach to the traveling salesman problem. IEEE Trans. Evol. Comput. **1**(1), 53–66 (1997)
4. Dorigo, M., Birattari, M., Stutzle, T.: Ant colony optimization. IEEE Comput. Intell. Mag. **1** (4), 28–39 (2006)
5. Bullnheimer, B., Kotsis, G., Strauß, C.: Parallelization strategies for the ant system. J. Econ. Integr. **12**(4), 419–432 (1998)
6. Talbi, E.G., Roux, O., Fonlupt, C., et al.: Parallel ant colonies for the quadratic assignment problem. Future Gener. Comput. Syst. **17**(4), 441–449 (2001)

A Reliable Method of Icing Detection for Transmission Lines

Zhao Guodong$^{(\boxtimes)}$, Li Pengfei, Fang Fan, Liu Xiaoyu,
and Zhang Yuewei

Harbin Engineering University, Harbin 150001, China
zhaoguodong@hrbeu.edu.cn

Abstract. The current ice-covering image processing method has poor fault-tolerance. And the classic algorithm using Hough transform linear fitting method to detect the conductor inclination is of low accuracy, in spite of the ability of suppressing interference and noise. In this paper, a new improved method was proposed, which is based on the analysis and studies of domestic and international methods for measurement of line ice thickness using image processing. The Hough transform was combined with the least-squares method to fit the edges of the covered wire. And fault-tolerance technology based on recovery blocks was used to solve the problem that the system fails due to data deviation from expectations. Experimental results show that compared with the traditional processing methods, the two proposed algorithms are capable to improve the system's fault-tolerance, this ensures high reliability and accuracy of the final measurement result. And it has great significance to study the image-based ice coating thickness detection algorithm.

Keywords: Ice thickness detection · Image processing · System reliability
Least square method

1 Introduction

As a basic component of the power grid, transmission lines make very important influence in term of the working status and stability. However, being affected by such natural disasters as ice and snow, the mechanical and electrical performance of the transmission lines dropped drastically, resulting in accidents such as broken ground lines, damage to fixtures and insulators, galloping of wires, collapse of towers, and interruption of power communication [1–3]. Therefore, the ice coating thickness detection of transmission lines has always been a major threat for the power system. The accuracy of the ice coating thickness monitoring results of the transmission lines plays a crucial role in the system's capacity to guide the deicing work of transmission line conductors accurately and reliably. In order to grasp the ice-coverage situation of transmission lines in real time, many researches have been made at home and abroad, on the on-line monitoring of ice transmission lines [4]. With the continuous development of information technology, the ice detection method for overhead transmission lines has a new automated method. Image processing-based detection system is the most ideal [5]. However, currently, most of the ice coating thickness detection

© Springer Nature Switzerland AG 2018
X. Sun et al. (Eds.): ICCCS 2018, LNCS 11063, pp. 194–206, 2018.
https://doi.org/10.1007/978-3-030-00006-6_17

algorithms, based on image processing, have suffered strong feature dependence of the ice coating image (the system is poorly tolerant to image data) and large errors in measurement results, thereby leading to poor system reliability and security. This leads to the reliability and security of the system can not bring the requirements of practical applications. In view of the above problems, the present research makes improvements from the following two aspects, thereby hoping to provide reference for relevant researchers.

(1) Apply software reliability fault tolerant technology to the system, and improve fault tolerance of the system's image data deviating from its expected design through software fault tolerance technology based on the recovery block method;

(2) In the detection of ice coating conductor inclination module, the traditional Hough transform linear fitting method and the least squares method are combined to improve the accuracy of the measurement results and the reliability of the detection system.

2   Software Reliability Design

The reliability design of software system refers to the application of various strategies and technical means in the process of software design, thus to make the system design is integrated with user needs (functionality, time-consuming), but also to meet the reliability requirements of the system. The techniques for improving system reliability include error avoidance and fault tolerance. Error avoidance refers to the prevention and avoidance of errors during the operation of the system; fault tolerance means: if the system deviates from the design requirements or the prescribed functions during the operation of the system, it will cause the system to fail and stop running. Redundancy can be used. Mutually shield the operation of their internal defect recovery system so that they can continue to provide services [6–8].

It has been proved from practices that taking effective measures in the software design phase is capable of improving the fault tolerance of the system, thus ensuring the reliability of the system in most effective and economical manner. Therefore, during the process of software system design, it is necessary to apply the reliability design to the system. The software reliability design techniques mainly include fault-tolerant design and error-detection design. The fault-tolerant design techniques will be used for improving system reliability herein.

According to different context in which the system may be wrong, the fault-tolerant system can be divided into the following stages: fault limitation, fault detection, fault masking, retry, diagnosis, reorganization, recovery, restart, repair, reconstruction [9, 10].

Among them, the fault limit is when the fault occurs, hoping to limit the scope of its impact, so as to limit the propagation of fault effects within a region; fault detection using parity, consistency check and protocol violations to detect system logic faults. Therefore, fault detection cannot provide tolerance for faults, but it only gives a warning notice in case of any fault. Therefore, fault detection cannot be called as fault tolerance. In this case, the fault tolerant technology of static redundancy and dynamic redundancy can be applied to implement system fault tolerance [11, 12].

Typical fault-tolerant technologies for software-oriented system faults are N version program design and recovery block methods [12]. N version programming is a static fault masking technique that employs a forward recovery strategy. The design concept is described as follows: for the same module, N teams develop programs independently with the same function based on the same need for different designs to perform a calculation at the same time, and then select by majority vote. This method is capable to shield accidental errors, therefore it is satisfied in real-time performance, but this method also requires a large number of developers, and result in higher cost of implementation. Generally, it is only applied in systems requiring high reliability. The recovery block method is a dynamic fault masking technique that employs a backward recovery strategy. This technique requires the provision of functionally identical master blocks and multiple spare blocks (Block A, Block B, Block C, etc.), and one block can be applied as a complete execution block. During the operation of the system, the main block is put into operation first, and after the end of the operation, a verification test is performed. If the test is not passed, the system is restored by the Block A after the scene is restored, and so on until a satisfactory result is identified.

In the processing of ice-covered images, the method using the N-version program design can ensure a higher reliability of the system, but the reliability is not high in the cost-effectiveness of changing the application scenario; the recovery block method requires validation results. Then the recovery block is executed, multiple backup blocks may need to be executed, therefore the real-time performance is slightly inferior to the N version program design method, but its cost is obviously reduced, and the reliability also meets the requirements of the system. Therefore, the recovery block method is used in this present research.

3   Ice Coating Image Preprocessing

The large noise of the ice-covered image and the inconsistent background will definitely affect the image processing. In the present research, the ice coating image is preprocessed to remove the noise points and interference areas in the image as much as possible. The purpose of separating the ice coating wire and the target background is maximum. The processing process mainly includes increasing the brightness and contrast, and graying processing, smooth processing technology in three stages. The pending image is shown in Fig. 1:

In the use of image enhancement technology to increase the brightness and contrast of the image, the feature area of the image is fully enhanced. in addition, some background areas that are not noticed are reduced and attenuated, thereby ensuring that the corresponding regional feature data is processed and analyzed at a later stage. The accuracy of the test. Further, it is necessary to convert the contrast-and brightness-enhanced color target image into a gray scale image. This method is greatly capable to reduce the amount of data calculation and ensures the efficiency of subsequent data processing.

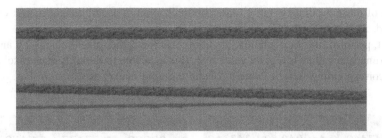

Fig. 1. Original ice coated image

Gaussian filtering is used for smoothing the gray scale image, which is a nonlinear filtering method. It employs a weighted average method to smooth the image, that is, the value of each pixel is obtained by weighting the pixel value itself and other pixel values in the neighborhood. When Gaussian filtering is applied, each pixel in the image needs to be scanned with a template (convolution, mask), and the weighted average gray value of pixels in the neighborhood determined by the template is applied to replace the value of the template center pixel.

According to the principle of two-dimensional normal distribution, it is available to derive this template. Normal distribution as a bell curve, the closer to the center, the greater the value, the smaller the contrary, so the two-dimensional normal distribution as a weight distribution model. The principle is shown in Fig. 2:

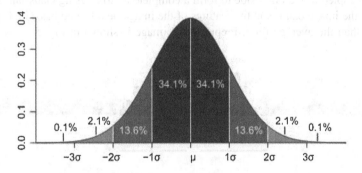

Fig. 2. Normal distribution map

Using the center point as the origin, the density function of the two-dimensional normal distribution is obtained, that is, the two-dimensional Gaussian function formula is shown in Eq. 1:

$$G(x, y) = \frac{1}{2\pi\sigma^2} e^{-(x^2 + y^2)/2\sigma^2} \tag{1}$$

According to this formula, the weight of each pixel can be calculated. Assuming $\sigma = 1.5$ and a fuzzy radius of 1, it is available to derive a weight matrix, but adding the weights of these 8 points is not 1. After normalization, a useful weight matrix can be achieved, as shown in the Fig. 3 shows.

Next, perform fuzzy calculation: assuming that the center pixel value is 25, and the surrounding blur radius is a pixel value of 1. it is available to multiply each pixel point by the corresponding weight value to obtain the final matrix as shown in Fig. 4.

0.0947416	0.118318	0.0947416
0.118318	0.147761	0.118318
0.0947416	0.118318	0.0947416

Fig. 3. Weight matrix diagram

1.32638	1.77477	1.51587
2.83963	3.69403	3.07627
3.22121	4.14113	3.4107

Fig. 4. The final weight matrix

Then add the 8 data as the value of the center pixel. If the original image is an RGB image, the values of the three channels can be separately calculated in a fuzzy manner. When the pixels on the boundary are blurred, only one point on the existing side will need to be copied to the other side to form a complete matrix. Using Gaussian filtering to smooth the image can retain the features of the image details, and has a higher noise reduction than the average filter. Preprocessed image is shown in Fig. 5:

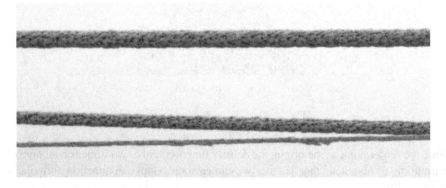

Fig. 5. Preprocessed ice coating image

By observing Fig. 5, after the pretreatment, the ice-covered conductor is more clearly segmented, and the noise of the image is also reduced, laying the foundation for the next thresholding process.

4 Threshold Treatment

4.1 The Concept of Image Thresholding

Image thresholding (binarization), also known as gray differentiation, is regarded as an important technique for image processing and has important applications in pattern recognition, optical character recognition, and medical imaging. The gray level of the general image is divided into only two gray values, that is, a gray value is set. If the gray level of the image itself is greater than that of the image, then it is a bright spot and the gray value is lower than the set value, so that it is Dark spots, so it is available to derive a binary image. In general, the binarization of the image is to set the grayscale of the point on the image to 0 or 255, which means that the whole image presents a clear black and white effect. That is, the 256 brightness level gray image is selected by an appropriate threshold to obtain a binarized image that can still reflect the overall image and local characteristics of the image. In digital image processing, binary image occupies a very important position. Especially in practical image processing, there are many systems constructed by binary image processing. To perform binary image processing and analysis, first of all, binarize the grayscale image to obtain a binarized image, which is conducive to further processing of the image. After the binarization process, the collection property of the image is only related to the position of the pixel with a value of 0 or 255, and no more multi-level values of pixels are involved, therefore the processing is simplified, and the amount of data processing and compression is small. In order to obtain an ideal binary image, closed and connected boundaries are generally applied in defining areas that do not overlap. All pixels whose gray levels are greater than or equal to the threshold are determined to belong to a specific object. The gray value is represented by 255. Otherwise, these pixels are excluded from the object area, and the gray value is 0, indicating the background or the exceptional object area. The mathematical principle is shown in Eq. 2. If a certain object has uniform gray values inside and it is in a uniform background with other levels of gray values, the threshold effect can be compared using the threshold method. If the difference between the object and the background is not reflected in the grayscale value (such as the texture is different), this difference feature can be converted to a grayscale difference, and then the threshold value is used for dividing the image, and the threshold value is dynamically adjusted to achieve the binary value of the image. Can dynamically observe the specific results of its segmented image.

$$g(x, y) = \begin{cases} 0 & f(x, y) < m \\ 255 & f(x, y) \geq m \end{cases} \tag{2}$$

Where: m means the binary threshold, f(x, y) means the gray value of the input image pixel coordinate (x, y), and g(x, y) refers to the gray of the output image pixel coordinate (x, y) Degrees. If the gray value of the image is less than the threshold m, let it be 0, and if the gray value of the image is higher than the threshold m, let it be 255.

Threshold is a scale that separates the target from the background. Choosing the appropriate threshold is to save the image information as much as possible, and to reduce the background and noise interference as much as possible. This is the principle of selecting the threshold. In practical applications, different methods may be taken according to the situation to determine the binarization threshold of this type of image. If the bivariate grayscale chart has a bimodal nature, then the principle of probability statistics can be applied in indentifying the optimal threshold to split the two clustered pixels in the binary image to achieve automatic threshold capture.

4.2   The Realization of Fault Tolerance Technology in Threshold Treatment

In the actual processing, because the image light field is not uniform, it may not be effective to handle the image binarization problem in a practical application. For example, in the present research, it is difficult to separate the target wire from the background with a fixed assignment using different types of ice-covered images. The magnitude of the binarization threshold often depends on whether or not the target is detected correctly. In general, the concentration map can be applied as the basis for selecting the critical value. If the concentration map exhibits a double peak shape, the valley between the two peaks is determined. The corresponding gray value is the appropriate binarization threshold, but if the image is located in a non-uniform light field when the image is captured, the object is assumed to be bright and the background is dark. At this time, only one binarization threshold is applied, it may cause objects in the background to become backgrounds, and the bright background may also turn into objects. Therefore, dynamic thresholds should be applied, that is, the critical values must be higher in bright places, and dark places. The critical value may be lower to derive a good binarization result. The above-mentioned fault tolerance technology of the recovery block is applied here to perform thresholding processing on the ice coating image. Thus to improve the adaptability of the algorithm to different types of pictures and improve the reliability of the system. It can be understood as the idea of a threshold parameter approximation. During the operation of the system, the main block deter-mined by the standard threshold is executed first, and then the result of the execution is verified and tested. If the test is not passed, the value of the parameter is modified to generate a backup block for the next execution of the system, and so on until it passes. Test until.

The specific implementation of the algorithm is described as follows:

(1) Find the minimum gray value and the maximum gray value in the image, respectively denoted as Zmin and Zmax, then the initial value of the threshold T0 is as the formula 3:

$$T_0 = \frac{Z_{min} + Z_{max}}{2} \tag{3}$$

(2) According to the threshold TK, the image is divided into two parts, the target and the background. The average gray values Z0 and ZG of the two parts are obtained as shown in formula 4 and formula 5 respectively:

$$Z_0 = \frac{\sum_{z(i,j) < T_K} Z(i,j) \times N(i,j))}{\sum_{z(i,j) < T_K} N(i,j))} \tag{4}$$

$$Z_0 = \frac{\sum_{z(i,j) > T_K} Z(i,j) \times N(i,j))}{\sum_{z(i,j) > T_K} N(i,j))} \tag{5}$$

Where: $z(i, j)$ is the gray value of the (i, j) point on the image; $N(i, j)$ is the weight coefficient of the (i, j) point, and generally $N(i, j)$ is z (The number of i, j).

(3) Use formula 6 to find the new threshold:

$$T_{K+1} = \frac{Z_0 + Z_G}{2} \tag{6}$$

If TK = TK + 1, it ends, otherwise K = K + 1, turn (2).

By consulting the data and experience, if the image to be processed is a histogram with double peaks, deep valleys, and a wide range of image dye values, this method can ensure accurate results and be strongly adaptable to images. At the same time, the method is capable of selecting new threshold according to the characteristics of the sub-image, and then using the new threshold to segment the image, after several cycles, to minimize the pixel image of the wrong segmentation. This method is suitable for many types of images to be processed. Change, the case of a larger range of threshold fluctuations. Figure 6 is the image after thresholding using this method.

It can be shown from observation the target wire (black area) is accurately selected, indicating that the thresholding process using this method is very good to separate the target wire from the background and facilitate subsequent processing. In addition, the use of fault-tolerant technology enables the system to process images beyond the design expectations, ensuring the reliability and safety of the system.

As shown in Fig. 6, there may be multiple wires in an ice-covered image, so after the image is binarized, different wires are separated from the image using the contour

Fig. 6. Image after threshold processing

extraction method. This technology is very mature. The sake of space is not detailed in the present research. Figure 7 directly shows the heaviest segmentation images:

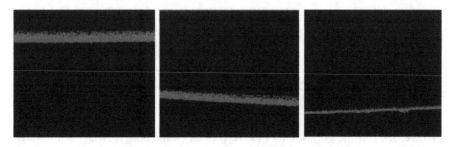

Fig. 7. Contour find the wire that is obtained after segmentation

5 Icing Wire Inclination Angle Calibration

In calculating the ice thickness of the target wire, the pixel difference in the vertical direction of the wire edge is often applied, instead of the ice coating thickness. However, the wire obtained by the division is often inclined due to problems such as the shooting angle. Therefore, it is necessary to straighten the wire by the image rotation technique before calculating the ice thickness. It is necessary to determine the angle of the wire to be tilted before the wire is straightened. The present research employs a Huff transform domain least-squares method combined with a straight line fitting method to measure the angle of inclination of the ice-covered wire, and then uses an image rotation technique to pull the slanted wire straight.

Assuming that the data set of a series of discrete data points on the edge of the collected wire is $M = (x_i, y_i)T$, and these data points are distributed around N straight lines. According to the Hough transform principle formula, its redefinition is expressed as formula 7:

$$\rho_k = x_i cos_k + y_i sin_k (k = 1, 2, \ldots, N) \tag{7}$$

Each fitted line can be represented using parameters (ρk, Θk);

Then, from the data set, the data points Wk near each fitted line (ρk, Θk) are found. Modify the above equation to the standard one-time one-time mode as formula 8:

$$y_i = a_k x_i + b_k \tag{8}$$

$a_k = \frac{cos_k}{sin_k}$, $b_k = \frac{\rho_k}{sin_k}$, calculate the distance from the point in W to the straight line determined by the above equation using Eq. 9:

$$d_{ki} = \frac{|a_k x_i + b_k - y_i|}{\sqrt{1 + a_k^2}} \tag{9}$$

It is needed to give the floating error (threshold) dk of this module in order, if: $d_{ki} < d_k$, then:

$$(x_i, y_i) \Rightarrow W_k\left(x_{kj}, y_{kj}\right);$$

W_k represents a set of data points near the k-th Hough transformation line that meets the floating error requirement. Finally, using point set Wk as the fitting data, respectively fitting each line, it is available to derive a_k, b_k; then determine the endpoint of straight line by the maximum and minimum value of x_{kj}, then it is allowable to determine the interval of each straight line segment, i.e.:

$$y_{kj} = a_k * x_{kj} + b_k, \left(x_{kj}\right)_{min} \leq x_{kj} \leq \left(x_{kj}\right)_{max} \qquad (10)$$

5.1 Experimental Data Analysis

Select the third image of Fig. 7, and collect a series of data points on the upper edge of the ice-covered wire, and obtain the coordinates of some points as shown in Table 1, where (x, y) represents the coordinates of the pixels of the discrete point in the image, respectively.

Table 1. Partial discrete point coordinates

1	2	3	4	5	6	7	8	9	10
(1, 798)	(16, 801)	(46, 800)	(241, 811)	(256, 812)	(301, 804)	(361, 820)	(706, 839)	(721, 843)	(766, 851)
11	12	13	14	15	16	17	18	19	20
(976, 854)	(1021, 849)	(1096, 868)	(1216, 872)	(1471, 890)	(1726, 905)	(1981, 914)	(2056, 930)	(2071, 936)	(2266, 946)
21	22	23	14	15	16	17	18	19	20
(2311, 946)	(2416, 950)	(2446, 947)	(2476, 960)	(2491, 969)	(2506, 967)	(2536, 976)	(2551, 978)	(2596, 980)	(2626, 986)

Hough transformation, least squares method, combined Hough transformation and least squares method are applied in straight line fitting to obtain the vector representation of the fitted line of the ice-covered wire, and the corresponding slope and intercept are shown in Table 2, and the fitting effect is shown in Fig. 8.

Through the analysis of the above experimental results, it is available to know that the edge of the ice-covered wire can be well fitted when the straight line is fitted with the Hough transform and the least-squares method, that is, the tilt angle of the ice-covered wire can be relatively accurately calculated. Because the interference point and noise were first removed by the Hough transform, then the least squares method was applied to obtain the best results, and the most accurate tilt angle was obtained. When the straight line is fitted, the least squares method is applied to directly fit the influence of interference points and noise. The Hough transform is not directly applied for fitting accuracy and the effective section of the straight line is not easily controlled. The

Table 2. The result of processing data

Method	Linear Vector	Slope	Intercept
Hough Transform	(0.997652, 0.0684885)	0.0686	787.093
Least Squares Method	(0.963252, 0.0864037)	0.0897	759.241
This article method	(0.989925, 0.0677108)	0.0684	787.357

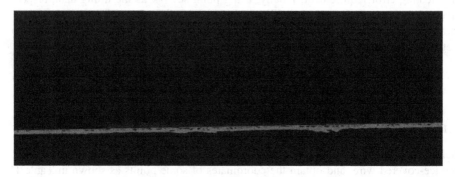

Fig. 8. Linear fitting effect diagram

method proposed in the present research makes full use of the strong anti-noise ability of the Hough transform algorithm and the high fitting precision of the least-squares method, resulting in more accurate measurement results.

5.2   Image Rotation and Ice Thickness Calculation

The image-spinning technology is used to straighten the ice-covered wire after obtaining the angle of inclination of the ice-covered wire, and the sum of the ice-covering thickness and the wire diameter is expressed by the average value of the distances between the pixel points in the vertical direction, and finally the ice coating of the wire is obtained. A ratio of the thickness to the diameter of the wire, when the diameter of the bare wire is known, the thickness of the ice coating can be calculated. The algorithm is described as follows:

Iterate over each column i $(i = 0, 1, \ldots, N)$ of the image and push the y coordinate corresponding to the pixel Point of the white (pixel value corresponding to the ice coating) into the stack points.

If the number of elements in the stack is greater than 5, proceed to the next step. Otherwise, perform the operation (2)

If a fault occurs in the data in the stack (points[i]-points(i−1) > 5), then the value in the fault (points[i]) is applied as the intermediate value to calculate the first one in the stack. The difference between the data and the last data and this data, the appropriate difference is pushed into the stack points_2, jump execution operation (2). Otherwise, perform the operation (4);

The difference between the first and last data in the stack is derived onto the stack points_2, and the jump is performed (2)

Remove the outliers in the stack points_2. Through experimental observation, it can be seen: if the ratio of the median value of the data in the stack and all the data is greater than 1.5 or less than 0.5, the data in the group is abnormal and is directly removed.

Find the average of all values in points_2, which is the sum of ice thickness and wire diameter.

5.3 Experimental Results and Analysis

The diameter of the wire is 15 mm according to the data of the high-voltage transmission line, therefore the corresponding ice coating thickness (excluding the diameter) of each wire in the image is as shown in Table 3:

Table 3. Measured thickness of ice covering (containing wire)

Wire	Measurement	Actual
Ice thickness (a)	23.86	25
Ice thickness (b)	21.19	22
Ice thickness (c)	8.43	9

It is shown from the test results in Fig. 3 that the model is correct and highly confident. It needs to be explained here that the method of calculating ice coating thickness based on image processing still is insufficient in on-site considerations. Although the proposed method is capable of increasing the system's adaptability to image data and improving the accuracy of calculation. However, since the two-dimensional map is employed to process the ice coating image, only the thickness of the wire ice coating in the horizontal direction is identified, while the non-uniformity of the ice coating along the cross section of the wire is neglected, which may cause the calculation error of the ice coating load within the interval. In addition, since the current picture is derived from a mobile camera, the distance between the wire and the camera will be, to a certain extent, influential to the proportion of the wire in the image. How to further improve the calculation accuracy under these influencing factors is the content to be studied in the next step. In addition, basing on the known thickness of ice coating, the density of ice coating can be obtained through image classification technology, and then the ice coating quality per unit length can be derived, which will make the ice coating detection system more reliable and safe.

6 Conclusions

The ice coating thickness calculation based on image processing is a new automated method for detecting the thickness of line ice. This kind of detection system can well solve the conventional over-manual monitoring problem. As long as the camera tool is set up at a fixed location, the ice coating thickness of the circuit can be automatically calculated and the guidance for deicing can be fed back to the power system. If the system is put into use, it will be capable of reducing the workload and material costs, and because the system is highly automated with negligible risk. However, the data of the image are obviously different, because of the influence of various factors such as region, season, and hardware, making the reliability of the system greatly affected. Existing research and some published papers are difficult to find. One way is that the system is also very adaptable to data that deviates from the design expectations. The accuracy of the measurement results cannot meet the needs of the power system. Therefore, the present research introduces software system fault-tolerance technology to improve the system's fault tolerance of image data, and combines the least squares method with Hough transform algorithm to improve the accuracy of straight line fitting. It is shown from the experimental results that the application of these two methods enhances the reliability and security of the system, and also improves the accuracy of measurement results greatly for the reference of researchers in related fields.

References

1. Jiang, X., Yi, H.: Ice Coating and Protection of Transmission Lines. China Electric Power Press, Beijing (2001)
2. Hu, Y.: Analysis and countermeasure discussion of large area ice disaster in power grid. High Voltage Eng. **34**(2), 215–219 (2008)
3. Huang, X., Liu, J., Gai, W., et al.: Present research situation of icing and snowing of overhead transmission lines in China and foreign countries. Power Syst. Technol. **32**(4), 23–28 (2008)
4. Wu, Y., Zhang, F., Feng, Q.: Research and application of on-line ice detection system in Guangdong power grid. Guangdong Electric Power (2009)
5. Li, Z., Hao, Ya., Li, L., et al.: Image recognition of ice thickness on transmission lines using remote system. High Volt. Eng. **37**(9), 2288–2293 (2011)
6. Xu, J., Tan, Q., et al.: Software fault tolerance technology for transient failure. Comput. Eng. Sci. **11**, 132–139 (2011)
7. Jiang, Y.: Embedded fault tolerant technology and application. Coal Mine Mechatron. **2011**(2), 119–120 (2011)
8. Ding, W., Guo, R., et al.: Fault-tolerant scheduling algorithm based on software fault-tolerance model in hard real-time systems. J. Comput. Res. Dev. **2011**(4), 691–698 (2011)
9. Huang, Y., Yu, Y., et al.: An aspect-oriented software fault tolerance enhancement tool. Comput. Appl. Technol. **2012**(2), 10–12 (2012)
10. Dong, L., Chunyuan, Z., et al.: Fault-tolerant real-time scheduling algorithm in software fault-tolerance model. J. Comput. Res. Dev. **2007**(9), 1495–1500 (2007)
11. Sun, P., Zhao, J., Zhang, W.: Software fault tolerance: technology and outlook. Comput. Eng. Sci. **2007**(8), 88–93 (2007)
12. Zhang, Y., Hong, B.: Research status and prospect of software fault tolerance technology. Comput. Appl. Res. **1999**(9), 1–3 (1999)

A Research About Trustworthiness Metric Method of SaaS Services Based on AHP

Tilei Gao[1,2], Tong Li[3], Rong Jiang[2], Ren Duan[2], Rui Zhu[1], and Ming Yang[2(✉)]

[1] School of Software, Yunnan University, Kunming 650091, China
[2] School of Information, Yunnan University of Finance and Economics, Kunming 650221, China
gtllei@ynufe.edu.cn
[3] Key Laboratory in Software Engineering of Yunnan Province, Kunming 650091, China

Abstract. Cloud computing, the internet of things (IoT), big data are the driving force for the transformation of the whole economy and cloud computing and services on cloud are also the foundations and infrastructure of the other two technologies. As the development of these technologies has brought us great changes in our life, challenges come as well. For the similar cloud services in functions in the cloud environment, it is a big problem to find the probable services to meet users' needs of security, reliability, easy of use and so on. To solve the problem mentioned above, a method of measuring the trustworthiness of SaaS services based on AHP is proposed, on the basis of the research on SaaS services and trusted computing. And also, a metric model for trustworthiness is built. In the end, a case study is put forward which proves the feasibility and usability of the method and model.

Keywords: AHP · SaaS services · Trusted computing

1 Introduction

Cloud computing, the Internet of things, big data are the driving forces for the transformation of the whole economy, and there is a progressive relationship among the three. Cloud computing is the infrastructure that plays a role in large data, Internet of things and other technologies [1]. The important reason for the rise of cloud computing is to save the cost of information by the sharing of information resources, and thus exclusive constraints under the traditional computing model is broken. In cloud computing, everything exists in the form of service and SaaS is the new form of software, whose target is to convert physical hardware and software assets into a paradigm. Under this paradigm, users and assets can achieve on-demand interaction, demand-resource binding, and on-demand operations. The abstraction layer provided by SaaS services enables people's concerns to be transferred from infrastructure and operations to the services [2].

The transformation of software drives the development of hardware at the same time. The combination of SaaS services and the Internet of things has opened up a new

X. Sun et al. (Eds.): ICCCS 2018, LNCS 11063, pp. 207–218, 2018.
https://doi.org/10.1007/978-3-030-00006-6_18

situation for the development of the Internet of things [3]: SaaS services provide communication and interoperability methods for the Internet of things, so as to solve the problems of communication between physical entities and the management of physical entities. On the other hand, The IoT component model is heterogeneous and multi-layered, and SaaS services can make up for the awkward situation that the traditional web service can't cope with. Nowadays, the research on Internet of things service is mainly focused on service design, service composition, reputation based on crowdsourcing and IoT itself [2]. Faced with more and more functionally similar SaaS services, how to measure and select the right services to achieve physical entity management and seamless docking has become a research topic that cannot be ignored.

In addition, affected by big data, it has become a developing direction to combine a large number of services into a consistent system. In 2008, the survey found that there were 5077 Web services [4] based on the web service description language (WSDL) on the Internet. And the number became 15000 on just one public website in 2016. At present, the popularity of cloud computing has promoted the rapid growth of services including web services and cloud services. In the age of smart phones, millions of mobile phone applications (App) can be downloaded from a cloud based application store. It is estimated that up to July 2015, 1,600,000 thousand Android applications and 1,500,000 thousand apple applications have been found. Finding the right service accurately and effectively from these large application libraries is becoming a huge challenge [5, 6].

Based on the above contents, this paper proposes a way to objectively and quantitatively measure SaaS services, so as to help users to have more sufficient and objective basis when choosing cloud services. The structure of the article is as follows: The second part introduces the research status of SaaS service concept and trustworthiness; the third part introduces the AHP based SaaS service trustworthiness measurement model; and the fourth part verifies the proposed measurement model through case analysis.

2   SaaS Service and Its Trustworthiness Research Status

At present, it is predicted that SaaS research has great commercial value, and has become the focus of attention of government, enterprises and research institutions, and has made some progress in basic theory, application research and practice. The achievements are mainly focused on the following three aspects: (1) clarification of SaaS service concept and Research on market development; (2) the analysis and design of SaaS service model in various information systems; (3) research on the theory and application of SaaS service in service customization, data security and so on.

2.1   The Concept of SaaS Services

In 1999, the concept of SaaS was first proposed by Keith Bennett in his service-oriented software papers [7]. In 2006, Frederick Chong proposed that SaaS was a new form of software which can be deployed as a hosted service and accessed through the internet and first proposed the four-level maturity model of SaaS, which provided a theoretical basis for the further clarifying of the concept of SaaS, the design principles and methods [8]. In September 2011, the definition of cloud computing was officially released by NIST as a standard (SP800-145) which gave the definition of SaaS services: they were software provided by service providers and used on cloud infrastructure by users and they could be accessed through a variety of clients and could be applied to a thin client interface such as browsers and e-mail. In the definition of SaaS service, it refers to a pattern that releases the functionality of the software as a "service". In this mode, people no longer need to buy software licenses, but buy the services that the software provides to the users to fulfill the needs of the enterprise production management. In this application mode, people gradually realize that software is not only a product in the sense of entity, but also may be added to the enterprise in the form of service. Sample Heading (Third Level). Only two levels of headings should be numbered. Lower level headings remain unnumbered; they are formatted as run-in headings.

2.2 Research on the Analysis and Design of the System Model of SaaS Services

In the aspect of development model, Professor Meng Xiaohua of Jinan University had put forward a seven layer model based on the traditional software development five-level model to meet the needs of SaaS software development [9]. It is the early study of SaaS service at the level of the development model; Yuan in his paper Research of online software system development solution based on SaaS [10] had studied the modeling methods, security handling and database design of SaaS software. At the database level, many researches have been done and data storage method of SaaS software and the way of expanding the data storage were the main direction, such as Jun [11] and Yu [12], both of whom have proposed a solution to the data structure of SaaS service.

2.3 Research on Service Customization and Data Security of SaaS Service

In literature [13] the key challenges of the current SaaS application development are pointed out on the basis of the analysis of the current research and application status of SaaS at home and abroad. Meanwhile, in Zhang Kun's paper Research on Data Combination Privacy Preservation Mechanism for SaaS [14], the performance of SaaS service is discussed. In literature [15], Shi et al. proposed a framework to support tenant business process customizing behavior modeling and verification, which put forward solutions in data security, application security, transmission security and many other aspects.

2.4 Research on SaaS Service Trustworthiness

The "trustworthiness" of software means that the behavior and results of the software system always conform to people's expectations and continue to provide services even when they are disturbed. The "trustworthiness" here emphasizes the predictability and controllability of behavior and results [16]. As a new application model for software, SaaS service has many differences with traditional software, but with the rapid development of science and technology, trustworthiness, the basic property of software, whose importance continuously increase under the new application model.

As early as the 90s of last century, several trust models were proposed to deal with trust relationships among entities in Internet such as Jøsang model [17], TEM model [18], Abdul-Rahman model [19], Beth model [20] and so on. These models provide functions to describe, quantify, convey trust information and integrate multiple trust information, and trust information operation is based on recommendation trust relationship among entities. However, the research on how the model can adapt to the dynamic changes of the trust relationship effectively is not enough. Therefore, they are not good enough to be used for trustworthiness metric of SaaS service.

In literature [21], trusted software requirements are defined from the perspective of software requirements and a formal definition of trusted requirements is implemented. In this paper to select the trustworthiness indexes of SaaS service, we draw lessons from the attributes of trusted requirement evaluation. These evaluation attributes in her paper are screened and seven indexes left.

SaaS service is bringing benefits to users, but meanwhile, as its complexity, it also poses challenges to developing technology and method, such as how to ensure the safety of user data, how to meet users' personalized needs, and how to objectively evaluate SaaS services, so as to facilitate users to find services that meet their needs. These are the problems to be solved in front of SaaS, and to some extent, these also hamper the development of SaaS. Now, user's experiences are more and more important and the ability to meet users' personalized requirements for services becomes the key point to software's success or not. This paper focuses on this problem. Based on the depth analysis of the trustworthiness of SaaS services and users' requirement, an easy to use and efficient service metric method is established to help users to make quick and correct decision for SaaS service.

3 Trustworthiness Metric Method of SaaS Services

3.1 AHP Structure Model

AHP (The analytic hierarchy process) is a combination of qualitative and quantitative evaluation decision making method, which is suitable for multi objective, multi element and multi-level problem solving [22, 23]. It can provide a suitable solution for decision making by quantitative comparison. Since the AHP has been put forward, it is widely used in multi index comprehensive measurement model. Its basic idea is the same as the thinking and judgment process of a complex decision making problem. First of all, decision problems are divided into three levels: the highest level is the target level, the middle level makes up of rules and the lower level is the plans. Straight lines are used to connect different layers, as is show in Fig. 1. These weights are usually qualitative in the person's mind, while in the AHP we have to give a quantitative method of gaining weight.

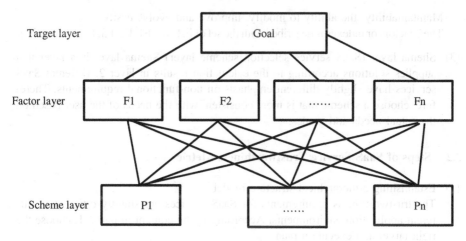

Fig. 1. AHP structure

When evaluating the trustworthiness of SaaS services, the key problem to be solved is to guarantee the objectivity of the measure process. In dealing with this problems, AHP method usually compares two factors at one time and after all factors finished, judgment matrix is built, which is used to evaluate the whole problem. This method can effectively reduce the influence of human subjective factors in the process of evaluation.

(1) Target layer (SaaS service trustworthiness metri) Target layer is the core of the entire AHP framework and also the subject and goal of the study. The core purpose of SaaS service trustworthiness is to give a quantitative trustworthiness measure for each service based on the real needs of the user. Therefore, user could choose the suitable SaaS service.

(2) Factor layer (SaaS service trustworthiness indexes layer) factor layer describes the set of factors that need to be considered. In the SaaS service trustworthiness assessment, it refers to the factors that affect the trustworthiness of the SaaS service. According to the description of quality indexes in the four common quality model of software: Boehem model, McCall model, ISO9126 model and ISO/IEC25010 [24], combined with the features of the SaaS service, 7 metrics that affect the trustworthiness of the SaaS service are summarized:

Availability: the ability to continue to provide specific functions in a specified environment.

Reliability: the ability to restore service within a specified time after a failure occurs.

Security: the ability to provide security requirements such as data confidentiality, integrity, controllability, and so on.

Real-time: the ability to response within the prescribed time

Easy-to-use: the ability to facilitate users to learn and use.

Compatibility: the ability to be used in different environments, also called portability.

Maintainability: the ability to modify, improve and evolve easily.

The 7 factors or indexes is described with the set of F, F = {F1, F2, F3, F4, F5, F6, F7 }.

(3) Shema layer (SaaS service selection scheme layer) Shema layer is a layer that supplies solutions according to the calculation results in layer 2. Different SaaS services have slightly different emphasis on non-functional requirements. Therefore, choose a scheme that is more consistent with the needs of the user based on the actual needs and grades.

3.2 Steps of SaaS Service Trustworthiness Metric

(1) Establishing a hierarchical structure model
The trustworthiness requirements for SaaS services are slightly different in different application environments. According to the content in part 3.1, choose the right target and execution plan.

(2) Establishing judgment matrix
In AHP, in order to make the judgment quantified, The key point is to try to make a quantitative description of the relative superiority of any of the two schemes. Generally speaking, result can always be found when comparing two factors in single plan and 1–9 scaling method is used to evaluate the relationship between every factor. Table 1 gives the criteria for comparison among the indexes. aij is supposed as some element in the judgment matrix.

Table 1. Index comparison standard

Scale	Definition and introduction
1	For SaaS service trustworthiness, two indexes have the same importance
3	For SaaS service trustworthiness, ai is a little more important
5	For SaaS service trustworthiness, ai is obviously important
7	For SaaS service trustworthiness, ai is very important
9	For SaaS service trustworthiness, ai is extremely important
2, 4, 6, 8	They are described as the scale of the tradeoff between the above criteria

(3) Computing weight vector and checking the consistency
Sum product method [25, 26] is used to calculate the maximum eigenvector ω_i and characteristic value λ_{max} in the matrix. Then CI (Consistency Index), RI, (Random Index) and CR (Consistency Ratio) are used to check the consistency. Formula (1) is the formula to check the consistency.

$$CR = \frac{CI}{RI}, CI = \frac{\lambda max - n}{n - 1} \qquad (1)$$

In the formula: The greater the value of CI in the matrix, the higher the degree of inconsistency of the matrix; n is the order of the judgement matrix; RI is an average random consistency index obtained by 1000 positive and negative matrices and the value is shown in Table 2. CR means Consistency Ratio. If CR < 0.1, it means he degree of inconsistency of the judgment matrix is within the allowable range and also means The result of the weight comparison of the trustworthiness index belongs to the reasonable range.

Table 2. Average random consistency index of matrix

n	1	2	3	4	5	6	7	8
RI	0	0	0.58	0.90	1.12	1.24	1.32	1.41
n	9	10	11	12	13	14	15	
RI	1.46	1.49	1.52	1.54	1.56	1.58	1.59	

Similarly, Sum product method is also used to calculate the maximum eigenvectors of the schema layer to target layer, which is marked as ω_j^i (i∈{A, R, S, RT, E, C, M}, j = 1,..., n, means the number of plans.)

(4) The total ranking of layers
The total ranking of layers is the value of calculating the relative importance of all factors to the highest level (total goal) of a certain level. In the process of SaaS service trustworthiness measure, formula (2) is used to calculate the ranking results.

$$\omega(P_j) = \sum_{i=1}^{7} \omega_i \times \omega_j^i \tag{2}$$

The greater the value of the $\omega(P_j)$, the higher the trustworthiness of the service j.

4 Case Study

In order to expand the business scale, some company is expected to improve the original online easy system. After research, it is decided to replace the traditional way with SaaS services. After screening, three products left, which marked as A, B and C. The functions of the three products are similar, and the differences lie in availability, reliability, compatibility and other non-functional requirements. By using the AHP method proposed in this paper, A quantitative measure of three products has been implemented to help the company choose the suitable service. The steps are as follows:

(1) Establishing a hierarchical structure model

A hierarchical model based on requirements and related indicators is shown in Fig. 2. The three products of A, B, C correspond to the P1, P2, P3 of the schema layer, respectively. In the index layer, A represents availability, R represents reliability, S represents security, RT represents real time, E is easy-to-use, C represents compatibility and M represents maintainability. The seven indexes makes up a index set I = {A, R, S, RT, E, C, M}.

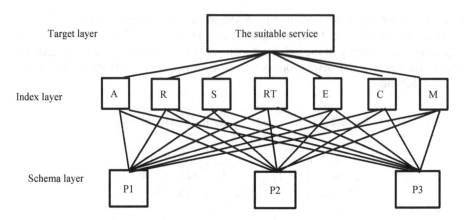

Fig. 2. SaaS service trustworthiness structure model

(2) Establishing judgement matrix

By consulting 12 professional personnel, an estimate is made. Draw the judgment matrix of the index layer by combining the opinions of 12 experts. The matrix is show in Table 3 and the judgment matrixes of product scheme relative to each index is shown in Table 4. In the table, Pij represents a comparison of the weight of the scheme i and the scheme j relative to a certain index.

Table 3. SaaS service trustworthiness index judgement matrix

Matrix	A	R	S	RT	E	C	M
A	1	2	1/2	5	7	5	3
R	1/2	1	1/2	5	7	6	3
S	2	2	1	7	9	9	5
RT	1/5	1/5	1/7	1	3	4	2
E	1/7	1/7	1/9	1/3	1	3	1/3

Table 4. Judgement matrix of different plans

A	P1	P2	P3	R	P1	P2	P3	S	P1	P2	P3
P1	1	3	5	P1	1	3	7	P1	1	8	8
P2	1/3	1	3	P2	1/3	1	5	P2	1/8	1	2
P3	1/5	1/3	1	P3	1/7	1/5	1	P3	1/8	1/2	1
RT	**P1**	**P2**	**P3**	**E**	**P1**	**P2**	**P3**	**C**	**P1**	**P2**	**P3**
P1	1	1/5	1/2	P1	1	1/3	1/7	P1	1	3	3
P2	5	1	5	P2	3	1	1/4	P2	1/3	1	1
P3	2	1/5	1	P3	7	4	1	P3	1/3	1	1

(continued)

Table 4. (*continued*)

A	P1	P2	P3	R	P1	P2	P3	S	P1	P2	P3
M	**P1**	**P2**	**P3**								
P1	1	4	3								
P2	1/4	1	1/2								
P3	1/3	2	1								

(3) Computing weight vector and checking the consistency

Sum product method is used to calculate the maximum eigenvector ωi and characteristic value λmax in the matrix and the results are:

$$\omega = (\omega 1, \omega 2, \omega 3, \omega 4, \omega 5, \omega 6, \omega 7)T = (0.231, 0.194, 0.353, 0.078, 0.038, 0.027, 0.080)T$$

$$\lambda max = 7.538$$

and then check the consistency with the formula (1), and the results are:

$$CI = (7.538 - 7)/(7 - 1) = 0.090$$
$$CR = CI/RI = 0.090/1.32 = 0.068 < 0.1$$

The result of calculation shows that the degree of inconsistency of the judgment matrix is within the allowable range, which is also means the weights of SaaS service trustworthiness indexes are within the allowable range.

Similarly, the maximum eigenvectors of the program layer to the target are obtained by the sum product method, respectively:

$$(\omega 1A, \omega 2A, \omega 3A) = (0.633, 0.260, 0.106)$$

$$(\omega 1R, \omega 2R, \omega 3R) = (0.643, 0.283, 0.074)$$

$$(\omega 1S, \omega 2S, \omega 3S) = (0.790, 0.129, 0.081)$$

$$(\omega 1RT, \omega 2RT, \omega 3RT) = (0.115, 0.703, 0.182)$$

$$(\omega 1E, \omega 2E, \omega 3E) = (0.085, 0.213, 0.701)$$

$$(\omega 1C, \omega 2C, \omega 3C) = (0.600, 0.200, 0.200)$$

$$(\omega 1M, \omega 2M, \omega 3M) = (0.623, 0.137, 0.722)$$

(4) The total ranking of layers

The results obtained from step 3 are substituted into the formula (2), and get the results:

$$\{\omega(P1),\ \omega(P2),\ \omega(P3)\} = \{0.628,\ 0.240,\ 0.133\}$$

The larger the value of $\omega(Pj)$ means the greater the weight of the schema j for SaaS service trustworthiness and the higher the trustworthiness is.

(5) Comparison of results

The comparison of the results of Table 5 shows that ,The SaaS services required by the business company are not sensitive in compatibility, ease of use, real-time, and maintainability in the attributes of trustworthiness, but care about the attributes of security, availability and reliability. Compare with the traditional software system, for services provided in cloud computing, users are still suspicious of their stability and security. In addition, by calculating, the results of the three plans are obvious, P1 > P2 > P3 and P1 is the most suitable service product for the company.

Table 5. Comparison of results

Indexes	Weights	Plan	Weights
availability	$\omega_1 = 0.231$	P1	$\omega(P1) = 0.628$
reliability	$\omega_2 = 0.194$	P2	$\omega(P2) = 0.240$
security	$\omega_3 = 0.353$	P3	$\omega(P3) = 0.133$
real-time	$\omega_4 = 0.078$		
easy-to-use	$\omega_5 = 0.038$		
compatibility	$\omega_6 = 0.027$		
maintainability	$\omega_7 = 0.080$		

5   Conclusion and Prospect

After ten years of effort, cloud computing has been accepted by most enterprises and users. It is expected that by 2030, 81% of the global IT workload will run on the cloud. Whether the advantages of cloud computing can be fully played will have a decisive impact on the development of the new economy. How to quantify and intuitively measure the trustworthiness of SaaS services, and how to select services that meet the needs of the users becomes an urgent question. In response to this problem, a measurement method for the trustworthiness of SaaS services is proposed, and a measure model is established based on AHP. This method combines qualitative and quantitative description and can deal with many practical problems and has a wide range of applications, and at the same time, its simplicity also reduces the use threshold for those who choose to use this method. Finally, the feasibility and usability of the method and model are verified by a case study. The disadvantage is that this method can only evaluate and measure the existing services, and help to choose a better solution. It cannot give the description of the shortage of the service itself, and cannot help improve the trustworthiness of the service. Moreover, the trustworthiness measurement of SaaS service is not an easy task and there is still a long way to go to perfect the method in the future. In practical applications, different application fields and scenes need specific analysis of specific problems. The methods and theories of SaaS service trustworthiness measurement can be gradually improved through continuous research and summary.

Acknowledgments. This work was supported by National Natural Science Foundation of China (Nos. 61379032, 61763048, 61263022, 61303234, 61662085), National Social Science Foundation of China (No. 12XTQ012), Science and Technology Foundation of Yunnan Province (No. 2017FB095), Yunnan Province Applied Basic Research Project (No. 2016FD060), Science Research Project of Yunnan Education (Nos. 2017ZZX001, 2017ZZX227), Key Project of Scientific Research of Yunnan Education (2015Z018), Provincial Scientific and Technological Innovation Team Project of Yunnan University (2017HC012), the 18th Yunnan Young and Middle-aged Academic and Technical Leaders Reserve Personnel Training Program (No. 2015HB038).

The authors would like to thank the anonymous reviewers and the editors for their suggestions.

References

1. Guojie, L.: Efforts to build a collaborative and win-win cloud computing environment. Commun. CCCF **3**, 7 (2017)
2. Bouguettaya, A., Singh, M., Huhns, M., et al.: A service computing manifesto: the next 10 years. Commun. ACM **4**(64), 72 (2017). https://doi.org/10.1145/2983528
3. Raggett, D.: The web of things: challenges and opportunities. Computer **48**(5), 26–32 (2015)
4. Al-Masri, E., Mahmoud, Q.H.: Investigating web services on the world wide web. In: International Conference of World Wide Web, pp. 795–804 (2008)
5. Blake, M.B., Nowlan, M.E.: Knowledge discovery in services (KDS): aggregating software services to discover enterprise mashups. IEEE Trans. Knowl. Data Eng. **23**(6), 889–901 (2010)
6. Yu, Q., Liu, X., Bouguettaya, A., et al.: Deploying and managing web services: Issues, solutions, and directions. Vldb J. **17**(3), 537–572 (2008)
7. Bennett, K., Layzell, P., Budgen, D., et al.: Service-based software: the future for flexible software. In: Software Engineering Conference, 2000. APSEC 2000. Proceedings. Seventh Asia-Pacific. IEEE, 214–221 (2002)
8. Chong, F., Carraro, G.: Architecture strategies for catching the long tail. Microsoft Corporation (2006)
9. Xiaohua, M., Chuankai, C.: Research of solution on transforming traditional software to SaaS. Microcomput. Appl. **31**(4), 7–10 (2012)
10. Zhijun, Y., Hongxia, X.: Research of online software system development solution based on SaaS. Comput. Eng. Des. **30**(11), 2714–2717 (2009)
11. Jun, Z., Haoyu, W., Chaojun, Y.: A comparative study of SaaS data layer scheme. J. Intell. **29**(21), 176–177 (2010)
12. Wenbin, Y., Xiaohui, H., Min, Y.: A solution of shared database and architecture's SaaS based on XML. Comput. Mod. **4**(4), 8–10 (2008)
13. Wei, C.: Research on Software Customization Technology for SaaS application. Shanghai Jiao Tong University (2011)
14. Shen, Z., Qingzhong, L., Yuliang, S.: Research on data combination privacy preservation mechanism for SaaS. Chin. J. Comput. **33**(11), 2044–2054 (2010)

15. Yuliang, S., Shuai, L., Qingzhong, L.: TLA based customization and verification mechanism of business process for SaaS. Chin. J. Comput. **33**(11), 2055–2067 (2010)
16. Liu, K.: Overview on major research plan of trustworthy software. Bulletin of National Natural Science Foundation of China (2008)
17. Jøsang, A.: An Algebra for assessing trust in certification chains network and distributed system security symposium. NDSS, San Diego, California, USA (1999)
18. Feng, X.U., et al.: Design of a trust valuation model in software service coordination. J. Softw. **14**(6), 1043–1051 (2003)
19. Abdul-Rahman, A., Hailes, S., et al.: A distributed trust model, vol. 35(3), pp. 4–60 (1997)
20. Beth, T., Borcherding, M., Klein, B.: Valuation of trust in open networks. In: Gollmann, D. (ed.) ESORICS 1994. LNCS, vol. 875, pp. 1–18. Springer, Heidelberg (1994). https://doi.org/10.1007/3-540-58618-0_53
21. Xuan, Z., Tong, L., Wang, X.: Formal analysis to non-functional requirements of trustworthy software. J. Softw. **26**(10), 2545–2566 (2015)
22. Lixia, W., Xiaozhou, F.: A new improved AHP algorithm research and application. Comput. Technol. Dev. **20**(12), 115–117 (2010)
23. Lei, W., Mengxing, H.: Research on evaluation of supplier based on gray AHP in cloud computing. Appl. Res. Comput. **30**(3), 742–744 (2013)
24. ISO/IEC. Systems and software engineering – Systems and software Quality Requirements and Evaluation (SQuaRE) – System and software quality models (2011)
25. Huanchen, Z., Shubai, X., Jinsheng, H.: AHP. Science Press, Beijing, China (1986)
26. Cuiping, W.: The optimization basis and properties of the sum-product method in AHP. Syst. Eng. Theory Pract. **19**(9), 113–115 (1999)

A Spectrum Sensing Algorithm Based on Information Geometry and K-medoids Clustering

Yonghua Wang[1,2]($\boxtimes$), Qiang Chen[1], Jiangfan Li[1], Pin Wan[1], and Shuiling Pang[1]

[1] School of Automation, Guangdong University of Technology, Guangzhou 510006, China
sjzwyh@163.com, bypb_chen@163.com, wanpin2@163.com, 1214999251@qq.com, 1024470491@qq.com
[2] Key Laboratory of Machine Intelligence and Advanced Computing, Sun Yat-Sen University, Ministry of Education, Guangzhou 510006, China

Abstract. In order to improve the performance of existing spectrum sensing methods in cognitive radios and solve the complex problem of decision threshold calculations. This paper uses the information geometry theory and combines the unsupervised learning method of K-medoids clustering to realize the spectrum sensing. Firstly, using the information geometry theory, the statistical characteristics of wireless spectrum signals received by secondary users are analyzed and transformed into geometric characteristics on statistical manifolds. Correspondingly, the sampled signal of the secondary user corresponds to the point on the statistical manifold, and the distance feature between different points is obtained by using a metric method on the manifold. Finally, the K-medoids clustering algorithm is used to classify the distance features and determine whether the primary user signal exists, and achieve the purpose of spectrum sensing. Simulation results show that the proposed method outperforms traditional spectrum sensing algorithms.

Keywords: Spectrum sensing · Information geometry · K-medoids clustering

1 Introduction

In order to solve the increasingly tense problem of wireless spectrum resources, the concept of cognitive radio is proposed, which can improve the utilization of spectrum resources [1]. Spectrum sensing has been widely studied as a core part of cognitive radio systems. The classic single-user spectrum sensing technology includes matched filter detection, energy detection (ED), and cyclostationary feature detection etc [2–4]. Affected by complex and varied wireless environments, including multipath fading, shadow effects, and hidden terminals etc, single-user spectrum sensing technologies have limitations and their perceived performance needs to be improved. Multi-user cooperative spectrum sensing technology can solve these problems well. Although spectrum sensing technology has been researched in depth, improving the performance of spectrum sensing is something that we always need to do, and there are some

X. Sun et al. (Eds.): ICCCS 2018, LNCS 11063, pp. 219–230, 2018.
https://doi.org/10.1007/978-3-030-00006-6_19

existing algorithms that have high complexity when calculating against the decision threshold. How to determine whether the primary user signal exists more accurately and quickly, and solve the problem that the threshold is difficult to calculate, so as to improve the performance of spectrum sensing, it still needs further study.

Information geometry originates from the study of the intrinsic geometrical properties of probability distribution manifolds and has evolved as a set of theoretical systems [5]. It provides a new idea for spectrum sensing problems. The concept of statistical manifold can be used to transform the problem of signal detection into a geometry problem on manifold. Using the geometric method, the problems of statistical detection can be analyzed more intuitively. Some scholars at home and abroad have studied the application of information geometry theory in some signal processing problems.

In [6, 7], using information geometry theory for radar signal detection. A Matrix Constant False Alarm Rate (CFAR) and a geodesic distance based distance detector were proposed, but the thresholds which were higher degree were calculated by simulation experiments. In [8], the information geometry method is applied to the spectrum sensing, which increases the measure of the manifold, and also gets the threshold through the simulation. In [9], the closed-form expression of the decision threshold obtained by the moment matching method has higher computational complexity. In spectrum sensing, the use of a fixed threshold method to determine whether the primary user exists will always have a bias and affect the detection performance. In [10], unsupervised learning based on K-means clustering is applied to spectrum sensing. The energy of the signal is used as a feature. The K-means clustering algorithm is used to classify the features and obtain a classifier. Then the cognitive signal is classified to achieve spectrum sensing.

Based on previous studies, this paper proposed a spectrum sensing algorithm based on information geometry and K-medoids clustering. Firstly, using the information geometric theory, the statistical characteristics of wireless spectrum signals received by secondary users are analyzed and transformed into geometric properties on statistical manifolds. The signal features of the wireless spectrum are represented by statistical distance features on the manifold. Finally, the K-medoids clustering algorithm is used to classify the distance features and determine whether the primary user signal exists or not, to realize the purpose of spectrum sensing.

2 System Scheme

2.1 Spectrum Sensing Scheme

In traditional spectrum sensing methods, threshold computation is often complex and can not be adaptive. Based on the K-medoids clustering algorithm, we classify the distance features on the manifold to determine whether the primary user exists. The entire spectrum sensing process includes two parts: the training part and the sensing part. Firstly, the distance feature of the priori information of the signal in the manifold is obtained by the information geometry method. The measurement metrics used in training and sensing need to be consistent. Then the K-medoids clustering algorithm is used to train the distance features to obtain a classifier. Finally, the distance feature calculated by the signal to be sensed is put into the classifier to detect whether the primary user signal exists. The overall spectrum sensing model is shown in Fig. 1.

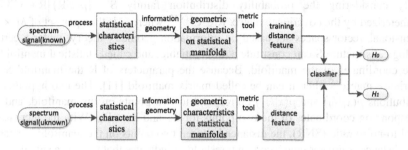

Fig. 1. Spectrum sensing based on K-mediods clustering algorithm

2.2   Signal Model

The detection of a primary user (PU) by a single secondary user (SU) in a cognitive radio network can be expressed as a binary hypothesis model in statistics:

$$x(n) = \begin{cases} w(n), & H_0 \\ s(n) + w(n), & H_1 \end{cases}, n = 1, 2, \ldots, N \tag{1}$$

Where $x(n)$ is the signal that the SU received at time n. $s(n)$ and $w(n)$ respectively represent the received signal and noise of the authorized user. It is assumed that the noise $w(n)$ is a Gauss white noise that is independent of the same distribution, the mean value is 0, the variance is σ_n^2, and $s(n)$ is the signal transmitted by PU. In the two case, the data $x(n)$ follows the distribution $\psi(0, R_n)$ and $\psi(0, (R_s + R_n))$, where R_n and R_s respectively represent the covariance matrix of the noise vector $w(n)$ and the random signal $s(n)$.

It is assuming that there are M SUs in the cognitive network, and the signals collected by M SUs constitute a vector matrix $X = [x_1, x_2, \ldots, x_M]$, where $x_i = x_i(1), x_i(2), \ldots, x_i(N)]^T$ denotes the signal received by the i-th SU, and N is the number of sample points. So, X is a matrix of $N \times M$ dimensions [8]:

$$X = [x_1, x_2, \ldots, x_M] = \begin{bmatrix} x_1(1), & x_2(1), & \cdots, & x_M(1) \\ x_1(2), & x_2(2), & \cdots, & x_M(2) \\ \vdots & \vdots & \ddots & \vdots \\ x_1(N), & x_2(N), & \cdots, & x_M(N) \end{bmatrix} \tag{2}$$

For any N-dimensional vector x, if it obeys the zero-mean Gauss distribution, its distribution expression is given by

$$p(x|\text{R}) = \frac{1}{\sqrt{(2\pi)^n \det \text{R}}} \exp\left(-\frac{1}{2} x^T \text{R}^{-1} x\right) \tag{3}$$

By considering the probability distribution family $S = \{p(x|\text{R}) \,|\, \text{R} \in \text{C}^{M \times M}\}$ parameterized by the covariance matrix $\text{R} \in \text{C}^{M \times M}$, where C is the open set of $M \times M$-dimensional vector spaces set based on information geometry theory, under a certain topological structure S can constitute a differentiable, and called statistical manifold, R is the coordinates of the manifold. Because the parameters of R the manifold S are covariance matrices, then it can be called matrix manifold [11]. The two hypothetical distributions $p(x|H_0)$ and $p(x|H_1)$ correspond to two points on the manifold, and the corresponding coordinates of the two points for R_w and $\text{R}_s + \text{R}_w$. With the increase of signal-to-noise ratio (SNR), the distance between two points on the manifold increases. If the distance is greater than a certain threshold, it indicates that there is a signal. If it is less than a certain threshold, it means that there is only noise.

3   System Analysis

3.1   Metric Tool

The distance between two probability distributions on a statistical manifold can be measured in various ways. Commonly used methods include geodesic distance and KLD. Geodesic distances are used for the manifold metrics used in this paper.

Due to the characteristics of manifold bending, defining the distance between two points on a manifold requires defining the length of the curve connecting two points. Consider an arbitrary curve $\theta(t)$ $(t_1 \leq t \leq t_2), \theta(t_1) = \theta_1, \theta(t_2) = \theta_2$ between two points θ_1 and θ_2 on any manifold, then the distance between θ_1 and θ_2 can be obtained along the curve $\theta(t)$:

$$D(\theta_1, \theta_2) \triangleq \int_{t_1}^{t_2} \sqrt{\left(\frac{d\theta}{dt}\right)^T G(\theta) \left(\frac{d\theta}{dt}\right)} \, dt \tag{4}$$

Where $G(\theta)$ is the fisher information matrix. It can be seen that the distance between θ_1 and θ_2 depends on the selection of $\theta(t)$. We call the geodesic curve the minimum distance, and the corresponding distance is called geodesic distance, which satisfies symmetry and trigonometric inequality.

The computation of geodesic distance from arbitrary probability distribution manifold is very complicated, which has a certain influence on its application. However, some scholars have also deduced the expression of geodesic distance on the manifold of common probability distribution. For multivariate Gaussian distribution families with the same mean but different covariance matrices, consider two members where the covariance matrix is Σ_1 and Σ_2, respectively, and the geodesic distances between them are given as follows [12]:

$$D(\Sigma_1, \Sigma_2) = \sqrt{\frac{1}{2}\mathrm{trlog}^2\left(\Sigma_1^{-\frac{1}{2}}\Sigma_2\Sigma_1^{-\frac{1}{2}}\right)} = \sqrt{\frac{1}{2}\sum_{j=1}^{M}\log^2\eta_j} \tag{5}$$

Where η_j denote the j eigenvalues of the matrix $\Sigma_1^{-\frac{1}{2}}\Sigma_2\Sigma_1^{-\frac{1}{2}}$.

3.2 Riemannian Mean

In the normed linear space, the midpoint calculation corresponds to the arithmetic mean. But on the manifold, it is found that the curvature is not constant and not positive, so the calculation of the midpoint must depend on the corresponding geometric mean rather than the arithmetic mean [13]. Using the geodesic distances we can define a mean [14] which is relative to a finite set of symmetric positive-definite (SPD) matrices $R_{b(b=1,2,...,B)}$ to be the SPD matrix $\bar{R}$ that minimizes

$$Q(\bar{R}) = \frac{1}{B}\sum_{b=1}^{B} D^2(R_b, \bar{R}) \tag{6}$$

that is,

$$\bar{R} = \mathrm{argmin}Q(\bar{R}) \tag{7}$$

For the matrix manifolds two points R_1 and R_2, $\bar{R}$ is equal to the midpoint of the geodesic line connecting R_1 and R_2, and the Riemannian mean can be written as

$$\bar{R} = R_1^{1/2}\left(R_1^{-1/2}R_2R_1^{-1/2}\right)^{1/2}R_1^{1/2} \tag{8}$$

For the case of B ($B > 2$) points, the Riemannian mean comparison is hard to find, in [15] and [16], by using the gradient descent algorithm is given the $\bar{R}$ iterative method, the iterative method of $\bar{R}$ is given by using the gradient descent algorithm, the final expression of the Riemannian mean is given by

$$\bar{R}_{u+1} = \bar{R}_u^{1/2}e^{\frac{\tau}{B}\sum_{b=1}^{B}\log\left(\bar{R}_u^{-1/2}R_b\bar{R}_u^{-1/2}\right)}\bar{R}_u^{1/2}, 0 \leq \tau \leq 1 \tag{9}$$

where τ is the iterative step (Table 1).

Robust Covariance Matrix Mean Estimation can be addressed by Riemannian center of mass, and Riemannian Mean happens to be Riemannian center of mass [17]. By using Riemannian mean we can better estimate the noise environment and thus improve the detection performance.

3.3 K-medoids Clustering Algorithm

Clustering is the process of dividing a similar object into clusters or classes in a certain way. The purpose of clustering is to make the differences in the objects within the cluster as small as possible, and the differences in objects between the clusters are as

Table 1. Calculate the Riemannian mean

	Algorithm 1: Gradient descent algorithm calculates the Riemannian mean value of the geodesic distance of the matrix
Input:	$R_{b(b=1,2,\ldots,B)}$ and τ
Initialize:	$\bar{R}_1 = R_1,\ u = 1$
Step 1:	Compute gradient of objective function $\nabla f = \sum_{b=1}^{B} \log\left(\bar{R}_u^{-1/2} R_b \bar{R}_u^{-1/2}\right)$
Step 2:	Compute $\bar{R}_{u+1} = \bar{R}_u^{1/2} e^{\frac{\tau \nabla f}{N}} \bar{R}_u^{-1/2}$
Step 3:	If $\bar{R}_{u+1}$ convergence, then the algorithm will stops; Otherwise, $u = u+1$, return to **Step 1**
Output:	Riemannian mean $\bar{R}$ for B matrices

large as possible. According to the actual situation of spectrum sensing, the training set needs to be divided into two categories, noise and signal. The process of obtaining the classifier through distance feature extraction is shown in Fig. 2. First, we get training sets by information geometry method, which are signal class and noise class, respectively. Then the classifier is obtained by the K-medoids clustering algorithm.

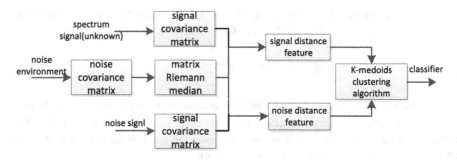

Fig. 2. Classifier model diagram

The K-medoids clustering algorithm calculates the clustering results by dividing, and implements the criterion of minimizing the sum of the differences between the data points and the center points of the clusters [18]. Before training, we first need the data $\bar{D}$ set of the signal and noise distance features obtained by the information geometry method:

$$\bar{D} = \{D^1, D^2, \ldots, D^L\} \tag{10}$$

where $D^l (l = 1, 2, \ldots L)$ is represented as one sample data and L represents the number of sample data of the training. The clustering algorithm can divide the unlabeled sample data into K non-overlapping clusters and find the corresponding center point M_k

of each cluster. Let C_k denote the set of training data belonging to class $k(k = 1, 2, \ldots, K)$ then:

$$C_k = \left\{ D^l | D^l \in \text{Cluster } k \forall l \right\} \tag{11}$$

In the K-medodis clustering algorithm, the center point of C_k can also be fixed as the sample data D^l under the condition of H_0, so M_1 can be defined as:

$$M_1 = \arg\min \sum\nolimits_{D^l | H_0} \left\| D^l - M_1^2 \right\| \tag{12}$$

The center point of the other cluster $C_k (k = 2, 3, \ldots, K)$ is defined as M_k:

$$M_k = \arg\min_{M_k \in C_k} \sum\nolimits_{D^l \in C_k} \left\| D^l - M_k^2 \right\| \tag{13}$$

The K non-overlapping clusters generated by the K-medoids clustering algorithm, such that the sum E of Euclidean distances between the data points of K clusters and their center points is minimum [19] (Table 2).

Table 2. K-medoids clustering algorithm

Algorithm 1: K-medoids clustering algorithm
Input: Training data: $\overline{D}$; the number of clusters:K.
Step 1: Initialize the centroid $M_1, M_2, \ldots, M_K$.
Step 2: Calculate the distance of each feature vector to each centroid and classify it into the nearest cluster.
Step 3: For the class $C_k(k = 2,3, \ldots, K)$, $M_k(k = 2,3, \ldots, K)$ is updated by equation(13).
Step 4: Calculate E. If E convergence then algorithm will stops; Otherwise, return to **Step 2**
Output: K clusters satisfying clustering criteria

$$E = \sum\nolimits_{k=1}^{K} \sum\nolimits_{D^l \in M_k} \left\| D^l - M_k^2 \right\| \tag{14}$$

After successful training, we can import test data using the following formula to test whether the primary user signal exists.

$$\frac{\left\| \hat{D} - M_1 \right\|}{\min_{k=2,3,\ldots,K} \left\| \hat{D} - M_k \right\|} \geq \gamma \tag{15}$$

where $\hat{D}$ represents the distance feature acquired by the spectrum signal to be perceived. As a test data, the parameter γ is given by the false alarm probability. If the equation is set up, it indicates the existence of PU. On the contrary, there is no PU.

4 Performance Evaluation

In this section, we evaluate the performance of the algorithm proposed and compare it with the CFAR method based on information geometry proposed in [6] and the maximum minimum eigenvalue (MME) method. The simulated PU signal selects the AM signal, and the noise is ideal Gauss white noise. Manifold metrics are calculated using geodesic distances. This method needs to train the sampled data first. In this simulation experiment, we obtained 1000 distance features through a feature extraction scheme, of which 500 were used as training data and 500 were perceived data.

First, we analyze the clustering effect of K-medoids clustering algorithm at different SNR, where the geodesic distance is used as a measure on the manifold. Setting the simulation parameters: $M = 5$, $N = 500$, SNR = -12 dB. Figure 3 shows the training samples of the signal and noise distance features obtained by the information geometry method.

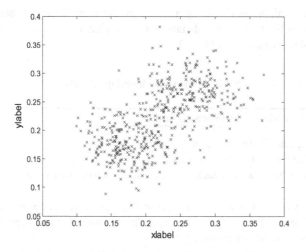

Fig. 3. Unlabeled data before the training

Figure 4 shows the training data after using the K-mediods clustering algorithm. At the same time, the centroid points of the two clusters are given. The blue point in the figure represents the noise feature, the red point represents the signal feature, and the black triangle represents the position of the center point after clustering.

The performance evaluation of the spectrum sensing method based on information geometry and K-medoids clustering is performed. In the figure, K-medoids represent the method proposed in this section. CFAR represents the use of geodesics in the constant false alarm rate detection model based on information geometry, MME represents the maximum and minimum eigenvalue algorithm.

Figure 5 shows simulation results with $M = 5$, $N = 500$, SNR = -12 dB and SNR = -14 dB. From Fig. 5, when the SNR is the same, the detection performance of K-medoids based sensing method is superior to the other two methods, and the two

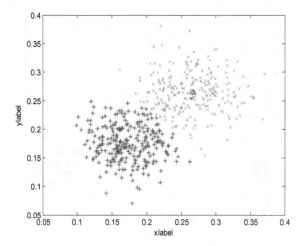

Fig. 4. Labeled data after the training

sensing methods based on information geometry have better detection performance than the traditional MME method. With the increase of SNR, the detection probabilities of the three detection methods have been improved.

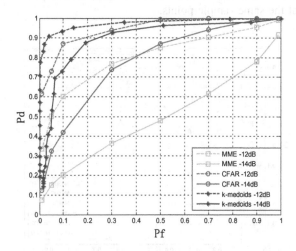

Fig. 5. The relationship between detection probability (P_d) and SNR

Figure 6 shows the simulation plot when $N = 500$, SNR $= -14$ dB, $M = 3$, $M = 5$, and $M = 7$, respectively. From Fig. 6, SUs has a certain influence on the detection probability. With the increase of the SUs, the P_d of the two sensing methods has been improved. When the SUs is the same, the detection method proposed in this paper is better than the CFAR method.

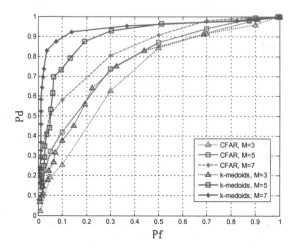

Fig. 6. The relationship between P_d and SUs

Figure 7 shows the simulation plot when $M = 5$, SNR $= -14$ dB, $N = 300$, $N = 500$, and $N = 700$. From Fig. 7, when the number of sampling points increases, the detection performance also increases. The K-medoids based information geometry method is superior to the CFAR method at the same sample points superior to the CFAR method at the same sample points.

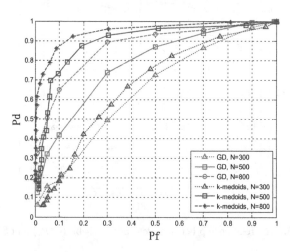

Fig. 7. Relationship between detection probability and sampling point

5   Conclusions

This paper proposes a spectrum sensing method based on K-medoids clustering algorithm and information geometry theory. In the feature extraction method, the information geometric theory is used to transform the distance feature on the manifold. Then use K-medoids clustering algorithm to analyze it to get the classifier, so as to achieve the purpose of spectrum sensing. Simulation results show that the method improves detection performance to some extent. The combination of clustering algorithm and information geometry theory has a certain application prospect in dealing with spectrum signal perception, and there are also some problems that need to be resolved.

Acknowledgments. This work was supported in part by special funds from the central finance to support the development of local universities under No. 400170044, the project supported by the State Key Laboratory of Management and Control for Complex Systems, Institute of Automation, Chinese Academy of Sciences under grant No. 20180106, the science and technology program of Guangdong Province under grant No. 2016B090918031, the degree and graduate education reform project of Guangdong Province under grant No. 2016JGXM_MS_26, the foundation of key laboratory of machine intelligence and advanced computing of the Ministry of Education under grant No. MSC-201706A and the higher education quality projects of Guangdong Province and Guangdong University of Technology.

References

1. Mitola, J., Maguire, G.Q.: Cognitive radio: making software radios more personal. IEEE Pers. Commun. **6**(4), 13–18 (1999)
2. Cabric, D., Tkachenko, A., Brodersen, R.: Spectrum sensing measurements of pilot, energy, and collaborative detection. In: IEEE Conference on Military Communications, pp. 2342–2348 (2006)
3. Urkowitz, H.: Energy detection of unknown deterministic signals. Proc. IEEE **55**(4), 523–531 (2005)
4. Oner, M., Jondral, F.: Cyclostationarity-based methods for the extraction of the channel allocation information in a spectrum pooling system. In: Radio and Wireless Conference, pp. 279–282 (2004)
5. Amari, S.: Information geometry of statistical inference - an overview. In: Proceedings of the Information Theory Workshop, pp. 86–89 (2002)
6. Liu, J.K., Wang, X.S., Tao, W., Long-Hai, Q.U.: Application of information geometry to target detection for pulsed-doppler radar. J. Natl. Univ. Def. Technology **33**(2), 77–80 (2011)
7. Zhao, X.G., Wang, S.Y.: Information geometry method to radar target detection. J. Signal Process. **31**, 631–637 (2015)
8. Chen, Q., Wan, P., Wang, Y., Li, J., Xiao, Y.: Research on cognitive radio spectrum sensing method based on information geometry. In: Sun, X., Chao, H.-C., You, X., Bertino, E. (eds.) ICCCS 2017. LNCS, vol. 10603, pp. 554–564. Springer, Cham (2017). https://doi.org/10.1007/978-3-319-68542-7_47
9. Lu, Q., Yang, S., Liu, F.: Wideband spectrum sensing based on riemannian distance for cognitive radio networks. Sensors **17**(4), 661 (2017)

230   Y. Wang et al.

10. Kumar, V., Kandpal, D.C.: K-mean clustering based cooperative spectrum sensing in generalized κ-μ fading channels. In: 22th National Conference on Communication (NCC), Guwahati, pp. 1–15. IEEE (2016)
11. Zhao, X., Wang, S.: An improved matrix CFAR detection method base on kl divergence. J. Electron. Inf. Technol. **38**, 934–940 (2016)
12. Calvo, M., Oller, J.M.: A distance between multivariate normal distributions based in an embedding into the siegel group. Academic Press, Inc. (1990)
13. Moakher, M., Batchelor, P.G.: Symmetric positive-definite matrices: from geometry to applications and visualization. In: Weickert, J., Hagen, H. (eds.) Visualization and Processing of Tensor Fields. Mathematics and Visualization. Springer, Heidelberg (2006). https://doi.org/10.1007/3-540-31272-2_17
14. Pennec, X.: Intrinsic statistics on Riemannian manifolds: basic tools for geometric measurements. J. Math. Imaging Vis. **25**(1), 127–154 (2006)
15. Lenglet, C., Rousson, M., Deriche, R., Faugeras, O.: Statistics on the manifold of multivariate normal distributions: theory and application to diffusion tensor MRI processing. J. Math. Imaging Vis. **25**(3), 423–444 (2006)
16. Moakher, M.: A differential geometric approach to the geometric mean of symmetric positive-definite matrices. SIAM J. Matrix Anal. Appl. **26**(3), 735–747 (2006)
17. Barbaresco, F.: Robust statistical radar processing in Fréchet metric space: OS-HDR-CFAR and OS-STAP processing in Siegel homogeneous bounded domains. In: International Radar Symposium, pp. 639–644. IEEE (2011)
18. Park, H.S., Jun, C.H.: A simple and fast algorithm for k-medoids clustering. Expert Syst. Appl. **36**(2), 3336–3341 (2009)
19. Thilina, K.M., Choi, K.W., Saquib, N., Hossain, E.: Machine learning techniques for cooperative spectrum sensing in cognitive radio networks. IEEE J. Sel. Areas Commun. **31**(11), 2209–2221 (2013)

A Spectrum Sensing Method Based on Null Space Pursuit Algorithm and FCM Clustering Algorithm

Yongwei Zhang[1], Yonghua Wang[1,2(✉)], Pin Wan[1],
Shunchao Zhang[1], and Nan Li[1]

[1] School of Automation, Guangdong University of Technology, Guangzhou
510006, China
gdut_zyw@163.com, sjzwyh@163.com, wanpin2@163.com,
gdut_zsc630@163.com, 2416672966@qq.com
[2] Key Laboratory of Machine Intelligence and Advanced Computing, Sun Yat-
Sen University, Ministry of Education, Guangzhou 510006, China

Abstract. In order to improve the sensing performance of spectrum sensing systems in complex environments. This paper proposes a spectrum sensing method based on Null Space Pursuit algorithm (NSP) and fuzzy c-means (FCM) clustering algorithm. The signal sensing by the spectrum system is first pre-processed using a Null Space Pursuit algorithm and the signal is decomposed into sub-signal components with more distinct features. In order to further improve the accuracy of feature estimation the IQ decomposition method is used to process the signal. Then extract the eigenvalues of the signals to form a two dimensional feature vector. Finally, these eigenvectors and the FCM clustering algorithm yield a classifier that uses the classifier to determine the state of the unknown spectrum. In the experimental part, we verify the method in different environments. Experimental results show that the method can effectively improve the sensing performance of spectrum sensing system compared to traditional spectrum sensing methods.

Keywords: Spectrum sensing · Null space pursuit · FCM clustering algorithm
Feature extraction · IQ decomposition

1 Introduction

With the gradual development of wireless networks, the demand for spectrum resources is increasing. However, research shows that the utilization of spectrum resources is low. The spectrum sensing technology in cognitive radio (CR) can effectively solve this problem. The purpose of spectrum sensing technology is to detect spectrum holes and improve spectrum utilization. The commonly used spectrum sensing methods mainly include energy detection, matched filter detection, cyclostationary feature detection, and spectrum sensing method based on a random matrix [1–3]. Matching filter detection and cyclostationary feature detection require prior information of the primary user (PU) and the complexity of the algorithm is large [4]. Energy detection does not require priori information and the complexity of the algorithm is low, so it is widely

© Springer Nature Switzerland AG 2018
X. Sun et al. (Eds.): ICCCS 2018, LNCS 11063, pp. 231–242, 2018.
https://doi.org/10.1007/978-3-030-00006-6_20

used in spectrum sensing. However, the energy detection is greatly affected by the noise, so the sensing performance is poor [5]. Literature [6] and [7] propose a spectrum sensing method based on eigenvalues of random matrices. This method first calculates the eigenvalues of the sampled signal covariance matrix, uses the eigenvalues as statistics, and then derives the corresponding threshold based on the random matrix theory to make the decision. Spectrum sensing method based on random matrix improves sensing performance of spectrum sensing system at low SNR by constructing different statistics. However, these methods have the problem of inaccurate threshold estimation, which affects the system sensing performance.

Spectrum sensing is a two-class problem. The clustering algorithm in machine learning can handle the two classification problems well. Therefore, spectrum sensing based on machine learning has gradually become a research hotspot. The literature [8] proposed a spectrum sensing method based on the k-means clustering algorithm. This method uses signal energy as a feature, and then uses the k-means clustering algorithm to train the classifier to judge the channel state. The literature [9] proposes a spectrum sensing method based on signal eigenvalues and clustering algorithms. This method mainly extracts the eigenvalues of the covariance matrix, then uses a k-means clustering algorithm to train the classifier and finally the classifier is used to determine whether the primary user exists. This method analyzes the experimental results under different features and different clustering algorithms. It solves the problem that the threshold in traditional spectrum sensing is difficult to determine. These methods can solve the problem of threshold derivation in traditional spectrum sensing and require user prior information. However, the noise in the actual environment will affect the effectiveness of the clustering algorithm, thus affecting the sensing performance of the entire system.

In order to improve the sensing performance of spectrum sensing systems in complex environments. This paper introduces a Null Space Pursuit algorithm to process the spectrum signal, decompose the complex spectrum signal into sub-signal components with more obvious features. In an actual environment, spectrum signals are usually non-stationary and non-linear. The essence of traditional short-time Fourier transform, Wigner-Ville distribution and wavelet transform is Fourier transform. These methods have some limitations in dealing with non-stationary, non-linear signals [10]. The empirical mode decomposition (EMD) algorithm proposed in the literature [11] decomposes the signal into the sum of Intrinsic modal function, which can better deal with non-stationary and non-linear signals. However, EMD algorithm should discard some useful high-frequency signals in denoising and EMD has not been well-reasoned in theory, so it has certain limitations. In order to make the spectrum sensing system have good sensing performance in a complex real environment, in this paper we introduce a NSP algorithm to process the spectrum signal. NSP algorithm decomposes a signal into a series of local narrow-band signals and residual signals based on a differential operator [12]. After the NSP algorithm has been processed, this paper also introduces the IQ decomposition method to process the decomposed signal matrix [13]. After the feature vector is extracted, the classifier is trained by the FCM clustering algorithm and finally the classifier is used to judge whether the main user exists. In the experimental part, MSE is used as the signal feature. Experimental results show that the spectrum sensing method based on the Null Space Pursuit algorithm has good performance.

2 Cooperative Spectrum Sensing System Model

In a cognitive radio network (CRN) secondary user (SU) spectrum sensing is susceptible to environmental factors, thereby reducing perceived performance. The cooperative spectrum sensing (CSS) technology can effectively solve this problem. Each SU in the CRN needs to transmit the sensed data to the fusion center (FC) and finally judged by the FC [14]. The system model shown in Fig. 1.

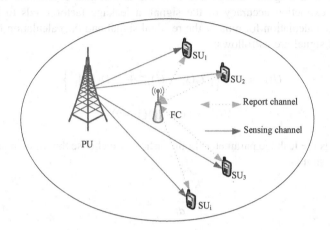

Fig. 1. System model

Assuming that H_0 indicates that PU does not exist, H_1 represents the existence of the PU. Based on this assumption, the signal received by the SU can be expressed in Eq. 1. Where $s_i(n)$ represents the signal of the PU, and $w_i(n)$ represents a Gaussian white noise with a mean of 0 and a variance of sigma σ^2 [14].

$$x_i(n) = \begin{cases} w_i(n), & H_0 \\ s_i(n) + w_i(n), & H_1 \end{cases} \tag{1}$$

The system's false alarm probability (P_f) and detection (P_d) probability can be defined as:

$$\begin{aligned} P_f &= P[H_1|H_0] \\ P_d &= P[H_1|H_1] \end{aligned} \tag{2}$$

3 Feature Extraction Based on NSP and IQ Decomposition

3.1 NSP Signal Decomposition

We assume that the spectrum signal can be expressed as $x_i(n) = V(n) + U(n)$. Where $U(n)$ is the residue component and $V(n)$ is the signal to be extracted. After operator T mapping can be obtained [12]:

$$T(x_i)(n) = U(n) \tag{3}$$

According to the literature [10], residual fraction $U(n)$ can be calculated by Eq. 4

$$\min_U \left\{ ||T_s(x_i - U)||^2 + \lambda ||D(U)||^2 \right\} \tag{4}$$

Where D is a diagonal matrix and λ is the Lagrangian coefficient. In order to improve the extraction accuracy of the signal, a leakage factor needs to be added. Therefore, the calculation formula of the residual signal and the calculation formula of the extracted signal are as follows:

$$U(t) = \min_U \left\{ ||T_s(x_i - U)||^2 + \lambda ||D(U)||^2 \right\} \tag{5}$$

$$V(t) = (x_i - U)(1 + \gamma) \tag{6}$$

Where λ is the leakage parameter. In this article, we choose the differential operator whose expression is:

$$T_s = \frac{d^2}{dt^2} + \alpha(n) \tag{7}$$

Where $\alpha(n)$ represents the square of the instantaneous frequency. $\frac{d^2}{dt^2}$ is a differential operator. Therefore, the Eq. 5 can be written as:

$$\min_{\alpha(n),U,\lambda_1,\gamma,\lambda_2} \left\{ \left\| \left(\frac{d^2}{dt^2} + \alpha(n) \right)(x_i - U) \right\|^2 + \lambda_1 \left(||U||^2 + \gamma ||x_i - U||^2 \right) + \lambda_2 ||D\alpha||^2 \right\} \tag{8}$$

Further calculations can lead to:

$$\min_{\alpha(n),U,\lambda_1,\gamma,\lambda_2} \left\{ ||(D + P_a)(x_i - U)||^2 + \lambda_1 \left(||U||^2 + \gamma ||x_i - U||^2 \right) + \lambda_2 ||D\alpha||^2 \right\} \tag{9}$$

Where P_α is a diagonal matrix and diagonal elements is α. Estimating α and U:

$$\hat{\alpha} = -\left(A^T A + \hat{\lambda}_2 D^T D \right)^{-1} A^T D \left(x_i - \hat{U} \right) \tag{10}$$

$$\hat{U} = \left(Q^T Q + (1 + \hat{\gamma}) \hat{\lambda}_1 I \right)^{-1} \left(Q^T Q S + \hat{\lambda}_1 \hat{\gamma} x_i \right) = M\left(\hat{\lambda}_1, \hat{\gamma} \right) \left(Q^T Q x_i + \hat{\lambda}_1 \hat{\gamma} x_i \right) \tag{11}$$

Where $Q = D + P_{\hat{\alpha}}$, $M\left(\hat{\lambda}_1, \hat{\gamma} \right) = \left(Q^T Q + \left(1 + \hat{\lambda} \right) \hat{\lambda}_1 I \right)^{-1}$. From the above expression, the value of α is determined by the parameter $\hat{\lambda}_2$. Experiments show that $\hat{\lambda}_2$ has little effect on the optimization problem and is generally set to a constant value. The value of $\widehat{U}$ is determined by the parameters $\hat{\lambda}_1$ and $\hat{\gamma}$. After some calculations, the parameters $\hat{\gamma}$ and $\hat{\lambda}_1$ can be derived from the following two equations, respectively.

$$\frac{\left(x_i - \widehat{U}\right)^T S}{\left\|x_i - \widehat{U}\right\|^2} = 1 + \gamma = 1 + \hat{\gamma} \tag{12}$$

$$\lambda_1 = \frac{1}{1 + \hat{\gamma}} \frac{x_i^T M(\lambda_1, \hat{\gamma})^T x_i}{x_i^T M(\lambda_1, \hat{\gamma})^T M(\lambda_1, \hat{\gamma}) x_i} \tag{13}$$

The specific steps of the Null Space Pursuit algorithm are as follows (Table 1):

Table 1. Null space pursuit algorithm

Algorithm 1: Null Space Pursuit algorithm
Input: Spectrum signal x_i, Set the initial value of parameters $\hat{\lambda}_2$, ε, λ_1^0 and γ^0
Step 1: Set $j = 0$, $\widehat{U}_j = 0$, $\lambda_1^j = \lambda_1^0$ and $\gamma^j = \gamma^0$
Step 2: Calculate the value of $\hat{\alpha}_j$ according to Eq. 10
Step 3: Calculate the value of λ_1^{j+1} according to Eq. 13
Step 4: Calculate the value of $\widehat{U}_{j+1}$ according to Eq. 11
Step 5: Calculate the value of γ^{j+1} according to Eq. 12
Step 6: If $\left\|\widehat{U}_{j+1} - \widehat{U}_j\right\| \geq \varepsilon\|x_i\|$, then let $j = j + 1$ and go back to **Step 2**
Step 7: According to Eq. 6, $\widehat{V}$ can be calculated
Step 8: **Output:** $\widehat{U}$, $\widehat{V}$

3.2 IQ Decomposition

After the above NSP process, the complex primary user signal can be effectively decomposed into more characteristic and low-complexity sub-signal matrices

$$\tilde{x}_i = \begin{bmatrix} \widehat{U} \\ \widehat{V} \end{bmatrix} \tag{14}$$

In this section, in order to more accurately acquire signal characteristics and improve the spectrum sensing performance in the case of a small number of collaborative users. We propose a feature extraction method combining the NSP algorithm with IQ decomposition. The $\tilde{x}_{i(i=1,2,3,\dots,M)}$ matrix will be decomposed into the $\tilde{x}_i^I$ matrix and the $\tilde{x}_i^Q$ matrix. The specific algorithm is as follows:

$$\tilde{x}_i^I = \begin{bmatrix} \widehat{U}^I \\ \widehat{V}^I \end{bmatrix} = \begin{cases} \widehat{U} \cdot \sin\left(\frac{2\pi f_c n}{f_s}\right) \\ \widehat{V} \cdot \sin\left(\frac{2\pi f_c n}{f_s}\right) \end{cases} \quad n = 1, 2, \ldots, N \tag{15}$$

$$\tilde{x}_i^Q = \begin{bmatrix} \widehat{U}^Q \\ \widehat{V}^Q \end{bmatrix} = \begin{cases} \widehat{U} \cdot \cos\left(\frac{2\pi f_c n}{f_s}\right) \\ \widehat{V} \cdot \cos\left(\frac{2\pi f_c n}{f_s}\right) \end{cases} \quad n = 1, 2, \ldots, N \tag{16}$$

Where f_c is the carrier frequency and f_s is the sampling frequency. After IQ decomposition, get two $2M \times N$ matrix, this matrix is as follows:

$$\mathbf{Y}^I = \begin{bmatrix} \widehat{U}_1^I \\ \widehat{V}_1^I \\ \vdots \\ \widehat{U}_M^I \\ \widehat{V}_M^I \end{bmatrix} = \begin{bmatrix} \widehat{U}_1^I(1) & \widehat{U}_1^I(2) & \cdots & \widehat{U}_1^I(N) \\ \widehat{V}_1^I(1) & \widehat{V}_1^I(2) & \cdots & \widehat{V}_1^I(N) \\ \vdots & \vdots & & \vdots \\ \widehat{U}_M^I(1) & \widehat{U}_M^I(2) & \cdots & \widehat{U}_M^I(N) \\ \widehat{V}_M^I(1) & \widehat{V}_M^I(2) & \cdots & \widehat{V}_M^I(N) \end{bmatrix} \tag{17}$$

$$\mathbf{Y}^Q = \begin{bmatrix} \widehat{U}_1^Q \\ \widehat{V}_1^Q \\ \vdots \\ \widehat{U}_M^Q \\ \widehat{V}_M^Q \end{bmatrix} = \begin{bmatrix} \widehat{U}_1^Q(1) & \widehat{U}_1^Q(2) & \cdots & \widehat{U}_1^Q(N) \\ \widehat{V}_1^Q(1) & \widehat{V}_1^Q(2) & \cdots & \widehat{V}_1^Q(N) \\ \vdots & \vdots & & \vdots \\ \widehat{U}_M^Q(1) & \widehat{U}_M^Q(2) & \cdots & \widehat{U}_M^Q(N) \\ \widehat{V}_M^Q(1) & \widehat{V}_M^Q(2) & \cdots & \widehat{V}_M^Q(N) \end{bmatrix} \tag{18}$$

After NSP and IQ decomposition, two new matrices $\mathbf{Y}^I$ and $\mathbf{Y}^Q$ are obtained, and then the corresponding covariance matrices are calculated respectively:

$$\mathbf{R}_{\mathbf{Y}^I} = \frac{1}{N} \mathbf{Y}^I \left(\mathbf{Y}^I\right)^T \tag{19}$$

$$\mathbf{R}_{\mathbf{Y}^Q} = \frac{1}{N} \mathbf{Y}^Q \left(\mathbf{Y}^Q\right)^T \tag{20}$$

According to the corresponding covariance matrix can be obtained $\eta_{u=1,2,\ldots,2M}$. Therefore, the MSE feature can be further calculated:

$$T = \eta_{max} - \frac{1}{2M} \sum_{u=1}^{2M} \eta_u \tag{21}$$

According to the above method T_1 and T_2 can be obtained. Finally, the features will form a two-dimensional feature vector $\mathbf{T} = [T_1, T_2]^T$. We used to represent signal characteristics.

4   Cooperative Spectrum Sensing Based on NSP and FCM Algorithm

In order to make the system have good sensing performance, we chose FCM algorithm as the clustering algorithm of the system. The FCM algorithm is an algorithm that determines which class a data point belongs to base on the fuzzy membership degree [15]. The objective function of FCM is the sum of squared error function. Assume that the training sample set is $\overline{T} = [T_1, T_2, \ldots, T_P]$. Considering that spectrum sensing is a two-class problem the training sample sets need to be divided into two categories. Assume that the degree of membership of each training sample j belong to a certain class i is u_{jc}. Then the objective functions and constraints of the FCM clustering algorithm can be expressed as:

$$J = \sum_{c=1}^{C} \sum_{j=1}^{P} u_{cj}^{m} ||T_j - \psi_c||^2 \qquad (22)$$

$$\sum_{c=1}^{C} u_{cj} = 1, j = 1, 2, \ldots, P \qquad (23)$$

Where P represents the number of classes of training samples. Divide the training feature vector into C classes, and let $\mathbb{C}_c$ represent the set of feature vectors belonging to the class $c = 1, 2, \ldots, C$. Let ψ_c denote the center of the corresponding class. u_{jc} indicate the degree of membership of the j-th feature value to the c-th class in the training sample $\overline{T}$. m represent the smoothing exponent of the FCM algorithm, generally m is greater than or equal to one. Add the constraints to the objective function using the Lagrangian multiplier method.

$$J = \sum_{c=1}^{C} \sum_{j=1}^{P} u_{jc}^{m} ||T_j - \psi_c||^2 + \lambda_1 \left(\sum_{c=1}^{C} u_{1c} - 1 \right) + \cdots + \lambda_j \left(\sum_{c=1}^{C} u_{jc} - 1 \right) + \cdots + \lambda_n \left(\sum_{c=1}^{C} u_{nc} - 1 \right) \quad (24)$$

Find derivatives of u_{jc} and ψ_c in equation

$$u_{jc} = \frac{1}{\sum_{k=1}^{C} \left(\frac{||T_{j-\psi_c}||}{||T_{j-\psi_k}||} \right)^{\left(\frac{2}{m-1} \right)}} \qquad (25)$$

$$\psi_c = \frac{\sum_{j=1}^{n} \left(x_j u_{jc}^{m} \right)}{\sum_{j=1}^{n} u_{jc}^{m}} \qquad (26)$$

Equations 25 and 26 are the iterative formulas for membership and clustering centers, respectively. After FCM algorithm training, we can use Eq. 27 to determine whether the primary user exists [8]

$$\frac{\left\| \hat{T}_j - \psi_1 \right\|}{min_{c=2,3,\ldots,C} \left\| \hat{T}_j - \psi_c \right\|} \geq \zeta \qquad (27)$$

Where $\widehat{T}$ represents the test set data, ζ is used to control the false alarm probability and detection probability of the system, and k is the number of clusters. In this paper, the value of C is 2 (Table 2).

Table 2. CSS based on NSP and FCM algorithm

Algorithm 1: CSS Based on NSP and FCM Algorithm	
Input:	Train data: $\widehat{T} = [T_1, T_2, \ldots, T_P]$ The number of categories: C the smooth number of FCM algorithm: m initial value of membership: u_{jc} Allowable error: ε
Step 1:	Calculate the cluster center c_j according to Eq. 26
Step 2:	Calculation error $v = \sum_{i=1}^{c} \left\| T_j - \psi_c \right\|^2$, If $v < \varepsilon$, the algorithm stops, otherwise continue to the fourth step
Step 3:	The new membership is calculated based on the value of the cluster center ψ_c and Eq. 25
Step 4:	Go to step (1) and continue until you reach the number of iterations
Step 5:	Output membership and clustering center
Step 6:	Import the test date $\widehat{T} = [T_1, T_2, \ldots, T_P]$
Step 7:	If $\dfrac{\left\| \widehat{T}_{-\psi_1} \right\|}{\min_{c=2,3,\ldots,C} \left\| \widehat{T}_{-\psi_c} \right\|} \geq \zeta$ **Output:** H_1, Else **Output:** H_0

5   Experiments

The result of cooperative spectrum sensing based on NSP and FCM clustering has been generated through simulation. The signal transmitted by the main user is the mixed signal $S(t) = \cos(t) + \cos(4t + 0.2t^2)$. Through the method described in this paper, 2000 feature vectors composed of MSEs are extracted, of which 1000 are used as training sets and the remaining 1000 are used for testing. The number of sampling points per SU is $N = 1000$.

5.1   Classification Effect Based on FCM Clustering Algorithm

Figure 2 shows 1000 unlabeled training feature vectors, 500 of which are feature vectors in the case of noise, and the rest are feature vectors in the presence of the PU.

Figure 3 shows the effect of training feature vectors classified by the FCM clustering algorithm. The blue dots in the figure represent the feature vectors classified as noise, and the red dots represent the feature vectors classified as signal plus noise. Triangles and circles respectively represent the center points within the corresponding class.

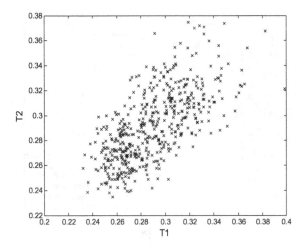

Fig. 2. Training feature vectors at SNR = 14 dB, $M = 2$

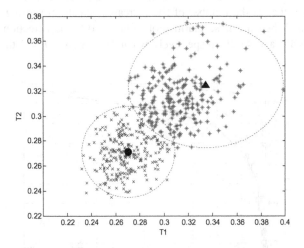

Fig. 3. Feature vectors classified by FCM algorithm

5.2 FCM Clustering Algorithm Under the Detection Performance

Figure 4 shows the sensing performance of various algorithms at different SNR. Compared with other algorithms, the proposed algorithm can effectively improve spectrum sensing performance. When SNR = −16 dB and the false alarm probability is 0.1, the detection probability increases by 44.4% compared to the IQMSE algorithm, and the detection probability increases by 24.1% when the false alarm probability is 0.2. When SNR = −14 dB and the false alarm probability is 0.1, the detection probability increases by 22.8% compared to the IQMSE algorithm, and the detection probability increases by 18.7% when the false alarm probability is 0.2.

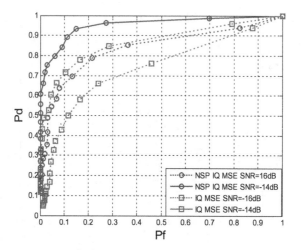

Fig. 4. ROC curves of different algorithms under different SNR with $M = 2$

Figure 5 shows the ROC curve for the number of different SUs at SNR = −16 dB. The results show that as the number of SU increases, spectrum sensing can be effectively improved. When the false alarm probability is 0.1, the detection performance increases by 18.4% and 46.1% respectively when $M = 3$ and $M = 4$ than $M = 2$.

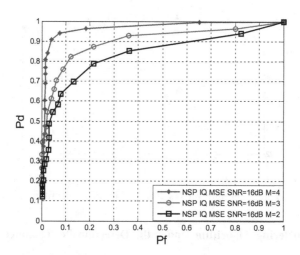

Fig. 5. ROC curves for different numbers of SU at SNR = −16 dB

6 Conclusions

In order to improve the sensing performance of spectrum sensing systems in complex environments. This paper proposes a spectrum sensing method based on NSP algorithm and FCM clustering algorithm. The spectrum signal is first processed by a NSP algorithm to decompose the complex signal into characteristic sub-signal components. In order to further improve the accuracy of the features, we also use the IQ decomposition method to further process the sub signal components. Then we use a FCM clustering algorithm to train the classifier. We use this classifier to determine whether the primary user signal exists. Experimental results show that the method has good sensing performance.

Acknowledgments. This work was supported in part by special funds from the central finance to support the development of local universities under No. 400170044, the project supported by the State Key Laboratory of Management and Control for Complex Systems, Institute of Automation, Chinese Academy of Sciences under grant No. 20180106, the science and technology program of Guangdong Province under grant No. 2016B090918031, the degree and graduate education reform project of Guangdong Province under grant No. 2016JGXM_MS_26, the foundation of key laboratory of machine intelligence and advanced computing of the Ministry of Education under grant No. MSC-201706A and the higher education quality projects of Guangdong Province and Guangdong University of Technology.

References

1. Zeng, Y., Liang, Y.C.: Eigenvalue-based spectrum sensing algorithms for cognitive radio. IEEE Trans. Commun. **57**(6), 1784–1793 (2008)
2. Xiao, L., Li, Y., Huang, X., Du, X.: Cloud-based malware detection game for mobile devices with offloading. IEEE Trans. Mob. Comput. **16**(10), 2742–2750 (2017)
3. Xiao, L., Xu, D., Xie, C., Mandayam, N.B., Poor, H.V.: Cloud storage defense against advanced persistent threats: a prospect theoretic study. IEEE J. Sel. Areas Commun. **35**(3), 534–544 (2017)
4. Cohen, D., Rebeiz, E., Jain, V., Eldar, Y.C.: Cyclostationary feature detection from sub-nyquist samples. In: IEEE International Workshop on Computational Advances in Multi-Sensor Adaptive Processing, pp. 333–336 (2011)
5. Atapattu, S., Tellambura, C., Jiang, H.: Energy detection based cooperative spectrum sensing in cognitive radio networks. IEEE Trans. Wirel. Commun. **10**(4), 1232–1241 (2011)
6. Cao, K.T., Yang, Z.: A novel cooperative spectrum sensing algorithm based on the maximum eigenvalue. J. Electr. Inf. Technol. **2**(5), 1367–1372 (2011)
7. Liu, N., Shi, H.S., Yang, B., Yuan, D.P.: Spectrum sensing method based on me-s-ed. Measurement & Control Technology (2016)
8. Kumar, V., Kandpal, D.C., Jain, M., Gangopadhyay, R., Debnath, S.: K-mean clustering based cooperative spectrum sensing in generalized κ-μ fading channels. In: Communication (2016)
9. Zhang, Y., Wan, P., Zhang, S., Wang, Y., Li, N.: A spectrum sensing method based on signal feature and clustering algorithm in cognitive wireless multimedia sensor networks. Adv. Multimedia **2017**(4), 1–10 (2017)
10. Griffin, D., Lim, J.S.: Signal estimation from modified short-time Fourier transform. IEEE Trans. Acoust. Speech Sig. Process. **32**(2), 236–243 (1984)
11. Boudraa, A.O., Cexus, J.C.: EMD-based signal filtering. IEEE Trans. Instrum. Meas. **56**(6), 2196–2202 (2007)
12. Peng, S., Hwang, W.L.: Null space pursuit: an operator-based approach to adaptive signal separation. IEEE Trans. Sig. Process. **58**(5), 2475–2483 (2010)

13. Song, Y., Zhou, Y.: An improved spectrum sensing algorithm based on random matrix theory. In: International Conference on Advanced Communication Technology, pp. 715–720 (2017)
14. Akyildiz, I.F., Lo, B.F., Balakrishnan, R.: Cooperative spectrum sensing in cognitive radio networks: a survey. Elsevier Science Publishers B. V. (2011)
15. Ahmed, M.N., Yamany, S.M., Mohamed, N., Farag, A.A., Moriarty, T.: A modified fuzzy C-means algorithm for bias field estimation and segmentation of MRI data. IEEE Trans. Med. Imaging 21(3), 193–199 (2002)

A Survey of Machine Learning-Based Resource Scheduling Algorithms in Cloud Computing Environment

Qi Liu[1](✉) and YingHang Jiang[2]

[1] Jiangsu Collaborative Innovation Center of Atmospheric Environment and
Equipment Technology (CICAEET), Nanjing University of Information Science
and Technology, Nanjing 210044, China
qi.liu@nuist.edu.cn
[2] School of Computer and Software, Nanjing University of Information Science
and Technology, Nanjing, China
jiangyinghang@foxmail.com

Abstract. As a new type of computing resource, cloud computing attracts more
and more users because it is convenient and quick service. The cloud server is
used by a large number of users, which brings about the problem of how to
reasonably schedule resources to ensure the load balance of the cloud environment. With the development of research, scholars have found that the simple
job scheduling of physical resources cannot meet the utilization of resources.
Connecting the characteristic of resource scheduling in cloud environment and
machine learning, researchers gradually abstract a resource scheduling problem
into a mathematical problem, and then combine machine learning with group
algorithm to put forward the intelligent algorithm which can optimize the
resource structure and the improve the resource utilization. In this survey, we
discuss several algorithms that use machine learning to solve resource
scheduling problems in a cloud environment. Experiments show that machine
learning can assist the cloud environment to achieve load balancing.

Keywords: Cloud computing · Resource scheduling · Machine learning
PSO · Reinforcement learning

1 Introduction

Cloud computing is a new type of computing model and service model which are paid
by amount. And it also can access configurable shared pool of computing resources
(The resources include network resources, server resources, storage resources, application resources, etc.) by using network. At the meantime, all the resources in the pool
can be accessed quickly, it just cost a little backstage management and has minimal
interaction with the suppliers to achieve rapid configuration or the release of resources
[1]. From the above definition of cloud computing, we realize that the essence of cloud
computing is to perform unified scheduling and management of resources in cloud
environment data center, while it provides services with fast and convenience for users

© Springer Nature Switzerland AG 2018
X. Sun et al. (Eds.): ICCCS 2018, LNCS 11063, pp. 243–252, 2018.
https://doi.org/10.1007/978-3-030-00006-6_21

to ensure load balance of cloud computing [2]. In other words, the main problem of cloud computing is resource scheduling.

The aim of resource scheduling is to optimize structure of resource and improve the rate of resource scheduling in cloud computing. What's more, the resource scheduling based on development of distributed computing [3, 4] and grid computing [5] has a great quantity of advantages. However, resource scheduling of distributed computing and grid computing has been relatively mature, so there is a certain reference to the research of resource scheduling in cloud environment. Meantime, resource in the cloud environment has its own characteristics, so it is necessary to study the resource scheduling algorithm and resource scheduling strategy [6] according to its characteristics. Table 1 explains the advantage and disadvantage about different kinds of cloud computing resource scheduling algorithm.

Table 1. Resource scheduling algorithms in Cloud computing

Algorithm classification	Advantages	Disadvantage
Traditional	Those algorithms are simple and easy to achieve	Poor performance when dealing with complex issues
Heuristic	These algorithms have great performance for optimal solution	They are easy to fall into early convergence and the sought solution is a local optimum

The traditional resource scheduling is the hardware resources [7] in management system, the common methods are Round Robin Scheduling Algorithm (RR), First In First Out Scheduling Algorithm (FIFO), etc. After introducing the cloud computing environment, if we insist using the method which use prior configured and fixed resource, load imbalance will be caused in cloud computing. What's more, the resources are wasted in shared pool and needs from the cloud users cannot be satisfied.

From results of current research scholars, the efficiency and energy consumption of cloud computing, the efficiency and fairness of cloud computing resource allocation are all affected by resource scheduling algorithm. And the dynamic resource scheduling of cloud computing has three significant features [8, 9].

1. Resource scheduling is oriented to heterogeneous platform or isomorphic platform. It needs to use virtualization technology to realize the deployment and operation of applications.
2. Achieve scalability of resource scheduling, through dynamically creating or destroying the lifecycle of a running task in a virtual machine.
3. Resource scheduling uses a relatively centralized way to manage large-scale physical resources into cloud servers, and then completes the unified supply of resources [10].

Therefore, it is necessary to design a dynamic resource scheduling with giving consideration to the features of dynamic resource scheduling, which realize efficient and dynamic resource scheduling of cloud computing. Nowadays, resource scheduling strategies and resource scheduling algorithms absorb the attention of scholars. The general idea of solving resource scheduling algorithm is as follows. Firstly, assign the scheduling problem to some known mathematical problem. Secondly, the model is created for settling this problem. Finally, settle this scheduling problem by using mathematical solving method. As a result, more and more intelligent algorithms are applied to the solution of resource scheduling problems, and it is greatly important to choose the best intelligent algorithms.

In this paper, we intend to investigate the algorithm of resource scheduling based on machine learning in the cloud computing. As we all known, machine learning is the best tool for cloud platform and a great number of algorithms is designed by machine learning which is easy to modify the knowledge base, expand the knowledge base and train many times to get better test results.

The remainder of this paper will be organized as follow. Traditional scheduling algorithm of machine learning is used in cloud computing, which will be presented in Sect. 2. While the heuristic intelligent scheduling algorithm of machine learning is introduced in Sect. 3, improved intelligent scheduling algorithm is the main part of this paper to introduce some popular algorithms in Sect. 4. Finally, in Sect. 5, we compare three algorithms of resource scheduling and give an evaluation about those algorithms.

2   Traditional Scheduling Algorithm of Machine Leaning

In this Section, we explain some algorithms about traditional resource scheduling how to work and participate the whole process. The problem of resource scheduling which is an allocation problem between virtual resource pool and physical resources focus on resource layer. As usual, the model of resource scheduling is divided into two stages. Figure 1 has vivid indicated those two stages [11].

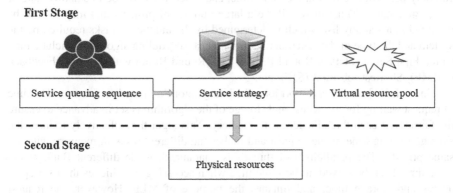

Fig. 1. Two stages of the resource scheduling model.

Resource scheduling achieve the first and second level in the cloud computing resource scheduling model. It first completes the dynamic matching of the cloud user's task request and the virtual machine resource, and then maps the physical machine based on the matching virtual machine. Figure 2 indicates the process of resource scheduling in cloud computing.

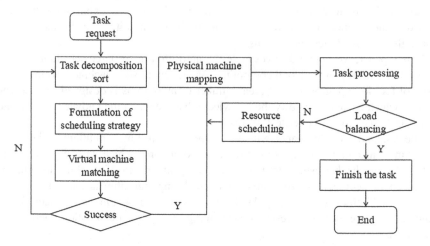

Fig. 2. The procedure of resource scheduling in cloud computing.

2.1   Task Scheduling Algorithm

The traditional scheduling algorithm is used in multichannel systems, and task scheduling algorithm is used to deal with batch jobs. After satisfying the condition of resource, task scheduling algorithms transfer task which maintain the reserve state into memory and generate corresponding processes. And then, according to selected of scheduling algorithm, provide corresponding resources for the process. That is, CPU can only perform one task at a certain time, and other tasks will be in standby state or congestion status. Thus, there will be a large number of projects that may wait to be executed in a standby list, which is determined by the number of tasks required by the system and the type of the scheduler. Common task scheduling algorithms include First Come First Serve (FCFS), Round Robin (RR), Round Robin with Multiple-Feedback (RRMF), Shortest job First (SJF), etc.

Jin et al. [11] proposes a short job scheduling algorithm based on fairness. The time of request waiting for the access and storage of the algorithm is set in advance to ensure the fairness of each thread's access to memory. This algorithm effectively reduces the average waiting time of the request and makes the different tasks in memory with the same priority. The parallelism of threads is guaranteed, while different Bank of the same thread can be served at the same time when accessing. It achieves the overlap of access and storage time, and finishes the purpose of MLP. However, the request waiting time of this algorithm needs to be set in advance and does not conform to most of the actual environment. Therefore, in the future work, they need to propose an adaptive maximum waiting time to set up the request.

2.2 Scheduler Based on Hadoop

The Fair scheduler, the FIFO scheduler and the Capacity scheduler are used in Hadoop [13]. Those schedulers and their applications will be introduced as follow.

The Fair Scheduler

The Fair scheduler provided by Facebook is suitable for multiuser shared cluster environments. This scheduler guarantees each job to get the same computing resources for a period of time. In order to solve the problem of data scheduling and resource utilization in MapReduce system, Liao et al. [12] proposed an effective resource waiting time fair scheduler, which could be allocated to the free slot for different tasks, and it was not illegal to coarse-grained fairness principle. At the same time, a scoring model considering data locality and resource utilization was put forward, so that each scheduling step in task determined the best task and improved the efficiency of MapReduce system. After analyzing this experimental results, the Fair scheduler is more fair and has better throughput than the other schedulers.

The FIFO Scheduler

The FIFO scheduler is a long used scheduler, which submits all users' operations to a queue and then Job Tracker chooses the jobs to be executed basis the order of the time of job submission. However, this kind of thought can handle the task of a single user. When facing different tasks of multi-user sharing the same platform, it can't meet the needs of different users, and the performance is very poor. Luo et al. [14] wanted to solve a problem which the existing FIFO scheduler could not monitor the wind power system in real time on the Hadoop platform. A FIFO scheduler based on double queues was designed. The main idea of this scheduler was to first use the soft real-time scheduling algorithm of EDF, then selected jobs according to the start time and priority of jobs, and finally, the jobs with early deadline would be given priority. Through simulation experiments, it was proved that the dual queue scheduler reduced the completion time of the work to a certain extent, and could realize the real-time job requirements.

3 Heuristic Intelligent Scheduling Algorithm of Machine Learning

Since the concept of heuristic algorithm is proposed, there are various versions of its definition. It is widely accepted by scholars that the heuristic algorithm is used as a technique to find the best solution to the premise that cost is small. But in most cases, the solution must be a feasible solution, but it may not be an optimal solution. The origin of heuristic algorithm is careful observation and deep understanding of the natural phenomena of organisms, the actual population situation formed between species, and the simulation of their behaviors or natural phenomena in the process of learning from nature. The main thought of this algorithm is strategy of 'winning the fittest', that is, selection and mutation, which can obtain different heuristic algorithms.

3.1 Ant Colony Optimization Algorithm

In 1992, an Italy scholar named Dorigo proposed a heuristic search algorithm based on ant colony, which simulated the foraging behavior of ant colony to find the best path.

This algorithm has diversity and positive feedback in the process of seeking the best path. Diversity is the ability of ant colony to search for food and to guarantee this behavior that does not circulate indefinitely. Positive-negative feedback is the learning and adaptation ability of ant colony foraging, which is a conscious algorithm to preserve some information about relative optimal path. Figure 3 is the process of describing ant colony to find an optimal path. At the beginning, the ant colony will send scouts to traverse each path and leave the pheromone on the connection node. Secondly, using its positive feedback in the process of ergodicity, the individual evolves gradually to the optimal solution. Gradual behavior is reflected in the concentration of volatile pheromone is automatic and gradual, which can avoid the excessive concentration of ant colony to the local optimal region. Finally, the ant colony will form the best path and save the path information.

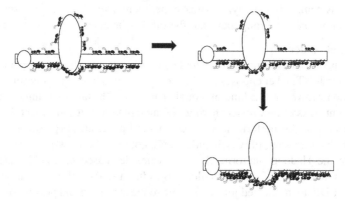

Fig. 3. The process of describing ant colony to find an optimal path.

Luo et al. [18] proposed two resource scheduling strategies, AC01 and ACO2, which were both introduced bi-directional ant mechanism to settle a problem of inefficient searching for effective resources because ants only relied on pheromone communication instead of direct communication. This mechanism would be divided into Forward-ant which searched nodes in the virtual machine resource and Back-ant which found the resources available and left the pheromone traces in the return path. In the process of mutual communication between two ants, the appropriate resources were quickly found to facilitate the Master node to allocate the virtual machine in time for the user's task. The experimental results proved that the time complexity of the algorithm was $O(k(m+n))$ and the time of Forward-ant found the nodes was $O(m)$. The time was obviously reduced and saved the time of distributing virtual machines.

3.2 Cat Swarm Optimization Algorithm

The cat swarm optimization algorithm is a new heuristic intelligent algorithm which has been proposed in recent years. Tsai et al. [17] proposed a virtual machine resource scheduling method based on the cat swarm optimization algorithm, which ensured the load balance of cloud computing and reduced the running cost of the cloud system.

Firstly, cat group was selected and population model was initialized basis state of resource and task. Then, combining the shortest time and the optimal load, the fitness function of the cat swarm optimization algorithm was constructed to guide the search direction of the cat group. Finally, the optimal resource scheduling scheme was found on the basis of search mode and tracking mode. Through CloudSim platform test, the cat swarm optimization algorithm avoided local optimization, improved the utilization rate of virtual machine resources, and integrated the advantages of genetic algorithm and particle swarm optimization.

4 Improved Intelligent Scheduling Algorithm of Machine Learning

In this Section, the optimized version of the heuristic intelligent algorithm is studied, which is based on the last section of the resource scheduling algorithm, adding priority, economic model and other conditions. In fact, the essence of algorithm is second kinds of algorithms. Starting from the reality of cloud computing resource scheduling, combining the actual application background with the second kinds of algorithms is the following common optimization heuristic resource scheduling algorithm, which plays a crucial role in improving the overall performance of cloud computing system.

4.1 Particle Swarm Optimization Algorithm

In 1995, when studying migratory routes and clustering of migratory birds in search of food, Dr. Kennedy and Dr. Eberhart [18] found that birds searching for food gradually approached the nearest food through repeated dispersion and polymerization. According to this phenomenon, they proposed a global particle search optimization algorithm. The algorithm is studied in detail in each particle velocity and trajectory of space motion process, combined with the particle history and population history to adjust their direction and speed, and to its own history and the optimal solutions of group optimal solution near optimal solution search [19]. Figure 4 is the model of particle swarm optimization algorithm. The advantages of particle swarm are low dependence on the target function and have strong adaptability. At the same time, the

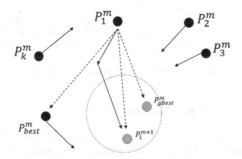

Fig. 4. Particle swarm optimization algorithm search model.

particle swarm also has shortcomings, it is not easy to determine the parameters of the algorithm and it is difficult to finish a solution in the discrete range [20].

The improved particle swarm optimization (PSO) algorithm was proposed by Jun et al. [21], which added the idea of dynamic multi group collaboration and variable particle reversed flight to the optimization algorithm. The dynamic multi group cooperative algorithm was used, which was divided into primary group and subgroup. Figure 5 shows the relationship between two groups. Among them, the focus of the main group was in the local search, and the subgroup focused on the global search. After continuous search of subgroups, the optimal resource was recommended to the main group, and the main group was selected from the optimal subgroup to evolve, and finally the global optimal solution was obtained. Through practice, we know that the dynamic multi group cooperation method improves the accuracy and speed of the optimization algorithm. The while variant particle retrograde flight avoids the situation of falling into the local optimal solution. However, the parameters set by this particle swarm optimization algorithm need to be discussed and the load is not balanced. In order to solve the two problems raised above, Yuan et al. [22] proposed a new algorithm to improve particle swarm optimization in cloud computing. First, the problem of scheduling resources was transformed into a corresponding mathematical model. Then the mathematical model was transformed into the corresponding eigenvalue of TSP problem. Finally, the optimized particle swarm was combined with the eigenvalue. To sum up, the problem of resource scheduling was finally abstracted as the process of particle swarm optimization. CloudSim was used to carry out the simulation experiment, and the performance was analyzed and verified. It was found that the best value of algorithm parameters could be determined by formula calculation and iterative algorithm.

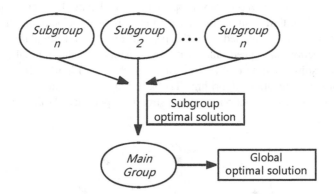

Fig. 5. The relationship between two groups.

4.2   Reinforcement Learning Algorithm

Peng et al. [23] put forward RP learning system and TS system based on strength learning on DRL-Cloud, modifying DQN training algorithm from standard intensity learning by using experience playback and target network. Learning in a changing environment generated the best time for decision making. With the rapid growth of mobile data traffic, the number of content access requests will also increase accordingly. Therefore, we need to unload the mobile data in the cellular network to reduce the load. So how many resources blocks the controller has to meet the actual needs is an urgent problem. Under the background mentioned above, Kumar et al. [24] proposed a reinforcement learning algorithm based on queuing model by using the model of the system, the use of three kinds of operation mode and the cache content management strategy to achieve the most efficient communication efficiency. Finally, the simulation analysis of Q learning algorithm a lot. It is concluded that the load on the resource block generated by the algorithm can satisfy the number of resource blocks required by the mobile operator.

5 Summary

In order to optimize the resource scheduling structure and improve the load balancing ability of the cloud environment, and the traditional resource scheduling method has been unable to meet the needs of users, people urgently need to use machine learning algorithm to solve the resource scheduling problem. In this survey, the traditional method of resource scheduling, second kinds of heuristic intelligent algorithms and third kinds of optimization algorithms are discussed in turn. First of all, the traditional resource scheduling method only uses simple first come first service and different schedulers to schedule small resources, which does not meet the actual needs. Secondly, the heuristic intelligent algorithm abstracts the problem of resource scheduling into mathematical problems, and then uses different machine learning algorithms to schedule them. But what kind of intelligent algorithm is better for the same mathematical problem and can only be tested by practice. Finally, the popular intelligent algorithm is able to solve the scheduling problem better by modifying the parameters in the algorithm or adjusting the design idea of the algorithm, making the algorithm and the actual mathematical problems more appropriate. The experiment shows that the last method of resource scheduling is more advantageous than other methods.

Acknowledgements. This work is supported by Marie Curie Fellowship (701697-CAR-MSCA-IF-EF- ST), the NSFC (61300238 and 61672295), the 2014 Project of six personnel in Jiangsu Province under Grant No. 2014-WLW-013, and the PAPD fund.

References

1. Mell, P., Grance, T.: The NIST definition of cloud computing. Commun. ACM **53**(6), 50 (2011)
2. Lin, W., Qi, D.: Survey of resource scheduling in cloud computing. Comput. Sci. **39**(10), 1–6 (2012)
3. Jiang, X.W., Fan, M.A.: Middleware and distributed computing. Comput. Appl. **22**(004), 5–8 (2002)
4. Arslan, M.Y., Singh, I., Singh, S., et al.: CWC: a distributed computing infrastructure using smartphones. IEEE Trans. Mobile Comput. **14**(8), 1587–1600 (2015)

5. Xiang, J.J.: Research on the key technologies of resource dynamic management in cloud computing environment. Adv. Mater. Res. **926–930**, 2618–2621 (2014)
6. Kim, B.G., Zhang, Y., et al.: Dynamic pricing and energy consumption scheduling with reinforcement learning. IEEE Trans. Smart Grid **7**(5), 2187–2198 (2016)
7. Feng, Y., Zheng, B., Li, Z.: Exploratory study of sorting particle swarm optimizer for multiobjective design optimization. Math. Comput. Model. **52**(11), 1966–1975 (2010)
8. Hou, Y., Lu, L., et al.: Enhanced particle swarm optimization algorithm and its application on economic dispatch of power systems. Proc. CSEE **24**(7), 69–70 (2007)
9. Liu, J., Fan, X., et al.: A new particle swarm optimization algorithm with dynamic adjustment of inertia weights. Comput. Eng. Appl. **43**(7), 69–70 (2007)
10. Shi, H., Bai, G., Tang, Z.: ACO algorithm-based parallel job scheduling investigation on Hadoop. Int. J. Digit. Content Technol. Appl. **5**(7), 283–289 (2011)
11. Jin, Y., Wu, J., et al.: Fairness-considered shortest job first strategy for memory scheduling. Comput. Eng. **38**(20), 243–246 (2012)
12. Liao, J., Zhang, L., et al.: Efficient and fair scheduler of multiple resources for MapReduce system. IET Softw. **10**(6), 182–188 (2016)
13. Berral, J., Poggi, N., Carrera, D., et al.: ALOJA: a framework for benchmarking and predictive analytics in Hadoop deployments. IEEE Trans. Emerg. Top. Comput. **PP**(99), 1 (2015)
14. Luo, X., Yue, L., et al.: Research on job scheduling algorithm on wind farms data center cloud platform based on Hadoop. Comput. Eng. Appl. **51**(15), 266–270 (2015)
15. Zhu, L., Li, Q., et al.: Study on cloud computing resource scheduling strategy based on the ant colony optimization algorithm. Int. J. Comput. Sci. Issues **9**(5), 54–58 (2012)
16. Guo, L., Zhao, S., et al.: Task scheduling optimization in cloud computing based on heuristic algorithm. J. Netw. **7**(3), 1–4 (2012)
17. Tsai, P.W., Pan, J.S., et al.: Parallel cat swarm optimization. In: International Conference on Machine Learning and Cybernetics, vol. 6, pp. 854–858. IEEE (2008)
18. Luo, Y., Yuan, X., et al.: An improved PSO algorithm for solving non-convex NLP/MINLP problems with equality constraints. Comput. Chem. Eng. **31**(3), 153–162 (2007)
19. Bonyadi, M.R., Michalewicz, Z.: Particle swarm optimization for single objective continuous space problems: a review. Evol. Comput. **25**(1), 1–54 (2017)
20. Gomathi, B., Krishnasamy, K.: Task scheduling algorithm based on hybrid particle swarm optimization in cloud computing environment. J. Theor. Appl. Inf. Technol. **7**(1), 575 (2013)
21. Jun, W., Zhang, M., et al.: Cloud computing resource schedule strategy based on MPSO algorithm. Comput. Eng. **37**(11), 43–44 (2011)
22. Yuan, H., Li, C., et al.: Optimal virtual machine resources scheduling based on improved particle swarm optimization in cloud computing. J. Softw. **9**(3), 705–708 (2014)
23. Peng, Z., Cui, D., et al.: Random task scheduling scheme based on reinforcement learning in cloud computing. Clust. Comput. **18**(4), 1595–1607 (2015)
24. Kumar, N., Swain, S.N., Murthy, C.S.R.: A novel distributed Q-learning based resource reservation framework for facilitating D2D content access requests in LTE-A networks. IEEE Trans. Netw. Serv. Manag. **PP**(99), 1 (2018)

A Trusted Computing Base for Information System Classified Protection

Hui Lu[1(✉)], Xiang Cui[1], Le Wang[1], Yu Jiang[1], and Ronglai Jia[2]

[1] Cyberspace Institute of Advanced Technology, Guangzhou University,
Guangzhou 510006, China
luhui@gzhu.edu.cn
[2] Research Center of Computer Network and Information Security Technology,
Harbin Institute of Technology, Harbin, Heilongjiang Province, China

Abstract. The 21st century is the age of information when information becomes an important strategic resource. Information security turns into one of the biggest issues facing computer technology today. Our computer systems face the risk of being plagued by powerful, feature-rich malware. Current malware exploit the vulnerabilities that are endemic to the huge computing base that needs to be trusted to secure our private information. This summary presents the trusted computing base (TCB) and the Trusted Computing Group (TCG). TCB is the collectivity of the computer's protector, which influences the security of system. The Trusted Computing Group (TCG) is an international industry standards group. There are extensive theories about information security and technology. Providing some technology and methods that can prevent you system from being attacked by malware and controlled by unauthorized persons. At last, we introduce efficient TCB reduction.

Keywords: Terms—Information security · Trusted computing base (TCB)
Trusted Computing Group (TCG) · TCB reduction

1 Introduction

The trusted computing base (TCB) of a computer system is the set of all hardware, firmware, and software components that are critical to its security, in the d sense that bugs or vulnerabilities occurring inside the TCB might jeopardize the security properties of the entire system. By contrast, parts of a computer system outside the TCB must not be able to misbehave in a way that would leak any more privileges than are granted to them in accordance to the security policy [1].

All of the operating system's security architecture is based on the conception of TCB. In order to maintain the compatibility of the applications, the practical security operation system is implemented by adding security mechanism on popular operation system at present.

The careful design and implementation of a system's trusted computing base is paramount to its overall security. Modern operating systems strive to reduce the size of the TCB so that an exhaustive examination of its code base (by means of manual or computer-assisted software audit or program verification) becomes feasible.

© Springer Nature Switzerland AG 2018
X. Sun et al. (Eds.): ICCCS 2018, LNCS 11063, pp. 253–262, 2018.
https://doi.org/10.1007/978-3-030-00006-6_22

The Trusted Computing Group (TCG) is an international industry standards group. The TCG develops specifications amongst it members. Upon completion, the TCG publishes the specifications for use and implementation by the industry [2].

The TCG publicizes the specifications and uses membership implementations as examples of the use of TCG Technology. The TCG is organized into a work group model whereby experts from each technology category can work together to develop the specifications. This fosters a neutral environment where competitors and collaborators can develop industry best capabilities that are vendor neutral and interoperable. TCG Incorporation and Benefits [3].

The TCG specifications for the TPM are large and complex, and as a result it seems inevitable that some security vulnerabilities will be present. In fact, given this complexity, it is rather surprising that more issues have not been identifed|in any event, detailed security analysis of the TCG specifications will remain an area of considerable importance for some time to come [4]. These security Issues includes: (1) use of cryptographic primitives; (2) an anonymity attack; (3) corrupt administrator attacks; (4) practical issues and so on.

2   The Brief History of Trusted Computing

The term trusted computing, as used here, is surprisingly recent, although some of the key ideas have been around for much longer. Two of the earliest papers to explore trusted computing were published as recently as 2000. As discussed by Pearson, the Trusted Computing Platform Alliance (TCPA), an industry alliance created to develop and standardise Trusted Platform technology, was formed in October 1999. The TCPA released the first specifications in early 2001, defining a fundamental component of a trusted platform, namely a Trusted Platform Module (TPM) [5]. A TPM is typically implemented as a chip mounted on a PC motherboard, and provides a foundation for all trusted functionality in the PC (in combination with the BIOS). The TCPA specifications are described in some detail in a book published in 2002.

The work of the TCPA was inherited by its successor body, the Trusted Computing Group (TCG), which is continuing to develop these specifications. An analysis of privacy issues relating to trusted computing, as defined by the TCG, has been provided by Reid, Gonzalez Nieto and Dawson.

3   Trusted-Computing Technology

3.1   Cryptographic Trusted Computing

Cryptographic TC technology protects data and programs on users' computers by sealing them in an encrypted virtual vault. If outside data or programs want access to the vault, they must pass muster with the TC system and obtain decryption keys. Only trusted processes would gain access to disk storage; the CPU memory space, including the stack and on-chip cache; and main memory [6].

TC systems don't actually decide whether code is safe. Instead, they identify users, their computing systems (based on a unique identifying digital signature), and the applications or data they want to run [7]. Trusted agents would provide much of the information. The agents identify the users and their computers to TC systems, which would then consult directory services to determine whether the users are authorized to run the applications or data on their systems, if the material is from a source deemed in advance to be trustworthy, and what level of access it should have to system resources.

3.2 Trusted-Computing Initiatives

The major TC initiatives differ primarily in where the encryption/decryption functionality occurs. In NGSCB and La Grande, it is incorporated into the main CPU, thereby avoiding the problem of unencrypted data going over the data bus to the dedicated processor [8]. However, this would require new CPUs that have the encryption/decryption functionality built in. In contrast, TCPA and Wave Systems' Embedded Application Security System (Embassy) move the workload from the CPU to a special-purpose chip.

3.3 Microsoft's NGSCB

Of the three major TC projects, NGSCB is closest to deployment.

Microsoft has not set an official release date for the technology. There had been speculation that it would ship with the next major Windows release, code-named Longhorn, in 2004. However, Mary Jo Foley, editor of the Microsoft Watch newsletter, said NGSCB probably won't appear until the 2006 release of Windows. Details of the technology are in the sidebar "Microsoft's Next-Generation Secure Computing Base" [9].

3.4 Intel's LaGrande

Intel has not issued any technical information on LaGrande and did not respond to requests for comments [10].

From available information, it appears that Intel will integrate LaGrande capabilities into future processors and chipsets. The technology would sandbox numerous risky processes by putting the CPU, chipset, I/O devices, and the graphics processor in an encryption-based security wrapper, as called for by NGSCB.

Rob Enderle, research fellow for the Giga Information Group, a market research firm, said LaGrande and NGSCB have a huge potential to stall the TC market because they would require a major, expensive, and timeconsuming redesign of the OS and microprocessor.

3.5 TCPA

The TCPA—formed in 1999 by Compaq Computer (now part of Hewlett-Packard), HP, IBM, Intel, and Microsoft—calls for creation of a trusted platform module, a motherboard-mounted cryptographic processor with a unique digital signature.

Some models of the IBM ThinkPad T30 high-end laptop use an Atmel processor based partly on TCPA. For example, the processor generates and stores digital certificates and private keys, and provides hardware support for multiple authentication schemes, as well as the encryption and decryption of files on demand.

3.6   Wave Systems' Embassy

Wave Systems' Embassy doesn't get the attention that the other initiatives do, but it's the only TC technology already in a desktop computer: NEC's Packard Bell Secure PC.

Embassy is an open-system hardware and software approach that uses HP's Ver-Secure Framework, a network-encryption system for secure transaction processing. Embassy's primary emphasis is enabling secure ecommerce transactions rather than providing a complete TC environment for PCs. It encrypts financial transactions over the network, rather than securing processes within the PC [11].

In Embassy's model, Integrated Technology Express makes a motherboard chip that handles the RSA encryption duties, Standard Microsystems supplies TC-capable I/O, and VeriSign contributes digital certification services.

4   An Execution Infrastructure for TCB Minimization

Today's popular operating systems run a daunting amount of code in the CPU's most privileged mode. The plethora of vulnerabilities in this code makes the compromise of systems commonplace, and its privileged status is inherited by the malware that invades it. The integrity and secrecy of every application is at risk in such an environment [12].

To address these problems, we propose Flicker, an architecture for isolating sensitive code execution using a minimal Trusted Computing Base (TCB). None of the software executing before Flicker begins can monitor or interfere with Flicker code execution, and all traces of Flicker code execution can be eliminated before regular execution resumes. For example, a Certi_cate Authority (CA) could sign certi-cates with its private key, even while keeping the key secret from an adversary that controls the BIOS, OS, and DMAenabled devices. Flicker can operate at any time and does not require a new OS or even a VMM, so the user's platform for non-sensitive operations remains unchanged.

Flicker depends on attestations composed of cryptographic hashes and digital signatures to allow a remote verifier to ascertain the identity of code that executes with Flicker's protections. We propose a mechanism called Seeing-is-Believing to allow the computer's owner to authenticate the physical identity of her computer, in addition to its digital identity represented in the attestation. This rules out the possibility of successful man-in-the middle or proxy attacks, and reduces the need for trusted third parties that are unavailable today [13].

Flicker provides strong isolation guarantees while requiring the application to trust as few as 250 additional lines of code for its secrecy and integrity. As a result, Flicker circumvents entire layers of legacy system software and eliminates reliance on their correctness for security properties (see Fig. 1). Once the TCB for code execution has been precisely de_ned and limited, formal assurance of both reliability and security properties enters the realm of possibility [14].

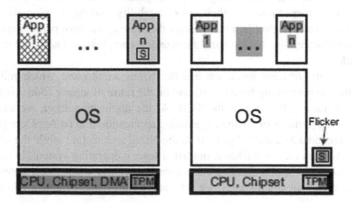

Fig. 1. On the left, a traditional computer with an application that executes sensitive code (S). On the right, Flicker protects the execution of the sensitive code. The shaded portions represent components that must be trusted; other applications are included on the left because many applications run with superuser privileges.

The use of Flicker, as well as the exact code executed (and its inputs and outputs), can be attested to an external party. For example, a piece of server code handling a user's password can execute in complete isolation from all other software on the server, and the server can convince the client that the secrecy of the password was preserved. Such _negrained attestations make a remote party's veri_cation much simpler, since the veri_er need only trust a small piece of code, instead of trusting Application X running alongside Application Y on top of OS Z with some number of device drivers installed. Also, the party using Flicker does not leak extraneous information about the system's software state [15].

To achieve these properties, Flicker utilizes hardware support for late launch and attestation recently introduced in commodity processors from AMD and Intel. These processors already ship with off-the-shelf computers and will soon become ubiquitous. Although current hardware still has a high overhead, we anticipate that future hardware performance will improve as these functions are increasingly used [16].

Attestation technologies potentially pose a risk to users' privacy. Flicker protects users' privacy by including only the code executed during a Flicker session in an attestation, instead of providing information about all software loaded for execution during the current boot cycle [17].

Motivated by our experience with Flicker on today's hardware, we offer suggestions to improve Flicker's performance that leverage existing processor technology, retain security, and improve performance.

5 Reducing TCB Complexity

The large size and high complexity of securitysensitive applications and systems software is a primary cause for their poor testability and high vulnerability. One approach to alleviate this problem is to extract the securitysensitive parts of application and systems software, thereby reducing the size and complexity of software that needs to be trusted.

At the system software level, we use the Nizza architecture which relies on a kernelized trusted computing base (TCB) and on the reuse of legacy code using trusted wrappers to minimize the size of the TCB. At the application level, we extract the security-sensitive portions of an already existing application into an AppCore [18]. The AppCore is executed as a trusted process in the Nizza architecture while the rest of the application executes on a virtualized, untrusted legacy operating system. In three case studies of real-world applications (e-commerce transaction client, VPN gateway and digital signatures in an email client), we achieved a considerable reduction in codesize and complexity.

At the system level, libraries, middleware and kernel also have grown similarly in functionality and size. For example, the X11 window server contains over 1.25 million lines of code. X11 executes with superuser privileges and it has been vulnerable to buffer overflow exploits in the past. A minimal functional configuration of the Linux kernel contains about 200,000 lines of code, and the whole kernel runs in privileged mode ($\times$86 architecture). The Linux kernel too suffers from a host of vulnerabilities including buffer overflow, privilege escalation and security bypass.

5.1 Nizza Architecture

Nizza is a design for a small, secure and generalpurpose platform supporting applications with high security requirements such as digital signatures and banking protocols while preserving the support for legacy code [19].

Figure 2 shows a sketch of the Nizza architecture. Nizza is composed of four major parts: a small kernel; an execution environment consisting of trusted components (such as a name-server and window manager); an untrusted legacy OS with its applications; and security-sensitive applications. In all figures, shaded boxes represent trusted components and plain boxes represent untrusted components.

5.2 Case Studies in Constructing Security-Sensitive Applications

Applications that perform security-sensitive tasks or handle security-sensitive data have to be trusted. Therefore, these applications should be as small and simple as possible, as long as they satisfy the functionality and security requirements. The large size of current application software code (e.g., 1 million lines of code in a browser) makes straightforward porting of existing applications an unattractive solution. The AppCore is then executed as a trusted process, while the rest of the application executes as an untrusted process.

The process of extracting an AppCore from an existing application can be broadly divided into three stages: (1) analysis of the application to identify security-sensitive

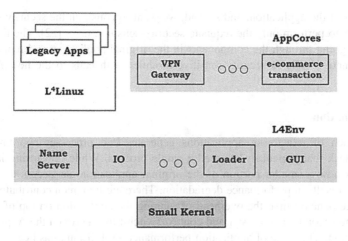

Fig. 2. Overview of the Nizza architecture. Shaded boxes represent trusted components.

components, (2) extracting the identified components and composing them into an AppCore and (3) modifying the original application to use the AppCore for security sensitive tasks [20] (Fig. 3).

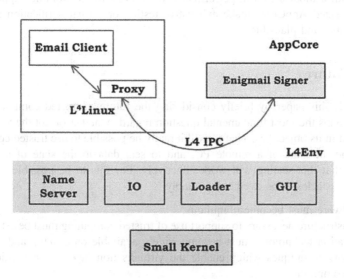

Fig. 3. AppCore for email client

The function of the analysis stage is to identify components that handle security-sensitive data or perform security- sensitive functions. In the next stage, we extract the security-sensitive components and integrate them into a standalone AppCore [21]. There are two factors that control component integration: First, to the greatest extent possible, we want to reuse the interfaces between the security-sensitive components and the rest of the application, and second, we want to constrain the security-sensitive components to perform only the requisite security-sensitive tasks [22]. The final stage consists of going through the components in the original application and replacing the existing function calls to security-sensitive modules with calls to the new AppCore [23].

5.3 Evaluation

Our approach of refactoring applications generates two processes coordinating to perform a task that previously required a single process. While refactoring improves security, as now a smaller portion of the original application has access to sensitive data, it also results in performance degradation. There are two main contributors to the performance penalty: first, the overhead of running the application on top of a virtual machine and second, data transfer and context switch times between the AppCore and the application. The issue of application performance on L4Linux has been addressed in detail in an earlier work. The conclusion was that performance penalty for most applications can be contained within the 5–10% range [24].

We implemented this approach for three real-world applications and found considerable reduction in code size and complexity (few tens of thousands of lines of code for AppCores compared to few hundred thousand lines of code for the current applications), with a modest loss in performance In contrast to "monolithic" applications, the smaller sized AppCores make exhaustive testing or formal verification and validation possible and plausible.

6 The Future

We conclude this paper by briefly considering the future of trusted computing technology. Perhaps the most fundamental question regards whether or not the technology will succeed in its objectives. That is, will it really be possible to use trusted computing to determine the state of a remote PC, and to seal data to the state of a PC with confidence that this sealing will work effectively. For this to be possible requires a number of obstacles to be overcome, notably:

- the hardware must become ubiquitous;
- the infrastructure necessary to support use of trusted computing must be established;
- virtualisation technology must become widely available on desktop and notebook PCs, using techniques which enable the virtualisation layer to be verified using trusted computing.

However, much greater support for trusted computing technology is emerging from the open source community, and from collaborative research projects such as OpenTC and EMSCB. Open source trusted virtualisation layers are being developed by both the Xen and L4 communities. Thus it may well be that open source users will be able to enjoy the benefits of trusted computing based security long before Windows users—we must wait and see!

Acknowledgment. This paper is supported by the National Natural Science Foundation of China under Grant No. 61572153 and the National Key research and Development Plan (Grant No. 2018YFB0803504).

References

1. Balfe, S., Gallery, E., Mitchell, C.J., Paterson, K.G.: Challenges for trusted computing. IEEE Secur. Priv. **6**(6), 60–66 (2008)
2. Balfe, S., Paterson, K.G.: Augmenting internet-based card not present transactions with trusted computing: an analysis. Technical report RHUL-MA-2006-9, Department of Mathematics, Royal Holloway, University of London (2005)
3. Barham, P., et al.: Xen and the art of virtualization. In: Proceedings of the 19th ACM Symposium on Operating Systems Principles (2003)
4. Garfinkel, T., Rosenblum, M., Boneh, D.: Flexible OS support and applications for trusted computing. In: The 9th Workshop on Hot Topics in Operating Systems, HotOS, Lihue, Hawaii, USA, pp. 145–150 (2003)
5. Trusted Computing Group (TCG): TPM Main Specification Version 1.2 rev. 103 (2007)
6. Trusted Computing Group. PC client specific TPM interface specification (TIS). Version 1.2, Revision 1.00. (2005)
7. Brumley, D., Song, D.: Privtrans: automatically partitioning programs for privilege separation. In: USENIX Security Symposium, San Diego, USA, pp. 57–72 (2004)
8. Kuhlmann, D., Landfermann, R., Ramasamy, H., Schunter, M., Ramunno, G., Vernizzi, D.: An open trusted computing architecture—secure virtual machines enabling user-defined policy enforcement (2006)
9. Sadeghi, A.-R., Stüble, C., Pohlmann, N.: European multilateral secure computing base| open trusted computing for you and me, White paper (2004)
10. McCune, J.M., Parno, B., Perrig, A., Reiter, M.K., Isozaki, H.: Flicker: an execution infrastructure for TCB minimization. In Proceedings of the ACM European Conference in Computer Systems (2008)
11. McCune, M., Parno, B., Perrig, A., Reiter, M.K., Seshadri, A.: How low can you go? Recommendations for hardware-supported minimal TCB code execution. In: ASPLOS (2008)
12. Engler, D., Chelf, B., Chou, A., Hallem, S.: Checking system rules using system-specific, programmer-written compiler extensions. In: Proceedings of the 4th Conference on Symposium on Operating System Design and Implementation, vol. 4. USENIX Association (2000)
13. Trusted Computing Group. Trusted platform module main specification. Version 1.2, Revision 94. (2006)
14. Singaravelu, L., Pu, C., Haertig, H., Helmuth, C.: Reducing TCB complexity for security-sensitive applications: three case studies. In: Proceedings of the ACM European Conference in Computer Systems (EuroSys) (2006)
15. Camenisch, J.: Better privacy for trusted computing platforms. In: Proceedings of the European Symposium on Research in Computer Security (ESORICS) (2004)
16. Anderson, D.P., Cobb, J., Korpela, E., Lebofsky, M., Werthimer, D.: SETI@ home: an experiment in public-resource computing. Commun. ACM **45**(11), 56–61 (2002)
17. Clarke, D., et al.: The untrusted computer problem and camera-based authentication. In: Mattern, F., Naghshineh, M. (eds.) Pervasive 2002. LNCS, vol. 2414, pp. 114–124. Springer, Heidelberg (2002). https://doi.org/10.1007/3-540-45866-2_10

18. Garfinkel, T., Pfaff, B., Chow, J., Rosenblum, M., Boneh, D.: Terra: a virtual machine-based platform for trusted computing. In: ACM SIGOPS Operating Systems Review, vol. 37, pp. 193–206. ACM (2003)
19. Brumley, D., Song, D.: Privtrans: automatically partitioning programs for privilege separation. In: Proceedings of USENIX Security Symposium (2004)
20. Garnkel, T., Pfa, B., Chow, J., Rosenblum, M., Boneh, D.: Terra: a virtual machine-based platform for trusted computing. In: Proceedings of the Symposium on Operating System Principles (2003)
21. Kauer, B.: OSLO: improving the security of trusted computing. In: Proceedings of the USENIX Security Symposium (2007)
22. Trusted Computing Group. Trusted platform module main specification, Part 1: Design principles, Part 2: TPM structures, Part 3: Commands. Version 1.2, Revision 103 (2007)
23. Sadeghi, A.R., Selhorst, M., Stüble, C., Wachsmann, C., Winandy, M.: TCG inside?: A note on TPM specification compliance. In: Proceedings of the First ACM Workshop on Scalable Trusted Computing, pp. 47–56. ACM (2006)
24. Datta, A., Franklin, J., Garg, D., Kaynar, D.: A logic of secure systems and its application to trusted computing. In: 2009 30th IEEE Symposium on Security and Privacy, pp. 221–236. IEEE (2009)

Address Allocation Scheme Based on Local MAC Address

Xinran Fan[1(✉)], Ting Ao[2], and Zhengyou Xia[1]

[1] College of Computer Science and Technology,
Nanjing University of Aeronautics and Astronautics, Nanjing 210016, China
xr.fan@nuaa.edu.cn
[2] Zhongxing Telecommunication Equipment Corporation, Nanjing 210016, China

Abstract. Virtualization and scale expansion in cloud data center result in sharp MAC address consumption which also expose some weaknesses in MAC address. The concept of local MAC address is proposed by IEEE standards organization to solve the limitation in traditional MAC address. In order to realize the automatic allocation of the local MAC address, we put forward two address allocation schemes which is appropriate for infrastructured network and ad-hoc network respectively. Our first scheme is a centralized management scheme which needs the usage of an address allocation device, while the other one is a distributed allocation scheme which is more suitable in wireless network without infrastructures. We simulate these two schemes based on OPNET and make an analysis on them. The results shows, our two schemes are feasible in different environment.

Keywords: Cloud computing · Virtualization · Local MAC address
Address allocation scheme · OPNET simulation

1 Introduction

With the rapid development of cloud computing, enterprises are adept to run their server applications in data center, which provide them with a large amount of computational and storage resources. NIST defines cloud computing [1] as a model for enabling ubiquitous, convenient, on-demand network access to a shared pool of configurable computing resources that can be rapidly provisioned and released with minimal management effort or service provider interaction. In Wikipedia [2], cloud computing is defined as a type of Internet-based computing that provides shared computer processing resources and data to computers and other devices on demand.

Virtualization, as one of the most important fundamental technologies in cloud computing, has been introduced into data center. By establishing a virtualized layer, such technology manages to provide system resources for higher layer while allocating various tasks to underlying physical resources [3] which tackling problem of how to allocate resources efficiently and dynamically. However, as each virtual machine has a global unique MAC address, the visualization

© Springer Nature Switzerland AG 2018
X. Sun et al. (Eds.): ICCCS 2018, LNCS 11063, pp. 263–274, 2018.
https://doi.org/10.1007/978-3-030-00006-6_23

of servers, storage and network has brought exponential growth of virtual facilities, which results in sharp consumption of MAC address.

In fact, the extensive use of visualization devices expose some shortcomings of MAC address. Firstly, the life cycle of MAC address assignment is permanent. Numerous virtualized devices in the data center will occupy too much MAC address space and work out it rapidly. Secondly, MAC address cannot·provide location information as it is a kind of one-dimensional address [4]. Last but not least, the current content addressable memory (CAM) which storing forwarding tables cannot match the growth rate of table length [5,6] with the fast growth of virtual devices. As a result, broadcast storm will happen once the data start to overflow.

To solve the problems discussed above, many new address structures are proposed, such as EUI-64 [7], Zonal [8], MOOSE [9], etc. And IEEE standards organization has proposed a concept of local MAC address, which is no longer the global unique 48-bit address but is locally used in local area network. This local MAC address is defined in IEEE802C standard and can be divided into three different formats, MA-L, MA-M and MA-S. Instead of burning in the hardware, the local MAC address is freely distributed within the local area network. Therefore, an allocation mechanism is necessary to ensure all the hosts in the cloud data center can get address automatically at the start.

The focus of our research is to assign the local MAC address effectively and reliably in the cloud data center. Considering the universal usage in different network environment, we propose two address allocation schemes which is appropriate for wired network and infrastructureless network respectively. The centralized scheme can avoid the problem of address confliction, while the distributed scheme is especially useful in the wireless network where the topology frequently changes. We have also simulated these two schemes based on OPNET and made a comparison between them.

2   Related Works

To deal with several challenges caused by the traditional MAC address as shown above, the local MAC address is proposed and is assigned dynamically through certain mechanisms. Several of researchers have proposed their schemes of dynamic address assignment, which ensure devices get address automatically.

In MOOSE (Multilevel Origin-Organized Scalable Ethernet) architecture [9], each switch selects an initial address during startup and then implements collision detection to deal with duplicated addresses caused by random address selection. Once the switch receives a frame from a different port with the record in forwarding table during start-up, the switch will send a unicast frame to ascertain whether the collision happened. If conflict exists, collision resolution program will send a frame to the recently found conflict switch indicating it should change its address. The MOOSE switch address allocation scheme is easy to implement but is also easy to cause address confliction.

DAC (generic and automatic address configuration for data center networks) [10] proposes a general solution that address can be automatically assigned in any structure of data center network, such as Portland, VL2 and DCell. DAC uses bottom-up approach to collect physical topology information and builds a tree based on a fixed node. It abstracts the device-to-logical ID mapping to the graph isomorphism (GI) problem [11] in graph theory, and then disseminates the logical ID using Logical ID Dissemination Protocol. Ultimately, every node acquires its own logical ID. Although this approach has universal applicability, applying this solution to practical work poses considerable challenges and has a great difficulty when solving GI problem.

ZigBee network [12] calculates distributed address blocks for every potential parent nodes via using four parameters: network depth, network max depth, network max children and max routers. Then each parent node makes use of its block to allocate addresses for its children nodes. The IDs are guaranteed to be unique within the network through this approach. However, it is possible to waste address because nodes distribution is uneven while address blocks assigned to parent nodes are fixed. It will happen that some parents dont have enough block space and others barely use their address blocks in the meanwhile.

Ali et al. [13] propose a distributed node address naming scheme based on cluster sensor network architecture. The scheme puts forward that the best number of members of each cluster is 16 based on the theory that optimal number of cluster heads should be 6% [14]. Accordingly, they use 4-bit address space to assign address for sensor nodes in each cluster. In order to maintain collision-free state, it requires the 4-bit allocated address of each new added node must satisfy the uniqueness within the cluster. Besides, two more bits are allocated to distinguish higher address for layer to layer communication. Although this scheme can allocate hierarchical address for nodes, the length of the address increases with the growing scale of network and it can be too long to manage.

3 Centralized Address Allocation Scheme

The first scheme we proposed is a centralized address allocation scheme, an address allocation server is required to centrally distribute and manage the local MAC address for devices in the local network. Different with the traditional centralized scheme, we propose that the server proactively distributes the available local address blocks to the network at regular intervals. In this way, the host does not need to generate a temp address at the very beginning and the server can assign addresses for multiple hosts at the same time. Our centralize allocation scheme can be divided into the following stages, address release and request, address approval and confirmation. The process can be simply depicted in the Fig. 1.

3.1 Address Release and Request

Initially, the server selects several consecutive available MAC addresses from its address pool and encapsulates them into the address release frame which will

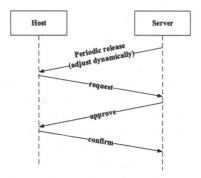

Fig. 1. Centralized address allocation.

broadcast to the network later. Specifically, the address pool consists of a group of available local MAC addresses, as well as four types of attributes, which is free, temporary, approved and formal.

After then, all the hosts without local address in the network will accept the address block released from server. Each host randomly selects an address from the block as its temporary local MAC address and then sends an address request frame to the server with the temporary address as the source address. However, multiple hosts may select the same address and generate confliction. Therefore, feature information is necessary for each device to distinguish the identity. The method to generate feature information is by concatenation of identity information (e.g. host name, CPU serial number, etc.) and one-byte random number.

3.2   Address Approval and Confirmation

The server may receive a large number of address request frames in a short time after release, including that several frames request for the same address. To avoid confliction, the server only approves the first arrival frame applying for a certain address. That will be conducted through address attributes, more specifically, the address is only available if its attributes is 'temporary'. If a frame with its requested address satisfying the conditions above, the server will reply an approval frame and update the related address attribute (i.e. from temporary to approval).

When a host receives an approval frame, it will check the feature information first to make sure that it is consistent with its own feature. If so, the host gets local MAC address successfully and responds a confirmation to server at once. Otherwise, the address has been occupied for others, thus the host should discard its temporary local MAC address and wait for the next round of address release. Figure 2 shows the procedure of the scheme.

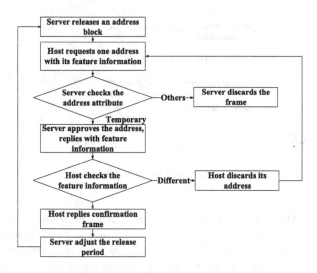

Fig. 2. Procedure of centralized scheme.

4   Distributed Address Allocation Scheme

Our second proposal is a distributed address allocation scheme in the wireless network without infrastructure. In this scheme, devices apply for the local MAC address from the neighboring nodes through broadcasting address request messages. Upon obtaining local address, the device will generate an address pool automatically and start to assign addresses for other nodes. Thus this scheme is hierarchical address allocation and is also point-to-point address allocation. The scheme can be divided into two stages, applying for the local address from the surrounding nodes, and generating address pool to assign addresses for other nodes.

4.1   Apply for the Local MAC Address

Address application program will be launched for every node without local address during the startup, and Fig. 3 is a schematic diagram showing the general steps to obtain address.

Initially, the device broadcasts an address request message to the surrounding nodes with a random address as the source address. The random address can be generated by concatenation of its feature information (e.g. host name) and a random number. The surrounding host will select an available address from its address pool once it receives a request message, and then reply it to the source device. If no address is available, no response will be sent. The address pool includes three types of address attributes which is free, temporary and formal.

The device may receive many responses after broadcasting request message, and it selects a local address according to the priority. The factors influent priority is the level of provider, the degree of trust with the provider and the

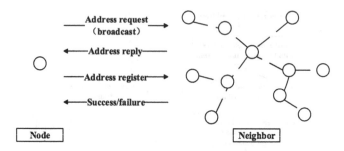

Fig. 3. Distributed address allocation.

response time. After then, the device sends a register frame to the provider with the selected address as its temporary local address. The provider will judge whether the registered address is legal through checking its attribute (i.e. should be temporary). Once the device receives a success message from the provider, it obtains the formal local MAC address successfully. Contrarily, if a failure message is arrival, then it will discard its temporary local address and apply for a new one. Figure 4 is a flow chart to depict the process.

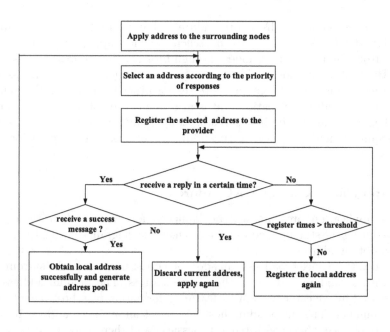

Fig. 4. Apply for the local MAC address.

4.2   Generate an Address Pool

Once the local MAC address is obtained, the device will generate its own address pool automatically according to the hierarchical address format, and provide addresses for the nodes applying for local address. In this way, a parent-child relationship can be established and a hierarchical structure can be formed in the whole network.

The hierarchical address format is consist of three parts (depicted in Fig. 5), in which high address is inherited from the parent, 8-bit allocation part is ranged from 0×00 to 0xFF, and the low address is all zero. Thus, the method to generate a consecutive address segment is to make a one-byte allocation bit based on the original local MAC address from the first non-zero bit. For example, if the local MAC address of a device is 0X1000, it will generate an address segment from 0X1-01-0 to 0X1-FF-0, which contains 255 available local addresses.

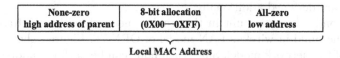

Fig. 5. Hierarchical address format.

Initially, 15 hosts are picked out as the first-level device by the administrator, and their local addresses are set as [0X1...0, 0XF...0]. After assigned address by the first-level device, the node becomes a second-level device and generates an address segment in the same way. By analogy, each device will generate an address segment. Depending on the length of different types of the local MAC address, the network can reach different maximum depths. For example, for the local address in MA-L format which is 24 bits, the network can reach a maximum depth of 4 layers.

5   Performance Evaluation

In this section, we evaluate the performance of the above two address allocation schemes using OPNET Modeler 14.5 for simulation.

5.1   Simulation Setup

We build two different network models for the two schemes. We build different scenarios representing different scales of the simulation system. Specifically, the number of the nodes without address is set to 50, 100, 200, 500 and 1000.

For the first scheme, the simulation model is built in LAN based on the built-in Ethernet model of OPNET. Figure 6(a) and (b) shows different scenarios of the network model. Devices involved in this scheme include client, address allocation

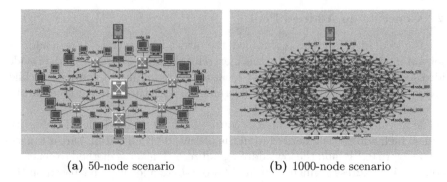

(a) 50-node scenario   (b) 1000-node scenario

Fig. 6. Example of network model in the centralized scheme.

server and switch. Among them, the switch is built-in bridge model, while client and server are designed additionally.

The second scheme is built in the wireless network without infrastructure, based on the build-in wireless LAN model of OPNET. Figure 7 shows different scenarios of the network model. Since each node can be both the address applier and provider, all the devices in network share the same node model similar to the Fig. 6(a). Figure 8 is the process model.

For both of the simulations, the address allocation related message is encapsulated in the data field of the second layer frame. In order to analyze and compare them better, all the simulation parameters are set to be the same. The data rate is set to 10 Mbps for both two schemes.

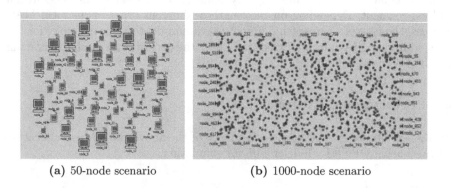

(a) 50-node scenario   (b) 1000-node scenario

Fig. 7. Example of network model in the distributed scheme.

5.2 Simulation Results Analysis

For both of the two schemes, we collect four performance indicators, including end to end delay, packet drop number, network traffic and allocation time.

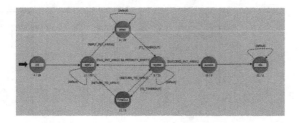

Fig. 8. Process model of address allocation.

Initially, we measure ETE delay in different scenarios, which is shown in Fig. 9(a) and (b). From the diagram, the delay increases and reaches a peak with the process of allocation, and then shows a gradual decline after the end of allocation. The delay in distributed scheme is almost 10 times longer than the centralized scheme with the peak value around 0.014 s in 1000-node scenario, and 0.0002 s within 200 nodes.

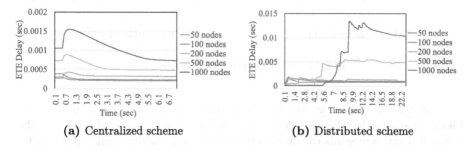

(a) Centralized scheme   **(b)** Distributed scheme

Fig. 9. ETE delay in two schemes.

Subsequently, we evaluate the packet drop number in the whole network during the address allocation. From Fig. 10(a) and (b), the larger of the network, the more packets are discarded. But the packet drop number is small in both two schemes, with the peak value of 3 packets in the centralized scheme and 2 packets in the distributed scheme. The result illustrates the network runs well in our two schemes.

Then, we analysis the traffic of the whole network for the two schemes. From the result of centralized scheme in Fig. 11(a), the traffic is proportional to the number of nodes, with a max value around 0.25 million bits per second in 1000-node scenario. On the other side, the distributed scheme shares a similar shape of traffic, but the traffic is much larger than the centralized scheme, with the peak value around 1.4 million bits per second. Considering our data rate is 10 million bits per second (10 mbps), the load of the network is not high.

272   X. Fan et al.

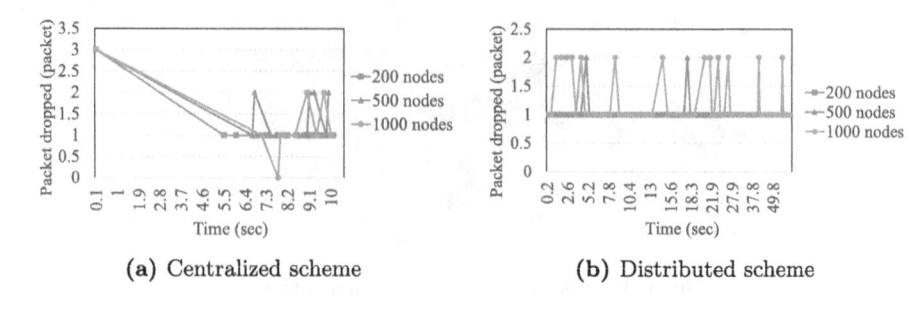

(a) Centralized scheme   **(b)** Distributed scheme

Fig. 10. Packet drop number in two schemes.

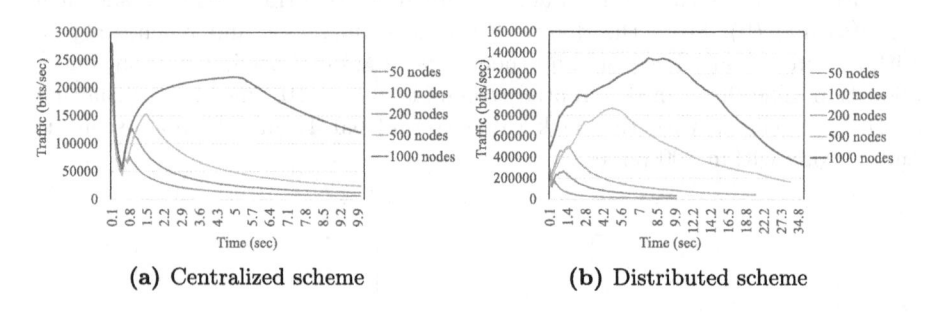

(a) Centralized scheme   **(b)** Distributed scheme

Fig. 11. Network traffic in two schemes.

Last but not least, we compare the allocation time of the two schemes. Figure 12 shows the average allocation time in different scales of network. The horizontal axis represents the number of nodes without address, and all the nodes apply for local addresses in the beginning. From the result, the allocation time of the two schemes is much similar in the small scale of network, but the distributed one experiences a sharp increase with the expansion of network. In the 1000-node scenario, the distributed scheme even takes about 10 s to get address, which is almost five times longer than the centralized one.

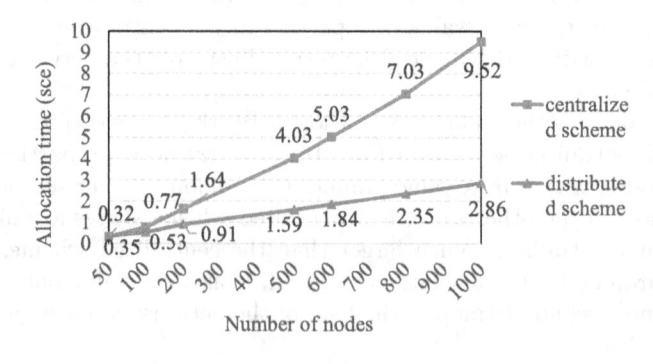

Fig. 12. Allocation time.

From the results above, we can conclude that the centralized scheme has a better performance in the large scale of network, with smaller delay, traffic and allocation time. For the distributed scheme, since the high collision of the wireless network, and the use of CSMA/CA brings high delay, the performance is not so good in the large data center.

6 Summary and Future Work

In this paper, we have presented a centralized and a distributed address allocation scheme, which is appropriate for infrastructured network and ad-hoc network respectively. We build network model, node model and process model for both of the two schemes in the simulation as required using OPNET. Additionally, we run each scheme in five scenarios with different scales of network separately, and make a comparison between them. From the simulation result, the centralized scheme has an advantage in the large data center with smaller delay, smaller traffic and less allocation time. However, the distributed scheme is available in ad-hoc network which does not need to maintain an extra allocation server. Thus, if the ad-hoc network is not so large, as shown in the simulation, the distributed scheme is recommended, while our centralized scheme can still perform well in the large scale of wired network.

In the future work, we plan to improve our distributed scheme in the large ad-hoc network, since the allocation time is so long and performance is not very good with the expansion of network. Additionally, information security will also be taken into account, in order to avoid some network attacks such as false address attack.

Acknowledgements. This paper was financially supported by the industrial-academic-research cooperation project-New type of MAC address control and self-adaptive technique research-from ZTE Corporation whose project number is 2015ZTE04-14.

References

1. Mell, P., Grance, T.: The NIST definition of cloud computing. Commun. ACM **53**(6), 50 (2011)
2. Cloud computing. https://en.wikipedia.org/wiki/Cloud-computing
3. R, Y., D, H.: KVM: Principles and Practices. China Machine Press (2013)
4. IEEE Standard for Local and metropolitan area networks: Media Access Control (MAC) Bridges, pp. 1–277. IEEE (2004)
5. Yu, F., Katz, R.H., Lakshman, T.V.: Efficient multimatch packet classification and lookup with TCAM. IEEE Micro **25**(1), 50 (2005)
6. Pagiamtzis, K., Sheikholeslami, A.: Content-addressable memory (CAM) circuits and architectures: a tutorial and survey. IEEE J. Solid-State Circ. **41**(3), 712–727 (2006)
7. Guideline for use of EUI. http://standards.ieee.org/develop/regauth/tut/eui64.pdf. Accessed 21 Mar 2017

8. Making Room for IEEE 802 Protocols in the Local Space. http://www.ieee802.org/1/files/public/docs2014/new-p802c-marks-LocalSpaceUse1114.pdf. Accessed 21 Mar 2017

9. Scott, M., Moore, A., Crowcroft, J.: Addressing the Scalability of Ethernet with MOOSE. In: DC CAVES Workshop (2010)

10. Chen, K., et al.: Generic and automatic address configuration for data center networks. In: ACM SIGCOMM Conference, pp. 39–50. ACM (2010)

11. McKay, B.D.: Practical graph isomorphism. J. Symb. Comput. **60**(1), 94–112 (2014)

12. Alliance, Z.B.: Zigbee specification. Technical report Document 053474r06, Version 1.0, ZigBee Alliance (2015)

13. Ali, M., Uzmi, Z.A.: An energy efficient node address naming scheme for wireless sensor networks. In: Proceedings of the International Networking and Communications Conference (INCC), pp. 25–30. IEEE (2004)

14. Heinzelman, W.B.: Application-specific protocol architectures for wireless networks. Massachusetts Institute of Technology (2000)

An Approach Based on Value Revision to Activity Recognition

Zhengguo Zhai[1], Yaqing Liu[1,2,3,4], Xiangxin Wang[1],
and Yu Jiang[2(✉)]

[1] School of Information Science and Technology, Dalian Maritime University,
Dalian, China
[2] College of Computer Science and Technology, Jilin University, Changchun,
China
jiangyu2011@jlu.edu.cn
[3] Artificial Intelligence Key Laboratory of Sichuan Province, Sichuan University
of Science and Engineering, Zigong, China
[4] Nanjing University of Information Science and Technology, Nanjing, China

Abstract. In recent years, activity recognition has attracted extensive attention and been applied in many areas including smart home, healthcare, energy saving, etc. A number of approaches for activity recognition have been proposed. However, the dispersion of values of run sensors imposes negative effect on activity recognition. In this paper, an approach based on value revision is proposed to recognize the activities of a resident. First, the time and the total duration that each sensor is run are calculated as sensor attributes in an activity record. Second, the start time, end time and duration of an activity record are extracted from a set of activity records as activity attributes. Third, the information gains of attributes are calculated to filter attributes which have low the information gains. Fourth, values of attributes of tested activity records are replaced with the most similar values of attributes of activity records of training dataset. Finally, classifiers are exploited to recognize daily activities. This paper validates the recognition of daily activities in two datasets by comparing the proposed approach and a previous approach. The results demonstrate that the proposed approach favourably outperforms previous approach.

Keywords: Information gain · Activity recognition · Sensors
Machine learning

1 Introduction

In recent years, activity recognition has attracted extensive attention and been applied in many areas including smart home, healthcare, energy saving, etc. In smart home, activity recognition is employed to reminder an accident which is prone to happen to a single resident. In healthcare application, activity recognition is employed to detect abnormal activity of an elderly people. In energy saving, energy, e.g. water, electricity can be saved effectively by recognizing activity of users.

Over the last decade, there has been considerable research on activity recognition. This research can be divided into three categories, depending on the method of activity

X. Sun et al. (Eds.): ICCCS 2018, LNCS 11063, pp. 275–284, 2018.
https://doi.org/10.1007/978-3-030-00006-6_24

detection. The first method is based on video cameras fixed in rooms [1]. Activities are recorded by the cameras, and activities are recognized by analysing the video recordings. However, the side effect is that the resident's privacy is compromised. The second method is based on wearable devices [2]. Residents are required to wear monitoring devices, and their activities are recorded by the devices in real time. Although this method protects the resident's privacy, wearing the devices is an extra burden. The third category is based on sensors [3–5] that are placed in various rooms. The resident's activities will activate a sequence of sensors. For example, "washing" will activate the sensors that are fixed in taps. In this manner, a resident not only has privacy protection but is also freed from wearing extra devices. Hence, the method based on sensors is increasingly popular.

Substantial effort has been expended on activity recognition [6, 7]. Most researchers have tried to introduce machine learning into their approaches. Some have employed time-series models to recognize activities, e.g., the Hidden Markov Model (HMM) [8–10] or Conditional Random Fields (CRF) [11–13]. The commonality of these approaches is that the order of activities and the order of sensor events are emphasized. However, time series models usually have poor robustness [14]. For instance, the daily order of a resident's activities is not always the same. For a single activity, the order of sensor events often changes. Further, the order of one resident's activities is different from that of another. To improve robustness, researchers exploit static classifiers for activity recognition, e.g., Naive Bayesian (NB) [15], Support Vector Machine (SVM) [16–19], etc. However, the result of activity recognition is undesirable. The dispersion of values of sensors disturbs classifiers. The durations and the frequencies of identical sensor vary with activity records even if these activity records have same activity label. The durations and the frequencies of identical sensor are dispersive. But, they are usually similar if activity records have same activity label. For instance, the durations of sensor "Toilet_Flus" are "280 min" and "272 min" in two activity records of activity label "Toileting". To improve the accuracy of activity recognition, we propose an approach based on value revision to activity recognition. First, durations and frequencies of sensors are selected according information gain of them. Second, durations or frequencies of test dataset are replaced with the most similar values of training dataset. Finally, classification is done.

The remainder of this paper is organized as follows: first, some terminologies are defined. Then, the proposed approach is described. Next, we validate the proposed approach and discuss the results. Finally, we introduce related work and conclude by summarizing our findings.

2 Terminologies

To represent the proposed approach well, some terminologies are defined in advance. For clarity, a segment of activity records is shown in Table 1. Throughout this manuscript, $\Omega = \{sn1, sn2, ..., snN\}$ is used to represent set of activity instances.

Table 1. A segment of activity record.

Activity	Start time of activity	End time of activity	Sensor	Start time of sensor	End time of sensor
Bathing	20:41:35	21:32:50	Toilet_Flush	20:51:52	21:05:20
			Sink_faucet_hot	20:51:58	20:52:05
			Closet	20:53:36	20:53:43
			Light_switch	20:53:49	21:21:43
			Shower_faucet	20:53:52	20:58:42
			Freezer	20:58:22	20:58:32
			Shower_faucet	20:58:43	21:06:09
			Medicine_cabinet	21:05:23	21:05:45
			Medicine_cabinet	21:05:46	21:18:55
			Cabinet	21:05:47	21:05:49

Definition 1. For an activity a, ai = (an, al, sh, eh, ad) is said to be an activity instance. al is the activity number of ai. al is the activity label of ai. sh is the start hour of ai. eh is the end hour of ai. ad is the duration of ai.

In Table 1, ai = (1, "Bathing", "20", "21", "51 min") is an activity instance of activity "Bathing".

Definition 2. For an activity instance ai and a sensor s, si = (ai.an, sn, sd, sf) is said to be a sensor instance of ai. sn is the name of s. sd is the total duration of s. sf is the frequency of s. SSIai is used to represent set of sensor instances of ai.

In Table 1, (1, "Light_switch", "28 min", 1) is an sensor instance of activity "Bathing". (1, "Shower_faucet", "13 min", 2) is another sensor instance.

Algorithm 1 is employed to calculate initial dataset according to set of activity instances.

Algorithm 1.

Input: SAI, set of activity instances.

Output: D, initial dataset.

1. for each ai=(an, al, sh, eh, ad) in SAI
2.   ar←((sn1,0), (sn2,0) ,..., (snN,0), (an,sh), (an,eh), (an,ad))
3.   for each (ai.an, sn, sd, sf) in SSIai
4.   replace tuple (sn, 0) of ar with (sn, sd/sf)
5.   end for
6.   D←D∪{ar}
7. end for
8. return D

---

3   The Proposed Approach

The proposed approach is introduced as follow.

Step1: For each a $\in$ A, calculate the information gain of a according to formula (1). For a given threshold α, only keep the attribute a whose information gain is greater than α.

Step2: For kept attribute set A*, build set aTra = {t.a}, where t $\in$ PTra and a $\in$ A* holds.

Step3: For each tes $\in$ PTes and each a $\in$ A*, replace tes.a with v* if tes.a $\notin$ aTra and $\forall$v' $\in$ aTra,|v'-tes.a| > |v*-tes.a|holds.

$$\mathbf{IG(T)} =$$
$$- \sum_{i=1}^{n} \mathbf{P(C_i)log_2 P(C_i)} + \mathbf{P(t)} \sum_{i=1}^{n} \mathbf{P(C_i|t)log_2 P(C_i|t)} + \qquad (1)$$
$$\mathbf{P(\bar{t})} \sum_{i=1}^{n} \mathbf{P(C_i|\bar{t})log_2 P(C_i|\bar{t})}$$

Our hierarchical temporal-spatial model is shown in Fig. 2. The raw data set is composed of a number of sensor records written in sequence of sensor runtime. The first task is to generate a set of activity records based on the raw data set. The activity record set is split into a training data set and a test data set in some proportion. The training and test data sets are clustered according to the tuples so, eo and u of each activity record. Algorithm 2 is executed to find an optimal alignment between the clusters of the training data set and those of the test data set. Finally, a classifier is used to recognize activity records in each corresponding cluster pair of test and training data sets.

4   Experiments

This section describes two independent experiments performed on two datasets. The two datasets were taken from the "single-resident apartment data" provided by Winona State University, US [20]. "single-resident apartment data" was collected from ten apartments, "hh102", "hh104", "hh107", "hh115", "hh116", "hh117", "hh118", "hh122" "hh123" and "hh124". Datasets "hh102" and "hh104" were used to validate the recognition of daily activities by comparing the hierarchical temporal-spatial ("ST") and single spatial ("SS") models for accuracy. The Naive Bayesian (NB), k-Nearest Neighbour (KNN), Supported Vector Machine (SVM) and Random Forest (RF) classifiers were employed to recognize activities. The threshold α is set to 0.01. Each validation was taken as a 10-fold cross validation.

4.1   Experiment

Experiment was performed on dataset "hh102". The details of data set "hh102" are displayed in Table 2. Ninety-seven sensors were fixed in the apartment. They were divided into battery-level sensors, magnetic-door sensors, light-switch sensors, light sensors, infrared-motion sensors, wide-area infrared-motion sensors and temperature sensors. Thirty activities were considered in the data set. The raw data set included

413142 sensor records. The activity data set included 2087 activity records. In our experiment, 5 activities were selected to test the proposed approach: "Bathing" ("B"), "Toileting" ("T"), "Going_out_to_work" ("G_o_t_w"), "Preparing_Breakfast" ("P_B"), "Doing_laundry" ("D_l"). 951 activity records were used.

Table 2. Description of dataset 1.

Sensors	Activity	Raw sensor records	Raw activity records	Selected activity	Selected activity records
97	30	413142	2087	12	951

Algorithm 2.

Input: PTra, training set

    PTes, initial test set

A, set of attributes.

Output: PTes, revised test set of activity records.

1. G←∅

2. for each a in A

3.   calculate the information gain of a, ga.

4.   if ga≥α then

5.   G←G∪{(a,ga)}

6.   end if

7. end for

8. ATra←∅

9. for each (a,ga) in G

10.   aTra←∅

11.   for each tra in PTra

12.   aTra←aTra∪{tra.a}

13.   end for

14.   ATra ←ATra∪{aTra}

15.end for

16.for each (a,ga) in G

17.   for each tes in PTes

18.   if tes.a∉aTra then

19.   replace tes.a with $v^* \in$ aTra, where $\forall v' \in$ aTra, $|v'\text{-tes.a}| > |v^*\text{-tes.a}|$ holds

20.   end if

21.   end for

22.end for

23.return PTes

• NB classifier

The accuracies of activity recognition of the NB classifier are displayed in Table 3 and Fig. 1. "SS" had an average accuracy of 0.6 and "ST" had an average accuracy of 0.74; "ST" was higher than "T" in average accuracy. In addition to the average, there were 9 activities in which "ST" had accuracies higher than "SS". In contrast, there were only 3 activities in which "SS" was higher than "ST". The higher accuracies are underlined in Table 3.

Table 3. Accuracies of activity recognition on dataset 1 when using classifier NB.

	B	T	G_o_t_w	P_b	D_l
A	0.389	0.512	1	0.643	0.263
P	0.5	0.81	1	0.714	0.526

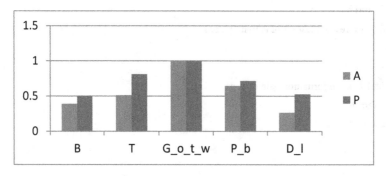

Fig. 1. Accuracies of NB in recognizing activities for dataset 1

• kNN classifier

The accuracies of activity recognition for the kNN classifier are displayed in Table 4 and Fig. 2. "SS" had an average accuracy of 0.66, and "ST" had an average accuracy of 0.73. "ST" was still higher than "SS" in average accuracy. In addition, there were 7 activities for which "ST" was higher than "SS". In contrast, there were 4 activities for which "SS" was higher than "ST".

Table 4. Accuracies of activity recognition on dataset 1 when using classifier kNN.

B	T	G_o_t_w	P_b	D_l
0.167	0.738	0.333	0.357	0.421
0.278	0.762	0.833	0.571	0.632

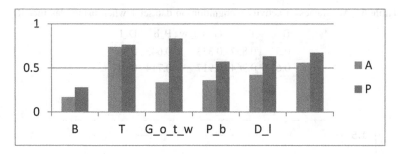

Fig. 2. Accuracies of KNN in recognizing activities for dataset 1

- SVM classifier

The accuracies of activity recognition for the J48 classifier are displayed in Table 5 and Fig. 3. "SS" had an average accuracy of 0.7 and "ST" had an average accuracy of 0.74. "ST" was still higher than "SS" in terms of average accuracy. In addition, there were 9 activities for which the accuracies of "ST" were higher than "SS". In contrast, there were only 3 activities for which "SS" was higher than "ST".

Table 5. Accuracies of activity recognition on dataset 1 when using classifier SVM.

B	T	G_o_t_w	P_b	D_l
0	0.929	0.583	0	0.105
0	0.917	0.75	0	0.105

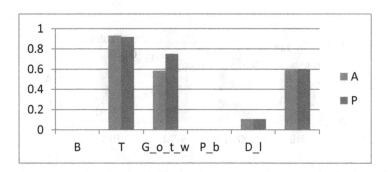

Fig. 3. Accuracies of SVM in recognizing activities for dataset 1

- RF classifier

The accuracies of activity recognition for the RF classifier are displayed in Table 6 and Fig. 4. "SS" had an average accuracy of 0.75, and "ST" had an average accuracy of 0.8. "ST" was higher than "SS" in average accuracy. In addition, there were 8 activities for which the accuracy of "ST" was higher than that of "SS". In contrast, there were 4 activities in which "SS" was higher than "ST".

Table 6. Accuracies of activity recognition on dataset 1 when using classifier RF.

B	T	G_o_t_w	P_b	D_l
0.5	0.857	0.333	0.643	0.368
0.611	0.964	0.917	0.714	0.947

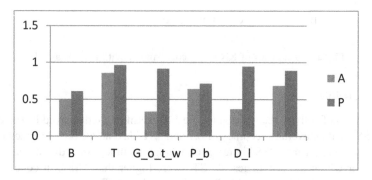

Fig. 4. Accuracies of RF in recognizing activities for dataset 1

4.2 Summary

The accuracies of activity recognition are displayed in Figs. 5 and 6. For each of the four classifiers, "P" was higher than "A" in average accuracy. RF had a higher average accuracy than other classifiers.

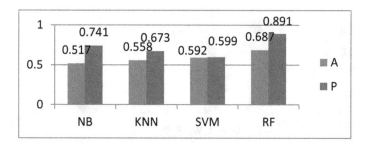

Fig. 5. Average recognition accuracies of four classifiers for dataset 1

As shown in Table 6, "ST" achieved an accuracy of 0.11 on activity "B" and 0.33 on "T_M", which are lowest of all accuracies. As shown in Table 7, most activity records of "B" were incorrectly labelled as "G" or "T". Most activity records of "T_M" were incorrectly labelled as "T". Incorrect labelling is explained as follow. First, there were few activity records for each of "B" (36 records) and "T_M" (24 records). These numbers were far less than the average of 80. Fewer activity records meant that the features of the activities were difficult to obtain adequately. Hence, "B" and "T_M"

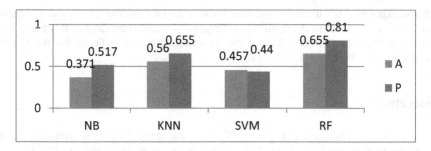

Fig. 6. Average recognition accuracies of four classifiers for dataset 2

have low accuracies. Because "Bath" is usually in "Toilet", most sensors for each activity are common to both. Hence, "Bath" is prone to be labelled as "Toilet". Because "Bath" is also tightly related to "Groom", "Bath" is prone to be labelled as "Groom".

Table 7. Recognition details of activities "B" and "T_M" for "ST" on data set "hh102".

	B	G	T_M	T	W_B_D	W_T
B	4	12	0	19	0	1
T_M	0	0	8	15	1	0

As shown in Table 7, "ST" achieved an accuracy of 0.08 on activity "P" and 0 on "T_M", which are lowest of all accuracies. As shown in Table 8, most activity records of "P" were incorrectly labelled as "W_O_C". Most activity records of "T_M" were incorrectly labelled as "T". "T_M" was incorrectly labelled for similar reasons. Activity "P" had only 13 activity records, far less than the average number, 93. Fewer activity records leads to low accuracy. In addition, "Phone" and "Computer" were placed in the table so that "P" was prone to be labelled as "W_O_C".

Table 8. Recognition details of activities "P" and "T_M" for "ST" on data set "hh104".

	S_O_O_B	E_M	D	C_D	P	T	W_O_C
P	1	0	1	1	1	2	7
T_M	0	1	0	0	0	11	0

5 Conclusions

To better aid elderly people by using context-aware services, this paper proposes a hierarchical temporal-spatial model for the activity recognition of a single resident. To validate the proposed model, naïve models were used for comparison in two experiments, each of which was performed to recognize twelve daily activities. The results show that the hierarchical temporal-spatial model outperforms the naïve spatial model, both in accuracy of individual activities and average accuracy.

Acknowledgments. We thank all reviewers for their useful comments to improve the paper. This work was supported by the Open Project Program of Artificial Intelligence Key Laboratory of Sichuan Province (2016RYJ01) and the Fundamental Research Funds for the Central Universities (NO. 3132016348, 3132018194).

References

1. Mccowan, I., Gatica-Perez, D., Bengio, S., et al.: Automatic analysis of multimodal group actions in meetings. IEEE Trans. Pattern Anal. Mach. Intell. **27**(3), 305–317 (2005)
2. Wang, L., Gu, T., Tao, X., et al.: Recognizing multi-user activities using wearable sensors in a smart home. Pervasive Mob. Comput. **7**(3), 287–298 (2011)
3. Wan, J., O'Grady, M.J., O'Hare, G.M.P.: Dynamic sensor event segmentation for real-time activity recognition in a smart home context. Pers. Ubiquit. Comput. **19**(2), 287–301 (2015)
4. Shen, J., Tan, H., Wang, J., Wang, J., Lee, S.: A novel routing protocol providing good transmission reliability in underwater sensor networks. J. Internet Technol. **16**(1), 171–178 (2015)
5. Xie, S., Wang, Y.: Construction of tree network with limited delivery latency in homogeneous wireless sensor networks. Wireless Pers. Commun. **7**(1), 231–246 (2014)
6. Benmansour, A., Bouchachia, A., Feham, M.: Human activity recognition in pervasive single resident smart homes: state of art. In: Proceedings of 12th International Symposium on Programming and Systems, IAlgiers, Algeria, p. 276 (2015)
7. Benmansour, A., Bouchachia, A., Feham, M.: Multioccupant activity recognition in pervasive smart home environments. ACM Comput. Surv. **48**(3), 1–36 (2015)
8. Kabir, M.H., Hoque, M.R., Thapa, K., et al.: Two-layer hidden Markov model for human activity recognition in home environments. Int. J. Distrib. Sens. Netw. **2016**, 15 (2016)
9. Sarkar, A.M.J.: Hidden Markov mined activity model for human activity recognition. Int. J. Distrib. Sens. Netw. **2**, 1–8 (2014)
10. Singla, G., Cook, D., Schmitter, E.M.: Recognizing independent and joint activities among multiple residents in smart environments. J. Ambient Intell. Hum. Comput. **1**(1), 57–63 (2010)
11. Chen, R., Tong, Y.: A two-stage method for solving multi-resident activity recognition in smart environments. Entropy **16**(4), 2184–2203 (2014)
12. Tong, Y., Chen, R., Gao, J.: Hidden state conditional random field for abnormal activity recognition in smart homes. Entropy **17**(3), 1358–1378 (2015)
13. Tong, Y., Chen, R.: Latent-dynamic conditional random fields for recognizing activities in smart homes. J. Ambient Intell. Smart Environ. **6**(1), 39–55 (2014)
14. Bourobou, S.T.M., Yoo, Y.: User activity recognition in smart homes using pattern clustering applied to temporal ANN algorithm. Sensors **15**(5), 11953–11971 (2015)
15. Cook, D., Schmitter-Edgecombe, M.: Assessing the quality of activities in a smart environment. Meth. Inf. Med. **48**(5), 480–485 (2009)
16. Wen, X., Shao, L., Xue, Y., Fang, W.: A rapid learning algorithm for vehicle classification. Inf. Sci. **295**(1), 395–406 (2015)
17. Yin, J., Yang, Q., Pan, J.J.: Sensor-based abnormal human-activity detection. IEEE Trans. Knowl. Data Eng. **20**(8), 1082–1090 (2008)
18. Gu, B., Sheng, V.S., Wang, Z., Ho, D., Osman, S., Li, S.: Incremental learning for v-support vector regression. Neural Netw. **67**(C), 140–150 (2015)
19. Gu, B., Sheng, V.S., Tay, K.Y., Romano, W., Li, S.: Incremental support vector learning for ordinal regression. IEEE Trans. Neural Netw. Learn. Syst. **26**(7), 1403–1416 (2015)
20. Cook, D., Crandall, A., Thomas, B., Krishnan, N.: CASAS: a smart home in a box. IEEE Comput. **46**(7), 62–69 (2013)

An Encryption Traffic Analysis Countermeasure Model Based on Game Theory

Xiangsong Gao[1], Hui Lu[2], Xiang Cui[2], and Le Wang[2(✉)]

[1] Institute of Computer Application, China Academy of Engineer Physics,
Mianyang 621900, China
nmbdc@live.cn
[2] Cyberspace Institute of Advanced Technology, Guangzhou University,
Guangzhou 510006, China
{luhui,cuixiang,wangle,tianzhihong}@gzhu.edu.cn

Abstract. With the development of network technologies, the proportion of encrypted traffic in cyberspace is increasing. This phenomenon directly leads to the increasingly challenging management and control of network traffic. The research on encrypted traffic analysis and monitoring at this stage has become an important direction. Based on game theory, this paper proposes a countermeasure model in the detection of encrypted traffic and expounds the key elements of the model. Finally, we will present a detailed analysis of the pay and benefits between the two sides of the game.

Keywords: Game theory · Encrypted traffic · Cyber confrontation

1 Introduction

Network security has always been a complex and difficult problem. All network security research has been devoted to finding some perfect methods to solve the threats and hidden dangers in cyberspace. Since many years ago, game theory has entered the field of view of researchers [1–9]. Especially in the establishment of cyber confrontation model, game theory shows its consistency with this direction [10–19].

Among many network security problems, the analysis of encrypted traffic has become an urgent problem to be solved [20, 21]. At this stage of the cyberspace, encrypted traffic is increasing rapidly. Specifically, 2017 encrypted traffic increased by more than 90% compared to 2016. In the website traffic, encrypted traffic in 2015 accounted for only 21%. In 2016, the website's encrypted traffic exceeded 40%. It is predicted that by 2019, encrypted traffic in cyberspace will be no less than 80% [22].

These data are all heralding a serious problem: all the ongoing activities in cyberspace and all the trends in cyberspace will become indistinguishable for everyone. This does not seem to be "hard" to the average user, but it is a fatal problem for telecommunications service providers, public security agencies and network regulators. When no one can promptly respond to activities that take place in cyberspace, and no one can alert some of the trends that appear in cyberspace, the cyberspace that was

X. Sun et al. (Eds.): ICCCS 2018, LNCS 11063, pp. 285–292, 2018.
https://doi.org/10.1007/978-3-030-00006-6_25

already in danger will become even more chaotic, and the already precarious network Space security will become even more nonsense.

In response to this grim situation, domestic and foreign researchers have also conducted research on encrypted traffic analysis in recent years. The paper [23] proposed a method to classify encrypted traffic based on deep learning technology that has recently become a topic. In addition, paper [24] further proposes context-based malware traffic identification. And for specific encrypted traffic identification, the paper [25] is a good example. It gives a recognition method based on the random forest algorithm in machine learning technology for the specific flow generated by a specific program. However, in the face of the complex and volatile situations in the cyber-space and the huge amount of active traffic, the cost of encrypted traffic analysis will be a factor that is hard to ignore.

Some researchers have already begun to study the application of game models in cyberspace security issues, among which the DDoS attacks are more widespread. The paper [26] uses game theory to model both the DDoS attack and defense. The performance of the strategy was evaluated quantitatively. Paper [27] proposes an auction theory based on game theory and proposes a model against the DDoS attacks in the network.

This paper will break away from the concrete technology and method. Starting from the game theory and introduce a confrontation model for encrypted traffic analysis in cyberspace. Based on this model, we describe the pay and benefits in encrypted traffic analysis. In Sect. 2, we introduce the model based on the theory of game theory. Some specific analysis of this model will be carried out in Sect. 3. In the fourth section, we will summarize the paper.

2   Encrypted Traffic Analysis Countermeasure Model

The game refers to a description of the strategic interaction between opposing, or co-operating, interests where the constraints and payoff for actions are taken into consideration. In a game, it contains the following elements: player, action, pay-off and strategy [28]. Next, we describe these factors in the game model of the application of the encrypted traffic analysis in the confrontation scenario.

2.1   Player

Player refers to the entity that makes an action decision in the game. It can be a person or a group of person, programs, and machines.

There are two players in this model proposed in this paper, and the two parties to the confrontation are defined as players. One of them is the generator of encrypted traffic, or the user. The other is an analyst of encrypted traffic. We assume that the generator of encrypted traffic wants the encrypted traffic generated by them to be covert, that is, the encrypted traffic cannot be identified. In contrast, encrypted traffic analysts will try to identify the specific encrypted traffic generated by the other party in the ocean of traffic.

Overall, the model is defined for the player collection as follows:

$$P = \{G, A\} \tag{1}$$

Between them, G represents the encrypted traffic generator and A represents the encrypted traffic analyzer.

2.2   LSTM-RNN

Strategy refers to the action plan that each player can choose. The confronting parties in the model proposed in this paper each have their own set of strategy: the encrypted traffic generator G can choose to impose different levels of traffic confusion on the encrypted traffic. Here we describe it as a level of con-fusion from 0 to 4 for a total of 5 levels. The greater the degree of confusion, the higher the concealment of the encrypted traffic generated by it, i.e., the more difficult it is to identify. Encrypted traffic analysts can choose to apply different levels of analysis to the monitoring traffic. Here we describe it as a five-level analysis method from 0 to 4. The larger the value, the greater the analysis strength. The higher the accuracy of the analysis, the easier it is to identify the encrypted traffic generated by the encrypted traffic generator. The number 0 means that no measures will be implemented.

Overall, the model's strategy set for the player is defined as follows:

$$S_G \in \{0, 1, 2, 3, 4\} \tag{2}$$

$$S_A \in \{0, 1, 2, 3, 4\} \tag{3}$$

S_G and S_A represent the policy sets of G and A, respectively.

2.3   Payoff

Payoff is a very important element of the game, it reflects the player's positive or negative benefits in the implementation of a strategy in the game.

In the model presented in this paper, we define the payoff of the encrypted traffic generator G as follows:

$$U_G(s_G, s_A) = \left(100 - \frac{s_A}{s_G + 1} \cdot 20\right) - s_G^2 \tag{4}$$

In contrast, the payoff of encrypted traffic analyzer A is as follows:

$$U_A(s_G, s_A) = \frac{s_A}{s_G + 1} \cdot 20 - s_A^2 \tag{5}$$

Here s_G and s_A represent the strategies chosen by G and A, respectively, and we have:

$$s_G \in S_G, s_A \in S_A \tag{6}$$

Table 1 shows the payoff combinations that the opposing parties achieve in all possible combinations of strategy choices. The ordered pairs of real numbers in its cells represent the payoff of encrypted traffic generator G and encrypted traffic analyzer A, respectively.

Table 1. Pay-off matrix

A's Strategy G's Strategy	0	1	2	3	4
0	100, 0	80, 19	60, 36	40, 51	20, 64
1	99, 0	89, 9	79, 16	69, 21	59, 24
2	96, 0	89.3, 5.7	82.7, 9.3	76, 11	69.3, 10.7
3	91, 0	86, 4	81, 6	76, 6	71, 4
4	84, 0	80, 3	76, 4	72, 3	68, 0

About the formula in payoff calculation:

$$\frac{s_A}{s_G + 1} \cdot 20 \tag{7}$$

It represents the reward on both sides of the encrypted traffic that was successfully identified when particular strategies are token. The other part, s2, represents the cost of both parties when implementing specific strategies. This is easy to understand: For encrypted traffic generators, confusion means increased computing and traffic, network bandwidth consumption, and increased network latency, which may be undesirable for encrypted traffic generators; for encrypted traffic analysts, the analysis of huge network traffic requires a lot of investment, and the increase of money and technology costs is inevitable.

3 Model Analysis

3.1 Classification

In this model proposed in this paper, the opposing parties know each other's strategy sets and their corresponding payoff, but obviously they do not know what actions the other party will take. In game theory, this is a typical Complete Information Game, which is different from the Perfect Information Game. In the latter, each party in the game can know the actions taken by all other players. Go is a typical Perfect Information Game. At the same time, the model proposed in this paper is still a one-shot game. That is to say, both sides need to decide their own strategy and take action at the same time, and this game has only one step. In game theory, we call it Static/Strategic

Game. It is distinguished from the Dynamic/Extensive Game, which requires the player to make multiple stages of decision making. In the same way, go is also a typical Dynamic/Extensive Game [28].

3.2   Iterative Deletion of Dominated Strategies

We mentioned in previous section that for a game model, payoff is a crucial element. The key to analyzing a game model is also boils down to how to choose the strategy that can maximize the benefits.

We first give the definition of Strictly Dominated Strategy: Player i's strategy s_i' is strictly dominated by player i's strategy s_i if

$$u_i(s_i, s_{-i}) > u_i(s_i', s_{-i}) \text{ for all } s_{-i} \tag{8}$$

Here s_{-i} stands for a choice for all except player i. Similarly, we also give the definition of Weakly Dominated Strategy: Player i's strategy s_i' is weekly dominated by player i's strategy s_i if

$$u_i(s_i, s_{-i}) \geq u_i(s_i', s_{-i}) \text{ for all } s_{-i} \tag{9}$$

$$u_i(s_i, s_{-i}) > u_i(s_i', s_{-i}) \text{ for some } s_{-i} \tag{10}$$

Obviously, whether strict or not, the dominated strategy is an option that any player should avoid because it always brings the worst payoff to the player. On the basis of game theory, there is such a conclusion: never choose strictly dominated strategies [29].

Based on this principle, we return to the game model proposed in this paper. By observing and calculating Table 2-1, we find that for encrypted traffic analyzer A, policy 0_A is a strictly dominated strategy. This also makes sense in common sense: If an encrypted traffic analyst does not make any effective analysis, he must have nothing to gain. As a rational player, the opposing parties know this, and the encrypted traffic analyzer's strategy 0_A is removed from the strategy set.

On this basis, observe and calculate all payoffs again. For the encrypted traffic generator G, the policy 0_G is not a dominated strategy, but as a rational player, he knows that the rational player A will not choose the strictly dominated strategy 0_A. Once 0_A is removed from the strategy set, for G, strategy 0_G becomes a weakly dominated strategy. In this case, the strategy 0_G is also eliminated as a dominated strategy. This is one step in the iteration deletion of dominated strategies. It assumes that each player is rationally involved in the game, and each iteration is based on a common knowledge. In the above analysis, "Strategy 0_A is a strictly dominated strategy and thus it will not be selected" is a common knowledge.

3.3 Best Response

Let's give the definition of Best Response: Player i's strategy $\hat{s}_i$ is a best response to the strategy s_{-i} of another players if

$$u_i(\hat{s}_i, s_{-i}) \geq u_i(s_i', s_{-i}) \quad \text{for all } s_i' \text{ is } S_i \tag{11}$$

or

$$\hat{s}_i \text{ solves } \max_{s_i}\{u_i(s_i, s_{-i})\} \tag{12}$$

Obviously, it's not wise to choose non-best response strategies because they are not always the best payoff for the player. There is also such a conclusion in the game theory foundation: Do not choose a strategy that is never a best response to any other's strategy [9].

Continuing to observe Table 2-1. For the encrypted traffic generator G, the best response to 1_A is 2_G, the best response to 2_A is 2_G, the best response to 3_A is 2_G or 3_G, and the best response to 4_A is 3_G. Then strategies 1_G and 4_G are removed from S_G.

Now for every rational player, "G will never choose strategy 1_G and 4_G" becomes a common knowledge. In this case, same to the principle of iteration deletion of dominated strategies, after the strategies 1_G and 4_G are eliminate. For encrypted traffic analyzer A, the best response to 2_G is 3_A and the best response to 3_G is 2_A or 3_A. Then strategies 1_A and 4_A are removed from S_A.

3.4 Nash Equilibrium

According to the two principles mentioned in this section, the strategy sets of the two parties are filtered iteratively. In the end, there will be only one strategy in the candidate strategy set for each other. This is the so-called Nash Equilibrium. Nash Equilibrium means that the players are playing a best response to each other, the opposing parties are not willing or will not easily change their strategic choices.

The model proposed in this paper has a Nash equilibrium: $(2_G, 3_A)$. At this time, the payoff of the two parties is:

$$u_G(2_G, 3_A) = 76 \tag{13}$$

$$u_A(2_G, 3_A) = 11 \tag{14}$$

4 Summary

For increasingly complex cyberspace and explosively increasing encrypted traffic, this paper discusses the possibility of game theory application and encrypted traffic analysis against this scenario from the perspective of game theory. And proposes a specific game model to detailed discussion and analysis.

We envisage that the future work should concentrate on improving and demonstrating the game model. In particular, the quantification of payoff and strategy still requires more detailed and in-depth study.

Acknowledgment. This paper is supported by the National Natural Science Foundation of China under Grant No. 61572153 and the National Key research and Development Plan (Grant No. 2018YFB0803504).

References

1. Myerson, R.B.: Game Theory: Analysis of Conflict. Harvard University Press, p. 1. Chapter-preview links, pp. vii–xi (1991)
2. Bellhouse, D.: The Problem of Waldegrave. Journal Électronique d'Histoire des Probabilités et de la Statistique **3**(2), 1–12 (2007)
3. Madison, J.: Vices of the Political System of the United States, April 1787
4. Screpanti, E., Zamagni, S.: An Outline of the History of Economic Thought, 2nd edn. Oxford University Press, Oxford (2005)
5. Kim, S.: Game theory applications in network design, p. 3. IGI Global, Hershey (2014)
6. Mirowski, P.: What were von neumann and morgenstern trying to accomplish? In: Weintraub, E.R. (ed.) Toward a History of Game Theory, pp. 113–147. Duke University Press, Durham (1992). ISBN 0-8223-1253-0
7. Leonard, R.: Von Neumann, Morgenstern, and the Creation of Game Theory. Cambridge University Press, New York (2010). ISBN 9780521562669
8. Owen, G.: Game Theory: Third Edition. Emerald Group Publishing, Owen, Guillermo, p. 11 (1995). ISBN 0-12-531151-6
9. Roy, S., Ellis, C., et al.: A survey of game theory as applied to network security. In: IEEE. Proceedings of the 43rd Hawaii International Conference on System Sciences, pp. 1–10 (2010)
10. Manshaei, M.H., Zhu, Q., Alpcan, T., et al.: Game theory meets network security and privacy. ACM Comput. Surv. **45**(3), 1–39 (2013)
11. Alazzawe, A., Nawaz, A., Bayaraktar, M.M.: Game theory and intrusion detection systems (2006). http://theory.stanford.edu/~iliano/courses/06S-GMUISA767/project/papers/alazzawe-mehmet-nawaz.pdf
12. Alpcan, T., Baser, T.: A game theoretic analysis of intrusion detection in access control systems. In: Proceedings of the 43rd IEEE Conference on Decision and Control (2004)
13. Alpcan, T., Baser, T.: An intrusion detection game with limited observations. In: Proceedings of the 12th International Symposium on Dynamic Games and Applications (2006)
14. Bloem, M., Alpcan, T., Basar, T.: Intrusion response as a resource allocation problem. In: IEEE Conference on Decision and Control (2006)
15. Bursztein, E., Goubault-Larrecq, J.: A logical framework for evaluating network resilience against faults and attacks. In: Cervesato, I. (ed.) ASIAN 2007. LNCS, vol. 4846, pp. 212–227. Springer, Heidelberg (2007). https://doi.org/10.1007/978-3-540-76929-3_20
16. Bush, G.W.: National strategy to secure cyberspace, office of the president (2003)
17. Carin, L., Cybenko, G., Hughes, J.: Quantitative evaluation of risk for investment efficient strategies in cybersecurity: The queries methodology. IEEE Computer (2008)
18. Chen, Z.: Modeling and defending against internet worm attacks. Ph. D. Dissertation at Georgia Institute of Technology (2007)

19. President's Information Technology Advisory Committee, Cyber Security: A crisis of prioritization (2005)
20. White, A.: Practical Analysis of Encrypted Network Traffic. Dissertations & Theses – Gradworks (2015)
21. Anderson, B., McGrew, D.: Machine learning for encrypted malware traffic classification: accounting for noisy labels and non-stationarity. In: ACM SIGKDD International Conference on Knowledge Discovery and Data Mining (KDD) (2017)
22. CISCO. Encrypted Traffic Analytics [R/OL] (2017)
23. Lotfollahi, M., Zade, R.S.H., et al.: Deep Packet: A Novel Approach for Encrypted Traffic Classification Using Deep Learning [J/OL] (2017)
24. Anderson, B., McGrew, D.: Identifying encrypted malware traffic with contextual flow data. In: ACM. Proceedings of the 2016 ACM Workshop on Artificial Intelligence and Security, pp. 35–46 (2016)
25. Deng, Z., Liu, Z.: The random forest based detection of shadowsock's traffic. In: 2017 IEEE 9th International Conference on Intelligent Human-Machine Systems and Cybernetics, pp. 75–78 (2017)
26. Liu, P., Zang, W., Yu, M.: Incentive-based modeling and inference of attacker intent, objectives, and strategies. ACM Trans. Inf. Syst. Secur. 8(01), 1–41 (2005)
27. Xu, J., Lee, W.: Sustaining availability of web services under distributed denial of service attack. IEEE Trans. Comput. 52(04), 195–208 (2003)
28. Osborne, M.J., Rubinstein, A.: A Course in Game Theory. MIT Press, Cambridge (1994)
29. Slantchev, B.L.: Game Theory: Dominance, Nash Equilibrium, Symmetry. Department of Political Science, University of California, San Diego (2008)

An Image Retrieval Technology Based on Morphology in Cloud Computing

Gui Liu[✉], Jianhua Yao, and Zhonghai Zhou

Jiangnan Institute of Computing Technology, Wuxi, Jiangsu, China
lgzhy@163.com

Abstract. In recent years, with the rapid development of computer network technology, the number of various multimedia data, including image data information, has increased rapidly. How to efficiently retrieve these image information and extract information from users in large amounts of image data efficiently and accurately has become a key issue in the field of information retrieval. The improvement of traditional algorithm of image retrieval is difficult to solve a series of problems such as massive data storage, computation and transmission. As a new computing model, cloud computing has a very important role in promoting the development of image retrieval. In this paper, image edge information is extracted by morphological method, and image retrieval is done as image shape feature. It solves the problem of poor edge detection by traditional methods. These features are extracted by the cloud computing platform of Hadoop, which can effectively improve the performance of image retrieval.

Keywords: Image retrieval · Feature extraction · Morphology
Hadoop · Cloud computing

1 Introduction

Screening out the message the users need from a huge source of information, especially image information, is one of the ways to solve the problem [1]. Content based image retrieval technology has become a hot topic in current research.

Shape is a very important visual content in images. It is one of the key information necessary for people to identify objects, and it is also one of the relatively difficult to describe image characteristics.

The image edge can express the basic shape of the image, which contains the rich inner information of the image. It is an important description method of the image shape feature. Therefore, the effect of image edge detection has a direct impact on the results of image retrieval.

The traditional edge detection methods mainly include Roberts operator, Sobel operator, Prewitt operator, Laplace operator, Canny operator and so on. The common problem of these methods is that the noise interference is very sensitive and the noise resistance performance is poor.

However, the actual processing images usually contain noise, and most of the traditional edge detection algorithms are difficult to resist the influence of noise. And

© Springer Nature Switzerland AG 2018
X. Sun et al. (Eds.): ICCCS 2018, LNCS 11063, pp. 293–302, 2018.
https://doi.org/10.1007/978-3-030-00006-6_26

generally, the noise is amplified in the process of edge detection to the image, and the calculation process is more complex.

In view of this situation, it is of great significance to find an algorithm which can effectively suppress noise and maximize the details of image edges [7]. Mathematical morphology [3, 5] is an emerging disciplines in the field of digital image processing. It has been widely applied in the fields of edge detection, shape recognition, image restoration and enhancement [6]. Aiming at the problem of poor edge detection in traditional methods, we use morphological method to extract image edge information as image shape feature for image retrieval, and then extract these features, so as to effectively improve the performance of image retrieval.

2   Image Feature Extraction Technology Based on Shape

Image feature extraction is the premise of content based image retrieval. There are many ways to express the image features.

In a broad sense, it can be divided into two categories: text-based features and low-level visual features. Shape feature is a very important visual content in the image, and it is one of the key information that people need to recognize objects.

Because human vision is not very sensitive to the rotation, scaling and displacement of objects, it often requires the expression of shape features to satisfy the invariance of rotation, zoom and displacement, which is also the difficulty of shape-based image retrieval.

At present, the description of shape feature can be divided into two categories: based on regional characteristics and boundary-based representation. The shape of the regional feature is the use of gray distribution information within the region, the main expression of the area, the center of gravity, centrifugal rate and shape invariant moment method.

Boundary feature shape is the shape edge information of the image, the expression method of edge curve, Fourier describes, edge direction histogram. Here we simply introduce two commonly used methods: the moment invariants and the histogram of the edge direction.

2.1   Moment Invariants

Moment is a rough feature obtained by finding and calculating all points in the region. In general, we define the (P, q) moment of an area of an image I (x, y) as follows:

$$m_{pq} = \sum_{(x,y)\in R} I(x,y)x^p y^q$$

Then, the definition of the central moment of the (P, q) order and the normalized center moment are as follows:

$$\mu_{pq} = \sum_{(x,y)\in R} I(x,y)(x-x_{avg})^p (y-y_{avg})^q$$

$$\eta_{pq} = \mu_{pq}/m_{00}^{(p+q)/2+1}$$

$$x_{avg} = m_{10}/m_{00}$$

$$y_{avg} = m_{01}/m_{00}$$

The moment invariants of Hu are computed by the linear combination of the higher moments of normalized centers moments. The obtained moment functions are invariant to image scaling, rotation and mirror mapping. The concrete formula is as follows:

$$h_1 = \eta_{02} + \eta_{20}$$

$$h_2 = (\eta_{02} - \eta_{20})^2 + 4\eta_{11}^2$$

$$h_3 = (\eta_{30} - 3\eta_{12})^2 + (3\eta_{21} - \eta_{03})^2$$

$$h_4 = (\eta_{12} + \eta_{30})^2 + (\eta_{03} + \eta_{21})^2$$

$$h_5 = (\eta_{30} - 3\eta_{12})(\eta_{12} + \eta_{30})\left[(\eta_{12} + \eta_{30})^2 - 3(\eta_{21} + \eta_{03})^2\right]$$
$$+ (3\eta_{21} - \eta_{03})(\eta_{03} + \eta_{21})\left[3(\eta_{12} + \eta_{30})^2 - (\eta_{03} + \eta_{21})^2\right]$$

$$h_6 = (\eta_{20} - \eta_{02})\left[(\eta_{12} + \eta_{30})^2 - (\eta_{21} + \eta_{03})^2\right] + 4\eta_{11}(\eta_{12} + \eta_{30})(\eta_{03} + \eta_{21})$$

$$h_7 = (3\eta_{21} - \eta_{03})(\eta_{30} + \eta_{12})\left[(\eta_{12} + \eta_{30})^2 - 3(\eta_{21} + \eta_{03})^2\right]$$
$$+ (3\eta_{12} - \eta_{03})(\eta_{03} + \eta_{21})\left[3(\eta_{12} + \eta_{30})^2 - (\eta_{03} + \eta_{21})^2\right]$$

2.2 Edge Direction Histogram

The edge direction histogram feature extraction method is a method of description based on boundary. Edge oriented histogram feature extraction is a shape description method based on boundary, which is a shape edge feature extraction method based on the theory of edge detection. The core idea is to express the shape information of the image by using the direction information of the edge pixels of the image. Therefore, the effect of early edge detection will affect the result of image feature extraction to a great extent.

The process of edge direction histogram extraction is that: first, edge detection is applied to extract the edge of image. Then, for each edge pixel, the direction angle of the edge point normal vector is calculated according to the gradient direction of the point in the image as follows:

$$\theta(x,y) = tan^{-1}[I(x,y+1) - I(x,y-1)]/[I(x+1,y) - I(x-1,y)]$$

The range of θ values obtained by this calculation is $[-\pi, \pi]$. In order to facilitate the expression and reduce the amount of computation and statistics of color histogram, we also need to quantify the value of θ and calculate the histogram of the edge direction of one dimension. That is:

$$His(k) = N \times Prob(K = k)$$

Here, N is the total number of edge pixels of all edges, and His can be understood as a one-dimensional array of K length, which is used to store the edge direction histogram feature vectors of the image. When we normalize it, we can make the shape feature scale invariable.

2.3   Extraction of Image Edge Feature Information by Morphological Algorithm

The image edge can express the basic shape of the image, which contains the rich inner information of the image. It is an important description method of the image shape feature. In this paper, we use morphological algorithm to extract image edge feature information, and then describe it by boundary histogram. Finally, we calculate the similarity distance based on histogram intersection algorithm for image retrieval.

Image Edge Extraction

Edge detection is a very important basis for image analysis, such as image segmentation, target area recognition and region shape extraction. The traditional edge detection methods mainly include Roberts operator, Sobel operator, Prewitt operator, Laplace operator, Canny operator and so on. However, the common problem of such methods is that it is very sensitive to noise interference and low noise performance. In order to solve the problem of poor edge detection in traditional methods, we use morphological method to extract image edge information.

First of all, we introduce three basic morphological edge detection operators, which are defined as follows:

Expansive edge detection operator:

$$G_1(x,y) = (f \oplus s)(x,y) - f(x,y) \tag{2.3.1}$$

Corrosion type edge detection operator

$$G_2(x,y) = f(x,y) - (f \ominus s)(x,y) \tag{2.3.2}$$

Expansion corrosion type edge detection operator (morphological gradient operator)

$$G_2(x,y) = (f \oplus s)(x,y) - (f \ominus s)(x,y) \tag{2.3.3}$$

In which $G(x,y)$ is the detected edge function, $f(x,y)$ is the input gray level image, $s(i,j)$ is the given structure element.

Morphological edge detection algorithm is to select clear structural elements and use morphological expansion, erosion, opening and closing operations and combination of these operations to achieve image processing, so as to get clear image edges. On the basis of the basic morphological edge operators, this paper uses a multi-structure and multi-scale adaptive morphological edge detection algorithm. The multi-structure elements are used as: $s_1 = [0\ 0\ 0;\ 1\ 1\ 1;\ 0\ 0\ 0]$, which are used to detect the horizontal direction edge of the image. $s_2 = [0\ 1\ 0;\ 0\ 1\ 0;\ 0\ 1\ 0]$, which is used to detect the vertical edge of the image; $s_3 = [0\ 0\ 1;\ 0\ 1\ 0;\ 1\ 0\ 0]$ and $s_4 = [1\ 0\ 0;\ 0\ 1\ 0;\ 0\ 0\ 1]$, which is used to detect two diagonal edges of the image. The large scale structure element is derived from the small scale structure element expansion operation, that is, $ns = \underbrace{s \oplus s \oplus \ldots \oplus s}_{n}$, $s = [0\ 1\ 0;\ 1\ 1\ 1;\ 0\ 1\ 0]$. Then the multi-structure and multi-scale edge detection operator can be obtained by 2.3.3.

$$E(x, y) = \sum_{i=1}^{4} \omega_i E_{fi}(x, y) + \sum_{j=1}^{3} \lambda_j E_{cj}(x, y) \qquad (2.3.4)$$

The $E_{fi}(x, y)$ and $E_{cj}(x, y)$ are the edge information extracted by the structural elements of different directions and scales, namely, $E_{fi}(x, y) = (f \oplus s_i)(x, y) - (f \ominus s_i)(x, y)$ and $E_{cj}(x, y) = (f \oplus js)(x, y) - (f \ominus js)(x, y)$, while ω_i and λ_j are their respective weight coefficients respectively.

The Implementation of the Algorithm
The implementation steps of the image retrieval algorithm based on the morphological edge operator are as follows.

The image edge detection is realized by multi-structure and multi-scale morphological edge detection algorithm, and the edge direction histogram is used.

Normalization of the edge orientation histogram information of each image is then stored into the image feature database in the form of feature vector, which is used as the shape feature information of the image.

Extract the shape feature information of the query image, match it in the image feature database according to the histogram intersection method, and then rank the matching results according to the size, and return the smallest N image as the retrieval result to the user.

Based on the above algorithms, still using the original image database experiments, selection of geometrical plane images as a sample image is analyzed respectively by the traditional image edge detection operator retrieval algorithm and the comparison algorithm based on morphological methods. We find that because of using morphological algorithm to extract the edges is more clearly and coherently, and the noise inhibition ability is stronger. Therefore, the retrieval efficiency of image retrieval algorithm based on this algorithm is much better than that of traditional edge detection operators, and effectively improves the performance of image retrieval.

3 Image Retrieval Based on Hadoop

Image data of all fields is growing rapidly, and the feature extraction data for retrieval of these images is also increasing. The traditional ways of image retrieval are to process and extract the image by single machine and single thread.

Then, the image feature extraction data are stored in the relational database, and the characteristics of the query image are compared with the whole library features by traversing the relational database, and the results are sorted and compared.

This way of processing single machine and single thread is obviously a drop in the rapid development of image data. Even through the multi-thread technology can not solve the problem of storage and processing efficiency of massive images.

With the rise of the concept of large data and the maturity of storage and processing technology, the use of Hadoop technology can not only solve the problem of storage and data transmission of massive images, but also can directly transplant the original image retrieval algorithm to parallel processing in a distributed environment, and relies on the parallel computing power of MapReduce cluster to achieve massive image retrieval [8].

Hadoop is a Java implementation of Google Map/Reduce [2] and GFS (GoogleFile System). It is a framework for running distributed applications on large scale common cluster computers. For a large file, Hadoop cuts it into blocks of size 16 MB–64 MB (Block). These Block are distributed on different nodes in the form of regular files. In this way, data security and reliability can be achieved.

Hadoop consists of two core elements: the bottom Hadoop Distributed File System (HDFS distributed file system), and the Map/Reduce engine for distributed computing. HDFS is the cornerstone of distributed computing, which uses a Master/Slave structure and consists of a NameNode and multiple DataNode. NameNode coordinates the user's access to the file, and the DataNode is responsible for the data storage. The principle is to split a complete file into multiple blocks (Block), each of which is stored in the disk of the data node respectively. HDFS provides a unified namespace that allows users to access HDFS like a single file system.

In the distributed image retrieval technology, the main work of data processing is the extraction of image features, the establishment of index and matching images [4].

3.1 Image Feature Extraction

The key to improve the speed of image processing is multi-node parallel processing. As shown in the Fig. 1, every node calls the local image for Map processing, that is, extracts the image features. After rearranging the processing results, the nodes are transferred to Reduce nodes in the form of (key, value) for subsequent processing. The actual steps are as follows:

The mass image distribution is stored in each DataNode in the HDFS system. Hadoop is the default input data in the text file, but saving the image files and ordinary files are not the same. So it needs to process images by implementing the Hadoop interface. This paper adopts HIPI image processing interface, using the class of CreateHipi and ImageBundh to process massive images into HIB files and DAT files.

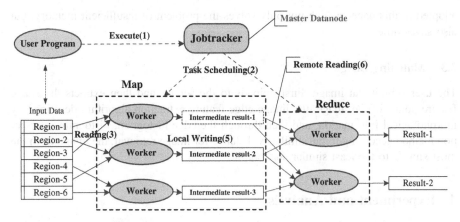

Fig. 1. Image feature extraction map-reduce parallel running framework

Write a distributed processing program. The job of Map is to extract the shape feature of the images and output it to Reduce by key value pair (image file identifier and feature point description). The job of Reduce is to output the same Key value, that is, the feature point of the same image.

With HIB file as input, the client submits the image feature extraction task to the master controller JobTracker, which distributes the task to the TaskTracker of each DataNode of the cluster, and each TaskTracker calls the image on the local DataNode to process.

3.2 Establish Index

There may be thousands of feature points in an image. Each feature point is represented by a 128 dimensional vector. If we want to do similarity computation with the feature library, the complexity is very high. In this paper, we get the class center after clustering by K-Means algorithm. K-Means algorithm is a classical clustering algorithm in data mining technology. The algorithm uses iterated update idea to cluster the clustering points into K classes.

The traditional way of clustering is to load characteristic data into memory, but when data volume is large, the algorithm is likely to have insufficient memory allocation during operation. Another way is to implement the algorithm by using the idea of batch loading and whole clustering, and limit the number of loading each time, then deal with a batch and release a batch. This method solves the memory problem, but it is too time-consuming. The distributed K-Means clustering algorithm is adopted in this paper, which not only solves the problem of insufficient memory, but also saves time.

The traditional way of clustering is to load characteristic data into memory, but when data volume is large, the algorithm is likely to have insufficient memory allocation during operation. Another way is to implement the algorithm by using the idea of batch loading and whole clustering, and limit the number of loading each time, then deal with a batch and release a batch. Although this method solves the memory problem, but it is too time-consuming, the distributed K-Means clustering algorithm is adopted in this paper, which not only solves the problem of insufficient memory, but also saves time.

3.3 Matching Image

The user submits an image. First uploads to the server, and then extracts the shape feature points of the image, the image edge feature extraction algorithm described by morphological information, and then through the edge histogram, histogram intersection method according to the similarity distance for image retrieval, the image from the most similar to the least similar sort output.

4 Experiment and Analysis

In order to verify the difference between using the Hadoop cloud computing platform and without using the Hadoop cloud computing platform, the following experiments are designed respectively.

We randomly choose some geometrical plane images as the sample images which were analyzed by image edge detection operator retrieval algorithm for feature extraction. On the same server, a method bases on using a Hadoop platform, and the other is only in accordance with common use. Then we extract shape feature to make 10 times the average precision query. And calculate the precision ratio and recall ratio of each method in different number of images return query results corresponding.

The two ways to retrieve the results are as shown in the following Figs. 2 and 3:

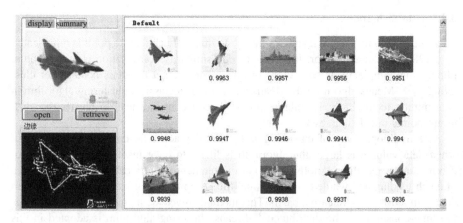

Fig. 2. Using the hadoop platform

It can be seen from the above results that the retrieval results of the image retrieval algorithms based on this algorithm are better because the edges extracted by morphological algorithms are more clear and coherent and have strong noise suppression ability. The retrieval results of Using the Hadoop platform and Without using the

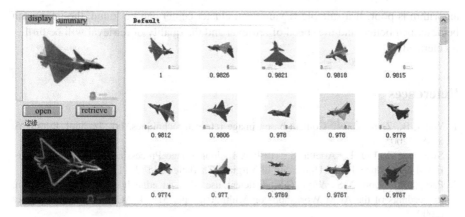

Fig. 3. Without using the hadoop platform

Hadoop platform are almost the same, so the retrieval time of two ways is compared, as shown in the following Fig. 4:

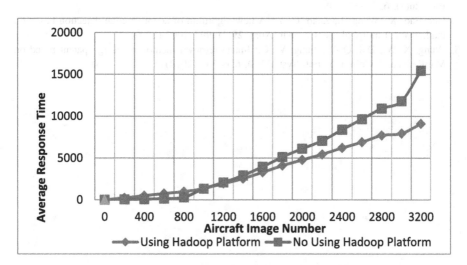

Fig. 4. Time consumption contrast

5 Concluding Remarks

Through the above analysis, the parallel computing technology based on Hadoop platform can greatly reduce the image processing time when the number of images to be retrieved is large, and the retrieval effect is almost the same as that without using the Hadoop platform. Because the K-Means algorithm first adopts the method of random selection of initial cluster centers, the noise and isolated vertex tolerance of the algorithm is poor. If a suitable K value and cluster center can be found, the image can be described better, and the speed of retrieval and the quality of retrieval will be further accelerated.

References

1. Wang, B., Zhao, Z.-W.: Content-based image retrieval techniques. Inf. Technol. Inform. **5**, 81–82 (2005)
2. Sweeney, C., Liu, L., Arietta, S.: HIPI: A Hadoop Image Processing Interface for Image-Based Mapreduce Tasks. University of Virgina, Charlattesville (2011)
3. Park, D.K., Jeon, Y.S., Won, C.S.: Efficient use of local edge histogram descriptor. In: Proceedings of the ACM Workshops on Multimedia, pp. 51–54. ACM Press, Los Angeles (2000)
4. Huiskes, M.J., Lew, M.S.: The MIR flickr retrieval evaluation. In: Proceedings of the 1st ACM International Conference on Multimedia Information Retrieval, pp. 39–43. ACM Press, New York (2008)
5. Wang, X.-P.: The Principle and Application of Morphological Image Analysis. Tsinghua University Press, Beijing (2008)
6. Maragos, P.: Tutorial on advances in morphological image processing and analysis. Optic. Eng. **26**(7), 623–632 (1987)
7. Guo-Bao, X., Wang, J., Zhao, G.-Y.: A new algorithm of adaptive edge detection based on mathematical morphology. Comput. Appl. **29**(4), 997–1002 (2009)
8. Wang, X.-W., Dai, Q.-Y., Jiang, W.-C.: Image retrieval method of design patent based on MapReduce. J. Chin. Comput. Syst. **33**(3), 626–632 (2012)

An Improved ICS Honeypot Based on SNAP7 and IMUNES

Chenpeng Ding[(⊠)], Jiangtao Zhai, and Yuewei Dai

School of Electronics and Information Engineering, Jiangsu University of
Science and Technology, Zhenjiang 212003, Jiangsu, China
dcp1092345323@163.com

Abstract. Honeypot, as an active defense technology, can make up for the low
efficiency of detection system for unknown threats and is of great significance
for the safety of industrial control network. At present, there are many defects in
industrial control system (ICS) honeypot, which can't support large-scale
deployment at the same time with high fraudulence and a certain degree of
interaction. In order to compensate for these defects, an improved honeypot
scheme has been proposed, which is based on the SNAP7 and IMUNES. The
proposed honeypot can be deployed rapidly, and also, through the use of
IMUNES and SNAP7 to achieve rapid construction of industrial control network "shadow" system, the system has the characteristics of light weight, high,
strong deceptive and a certain degree of interaction. With scalability, it is easy to
achieve docking industrial control Honeynet and computer network.

Keywords: SNAP7 · IMUNES · Honeypot · Industrial control system (ICS)
Information security

1 Introduction

With the widely usage of Internet in industrial control system, various security incidents such as Stuxnet, Duqu [1], and fire virus [2] attack are increasing. The safety of
the industrial control network is greatly threatened. At present, the protection for
industrial control network is mainly from the traditional Internet technology methods,
including firewall, IDS [3–5] and so on. Such methods are not effective enough to
detect unknown threats and can't meet the needs of industrial control network security
protection. Honeypot network is a kind of active defense technology, which is virtual
based on real system, and there is no network system for any business use. By
deploying such security resources, the attackers are enticed to illegally use them to
capture and analyze the attacks. The security of the industrial control network can be
effectively improved by deploying a honeypot system in the industrial control network.
According to the interactive level of the honeypot, it can be divided into three types:
low interaction, medium interaction and high interaction. The higher of the interaction,
the more security of the honeypot. Also, the complex of the honeypot is increasing.

At present, there are few researches on honeypot related to industrial control network. The existing mainstream industrial honeypot, such as conpot [6], which is a low
level interaction honeypot. The industrial PLC fingerprint of which is imperfect and

© Springer Nature Switzerland AG 2018
X. Sun et al. (Eds.): ICCCS 2018, LNCS 11063, pp. 303–313, 2018.
https://doi.org/10.1007/978-3-030-00006-6_27

easily to be identified by attackers. The medium interactive honeypot, such as CryPLH [7] can support data reading, SNMP and WEB protocol. However, its TCP/IP operation system fingerprints are different from the real PLC fingerprints, which will make it recognized by attackers with tools such as nmap, plcscan and so on. Stephan [8] developed the first high-interactive honeypot XPOT which can support higher level PLC program interaction, but the researchers did not consider the situation of large-scale deployment. Based on this, a fast deployment and medium-interactive method of intercommunication industrial control honeynet is proposed in this paper. The main contributions of this paper can be concluded as: (1) Compared with the traditional ICS honeypot that based on virtual machine, the proposed scheme based on Docker container with the platform of IMUNES. This will reduce the resource consumption of the host, at the same time it supports one click deployment, more convenient. (2) According to the defects that the fingerprint of CryPLH system are easy to be identified by Nmap and PLCscan, the fingerprint of SNAP7 [9] is improved, which makes the fingerprint of the ICS honeypot same to the real PLC. Also, our scheme supports the function of data read-write, PLC switch controlling and so on. (3) A convenient method to achieve docking with ICS Honeynet and computer network is built, unlike the construction of traditional Honeynet which focuses on industrial control layer, it embodies the integrity of the industrial control network and can improve the extensibility of the industrial control Honeynet by combining the relatively mature honeypot technology.

2 Related Works

The current mainstream industrial honeypot technology is adopted to simulate the industrial PLC and industrial control system with Modbus and other common protocols. Deploying them in network together [10], recording and scanning attack process of the system and the corresponding IP, in order to study the defense of industrial control system. Document [11] analyzes the threat source and attack process of the industrial control system by deploying an industrial control honeypot network. However, the deployment process includes the deployment of real PLC, which costs too much. The existing deployment of industrial honeypot network mostly uses the Internet honeypot technology, and the third generation Honeynet structure is used to deploy honeypot network which consumes too much resources and is difficult to deploy in large quantities. The CrySyS Lab built a Medium interactive ICS honeypot with S7, SNMP and other protocols included. However, the whole system is built on the basis of Vmware ESXI server, which greatly consumes the physical machine resources so that it can't be deployed with many destinations. Different from the above, a new Docker container technology is used to deploy the industrial honeypot network to make the Honeynet lighter, more convenient and quick to deploy.

The first highly interactive industrial honeypot XPOT [8] developed by StephanLua and others provided the highest level of PLC program interaction, which is a major breakthrough in ICS honeypot field. However, as it is not an open source project, the researcher cannot undertake further analysis and research, which also makes the large-scale deployment of it is impossible.

The open source project——Conpot is a low interactive honeypot technology on the server side of the industrial control system, which is widely used on the basis of its easy to arrange and modify features. But it can only provide interaction to read the list of system status. Also, the SIEMENS PLC fingerprint set simulated by Conpot is too limited and it is very easy to be recognized by experienced attackers. An Experiment using IMUNES and Conpot to emulate Honeypot Control Networks, proposed by Stipe *et al.* [12], no longer depend on the VMware virtual machine with the bottom of the Docker container to make the deployment of a large number of PLC nodes become more convenient and fast. However, because of the limitation of Conpot, the interactivity of the industrial control Honeynet is not high, and it is also easily recognized by the attacker too.

In order to take into account of the performance both interaction and deployment, this paper used the method of IMUNES to build the industrial Honeynet project, combined with the SNAP7 and SNMP protocol to build the industrial Honeynet. The functions of PLC control, data reading and writing, module movement have been added, which makes improve its interactivity level. At the same time, IMUNES based on the Docker container makes the system deployment more lightweight and convenient. Different from CryPLH, this article is aimed at the defects that the system fingerprint can be identified by sniffer tools such as Nmap, PLCscan etc. In this paper, the SNAP7 is improved and the fingerprint information is also perfected. It makes the system fingerprint information has no different from real PLC. This will lead to the honeypot system more fraudulent.

At present, the research on the technology of industrial control honeypot is mainly focused on the simulation of the industrial control layer network. It can't fully reflect the characteristics of the industrial control network, and not combine the existing relatively mature Internet honeypot technologies. Therefore, based on IMUNES, a convenient way to connect industrial control Honeynet to computer network is proposed, which increases the scalability of Honeynet deployment and makes the industrial Honeynet more flexible and diverse.

3   The Proposed Scheme

3.1   The Design of a Single Honeypot Node

In order to make the honeypot system has a certain degree of interactivity, the SNAP7 project is used to construct the honeypot system. The SNAP7 is a SIEMENS S7 protocol tool and it is an open source project, through the relevant reply command constructed in the S7 protocol, it will be packaged into a protocol data unit to realize the communication between SIEMENS PLC. The functions it supported include data read and write, cyclic data read and write, directory information read, system information read, mobile processing module, PLC control (stop/restart operation), date and time read.

In terms of the deception of honeypot, the SNAP7 project is defective. Because its unique system fingerprint is different from the real PLC devices, which makes it can be identified by Nmap, PLCscan and other scanning tools easily. The experienced attackers can identify it as a fake industrial control system. Because of this, the CryPLH exposes these shortcomings. To Aim at this point, the SNAP7 server has been improved and the fingerprint also be perfected. It makes the fingerprint information the same as the real PLC device system. The specific fingerprint information contrast diagram shows the following (Figs. 1 and 2).

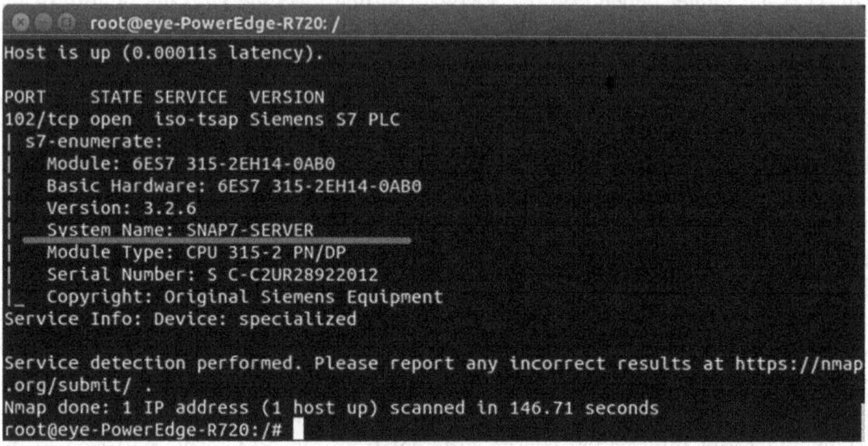

```
root@eye-PowerEdge-R720: /
Host is up (0.00011s latency).

PORT    STATE SERVICE  VERSION
102/tcp open  iso-tsap Siemens S7 PLC
| s7-enumerate:
|   Module: 6ES7 315-2EH14-0AB0
|   Basic Hardware: 6ES7 315-2EH14-0AB0
|   Version: 3.2.6
|   System Name: SNAP7-SERVER
|   Module Type: CPU 315-2 PN/DP
|   Serial Number: S C-C2UR28922012
|_  Copyright: Original Siemens Equipment
Service Info: Device: specialized

Service detection performed. Please report any incorrect results at https://nmap
.org/submit/ .
Nmap done: 1 IP address (1 host up) scanned in 146.71 seconds
root@eye-PowerEdge-R720:/#
```

Fig. 1. The original SNAP7 server

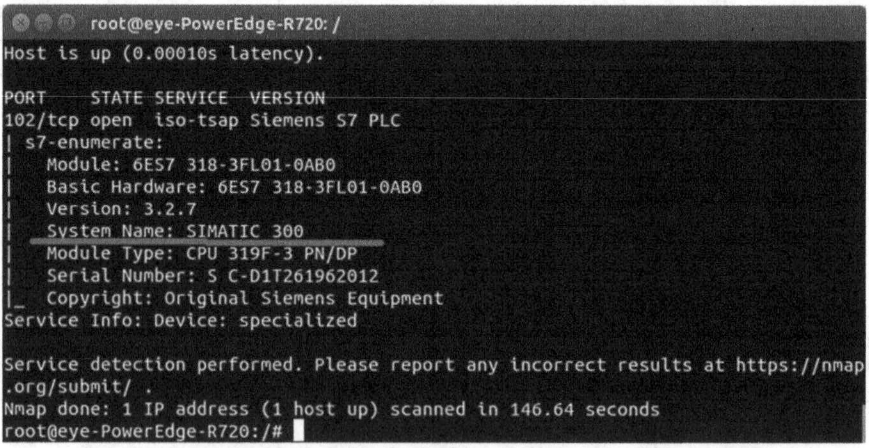

```
root@eye-PowerEdge-R720: /
Host is up (0.00010s latency).

PORT    STATE SERVICE  VERSION
102/tcp open  iso-tsap Siemens S7 PLC
| s7-enumerate:
|   Module: 6ES7 318-3FL01-0AB0
|   Basic Hardware: 6ES7 318-3FL01-0AB0
|   Version: 3.2.7
|   System Name: SIMATIC 300
|   Module Type: CPU 319F-3 PN/DP
|   Serial Number: S C-D1T261962012
|_  Copyright: Original Siemens Equipment
Service Info: Device: specialized

Service detection performed. Please report any incorrect results at https://nmap
.org/submit/ .
Nmap done: 1 IP address (1 host up) scanned in 146.64 seconds
root@eye-PowerEdge-R720:/#
```

Fig. 2. The improved SNAP7 test

In order to make the honeypot system more fraudulent, the SNMP services are added to a single honeypot system to act as a monitoring function in the industrial control system. It provides PLC device information, the access information and so on. Different from the CryPLH, the real SNMP services will make the honeypot looks more real. In this paper, an experiment is done to verify it. The Nmap and SNMP walk are respectively used to scan the single node honeypot that runs SNPA7 services and SNMP services. Compared with the fingerprint information map of ICS device searched by Shodan search engine [13], it can be found that the system information is basically the same. This verifies the effectiveness of our scheme (Figs. 3 and 4).

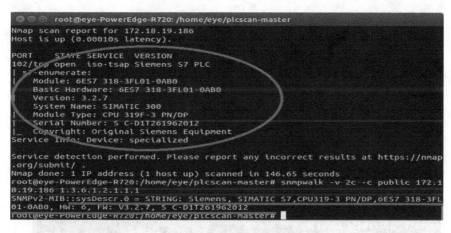

Fig. 3. The scanning results by Nmap and snmpwalk.

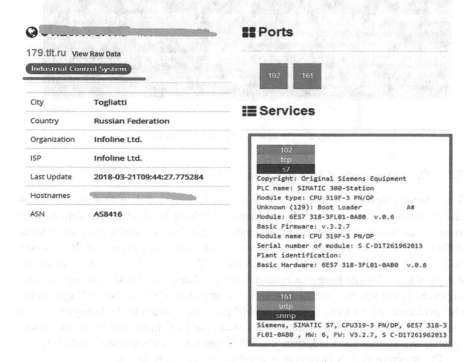

Fig. 4. The information of an industrial control system scanned by the Shodan engine.

In order to test the interaction of the honeypot, a software of the STEP7 series was used. The function of data read and write and the PLC control (stop/restart operation) were tested successfully. The test results are as follows in Fig. 5.

Fig. 5. The results of functional testing.

3.2 The Framework of Our ICS Honeynet

The scheme proposed by this paper is based on IMUNES. It is a network simulation and emulator running on FreeBSD and Linux, and also it is a light weight virtualization system. All nodes in it are based on customizable Docker mirror [14] to simulate different roles, such as routers, switches and Linux hosts and servers et al. It can easily build network and manage later stage through GUI interface. In order to make the design of the industrial honeypot system more fraudulent, the SNAP7 project has been improved in our scheme and the fingerprint information of SIEMENS PLC system has also perfected. At the same time, the SNMP protocol is added to the honeypot system to simulate the information management function of PLC in the real industrial control system, which makes the industrial control Honeynet constructed more truthfully.

The structure of ICS Honeynet is designed as shown in Fig. 6.

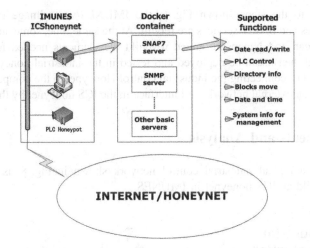

Fig. 6. The system architecture diagram.

In Fig. 6. each honeypot in the industrial control Honeynet built on IMUNES is acted by virtual nodes. Each virtual node is a Docker container running on the basis of the mirror. The SNAP7 server process running in each container acts as SIEMENS PLC honeypot. The SNMP server process provides PLC information and acts as a monitoring function in the real industrial control system. It calls each container node to form industrial control Honeynet, and then connects with the computer network or the Internet honeypot network through external interfaces, thus, a complete industrial control honeynet is formed.

3.3 The Construction of ICS Honeynet

The block diagram of the industrial control Honeynet based on IMUNES is shown in Fig. 7.

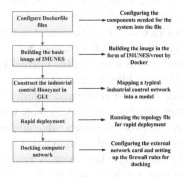

Fig. 7. The system construction flow chart

According to the steps shown Fig. 6, the IMUNES/vroot image that contains SNAP7 services and SNMP services are rebuilt. At the same time, some auxiliary tools such as PLCscan and Nmap are added to build the elements needed for industrial Honeynet. And then it can be deployed and tested in the industrial honeynet.

The method of connecting the industrial control Honeynet to the computer network is to configure an external network card interface in the ICS honeynet by the IMUNES.

4   Experiments and Analysis

In this paper, a typical industrial control network shown in Fig. 8. is used as an example to build an ICS honeynet in IMUNES.

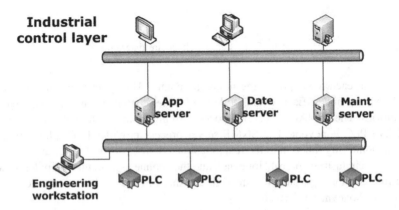

Fig. 8.   The typical industrial control network layer.

It maps to the miniature model in IMUNES as shown in Fig. 9.

In Fig. 9. the initialized node is used as the host to simulate the PG and the engineer station in the PLC network. The honeypot which runs the SNAP7 service terminal and the SNMP server side can be used to simulate the PLC device to access the network. Here, the configured honeypot network is tested, and the PLC honeypot node is scanned by the scanning tool PLCscan at the engineer station, as shown in Fig. 10.

From Fig. 10. it can be seen that the PLC honeypot node responds to the request for the read state information and returns a set of PLC internal information, including the CPU model, the SIEMENS system identity, and so on.

Next, an external network card in a configured industrial honeynet is built. In the external network, the Internet honeypot network is built with the tool Honeyd to do docking experiments. The two network segments are configured to be 10.0.2.0/24 and 10.0.3.0/24. The docking results are tested as shown in Fig. 11.

It can be seen from the above test that there is no problem in the connection between the two virtual network segments and the industrial control honeynet. The Honeyd honeypot technology is effectively combined with the industrial control honeynet based on the IMUNES. The method proposed in this paper is feasible to

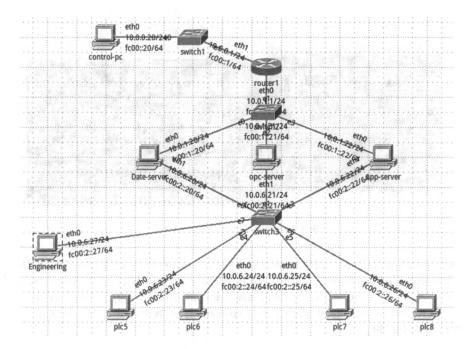

Fig. 9. The model diagram.

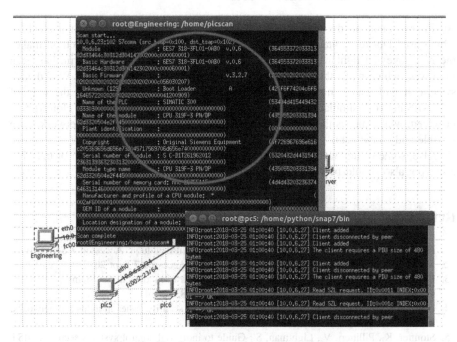

Fig. 10. The Scanning results by using PLCscan.

Fig. 11. The Nmap scan experiment.

connect the industrial control Honeynet with the computer network based on IMUNES. The purpose of combining industrial control Honeynet and Internet honeypot technology has also realized, which will make the industrial control Honeynet more complete, and enhance the flexibility and expansibility of the industrial honeypot in the process of building.

5   Conclusions and Future Works

An improvement on the traditional honeypot network based on the virtual machine which used Docker container is proposed in this paper. The proposed method makes the ICS honeynet light weight. Also, the SNAP7 server and the fingerprint has been improved, which made the fingerprint of our method the same as the real PLC device system. It will lead it not easy to be identified by the attackers. With the help of IMUNES network simulator, a way of docking management of industrial Honeynet is provided, which makes the configuration of industrial control honeypot network more flexible and convenient.

Also, some of this work can be improved, for example, the interaction of the PLC honeypot also should be improved in future.

References

1. Duqu. http://www.crysys.hu/publications/files/bencsathPBFIlduqu. Accessed 7 Sept 2017
2. SkyWiper. http://www.crysys.hu/skywiper/skywiper. Accessed 7 Sept 2017
3. Butun, I., Morgera, S., Sankar, R.: A survey of intrusion detection systems in wireless sensor networks. IEEE Commun. Surv. 1(16), 266–282 (2014)
4. Cheminod, M., Durante, I., Valenzano, A.: Review of security issues in industrial networks. IEEE Trans. Ind. Inform. 1(6), 277–293 (2013)
5. Stouffer, K., Pillitteri, V., Lightman, S.: Guide to industrial control systems security. NIST Spec. Publ. 1(8), 80–82 (2015)

6. The conpot project. http://www.conpot.org. Accessed 12 Nov 2017
7. Buza, D.I., Juhász, F., Miru, G., Félegyházi, M., Holczer, T.: CryPLH: protecting smart energy systems from targeted attacks with a PLC honeypot. In: Cuellar, J. (ed.) SmartGridSec 2014. LNCS, vol. 8448, pp. 181–192. Springer, Cham (2014). https://doi.org/10.1007/978-3-319-10329-7_12
8. Stephan, L., Johannes, K., Stephan, A.: POSTER: towards highly interactive honeypots for industrial control systems. Comput. Commun. Secur. **10**(16), 1823–1825 (2016)
9. SNAP7. https://snap7.sourceforge.net. Accessed 9 Mar 2018
10. Kriaa, S., Pietre-Cambacedes, L., Bouissou, M.: A survey of approaches combining safety and security for industrial control system. Reliab. Eng. Syst. Saf. **139**, 156–178 (2015)
11. Wilhiot, K.: Who's really attacking your ICS equipment. Trend Micro Incorporated (2013)
12. Stipe, K., Stjepan, G., Miljenko, M.: An experiment in using IMUNES and conpot to emulate honeypot control networks. In: IEEE Information and Communication Technology (2017)
13. Bodenheim, R., Butts, J., Dunlap, S., Mullins, S.: Evaluation of the ability of the Shodan search engine to identify Internet-facing industrial control devices. Int. J. Crit. Infrastruct. Prot. **2**(7), 114–123 (2014)
14. Merkel, D.: Docker: lightweight linux containers for consistent development and deployment. Linux J. **2**, 239 (2014)

Analysis of Dynamic Change Regulation of Water and Salt in Saline-Alkali Land Based on Big Data

Rui Zhao, Pingzeng Liu[✉], He Li, Xueru Yu, and Xue Wang

College of Information Science and Engineering, Shandong Agricultural
University, Tai'an 271018, China
lpz8565@126.com

Abstract. With the rapid development of the "Internet plus", the monitoring service of saline-alkali land has undergone profound changes, intelligent technologies such as big data, cloud computing and data mining are gradually being applied to analyze the changing trend of saline-alkaline lands. In order to study the dynamic changes rule of saline-alkali land, using the synchronous monitoring system of the Internet of things to monitor soil moisture, salt content and other relevant data continuously. Then taking the soil of Yong'an town in Kenli County as the research object, the change trend and correlation of the key factors such as soil temperature, salt and water and pH are studied. The results show that the soil water content and salt content had a relatively obvious seasonal change. The soil was alkaline soil, and the change of pH value was not obvious with the season. Correlation analysis shows that there is a significant positive correlation between water content and salt content in most months, and correlations between the two factors and the other soil factors are different. Through the research on the trend and correlation of key factors such as soil water and salt, revealed the factors that affect the change of water content and salt content in the area which provided reference for the improvement of soil salinization in the next step.

Keywords: Saline-alkali land · Water and salt dynamics · Big data
Change regulation

1 Introduction

With the continuous popularization of the Internet and information technology, the amount of data generated by various industries has grown exponentially. These data far exceed the scope that manpower can handle, and big data technology has emerged. "Big data" refers to a data set that cannot be captured, managed, and processed using conventional software tools within an affordable time frame [1]. With the improvement of the level of China's agricultural informatization, big data has gradually appeared in various fields of agriculture, especially in improving the cultivation environment of crops and increasing national food production security [2–4]. As an important reserve cultivated land resource in China, saline-alkali land has great potential for production. However, at the present stage, saline-alkali soils generally have the characteristics of

© Springer Nature Switzerland AG 2018
X. Sun et al. (Eds.): ICCCS 2018, LNCS 11063, pp. 314–325, 2018.
https://doi.org/10.1007/978-3-030-00006-6_28

scarcity of fresh water resources and soil infiltration, which directly affects agricultural production [5, 6]. Reforming the use of saline-alkali wasteland and increasing the production capacity of low and medium yield fields have become increasingly important. This has important implications for improving the human living environment and elevating economic and environmental development to the path of sustainable development. The rapid development of internet plus and various new and high technologies has brought big data for the management of saline-alkali land. Big data has a large amount of data, many types of changes, and a large degree of redundancy. The management of saline-alkali lands should analyze and excavate large amounts of big data generated in saline-alkali lands through emerging technologies to obtain its own unique value attributes and decision-making advantages.

The soil water and salt dynamics are the theoretical basis for understanding the evolution of soil saline soil and preventing secondary salinization of soil [7–9]. Correct understanding of the relationship between water and salt and their changing rules is the key to regulating the movement of water and salt. It can be soil. The dynamic monitoring of salinization provides a theoretical basis. Based on the above importance, scholars at home and abroad have done extensive research on the dynamic changes of soil water and salt. There are some scholars have studied the changes of soil water and salt in different planting areas: Ying et al. observed the dynamics of water and salt in the soil of Robinia pseudoacacia forest land, and found that the water and salt content in different soil layers showed significant seasonal changes with local rainfall [10]; Zhang et al. have shown that the changes in water content and salinity in cotton fields are mainly affected by factors such as rainfall, evaporation, soil structure, and vegetation cover [11]; Hammecker et al. found that the accumulation of salt solution in rice fields mainly occurred during the rainy season [12]. Some scholars have studied the regulations of soil water and salt changes under the implementation of different technologies: Xu Wei et al. studied the effect of drip irrigation on soil water and salt changes. With the increase of irrigation time and irrigation volume, the overall water and salt content of the upper layer showed a downward trend. After the completion of the irrigation period, the salt content gradually recovered [13]. Liu et al. have found that the technology of underground drain drainage and drainage can effectively control the groundwater level, which has the ability to enhance salt precipitation in precipitation and reduce the ability of the groundwater table to inhibit salt return [14]. Some scholars use different models to study soil water and salt changes: Liang et al. used the Hydrus-2D model to conduct numerical simulation analysis on the salt and water transport regulations in saline-alkali land, and determined a reasonable saline-alkali land improvement measure [15]; Hasan and Tiyip established a BP neural network model for soil salinity inversion to simulate changes in soil salinity for prediction of salinized soil information [16]. The "internet plus" era gave birth to the scientific management of saline-alkaline land. With the continuous improvement of data mining and analysis technologies, the introduction of big data technology can improve the accuracy of water and salt dynamic analysis to some extent, and at the same time provide the saline-alkali land improvement and treatment. The data support ensures the continuity of the analysis process, truly realizes the scientific governance of saline-alkali land, and solves the key issues of mass data analysis.

Relevant literature studies have shown that, on the one hand, the results of dynamic analysis of salt and water in saline-alkali land based on big data are relatively less; on the other hand, systematic research on water and salt conditions of saline-alkaline soil around the Bohai Sea is still insufficient, and it is difficult to meet the efficient economic development of the Yellow River Delta and the current Demand for the construction of "Bohai Sea Granary", the related research on soil water and salt dynamic changes in this area still needs further exploration. Therefore, this paper conducts the water and salt dynamic test on the saline-alkali wasteland in the "Bohai Sea Granary Technology Demonstration Project" through a self-developed synchronous salt-alkali water and salt dynamic internet of things detection system. The IoT technology combined with various types of sensors can provide a large number of sources for large-scale data acquisition for saline-alkaline water and salt environment monitoring. It is proposed to explore the seasonal distribution of soil factors, in order to provide soil improvement, agricultural development, and ecological environment construction in the region with theoretical basis of science.

2 Data and Methods

2.1 Survey of the Research Area

Kenli County is located at the mouth of the Yellow River Delta, and the Yellow River runs through the sea from the southwest to the northeast of the county. The geographical position is 37°24′ to 38°10′N, and 118°15′ to 119°19′E. In the temperate monsoon climate zone, there is dry and cold in winter and there is hot and humid in summer, the spatial and temporal distribution of precipitation is uneven. Precipitation is mainly concentrated in July–August, and the difference in evaporation is larger than that in the year. Spring is as high as 7.6. The county is located in the southwest and northeast, with a vertical distance of 55.5 km from north to south and 96.2 km from east to west. The main types of landforms are beach areas, micro-slope lands and flood plains. The terrain is slightly fan-shaped from southwest to northeast. The county has a shallow depth of groundwater and a high degree of mineralization. It is brackish and brackish in most areas and cannot be used for agricultural irrigation and drinking. Due to the low-lying terrain and poor drainage, coupled with lateral seepage of the Yellow River and seawater infiltration, soil salinization is common. The soil type is dominated by salinized fluvo-aquic soil and saline soil. The area of saline-alkali soil is large, which has a serious impact on agricultural production.

2.2 Data Preprocessing

In order to study the dynamic changes of water and salt in saline-alkali soil, a synchronous detection system for water and salt dynamic internet of things in saline-alkali soil was designed and developed according to the architecture of the Internet of things. It adopts synchronous method to realize the timing, synchronization, and automatic collection of soil environmental data in multiple areas of saline-alkali soil, and carries out water and salt dynamic detection. The system focuses on comprehensive sensing, stable transmission, and intelligent applications. Its structure is simple and reliable. The information detection is synchronous, automatic, stable, and the cost is reasonable and easy to deploy. It fully compensates for the existing defects in the water and salt information acquisition in the current saline-alkali land. By measuring high precision and reliable performance of the soil pH sensors, soil moisture sensors, soil temperature sensors, soil salinity sensors, groundwater level sensors and other sensor networks, collecting soil pH, humidity, temperature, salinity, groundwater level and other information in real time, automatically set the data transmission frequency, by the intelligent processing platform through data checking, data denoising method for data preprocessing into the database.

This article selects the data collected at the collection sites in Yong'an Town, Kenli County from September 2014 to April 2016. Due to the influence of certain uncertainties, the data for May and June 2015 were lost. The abnormal data was cleaned and a total of 2664 data were retained. Matlab and SPSS are used for data processing and analysis, in order to eliminate the influence of different data dimensions on the experimental results; the regularization method is first used to standardize the collected data. Then use the software to perform descriptive statistical analysis of the mean, standard deviation, coefficient of variation and so on, and carry out correlation determination between factors.

2.3 Method

Dynamic Analysis. Dynamic analysis is the analysis of the actual process of water and salt changes, including the analysis of the variables in the course of a certain period of time, variables in the process of mutual influence and mutual restraint between relationships. Because the data acquisition is a dynamic process, the dynamic analysis method takes the experimental change as a continuous process to look at the analysis and analyzes the collected data for dynamic time changes. Study monthly changes in soil temperature, water content and salt content, etc.

Correlation Analysis. Correlation analysis determines whether variables are interdependent based on quantitative analysis of the relationship between data. This method determines the specific manifestations of the relationship, it grasps the direction and the close degree of the correlation, so as to make decisions based on the analysis results or provide reference for further statistical analysis. In this paper, Pearson correlation coefficient method is used to describe the degree of linear correlation between the two variables, the greater the correlation coefficient, the stronger the correlation.

3 Results and Analysis

In this chapter, the soil temperature, volumetric water content, salinity and pH data were studied based on the monthly scale. First, the dynamic trend of data in different months was analyzed. Then, the Pearson coefficient method was used to study the correlation between different month factors. Finally, conclusions were drawn from the experimental results.

3.1 Dynamic Analysis of Soil Temperature

The dynamic change trend of soil temperature in each month of the test site is shown in Fig. 1. Through the statistical analysis of soil temperature data for each month, it can be seen that the soil temperature is within the range of 0–30 °C, and shows the trend of high temperature in summer and low temperature in winter. The highest soil temperature is 28.87 °C in July 2015 while the minimum soil temperature is 1.15 °C in January 2015. The lowest temperature in 2016 appeared in February at 5.74 °C, which is 4.59 °C higher than in 2015.

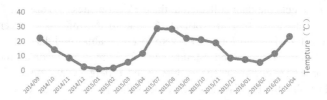

Fig. 1. Dynamic trend of average soil temperature.

According to other statistics, the coefficient of variation of soil temperature is 0.01 to 0.56, of which the coefficient of variation in February 2015 is as high as 56%, indicating that this month has a strong variability. The temperature range in March 2015 reached 10.5 °C, and the temperature ranges in November 2014, April 2015, and October–December 2015 were all above 8 °C, indicating that the relative changes in temperature in winter and spring are larger. The relative range is in the range of 0.03 to 1.93. The degree of numerical dispersion is different from month to month, and the degree of dispersion in winter is greater. The statistics of soil temperature characteristics for some months are shown in Table 1.

3.2 Dynamic Analysis of Soil Water and Salt

The dynamic changes of soil salt and water in each month of the test site are shown in Fig. 2. Through the study of the dynamic changes of the volumetric moisture content in the test soil, it was found that the peak volume of soil volumetric water content appeared in September 2014, with a maximum of 32.97%/vol. At the same time, the volumetric moisture content in the months of July, August and September of 2015 was also high, at 31.76%/vol, 30.50%/vol, and 30.84%/vol, respectively, while the lowest value was 11.69%/vol in February of 2016. In general, soil volumetric water content is high and stable, mostly concentrated in the range of 25–35%/vol. Soil in this layer is less affected by temperature and precipitation. Although it is also characterized by small water content in winter and large water content in summer, it is not obvious with seasonal changes.

Through the study of the dynamic changes of soil salinity in the test site, it was found that in July 2015 as the boundary point, the previous salt content was between 0.5 and 2 mol/l, but the subsequent salt content was between 0.02 and 0.05 mol/l with

Table 1. Soil temperature statistical characteristics analysis.

Project		Mean	Standard deviation	Variation coefficient	Maximum	Minimum	Range	Relative range
2014	Sept	22.28	0.71	0.03	23.28	20.85	2.43	0.11
	Oct	14.31	0.72	0.05	16.94	13.36	3.58	0.25
	Nov	8.46	1.58	0.19	14.5	6.43	8.13	0.96
	Dec	2.5	0.8	0.3	6.2	1.9	4.3	1.7
2015	Jan	1.15	0.06	0.05	1.25	0.99	0.26	0.23
	Feb	1.78	0.99	0.56	4.24	0.8	3.44	1.93
	Mar	5.73	2.59	0.45	13.1	2.54	10.5	1.84
	Apr	11.74	2.61	0.22	16.9	7.53	9.34	0.79
	Jul	28.87	2.2	0.08	33.49	26.57	6.92	0.24
	Aug	28.52	0.33	0.01	28.94	28.04	0.9	0.03
	Sept	22.25	1.13	0.05	26.85	20.44	6.41	0.29
	Oct	21.34	2.66	0.12	26.57	17.58	8.99	0.42
	Nov	19.18	1.59	0.08	24.53	15.72	8.81	0.46
	Dec	8.6	1.2	0.1	16	6.3	10	1.2

Fig. 2. Dynamic change of soil average water and salt.

a slight upward trend. This shows that after the middle two months, the improvement measures of the saline-alkali land reduced the soil salinity. From the early stage, the salt content in soil shows a certain variation with the soil moisture content. With the increase of soil moisture content, the salt content will also increase, with the characteristics of "salt goes with water and salt goes with water" [17–19]. However, due to the temperature drop, the soil freezes, the internal activities are basically weakened, and the soil salt content remains basically unchanged in winter.

From the statistics of some months, the volumetric moisture content of the soil remains relatively stable with a maximum of 36.24%/vol and a minimum of 24.16%/vol, and coefficient of variation between 0 and 0.05. The variation is very small, with weak variability. The relative range is between 0 and 0.16. The statistical characteristics data of soil volume moisture in some months are shown in Table 2.

Table 2. Soil moisture statistical characteristics analysis.

Project		Mean	Standard deviation	Variation coefficient	Maximum	Minimum	Range	Relative range
2014	Sept	32.97	1.76	0.05	36.24	31.28	4.95	0.15
	Oct	28.57	0.11	0.01	28.95	28.48	0.47	0.02
	Nov	28.92	0.79	0.03	32.96	28.28	4.68	0.16
	Dec	27.44	0.98	0.04	30.56	26.77	3.79	0.14
2015	Jan	27.69	1.12	0.04	30	25.9	4.09	0.15
	Feb	26.47	0.65	0.02	28.53	25.85	2.67	0.1
	Mar	26.85	0.42	0.02	28.01	26.28	1.73	0.06
	Apr	29.08	0.87	0.03	33.14	27.36	5.78	0.2
	Jul	31.76	0.5	0.02	32.87	30.81	2.06	0.06
	Aug	30.5	0.01	0	30.52	30.49	0.04	0
	Sept	30.84	0.86	0.03	34.19	30.27	3.92	0.13
	Oct	29.35	0.45	0.02	30.04	28.43	1.6	0.05
	Nov	29.42	0.33	0.01	31.19	28.77	2.42	0.08
	Dec	25.9	0.78	0.03	28.34	24.16	4.18	0.16

The coefficient of variation of soil salinity was between 0.07 and 0.42, of which, in January, March and April of 2015, it was a weak variability, and in December 2014, the variability was as high as 42%. And the highest salt content in this month was 1.44 mol/l, the lowest was 0.42 mol/l, and the relative extreme was as high as 1.66. The statistical characteristics of soil salinity in some months are shown in Table 3.

Table 3. Soil salt content statistical characteristics analysis.

Project		Mean	Standard deviation	Variation coefficient	Maximum	Minimum	Range	Relative range
2014	Sept	1.94	0.41	0.21	2.26	0.93	1.33	0.68
	Oct	0.91	0.25	0.28	1.95	0.74	1.21	1.32
	Nov	1.29	0.32	0.25	2.34	0.84	1.5	1.16
	Dec	0.61	0.25	0.42	1.44	0.42	1.02	1.66
2015	Jan	0.63	0.04	0.07	0.74	0.52	0.22	0.35
	Feb	0.53	0.07	0.14	0.64	0.32	0.32	0.6
	Mar	0.61	0.04	0.07	0.74	0.43	0.31	0.5
	Apr	0.66	0.05	0.08	0.83	0.61	0.22	0.33

3.3 Dynamic Analysis of PH

The trend of soil pH changes at each month of the test site is shown in Fig. 3. The pH value of the soil in the test site was concentrated between 7 and 8.5, belonging to alkaline soil. Because the salt content was too high in some months, the pH was low, indicating that the soil water-soluble salt contained more acidic ions. The pH did not change significantly with the season, and the difference was not significant in each month. The highest value occurred in November 2015 and the soil pH was 8.4. The lowest value was observed in October 2014 and the pH value was 5.63.

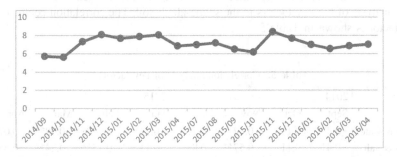

Fig. 3. Dynamic trend of average soil pH value.

From the statistical data of soil pH in some months, the highest value is 10 and the lowest value is 5.13. The difference in soil salt content leads to the difference in pH values in each month. The coefficient of variation is between 0.02 and 0.2, and the variation is relatively small. The relative range is between 0.13 and 0.52. The degree of numerical dispersion is different from month to month, and the degree of dispersion in December is relatively high. The soil pH statistics for some months are shown in Table 4.

Table 4. Soil pH value statistical analysis.

Project		Mean	Standard deviation	Variation coefficient	Maximum	Minimum	Range	Relative range
2014	Sept	5.72	0.12	0.02	5.97	5.13	0.84	0.15
	Oct	5.63	0.64	0.11	7.4	5.09	2.31	0.41
	Nov	7.33	0.75	0.1	8.19	5.11	3.08	0.42
	Dec	8.1	1.1	0.1	9.8	5.1	4.6	0.6
2015	Jan	7.69	0.66	0.09	8.91	6.01	2.9	0.34
	Feb	7.88	0.72	0.09	9.1	6.02	3.08	0.39
	Mar	8.06	0.53	0.06	8.96	6.77	2.19	0.27
	Apr	6.86	0.64	0.09	8.21	6.01	2.2	0.32
	Jul	6.99	0.7	0.1	8.46	6.01	2.45	0.35
	Aug	7.19	0.53	0.07	7.91	6.05	1.86	0.25
	Sept	6.49	0.81	0.12	7.7	5.03	2.67	0.41
	Oct	6.18	0.18	0.03	6.78	6	0.78	0.13
	Nov	8.4	1.24	0.15	9.92	6	3.92	0.47
	Dec	7.68	1.55	0.2	10	6	4	0.52

3.4   Correlation Analysis

The key soil factors obtained through the synchronous monitoring system of the Internet of things include soil temperature, soil volumetric water content, soil pH and soil salinity. The data from September 2014 to April 2015 are selected for the correlation analysis of the key factors in the saline-alkali soil. The correlation coefficient of each factor is shown in Table 5.

Table 5. Correlation analysis of key factors.

Project	2014				2015			
	Sept	Oct	Nov	Dec	Jan	Feb	Mar	Apr
Temp & water	−0.47**	0.19	0.07	0.27**	0.24**	0.63**	0.98**	0.07
Temp & salt	−0.41**	0.11	0.57**	0.83**	−0.11*	0.75**	0.24**	−0.65**
Temp & pH	0	0.11	−0.29**	−0.45**	−0.17**	−0.48**	−0.43**	−0.33**
Water & salt	0.45**	0.84**	−0.15	0.5**	0.24**	0.48**	0.25**	0.61**
Water & pH	0.01	0.67**	−0.74**	−0.54**	−0.22**	−0.78**	−0.35**	−0.44**
Salt & pH	−0.48**	0.82**	0.06	−0.56**	−0.17**	−0.32**	−0.35**	0.1

Note: '***' represents 99% significant levels of correlation; '**' represents 95% significant levels of correlation; '*' represents 90% significant levels of correlation.

Soil temperature had a positive correlation with soil volumetric water content. Only in September 2014, there is a negative correlation between soil temperature and soil moisture. That is to say, with the increase of soil temperature, soil volumetric water content is decreasing, which indicates that evaporation in September 2014 was greater than rainfall; with the increase of soil temperature, the volumetric water content of soil is increasing, which may be related to the increase of spring rainfall. The most relevant months were September 2014, and from December 2014 to March 2015. The highest correlation coefficient was 0.98 in March 2015.

There was a significant positive correlation between soil temperature and salinity. Only in September, January and April were significantly negatively correlated. The months with positive correlation coefficients were November, December, and February, and the correlation coefficients were 0.57, 0.83, and 0.75. The salt in the soil moves with the water and the soil temperature in winter increases. As the soil moisture evaporates, the salt is transported to the surface of the soil and the detected salt content increases.

There was a significant negative correlation between soil temperature and pH, and the maximum correlation coefficient was −0.48. The increase in temperature caused a shift in the dissociation equilibrium of the soil solution and a change in the relative pH value. There is a significant positive correlation between water and salt, indicating that irrigation and precipitation infiltration of water will bring salt into the soil, with the characteristics of salt with water, the correlation coefficient between 0.25–0.61.

Soil moisture content affects the distribution of ions in the solid phase, as well as the degree of dissociation of adsorbed ions on the colloidal particles, thus affecting soil pH [20]. The increase in water content will dilute the soil, lower the clay concentration, and decrease the pH of the alkaline soil, so the overall negative correlation between the two, the highest negative correlation coefficient is −0.78.

The overall soil pH value decreased with the increase of soil salt content. The soil pH value was significantly negatively correlated with the ratio of NO_3-, SO_4^{2-}, Cl^- in total salt while the increase of the ratio of Ca^{2+}, Mg^{2+} and Na^+ in total salt is the reason for the increase of soil pH. The content of metal anions in the Yong'an Town area, Kenli County, from December 2014 to March 2015 was high, so the increase in total salt content led to a drop in pH value. There is a significant positive correlation in October 2014, with a correlation coefficient of 0.82.

4 Conclusion

Combined with the requirements for the detection and management of saline-alkali lands, we detect water and salt information real-timely, synchronously and automatically. Based on big data, trend analysis and correlation analysis of water and salt data were carried out to understand and judge the trend and rule of salt and water change in saline alkali soil. The main conclusions are as follows:

(1) The correlation between soil temperature, pH, water content, and salt content in Yong'an Town, Kenli County can all reach significant levels. From September to March of the correlation analysis, we can see that as the temperature rises and the soil volumetric water content increases, the salt content rises and there is a characteristic that "salt comes with water". In most months, soil pH decreased with the increase of temperature, water content, and salt content, and negatively correlated with the latter three. The above correlations are different at different times. Through comprehensive factor analysis, it can provide a reasonable reference for the adjustment of water and salt balance in each season.

(2) While fully understanding the salt and water regulations of salt and alkali changes, it is particularly important to regulate water and salt changes through various measures. It is recommended that Yong'an Town of Kenli County be reasonably applied with chemical fertilizers to avoid excessive use of nitrogen-containing alkaline fertilizers such as urea and ammonium bicarbonate, and that neutral and acidic fertilizers should be preferred which can not only neutralize the alkalinity of soil, change the composition of soil salt, but also maintain the balance of soil nutrients, and continuously improve soil buffering capacity and soil fertility. Halophytes can be cultivated to improve the soil environment, and a large amount of irrigation water is used to leach soluble salts and alkalis from the soil, and combined with other agro-agricultural measures to improve cropping environment. It will relieve the phenomenon of soil salinization in the Bohai Sea region and provide a strong guarantee for the increase of grain output and income.

(3) The research uses big data to carry out the trend analysis of water and salt data and explore the regulation, so as to provide data support for the scientific and rational

improvement of salt and alkali land improvement, so as to provide data support for scientific and rational improvement of saline-alkali soil. On the basis of big data analysis and information mining, the management of saline-alkali land will be more effective, more targeted and more targeted.

Acknowledgements. This work was financially supported by the following project:

(1) The Independent Innovation and Achievement Transformation of Shandong Province under Grant No. 2014ZZCX07106.

(2) Science and Technology development Program of Shandong Province under Grant No. 2014GNC110012.

References

1. Manyika, J., Chui, M., Brown B.: Big data: the next frontier for innovation, competition, and productivity. Analytics (2011)
2. Shi-Wei, X.U., Wang, D.J., Zhe-Min, L.I.: Application research on big data promote agricultural modernization. Sci. Agric. Sin. **48**, 3429–3438 (2015)
3. Liu, P., Wang, X., Wen, F.: Development and application of big data platform for "Bohai granary". Wireless Pers. Commun. **6**, 1–19 (2018)
4. Yang, Y.: Crop monitoring and early warning of big data era. Chin. Comput. Commun. (2017)
5. Liu, Y., He, W., He, J.: Progress of improvement and utilization of saline-alkali land. J. Agric. Sci. **73**(73), 89–92 (2007)
6. Chen, S.Q.: Control and development of Saline-alkali soil in Binzhou. J. Hebei Agric. Sci. (2009)
7. Song, J.R., Yang, J., Wang, Y.M.: Exploration of the Reason and improvement measures of saline-alkali soil in the Yellow river delta. J. Anhui Agric. Sci. (2017)
8. Tulake, G., Xin-Guo, L.I., Tuerdi, A.: Analysis of soil salinity characteristics of oasis in the lower reaches of the Kaidu River. Agric. Res. Arid Areas (2014)
9. Sun, L., Luo, Y.: Study on the evolution trends of soil salinity in cotton field under long-term drip irrigation. Res. Soil Water Conserv. (2013)
10. Ying, F.U., Suyan, L.I., Sun, X.: Soil water and salt dynamic variation in Robinia Pseudoacacia planting area of coastal saline-alkali area in Tianjin City. Bull. Soil Water Conserv. (2015)
11. Zhang, Q., Hong, Q.I., Feng, G.Y.: A study on variation of water and salinity and its influence on cotton growth and development in coastal saline fields. J. Agric. Univ. Hebei **37**(1), 6–10 (2014)
12. Hammecker, C., Maeght, J.L., Grünberger, O.: Quantification and modelling of water flow in rain-fed paddy fields in NE Thailand: evidence of soil salinization under submerged conditions by artesian groundwater. J. Hydrol. **456–457**(5), 68–78 (2012)
13. Ji, X.U., Shi, K.B., Wang, C.F.: Experimental analysis on saline-alkali soil drip irrigation soil water and salt. Water Conserv. Sci. Technol. Econ. **18**, 53–55 (2012)
14. Liu, H.T., Tan, L.M., Shu-Hui, Y.U.: Response of water and salt movement to subsurface pipe drainage system in sa-line-alkali coastal areas of Hebei Province. Chin. J. Eco-Agric. **20**(12), 1693–1699 (2013)

15. Liang, L.I., Mei-Yan, L.I., Zhang, J.J.: The moving rule of salt and water in cultivated land and saline wasteland based on HYDRUS-2D model. Agric. Res. Arid Areas **32**(1), 66–71 (2014)
16. Hasan, T., Tiyip, T.: Mamatsawut: study on the saline-alkali soil salinity inversion model in the arid regions based on BP neural network. Environ. Pollut. Control **33**(2), 23–24 (2011)
17. Yang, D., Xinju, L I., Kong, X.: Effects of different straw returning modes on the water and salt movement in the coastal saline soil. Res. Soil Water Conserv. (2017)
18. Xie, X., Pu, L., Zhu, M.: Evolution and prospects in modeling of water and salt transport in soils. Sci. Geogr. Sin. (2016)
19. Li, J., Pu, L., Zhu, M.: The present situation and hot issues in the salt-affected soil research. Acta Geogr. Sin. **67**(9), 1233–1245 (2012)
20. Wang, M., Zhang, Q.W., Yang, Z.L.: Dynamic changes of soil pH and its influencing factors in the process of dry and wet alternation in the Yellow River irrigation area of Ningxia. J. Nucl. Agric. Sci. **28**(4), 720–726 (2014)

Analysis of LSTM-RNN Based on Attack Type of KDD-99 Dataset

Chaochao Luo[1], Le Wang[2(✉)], and Hui Lu[2]

[1] Institute of Computer Application, China Academy of Engineer Physics,
Beijing, China
luochaochao17@gscaep.ac.cn
[2] Cyberspace Institute of Advanced Technology, Guangzhou University,
Guangzhou, China
{wangle,luhui}@gzhu.edu.cn

Abstract. Method and model of machine learning have applied to many industry fields. Employing RNN to detect and recognize network events and intrusions is extensively studied. This paper divides KDD-99 dataset into 4 subsets according to data item's 'attack type' field. And then, LSTM-RNN is trained and verified on each subset in order to optimize model parameters. Experiments show the strategy of training for LSTM-RNN could boost model accuracy.

Keywords: KDD-99 · RNN · LSTM

1 Introduction

Artificial intelligence is still in its infancy in the field of security. The heat flow of machine learning has made its development in various directions in the field of security. In network security, the most common intrusion detection and pattern recognition have also become a hot area. Automatic offensive and defensive technology is bound to be an inevitable trend in the development of network security. Our main task is to automatically identify and generate intrusion responses in the network automatic offensive and defensive systems. The data in the network flow is very complicated, and it is very difficult to discriminate attacks. The traditional machine learning mode has a good performance in intrusion detection, such as artificial neural networks (ANN) [1–5], Self-Organized Maps (SOM) [6–10], K-Means [11–14], Apriori [15, 16], naive-Bayesian (NB) [17–20], etc. However, it is more convenient and efficient to learn features by using deep learning neural networks [21–25]. The complex feature learning of data streams is the key to the whole system. In this paper, RNN (Recurrent Neural Network) model and KDD 99 dataset [26] for preliminary experiments and network optimization.

The rest of the paper is organized in four sections. In Sect. 2, we review several related work. Section 3 presents an overview of LSTM-RNN (Recurrent Neural Network) and the KDD 99 dataset. We will report our experiments in Sect. 4. Section 5 will show our conclusion and future work.

© Springer Nature Switzerland AG 2018
X. Sun et al. (Eds.): ICCCS 2018, LNCS 11063, pp. 326–333, 2018.
https://doi.org/10.1007/978-3-030-00006-6_29

2 Related Work

In this section, we mainly discuss some related work, it is worth noting that because of the limited level, we are discussing only a very small part of all the research in this field. There are many published data sets about cybersecurity, each with different data types and characteristics, and the results will be quite different. Here, we only discuss work that is also based on the KDD 99 dataset.

The related work using Sparse Auto-Encoder [27] as the basic model has a good effect. This work uses the most basic pattern of deep learning that divides the system into two major parts, a self-learning part and a fine-tuning part, starting with a network of self-learning using unlabeled data and then using the tape Tagged data to fine-tune the entire system from top to bottom and achieved good results. However, the entire dataset used for the KDD 99 dataset in this work was processed without subdividing the dataset. R. S. Naoum's work in [28] has used ANN (Artificial Neural Network) as the model. He used the unlabeled data to do experiments and yielded good results. In recent related work, some classifiers do not use the entire dataset to model training, but select some valid features to test. Among them, the most obvious effect is [29, 30].

3 KDD 99 Dataset and LSTM-RNN

3.1 Subsets of KDD-99

The Lincoln Labs modeled the US Air Force LAN network environment in 1988, collecting nine weeks of network connectivity and system auditing data, simulating various types of users, different types of network traffic, and attacks to make it look like a real Network environment [31]. A network connection is defined as a sequence of TCP packets from start to finish over a period of time, and data is passed from the source IP address to the destination IP address under a predefined protocol during this time. Each network connection is marked as "normal" or "attack", in which the attack types are subdivided into four categories, a total of 39 attack types, of which 22 attack types appear in the training-set, another 17 unknown attack types appear in the test-set, as shown in Table 1.

Table 1. Attack type of KDD 99

Dos	R2 l	U2r	Probe
Back	ftp_write	buffer_overflow	Ipsweep
Land	Imap	Loadmodule	Nmap
Neptune	Multihop	Perl	Portsweep
Pod	Phf	rootkit	satan
Smurf	Spy		
Teardrop	Warezclient		
	Warezmaster		
	guess_passwd		

Subsequently, Prof Sal Stolfo and Prof Wenke Lee at Columbia University performed characterization and preprocessing of the raw data to form the KDD 99 dataset, where each link was described by 41 features [32].

3.2   LSTM-RNN

RNN (Recurrent Neural Network) is the traditional neural network added with "memory" component. In the traditional neural network model, the data $(x_1, x_2, x_3, \ldots, x_m)$ input to the sequence are separately calculated $(o_1, o_2, o_3, \ldots, o_m)$. The calculated value of the state also depends on the result of the previous step, therefore, the result of o_2 is actually based on x_2 and o_1. RNN model diagram shown in Fig. 1.

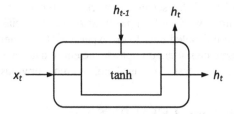

Fig. 1. The input and output of RNN

The forward propagation formula can be expressed in formula (1–4):

$$\partial_t = b + Wh_{t-1} + Ux_t \tag{1}$$

$$h_t = tanh(\partial_t) \tag{2}$$

$$o_t = c + Vh_t \tag{3}$$

$$y'_t = soft\,max(o_t) \tag{4}$$

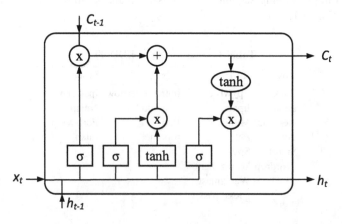

Fig. 2. The input, output and data flow relationship of LSTM-RNN

X_t is the input at time t, h_t is the hidden layer state at time t, ot represents the output at time t, and y'_t represents the normalized prediction.

Comparing to ordinary RNN, the most difference in LSTM-RNN is the extra three gate controller: input gate, output gate, forget gate (in Fig. 2).

The characteristic of LSTM-RNN is to add a memory cell C_t to maintain long-term memory based on the original short-term memory cell h_t, and to add a linear connection to the original RNN structure instead of a simple non-linear connection superposition, So that long-term information can be better spread.

4   Experiments and Results

The experimental model is based on LSTM-RNN as the main neural network model, which joined the Gradient Descent algorithm to correct the learning process error. KDD 99 dataset is divided into two parts - training set and testing set, first we preprocess the data set, and count the four major types of attacks separately. The model were used to train and test under the four types of attack, the results shown in Table 2.

Table 2. Statistics table of the four types of attack

Attack type	Dos	Probe	U2r	R2l
Normal in training set	7204	20204	86	7338
Normal in test set	1490	1582	78	1507
Attack in training set	3593	10102	43	3669
Attack in test set	2537	2651	120	2637
Attack identified to be attack	2533	2585	120	2637
Attack identified to be normal	4	66	0	0
Normal identified to be attack	694	451	2	1367
Normal identified to be normal	796	1131	76	140

We then subdivided the 41 features in the KDD 99 dataset into 3 major categories: basic features, content-based features, traffic-based features, and then screened new training and testing datasets based on three different kinds of combinations (Figs. 3 and 4).

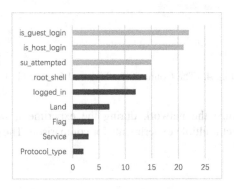

Fig. 3. The Count of Basic Featrue (BF, gray colur) and Content-based Featrue (CF, dark)

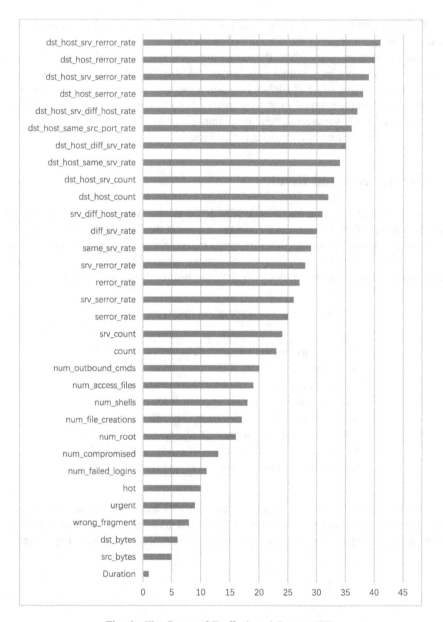

Fig. 4. The Count of Traffic-based Feature (TF)

In order to optimize the network during the experiment, we also changed the learning rate to conduct multiple experiments for comparison. The experimental results are shown in Table 3.

Table 3. Table of experimental results

Input	Learning Rate	Test-accuracy	Train-accuracy
BF + CF + TF	0.1	0.9788	1
	0.01	0.9613	0.99–1
	0.001	0.9454	0.94–0.96
	0.0001	0.8853	0.83–0.85
BF + CF	0.1	0.9035	0.99–1
	0.01	0.9341	0.96–0.98
	0.001	0.9314	0.95–0.96
	0.0001	0.9052	0.88–0.93
BF + TF	0.1	0.9993	1
	0.01	0.9912	0.99–1
	0.001	0.943	0.92–0.94
	0.0001	0.8029	0.81–0.84

5 Conclusion and Future Work

The experiment in this article as a preliminary test, basically achieved the intended purpose. We use the KDD 99 dataset for training and testing. The advantage is that our experiments are grouped and compared multiple times, the characteristics of each data are categorized before training and testing, so that irrelevant features can be reduced for experimental models Influence and improve the recognition accuracy of the whole model. It can be seen from the experimental results that such a sub-method is effective. Next we will modify and optimize the model, use more network models to test, and combine multiple networks to optimize the overall system.

Acknowledgment. This paper is supported by the National Natural Science Foundation of China under Grant No. 61572153 and the National Key research and Development Plan (Grant No. 2018YFB0803504).

References

1. Ripley, B.D.: Pattern Recognition and Neural Networks. Cambridge University Press, Cambridge (2007). ISBN 978-0-521-71770-0
2. Siegelmann, H.T., Sontag, E.D.: Analog computation via neural networks. Theor. Comput. Sci. **131**(2), 331–360 (1994). https://doi.org/10.1016/0304-3975(94)90178-3
3. Wasserman, P.D.: Advanced methods in neural computing. Van Nostrand Reinhold (1993). ISBN 0442004613. OCLC 27429729
4. Kruse, R., Borgelt, C., Klawonn, F., Moewes, C., Steinbrecher, M., Held, P.: Computational intelligence: a methodological introduction. Springer (2013). ISBN 9781447150121. OCLC 837524179
5. Borgelt, C.: Neuro-Fuzzy-Systeme: von den Grundlagen künstlicher Neuronaler Netze zur Kopplung mit Fuzzy-Systemen. Vieweg (2003). ISBN 9783528252656. OCLC 76538146
6. Kohonen, T., Honkela, T.: Kohonen network. Scholarpedia **2**, 1568 (2007)

7. Kohonen, T.: Self-organized formation of topologically correct feature maps. Biol. Cybern. **43**(1), 59–69 (1982). https://doi.org/10.1007/bf00337288
8. Von der Malsburg, C.: Self-organization of orientation sensitive cells in the striate cortex. Kybernetik **14**, 85–100 (1973). https://doi.org/10.1007/bf00288907
9. Turing, A.: The chemical basis of morphogenesis. Phil. Trans. R. Soc. **237**, 5–72 (1952)
10. Ultsch, A., Siemon, H.P.: Kohonen's self organizing feature maps for exploratory data analysis. In: Widrow, B., Angeniol, B. (eds.) Proceedings of the International Neural Network Conference (INNC-90), Paris, France, 9–13 July 1990, pp. 305–308. Kluwer, Dordrecht (1990). ISBN 978-0-7923-0831-7
11. Arthur, D., Vassilvitskii, S.: K-means ++: the advantages of careful seeding. In: Proceedings of the Eighteenth Annual ACM-SIAM Symposium on Discrete Algorithms, SODA 2007, pp. 1027–1035 (2007)
12. Lloyd, S.P.: Least squares quantization in PCM. IEEE Trans. Inf. Theory **28**, 129–137 (1982)
13. Seber, G.A.F.: Multivariate Observations. Wiley, Hoboken (1984)
14. Spath, H.: Cluster Dissection and Analysis: Theory, FORTRAN Programs, Examples. Translated by J. Goldschmidt. Halsted Press, New York (1985)
15. Agrawal, R., Srikant, R.: Fast algorithms for mining association rules. In: Proceedings of the 20th International Conference on Very Large Data Bases, VLDB, Santiago, Chile, pp. 487–499, September 1994
16. Bayardo Jr., R.J.: Efficiently mining long patterns from databases. ACM SIGMOD Record **27**(2), 85–93 (1998)
17. Russell, S., Norvig, P.: Artificial Intelligence: A Modern Approach, 2nd edn. Prentice Hall, Upper Saddle River (2003). ISBN 978-0137903955
18. Rennie, J., Shih, L., Teevan, J., Karger, D.: Tackling the poor assumptions of Naive Bayes classifiers. In: ICML (2003)
19. Rish, I.: An empirical study of the naive Bayes classifier. In: IJCAI Workshop on Empirical Methods in AI (2001)
20. Hand, D.J., Yu, K.: Idiot's Bayes—not so stupid after all? Int. Stat. Rev. **69**(3), 385–399 (2001). https://doi.org/10.2307/1403452. ISSN 0306-7734
21. Bengio, Y., Courville, A., Vincent, P.: Representation learning: a review and new perspectives. IEEE Trans. Pattern Anal. Mach. Intell. **35**(8), 1798–1828 (2013). arXiv:1206. 5538, https://doi.org/10.1109/tpami.2013.50
22. Schmidhuber, J.: Deep learning in neural networks: an overview. Neural Netw. **61**, 85–117 (2015). arXiv:1404.7828, https://doi.org/10.1016/j.neunet.2014.09.003. PMID 25462637
23. Bengio, Y., LeCun, Y., Hinton, G.: Deep learning. Nature **521**(7553), 436–444 (2015). https://doi.org/10.1038/nature14539. PMID 26017442
24. Ghasemi, F., Mehridehnavi, A.R., Fassihi, A., Perez-Sanchez, H.: Deep neural network in biological activity prediction using deep belief network. Appl. Soft Comput. **62**, 251 (2017). https://doi.org/10.1016/j.asoc.2017.09.040
25. Ciresan, D., Meier, U., Schmidhuber, J.: Multi-column deep neural networks for image classification. In: 2012 IEEE Conference on Computer Vision and Pattern Recognition, pp. 3642–3649 (2012). arXiv:1202.2745, https://doi.org/10.1109/cvpr.2012.6248110. ISBN 978-1-4673-1228-8
26. The UCI KDD Archive Information and Computer Science University of California, Irvine, CA 92697-3425 (1999)
27. Javaid, A., Niyaz, Q., Sun, W., et al.: A deep learning approach for network intrusion detection system. In: EAI International Conference on Bio-Inspired Information and Communications Technologies. ICST (Institute for Computer Sciences, Social-Informatics and Telecommunications Engineering), pp. 21–26 (2016)

28. Naoum, R.S., Abid, N.A., Al-Sultani, Z.N.: An enhanced resilient backpropagation artificial neural network for intrusion detection system. Int. J. Comput. Sci. Netw. Secur. **12**(3), 11–16 (2012)
29. Chae, H.-S., Jo, B.-O., Choi, S.-H., Park, T.-K.: Feature Selection for Intrusion Detection using NSL-KDD. In: Recent Advances in Computer Science, pp. 184–187 (2013)
30. Thaseen, S., Kumar, C.A.: An analysis of supervised tree based classifiers for intrusion detection system. In: 2013 International Conference on Pattern Recognition, Informatics and Mobile Engineering (PRIME), pp. 294–299. IEEE (2013)
31. Mikolov, T., et al.: Recurrent neural network based language model. In: Interspeech, vol. 2 (2010)
32. KDD Cup 99. http://kdd.ics.uci.edu/databases/kddcup99/kddcup99.html

Analysis of Price Fluctuation Characteristics and Influencing Factors of Garlic Based on HP Filter Method

Guojing Wu[1], Pingzeng Liu[1(✉)], Weijie Chen[1], and Wei Han[2]

[1] College of Information Science and Engineering, Shandong Agricultural
University, Tai'an 271000, China
lpz8565@126.com
[2] Career Technical Colleges, Laiwu 271100, China

Abstract. In order to analyze the fluctuation regulation of garlic price from a large number of garlic prices data, this paper makes an in-depth analysis of the garlic price data by using the HP filtering analysis method. Firstly analyzing the seasonal effect on garlic price volatility using CensusX12 seasonal adjustment method; secondly, the monthly data of garlic price in Shandong garlic wholesale market from January 2010 to December 2017 was decomposed by HP filtering. So the original sequence, the long-term trend sequence, and the cyclic variation sequence were obtained after the garlic price season was adjusted. Since January 2010, the fluctuation of garlic monthly prices can be divided into 5 cycles. After sorting out the regulation of garlic price and consulting a lot of data, it is concluded that the price of garlic is affected by planting area and natural conditions, and it is easy to cause market speculation and blindly follow suit.

Keywords: HP filtering · Garlic · Price fluctuation

1 Introduction

Since the beginning of the 21st century, the fluctuation of agricultural product prices in China has aroused people's widespread concern; the most significant is the price of garlic. It shows that the price of garlic rose constantly from 2004 to 2006 provided by the agricultural database Burick data, which stimulated the enthusiasm of planting garlic farmers, planting area, and garlic prices dropped sharply in 2007 until a serious reduction in 2010 garlic prices soared to 13 yuan/kg. As the price continued to decrease, planting area reduced rapidly by 2014, in 2015, garlic prices have risen by a certain margin. Then after entering 2017, garlic prices have once again become loose. Because of the initial stage of agricultural big data in China, the analysis of garlic price data is not thorough enough, which leads to the blindly following of garlic production. The price of garlic is like a roller coaster, which has a huge negative impact on the whole agriculture. This paper makes an in-depth study on the cyclical characteristics of garlic prices, which is of great significance to the reduction of the negative effects of garlic price fluctuation. This paper makes an in-depth study on the cyclical

X. Sun et al. (Eds.): ICCCS 2018, LNCS 11063, pp. 334–342, 2018.
https://doi.org/10.1007/978-3-030-00006-6_30

characteristics of garlic prices, which is of great significance to the reduction of the negative effects of garlic price fluctuation.

Scholars at home and abroad have made a lot of related research on the fluctuation characteristics of agricultural products price. Fang and Song [1] used unit root test, cointegration test and error analysis to analyze the factors affecting the price fluctuation of agricultural products from January 2011 to February 2013. You and Chun-Jie [2] decomposed the fruit price index series of 2001–2011 years into the trend value series and the fluctuation value series using the HP filter decomposition model, studied the rule and frequency of price fluctuation in the past eleven years, and put forward the suggestion of agricultural product price regulation accordingly. Xu et al. [3] to divided the total price fluctuation of agricultural products into 5 cycles in the past 2006 years using HP filter, and found that the price fluctuation cycle of agricultural products is not repeatable and asymmetric. Hou [4] analyzed the Hainan vegetable price index data of the first quarter of 2006 to the third quarter of 2014 using HP filtering model, found out the law of vegetable price fluctuations and put forward measures to stabilize the price of vegetables. Li et al. [5] decomposed the price of 28 kinds of aquatic products in our country by X12 seasonal decomposition and HP filtering, which were decomposed into trend fluctuation, periodic fluctuation, seasonal fluctuation and random fluctuation. The fluctuation periods and changing rules of their prices are analyzed. Tang [6] used time series analysis to analyze egg prices from 2000 to 2015, and divided them into six fluctuation periods. The Holter - Winter seasonal product model was used to predict the price of eggs from July 2015 to June 2016. Zheng et al. [7] used the H-P filter decomposition model to divide the vegetable prices in Hebei from 1995 to 2014. The fluctuation of vegetable prices in Hebei province is seasonal and cyclical, and the main influencing factors of price are analyzed through factor analysis. Li [8], etc. analyzed the fluctuation characteristic of garlic price using CF filter and constructed the VAR model to analyze the influence factors of the price change of garlic. Zhang et al. [9] analyzed the fluctuation characteristics of garlic quarterly wholesale price data in eight years by H-P filter and concluded that hot money is not the main reason for the fluctuation of garlic prices. Avoid blindly following and guarantee the balance of supply and demand.

This article uses HP filtering to study the monthly fluctuations and the volatility cycle. in the price of garlic in January 2010–December 2017 in Shandong Province and puts forward the effective method to reduce the garlic price volatility and stable price of garlic by the frequency of price fluctuations, fluctuation cycles, and fluctuations. In addition, the state is paying more and more attention to the development of agriculture. The Department of Agriculture of Shandong Province and Shandong Agricultural University jointly built the garlic big data analysis and visualization platform—the garlic industry chain big data platform. In the platform, the analysis process and conclusion of this paper are also reflected.

2 Selection and Method of Data and Materials

2.1 Data Material

Shandong is the main producing area of garlic in China. It is the distributing center of garlic and the wind vane of garlic price. Its garlic occupies more than 70% of the domestic market share. [10] Based on the average wholesale price of Shandong rose from 2010 to 2017, this paper explores the fluctuation rule of price, so as to provide a reliable basis for the regulation and prediction of garlic price. Data processing uses Excel and e-views9.0 software.

2.2 Research Methods

The Censusx12 Seasonal Adjustment Method

The CensusX12 seasonally adjusted method is a standard way for US official to adjust seasonal data of published economic events. Generally speaking, the change of economic time series is usually formed by Trend, Cycle, Seasonal and Irregular [11]. This structural model mainly represents the sequence by decomposing the time series into components with real economic meaning. The description of economic variables is clearer and more flexible, and it is more accurate to express the characteristics of sequence changes [12]. Eliminating seasonal variation elements from time series shows the real objective rules and trends of time series. It mainly includes: multiplication, addition, pseudo plus and logarithmic addition models are not allowed to have zero and negative numbers in time series when seasonally adjusting:

Addition mode: $Y_t = TC_t + S_t + I_t$;
Multiplication mode: $Y_t = TC_t * S_t * I_t$;
Logarithmic addition model: $\ln Y_t = \ln TC_t + \ln S_t + \ln I_t$
Pseudo addition model: $Y_t = TC_t(S_t + I_t - 1)$

The HP Filtering Analysis

The HP filtering analysis was proposed by Hodrick & Prescott in 1980 to study the economic boom of the United States after the study of World War II. Later, this method was widely used in the analysis of macroeconomic trends. Different from the phase average method, the HP filter analysis method does not depend on the determination of the economic cycle peaks and troughs. The use of more flexible methods can be seen as an approximate high-pass filter. The principle can be expressed as: Assume that the economic time series is $Y = \{y_1, y_2, \ldots, y_n\}$ and the trend element is $G = \{g_1, g_2, \ldots, g_n\}$, n is the capacity of the sample. HP filtering can decompose y_t into: $Y_t = g_t + c_t$, g_t and c_t are both unobservable values. It is generally believed that the partial trend G that cannot be observed in the time series Y is often defined as the solution to the smallest problem in formula one:

$$\min \{\textstyle\sum_{t=1}^{n}(y_t - g_t)^2 + \lambda\sum_{t=1}^{n}[B(L)g_t]^2\} \qquad (1)$$

B (L) = (L^ (−1) −1) − (1−L) is brought into the above formula, and then the conclusion is obtained:

$$\min \{\textstyle\sum_{t=1}^{n}(y_t - g_t)^2 + \lambda\sum_{t=1}^{n}[(g_{t+1} - g_t) - (g_t - g_{t-1})]^2\} \qquad (2)$$

The minimization problem with $[c (L) Y_t^T]^2$ to adjust the trend, and increases with the increase of. Ravn in 1997 on how to adjust the filter component so that it can accurately measure the business cycle, that is how to select the problem. =0, meet the minimization problem trend is equal to the sequence of $\{Y_t\}$; the greater estimated trend is more smooth; tends to infinity, the trend will be close to linear function estimation. In general, the use of annual data, =100; in the use of monthly data, value for 14400.

3 Results and Analysis

3.1 Monthly Wholesale Price Fluctuation Analysis of Garlic

According to the price change chart of garlic prices collected from the garlic wholesale market, it can be clearly seen that in January 2010–July 2011, garlic prices fluctuate drastically, and the price difference reached around 10 yuan/kg. Then, from July 2011 to April 2012, the trend of garlic prices changed smoothly. After June 2012 and April 2013, the price of garlic increased slightly, and the average price was about 4–5 yuan/kg. After June 2013, the price of garlic dropped again and did not rise until June 2015. By January 2017, the price of garlic rose to 15 yuan/kg, and prices dropped again. By June, the seasonal price of new garlic was as low as 4 yuan/kg. Judging from the overall price fluctuations, the price of garlic has risen and fell, and the cycle has changed (Fig. 1).

3.2 Analysis of Seasonal Adjustment Results

Adjustments to certain economic indicators due to seasonally-related peaks or troughs can be expected. Seasonal adjustments to economic indicators can help pinpoint potential trends by deducting current changes over the past few years. The average change in the price can indicate whether this increase or decrease is unusual or purely a seasonal phenomenon. Figure 2 is the seasonal variation of garlic initial price and seasonally adjusted price trend chart, which is seasonally adjusted by the seasonal adjustment method of CensusX12 in Shandong province through Eviews9.0 and CensusX12 seasonal adjustment method. DS expresses the trend of the initial price of garlic, and DS_SA shows the trend of garlic price change after seasonally adjusted. It can be drawn from the graph that there are large deviations between the two curves from April 2010 to August 2010, 2011 to 2012 and January 2013 to June 2015. The season has a more significant impact on garlic prices, and the effect is different at different time. During the study period, we can see that the price of garlic wholesale market in China shows a state of basic supply and demand fluctuation.

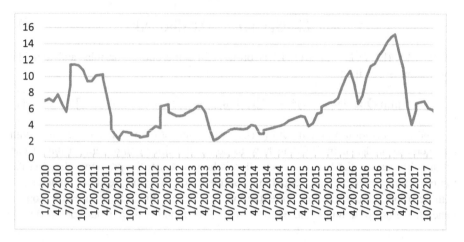

Fig. 1. Price trend of garlic rose market from january 2010 to december 2017

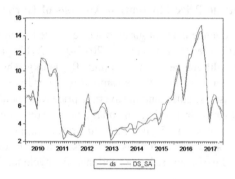

Fig. 2. 2010–2017 of the monthly price and seasonal adjustment of garlic wholesale market in Shandong Province

3.3   Seasonal Factor Analysis and Analysis of Irregular Factor Sequences

The Fig. 3 shows that seasonal fluctuation characteristics of garlic are more obvious. During the research period, the highest seasonal value of garlic shows a "U-shaped" trend. From the figure, we can see that the garlic price is at the lowest level every year during the new garlic harvest season. On the whole, the price of garlic rose from January to March every year. In March garlic prices began to decline until the price of garlic dropped to the lowest point in June. After June, garlic prices began to rise. Before and after New Year's Day, garlic prices fell again to a certain extent, until a new round of price increases in November, during the Spring Festival, prices rose to the highest point of the year, the changes of trend in the four years of 2010–2013 is most obvious. After 2014, the downward trend of garlic prices before and after New Year's Day is no longer obvious. After a slight change, it has risen to high levels before and after the Spring Festival. Through the analysis of Fig. 3, it can be clearly demonstrated that supply and demand is an important factor affecting garlic prices.

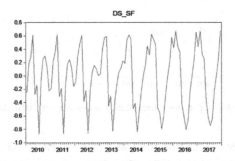

Fig. 3. Garlic price seasonal factor series for 2010–2017

According to Fig. 4, we can see that the irregular price of garlic prices is between 2010 and 2013 and 2016 to 2017, which shows that garlic prices fluctuate drastically. In 2013, 2016 and 2017, the price of irregular components was negative, and the trend was obvious, especially in 2017, the price fell to the low. After 2009–2010 years of speculators, it was found that the price of garlic increased by 2009–2010 years of speculators, which stimulated farmers' enthusiasm for garlic planting. [13] In 2011, the price of garlic began to decline, the price continued to decline, and the planting area was reduced accordingly. Under the influence of unfavorable natural factors such as heavy precipitation in 2012, garlic was severely reduced and the supply of the market was insufficient, making the price of garlic pick up. This is also one of the important factors of the peak in Fig. 4. The price falls to rise up to 2016, there is a big wave again in Fig. 4, which is due to the price of garlic in recent years is not impressive, the farmers planting enthusiasm weakened, garlic planting area decreased year by year. In early 2016, garlic producing areas in north suffered a snow disaster in a large range, which caused large-scale production cuts in the main garlic producing areas, resulting in market supply shortage, and some of the dealers were selling goods. So many factors caused garlic prices to rise sharply in 2016. This price also contributed to the dramatic increase of garlic planting area in autumn 2016, with the natural conditions of this season, in 2017, garlic had a bumper harvest, and the price dropped again. It can be seen that the price of garlic is not only affected by the planting area, natural conditions and dealers' hype are also important factors that affect the fluctuation of garlic prices.

3.4 HP Filter Analysis

In the Trend Fluctuation Graph in Fig. 5, the DS_SA curve represents the Original garlic price sequence after Seasonal adjustment; the Trend curve shows the long-term trend sequence of the garlic wholesale price index change. The Cycle curve shows the cyclic variation sequence of the garlic wholesale price index. It can be clearly seen in the figure that the Trend curve is much flatter than the DS_SA curve, and the garlic

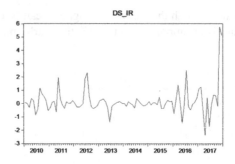

Fig. 4. Garlic price irregularity sequence for 2010–2017

price shows a flat trend of first decrease and then increase, and the garlic price as a whole shows a growth state over time, garlic prices have shown an increase over time as a whole, but garlic prices have weakened in the following year. The cycle of garlic price fluctuations can be divided by the year from peak to peak. HP filter analysis results show that China's garlic price fluctuation cycle is generally 3–4 years. If the peak wave crest is a complete wave period, the result is shown in Table 1.

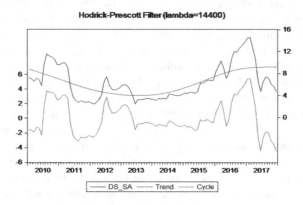

Fig. 5. HP filter for monthly prices of garlic

From the analysis of Table 1, from January 2010 to December 2017, the fluctuation cycle of garlic prices is short, to a certain extent, the stability of the garlic market is poor and the risk of price fluctuation is high. The volatility period from July 2012 to February 2013 and February 2016 to November 2016 is relatively short. The volatility period from July 2010 to June 2012, March 2013 to January 2016 and December 2016 to July 2017 was relatively long, which fully demonstrated the cyclical characteristics of garlic price fluctuation.

Table 1. Cycle characteristics of garlic monthly price fluctuation

Periodic number	Starting and finishing time	Wave length (month)	Trough time	Periodic wave type
一	2010/7/1–2012/6/1	18	2011/7/1	Sharp decline Sharp rise
二	2012/7/1–2013/2/1	6	2012/9/1	Sharp decline Slow rise
三	2013/3/1–2016/1/1	35	2013/5/1	Sharp decline Slow rise
四	2016/2/1–2016/11/1	9	2016/4/1	Sharp decline Sharp rise
五	2016/12/1–2017/7/1	16	2017/5/1	Sharp decline Sharp rise

4   Summary and Suggestion

4.1   Conclusion

In this paper, the HP filtering method is used to analyze the monthly price index of garlic market, and the characteristics of the overall price rising trend of the garlic market in Shandong province are analyzed. It is concluded that the price of garlic wholesale market in Shandong province shows a state of basically consistent fluctuation in supply and demand on the whole.

(1) The price of garlic wholesale market in Shandong province shows a state of basically consistent fluctuation in supply and demand on the whole;
(2) The fluctuation trend of garlic prices has a periodic characteristic, and the fluctuation curve shows a number of inverted "U" structures;
(3) The cycle of garlic price fluctuation is generally 3 to 4 years.

4.2   Expectations

But in this paper, we only analyze the fluctuation rule of garlic price in the past, and we cannot predict the price of garlic further. In future research, it should be combined with other models, and derive more valuable information from the previous garlic price data.

Acknowledgments. This work was financially supported by the following project:

(1) Shandong independent innovation and achievements transformation project (2014ZZCX07106).

(2) The research project "Intelligent agricultural system research and development of facility vegetable industry chain" of Shan-dong Province Major Agricultural Technological Innovation Project in 2017.

(3) Monitoring and statistics project of agricultural and rural resources of the Ministry of Agriculture.

References

1. Fang, Y., Song, J.Y.: An empirical analysis of the price fluctuation of agricultural products in China – based on HP filtering and cointegration test. Price: Theory Pract. (06), 62–63 (2013)
2. You, H.U., Chun-Jie, Q.I.: Analysis on price volatility of agricultural products based on HP filter model——a case study of fruits. J. Huazhong Agric. Univ. (2014)
3. Xu, X.G., Lou, X.C., Shen, J.: Historical review of China's agricultural product price fluctuations and its inspiration. Chin. Price (05), 22–25 (2008)
4. Hou, Y.Y.: Analysis of sea squash vegetable price fluctuation based on HP filter model. Guangdong Agric. Sci. **42**(19), 173–180 (2015)
5. Li, H.S., Shen, C., Kong, F.T.: Study on the decomposition of aquatic products price fluctuation based on X12-HP model. Guangdong Agric. Sci. **43**(11), 175–183 (2016)
6. Tang, J.Q.: China's egg price fluctuation cycle identification and short-term prediction. Chin. Anim. Husb. Mag. **53**(05), 142–148 (2017)
7. Zheng, S., Song, Y., Zong, Y.X., Zhao, B.H.: Analysis on period of vegetable price fluctuation and influencing factors in Hebei Province——based on H-P filtering and VAR model analysis. J. Jiangsu Agric. Sci. **45**(19), 350–357 (2017)
8. Li, J.D., Zhang, J.G.: Factors China fluctuation characteristics of a small variety of prices of agricultural products and its effect – Based on the analysis of 2005–2014 garlic price data of the empirical. J. Hunan Agric. Univ. (Soc. Sci.) **16**(04), 8–15 (2015)
9. Zhang, L.X., Zhang, X.C., Chen, S.T.: Does hot money impact fluctuation of agricultural product price——case of fluctuations in garlic prices. J. Agrotech. Econ. (12), 60–67 (2010)
10. Cai-Cai, L.I., Qin, N., Zhou, Y.: Characteristics of and factors affecting garlic price fluctuations in Shandong. Fujian J. Agric. Sci. (2017)
11. Liang, J.F., Fang, W., Wan, Z.: Analysis on fluctuation trend and temporal characteristics of pig price in Guangdong based——CensusX12 and H-P model. J. Guangdong Agric. Sci. **42**(23), 226–231 (2015)
12. Chen, F., Gao, T.M.: The application of structural time series model in seasonal adjustment – comparison and analysis of X-12 seasonal adjustment method. Syst. Eng. Theory Pract. (11), 7–14 (2007)
13. Jiang H., Wei H.: The cause of the price fluctuation of garlic in China and its policy regulation and control research. Price: Theory Pract. (10) 112–115 (2016)

Application of Extensible Mind Mapping in Retirement Paradox Solution

Wenjun Hong, Rui Fan$^{(\boxtimes)}$, Bifeng Guo, Yongzhao Feng, Fuyu Ma,
and Shunliang Ye

Faculty of Software, Guangdong Ocean University, Zhanjiang, China
455485327@qq.com, 1037486652@qq.com,
1544266684@qq.com, 452388727@qq.com, 756323372@qq.com,
fanrui@gdou.edu.cn

Abstract. With the development of society, the problem of population ageing becomes increasingly in our life. However, there is a contradictory problem that population ageing brings much pressure to economy while delay of retirement age makes employment pressure more severe. In order to solve the problem, we put up with a new innovative thought and perform an innovative thinking in combination with Extensive mind mapping, giving some suggestions to population ageing problem.

Keywords: Extenics · Mind mapping · Retirement age · Social production

1 Introduction

To find out the solution to population ageing becomes a global problem. Taking China as an example, China is in the midst of an aging population at present [1] and the labor force participation rate also shows a trend of rapid decline [2]. It is reported that China is now in a situation of "aging before getting rich" [3]. Delaying the retirement age becomes an irresistible trend [4]. Now there are some experts studying the optimal retirement age [5]. However, no one solves this problem with the principle of Extenics theory [6]. Extenics is a subject originated in China and is used to solve contradictory problem [7]. Our team is committed to the study of Extenics and has made the following contributions. Up to now, our team has developed an web-based extension innovative service software [8]. In addition, we have developed the extension innovation software service architecture [9], but it can not clearly reflect the whole thinking process of people. However, adaptive extension innovation software model [10] provides us with a new idea. In the way of combining the principle of extension theory and mind mapping [11], it shows the whole procedure of thinking clearly by pictures. We want a mind-mapping software that allows people to change lines and shapes flexibly, and to help people solve problems by combining the principles of Extenics, whose model is shown in Fig. 1.

From the Fig. 1, a kernel problem is separated into two sub-problems. While one of the sub problems was identified as a kernel problem, the problem modeling solving process of the problem was displayed in the mind mapping. We used table to describe

X. Sun et al. (Eds.): ICCCS 2018, LNCS 11063, pp. 343–352, 2018.
https://doi.org/10.1007/978-3-030-00006-6_31

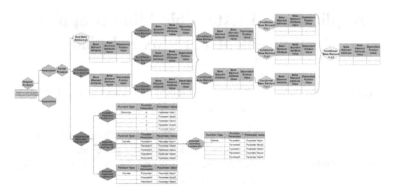

Fig. 1. Extensible mind mapping with flexible software

goal base elements, conditional base elements and comprehensive dependent functions in kernel problems. The contents of base elements included base element attribute, base element attribute value and dependent function value. And the comprehensive dependent function is composed of finite extended dependent functions, which expands the three attributes including function type, function parameter and parameter value. At the same time, we can see that the relationship between kernel problem and original problem has been identified in the gray figure of the graph. In extensible analysis, we can extend more conditional base element. After screening these conditional base element, we select some base elements with greater comprehensive dependent function value and carry out extensible transformation. After the extensible transformation of these base elements, we choose the final base element to solve the kernel problem by the superiority evaluation.

2 Procedures of Solving the Problem

2.1 Problem Modeling

Finding an optimal retirement age is essential, which will not only reduce the burden of social pension, but also it avoids the severe employment pressure. First, we set up an extension model for the original problem. By looking up the relevant information, the original problem is decomposed into two sub-problems, which are the problem of pension system and labor demand. Pension system problems, such as the limited pension funds, if there are too many people in retirement, there will be huge social and economic pressure. The problem of Labour demand limits the retirement age. They are two factors that affect the retirement age. The modeling process of the original problem is shown in Fig. 2 through the way of mind mapping.

As can be seen from Fig. 2, a kernel problem modeling is presented through the mind mapping of the goal base element, conditional base element and integrated dependent function. By referring to the relevant data, three primitive properties including per capita pension, life expectancy and retirement age are listed in the corresponding form. We analyze the current situation of China from the above three

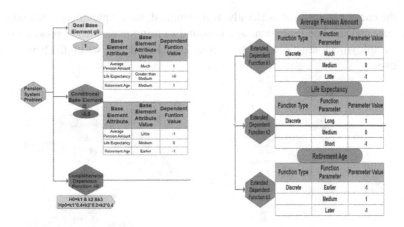

Fig. 2. Modeling of sub-problem pension system

aspects and find out new solutions through extension. Comparing with the pension amount of the developed countries, we found that the per capita pension in China is still at a low level. Comparing life expectancy with other countries in the world, China's life expectancy is at a moderate level [12]. For the above three primitive properties, we set up three discrete dependent functions to describe the contradiction caused by the current retirement age. First, the basic element of the first kernel issue is established.

$$L1 = \begin{bmatrix} PensionSys, & AvgPA & Little \\ & LifeExp & Medium \\ & RetAge & Earlier \end{bmatrix} \qquad G1 = \begin{bmatrix} PensionSys, & AvgPA & Much \\ & LifeExp & GreaterthanMedium \\ & RetAge & Medium \end{bmatrix}$$

For the primitive properties of kernel issue 1, per capita pension, life expectancy and retirement age, we have established three discrete dependent functions, k1(x), k2 (x) and k3(x) are shown below.

$$k1 = \begin{cases} Much, & 1 \\ Medium, & 0 \\ Little, & -1 \end{cases} \qquad k2 = \begin{cases} Long, & 1 \\ Medium, & 0 \\ Short, & -1 \end{cases} \qquad k3 = \begin{cases} Earlier, & -1 \\ Medium, & 1 \\ Later, & -1 \end{cases}$$

According to the above three discrete dependent functions, we can find the corresponding values from formula 1, formula 2 and formula 3. The associated function values of k1, k2 and k3 are negative 1, greater than or equal to 0 and negative 1. Therefore, the basic element attribute and the retirement age group attribute are incompatible and need to be extended.

From Fig. 3, we can see the modeling process of the second kernel problem and its goal primitives, conditional primitives, and integrated dependent functions. By referring to literature and research reports, the selection of labor demand and the number of existing labor force as the base element attribute. China's demand for Labour is already saturated, and the retirement age will not increase the demand for Labour. On the other hand, the current labor force is already over-saturated, the employment situation is not optimistic, and the late retirement age is bound to bring even greater pressure on the serious employment situation. For the second kernel issue, we set up the base element as follows.

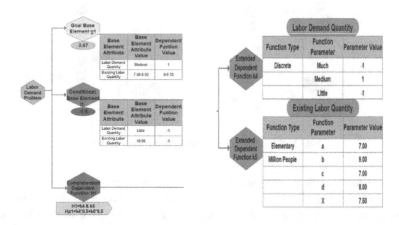

Fig. 3. Modeling of sub-problem labor demand

$$L2 = \begin{bmatrix} Labor, & DemandQuantity & Little \\ & ExistingQuantity & 10.00 \end{bmatrix} \quad G2 = \begin{bmatrix} Labor, & DemandQuantity & Medium \\ & ExistingQuantity & 7.00-8.00 \end{bmatrix}$$

For the labor demand primitives, we set up a discrete dependent function, k4(x), as shown below.

$$k4 = \begin{cases} Much, & -1 \\ Medium, & 1 \\ Little, & -1 \end{cases}$$

According to function 4, we find the discrete dependent k4 = −1. Therefore, the basic element attribute of labor demand in the second is incompatible.

For the existing labor quantity primitives, we have established an elementary dependent function k5(x). According to the extension principle, the form of elementary dependent function is shown in formula 5 and formula 6.

$$k5(x) = \begin{cases} \frac{\rho(x,x0,X)}{D(x,X0,X)} & D(x,X0,X) \neq 0, x \in X \\ -\rho(x,x0,X0)+1 & D(x,X0,X) = 0, x \in X0 \\ 0 & D(x,X0,X) = 0, x \notin X0, x \in X \end{cases}$$

$$D(x,X0,X) = \rho(x,X) - \rho(x,X0)$$

The relevant function procedure for calculating the number of existing labor force is as follows.

$$\rho(x, X0) = \left| x - \frac{7.00 + 8.00}{2} \right| - \frac{8.00 - 7.00}{2} = |x - 7.50| - 0.50$$

$$\rho(x, X) = \left| x - \frac{7.00 + 9.00}{2} \right| - \frac{9.00 - 7.00}{2} = |x - 8.00| - 1.00$$

According to the formula above, we calculated the dependent function value k5 (x) = −1, knowing that this is an incompatible problem.

2.2 Extensible Analysis

From the mind map, we already know the contradictory attributes of the primitive. Then use the method of extension analysis to think in a divergent way. For the first kernel issue, we propose five solutions to the problem by changing the conditional primitives shown as follows.

$$L1.a = \begin{bmatrix} PensionSys, & AvgPA & Much \\ & LifeExp & Medium \\ & RetAge & Earlier \end{bmatrix} \quad L1.b = \begin{bmatrix} PensionSys, & AvgPA & Medium \\ & LifeExp & Medium \\ & RetAge & Earlier \end{bmatrix}$$

$$L1.c = \begin{bmatrix} PensionSys, & AvgPA & Much \\ & LifeExp & Medium \\ & RetAge & Earlier \end{bmatrix} \quad L1.d = \begin{bmatrix} PensionSys, & AvgPA & Medium \\ & LifeExp & Medium \\ & RetAge & Earlier \end{bmatrix}$$

$$L1.e = \begin{bmatrix} PensionSys, & AvgPA & Little \\ & LifeExp & Medium \\ & RetAge & Medium \end{bmatrix}$$

We expand the attributes, the five elements were L1. A, to improve the endowment insurance, L1. B, limit the age pension, L1. C, a tax increase, L1. D, appropriation of other state spending, L1. E, delay retirement age. Their integrated dependent function values are 0, −0.4, 0, −0.4, 0. The detailed description is shown below.

The endowment insurance of pay endowment insurance: people is part of the pension, improving the endowment insurance of pay to increase the total amount of social endowment, and with the increase of life expectancy, residents of pension extend, can not only solve the problem of less per capita pension, unapt make the residents feel cheated.

Limit the age of pensionable age: it stipulates that residents can only receive a pension of 15 years after retirement, which is equivalent to not increasing the number of elderly people, and will not increase the pressure on social pension. However, after the residents have passed the pension age, they have neither the capacity to work nor the income to make their lives unsustainable.

Increasing tax: tax is one of the country's main source of income, increase residents can increase national income tax, countries with more money, social endowment parts can also be assigned to the more amount, so as to solve the problem of less per capita pension.

Appropriation of other state financial expenditures: the provision of funds for other purposes in the state budget to the social endowment to increase the total amount of social endowment. Countries, however, every aspect of funds will be occupied a certain proportion, misappropriate the funds for other purposes to fill the gaps in social pension, is bound to make a country other aspects cannot be normal operation, with dysfunctional in the affairs of their country.

Postponing five years of retirement:A delay of five years would allow residents to extend their working lives, extend the number of years they earn, extend the number of years they pay taxes, and reduce the number of pensioners.

For kernel problem 2, the conditional primitives are extended to five primitive properties. They are L2. A, adding jobs, L2. B, prohibiting the use of scientific and technological production, L2. C, prohibiting the company from laying off workers, L2. D, early retirement, L2. E, transferring labor to foreign countries. Their integrated dependent function values are 0, −1, −1, −0.33, 0.04.

$$L2.a = \begin{bmatrix} Labor, & DemandQuantity & Medium \\ & ExistingQuantity & 10.00 \end{bmatrix} \quad L2.b = \begin{bmatrix} Labor, & DemandQuantity & Much \\ & ExistingQuantity & 10.00 \end{bmatrix}$$

$$L2.c = \begin{bmatrix} Labor, & DemandQuantity & Much \\ & ExistingQuantity & 10.00 \end{bmatrix} \quad L2.d = \begin{bmatrix} Labor, & DemandQuantity & Little \\ & ExistingQuantity & 8.00 \end{bmatrix}$$

$$L2.e = \begin{bmatrix} Labor, & DemandQuantity & Little \\ & ExistingQuantity & 7.70 \end{bmatrix}$$

Job position creation: countries increase labor demand by increasing national infrastructure.

It is forbidden to use scientific and technological production: by prohibiting enterprises from using high-tech technology, all products are produced in the most primitive way. However, this method will lead to a decrease in social productivity and will bring the country's scientific and technological level to a standstill, which is not conducive to the improvement of comprehensive national strength.

The company is prohibited from cutting staff: this method can reduce the unemployment rate, but it will lead to the employee's unthinking, which is not good for the company's development.

Early retirement: early retirement can reduce the number of existing workers, but it will increase the number of pensioners and put severe pressure on the social economy.

Moving labor abroad: this approach reduces the amount of labor available in our country. The extension analysis process is shown in Fig. 4.

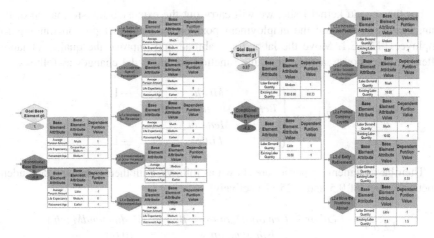

Fig. 4. Extensible analysis

2.3 Extensible Transformation

Based on the analysis of extension base element in the extension analysis, the extended primitives with the value less than 0 are excluded. In the first kernel issue, the age and appropriation of the state's other fiscal expenditure were excluded. In the second kernel issue, the use of technology was banned, and companies were barred from cutting jobs and early retirement.

In the first kernel issue, the selected scheme can be expanded by extension, L1. A. 1, while raising the pension insurance premium and extending the life of the pension insurance. 1. On the basis of increasing tax revenue, we will increase the amount of tax payable. L1. 1, 10 years of retirement. After the above extension transformation, the function parameters of the dependent function are changed as follows.

$$k1.1 = \begin{cases} GreaterthanMore & 3 \\ More & 2 \\ Much & 1 \\ Medium & 0 \\ Little & -1 \end{cases} \qquad k3.1 = \begin{cases} Earlier & -1 \\ Medium & 1 \\ BetweenMediumandLater & 4 \\ Later & -1 \end{cases}$$

Their primitive properties are shown below, and the values of the composite dependent functions are 0.4, 0.8, and 1.2.

$$L1.a.1 = \begin{bmatrix} PensionSys, & AvgPA & More \\ & LifeExp & Medium \\ & RetAge & Earlier \end{bmatrix} \quad L1.c.1 = \begin{bmatrix} PensionSys, & AvgPA & GreaterthanMore \\ & LifeExp & Medium \\ & RetAge & Earlier \end{bmatrix}$$

$$L1.e.1 = \begin{bmatrix} PensionSys, & AvgPA & Little \\ & LifeExp & Medium \\ & RetAge & BetweenMediumandLater \end{bmatrix}$$

For the second kernel issue, we will carry out the extension transformation of the plan, L2. A. 1, increase the employment position, and conduct pre-job training for employees. L2. E.1. Move the labor force abroad and improve the quality of labor. After the extension transformation, the function parameter k4 changes as follows.

$$k4.1 = \begin{cases} Much & -1 \\ BetweenMediumandMuch & 2 \\ Medium & 1 \\ Little & -1 \end{cases}$$

Their base element properties are shown as follows, with their combined dependent function values of 0.5 and 0.25 respectively.

$$L2.a.1 = \begin{bmatrix} Labor, & DemandQuantity & BetweenMediumandMuch \\ & ExistingQuantity & 10.00 \end{bmatrix}$$

$$L2.e.1 = \begin{bmatrix} Labor, & DemandQuantity & Little \\ & ExistingQuantity & 7.50 \end{bmatrix}$$

The extension transformation process of two kernel problems is shown below (Fig. 5).

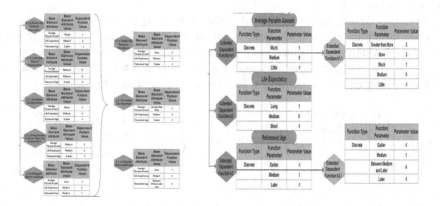

Fig. 5. Extensible transformation

2.4   Superiority Evaluation

After analysis, we chose to solve the two kernel problems with the most advantageous solution. The first kernel option, L1. E. 1, the second kernel option, L2. A. 1, their associated function values are as follows.

$$H1 = \begin{bmatrix} PensionSys, & AvgPA & -1 \\ & LifeExp & 0 \\ & RetAge & 4 \end{bmatrix} \quad H2 = \begin{bmatrix} Labor, & DemandQuantity & -1 \\ & ExistingQuantity & 1.50 \end{bmatrix}$$

$$Y(H) = H1(k) \wedge H2(k)$$
$$= k1 \wedge k2 \wedge k3 \wedge k4 \wedge k5$$
$$> 0$$

Therefore, the solution for the first kernel problem is to extend ten years for retirement. And the solution for the second kernel is to move the labor abroad so that the quality of the productivity can be modified. The procedure of the optimization is as Fig. 6.

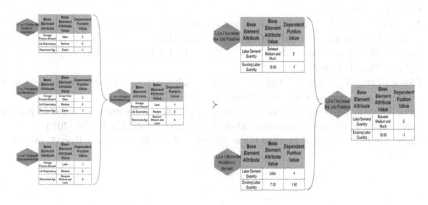

Fig. 6. Superiority evaluation

3 Conclusion and Future Work

Population aging is a problem from all over the world. But the situation in China is different from other counties. China is confronting a circumstance of aging before getting rich. Aging population is more than labor number which brings forth burden in raising the old. Of course, postponing retirement is one of the solution. However, postponing retirement might aggravate the competition pressure in job market.

The produce of applying Extenics is quite obvious by utilizing this software, which is a part of the software functions developed. Besides, the software can provide online Extenics education and exchange. And We will continue working on the whole probing of problem solving by human to achieve Artificial intelligence applied Extenics.

Acknowledgements. The research is supported by Guangdong Provincial Science and Technology Project (2014A040402010) and Guangdong Province Innovation and Entrepreneurship Training Program for College Students(201710566036).

References

1. Zhai, Z., Jiaju, C., Li, L.: China's population aging trend, new features and corresponding pension policies. Shandong Univ. Acad. J. (Philos. Soc. Sci Version) **1**(3), 27–35 (2016)
2. Wang, Y., Tong, Y.: The impact of China's aging population on labor participation rate. Cap. Econ. Trade Univ. Acad. J. **17**(1), 61–67 (2015)
3. Shi, X.: Preparing for "not rich first", achieving a decent retirement life. Public Financ. Advis. (9), 26–27 (2016)
4. Yin, S.: Research on the retirement age in the context of population aging. Hunan Ind. Prof. Technol. Coll. Acad. J. **15**(4), 34–36 (2015)
5. Xiong, X.: Study on Optimal Retirement Age Based on Personal Utility and Health and Empirical Analysis. Xiamen University (2014)
6. Yang, C., Wang, G., et al.: A new cross discipline——extenics. China Sci. Found. (Engl. Ed.) **13**(1), 55–61 (2005)
7. Cai, W., Yang, C.Y., Bin, H.E.: Several problems on the research of extenics. J. Guangdong Univ. Technol. (2001)
8. Yan, S., Fan, R., Chen, Y., et al.: Research on web services-based extenics aided innovation system. Procedia Comput. Sci. **107**(C), 103–110 (2017)
9. Fan, R.: Modelling Extenics Innovation Software by Intelligent Service Components. Open Cybern. Syst. J. **8**, 1–7 (2014)
10. Fan, R., Peng, Y., Chen, Y., et al.: A method for self-adaptive software formal modeling by extenics. CAAI Trans. Intell. Syst. **10**(6), 901–911 (2015)
11. Deng, Q., Wu, Y., Weng, Y.: The method and application of the extension mind map for the construction of the system structure. Math. Pract. Underst. **45**(12), 94–99 (2015)
12. Zhao, Y.: The ranking of average life expectancy of countries. Encycl. Knowl. (6), 43–45 (2014)

Big Data Equi-Join Optimization Algorithms on Spark Cloud Computing Platform

Sihui Li[✉] and Wei Xu

Beijing Jiaotong University, Beijing 100044, China
16120386@bjtu.edu.cn

Abstract. On Spark cloud computing platform, the conventional big data equi-join algorithms cannot meet the performance requirements well and the procedure of it is very time-consuming, so the efficiency of big data equi-join is a burning challenge. To overcome it, in this paper, we propose Compressed Bloom Filter Join algorithm, an efficient algorithm filters out most of invalid connections which cannot meet the criteria to reduce network overhead, and it constructs static one-dimensional bit array to improve join performance. Moreover, Compressed Bloom Filter Join Extension algorithm, an extended optimization based on Compressed Bloom Filter Join algorithm, produces a dynamic two-dimensional bit array to filter out invalid records, and it can further accelerate the process of data join when the data size is unknown. Experimental results show that the performance of two optimization algorithms which can reduce time consumption and the data size of Shuffle stage are better than Hash Join and Broadcast Join on Spark cloud computing platform.

Keywords: Big data equi-join · Compressed Bloom Filter · Join performance Spark cloud computing platform

1 Introduction

In the ear of big data, the data has the characteristics of large volume, fast generation and various kinds. In order to handle massive data better, the concept of cloud computing emerges as the times require. Spark, a new cloud computing platform, has good performance in both execution efficiency and development efficiency.

The Spark cloud computing platform is mainly comprised of four parts: Spark SQL, Spark Streaming, GraphX and MLlib [1]. Spark SQL plays an important role in the Spark cloud computing platform, and equi-join is an operation with high frequency and execution cost in big data processing in Spark SQL [2]. It can influence the performance of Spark distributed computing framework greatly. Broadcast Join and Hash Join, provided by Spark cloud computing platform, are the most commonly join methods used. Broadcast Join is suitable for equi-join of the big table and small table because of broadcasting a data which to be joined [3]. Hash Join is used for big table join, but it can bring significant network traffic and a high disk I/O when the joined date is too large [4]. Therefore, how to improve the performance of big data equi-join is a challenge on Spark cloud computing platform.

X. Sun et al. (Eds.): ICCCS 2018, LNCS 11063, pp. 353–363, 2018.
https://doi.org/10.1007/978-3-030-00006-6_32

Many studies have been presented for big data join optimization on Spark cloud computing platform. Sun [5] proposes an algorithm using Bit-map compress algorithm to improve join performance, but the performance of this algorithm is not significant, because of non-ideal filter stage. Lin et al. propose a multi-join algorithm which divides join tasks into many join subtasks based on presorting [6], and it makes the same tuples in a node to save time and increase efficiency. An efficient algorithm, based on Bloom Filter, is presented in [7] which has a better effect in filter stage, but its generated bit array is large. Reference [8, 9] study the efficient equi-join algorithms based on Bloom Filter, however, the latter has not an obvious improved because of the size of the bit array. Ramesh et al. [7] extend Bloom Join algorithm to reduce the network overhead by using the statistical information of the database.

In k Nearest Neighbor Joins [10], it is designed to reducing both the shuffling and computational costs by exploiting pruning rules. Blanas et al. [11] propose an optimization algorithm based on Broadcast Join. When a small dataset and a big data set are joined, the big data set will filter invalid records by small dataset which is broadcast to each node. However, this algorithm is only suitable for the join of big data set and small data set. Reference [12, 13] also research the equi-join optimization algorithm in Spark, and the algorithm filters data which to be joined by Bloom Filter, but the consumption of broadcast operation is large. In order to solve the inefficient joining operation, Liu et al. [14] devise an efficient algorithm named Bloom Filter Repartitioning to filter out most of the invalid records. Reference [15] presents a load balancing join algorithm, and it uses sampling method to detect the useless data in the join operation to reduce negative influence so as to realize load balancing.

On the basis of Broadcast Join, Hash Join and other existing optimization algorithms, we propose two new equi-join optimization algorithms to improve the performance of data join in this paper, Compressed Bloom Filter Join (CBF Join) algorithm and Compressed Bloom Filter Join Extension (CBF-extension) algorithm. CBF Join algorithm is designed for big data equi-join in Spark, it filters out the records which do not meet conditions to reduce the data size of Shuffle stage firstly to improve the join performance. CBF-extension algorithm is presented for the situation of unknown data join size, which can improve the join performance by generating two-dimensional bit array dynamically.

The contribution of this paper can be summarized as follows:

(1) We propose an efficient big data equi-join optimization algorithm to reduce network overhead to accelerate the data join process;
(2) We further design a extended optimization algorithm to improve performance when the data size is unknown;
(3) We evaluate the proposed algorithms with the datasets from an Internet company. The results show that our algorithms outperform their alternatives in all experiments.

The remainder of this paper is organized as follows. Section 2 describes Compressed Bloom Filter Join algorithm and Compressed Bloom Filter Join Extension algorithm. Section 3 presents the performance evaluation. Finally, we conclude this paper and discuss future work in Sect. 4.

2 Compressed Bloom Filter Join Algorithm and Extension Algorithm

In the Spark cloud computing platform, Hash Join and Broadcast Join, commonly used methods, have some limitations in time consumption and network overhead. In this section, an equi-join optimization algorithm based on Compressed Bloom Filter, called Compressed Bloom Filter Join (CBF Join), is proposed to solve the defect of big data equi-join operation firstly. The main feasible idea is to reduce a majority of the key/value date pairs that do not participate in the join stage, and the aim is to improve the performance of equi-join operation according to reduce the data size of Shuffle stage. When the selection rate is very low, the filtered data can even be broadcast to each node directly, thus algorithm can be converted to a highly efficient Broadcast Join. And then, an extension algorithm based on CBF Join is designed to solve the unknown size of data, which called Compressed Bloom Filter Join Extension Algorithm (CBF-extension). The unknown size of data means that the data size is difficult or inconvenient to calculation, or the data size is inaccuracy due to the dynamical growing of data size. The core concept is dynamically generating two-dimensional bit array to filter big table when the data size is unknown, and executing join operation after filtering most of invalid data.

2.1 Compressed Bloom Filter Join Algorithm

CBF Join algorithm is divided into two stages: the bit array generation stage and join operation stage. In the first stage, the bit array generation stage consists of three parts: the whole generation phase of the bit array, the partition generation phase of the bit array, the broadcast phase of the bit array. Figure 1 shows the flowchart of the first stage, where KeyA and KeyB represent the join property sets of TableA and TableB, respectively.

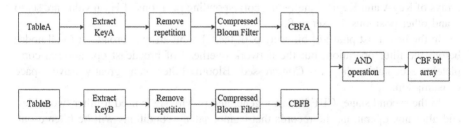

Fig. 1. First stage algorithm flowchart of CBF Join

In the whole generation phase of the bit array part, CBF bit array is generated according to the value of the join properties of the two big tables. Firstly, the join properties of TableA and TableB are extracted to generate two new RDDs, called KeyA and KeyB. Secondly, KeyA and KeyB are removed repetition to DistinctKeyA and DistinctKeyB separately, which are the non-repeating RDD. Then DistinctKeyA and DistinctKeyB are compressed to generate bit array CBFA and CBFB by

Compressed Bloom Filter. Finally, CBF Join gets the final CBF bit array after doing AND operation and compression, and broadcasts final CBF bit array to all nodes in the cluster. Figure 2 shows the whole generation of CBF bit array.

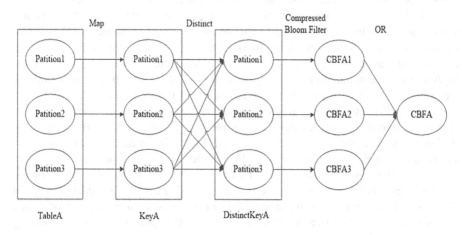

Fig. 2. Bit array generate flowchart of CBF join

In the partition generation phase of the bit array part, the most important stage is to generate CBF bit array by DistinctKeyA and DistinctKeyB. In Spark, an RDD usually contains multiple partitions, and in the stage of generating CBF bit array, each RDD partition generates a bit array firstly, such as CBFA1, CBFA2, CBFA3 which are shown in Fig. 2, then the all generated bit arrays are executed or operated to get corresponding bit arrays. Before generating bit arrays, CBF Join needs to select K independent Hash functions and the value of K is determined by the size of the joined table, then the K independent Hash functions will be used to calculate all generated bit arrays of KeyA and KeyB. Finally, the corresponding positions of Hash value are set to 1 and other positions are set to 0.

In the broadcast phase of bit array part, the CBF bit array is broadcast to all nodes before the filter operation, but the network overhead of broadcast operation is completely acceptable due to Compressed Bloom Filter can greatly save space consumption.

In the second stage, CBF bit array generated previously is used to filter two tables, and after this operation, the records that cannot satisfy conditions will be filtered out. The flowchart of the second stage is as shown in Fig. 3. In the filtering operation, CBF Join checks whether the value of k positions is 1 according to the k values of the first stage. If these positions of a record are not all 1, then this record will be filtered out. In the join operation, CBF Join calculates the size of the filtered table, if the size exceeds a certain threshold, then Hash Join will be executed to get the final result. If the size is smaller then threshold, then Broadcast Join will be executed to get the final result.

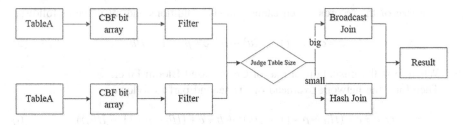

Fig. 3. Second stage algorithm flowchart of CBF join

2.2 Compressed Bloom Filter Join Algorithm Performance Analysis

The network overhead of the equi-join algorithms is analyzed in this section. The network overhead of Hash Join as follows,

$$O(a * c + b * c) \tag{1}$$

where a represents the number of records in TableA, b and c denotes the number of records in TableB, and the average size of a record respectively.

The network overhead of Broadcast Join as follows,

$$N * Min(a, b) * c \tag{2}$$

where N denotes the number of compute nodes.

The network overhead of CBF Join algorithm is made up of two parts. The first part is the cost of Distinct operation and bit array combined. The cost of Distinct operation is related to the repetition rate of data sets, and the repetition rate of join properties which used in this paper is high, so the network overhead of this part is small and negligible. In the combination of the bit array, k bit arrays whose size are M bit need to be transferred from Executor node to Driver node, so that the network overhead is M * k bit. After generating bit arrays, bit arrays need to be broadcast to all compute nodes, and the network overhead of broadcasting is M * N bit. Therefore, the network overhead of the first part as follows,

$$2 * K * M + N * M \tag{3}$$

The cost of executing Hash Join or Broadcast Join after filtering tables is calculated in the network overhead of the second part. The above information shows that the network overhead of Hash Join is greater than Broadcast Join, so Hash join operation is chosen to analyze the cost of CBF Join considering the worst case. The data of Shuffle stage consists of the records of satisfying conditions and records which are misjudged. And the size of the records of satisfying conditions as follows,

$$a * c * Ha + b * c * Hb \tag{4}$$

where Ha and Hb represent the percentage of records in TableA and TableB which satisfy conditions respectively.

The size of the records which cannot satisfy conditions and misjudge as follows,

$$a * c * p * (1 - Ha) + b * c * p * (1 - Hb) \tag{5}$$

Where p is the misjudgment rate of Compressed Bloom Filter.
Therefore, the network overhead of the second part as follows,

$$O(a * c * (Ha + p * (1 - Ha)) + b * c * (Hb + p * (1 - Hb))) \tag{6}$$

and the whole network overhead of CBF Join algorithm as follows,

$$2 * K * M + N * M + O(a * c * (Ha + p * (1 - Ha)) + b * c * (Hb + p * (1 - Hb))) \tag{7}$$

Comparing and analyzing the network overhead of three equi-join algorithms, it can be demonstrated that Broadcast Join has the largest network overhead, so that Broadcast is usually given up in big data equi-join operation. And the network overhead of Hash Join is related to the size of the original data table, when the data size of the original table is too large, the time consumption is very high. In the result of CBF Join, D and 2 * M * k are relatively small, and the misjudgment rate of Compressed Bloom Filter p is also small, so Ha and Hb have great influence on the network overhead of CBF Join. When the percentage of records satisfying conditions is not particularly high, namely Ha and Hb is relatively small, the performance of CBF Join has a great improvement than Hash Join.

2.3   Compressed Bloom Filter Join Extension Algorithm

CBF-extension algorithm is also divided into two stages, in the first stage, the generated bit array part of CBF-extension is the same as CBF Join, but CBF-extension can get corresponding bit array CBFeA and CBFeB dynamically even if the number of Hash functions is unknown. Figure 4 shows the flowchart of the first stage, and then CBFeA and CBFeB bit arrays are discussed how to dynamically generate.

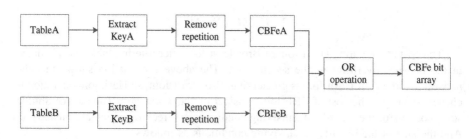

Fig. 4. First stage algorithm flowchart of CBF-extension

The length of bit array is dynamically growing, and using a Bloom Filter bit array which can handle fewer records to process generated bit arrays firstly. The size of handled data assume to be d, then CBF-extension selects k independent Hash functions to calculate all partition bit arrays of KeyA and KeyB. When the number of handled records reach the limit, the same k Hash functions are utilized to generate new bit array with the same length as the initial bit array, and then generate S final bit arrays by continuing to calculate. Eventually, S final bit array can be generated a two-dimensional bit array with S * L.

In the second stage, previously generated CBFe bit arrays are used to filter two tables, and after this operation, the records that cannot satisfy conditions will be filtered out. In the filter stage, CBF-extension needs to compare the data to CBFe two-dimensional bit array for each row in turn. If the value of k positions are all 1 in a row, then this record will be filtered and the latter rows need not be compared.

When the table size is known, CBF Join can not ensure the number of Hash functions to make the algorithm unusable, but CBF Join and CBF-extension are the same network overhead in the suitable scenario, respectively. The network overhead of CBF-extension as follows,

$$2 * K * M + N * M + O(a * c * (Ha + p * (1 - Ha)) + b * c * (Hb + p * (1 - Hb)))$$
(8)

3 Experimental Evaluation

3.1 Experimental Setup

Experiments are implemented in Hadoop and Spark respectively, and they are built on the same cluster with 7 nodes including client, which are configured with 7 same physical machines. Table 1 shows the information of the experimental configuration, and the size of data set used in experiments is displayed in Table 2.

Table 1. The information of the experimental configuation

Hardware	Information	Software	Information
Operating system	CenOs release 6.5 (Final) x86_64	Java JDK	1.7.0_79
CPU basic frequency	3.2 GHZ	Hadoop	2.7.1
The number of CPU kernel	8 kernels	Scala	2.10.4
Memory	32 G	Spark	1.6.2
Hard disk	2 T/7200 turns	Network	1000 M

The experiment adopts Hash Join provided by Spark cloud computing platform and CBF Join to process data sets, separately, and validates the performance of CBF Join is higher than Hash Join. In each experiment, five groups of data sets with different size are selected to join. In order to avoid the Broadcast Hash is executed in join stage, the automatic broadcast function is disabled by setting parameters and the same parameters

Table 2. The size of experimental datasets

Dataset	The size of dataset	Dataset	The size of datasize
1	1 G	4	20 G
2	5 G	5	40 G
3	10 G		

are used in other experiments. In the experiment, the misjudgment rate is about 0.8%, and the size of bit array is about 10 M when the max size of join data is 40G. Therefore, the network overhead of broadcasting stage is acceptable.

3.2 CBF Join Experimental Results

First of all, the experiment compares the data size of Shuffle stage between Hash Join and CBF Join. Tables 3 and Table 4 show the write data size and read data size in Shuffle stage between Hash Join and CBF Join, respectively.

Table 3. Comparison of the write data size in shuffle stage

Dataset	Hash Join	CBF Join
1	40.02 MB	201.9 KB
2	200.4 MB	1098 KB
3	407.3 MB	2116 KB
4	820.9 MB	4283 KB
5	1660 MB	8617 KB

Table 4. Comparison of the read data size in shuffle stage

Dataset	Hash Join	CBF Join
1	60.21 MB	312.7 KB
2	307.6 MB	1573 KB
3	611.1 MB	3155 KB
4	1225 MB	6342 KB
5	2479 MB	12706 KB

In Tables 3 and 4, the data size of CBF Join is considerably lower than Hash Join both in Shuffle write and Shuffle read part. In CBF Join, the data size of Shuffle stage is only about 0.5% of Hash Join, so that the effect of filter operation is obvious on data sets used in experiments.

Figure 5 shows the time consumption comparison of two join algorithms, where CBF Join1 represents the stage of generating bit array and broadcasting, CBF Join2 denotes the stage of filtering join table and executing join operation. As shown in Fig. 5, the time consumption of executing join operation after filter stage in CBF Join is less than that of Hash Join, and it is only 1/3 of Hash Join. But CBF Join has a stage of generating bit array, the time consumption of this stage is less than the stage of joining and filtering in Fig. 5, Thus, the time consumption of CBF Join is less than Hash Join while doing big table equi-join operation.

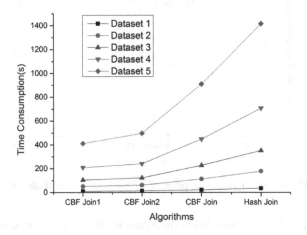

Fig. 5. The time consumption of CBF Join and Hash Join

3.3 CBF-Extension Experimental Results

Experiments validate the performance of CBF-extension is better than Hash Join when the size of date is unknown. The experimental parameter is the same as that of CBF Join. Since the data size of CBF-extension and CBF Join in Shuffle stage is only related to data sets and misjudgment rate, the values of misjudgment rate and data set are the same as the above experiments, and the data size of CBF-extension in Shuffle stage is equal to that of CBF Join, and it is about 0.5% of Hash Join. The effect of filtering is very obvious in the data sets used in experiments.

Table 5 and Fig. 6 shows the time consumption of equi-join operation when the data size is unknown, Where CBF-extension1 represents the time consumption of generating and broadcasting bit arrays stage, CBF-extension2 denotes the time consumption of filtering and joining stage, and CBF-extension is the total time consumption.

Table 5. The comparison of CBF-extension and Hash Join about time consumption

Dataset	CBF-extension1	CBF-extension2	CBF-extension	Hash Join
1	10 s	16 s	26 s	35 s
2	51 s	73 s	124 s	178 s
3	106 s	143 s	249 s	351 s
4	209 s	279 s	488 s	708 s
5	413 s	577 s	990 s	1416 s

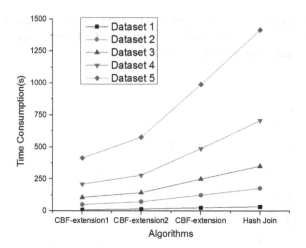

Fig. 6. The time consumption of CBF-extension and Hash Join

The Table 5 and Fig. 6 show that the time consumption of CBF-extension is less than Hash Join when the data size is unknown. However, the time consumption of the first stage is basically equal to that of CBF Join comparing to CBF Join, and the time consumption of the second stage of CBF-extension is slightly higher than that of CBF Join. Thus, CBF Join should be chosen preferentially when the data size is known, and CBF-extension should be chosen when the date size is unknown or inconvenient calculated.

In conclusion, CBF Join algorithm is obviously better than Hash Join algorithm in the network overhead through filtering table previously. When the data size is unknown, CBF-extension algorithm can also reduce the time consumption, and remedy the defect of CBF Join algorithm that cannot be used in the unknown data size.

4   Conclusion and Future Work

In this paper, we have proposed two kinds of big data equi-join optimization algorithms, CBF Join algorithm and CBF-extension algorithm, which are designed to solving the low performance of big data equi-join algorithm provided by Spark cloud computing platform. CBF Join has filtered tables and generated bit arrays by using Compressed Bloom Filter to reduce the data size of join stage, that can improve the effect of the join operation. In the experimental section, results have proved that the performance of CBF Join was better than Hash Join and Broadcast Join in the normal big data equi-join. When the data size was unknown, CBF-extension was adopted to use two-dimensional bit array dynamically to improve the performance of join operation, and the time consumption of CBF-extension was only 1/3 of Hash Join.

In the future, we will focus on increasing the bigger data size and improving the effect of filter operation by combining with the two equi-join optimization algorithm proposed in this paper, so as to enhance the performance of the big data equi-join operation in the Spark cloud computing platform.

References

1. Xin, R.: Spark and Scala (keynote). In: ACM SIGPLAN International Symposium on Scala, p. 1. ACM (2017)
2. Cui, Y., Li, G., Cheng, H., Wang, D.: Indexing for large scale data querying based on Spark SQL. In: IEEE International Conference on E-Business Engineering, pp. 103–108. IEEE (2017)
3. Zhang, J., Yang, Q., Shang, H., Zhang, H., Lin, Y., Zhou, R.: Performance evaluation for distributed join based on MapReduce. In: International Conference on Cloud Computing and Big Data, pp. 295–301. IEEE (2017)
4. Guo-Hua, L.I., Ren, Y.Q., Luo, C., Huang, J., Deng, Y.D.: Optimization of GPU-based main-memory hash join. In: IEEE International Conference on Computational Modeling, Simulation and Applied Mathematics (2017)
5. Sun, H.: Join processing and optimizing on large datasets based on hadoop framework (in Chinese). Dissertation, Nanjing University of Posts and Telecommunications (2013)
6. Lin, Y., Agrawal, D., Chen, C., Ooi, B.C., Wu, S.: Llama: leveraging columnar storage for scalable join processing in the MapReduce framework. In: ACM SIGMOD International Conference on Management of Data, pp. 961–972. ACM (2011)
7. Ramesh, S., Papapetrou, O., Siberski, W.: Optimizing distributed joins with bloom filters. In: Parashar, M., Aggarwal, S.K. (eds.) ICDCIT 2008. LNCS, vol. 5375, pp. 145–156. Springer, Heidelberg (2008). https://doi.org/10.1007/978-3-540-89737-8_15
8. Zhang, C.C.: Design and optimize big-data join algorithms using MapReduce (in Chinese). Dissertation, University of Science and Technology of China (2014)
9. Huang, L.: Research on join query processing and optimization techniques in cloud computing environment (in Chinese). Dissertation, Liaoning University (2014)
10. Wei, L., Shen, Y., Su, C., Ooi, B.C.: Efficient processing of k nearest neighbor joins using MapReduce. Proc. VLDB Endow. 5(10), 1016–1027 (2012)
11. Blanas, S., Patel, J.M., Ercegovac, V., Rao, J., Shekita, E.J., Tian, Y.: A comparison of join algorithms for log processing in MaPreduce. In: Proceedings of the 2010 ACM SIGMOD International Conference on Management of data, pp. 975–986. ACM (2010)
12. Zhang, L.: Research on query analysis and optimization based on spark system (in Chinese). Dissertation, Beijing Jiaotong University (2016)
13. Zhou, S.W.: Optimizing big data equi-join in spark and its application in analysis of network traffic data (in Chinese). Dissertation, South China University of Technology (2015)
14. Liu, R.C., Zhou, M.Q., Xing-Jie, P.I., Zhao, X.: Optimization of the equi-join problem based on big data in spark. Mod. Comput. 8, 3–6 (2017)
15. Zhong-Kui, H.U., Bo, Q.U., Huang, B., Wen-Yang, L.I.: A load balanced equi-join algorithm based on virtual processor range partition. Mod. Comput. (2016)

Blocking Time-Based MPTCP Scheduler for Heterogeneous Networks

Chen Ling[1], Wensheng Tang[1(✉)], Pingping Dong[1], Wenjun Yang[1],
Xiaoping Lou[1], and Hangjun Zhou[2]

[1] College of Information Science and Engineering, Hunan Normal University,
Changsha 410081, China
Tangws@hunnu.edu.cn
[2] Hunan University of Finance and Economy, Changsha 410081, China

Abstract. In order to solve the problem of buffer congestion caused by multipath transmission, we present Blocking Time-based MPTCP (MPTCP-BT) in heterogeneous network. The proposed algorithm designs a new metric path blocking delay (PBD) and compared it with the receiver buffer to determine whether using a path would cause blocking, and then selects specific subflows set to transfer data. Our evaluation proves that MPTCP-BT allows a reduce by 9.45% in average completion time and decreasing number of out-of-order (OFO) packets by 58.5% as compared against default MPTCP and other schedulers. The experimental results show that the MPTCP-BT algorithm reduces the OFO packets in receiving terminal and improves the throughput.

Keywords: MPTCP protocol · Packet scheduling
Receive buffer blocking · RTT

1 Introduction

With the rapid development of communication technology, more and more communication devices usually are equipped with multiple interfaces and include heterogeneous wireless network access (commonly 3/4G and WIFI). However, the traditional TCP protocol can only use a path between the end system to transmit data, in order to fully utilize the bandwidth resources of the host terminal, MPTCP (multi-path TCP) is proposed [11], which is a TCP extension version. MPTCP provides concurrent data transmission over multiple paths and supports compatibility with a single TCP. Thus, MPTCP can improve the throughput of the network. However, the performance of MPTCP is challenging with heterogeneous network and the limited receiver buffer, which causes packet reordering leading to head-of-line (HOL) blocking at the receiver. This problem has been attracting significant attention [6,8,9].

To solve the problem of HOL-blocking, the researchers mainly studied from three aspects: buffer size settings, congestion control methods, and data scheduling algorithm [1–4,13]. The MPTCP scheduling algorithm should be considered

© Springer Nature Switzerland AG 2018
X. Sun et al. (Eds.): ICCCS 2018, LNCS 11063, pp. 364–375, 2018.
https://doi.org/10.1007/978-3-030-00006-6_33

in order to maintain packets arrive at the receiver. Currently, Round-Robin is a basic scheduling algorithm that MPTCP has implemented in the Linux kernel that is based on Round-Trip Time (RTT). Round-Robin starts by filling the congestion window (CWND) of all the subflows. Thus, the data is simply scheduled between the multiple paths, lead to the packets out-of-order at receiver. Considering the difference between paths, Delay-Aware Packet Scheduler (DAPS) [10] and Out-of-order Transmission for In-order Arrival Scheduler (OTIAS) [14] are proposed. The design objective of DAPS is to make segments arrive in order by proactively determining which subflows the next segments should be sent over according to both the congestion window and forward delays of each subflow. However, the proactive method is insensitive to the changes in link characteristics, i.e., it cannot timely adjust scheduling policy when the delay and CWND of each subflow changed. OTIAS plans to scheduling more packets on a subflow than what it can currently send, yet the traffic on subflow with lowest RTT will overload if RTT difference among each subflow is too large.

With these above analyses, we conclude that most of proposed path scheduling algorithms which proactively schedule packet for in-order cannot effectively achieve their performance when the link state changes. Furthermore, both RTT and CWND are important parameters to measure the performance of each MPTCP subflow. It is insufficient to design the path scheduling algorithm only using RTT as a metric in the above literatures. In this paper, we firstly present a new metric PBD to identify the quality of each MPTCP subflow based on subflow's RTT, its CWND, the time per-packet sent. And then we present MPTCP-BT which takes new method towards preventing HOL-blocking. The key idea behind MPTCP-BT is that MPTCP calculates the amount of data that each subflow can transmit during the maximum PBD period, and then dynamically adjusts the subflow set to ensure that the total amount of data transferred over these subflows will not exceed the receiver buffer.

The remainder of this paper is organized as follows. Section 2 discusses the design motivation of this paper. Section 3 describes the details of MPTCP-BT. Section 4 presents the evaluation of MPTCP-BT in Simulator-3(ns3). Finally, Sect. 5 concludes this paper.

2 Motivation

MPTCP is an extension for the traditional TCP protocol. It implemented concurrent multiple transfer by establishing multiple TCP transmission paths at the same time. As shown in the protocol model of Fig. 1 [12], the control module of MPTCP manages multiple TCP connection to provide a reliable service. In other words, the data should arrive in order at receiver buffer and then deliver to the upper level to complete the transmission. However, in a heterogeneous MPTCP network, there is a difference in the path transmission delay if the data packet cannot be order arrival, however the receiver buffer size is limited, when the receiver buffer is full of a large number of OFO packets, it will cause HOL-blocking phenomenon.

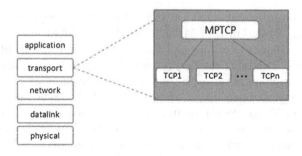

Fig. 1. The protocol model of MPTCP

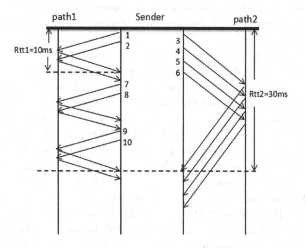

Fig. 2. Scheduling sequence diagram of polling algorithm

As described above, we will analyze the details about how Round-Robin scheduler caused HOL-blocking. As shown in Fig. 2, there are two paths: path 1 and path 2. The initial CWND of path 1 and path 2 is 2 and 4, respectively. The RTT over these two paths is 10 ms and 30 ms, i.e., the time required to send 3 rounds of data over path1 is the same as the time required to send 1round of packets over path 2. Under the control of Round-Robin, path1 firstly sends packet 1-2, and then path 2 sends packet 3-6. Whenever the sender receives the ACK returned by packets 1 and 2, path 1 begins to send packet 7-8. This will cause packet 7-8 to arrive at the receiver before packet 3-6. In addition, the subsequent rounds of data transmission over path1 will still arrive at the receiver as early as the packet 3-6. Therefore, OFO packets always occupy the memory of the receiver, causing the HOL-blocking.

To eliminate the impact of HOL-blocking on the performance of MPTCP, some researchers have tackled the problem of solving packets out of order [5,7]. Both DAPS and OTIAS algorithms are based on pre-allocation to allow the data to reach the receiver as much as possible in order, thereby reducing HOL blocking. DAPS and OTIAS use forward transmission delay, namely the time from the sender to the receiver as a metric to measure quality of each path and then schedule packets over paths according to the quality of these paths. For the calculation of the forward transmission delay, the above algorithm uses RTT/2 to approximately estimate its value. We believe that this cannot accurately reflect the quality of the path. RTT embodies the path transmission speed and is a key factor in evaluating the path quality. CWND of the each path is also an important indicator that reflects the amount of data the path can send. In this paper, we propose a new metric PBD to measure the quality of the path by combining the values of RTT and CWND. As shown in Fig. 3, the time for the sender to start sending data is t_s, the current time is t_i, and the PBD calculation formula for each path is as follows:

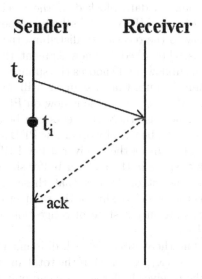

Fig. 3. The round model mentioned in TCP

(1) If there are no data packets are transmitted over this path and the corresponding cwnd is available, $PBD = RTT$.
(2) If there are packets being transmitted over this path and the cwnd is available, $PBD = RTT - (t_i - t_s)$.
(3) If there are packets being transmitted over this path and the cwnd is available, $PBD = RTT - (t_i - t_s) + RTT$.

Because the mass difference between each subflow of MPTCP, it will cause the packets out-of-order arrive at the receiver. In other words, whether it will cause blocking depends mainly on the path with the worst quality. If the path with the largest PBD does not cause blocking, data transmission over other paths will not cause HOL-blocking. In addition, if the total amount of data sent over all subflows within a certain period of time is less than the receiver buffer, it will decrease the number of OFO packets and significantly reduce the occurrence of HOL-blocking. Therefore, we proposed MPTCP-BT, which calculates the amount of data that each subflow can send in the maximum path blocking delay, and then select the appropriate number of subflows for data transmission according to the receiver buffer.

3 Operation of MPTCP-BT Scheduling

Based on the above analyses, we proposed a new scheduling policy, MPTCP-BT to minimize HOL-blocking in heterogeneous networks. MPTCP - BT initially analyzes the CWND of each path, combines the forecast to maximum blocking time delay and the amount of data blocked at the receiver during the maximum block time delay. Finally, MPTCP-BT schedules the subflow that will not generate the zero window to the receiver to distribute the packets.

In this paper, when asked to schedule a new segment, the algorithm calculates its PBD if sent over each subflow, and chooses the subflow with the highest PBD (PBD_{max}).The algorithm assumes that a segment will stay space in MPTCP's send window for at least PBD_{max} if it is sent now on PBD_{max}'s subflow. It's a conservative assumption, because these segments can be acknowledged earlier. The available send window can be used by other low PBD's subflows. This means that HOL-blocking would occur at the receiver if low PBD's subflows were not able to send due to lack of space in the receiver buffer size of PBDmax subflows. Thus, we calculate the amount of data X that these paths can send during PBD_{max}, and check whether this blocking of the receiver buffer. To estimate X, we assume that all paths are in the state of congestion avoidance, its CWND grows by 1 for every PBD.

As an example, assume there subflows with different PBD($PBD_i \in \{PBD_1,$ $PBD_2, PBD_3\}$) and X($X_i \in \{X_1, X_2, X_3\}$), if the total amount of data by PBD1-PBD3 is greater than the receiver buffer size, we can only use PBD1 and PBD2 for transmission. Doing so enables the data scheduling to effectively avoid the receiver blocking on the basis of sequential arrival. Algorithm 1 shows the main loop of the MPTCP-BT mechanism.

4 Performance Evaluation in MPTCP-BT

The experiment was implemented using Network Simulator NS-3 and compared with Round-Robin, DAPS and OITAS. Experimental performance indicators include completion time of data segment and OFO queue in receiver buffer. The network transmission completion time selected four parameters: long and short subflow, receiver buffer, bandwidth and RTT.

Table 1. *

Algorithm1: MPTCP-BT Schedule
1: for all subflow i do
2: if subflow i have space of CWND
3: then $PBD = RTT - (ti - ts)$
4: else $PBD = RTT - (t_i - t_s) + RTT'$
5: sort paths by Pb, $F' = \{F'_1, F'_2, ..., F'_N\}$
6: end for
7: for all F_i do
8: calculate $PBD = \frac{PBD_{max}}{PBD_{n-1}}$
9: calculate $X = MSS \times \left[CWND + \frac{PBD-1}{2}\right] \times PBD$
10: calculate $N = X_i + X_{i+1}$
11: if ($N >$buffer size) then
12: choose $P = \{P_1, P_2, ..., P_N\}$ for scheduled
13: end for

4.1   Experimental Environment Setup

The experimental topology is shown in Fig. 4. Under a heterogeneous network, both the sender and the receiver are equipped with multiple radio interfaces. Among them, S_i and R_i (i=1, 2,..., N) represent the interfaces of the sender and the receiver respectively, they are connected by n routers so that there are n available connections.

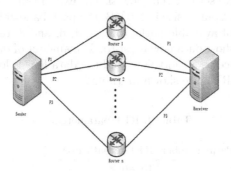

Fig. 4. Network Topology

A. Throughput. The experiment aims to make full use of network resources and reduce HOL-blocking to improve throughput. Throughput is the amount of data that passes through a network in a unit of time, its calculation formula is as follows:

$$throughput = \frac{actual\_amount\_of\_data}{transmission\_data\_completion\_time} \tag{1}$$

The completion time of the transmitted data can directly determine the network throughput. The shorter the completion time of data transmission is, the higher the throughput of the network is.

B.Out-of-order Packets at the Receiver. In a single transmission, the main reason for the existence of OFO packets is the loss of packets. Even if the packet loss rate of the link is low in multi-path transmission, a large amount of out-of-order packets will be generated. The reason is the link difference among multiple links, especially the RTT difference. The post-sequence data packet transmitted by the fast subflow may arrive at the receiver buffer first, and it needs to wait for the pre-sequence data that is transmitted on the slow subflow, thereby causing an OFO packet. The OFO packets at the receiver cannot be delivered to the upper layer and must be stored in the buffer, which causes a series of problems such as the HOL-blocking and slow growth of the sending and receiving windows. Because the increased end-to-end delays will affect user's experience, OFO packets are also an important performance indicator each algorithm should consider. In summary, this paper evaluates MPTCP-BT and compares it with other algorithms in terms of reducing the number of OFO packets at the receiver and the completion time of data transmission.

4.2   Impact of Data Stream

In order to explore the performance of these algorithms during long and short flows transmission, we set different flow size as experimental parameters in this scenario. The receiver buffer size is 100 KB, the path bandwidth is 10 Mbps, and we set the number of available paths to 2, 3, 4, 6, and 8, respectively. Among them, the long and short data flow is set to: The amount of data transferred less than 800 KB is defined as a short flow, and the data flow is longer than 800 KB. The parameters for RTT are shown in Table 2.

Table 2. RTT parameters.

Paths number	RTT of path(ms)
2	10, 20
3	10, 20, 30
4	10, 20, 30, 40
6	10, 20, 30, 40, 50, 60
8	10, 20, 30, 40, 50, 60, 70, 80

As shown in Fig. 5, the completion time of the MPTCP-BT and the three contrast algorithms are compared in the long and short data flow respectively. The completion time of MPTCP-BT is less than the other three algorithms in both the long flow and the short flow. Especially in Fig. 5(b), the advantage of the MPTCP-BT scheduling algorithm is obvious for the long flow, because MPTCP-BT evaluates each path based on the estimated PBD and uses only the set of paths that do not cause the zero windows of the receiver, and discards the path with poor link performance, the data transmission time of the algorithm is shortened.

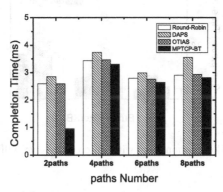

(a) Short flow Completion time

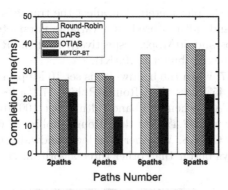

(b) Long flow Completion time

Fig. 5. Completion time with different receive buffer sizes data stream

4.3   Impact of Receiver Buffer

In order to explore the performance of these algorithms in different receiver buffer size, the receiver buffer size is used as the variable parameter. In the first scenario, the buffer size is 50 KB; the second scenario, the buffer size is 100 KB. And the RTT of path are the same of 2 scenario; the bandwidth is 10 Mbps. As shown in Fig. 6, the MPTCP-BT algorithm has the best performance compared to other schedulers, that is because MPTCP-BT can adapt the size of the receiver cache of different mobile devices and selects a path set whose estimated data amount is smaller than the receiving buffer for data allocation.

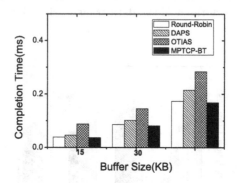

Fig. 6. Completion time with different receive buffer sizes

4.4   Impact of Bandwidth

Bandwidth is one of the parameters that affect the transmission of MPTCP. In this scenario, the bandwidth is used as a variable parameter. The bandwidth of 2 paths is 10 Mbps and 50 Mbps, respectively. And the RTT of path are the same of 2 path; the receive buffer is 100 KB.

As shown in Fig. 7, when the bandwidth is set 10 Mbps, the completion time of MPTCP-BT is 9.45% less than Round-Robin, 17.1% less than DAPS, and 53.7% less than OITAS; when the bandwidth is set 100Mbps, MPTCP-BT is completed. The time was 48.4% less than Round-Robin, 87.6% less than DAPS and 87.7% less than OITAS. Whether it is low bandwidth or high bandwidth, MPTCP-BT is always better than other three algorithms.

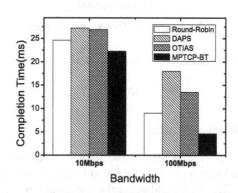

Fig. 7. Completion time with different bandwidth

4.5   Impact of RTT

The path RTT is the decisive factor to evaluate the path performance, and literature [8] shows that the RTT difference can be generated by the throughput difference between paths. Therefore, we investigate the effect of RTT difference on the Round-Robin, DAPS and OITAS with MPTCP-BT. There are 2 scenarios in this experiment, and 8 paths are respectively established. The path bandwidth is 10 Mbps, and the receiver buffer size is 100 KB. The parameters for RTT are shown in Table 3.

Figure 8 shows the completion time of MPTCP-BT algorithm transmission data is 39.9% lower than that of DAPS and 37.7% lower than OITAS for RTT_1; the completion time of MPTCP-BT algorithm is higher than that of DAPS for RTT_2. It was reduced by 56.9%, which is a reduction of 34.3% over OITAS. It can be seen that the greater the RTT difference, the better performance of the MPTCP-BT algorithm.

Table 3. RTT parameters.

Scenarios	RTT of path(ms)
1	10, 50, 90, 130, 170, 210, 250, 290
2	5, 10, 15, 20, 25, 30, 35, 40

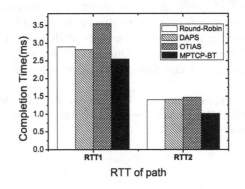

Fig. 8. Completion time with different RTT

4.6   Number of Out of Order Packets at Receiver Buffer

Figure 9 shows the OFO buffer size with MPTCP-BT, Round-Robin, DAPS and OITAS. Round-Robin algorithm causes most OFO packets in the receiver due to it cannot fully utilize the RTT of path. MPTCP-BT receiver's OFO packet size is reduced by 58.5% over Round-Robin, 15.7% over DAPS, and 34.9% less than OITAS.

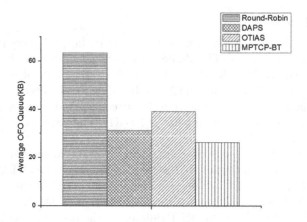

Fig. 9. OFO queue during data

5   Conclusions

We argued for algorithms that have been proposed to solve HOL-blocking and presented MPTCP-BT to implement the performance gain of MPTCP. In this paper, we conduct extensive experiments to evaluate different application performance metrics, e.g., average completion time, the number of OFO packets in receiver buffer. Finally, compared with MPTCP, DAPS and OTIAS, the test results show that MPTCP-BT greatly improve the performance with different scenarios. Specially, our contribution enables a lower OFO occupancy of the receiver's buffer, resulting in reduced occurrence of HOL-blocking and decreased completion time of each application. Our further investigation will focus on exploring the implement in Linux kernel to address some practical problems.

Acknowledgement. Project supported by National Natural Science Foundation of China (61602172, 61602171), Hunan Provincial Higher Education Teaching Reform Research Project (Grant No. 564).

References

1. Barré, S.: Implementation and assessment of modern host-based multipath solutions. Ph.D thesis. Universite catholique de Louvain (2011)
2. Bonaventure, O., De Coninck, Q., Baerts, M., Duchene, F., Hesmans, B.: Improving multipath tcp backup subflows. IETF, Individual Submission, Internet Draft draft-bonaventure-mptcpbackup-00 (2015)
3. Choi, K.W., Cho, Y.S., Lee, J.W., Cho, S.M., Choi, J.: Optimal load balancing scheduler for mptcp-based bandwidth aggregation in heterogeneous wireless environments. Comput. Commun. **112**, 116–130 (2017)
4. Halepoto, I.A., Lau, F.C.M., Niu, Z.: Management of buffer space for the concurrent multipath transfer over dissimilar paths. IEEE (2015)

5. He, S., Xie, K., Zhang, D.: Completion time-aware flow scheduling in heterogenous networks. In: Wang, G., Zomaya, A., Perez, G.M., Li, K. (eds.) ICA3PP 2015. LNCS, vol. 9528, pp. 492–507. Springer, Cham (2015). https://doi.org/10.1007/978-3-319-27119-4_34
6. Kim, J., Oh, B.H., Lee, J.: Receive buffer based path management for MPTCP in heterogeneous networks. In: Integrated Network and Service Management, pp. 648–651 (2017)
7. Le, T.A., Bui, L.X.: Forward delay-based packet scheduling algorithm for multipath TCP. Mob. Netw. Appl. **23**(1), 4–12 (2015)
8. Oh, B.H., Lee, J.: Constraint-Based Proactive Scheduling for MPTCP in Wireless Networks, pp. 548–563. Elsevier, New York (2015)
9. Paasch, C., Ferlin, S., Alay, O., Bonaventure, O.: Experimental evaluation of multipath TCP schedulers. In: Proceedings of the 2014 ACM SIGCOMM Workshop on Capacity Sharing Workshop, pp. 27–32 (2014)
10. Sarwar, G., Boreli, R., Lochin, E., Mifdaoui, A., Smith, G.: Mitigating receiver's buffer blocking by delay aware packet scheduling in multipath data transfer. In: International Conference on Advanced Information NETWORKING and Applications Workshops, pp. 1119–1124 (2013)
11. Wischik, D., Raiciu, C., Greenhalgh, A., Handley, M.: Design, implementation and evaluation of congestion control for multipath TCP. In: USENIX Conference on Networked Systems Design and Implementation, pp. 99–112 (2011)
12. Xue, K., Ke, C., Dan, N., et al.: Survey of MPTCP-based multipath transmission optimization. J. Comput. Res. Dev. **53**(11), 2512–2529 (2016)
13. Yang, F., Amer, P.: Work in progress: using one-way communication delay for in-order arrival MPTCP scheduling. In: International Conference on Communications and NETWORKING in China, pp. 122–125 (2015)
14. Yang, F., Wang, Q., Amer, P.D.: Out-of-order transmission for in-order arrival scheduling for multipath TCP. In: International Conference on Advanced Information NETWORKING and Applications Workshops, pp. 749–752 (2014)

Cloud Computing Data Security Protection Strategy

Yu Wei[1,2] and Yongsheng Zhang[1,2(✉)]

[1] School of Information Science and Engineering, Shandong Normal University,
Jinan 250358, China
2515868427@qq.com, zhangys@sdnu.edu.cn
[2] Shandong Provincial Key Laboratory for Novel Distributed Computer
Software Technology, Jinan 250358, China

Abstract. Cloud computing is a computing model that has emerged in recent years. It is of great significance for promoting massive information data calculations. We store large amounts of data in the cloud and use algorithms to make huge computations on large-scale data centers on the Internet. Big data cloud computing resources have a huge amount of information, which can provide convenient and fast computing while being a new type of storage. Due to the large amount of data that needs to be processed by cloud computing, many information processing methods are involved, and customer privacy data is difficult to be effectively protected in the cloud computing environment. Therefore, the protection of information security in the cloud computing environment becomes more important. Based on the analysis of the data security problems in the big data cloud computing environment, this paper analyzes the security protection of big data cloud computing data, which is of great significance for promoting the establishment of a complete data security system, and can also be further promoted the useful of cloud computing.

Keywords: Cloud computing · Data security · Privacy protection

1 Cloud Computing Overview

Cloud computing systems are generally composed of hardware and software systems of one or more data centers within a single organization, sharing the resources of data centers among multiple users or applications. In layman's terms, cloud computing is like a large-scale resource pool. Resources in the pool are abstract and virtualized, and the functions of computing, storage, platforms, and services can be implemented in the pool. Cloud computing resources can be shared among multiple tenants, scheduling and optimization can be facilitated for centralized resource management, low cost and energy consumption, and improved resource utilization. Because of the unpredictability of user requests, cloud computing can dynamically adjust the number of resource usages for supporting users, and the system responds to load changes by increasing or decreasing resources.

Cloud computing adopts resource sharing technology, which separates ownership and management of data and supports data virtualization, multi-tenancy and cross-

© Springer Nature Switzerland AG 2018
X. Sun et al. (Eds.): ICCCS 2018, LNCS 11063, pp. 376–386, 2018.
https://doi.org/10.1007/978-3-030-00006-6_34

domain services. The resources of cloud computing systems are very concentrated and the architecture is highly complex. Therefore, there are many issues that need to be studied in terms of technology and management in cloud computing security, such as cloud computing security architecture model, data security, cloud computing mode encryption method, privacy protection scheme, access control and authentication, virtualization security, and more. Tenant isolation, cross-domain service security, etc.

The cloud computing facility architecture can be decomposed into a core service layer, a quality assurance layer, and a user access layer [1].

The core service layer meets the diverse application needs of users. The core service layer is divided into Infrastructure as a Service (IaaS), Platform as a Service (PaaS), and Software as a Service (SaaS). The most basic category is Infrastructure as a Service. IaaS is an efficient use of underlying hardware resources, including processing, storage, networking, and other basic computing resources. Users can deploy and run software on them, including operating systems and applications. Users do not have to take responsibility for managing the cloud computing infrastructure, but can control the corresponding applications. Platform-as-a-service provides users with the resources and software platforms needed for application operations, including middleware services, information services, integration services, and messaging services, to reduce users' work complexity [2]. Software-as-a-service provides users with services that run on the cloud infrastructure and users can access them through various clients. For ordinary users, software as a service migrates desktop applications to the Internet, enabling ubiquitous access to applications. The cloud computing service structure is shown in Fig. 1.

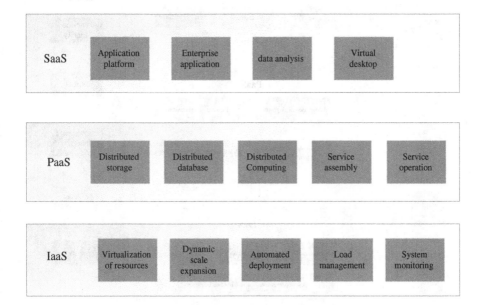

Fig. 1. Cloud computing service architecture model

The quality assurance layer guarantees the reliability, security, service quality, and scalability of the core service layer. The cloud infrastructure needs to provide users with highly reliable, highly available, and low-cost personalized services. The service level agreement (SLA) enables the service providers and users to agree on the quality of service requirements. Security and privacy protection technologies in the cloud computing environment (such as data isolation, privacy protection, access control, etc.) are the key to ensure that cloud computing is widely used.

The user access layer implements ubiquitous access to cloud computing services. Users can use cloud resources and services through a variety of terminal devices. The general form of access to resources is command line, web, API, and Widget, which greatly improves user productivity.

The core service layer, quality assurance layer, and user access layer form a complete cloud infrastructure architecture to ensure the reliability, availability, and security of cloud computing, and provide resources to the outside world according to user requirements. The cloud system architecture is shown in Fig. 2.

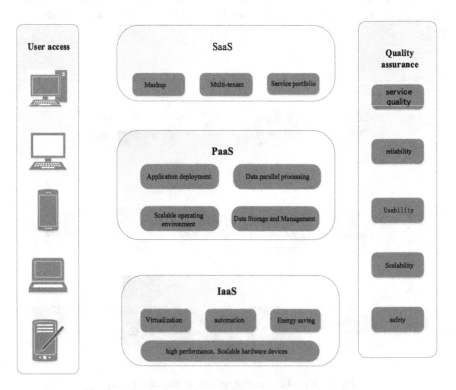

Fig. 2. Cloud infrastructure architecture and core technology

2　The Characteristics of Cloud Computing

Cloud computing can store data in the cloud. The characteristics of cloud computing are as follows:

(1) The cloud computing system can effectively handle the detection and recovery of failed nodes. When any node failure is detected, other nodes can seamlessly connect and automatically take over the calculation tasks of the failed node. After the failed node recovers, it can be automatically configured without administrators manually. Joining the cluster, using cloud computing is more reliable than using local computing.

(2) The system is dynamically scalable. Scalable software systems can respond to load changes through resource increase or decrease. User requests within the Internet are unpredictable, and the scale reached during the peak period is bursty. The cloud computing system supports users' dynamic adjustment of resource usage. Meet the needs of applications and user scale growth.

(3) On-demand service. Cloud computing adopts a service-oriented and on-demand billing business model. Users pay according to the actual use of cloud services, and how much they buy is not wasted.

(4) Virtualization of resources. Cloud computing allows users to use various terminals to obtain application services anytime, anywhere, without worrying about the specific location of applications running, thereby reducing the degree of coupling between users and resources.

(5) Versatility. Cloud computing is not targeted to specific applications. Under the cloud's support, it can create ever-changing applications. The same cloud can support different applications at the same time.

(6) Extremely cheap. The cloud can use extremely inexpensive nodes to form the cloud. The cloud's automated centralized management eliminates the burden of high-cost data center management costs on a large number of enterprises, and cloud computing greatly increases resource utilization [2].

(7) System Security Vulnerabilities. Due to the complex services of cloud computing systems and the varying levels of management and service levels of many service providers, there are always insecure interfaces and APIs. Other security vulnerabilities in the system can also amplify the risks due to the scale effect of cloud computing.

(8) Insider threats: Inadvertent or intentional disclosure of information by insiders of service providers often makes security strategies against external attacks difficult to achieve. This has become an important issue in the current cloud computing security.

(9) Multi-tenancy and cross-domain sharing: Multi-tenant isolation and multi-user security needs are ensured; cross-domain sharing makes service authorization and access control more complex, and trust transfer between cloud computing entities needs to be revisited.

3 The Status of Cloud Computing Research

In the face of continuous security incidents from Cloud Service Providers (CSP), concerns about the security and privacy of user data in cloud storage environments are increasing. Once the data is stored in the cloud, the user loses absolute control over the data, and part of the control rights is transferred to the CSP. This gives illegal elements to destroy and tamper with the user's data through illegal means, and steals the user's private data. Opportunity. In order to protect the uploaded data from being maliciously stolen, destroyed, or tampered with, it is a feasible method to store data in the form of encryption to the cloud [3].

From the current research situation, confidentiality and integrity of private data in cloud storage are urgently studied. The current generation of privacy data integrity verification and verification information requires more complex signature operations and data structures. In the process of sexual detection, the client needs to participate in too many calculations, which increases the calculation and communication expenses of the client. It is not suitable for the architecture of the cloud platform. The performance needs to be improved. Most methods do not support public verification, and do not support data. Dynamic operations, including insertions, deletions, and modifications [4].

With the further application of cloud computing and the increase in the number of vendors providing cloud computing services, cloud computing data security prevention capabilities and risk processing capabilities have gradually become an important factor in the future development of cloud computing. Cloud computing breaks through the space constraints and enables computing services to be distributed everywhere. Therefore, in the cloud computing environment, the specific location of data storage and transmission greatly increases the risk of data transmission. The traditional improper handling of data often causes many unnecessary losses to users. In a comprehensive view, the lack of key technologies for cloud computing is an important factor affecting the further promotion and development of cloud computing technologies. It is a concrete manifestation of cloud computing in social applications.

4 The Existence of Data Security Problems in Cloud Computing Environment

Cloud computing brings many advantages, but it will inevitably lead to data security problems. The fundamental goal of cloud computing data security is to ensure that data security is not tampered with during data generation, transmission, storage, and access. The big data cloud is just a virtual concept. We only know that it is a huge pool of resources, but we don't know where the data is. We ask who will manipulate the data after the request is made and where we go after the data is used. Due to the existence of these unknown factors, we must pay attention to big data cloud computing, otherwise it may lead to the user's information being stolen, causing incalculable losses. To ensure the storage security of user data in the cloud environment, we must not only consider traditional information security, storage encryption and other technologies, but also need to consider the security issues caused by the uniqueness of the cloud environment.

4.1 Data Sharing Security Issues

An effective way to solve the privacy information leakage is to encrypt the privacy information. In the traditional data calculation methods, symmetrical or asymmetric encryption algorithms are generally selected. In the cloud computing, the data owner and the user are inconsistent. If you choose the symmetric encryption algorithm, Users can't get control over data and heavy key management issues. If you use asymmetric encryption algorithms, you need public key infrastructure support. Obviously this is a very dangerous practice. Usually in cloud computing data sharing The method of re-encrypting data with a third-party proxy and the attribute encryption algorithm based on the characteristics of the user identity attribute are used to solve this problem [5].

Domestic and foreign experts still have flaws in the proposed solutions to these two problems. The main manifestations are: When the data owner uploads the ciphertext to the cloud server, the user identity information of the ciphertext sharing data changes and the ciphertext data sharing strategy is updated., it will cause extremely complex data management problems for third-party agents, resulting in the risk of leakage of user privacy data.

4.2 Data Segregation Security

Data isolation is an important issue concerning data security in cloud computing. From the viewpoint of data usage and processing flow, there may be data isolation and security problems in data sharing operations. Cloud computing is like a huge resource sharing pool. If users do not encrypt the data transmission process during data sharing operations, the data is encrypted. The processing is not tight enough. When the data is connected to an external computer, it is necessary to share the advantages of resources, which will provide convenience for hackers and cause data leakage or loss of users. Currently, cloud computing systems still lack a sound isolation system. In a collective office environment, data must be shared, data in transmission cannot be encrypted, data is not completely isolated from external computers, and security in data transmission is reduced. Illegal molecules are easily The sharing link steals data and causes the disclosure of encrypted information.

4.3 Access Control Technology

In order to better protect the user's privacy information, we propose fine-grained and dynamically changing permission requirements, and the access authorization for data is refined to the file level. Authorization is the process of authorization for specifying key-encrypted data [6]. Users in cloud computing The dynamic changes, so that the file's authorization also dynamically increase or decrease.

Data access control algorithms in cloud computing include key policy KP-ABE and ciphertext policy CP-ABE algorithms. This algorithm not only breaks away from PKI constraints, but also reduces the burden of key management in ciphertext access control. Therefore, ABE has been applied to the system. However, because of the large overhead and low efficiency of ABE encryption, a large number of operations will occur when a ciphertext update operation occurs. Therefore, dynamic management of multi-level access control is a place to be improved. The access control in the calculation lacks the control over the write ciphertext data and fails to achieve comprehensive cloud storage security protection.

4.4 Data Damage

Under the influence of the big data cloud computing environment, the data processing process is relatively complicated. To ensure the security of data, we must do preventive work at the root of the data. After the data is read and applied, it can be completely cleaned up so that leakage can be avoided. If some data cannot be destroyed at the terminal, then the data will be leaked and stolen. Under the influence of big data cloud computing, it takes a certain amount of time to implement data destruction. Usually, it takes more than ten minutes [7]. However, during this time period, data may be stolen, making it difficult to clear and destroy data. Therefore, in the process of actual destruction of data, if it takes a long time, the invasion status may be destroyed, which will lead to data remnants, providing opportunities for intruders and failing to ensure the security of data information.

5 Data Security Protection Strategy in Cloud Computing Environment

Although there are still some data security problems in cloud computing, the advantages brought by cloud computing are beyond doubt. For the current security problems in the big data cloud computing environment, security protection should be implemented in a timely manner to ensure data security and make big data real. The role of promoting people's work efficiency.

5.1 Encrypt Static Data

The overall principle of cloud computing is "resource sharing", which makes cloud storage cloud service providers not necessarily all legal. To achieve effective avoidance due to the risk of cloud computing service providers posing a risk of data leakage, users should adopt encryption to effectively protect static data and files in the database [8]. In terms of the IaaS environment, the means available to users mainly include:

(1) Use a cloud computing service provider's own encryption system;
(2) Encrypt the file using a third-party password system.

Taking the PaaS environment as an example, users can also use the encryption services provided by the cloud computing service provider to customers. When encrypting and transmitting user data, the commonly used technologies are mainly IPSec VPN, SSL, etc. These technologies have proved to be able to greatly improve the security of data during network transmission.

In terms of cloud storage security services, to achieve this, cloud computing should effectively encrypt and store data in the form of cryptographic services. Its purpose is to effectively prevent malicious disclosure of data. The use of appropriate encryption algorithms is also an effective security measure. At present, the commonly used international general algorithms are mainly AES, 3DES and so on. In this regard, users should make choices based on their actual conditions to improve security. It is also very important to manage the encryption key effectively. As a user, it is necessary to implement the standardization of user key management and distribution mechanisms in order to achieve the purpose of managing data securely.

5.2 Improve Data Encryption Technology for Big Data Cloud Computing

The use of attribute-based encryption mainly includes key policies and ciphertext policies. It is usually in the user query class to use key policies, such as video on demand. The ciphertext strategy determines the access control strategy, which is usually used in access control processes such as social networking sites. By using attribute-based encryption in cloud storage sharing operations, time and user information can be added in ciphertext, and users can apply for log services at different time periods [6].

Under the influence of the big data cloud computing environment, the data has social public attributes, and users cannot determine whether the data provider has properly stored its own data information. In the process of sharing data, it is necessary to fully consider the encryption of data information. For example, if both parties A and B share information, but they do not want the key pa to be delivered to Party B, this time they can use proxy re-encryption to resolve the related issues. Proxy re-encryption can set decryption instead of actual operation. When A and B company keys are calculated, the key RK is converted. Through key conversion, the private key pa can be converted to encrypt the ciphertext to be the public key pa encrypted cipher text. In the process of transforming the data information, the original party password is not decrypted. After the pass, the secret key can only be Party B decrypts the ciphertext. In summary, the design process of the public key system is shown in Fig. 3.

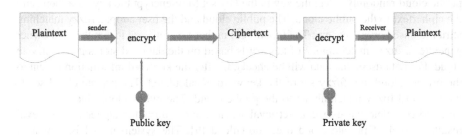

Fig. 3. Public key system

5.3   Research on Data Recovery Technology in Cloud Storage Environment

The data redundancy storage mainly includes copy redundancy and encoding redundancy. Among them, the code redundancy recovery method is mainly used for recovery when data is damaged in the cloud data access process; the copy redundancy recovery method is mainly used for recovery when the data is damaged after the cloud data storage. One of the most common methods of coding redundancy recovery is the RS erasure code redundancy method. The principle is: the n file block data is generated as n + m coded data blocks, and the erasure code data redundancy is k. (k = m/n), then store n + m redundant coded data in multiple cloud storage sites, where any n blocks can recover the original data [10]. Because there are multiple erasure code encoding methods, the redundant method of erasure codes is an open platform, and many algorithms can be introduced into cloud storage.

Aiming at the characteristics of cloud storage, we study the encoding algorithms and replica redundancy methods that are suitable for cloud storage, and propose an efficient and effective data recovery method based on these two methods, so that when the integrity of data is destroyed, Recover quickly to ensure data availability and integrity [7].

5.4   System Model

According to the analysis, we found that the key to cloud computing security technology lies in the difficulty of resisting the collusion attack between the cloud server and the user. The private cloud is a trusted party, but subject to the limitation of the use domain, the public cloud is a semi-trusted party. Therefore, the security model in the article We divide the cloud into a trusted private cloud and a semi-trusted public cloud, together with the owner of the data and the users of the data sharing. The data storage encrypts the data that needs the cloud storage service and uploads it to the cloud [8]. The server, ciphertext data $C = \{C_1, C_2 \ldots C_n\}$, in order to adapt to the dynamic changes in the characteristics of cloud users, the realization of dynamic security based on attribute-based shared security control and user fine-grained access control, data owner and private cloud Adopting a symmetric cryptosystem, the private cloud and the public cloud randomly select the key in the key set to re-encrypt the key, and then send the ciphertext to the public cloud. The public cloud and the user adopt a fuzzy matching attribute-based cryptosystem; The function of cipher text retrieval is that the data owner generates a fuzzy matching set of keywords based on the data and stores it in a private cloud. For data users, the data will be checked. After the keyword information is sent to the private cloud, the fuzzy set of the keyword is calculated. The private cloud sends the keyword fuzzy matching set to the public cloud. The public cloud finally uses the index to complete the user data retrieval service, and returns the cipher text retrieval result. A total of private cloud users download [9]. The system model is shown in Fig. 4.

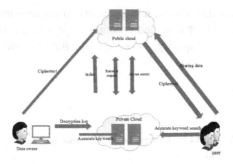

Fig. 4. System model diagram

5.5 Make Data Backup

In view of the portability of current mobile devices in data storage and backup, data protection for mobile devices should be taken into account when protecting data in the context of big data cloud computing environments, so as to prevent them from being damaged by external forces during use. The phenomenon of data loss, once the data can not be restored, will bring huge losses to the user. In order to avoid this situation, we must make a safe backup of the data. Although the user's data can be uploaded to the cloud server to ensure its backup reliability, the cloud server is not absolutely secure, making the data backup a planning solution. It is necessary to establish a safe and reliable data backup strategy to improve the safety and reliability of data backup [10]. In the mobile environment, the user's data covers video, audio, and text. The user terminal must fully prepare for data backup. In the process of data backup transmission, cipher text transmission is used. This method consumes a lot of data. As time affects the cloud storage and terminal battery life, it should also increase scientific and technological research and development to develop a practical and feasible solution [11].

6 Conclusions

The future of cloud computing security depends on research in the following areas:

(1) The expansion of the application model: providing "cloud computing security components", using the powerful computing capabilities provided by cloud computing, to solve their own security problems;

(2) Advances in technology: privacy-protected access control and identity authentication, homomorphic encryption, secure cloud outsourcing, secure multi-party computing, and quantum homomorphic encryption;

(3) Specifications at the management level;

(4) The maturity of commercial application practice.

As a new computing model, cloud computing uses the transmission capabilities of high-speed Internet to give users unprecedented computing power. Cloud computing not only reduces computing costs, but also promotes the development of Internet technology. To ensure data security, it is necessary to improve the network protection system, and strengthen data sharing and isolation, improve data encryption algorithms, ensure data security and data quality, and soon In the future, cloud computing will have better development.

References

1. Gong, C.C., Xiao, Y., Li, M.F.: Review of cloud computing security research. J. Shenyang Aerosp. Univ. **34**(4), 1–17 (2017)
2. Yang, X.: Improvements and applications of the range and efficiency of homomorphic encryption algorithms. Comput. Eng. Des. **38**(2), 318–322 (2017)
3. Xin, S.Y., Zhao, Y., Lin, L.: Research on the trustworthy proof method of IaaS environment. Comput. Eng. **38**(5), 117–119 (2012)
4. Feng, H.Y., Zhao, F.Y.: Research on dynamic data integrity detection supported in cloud storage services. J. Small Microcomput. Syst. **35**(2), 239–243 (2014)
5. Xin, M.Y., Fan, L.: Research on data security strategy in cloud computing environment. J. Chifeng Univ. (Nat. Sci. Ed.) **33**(22), 26–27 (2017)
6. Wu, Y.M., Xu, J., Pan, X.: Application of OGSA-DAI 4.0 in scientific data sharing platform. Comput. Appl. Softw. **29**(1), 131–133 (2012)
7. Wang, X.R.: Data security analysis under big data cloud computing environment. Intell. Comput. Appl. **7**(6), 171–172 (2017)
8. Xie, J.L.: Research on data security in cloud computing. Decis. Inf. (36), 307 (2017)
9. Yang, C.: Big data and cloud computing: innovation opportunities and challenges. Int. J. Digit. Earth **10**(1), 13–53 (2017)
10. Meng, L.J.: Research on cloud storage and data recovery based on cloud platform. Comput. Knowl. Technol. (14), 3230–3232 (2016)
11. Kuang, S.H., Li, B.: Analysis of cloud computing architecture and application examples. Comput. Digit. Eng. **38**(3), 60–63 (2010)

Clustering Model Based on RBM Encoding in Big Data

Lina Yuan[1], Xinfeng Xiao[2], FuFang Li[3(✉)], and Ningning Deng[1]

[1] South China Institute of Software Engineering, GU Guangzhou University,
Conghua, Guangzhou 510990, China
18971656@qq.com, 17181547@qq.com
[2] Department of Mechanical and Electric Engineering, Guangdong Polytechnic
of Environmental Protection Engineering, Foshan 528216, Guangdong, China
85043766@qq.com
[3] School of Computer Scuence and Educational Software,
Guangzhou University, Guangzhou 510006, China
lffgz@163.com

Abstract. In this paper, a clustering model based on deep learning RBM encoding is proposed for the further data mining of the massive, complex and high-dimensional data. This model includes two major parts: pre-training and fine-tuning & optimization. In the pre-training part, proper parameters are adopted for RBM encoding to reduce the high-dimensional and large-scaled data, and then pre-clustering is done with k-means and other algorithms. The fine-tuning & optimization part is developed from the deep structure of pre-training to form a deep fine-tuning, and network is initialized with the parameters generated from the pre-training, and then the initial clustering center generated from pre-training process is further clustered and optimized. At the same time, encoding features are optimized and the final clustering center and membership matrix are obtained. In order to validate this model, some data are selected from the UCI dataset for clustering comparison. It is indicated in the data analysis that this clustering model based on RBM encoding has little impact on the clustering effect, but the execution is more efficient.

Keywords: Clustering model · RBM encoding · Big data

1 Introduction

Since the 20th century, the informatization has been developed rapidly in the governments and various industries, and a large amount of data has been accumulated [1, 2]. With the extensive application of technologies, such as Internet of Things and big data, the data volume has been exponentially increasing and the data structure is complex and correlated. However, how to mine these massive and complex big data and obtain the maximum commercial value stands as a serious challenge. Machine learning, especially deep learning and clustering, will be the key to unlocking big data treasures.

Deep learning will carry out feature learning mainly through establishing and simulating the human brain, and will learn an incremental abstract feature with minimal human effort [3, 4]. Deep learning is a kind of unsupervised learning, which is mainly used to find the distributed feature expression of data, and the low-level feature are combined to construct more abstract high-level features, thereby expressing its attribute feature or classification. Deep learning can efficiently achieve dimensionality reduction through encoding.

Clustering is the process of dividing a collection of physical or abstract objects into similar object classification [5, 6]. Each object classification is a cluster, in which the objects in the same cluster have higher similarity, and the objects in different clusters have higher dissimilarity. Clustering does not know the classification information about the target data in advance, but divides the data classification directly by some measures, which is a typically unsupervised learning technique [7, 8].

With the continuous emergence of images, texts and some high-dimensional big data, traditional clustering algorithms are unable to deal with the dimensionality reduction efficiently, but deep learning has advantages in this respect, so the deep learning and clustering will be jointly studied in this paper.

2   Profile of Deep Learning and RBM

Deep learning is to learn more valuable features by establishing a machine learning model with many hidden layers and massive training data so as to improve the accuracy of classification or prediction. Therefore, the "deep model" is the means, and "feature learning" is the purpose. As compared with the traditional shallow learning, deep learning focuses more on the depth of the model structure, usually having six or seven, or even ten layers of hidden nodes; big data is used to learn features, and classification or forecast is easier through layer-by-layer feature transformation.

The common method of deep learning is to use deep neural network structure for feature learning. The common network models include: Boltzmann model, restricted Boltzmann model, automatic coder model and some mixed models. As the restricted Boltzmann model is used in this experiment, this paper will mainly focus on this structure.

Restricted Boltzmann Machine (RBM) is a randomly generated neural network that learns the probability distribution from the input dataset [3, 4]. The network is composed of some visible units (visible variables, namely, data samples) and some hidden units (hidden variables), and both visible variables and hidden variables are binary variables, whose state is {0, 1}. The entire network is a bipartite graph. There is no connection between nodes in the same layer, but there is a connection between nodes in two adjacent layers and the unit nodes in the same layer are independent each other. Bengio and Roux have theoretically proved that RBM can express arbitrary discrete distributions if the number of nodes in hidden layer is large enough. Restricted Boltzmann Machine is an undirected graph model, and its structure is shown in Fig. 1 below:

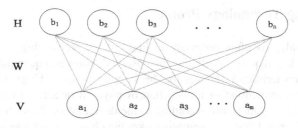

Fig. 1. RBM structure

In Fig. 1, V means the visible layer of the input data node, with m unit nodes, H means the hidden layer of the feature extraction node, with n unit nodes, and W is the connection weight between the two layers. For the above RBM model, the energy function between the input vector V and the hidden layer vector H is:

$$E_\beta(v,h) = -\sum_{i=1}^{m} a_i v_i - \sum_{j=1}^{n} b_j h_j - \sum_{i=1}^{m}\sum_{j=1}^{n} v_j w_{ij} h_j$$

Where, β, a_i, b_j and w_{ij} parameters means, a_i is the offset parameter of the visible layer unit i, b_j is the offset parameter of the hidden layer unit j, w_{ij} is the weight between the visible layer unit i and the hidden layer unit j. Using this energy formula, the joint probability distribution of (v, h) can be defined: $P_\beta(v,h) = \frac{1}{z_\beta}e^{-E_\beta}(v,h)$, where, z_β is the normalization factor.

$$z_\beta = \sum_{v,h} \theta^{-E_\beta}(v,\ h)$$

Knowing the joint probability distribution, the probability distribution of the visible and hidden data can be defined:

$$P_\beta(v) = \sum_h P_\beta(v,h) = \frac{1}{z_\beta}\sum_h e^{-E_\beta}(v,\ h),$$

$$P_\beta(h) = \sum_v P_\beta(v,h) = \frac{1}{z_\beta}\sum_v e^{-E_\beta}(v,h).$$

Thus, if the visible layer state is given, the probability of a unit in the hidden layer being activated will be: $P_\beta(h_j = 1|v) = \sigma(b_j + \sum_i v_i w_{ij})$.

If the hidden layer state is given, the probability of a neuron in the visible layer being activated will be: $P_\beta(v_i = 1|h) = \sigma(a_j + \sum_j h_j w_{ij})$.

The main purpose of RBM training is to get the value of the parameter $\beta = \{a_i, b_j, w_{ij}\}$ on the basis of sampling data so as to determine the distribution of the training data and maximize the possible fitting input data. Optimal parameter β can be calculated through maximum likelihood estimation.

3 Clustering Technology Profile

In the real world, it is often necessary to find out the relationship between various things, namely, it is required to digitize the observed things and quantitatively express the various characteristics in figures for the samples of such things. Clustering is a process of grouping or dividing a collection of physical or abstract sample sets into subsets or clusters automatically according to the degree of similarity between objects without any guidance. Clustering analysis makes the objects in each cluster have higher similarity, while the objects in different clusters have higher dissimilarity. Clustering analysis is to search the valuable connection between data objects from given data set, and is a way to simplify data through data modeling. Clustering analysis is also an unsupervised learning technique that does not require priori knowledge. Reasonable clustering division depends on the description of the similarity between the samples, whereas the methods of describing the similarity between the various samples are mainly relied on distance and similarity coefficient. According to the main idea of clustering analysis method, the clustering methods include division method, level method, density method, grid method and model method.

4 Clustering Model Combined with Deep Learning

With the rapid development of big data in various fields, there emerges dimensional disaster in the respects of feature learning and clustering in big data processing. In the past, the solution for high-dimensional data was to learn the features and reduce the size of the original data to be counted. However, at present, the traditional method of feature learning is unable to efficiently reflect the deep features of big data. Deep learning uses deep structure for feature abstraction, so its hierarchical feature learning mode can find data distribution features and patterns in a deeper level. It has good distributed performance and is suitable for big data and distributed computing. Therefore, a clustering model based on deep learning, which is suitable for big data processing, is proposed in this paper to adapt to the big data processing in a more efficient manner. This clustering model includes two major parts: pre-training and fine-tuning & optimization. The model of pre-training part is shown in Fig. 2:

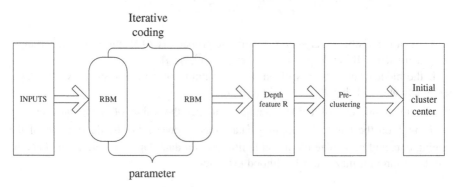

Fig. 2. Pre-training model

The pre-training part mainly includes unsupervised deep learning structure layer and pre-clustering layer. The data is entered through the INPUTS layer, and then the simple and effective Depth feature R is effectively learned from the unsupervised deep learning structure. Moreover, the distribution parameter of the input data is also obtained, and then pre-clustering is performed on the Depth feature R through the pre-clustering layer to get the initial clustering center and membership matrix. Among them, the unsupervised deep learning structure in pre-training part could take on the deep Boltzmann model, deep restricted Boltzmann model, deep automatic coder model or some mixed models.

In this paper, deep Restricted Boltzmann Machine (RBM) model is adopted for encoding in the pre-training part. The commonly used simple clustering algorithm (for example, k-means) is employed in the pre-clustering. The RBM includes a visible layer and a hidden layer, in which, the visible layer is the input sample data, and the hidden layer is the sampling data of the input sample. Given a training sample $x = \{X_1, X_2.. X_n\}$, the m-dimensional code $y = \{y_1, y_2..y_m\}$ of the sample is obtained by RBM, that is, the m-dimensional feature is extracted. The encoding process is shown in Fig. 3 below:

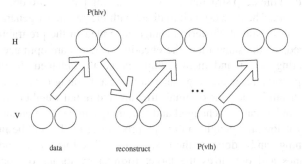

Fig. 3. RBM procedure

In RBM, the unit nodes in the same layer are independent each other. That is, given the state of the visible layer node v, the hidden layer h can be gotten by P(h|v), and after the hidden layer is gotten, the visible layer can be acquired by P(h|v). After training, if the data obtained from the hidden layer are consistent with the previously input data, the sampled hidden layer is an additional expression of the visible layer data, so the RBM encoding of the input data is obtained.

In the clustering process of high-dimensional and large-scale data, first, the proper data parameters are selected for RBM feature encoding to reduce the size of statistical data, and then k-means and other algorithms are used for clustering. A random simulated sampling Gibbs method is used in RBM training, which can extract random samples representing their own distribution and can express most of the data distribution.

The fine-tuning & optimization part is also composed of a deep learning structure and final clustering layer, and the difference lies in the fine-tuning & optimization on the fine-tuning part after pre-training, which is shown in Fig. 4:

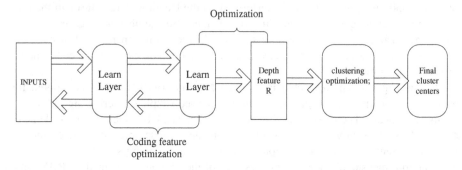

Fig. 4. Fine-tuning & optimization model

The original data are input into the fine-tuning & optimizing part through the input data layer and then the deep structure in the pre-training part is unfolded to form a deep fine-tuning structure. The network is initialized with the parameter generated in the pre-training, and then the initial clustering center generated in the pre-training process is further optimized. At the same time, the encoding features are optimized, and finally, the final clustering center and membership matrix are obtained. In the fine-tuning process of deep structure, if the original data and the training data of the pre-training model have high similarities, the original structure and initial weight of the pre-training model can be kept basically unchanged and retraining can be done on the new data set. If the similarity is low, the weights in the preprocessing model will be fully initialized and then retraining can be done on the new data set. The fine-tuning and optimization part mainly tunes and optimizes the target formula by means of continuous cross iteration. When the number of iterations reaches the pre-set value or the target function value is less than a certain threshold, the fine-tuning is stopped.

For high-dimensional data, the number of nodes in the hidden layer can be set to be smaller than the number of nodes in the visible layer, which can reduce the original data and remove redundant data.

The entire process of this model is an unsupervised learning process, and the deep structure and clustering are jointly processed, which is particularly suitable for the big data field.

The target formula for fine-tuning part is the combination of two parts, namely, likelihood probability function plus the within-classification distance:

$$
f = e * \left(-\sum_i x_i \log f_i(R(x_i, w_i)) - \sum_i (1 - x_i) \log(1 - f_i(R(x_i, w_i))) \right) + (1 - e)
$$
$$
* \sum_{i=1}^{N} \sum_{j=1}^{C} \sqrt{\left(R(x_i, w_i) - c_j^2 \right)}
$$

R (…) means the original data encoding, namely, the new features after learning; f (R (…)) means the reconstruction of the original data, namely, the decoded data. Parameter e is the adjustment factor. If likelihood probability value of reconstructed data is much larger than the within-classification distance, fine-tuning effect is very little. Therefore, the value range of adjustment factor is between 0 and 1. Likelihood probability function is a convergent function. For the sum of within-classification distance, in case of a known clustering center, the target function f is a simple function for the derivative of the parameter membership W. Therefore, the target function is also convergent.

5   Experimental Results and Analysis

A clustering model based on RMB encoding is proposed in this paper. In order to test the effect of this model, a verification experiment is carried out.

5.1   Experimental Parameters

The learning rate can determine how fast the parameter moves to its optimum value. If the learning rate is over-large, the optimization efficiency may exceed the optimal value; if the learning rate is over-small, the optimization efficiency may be too low and long time algorithm is unable to be converged. It is indicated in Hinton's experience that if the learning rate is set over-large, the reconstruction error will be substantially increased accordingly, and the weight will also be larger, so the learning rate is usually set as 0.1 or 0.06, of course, the learning rate can be adjusted according to the actual situation. For the initial value of the weight parameter W, it is usually set to a random number close to the positive distribution N (0, 0.01), and offset parameter a in the visible layer and offset parameter b in the hidden layer can be set as 0 respectively.

In this experiment, in order to test the effect difference of RBM coding of the clustering model under different parameters, the node in hidden layer is set to be 3/4 of that in visible layer, the learning rate parameters are set 0.1 and 0.06 respectively, and the number of iterations is 18 times and 32 times separately.

5.2   Experimental Data Sets

Twenty data of various high and low dimensions in UCI dataset are selected as the data in this experiment. The data sample point has 2458285 data maximally or only 24 minimally; 617 dimensions as the maximum or 4 dimensions as the minimum. The specific experimental data is shown in Table 1 as below:

Table 1. Experimental data information

Data sets	The number of data sample point	Attribute	The number of categories
Sponge	76	45	2
Water treatment plant	527	38	3
University	285	17	2
US census data	2458285	68	20
Plants	22632	70	5
Computer hardware	209	9	2
Dresses_attribute_sales	501	13	6
Wholesale customers	440	8	2
Stoneflakes	79	8	2
Wiki4HE	913	53	2
Iris	150	4	3
Isolet	7797	617	26
Flags	194	30	5
Lenses	24	4	3
Letter recognition	20000	16	4
Musk(version 2)	6598	168	2
Zoo	101	17	2
Anuran calls	7195	22	4
Wine	178	13	2
Yeast	1484	8	6

5.3   Experimental Results Analysis

In this experiment, firstly, the above UCI datasets are all run twenty times in the k-means algorithm, and the final average after twenty times running is taken as its accuracy. Secondly, the RBM encoding is done for the above data set, and then it is run twenty times in the k-means algorithm, continuing to take the final average after twenty times running as its accuracy. Thirdly, the learning rate is set as 0.06 and 0.1 respectively, and the number of iterations is set as 18 times and 32 times separately for comparing their accuracy effect. As the experimental results for learning rate at 0.06 and 0.1 are similar, only the comparison results at learning rate of 0.1 is listed here, which is shown in Table 2:

It is found in the experimental results that the experimental results at learning rates of 0.06 and 0.1 are similar and have little effect, and the number of iterations has a certain impact on the data RBM coding, but it has little effect on the clustering effect and so does on the clustering data accuracy. There are only five pieces of experimental data whose accuracy after encoding 32 times iterations is greater than that before encoding, the reason being that these five data have more redundancy, and the dimension is reduced after the RBM encoding, so accuracy is improved due to a clearer data structure, while the accuracy of other data is not lifted due to less redundancy.

Table 2. k-means clustering results at learning rate 0.1

Datasets	Algorithm			
	18		32	
	Before coding	After coding	Before coding	After coding
Sponge	0.7933	0.7924	0.7933	0.7912
Water treatment plant	0.8531	0.8516	0.8531	0.8514
University	0.5960	0.6028	0.5921	0.6098
US Census Data	0.7124	0.7243	0.7256	0.7309
Plants	0.7256	0.7321	0.7432	0.7562
Computer hardware	0.6822	0.6075	0.6822	0.6235
Dresses_attribute_sales	0.7567	0.8468	0.8448	0.6787
Wholesale customers	0.5089	0.4765	0.4987	0.4856
Stoneflakes	0.7085	0.7234	0.7542	0.7343
Wiki4HE	0.5484	0.5466	0.5466	0.5426
Iris	0.7711	0.8623	0.8912	0.8734
Isolet	0.5567	0.3546	0.5498	0.3745
Flags	0.5548	0.5548	0.5836	0.5739
Lenses	0.7653	0.8012	0.8123	0.7987
Letter recognition	0.7975	0.7125	0.7865	0.7189
Musk(version 2)	0.5513	0.6632	0.5593	0.6680
Zoo	0.6822	0.6122	0.6822	0.6822
Anuran calls	0.5346	0.5167	0.5346	0.5143
Wine	0.7233	0.6373	0.7254	0.7267
Yeast	0.4216	0.4134	0.4287	0.4112

In addition, the average execution time of twenty times running for eight data clustering in UCI dataset before and after RBM encoding is recorded during the experiment, in which, the learning rate of RBM encoding is set as 0.1 and the number of iterations is set at 32 times. The comparison shows that the average execution time of clustering after RBM encoding is less than that before RBM encoding, which is shown in Fig. 5 below:

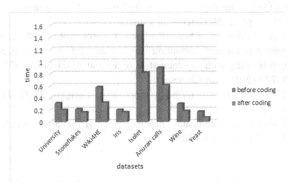

Fig. 5. Comparison chart of clustering execution timer before and after RBM encoding

6 Conclusions

In this paper, a clustering model based on Restricted Boltzmann Machine (RBM) is proposed to deal with the big data mining issue that is currently in dimensional disaster, and this model is characterized as the combination of traditional clustering and machine learning that is suitable for dimensionality reduction. This model includes two parts: pre-training and fine-tuning & optimization. In the pre-training part, the data size of the high-dimensional big data is reduced by RBM coding, and then the traditional clustering algorithm is used for pre-clustering. In the fine-tuning & optimization part, the deep fine-tuning is done to further optimize encoding features and clustering. In addition, the model is validated through experiment, and some data are selected from the UCI dataset for the comparison between the traditional clustering and subject clustering proposed in this model. It is indicated in the data analysis that the clustering model based on RBM has little impact on the clustering effect, but the execution is more efficient.

Acknowledgments. We would like to thank the anonymous referees for their careful readings of the manuscripts and many useful suggestions. This work has been co-supported by: Natural Science Foundation of China under Grant No. 61472092; Guangdong Provincial Science and Technology Plan Fund with grant No. 2013B010401037; Natural Science Foundation of Guangdong Province under Grant No. S2011040003843; GuangZhou Municipal High School Science Research Fund under grant No. 1201421317; State Scholarship Fund by China Scholarship Council under Grant No. [2013]3018-201308440096; and Yuexiu District Science and Technology Plan Fund of GuangZhou City with grant No. 2013-GX-005.

References

1. Jinjia, W., et al.: The study of deep learning under big data. High Technol. Lett. **27**(1), 27–37 (2017). (in Chinese)
2. Weng, S.: The construction of the cognitive modeling for deep learning based on the micro-MOOC learning system. Mod. Educ. Technol. **27**(6), 87–93 (2017). (in Chinese)
3. Cai, H.: Research of clustering algorithms in big data analysis. Hehui University Of Science Technology, An Hui, pp. 1–33 (2016). (in Chinese)
4. Qi, Y.: Research of key technologies of clustering based on deep learning. Southwest Jiaotong University, Si Chuan, pp. 1–58 (2016). (in Chinese)
5. Li, F., Xie, D., Qi, D., Xie, G., Chen, W., Peng, L.: Research on effective and intelligent resource management in internet computing. Appl. Math. Inf. Sci. **8**(2), 625–631 (2014)
6. Ma, S.: ETc. Deep learning with big data: state of art and development. CAAI Trans. Intell. Syst. **11**(6), 728–740 (2016). (in Chinese)
7. Zhang, J.: ETc. Review of deep learning. Appl. Res. Comput. **35**(7), 27–37 (2018). (in Chinese)
8. Keguang, Y.: Research on incremental clustering method for large dataset. Mod. Electron. Tech. **40**(9), 176–182 (2017). (in Chinese)

Criteria Interdependence in Fuzzy Multi-criteria Decision Making: A Survey

Le Sun[1($\boxtimes$)] and Jinyuan He[2]

[1] School of Computer and Software, Nanjing University of Information Science and Technology, Nanjing, China
sunle2009@gmail.com
[2] Centre for Applied Informatics, Victoria University, Melbourne, Australia
jinyuan.he@live.vu.edu.au

Abstract. In this paper, we investigate how Bonferroni mean (BM) operator models criteria interdependence in fuzzy multi-criteria decision making problems. We first study definitions of different types of fuzzy sets proposed in 1960s–2010s; we then introduce definitions of aggregation functions and the Bonferroni mean operator; we finally survey the work of modeling criteria interdependence by using BM and its extensions.

Keywords: Fuzzy multi-criteria decision making
Criteria interdependence · Bonferroni Mean

1 Introduction

Multi-criteria factors are key components in various areas of Information Technology, like multi-criteria decision making, information fusion, case-based reasoning, and pattern recognition [25]. Aggregation operations are required to operate multi-criteria according to different types of criteria relations. Though we can recognize a few of relations between criteria based on our knowledge and experience, there are still a large number of criterion relations that are not definite and cannot be recognized easily [12]. However, we can identify them by using other technical methods, e.g. determining criterion correlations based on a great deal of criterion performance samples.

Bonferroni mean (BM) operator is recently extended to solve multi-criteria problems by Yager [25]. It has been proved to be a meaningful aggregation function to model homogeneous criteria relations in decision making problems [7].

In this paper, we investigate how BM models criteria interdependence in fuzzy multi-criteria decision making problems. We first study definitions of different types of fuzzy sets proposed in 1960s−2010s (Sect. 2); then we introduce definitions of aggregation functions and the Bonferroni mean operator (Sect. 3); we survey the work of criteria interdependence modeling by using BM and its extensions in Sect. 4; Sect. 5 concludes this paper.

© Springer Nature Switzerland AG 2018
X. Sun et al. (Eds.): ICCCS 2018, LNCS 11063, pp. 397–407, 2018.
https://doi.org/10.1007/978-3-030-00006-6_36

2 Definitions of Fuzzy Sets

We summarize definitions of fuzzy sets proposed in 1960s–2010s. Table 1 shows an overview of these fuzzy sets. Columns of Table 1 represent names of fuzzy sets (FuzzySet), abbreviations in this paper (Abbr.), authors (Author), publication papers (Paper), publication years (Year), and definitions (Defs).

Table 1. Definitions of fuzzy sets in 1960s–2010s

FuzzySet	Abbr.	Author	Paper	Year	Definitions
Type-1	T1-FS	Zadeh	[27]	1965	Definition 1
General Type-2	GT2-FS	Zadeh	[11]	1975	Definition 2
Interval valued type-2	IV-FS	Zadeh	[11]	1975	Definitions 3 and 4
Intuition-istic	IFS	Atanassov	[2]	1986	Definition 5
Interval-valued intuitionistic	IVI-FS	Atanassov	[1]	1989	Definition 7
Fuzzy multiset	FM	Yager	[24]	1986	Definition 8
Hesitant	HFS	Torra	[20]	2010	Definitions 9 and 10
Pythagorean	PFS	Yager	[19]	2013	Definition 11
Probabilistic hesitant fuzzy set	PHFS	Zhu and Zhang	[28]	2017	Definition 12

We give detailed definitions of fuzzy sets in Table 1 as below.
Definition 1 [27] defines type-1 fuzzy sets (T1-FSs).

Definition 1. *Assume X be a space of n objects: $X = \{x_1, ..., x_n\}$, a fuzzy set A of X is characterized by a membership function $\mu_A : X \to [0,1]$, where $\mu_A(x)$ represents the degree of membership of x in A.*

Mendel [17] identified four types of uncertainties that cannot be processed by T1-FSs, which are: (1) uncertain meanings of words in fuzzy rules; (2) in cases of group decision making, uncertain consequents may associate with a frequency distribution; (3) noises in activating measurements of a T1-FS cause uncertainties; and (4) noises in data for tuning parameters of T1-FS. Zadeh [11] proposed General Type-2 fuzzy sets (GT2-FSs) to complement the inability of T1-FS by introducing fuzzy membership functions into GT2-FSs, which is defined by Definition 2 [17].

Definition 2. *A type-2 fuzzy set $\overline{A}$ of X is denoted by Eq. 1.*

$$\overline{A} = \int_{x \in X} \int_{u \in J_x} \mu_{\overline{A}}(x,u)/(x,u), J_x \subseteq [0,1] \tag{1}$$

where $\mu_{\overline{A}}(x,u) \in [0,1]$ and $\int \int$ is unions over x and u.

In [17], Mendel summarized difficulties of using GT2-FSs in 2002: (1) it is difficult to draw GT2FS because of its three-dimensional form; (2) there has not been precisely defined mathematical terms to model and represent GT2FS; (3) derivations of the union, intersection and complement of GT2FS are difficult and ad hoc; and (4) processing GT2FS requires more time complexity than processing T1FS. He [17] also discussed the general application domains of GT2FS, which are (1) the mathematical description of time-variabilities of a data-generating system is unknown; (2) the mathematical description of nonstationarities of measurement noises is unknown; (3) the mathematical description of nonstationarities of features' statistical attributes is unknown; (4) existing uncertainties of expert knowledge from questionnaires; and (5) existing linguistic terms having a nonmeasurable domain.

Interval-valued fuzzy sets (IV-FSs) generalize GT2-FSs by accounting for an observation that we cannot always assume the membership degree of x is exactly given, so we define a second uncertainty – the membership degree of x – being not a crisp number, but an interval. In the past 15 years, because of the time complexity of processing a GT2-FS, most researchers explore applications of IV-FSs, where the operations of IV-FSs are more manageable and practical. A IV-FS is a special case of GT2-FS, which is defined by Definition 3.

Definition 3. *A general type-2 fuzzy set $\widetilde{A}$ is an interval-valued fuzzy set if $\mu_{\widetilde{A}}(x, u) = 1$ for all $x \in X$ and $u \in J_x \subseteq [0, 1]$, which is denoted by Eq. 2.*

$$\widetilde{A} = \int_{x \in X} \int_{u \in J_x} 1/(x, u) \qquad (2)$$

Another description of IV-FSs is shown in Definition 4 [1].

Definition 4. *An IV-FS $\widetilde{A}$ over a universe X is characterized by a function $J_{\widetilde{A}}(x) \in INT$, where $x \in X$ and $INT \subseteq [0, 1]$.*

Intuitionistic fuzzy sets (I-FSs) was proposed by Atanassov [2] to deal with uncertainties in situations that insufficient information available to establish membership functions. I-FSs is defined in Definition 5.

Definition 5. *An intuitionistic fuzzy set $\breve{A}$ is defined by Eq. 3.*

$$\breve{A} = \int_{x \in X} (x, v_{\breve{A}}(x), \mu_{\breve{A}}(x))/x \qquad (3)$$

where $v_{\breve{A}}(x) \in [0, 1]$ and $\mu_{\breve{A}}(x) \in [0, 1]$ represent the non-membership degree and membership degree of x belonging to $\breve{A}$ respectively, and $v_{\breve{A}}(x) + \mu_{\breve{A}}(x) \leq 1$. Value $\pi_{\breve{A}}(x) = 1 - v_{\breve{A}}(x) - \mu_{\breve{A}}(x)$ denotes the degree of hesitancy of x belonging to $\breve{A}$.

I-FSs are isomorphic to IV-FSs. Atanassov introduced maps (Definition 6) between I-FSs and IV-FSs [2], and proposed interval-valued intuitionistic fuzzy sets (IVI-FSs) (Definition 7) [1] based on these maps.

Definition 6. *Let f and g be two maps:*

- *f maps an IV-FS $\widetilde{A}$ to an I-FS $\breve{A}$: $\breve{A} = f(\widetilde{A})$, where $\mu_{\widetilde{A}}(x) = inf J_{\widetilde{A}}(x)$ and $v_{\widetilde{A}}(x) = sup J_{\widetilde{A}}(x)$.*

- g *maps an I-FS $\check{A}$ to an IV-FS $\widetilde{A}$: $\widetilde{A} = g(\check{A})$, where $J_{\check{A}}(x) = [\mu_{\widetilde{A}}(x), 1 - v_{\widetilde{A}}(x)]$.*

Definition 7. *An interval-valued intuitionistic fuzzy set $\widehat{A}$ over X is defined as $\widehat{A} = \{\langle x, \mu_{\widehat{A}(x)}, v_{\widehat{A}}(x) \rangle\}$, where $x \in X$, $\mu_{\widehat{A}} \in [0,1]$, $v_{\widehat{A}} \in [0,1]$, and $\mu_{\widehat{A}} + v_{\widehat{A}} \leq 1$.*

Fuzzy multisets (FM) is a generalization of fuzzy sets and multisets. Multisets allow multiple occurrences of an element in a set, e.g. $M = \{e, e, f, g, g, g\}$ is a multiset of a universe $X = \{e, f, g, h\}$. Each multiset is associated with a function *count* over X, e.g. $count_M(e) = 2$, $count_M(f) = 1$, $count_M(g) = 3$ and $count_M(h) = 0$. A fuzzy multiset is defined by Definition 8.

Definition 8. *A fuzzy multiset assigns a membership value to each element in a multiset.*

For example, $\widetilde{M} = \{(e, 0.4), (e, 0.5), (f, 0.3), (g, 0.7), (g, 0.8), (g, 0.2)\}$ is a fuzzy multiset over X.

Hesitant fuzzy sets (HFSs) are proposed by Torra [20], which assign a set of possible membership values to each element x in X, rather than assigning an interval value or a possibility distribution. HFSs are defined in Definition 9.

Definition 9. *A hesitant fuzzy set A' of X is characterized by a membership function $h_{A'}(X) \subseteq [0,1]$.*

Given a set of fuzzy sets M of X, which is associated with a set of membership functions $M = \{\mu_1, ..., \mu_N\}$, a hesitant fuzzy set can be defined in terms of the union of memberships of M (Definition 10) [20].

Definition 10. *The hesitant fuzzy set of M is defined as $h_M(x) = \{\mu_1(x), ..., \mu_N(x)\}$.*

Yager [19] proposed Pythagorean fuzzy sets (PFSs) that are a generalization of intuitionistic fuzzy sets. We can use PFS in situations where we cannot use intuitionistic fuzzy sets. PFSs involve pythagorean membership grades that are formally defined by Definition 11 [19].

Definition 11. *Given a pair $(r(x), d(x))$, where $\forall x \in X$, $r(x) \in [0,1]$ is the commitment strength at x, and $d(x) \in [0,1]$ is the commitment direction at x. A Pythagorean Fuzzy Set A_{PFS} is defined as $A_{PFS} = \{(x, A_Y(x), A_N(x)) | x \in X\}$, where $A_Y(x)$ and $A_N(x)$ represent the membership degree of x in A and non-membership degree of x in A respectively, and A_Y and A_N are Pythagorean complements with respect to $r(x)$, i.e. $A_Y^2(x) + A_N^2(x) = r^2(x)$.*

Probabilistic hesitant fuzzy set (PHFS) is proposed in 2014 [28]. It improves HFSs by solving some problems to avoid information loss. Three main problems it solves are [28]: (1) the sum of occurrence probability of different memberships of an element may be less than 1; (2) the occurrence probability of an element membership may be irrational number; and (3) it is difficult to use the complex expression of fuzzy multisets. The definition of Probabilistic hesitant fuzzy element (PHFS) is shown in Definition 12.

Definition 12. *Given a crisp set X, a probabilistic hesitant fuzzy set (PHFS) is defined as $H = \{x, h_x(p_x) | x \in X\}$, where $h_x \in [0,1]$ is a set of membership degrees of $x \in X$, and $p_x \in [0,1]$ is a set of frequencies of h_x. We call $h_x(p_x)$ as the probabilistic hesitant fuzzy element (PHFE).*

3   Background: Aggregation Functions and Bonferroni Means

A multi-criteria decision making (MCDM) problem [25] is to select one alternative from a set of alternatives $A = \{a_1, ..., a_m\}$ based on satisfaction degrees of each alternative with respect to a set of criteria $C = \{c_1, ..., c_n\}$. The satisfaction degree of a_i with respect to c_j is represented by $S_j(i)$. An MCDM method uses a pointwise valuation function to valuate a_i with respect to n criteria in C, which is defined as $D(a_i) = f(c_1, ..., c_j, ..., c_m)$. The selection result is a_i with the largest valuation D. Function f is an aggregation function that has three significant properties: (1) indifference: $D(a_i)$ only depends on the satisfaction degree of $c_j, \forall c_j \in C$, but not depends on satisfaction degrees by any of the other alternatives; (2) monotonicity: if a_i and a_k are two alternatives and $S_j(i) \geq S_j(k)$ for all $c_j \in C$, then $D(a_i) \geq D(a_k)$; (3) grounding: if $S_j(i) = 0, \forall c_j \in C$, then $D_{a_i} = 0$; and if $S_j(i) = 1, \forall c_j \in C$, then $D_{a_i} = 1$. We formally define an aggregation function in Definition 13.

Definition 13. *Let $I = [0,1]$, then an aggregation function f is a mapping $f : I^n \to I$, where $f(0, ..., 0) = 0$, $f(1, ..., 1) = 1$, and $f(g_1, ..., g_n) \geq f(h_1, ..., h_n)$ if $g_i \geq h_i$, for $\forall i$.*

Bonferroni mean (BM) operator [6] is an important aggregation operator that models criterion relations (Definition 14).

Definition 14. *Let $C = \{c_1, ..., c_n\}$ be a collection of values that $c_i \in [0,1]$, and two values $p, q \geq 0$. Then the general Bonferroni mean of C with respect to p, q is represented by Formula 4:*

$$B^{p,q}(a_1, ..., a_n) = (\frac{1}{n} \frac{1}{n-1} \sum_{i,j=1; i \neq j}^{n} a_i^p a_j^q)^{\frac{1}{p+q}} \qquad (4)$$

BM has the following properties: $B^{p,q}(0, ..., 0) = 0$, $B^{p,q}(1, ..., 1) = 1$ and $B^{p,q}(g_1, ..., g_n) \geq B^{p,q}(h_1, ..., h_n)$ if $g_i \geq h_i$ for all i. Therefore, BM is an aggregation function. It is also a mean type aggregation operator [25].

We investigate a special case of BM with $p = q = 1$. Let c_i denote the satisfaction degree of an alternative with respect to criterion i, $BM^{1,1}$ can be represented by formula 5.

$$B(c_1, ..., c_n) = (\frac{1}{n} \sum_{i=1}^{n} u_i c_i)^{\frac{1}{2}} \qquad (5)$$

where u_i represents the average satisfaction degree to all criteria other than i.

4 Criterion Correlations Based on Bonferroni Means

Dutta et al. [8] considered the importance and concept of heterogeneous interrelationships among attributes in group decision making. They defined that an "heterogeneous interrelationship" means in an attribute set $A = \{A_1, A_2, ..., A_n\}$, some attributes $A_i \subset A$ are dependent with a subset $B_i \subset A/A_i)$, while $C_i = A/(A_i \cup B_i)$ are independent with the other attributes. They defined an extended Bonferroni mean (EBM) operator to measure heterogeneous interrelationships among attributes. They extended EBM operator to linguistic 2-tuple fuzzy numbers, and defined three aggregation operators: 2-tuple linguistic EBM, weighted 2-tuple linguistic EBM, and linguistic weighted 2-tuple linguistic EBM.

Yu et al. [26] pointed out the advantages of using the Heronian mean (HM) to model interrelationships between attributes compared with BM operators. Based on Yu's theory, Liu et al. [12] extended HM to intuitionistic fuzzy numbers. One drawback of HM is it does not have the generality of IFNs as it is only based on Algebraic operations rather than based on the general Archimedean t-conorm and t-norm. Therefore, Liu et al. [12] combined the HM with the Archimedean t-conorm and t-norm to model attribute interrelationships in MADM problems. They defined the intuitionistic fuzzy Archimedean Heronian aggregation (IFAHA) operator and the intuitionistic fuzzy weight Archimedean Heronian aggregation (IFWAHA) operator, and discussed properties of these operators.

Zhang et al. [29] improved the Analytic Hierarchy Process (AHP) with intuitionistic multiplicative preferences (IMRPs) in multi-criteria group decision makings (MCGDMs). The authors developed an intuitionistic multiplicative group AHP (IMGAHP) that uses IMPRs to capture experts' preference expressions. The proposed IMGAHP can simultaneously capture decision makers' preferred and nonpreferred judgments on compared objects. Zhang et al. [29] developed a method for the consistency checking and improvement of IMPRs. They used an induced ordered weighted geometric averaging (IOWGA) operator to fuse IMPRs of different experts (Tables 2 and 3).

The Bonferroni mean (BM) [6] is an averaging aggregation function that is capable of modeling homogeneous relations among attributes in decision-making problems, which is based on an assumption that each attribute is related to all the other attributes [23]. Extended BM (EBM) was proposed by Dutta et al. [8] to model heterogeneous interrelations among attributes, that is, some of attributes are interrelated with a non-empty subset of the remaining attributes, and other attributes may be independent with the remaining attributes. Overall, EBM is a combination of averaging and conjunctive functions, and it can model both heterogeneous interrelationships among attributes and aggregation operations of independent attributes. Based on these capabilities of EBM, Chen et al. [7] designed the generalized EBM (GEBM), and defined a composite aggregation function to investigate the aggregation mechanism of EBMs. They also analyzed the properties of GEBMs.

Liu et al. [15] extended the power Bonferroni mean (PBM) operator to operate interval-valued intuitionistic fuzzy numbers (IVIFNs). They defined four aggregation operators for IVIFNs: the power Bonferroni mean operator

Table 2. Overview of fuzzy decision making techniques

Work	Year	Issues	Methods	Validate
[25]	2009	Use BM to measure criteria interrelationship	Extend BM to MCDM; combine BM with OWA; combine BM with Choquet integral	NA
[4]	2010	Generalized BM (GBM)	Propose generalized BM (GBM) in general MADM problems	NA
[23]	2011	Extend BM to IFSs	Define intuitionistic fuzzy BM	Case study
[22]	2011	Extend BM to IVIFSs	Define IVIFS BM	Case study
[26]	2012	Advantages of Heronian mean (HM) compared with BM, PA, and fuzzy measure	Extend HM to IVFSs	Case study
[30]	2012	Extend geometric Bonferroni mean (GeoBM) to hesitant fuzzy environment	Propose GeoBM for HFSs	Case study
[21]	2013	Extend Geometric BM (GeoBM) in IFSs	Combine geometric means with BMs for IFNs	Case study
[31]	2013	Extend generalized Bonferroni mean (GBM) to hesitant fuzzy environment	Propose GBM for HFSs	Case study
[3]	2013	Drawbacks of old extension of generalized Bonferroni mean (GBM) to IFSs	New extension of GBM to IFSs	Case study
[18]	2015	Study correlation coefficients of HFSs	Propose Shapley weighted correlation coefficients of HFSs based on fuzzy measure	Cast study
[8]	2015	Heterogeneous interrelationship among attributes	Define heterogeneous interrelationship among attributes; define EBM; apply EBM to linguistic 2-tuples	Case studies
[9]	2015	Interactions between membership functions and non-membership functions between different IFNs	Develop intuitionistic fuzzy interaction BM and weighted intuitionistic fuzzy interaction BM	Case studies
[10]	2015	Unduly high or unduly low arguments in ranking of HF elements; interrelationships between input values of hesitant fuzzy MADMs	Define the ith order polymerization degree function; combine power average operators with the Bonferroni mean in hesitant fuzzy environments	Case study

Table 3. Overview of fuzzy decision making techniques (continue)

Work	Year	Issues	Methods	Validate
[5]	2016	Continuous aggregations, multiple comparisons between each argument and distance measures	Develop new aggregation operators based on BMs, OWA operators and distance measures; establish relationships and groups of experts using Moore's families and Galois lattice based on dissimilarity and fuzzy relationships and the maximum similarities of sub-relations	Case study
[7]	2016	Capture both heterogeneous and homogeneous attribute interrelationships; GEBM aggregation	Generalize EBM to GEBM; define a composite aggregation function for GEBMs; explore properties of GEBMs	Case study
[12]	2017	Use HM to replace BM to process attribute interactions in IFSs	Construct intuitionistic fuzzy HM operators based on Archimedean t-conorm and t-norm	Case study
[29]	2017	Lack a multiplicative preference relation to denote the preferred and nonpreferred intensity, and the hesitancy of one object over another in AHP	Define acceptably consistent IMPRs; interactively adjust an inconsistent IMPR; integrate acceptably consistent IMPRs	Case study
[15]	2017	Extend PBM operator to IVIFNs	Propose power Bonferroni mean operator, weighted PBM operator, power geometric BM operator, and weighted power geometric BM operator	Case study
[14]	2017	Extend ParBM and PGBM to IFNs	Propose interaction PBM operator, weighted interaction PBM operator, interaction PGBM operator and weighted interaction PGBM operator for IFNs	Experiments
[13]	2017	Extend PA and HM to IVIFNs	Propose two aggregation operators and a similarity measure for IVIFNs	Case study
[16]	2018	Extend BM to q-ROFs	Propose four aggregation operators	Case study

(IVIFPBM), the weighted PBM operator (IVIFWPBM), the power geometric BM operator (IVIFPGBM), and the weighted power geometric BM operator (IVIFWPGBM).

Liu et al. [14] extended the partitioned Bonferroni mean (ParBM) and the partitioned geometric Bonferroni mean (PGBM) operators to intuitionistic fuzzy numbers (IFNs). They defined four operators for IFNs: interaction PBM (IFIPBM), weighted interaction PBM (IFWIPBM), interaction PGBM (IFIPGBM) and weighted interaction PGBM (IFWIPGBM) operators.

Liu [13] extended the combination of power average operator (PA) and Heronian mean operator (HM) to operate IVIFNs. He defined two operators for IVIFNs: interval-valued intuitionistic fuzzy power Heronian aggregation (IVIF-PHA) and interval-valued intuitionistic fuzzy power weight Heronian aggregation (IVIFPWHA) operators. In addition, he proposed a new similarity function of IVIFNs to calculate support degrees in power weighting.

Liu et al. [16] extended BM to q-ROFs to q-rung orthopair fuzzy sets (q-ROFs) for MAGDM. They defined for aggregation operators for q-ROFs: q-rung orthopair fuzzy BM (q-ROFBM), q-rung orthopair fuzzy weighted BM, q-rung orthopair fuzzy geometric BM (q-ROFGBM), and q-rung orthopair fuzzy weighted geometric BM (q-ROFWGBM) operators.

5 Conclusion

In this paper, we investigated how Bonferroni mean (BM) operator models criteria interdependence in fuzzy multi-criteria decision making problems. We studied definitions of different types of fuzzy sets proposed in 1960s–2010s; we then introduced definitions of aggregation functions and the Bonferroni mean operator; at last we surveyed the work of modeling criteria interdependence by using BM and its different types of extensions.

Acknowledgment. This work is partially supported by the National Natural Science Foundation of China (Grants No 61702274) and the Natural Science Foundation of Jiangsu Province (Grants No BK20170958).

References

1. Atanassov, K., Gargov, G.: Interval valued intuitionistic fuzzy sets. Fuzzy Sets Syst. **31**(3), 343–349 (1989)
2. Atanassov, K.T.: Intuitionistic fuzzy sets. Fuzzy Sets Syst. **20**(1), 87–96 (1986). https://doi.org/10.1016/S0165-0114(86)80034-3
3. Beliakov, G., James, S.: On extending generalized Bonferroni means to Atanassov orthopairs in decision making contexts. Fuzzy Sets Syst. **211**, 84–98 (2013)
4. Beliakov, G., James, S., Mordelová, J., Rückschlossová, T., Yager, R.R.: Generalized Bonferroni mean operators in multi-criteria aggregation. Fuzzy Sets Syst. **161**(17), 2227–2242 (2010)
5. Blanco-Mesa, F., Merigó, J.M., Kacprzyk, J.: Bonferroni means with distance measures and the adequacy coefficient in entrepreneurial group theory. Knowl. Based Syst. **111**, 217–227 (2016)

6. Bonferroni, C.: Sulle medie multiple di potenze. Boll. Unione Mat. Ital. **5**(3–4), 267–270 (1950)
7. Chen, Z.S., Chin, K.S., Li, Y.L., Yang, Y.: On generalized extended Bonferroni means for decision making. IEEE Trans. Fuzzy Syst. **24**(6), 1525–1543 (2016)
8. Dutta, B., Guha, D., Mesiar, R.: A model based on linguistic 2-tuples for dealing with heterogeneous relationship among attributes in multi-expert decision making. IEEE Trans. Fuzzy Syst. **23**(5), 1817–1831 (2015). https://doi.org/10.1109/TFUZZ.2014.2379291
9. He, Y., He, Z., Chen, H.: Intuitionistic fuzzy interaction bonferroni means and its application to multiple attribute decision making. IEEE Trans. Cybern. **45**(1), 116–128 (2015). https://doi.org/10.1109/TCYB.2014.2320910
10. He, Y., He, Z., Wang, G., Chen, H.: Hesitant fuzzy power Bonferroni means and their application to multiple attribute decision making. IEEE Trans. Fuzzy Syst. **23**(5), 1655–1668 (2015). https://doi.org/10.1109/TFUZZ.2014.2372074
11. Zadeh, L.A.: The concept of a linguistic variable and its application to approximate reasoning-I. Inf. Sci. **8**(3), 199–249 (1975). https://doi.org/10.1016/0020-0255(75)90036-5
12. Liu, P., Chen, S.M.: Group decision making based on heronian aggregation operators of intuitionistic fuzzy numbers. IEEE Trans. Cybern. **47**(9), 2514–2530 (2017). https://doi.org/10.1109/TCYB.2016.2634599
13. Liu, P.: Multiple attribute group decision making method based on interval-valued intuitionistic fuzzy power Heronian aggregation operators. Comput. Ind. Eng. **108**, 199–212 (2017)
14. Liu, P., Chen, S.M., Liu, J.: Multiple attribute group decision making based on intuitionistic fuzzy interaction partitioned Bonferroni mean operators. Inf. Sci. **411**, 98–121 (2017)
15. Liu, P., Li, H.: Interval-valued intuitionistic fuzzy power Bonferroni aggregation operators and their application to group decision making. Cogn. Comput. **9**(4), 494–512 (2017)
16. Liu, P., Liu, J.: Some q-Rung Orthopai fuzzy Bonferroni mean operators and their application to multi-attribute group decision making. Int. J. Intell. Syst. **33**(2), 315–347 (2018)
17. Mendel, J.M., John, R.I.B.: Type-2 fuzzy sets made simple. IEEE Trans. Fuzzy Syst. **10**(2), 117–127 (2002). https://doi.org/10.1109/91.995115
18. Meng, F., Chen, X.: Correlation coefficients of hesitant fuzzy sets and their application based on fuzzy measures. Cognit. Comput. **7**(4), 445–463 (2015). https://doi.org/10.1007/s12559-014-9313-9
19. Yager, R.R.: Pythagorean fuzzy subsets. In: 2013 Joint IFSA World Congress and NAFIPS Annual Meeting (IFSA/NAFIPS), pp. 57–61, June 2013. https://doi.org/10.1109/IFSA-NAFIPS.2013.6608375
20. Torra, V.: Hesitant fuzzy sets. Int. J. Intell. Syst. **25**(6), 529–539 (2010)
21. Xia, M., Xu, Z., Zhu, B.: Geometric Bonferroni means with their application in multi-criteria decision making. Knowl. Based Syst. **40**, 88–100 (2013)
22. Xu, Z., Chen, Q.: A multi-criteria decision making procedure based on interval-valued intuitionistic fuzzy Bonferroni means. J. Syst. Sci. Syst. Eng. **20**(2), 217–228 (2011)
23. Xu, Z., Yager, R.R.: Intuitionistic fuzzy Bonferroni means. IEEE Trans. Syst. Man Cybern. Part B (Cybern.) **41**(2), 568–578 (2011)
24. Yager, R.R.: On the theory of bags. Int. J. Gen. Syst. **13**(1), 23–37 (1986)
25. Yager, R.R.: On generalized Bonferroni mean operators for multi-criteria aggregation. Int. J. Approx. Reason. **50**(8), 1279–1286 (2009)

26. Yu, D., Wu, Y.: Interval-valued intuitionistic fuzzy Heronian mean operators and their application in multi-criteria decision making. Afr. J. Bus. Manag. **6**(11), 4158 (2012)
27. Zadeh, L.: Fuzzy sets. Inf. Control **8**(3), 338–353 (1965). https://doi.org/10.1016/S0019-9958(65)90241-X
28. Zhang, S., Xu, Z., He, Y.: Operations and integrations of probabilistic hesitant fuzzy information in decision making. Inf. Fusion **38**, 1–11 (2017)
29. Zhang, Z., Pedrycz, W.: Intuitionistic multiplicative group analytic hierarchy process and its use in multicriteria group decision-making. IEEE Trans. Cybern. **48**, 1950–1962 (2017)
30. Zhu, B., Xu, Z., Xia, M.: Hesitant fuzzy geometric Bonferroni means. Inf. Sci. **205**, 72–85 (2012). https://doi.org/10.1016/j.ins.2012.01.048
31. Zhu, B., Xu, Z.: Hesitant fuzzy Bonferroni means for multi-criteria decision making. J. Oper. Res. Soc. **64**(12), 1831–1840 (2013)

DBHUB: A Lightweight Middleware for Accessing Heterogeneous Database Systems

Dingding Li[1(✉)], Wande Chen[1], Mingming Pan[1], He Li[2], Hai Liu[1], and Yong Tang[1]

[1] School of Computer Science, South China Normal University, GuangZhou 510631, Guangdong, China
dingdingli@m.scnu.edu.cn
[2] Department of Information and Electronic Engineering, Muroran Institute of Technology, Muroran 050-8585, Japan
heli@mmm.muroran-it.ac.jp

Abstract. Traditional relational database management system (RDBMS) has the capability of full transaction processing but introduces the unnecessary overhead for dealing with the unstructured data in several big data scenarios. In contrast, the NoSQL systems can query the unstructured data with higher space-time efficiency, but most of them are lacking the function of transaction processing. To bridge the gap, we propose DBHUB, a lightweight middleware to combine the advantages of both sides. DBHUB provides the compatible APIs to upper applications and detects the received queries to extract the unstructured data automatically. In general, DBHUB handles the write query with RDBMS's storage engine and serves the read query by NoSQL's routine. We implement DBHUB in a practical system which including InnoDB in MySQL and MongoDB. The experimental results show that DBHUB can effectively accelerate the read query on unstructured data against the single RDBMS one. Meanwhile, the write query incurs mild overhead due to the write amplifications on heterogeneous databases.

Keywords: Big data · Database · RDBMS · NoSQL

1 Introduction

Unstructured data, such as documents, audio and video files, is pervasive in the modern applications [7]. To persist them reliably, at one time the back-end of these applications usually uses the traditional database system, namely RDBMS, to play the role of backing storage [9]. However, since the typical RDBMS is general-purpose and complicated, deploying it to operate the various unstructured data is usually squandering the underlying hardware resource as well as the maintenance cost [4]. To relieve such issue, recently there are many

© Springer Nature Switzerland AG 2018
X. Sun et al. (Eds.): ICCCS 2018, LNCS 11063, pp. 408–419, 2018.
https://doi.org/10.1007/978-3-030-00006-6_37

NoSQL systems, which are often treated as the subset of a typical RDBMS, to be tailor-made for operating the specific unstructured data while running separately. Therefore, NoSQL system is much lightweight and simple than an original RDBMS, and shows higher performance, better scalability and lower maintenance cost [3]. However, NoSQL system often disables the capability of transaction processing to obtain its simplicity [2]. Considering the requirement of transaction processing is still indispensable among many scenarios, such as financial transaction and multi-player on-line game, NoSQL systems are frustrated on their usages [6]. Besides, accessing NoSQL system requires the applications to modify their codes, because this kind of new database system exports the completely different interface upward with traditional RDBMS [8].

To strike the balance between the two poles, we propose DBHUB, a lightweight middleware to combine the advantages of RDBMS and NoSQL databases. Rather than designing a new database system, DBHUB is built around the original RDBMS and NoSQL systems. Therefore there is no intrusive modifications on these complicated systems. On the other hand, due to reservation on the traditional database interface, such as JDBC (Java DataBase Connectivity) or ODBC (Open DataBase Connectivity), the applications upon DBHUB are also no need to modify their codes. These guarantee DBHUB a drop-in solution, which is highly desirable in practice.

A main challenge of DBHUB is performance, since each user query from the upper application is involved in the coordination of DBHUB. To relieve such issue, DBHUB uses a pass-through transaction framework to deal with the user transaction commitment but still enforces the strong-consistency method to synchronize the heterogeneous databases. After several specific improvements applied in DBHUB, the performance loss due to the strong-consistency in transaction commitment is mild, only incurring up to 7% overhead versus the single RDBMS instance.

In summary, we have made the following contributions in this paper:

1. A middleware-based method called DBHUB is designed to combine the advantages of RDBMS and NoSQL systems;
2. We implement DBHUB in a practical system and apply several techniques to improve its performance;
3. Finally, extensive experiments are conducted to justify DBHUB advantages and its associated cost.

The rest of this paper is organized as follows. In Sect. 2 we show the design of DBHUB and propose its implementation in Sect. 3. In Sect. 4 we introduce the experiment configuration and result. The related work is discussed in Sect. 5. Finally, we conclude the paper and talk about the future work in Sect. 6.

2   Design

In this section we first describe the goals of DBHUB and then show the overview of its architecture. Finally, we discuss the techniques DBHUB used specifically.

2.1 Goals

According to the motivation of this paper, we should obtain the following goals
on DBHUB design:

- *High-performance*: DBHUB should operate the unstructured data as high-efficient, both in temporal and spatial;
- *Transaction-compatible*:DBHUB must support the capability of transaction processing to overcome the deficiency of NoSQL systems, meanwhile, the ACID features are also required to be maintained;
- *Simplicity*: DBHUB should keep its design simply, since a over-sized code base violates the original intention of NoSQL systems.

2.2 Overview

Figure 1 shows the architecture of DBHUB. It leverages the original database
systems to achieve both goals of *High-performance* and *Transaction-compatible*,
namely, a modern NoSQL system is deployed to serve the read queries while
another typical RDBMS is responsible for receiving the write queries, which are
the committed user transactions.

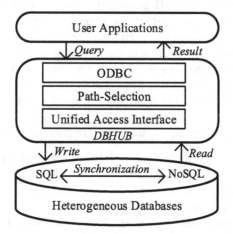

Fig. 1. Three layers constitute the architecture of DBHUB: (1) user applications; (2)
DBHUB middleware and (3) the heterogeneous databases. Since read queries only
target on the NoSQL system for higher efficiency, a synchronization process is required
to be deployed between the systems of SQL and NoSQL to eliminate the inconsistency
issue.

To NoSQL systems, they provide the specific improvements on operating
the unstructured data. Taking MongoDB as an example, a *direct mapping* technique is used in its storage engine, which maps the unstructured data directly
to the underlying file system, to bypass the intervention of operating system

(OS) kernel, forms a in-memory read cache for the incoming user queries and hence excludes the following disk accesses. In addition, MongoDB employs the fine-grained allocation strategy to fit the various unstructured data in memory, especially for the document type. Not like the traditional table-level memory management on typical RDBMSs, MongoDB designs the row-level memory subsystem to obtain the more lightweight and higher efficient operations on the unstructured data. Due to the irregular access characteristic of unstructured data, this can greatly relieve the costs of CPU and memory for running the NoSQL system.

For achieving the goal *Transaction-compatible*, a typical RDBMS, such as InnoDB in MySQL or PostgreSQL, is enough to be qualified. However, due to the different storage engines of the two databases, user committed transactions are only stored in the RDBMS and the NoSQL system cannot perceive the modifications directly. As a result, any read queries arriving in NoSQL engine lead to a stale item returning or nothing. To solve this inconsistency issue, DBHUB proposes an explicit synchronization process to enforce the data strong-consistency between the underlying heterogeneous database systems.

Specifically, a detail procedure of the write user query or a user transaction in DBHUB is described as follows by referring Fig. 1:

1. An user application invokes ODBC to commit a transaction, denoted by Q_W, to the backing database;
2. DBHUB receives Q_W and then analyzes its contents, in which the involved fields (denoted by $\{F_W\}$) of the underlying RDBMS will be detected;
3. If a set of $\{F_W\}$, denoted by $\{f_w\}$, are the fields to store the unstructured data, then *Path-Selection* in DBHUB forks a new query, denoted by q_w which only includes the $\{f_w\}$ data, to be delivered to the NoSQL system. Meanwhile, $\{Q_W\}$ is still sent to RDBMS;
4. After both $\{Q_W\}$ and $\{q_w\}$ completed successfully, *Path-Selection* returns the acknowledgment to user application;
5. In step 4, any delays or losses on the return of $\{Q_W\}$ or $\{q_w\}$ result in that *Path-Selection* cannot receive the acknowledgment of $\{Q_W\}$ or $\{q_w\}$ in time. In this case, DBHUB waits T seconds and retries to send $\{Q_W\}$ or $\{q_w\}$ if the corresponding acknowledgment didn't return during T.

On the other hand, the procedure of a read user query in DBHUB is described as follows:

1. An user application invokes ODBC to send the user query, denoted by Q_R, to the backing database;
2. DBHUB receives Q_R and then analyzes its contents, in which the involved fields (denoted by F_R) of the underlying RDBMS will be detected;
3. If a set of $\{F_R\}$, denoted by $\{f_r\}$, are the fields of the unstructured data, then *Path-Selection* in DBHUB forks a new query, denoted by q_r which only targets on $\{f_r\}$, to be delivered to the NoSQL system. Meanwhile, the remaining query, namely $\{Q_R - q_r\}$ (denoted by Z_r), is still sent to RDBMS;

4. After both $\{Z_r\}$ and $\{q_r\}$ completed successfully, *Path-Selection* returns the unified read result to the user application;

5. In step 4, any delays or losses on the return of $\{Z_r\}$ or $\{q_r\}$ result in that *Path-Selection* cannot receive the read results in time. In this case, DBHUB waits t seconds and retries to send $\{Z_r\}$ or $\{q_r\}$ if the corresponding read query didn't return during t.

In summary, with this arrangement the underlying heterogeneous databases have the redundancy on the unstructured data, one is on the RDBMS, the other is on the NoSQL system. However, two performance issues arise due to: (1) DBHUB intercepting the user query and then extracting the unstructured data; (2) DBHUB forking the user query either to cause the data inconsistency or to get the full query data, which inevitably enforces costs on the transaction commitment and read query respectively.

2.3   Techniques of DBHUB

Field-Binding. To achieve the goal of *High-performance*, a technique called *field-binding* is used to improve the procedure of user query extraction, in which a process is launched to detect the unstructured data from user query.

According to the user scenario, DBAs (Database Administrators) define several specific fields in the backing RDBMS to store the user data. Therefore, DBHUB leverages the built-in semantics of these fields to recognize the unstructured data which contained in the user transactions. Namely, DBHUB directly extracts the unstructured fields according to the predefined data tables in RDBMS. For example, a table denoted by P in a RDBMS contains N fields, in which M fields are the unstructured type ($M \leq N$). After a user transaction Q_W is issued, DBHUB middleware intercepts Q_W and then uses the predefined rule to extract M directly, rather than a process to check Q_W which consumes the CPU resources.

Lightweight Transactions. As Fig. 2 showing, in order to maintain transaction consistency, DBHUB first makes data generated or changed by RDBMS and then passes this increment to NoSQL database simultaneously. The process of verification is also required to ensure these data arriving on NoSQL system. The specific process is described as follows:

1. At the beginning of system running, DBHUB builds the connection pool for users;

2. When receiving the transaction t submitted by user, RDBMS uses the connection pool to get the related data, marked as $Data_{trans}$, and then connects the NoSQL connection pool, then $Data_{trans}$ will be redundantly written to the NoSQL system;

3. If step 2 is completed successfully, then an acknowledgment is returned to the upper application; If t fails to submit, RDBMS leverages its own storage engine to roll back t immediately.

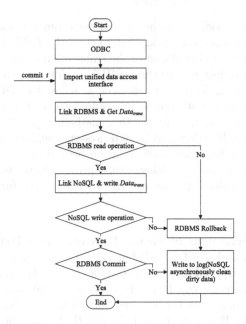

Fig. 2. Transaction framework in DBHUB.

2.4 Discussion

How to Deal with Query Cache Invalidation on DBHUB? When the
internal data of DBHUB is updating or the user query does not hit in the memory
of NoSQL system, the corresponding part of the query cache will be invalidated.
This divides into two cases: (1) cache invalidation on RDBMS and (2) NoSQL
system. To deal with the former case, DBHUB allows the user query to find its
target data into the underlying storage engine. To the latter one, it indicates
that the update have been stored in the RDBMS but they are still not reflected
in the NoSQL part. In such case, DBHUB redirects the related user query from
the NoSQL system to the RDBMS.

**How to Improve the Performance of Transaction Commitment on
DBHUB?** As Sect. 2.3 described, the transaction commitment of DBHUB is
not only required to be submitted to RDBMS, but also a portion of them is
needed to synchronized to the NoSQL system, resulting in a certain of performance penalty. To deal with this issue, DBHUB uses the following improvements
to accelerate the process of double writes.

First, after user transaction, denoted by Q_W, is committed to RDBMS, then
DBHUB copies the unstructured portion q_w only into the memory of NoSQL system, rather than waits for q_w being stored in the disk. In such a way, DBHUB can
eliminate one disk I/O interaction in the procedure of transaction commitment.
Although the NoSQL system has not yet persisted the q_w when an unexpected

event occurred, it is inviolate to the system consistency because the restarted NoSQL system can restore the updated data from the RDBMS.

Second, a large proportion of cost of the transaction commitment in DBHUB is the communication delays from the DBHUB middleware to the RDBMS and NoSQL system. One optional improvement is using RDMA (Remote Direct Memory Access) to pass data but it is required to modify the codes of both RDBMS and NoSQL system. The another method is put three units, namely DBHUB middleware, RDBMS and NoSQL system, into one physical machine, and then enforces the hardware-level isolation between them by virtualization. As a result, the communication delays are improved. Extra techniques, such as the inter-domain transferring system, can be exploited to further improve the performance.

What Is the Mechanism of Crash Recovery in DBHUB? When the underlying physical nodes of DBHUB fail to run or suffer a crash, a mechanism of crash recovery is required for the failed nodes. DBHUB can capture all transaction requests, which are sent to the heterogeneous databases, and then store them in a specific format as the log file (including all operations of RDBMS and NoSQL system). If a transaction fails, DBHUB scans the log file reversely, undoes operations which are finished in the failed transaction. If system incurs a *failure-stop* event, such as power out-stage, DBHUB can scan the log file forward, to find the transactions which are committed before the failure point, then marks it as a redo queue. To the transactions that have not been completed, DBHUB marks it as a undo queue. If reasons which lead the data loss are hardware-level, DBHUB should load the most recent replicas from the backups or checkpoints, in order to restore the data as much as possible. As far as we know, most of organizations and enterprises have been deployed the duplexed backup sets to provide the data reliability.

3   Implementation

Scholat.com[1] is an academic social network platform, in which the storage data is divided into the structured and unstructured data. Of them, the structure data is often lightweight, which is accounted for the small storage space and consumes mild costs on CPU and disk. Specifically, the unstructured data in Scholat.com refers to those data which are not very convenient to be presented or stored by the two-dimensional logic of RDBMS, and it is characterized by the large consumptions on both CPU and storage. The volume of unstructured data on Scholat.com accounts for more than 80%.

Currently, Scholat.com uses the InnoDB storage engine of MySQL server to manage and store these data indiscriminately, but it is always too slow to process the intensive message text as well as the user upload files, according to the recent user feed-back report. Moreover, the number of Scholat.com user

---

[1] http://www.scholat.com/.

is higher than we expected, which makes the requirement imperative on system scalability, hence, we decide to deploy MongoDB[2] to improve this problem. But MongoDB only reaches the weak consistency in the transaction processing. Therefore, Scholat.com prefers to a solution of the heterogeneous database systems, maintaining the capability of transaction process on MySQL server while improving the access of unstructured data with MongoDB.

Here takes the related table on the on-line course of Scholat.com as an example to illustrate the implementation of DBHUB. A table in the original InnoDB called *course*, which stores the basic information of a course created by a certain user, such as the course introduction and outline. Another table, called *course-notice*, stores the specific information of the associated announcements. Besides, a table called *course-resource*, stores the path of the related resource files, such as slides. The method to separate their unstructured data is described as follows: (1) we create the replicas of the unstructured data in MongoDB, including course introductions, syllabuses, announcements, pictures from the relevant tables; (2) we merge the table to remove the redundant fields, and then generate a new table called *course_sum* which is reserved in MySQL and available for users to query the structured data correctly.

In order to guarantee the consistency of transaction commitment in DBHUB, we write three tables' key fields to MongoDB redundantly through our middleware. In addition, for the informational unstructured data such as course introduction and outline, we store them directly into MongoDB by using the BSON format. GridFS format is also used to store file data such as images and course resource file, while the *files* field of GridFS stores the meta-data information, and its specific content is stored in the *chunks* field. If the size of the stored file is too large, DBHUB splits it into many blocks, and preserves the offset of file block in the original file to the *file* field. When the amount of data are stored in these chunks, MongoDB uses the auto-fragmentation mechanism to reduce server pressure.

4 Evaluation

4.1 Experimental Setup

The experiment is divided into three parts. The first one is the performance comparison of transaction commitment between the original MySQL server and DBHUB, with the data size increasing. The second one is the read performance comparison of the unstructured data between the original MySQL server, MongoDB and DBHUB. During the test procedure, the size of each read is also varied. The third experiment is the performance comparison of the mixture workload, in which the queries of read and write account for about 50% respectively. Experimental results are shown in Figs. 3, 4 and 5 respectively. The experimental configurations are: Windows 10 Pro, 6G DDR3 memory, Intel i5 processor, a SSD 256 GB and a hard disk 500 GB. The versions of MongoDB and MySQL are 3.2.9 and 5.7.12 respectively.

---

[2] https://www.mongodb.com/cn.

4.2   Results

Figure 3 shows the performance comparison of transaction commitment between MySQL and DBHUB. It can be seen that the MySQL write operation grows linearly as the amount of data grows, but the performance growth trend slows as close to ten millions of all data volumes. The time overhead of DBHUB is slightly larger than MySQL, but their curves are almost same, because the DBHUB middleware consumes a little extra CPU cycles. Although there is a performance loss, but it is restrained in a reasonable range.

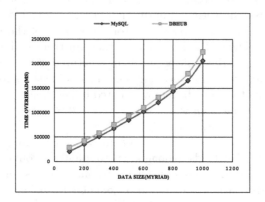

Fig. 3. Performance of transaction commitment.

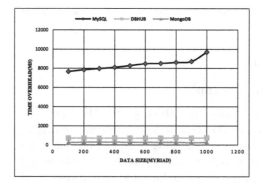

Fig. 4. Performance of read query.

Figure 4 shows the read performance. Although the time overhead of DBHUB is slightly larger than the single MongoDB, both of them are close to each other. On the other side, due to the interception of middleware, there is a slight loss of performance on DBHUB. However, both DBHUB and MongoDB are better than

MySQL. Furthermore it can be also found that the read performance of MySQL did not show scalability with the amount of data approaching to ten million levels. Besides, its performance loss is larger, which manifests the deficiency of MySQL when dealing with the massive unstructured data.

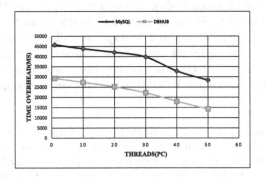

Fig. 5. Performance of read-write mixture workload.

As Fig. 5 showing, with the number of client thread increased, both of DBHUB and MySQL have the decreasing trend on the time overhead. Compared with the previous solution on Scholat.com, both performances of read and write on DBHUB have been improved significantly. It indicates that DBHUB has the better performance scalability when it is required to handle the intensive user requests.

5   Related Work

Aguilera et al. propose Yesquel [1], a system that provides performance and scalability comparable to NoSQL with all the features of a typical RDBMS. Yesquel is a scalable SQL storage for Web applications, not like a typical database for the general purpose. Compared with DBHUB, Yesquel is a brand new database software. Although it is open-sourced, its reliability has not been verified with the realistic scenarios.

Unity [5] is an integrated and virtualized system, allowing SQL queries to across multiple database sources and uses its internal query engines to connect the different database sources. Compared with Unity, DBHUB mainly targets on the lightweight transaction commitment framework. Theoretically, Unity can achieve better transaction performance, but without the support to access the underlying heterogeneous databases transparently.

A hybrid cloud storage systems called e-government [10], use cloud technology to combine the features of MySQL and MongoDB. Compared it with DBHUB, this kind of system is more suitable for the field of e-government, and its functionality is slightly limited.

6 Conclusion

We propose DBHUB, a lightweight middleware to combine both systems of RDBMS and NoSQL. Rather than a new database design from the scratch, DBHUB leverages the existed RDBMS and NoSQL system to achieve both goals of transaction-compliance and high-performance for operating the unstructured data. Thus, in DBHUB there are no intrusive modifications to the original system. We implement DBHUB in a practical system called Scholat.com and conduct the experiments to verify its correctness, simplicity and high-performance. The results show that DBHUB can operate the unstructured data as higher efficiency versus the traditional RDBMS while support the transaction commitment.

Acknowledgements. This work was funded by the National Natural Science Foundation of China under grant number 61502180 and 61772211, by the Natural Science Foundation of Guangdong Province, China under grant number 2017A030303074 and 2016A030313441, by the Pearl River S&T Nova Program of Guangzhou under grant number 201710010189. We would like to thank Mr.Yijie Zhong for his wonderful work to improve this paper.

References

1. Aguilera, M.K., Leners, J.B., Walfish, M.: Yesquel: scalable SQL storage for web applications. In: Proceedings of the 25th Symposium on Operating Systems Principles (SOSP 2015), pp. 245–262. ACM, New York (2015)
2. Dashti, M., Basil John, S., Shaikhha, A., Koch, C.: Transaction repair for multi-version concurrency control. In: Proceedings of the 2017 ACM International Conference on Management of Data (SIGMOD 2017), pp. 235–250. ACM, New York (2017)
3. Dayan, N., Athanassoulis, M., Idreos, S.: Monkey: optimal navigable key-value store. In: Proceedings of the 2017 ACM International Conference on Management of Data (SIGMOD 2017), pp. 79–94. ACM, New York (2017)
4. Gessert, F., Schaarschmidt, M., Wingerath, W., Witt, E., Yoneki, E., Ritter, N.: Quaestor: query web caching for database-as-a-service providers. Proc. VLDB Endow. **10**(12), 1670–1681 (2017)
5. Lawrence, R.: Integration and virtualization of relational SQL and NoSQL systems including MySQL and MongoDB. In: 2014 International Conference on Computational Science and Computational Intelligence, vol. 1, pp. 285–290, March 2014
6. Lim, H., Kaminsky, M., Andersen, D.G.: Cicada: dependably fast multi-core in-memory transactions. In: Proceedings of the 2017 ACM International Conference on Management of Data (SIGMOD 2017), pp. 21–35. ACM, New York (2017)
7. Ramakrishnan, R., et al.: Azure data lake store: a hyperscale distributed file service for big data analytics. In: Proceedings of the 2017 ACM International Conference on Management of Data (SIGMOD 2017), pp. 51–63. ACM, New York (2017)
8. Sun, K., Fryer, D., Chu, J., Lakier, M., Brown, A.D., Goel, A.: Spiffy: enabling file-system aware storage applications. In: 16th USENIX Conference on File and Storage Technologies (FAST 2018), pp. 91–104. USENIX Association, Oakland (2018)

9. Tang, Y., Chen, L., Liu, J., Li, D.: Speeding up virtualized transaction logging with vTrans. In: 2016 IEEE 22nd International Conference on Parallel and Distributed Systems (ICPADS 2016), pp. 916–923, December 2016
10. Wu, C.: A NoSQL-SQL hybrid organization and management approach for real-time geospatial data: a case study of public security video surveillance. ISPRS Int. J. Geo-Inf. **6**(1), 21 (2017)

Design a New Dual Polarized Antenna Using Metallic Loop and Annular-Ring Slot

Qingyuan Fang$^{(\boxtimes)}$, Zhiwei Gao, and Shugang Jiang

School of Information Science and Technology, Shijiazhuang Tiedao University,
Shijiazhuang, China
617140612@qq.com, gao_zhiwei@163.com, 499283062@qq.com

Abstract. The dual polarized antenna is the key component of the fully polarized electronic system, which can sense the polarization information of the electromagnetic wave. This paper presents a low cost dual polarized antenna composed of a metallic loop antenna and an annular-ring slot antenna. The metallic loop antenna is a current radiator and the annular-ring slot antenna can be regarded as a magnetic current radiator. A dual linearly polarized antenna is realized by using complementary loop antenna. Compact antenna structure together with simple coaxial probes feeding substantially decrease the antenna cost. Simulated results indicate that the proposed antenna has an impedance band width of 4.61%, higher antenna gain than 6 dB and broad beam width.

Keywords: Dual polarized antenna · Loop antenna · Annual-ring antenna

1 Introduction

The dual-polarized antenna devices capable of sensing electromagnetic polarization information have better performance than traditional single polarized electronic devices. Dual polarized antenna is the key components in communication system, and its function is to realize the full polarization signal processing algorithm through radiation or receiving two orthogonal polarization components of electromagnetic wave. Thus it is widely applied in radar system for target detection, localization and recognition according to the polarization information of targets. Dozens even hundreds of dual polarized antenna elements are required in large phased array antenna in radar system, thus the cost as well as the structure complexity of each antenna element should be strictly controlled. The design and implementation of dual-polarized antenna has become a hotspot in the field of antenna technology [1, 2]. However, simple antenna configuration and compact feeding network together with low cost generally can not be fulfilled at the same time [3, 4]. Hence dual polarized antenna with simple structure and low cost is more competitive than other candidates in large phased array antenna.

Dipole antenna is one of the most common linearly polarized antennas in realizing one of the polarization in dual polarized antenna. Compared with wire dipole antenna, dipole antenna with square loops has a much wider impedance bandwidth [4]. Large loop antenna has reasonable radiation resistance compared with small loop antenna [5]. Loop antennas working as magnetic dipole, which can achieve horizontal polarization and unidirectional radiation, are widely used in base station [6]. By adding interlaced

© Springer Nature Switzerland AG 2018
X. Sun et al. (Eds.): ICCCS 2018, LNCS 11063, pp. 420–426, 2018.
https://doi.org/10.1007/978-3-030-00006-6_38

coupling lines, the current along the loop remains in phase and uniform at each section and then yields unidirectional radiation pattern. Current along the loop without inter-laced coupling lines become non-uniform with the phase shift and has same direction at both the top and bottom edges generating a maximum radiation in the broadside. For phased array antenna in radar system, each antenna element is usually required to radiate in the broadside of antenna plane. Accordingly, a large metallic loop antenna that provides in phase currents at both side of the metallic loop can satisfy the requirements of phased array antenna. Therefore metallic loop antenna employing dipole or monopole configurations can be good choices in realizing one polarization of the dual polarized antenna element [7].

Since metallic loop antenna is a good choice for application of one polarization in dual polarized antenna, annular-ring slot antenna taken as the complementation of metallic loop antenna can also be employed to achieve another polarization. Besides, annular-ring slot is widely used in linear polarized antenna [8], circular polarized antenna [9] and even polarization reconfigurable antenna [10]. Different polarization can be generated by controlling the feeding network of annular-ring slot antenna.

In this paper a dual polarized antenna based on a metallic loop and an annual-ring slot is presented. The metallic loop antenna is fed by a coaxial probe and the annual-ring slot is excited by a microstrip line. Complementary radiators generating similar antenna radiation pattern are preferred to hybrid radiators with different antenna con-figurations in dual polarized antenna. Unidirectional radiation patterns are obtained through utilizing metallic reflector located below the antenna. Due to the simple metallic loop and annual-ring slot structure as well as the succinct feeding network, the manufacturing complexity and antenna cost is decreased so that this dual polarized antenna could be a better choice to other antennas in realizing large phase array antenna.

2   Antenna Design

2.1   Architecture

As shown in Fig. 1 the proposed antenna configuration are totally three layers in the presented antenna, in which an annular-ring slot is etched on the top layer, a metallic loop is printed on the middle layer and a metallic reflector used for obtaining unidi-rectional radiation pattern is used as the bottom layer. Substrates used in the top and middle layers are Rogers RT5880 with dielectric constant 2.2 and thickness 1.00 mm. Four shorting pins around the corners of substrate are used to connect the ground plane on the top layer with the metallic reflector as well as to support and fix the three layers of antenna. The annular-ring slot on the top layer is fed by a microstrip line and the metallic loop on the middle layer is excited by a coaxial probe. The annular-ring slot can be taken as a magnetic current radiator and the metallic loop can be regarded as a current radiator. Both of the radiators are linearly polarized antennas and have orthogonal polarizations via exciting from orthogonal ports. So a dual polarized antenna is created through two linearly polarized annular-ring slot antenna together with the metallic loop antenna.

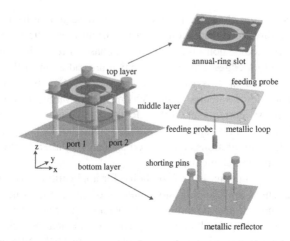

Fig. 1. The antenna configuration with detached antenna structure

The detailed antenna structure and dimension is illustrated in Fig. 2. As shown in Fig. 2(a) the distance between the annual-ring slot and metallic loop is h1 6 mm, and that between the metallic loop and metallic reflector is h2 8.00 mm. The square substrates used in the top and middle layer have same length l 28.00 mm while the metallic reflector has length l_r 45.00 mm.

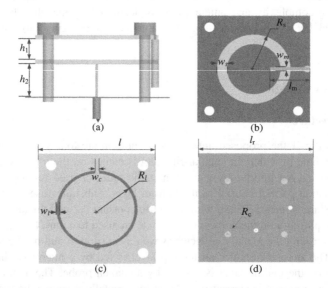

Fig. 2. The antenna detailed structure and parameters. (a) side view (b) the top layer (c) the middle layer (d) the bottom layer

Both of the linearly polarized antennas are excited through coaxial probes. The difference is that the metallic loop is directly connected to the coaxial probe while the annual-ring slot is excited via a microstrip line which is connected to the coaxial probe. As shown in Fig. 2(c), the metallic loop with radius R_1 9.00 mm and width w_1 0.70 mm is an open loop (gap width w_c 1.00 mm) to expand the antenna impedance bandwidth. The metallic loop works as a monopole antenna and gets an unidirectional radiation pattern through employing the metallic reflector located under the antenna plane. The other polarization of the dual polarized antenna is realized by adopting an annual-ring slot antenna which can be taken as the complementation of metallic loop antenna. The annual-ring slot with radius Rs 6.60 mm and width w_s 2.50 mm is fed through a microstrip line with length l_m 10.00 mm and width w_m 1 mm. The ground plane on the top layer is shorted to the bottom reflector via four shorting pins with radius R_c 1.25 mm. Likewise, the annual-ring slot antenna also obtained an unidirectional radiation pattern through the metallic reflector.

2.2   Parameters Discussion

Critical parameters of proposed antenna are studied using electromagnetic simulation software CST Microwave Studio in this section. In this dual polarized antenna four shorting pins are exploited to improve the impedance matching and bandwidth of the annual-ring slot antenna. Three cases about the shorting pins are exhibited in Fig. 3 that are with shorting pins in Fig. 3(a), without shorting pins in Fig. 3(b) and pins using FR4 material (dielectric constant 2.2) in Fig. 3(c).

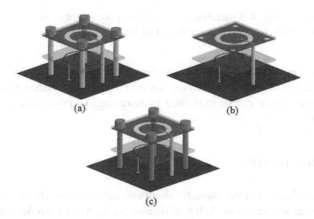

Fig. 3. Antenna models. (a) with shorting pins (b) without shorting pins (c) with pins made of FR4

The cutting off the metallic loop can also improve the impedance bandwidth of the antenna. The simulated refection coefficient and transmission coefficient of the proposed antenna is shown in Fig. 4 when the metallic loop antenna is and isn't cut off.

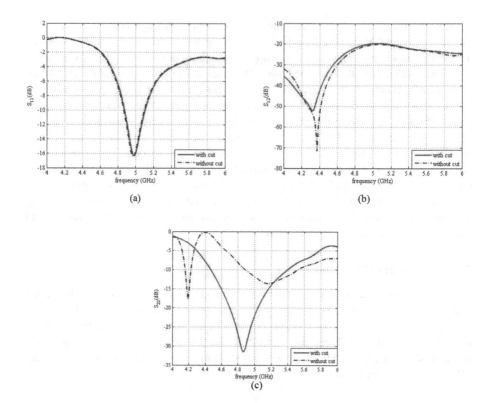

Fig. 4. Simulation results of S parameters. (a) reflection coefficient of port 1 (b) transmission coefficient between ports (c) reflection coefficient of port 2

Noticed in Fig. 4 that the cut in metallic loop will significantly improve the reflection coefficient of port 2 and almost has no effect on the reflection coefficient of port 1. This phenomenon can be explained by resorting to analyze electric currents on the metallic loop.

3   Simulation Results

In this section the dual polarized antenna is simulated and analyzed. The simulation results of S parameters are shown in Fig. 5. It is illustrated in Fig. 5 that the reflection coefficient of metallic loop (port 1) is below −10 dB from 4.87 GHz to 5.10 GHz. The metallic loop has an impedance bandwidth of 4.61%. However, the annual-ring slot antenna obviously has much broader bandwidth of 18.84% that is from 4.47 GHz to 5.40 GHz. The isolation between two ports is higher than 20 dB in the whole working frequency band and could be increased by amending the shorting pins or revising the slot shape.

The simulated antenna gain of metallic loop at 4.90 GHz, 5.00 GHz and 5.10 GHz is 6.16 dBi, 6.10 dBi and 6.09 dBi, respectively. The antenna gain of annual-ring slot at aforementioned frequencies is 7.01 dBi, 7.30 dBi and 7.52 dBi, respectively. The

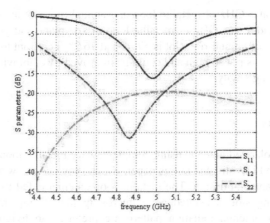

Fig. 5. Simulation results of proposed dual polarized antenna.

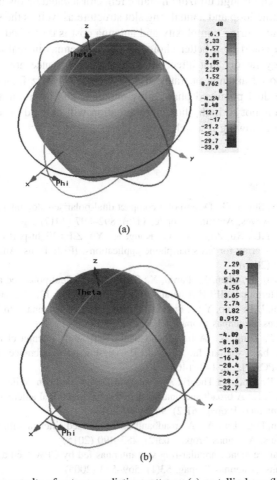

(a)

(b)

Fig. 6. Simulation results of antenna radiation patterns. (a) metallic loop (b) annual-ring slot

radiation patterns at 5 GHz of metallic loop and annual-ring slot are shown in Fig. 6. The 3 dB beam width at 5 GHz of metallic loop in xoz plane and yoz plane is 83.7° and 56.5°, and that of annual-ring slot is 57.5° and 76.2°. The front to back (F/B) ratio of proposed antenna is not so high and could be improved by employing other shape of reflector or reflecting cavity.

4   Conclusions

A low cost dual polarized antenna using complementary metallic loop and annual-ring slot is proposed and investigated in this paper, which provides a new technical way for dual polarization antenna design. The metallic loop antenna is fed by a coaxial probe and the annual-ring slot is excited by a microstrip line. Complementary radiators generating similar antenna radiation pattern are preferred to hybrid radiators with different antenna configurations in dual polarized antenna. Unidirectional radiation patterns are obtained through utilizing metallic reflector located below the antenna. Due to the simple metallic loop and annual-ring slot structure as well as the succinct feeding network, the manufacturing complexity and antenna cost is decreased so that this dual polarized antenna could be a better choice to other antennas in realizing large phase array antenna. Key factors that affect the antenna performance are studied and discussed. The proposed antenna operates in 4.87 GHz–5.10 GHz frequency range and can be applied in dual polarized phase array antenna. The isolation and F/B ratio of proposed antenna is not so high, thus more attention will be paid on improving these two factors in the following research work.

References

1. Hu, L., Ying, L., Shuxi, G.: Design of a compact dual-polarised slot antenna with enhanced gain. IET Microwaves, Antennas Propag. **11**(6), 892–897 (2017)
2. Li, M.Y., Ban, Y.L., Xu, Z.Q., Wu, G., Kang, K., Yu, Z.F.: Eight-port orthogonally dual-polarized antenna array for 5G smartphone applications. IEEE Trans. Antennas Propag. **64**(9), 3820–3830 (2016)
3. Falade, O.P., Gao, Y., Chen, X., Parini, X.: Stacked-patch dual-polarized antenna for triple-band handheld terminals. IEEE Antennas Wirel. Propag. Lett. **12**, 202–205 (2013)
4. Chu, Q.X., Wen, D.L., Luo, Y.: A broadband dual-polarized antenna with Y-shaped feeding lines. IEEE Trans. Antennas Propag. **63**(2), 271–350 (2015)
5. Bao, Z., Nie, Z., Zong, X.: A broadband dual-polarization antenna element for wireless communication base station. In: 2012 IEEE Asia-Pacific Conference on Antennas and Propagation (APCAP), pp. 144–146 (2012)
6. Constantine, A.B.: Antenna Theory: Analysis and Design, 3rd edn. Wiley, Hoboken (2005)
7. Quan, X.L., Li, R.L.: A broadband dual-polarized omnidirectional antenna for base stations. IEEE Trans. Antennas Propag. **61**(2), 943–947 (2013)
8. Chu, Q.X., Wen, D.L., Luo, Y.: A broadband dual-polarized antenna with Y-shaped feeding lines. IEEE Trans. Antennas Propag. **63**(2), 483–490 (2015)
9. Chen, J.S.: Dual-frequency annular-ring slot antennas fed by CPW feed and microstrip line feed. IEEE Trans. Antennas Propag. **53**(1), 569–573 (2005)
10. Wong, K.L., Huang, C.C., Chen, W.S.: Printed ring slot antenna for circular polarization. IEEE Trans. Antennas Propag. **50**(1), 75–77 (2002)

Design and Implementation of Web Crawler Based on Coroutine Model

Renshuang Ding$^{(\boxtimes)}$ and Meihua Wang

School of Information Science and Engineering,
Hebei University of Science and Technology,
Shijiazhuang 050024, People's Republic of China
abc618382@126.com

Abstract. Web crawler is widely used in Chinese information processing. According to the problem to be dealt with, crawling related domains data, it provides the basis for subsequent Chinese information processing. The traditional multi-threaded model has obvious limitations and deficiencies when dealing with high concurrency and large number of I/O blocking operations. To solve the above problems, this paper proposes a solution based on the coroutine model. In this paper, the basic principles and implementation methods of coroutine are discussed in detail, then give a complete implementation of web crawler based on coroutine. Experimental results had shown that our scheme can effectively reduce system load and improve web crawler crawling efficiency.

Keywords: Coroutine · Crawler · Multithread · Block

1 Introduction

In recent years, with the development of the Internet, especially the development of the mobile Internet and social networks, the Internet data has shown explosive growth. According to statistics, China's webpage size has generally doubled each year with 2003 as the benchmark. By 2010, the number of web pages in China's Internet has exceeded 60 billion. In accordance with this growth rate, the amount of data generated in the new year is close to or even more than the sum of all data in previous years. There is a lot of useful information resources hidden under these massive amounts of information. How to extract and use these information resources efficiently, accurately and quickly, and provide data bases for analysis and calculation in specific scientific research and engineering practice and other technical fields are getting more and more attention.

A web crawler [1], also known as a web spider, is a web application that can be programmed to automatically extract internet resources A web crawler begins with a list of unified resource addresses called seeds. When the web crawler accesses these unified resource locators, all hyperlinks on the page are identified and written to a "list to be accessed". Each URL on this list is traversed according to a set of algorithmic policies until some predetermined stopping criterion is met.

X. Sun et al. (Eds.): ICCCS 2018, LNCS 11063, pp. 427–435, 2018.
https://doi.org/10.1007/978-3-030-00006-6_39

2 Related Work

The web crawler has a long history, the related technology is relatively mature, the programming model has also experienced the continuous evolution along with the development of the technology. This section firstly introduces the requirements of compiling web crawlers according to the specific tasks of NLP [2] competition, and then analyzes and compares the commonly used web crawler programming models. Finally, the author gives the basis for choosing the coroutine web crawler programming model.

2.1 Presentation of Requirements

In the process of classifying a given lexical group, we use a combination of various algorithms to complete the final classification requirements, one of which is based on wordnet [3]. Because wordnet is mainly characterized by English vocabulary, we have decided to write a web crawler program to convert the Chinese vocabulary equivalence of data sets into English vocabulary sets. Therefore, writing web crawler application is the basis of the follow-up work.

2.2 Programming Model Based on Multi-process

With the development of the Internet, the application of the web crawler becomes more and more popular, which is influenced by the early web application based on the multi-process CGI computing model. The original web crawler also used a similar multi-process programming model. Based on the multi-process programming model, The advantage of this model is that programming is relatively easy, usually do not need to consider the problem of locking and synchronization competing access resources; at the same time, because the process has the isolation characteristic which the kernel guarantees, thus brings the relatively strong program fault-tolerant ability, the crash of one process will not affect the normal operation of the other process. But the multi-process programming model is based on inter-process call, and the shared memory, semaphore and other IPC technologies are used in the data sharing between the processes. The switching between processes and the mutual communication consume more resources, and the pressure on the system is also great.

2.3 Programming Model Based on Multithreading

With the development of computer hardware and software, the emergence of hyper-threaded multi-core CPU and the improvement of multi-thread support at operating system level. Multithreading programming model has gradually become the main solution for writing concurrent data processing. The advantage of multithread programming model is that thread can be created quickly and the same virtual address space can be shared between threads. This programming model enables convenient and efficient data sharing, because there is no need to switch address space, do not change registers, do not need to refresh the TLB and other operations, this approach results in less context switching overhead. The above advantages make the multithreaded programming model gradually become the mainstream solution in the writing of web crawler applications.

2.4 Limitations of Existing Programming Models

The scheduling of processes and threads is implemented with the help of the operating system. The kernel saves the context of the current execution environment, and then schedules the next execution environment to resume execution again from the last pause. The duration of the instruction running on the CPU is allocated by the operating system kernel according to the algorithm, and the current execution environment will be forced to suspend by the operating system.

With the development of the Internet, the scale of the network expands in geometric multiples. The traditional network crawler based on multithreading programming model meets more and more problems and challenges. The first and foremost is that the frequent switching between threads causes system performance bumps and drops. The number of concurrent threads on a single computer increases by more than one order of magnitude, and thread scheduling leads to a gradual increase in the kernel-level context switching pressure with the increase in the number of concurrency.

Many scholars began to explore and study the calculation model of alternative multi thread, such as Li [4] in 2007 found that the thread context switch on the system operation efficiency as the system load increases, in high concurrency conditions, context switching will gradually become the main factors affecting the performance. In 2008, Yin et al. [5] made a comparison between synchronous model and asynchronous model in high concurrency processing environment. It was found that the asynchronous model was relatively synchronous model, and the performance and extensibility of asynchronous model were greatly improved. Zhou et al. [6] put forward in 2009 that under the concurrent processing environment, the non-blocking asynchronous I/O model has the characteristics of strong expansibility and short response time, and is the first choice of high performance network programming. When Shaver and others [7] proposed high concurrency in 2012, the coroutine programming model is a better choice.

From the above work, with the development of technology, the web crawler programming model evolves from an initial multi-process model to a multi-threaded model, and in recent years, with the increase of data scale and further research, then, the asynchronous nonblocking model based on coroutine continues to evolve from multithread model. Compared to the multi-threaded model, the coroutine-based asynchronous model has less performance loss in high-concurrency processing environments, and CPU processing power and network utilization are further improved.

2.5 Technical Basis of Coroutine

The concept of coroutine was first put forward by conway et al. [8]. Later, Professor Donald Knuth gave a relatively complete and accurate definition of coroutine: the subroutine is a special case of the correlator [9]. The creation of the correlator is realized in the user-level by saving the state of the stack. The creation of coroutine is very fast without kernel involvement, because coroutine uses fewer resources than threads to implement coroutine through stacks in the user-level.

The essential difference between coroutine and processes and threads lies in the way scheduling is implemented. The compiler places scheduling instructions in machine code along with other instructions written by the user. The location of the return and reentry of the instruction is specified by the yield keyword in the code during the programming period, and the scheduled operation is completed in the user-level, while the scheduling of the process and thread belongs to the operating system level and is completed by the instruction located in the kernel mentality.

3   Application of Crawler System Based on Coroutine

In this section, we first introduces the overall system processing flow for participation in the NLP Chinese lexical semantic classification competition, and then give the detailed design and implementation of the web crawler based on the coroutine model.

3.1   Integral Process

In the task of semantic relation classification of NLP Chinese vocabulary, we design and implement the system using a combination of various algorithms and strategies. When we build the processing scheme based on wordnet, we wrote a web crawler program and used online dictionaries to convert Chinese vocabulary in input data set into corresponding English output based on HTML format. Then write another program to parse and extract the results of the crawl through the Beautiful Soup extension package and extract the corresponding English interpretations. As the basic data of the follow-up work, we design and write a classification algorithm, use the wordnet toolkit to classify the English words obtained, and then write a corresponding mapping algorithm to derive the classification results of Chinese words from the classification results of English words. The overall processing flow of the system is shown in Fig. 1.

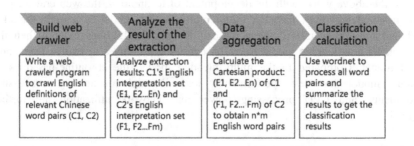

Build web crawler	Analyze the result of the extraction	Data aggregation	Classification calculation
Write a web crawler program to crawl English definitions of relevant Chinese word pairs (C1, C2)	Analyze extraction results: C1's English interpretation set (E1, E2...En) and C2's English interpretation set (F1, F2...Fm)	Calculate the Cartesian product: (E1, E2...En) of C1 and (F1, F2... Fm) of C2 to obtain n*m English word pairs	Use wordnet to process all word pairs and summarize the results to get the classification results

Fig. 1. Overall processing flow of the system

3.2   Detailed Design and Implementation

Ubuntu 14.04 LTS 64-bit operating system is chosen as the basic computing platform. The development and running environment mainly includes: Python 3.5, Beautiful Soup, WordNet and PyCharm etc. Writing coroutine-based web crawlers using Python and the standard library asyncio that supports asynchronous IO.

Based on the coroutine model, we designed and implemented a web crawler. First, the asyncio [9] standard library is used to create the EventLoop. Then the crawler program reads the list of urls to be crawled to build the coroutine task group, and then puts the coroutine task group into EventLoop to be executed. EventLoop will be scheduled according to the specific code executed by the coroutine, ensuring that the rest of the coroutine can continue to execute in the case of partial coroutine blocking, that is, the entire task group can move forward. The detailed process is shown in Figs. 2 and 3:

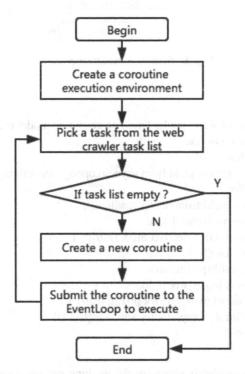

Fig. 2. Coroutine overall execution process

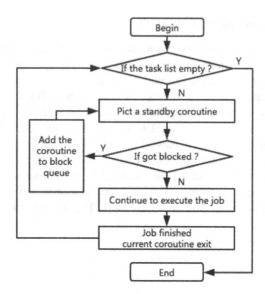

Fig. 3. Eventloop execution process

The main code of web crawler based on coroutine model is as follows:

```
1.  @asyncio.coroutine
2.  def crawler01(p01):
3.     reader, writer = yield from asyncio.open_connection(p01, 80)
4.     while True:
5.         line = yield from reader.readline( )
6.         if line == b'\r\n'  break
7.         result += line.decode('utf-8').rstrip( )
8.     writer.close()
9.     write_result(p01,result)
10. loop = asyncio.get_event_loop( )
11. tasks = [ crawler01(p01) for p01 in list01 ]
12. loop.run_until_complete(asyncio.wait(tasks))
13. loop.close( )
```

The above code completely expresses the working process based on the coroutine programming model. The overall processing flow is coordinated by the following components.

The first line @asyncio.coroutine is the decorator statement of Python, marking the function crawler01() as coroutine, and then putting the coroutine into EventLoop.

The tenth line asyncio.get_event_loop() is used to create an EventLoop.

Line 11 reads the url list to crawl to create a task list.

Line 12 build the coroutine task group based on the url task list and put it into the EventLoop execution.

Line 5 line = yield from reader.readline () crawls the specified url data through an open network connection, which is a very typical I/O blocking operation. The current coroutine code uses the yield from keyword to notify EventLoop, suspend the current coroutine and select the next coroutine in the ready state to continue running.

4   Results and Analysis

Based on the above analysis, this section tests web crawlers based on multithread model and coroutine model. The specific experimental environment is Intel Core i5 2.6 GHz CPU, 4G RAM, 100 M wired network and Ubuntu 14.04 LTS 64-bit operating system. The test mainly starts from two aspects of memory occupancy and CPU occupancy ratio, and makes a comparative analysis of different implementation schemes. Specific data are shown in Figs. 4 and 5:

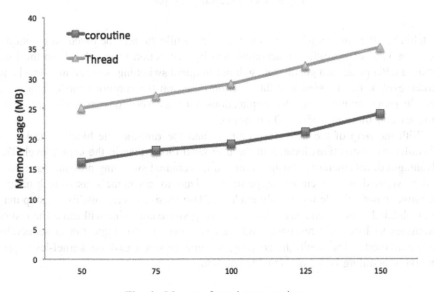

Fig. 4. Memory footprint comparison

From the aspect of memory occupation, we can observe that the scheme based on multithread model has a linear relationship between memory occupancy and concurrent number, and the scheme based on coroutine model, with the increase of concurrent number, the memory usage is obviously better than the former. At the same time, we also observed that the memory footprint of the scheme based on coroutine is better than that of the scheme based on multi-thread under the same number of concurrency.

From the point of view of CPU occupancy, we can see from Fig. 5 that the multithreading model can be used to increase the overhead of scheduling and context

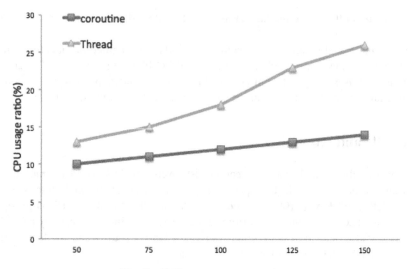

Fig. 5. CPU occupancy comparison

switching as the number of concurrent increases, while the scheme based on coroutine, the same kind of operation is accomplished by instruction in user-level, so the load curve of CPU presents a gentle state without frequent switching between user-level and kernel-level. It can be seen that the solution based on the coroutine model is a more suitable programming mode for applications such as web crawlers with large concurrency and more intensive I/O operations.

With the help of the language compiler and the runtime, the blocking tasks are scheduled by instructions located in the user-level rather than in the kernel-level. The advantages of less memory consumption and less context switching pressure have been further verified in the current experiments. Due to coroutine's user-level nature, coroutine is not suitable for heavily loaded CPU-intensive operations. EventLoop may be invalidated under such a scenario. A non-responsive coroutine will cause the rest of coroutines to lose their response, and then degenerate into single thread sequential execution mode. The multi-thread programming model based on kernel-level preemptive scheduling is a more suitable solution.

5   Conclusion

Combined with the task of NLP competition, this paper analyzes some of the deficiencies of the web crawler solution based on the multi-thread model in the face of high concurrent and intensive I/O application scenarios, and proposes a web crawler solution based on the coroutine model. On the basis of the above, we conducted in-depth analysis and research and programming. During the implementation process, we compared the experiments with the multi-threaded model. The results show that the scheme based on the coroutine model can significantly reduce the system load pressure and thus improve the web crawler crawling efficiency.

References

1. Network crawler. https://en.wikipedia.org/wiki/networkcrawler. Accessed 1 Feb 2018
2. Hua, B.L.: Research on knowledge extraction system architecture based on NLP. New Library Information Technology, pp. 38–41 (2007)
3. WordNet structure and relations. http://wordnet.princeton.edu/. Accessed 1 Feb 2018
4. Li, X.M., Yan, H.F., Wang, J.M.: Search Engine: Principle, Technology and System. Science China Press, Beijing (2012)
5. Yin, J., Yin, Z.B., Huang, H.: Analysis and solution of the bottleneck of web reptilian efficiency. J. Comput. Appl. **28**(5), 1114–1119 (2008)
6. Zhou, D.M., Li, Z.J.: High-performance web reptiles: a review of research. Comput. Sci. **36**(8), 26–29 (2009)
7. Shaver, C., Lee, E.A.: The coroutine model of computation. In: Proceedings of the International Conference on Model Driven Engineering Languages and Systems, pp. 319–334 (2012)
8. Document of Beautiful Soup. https://www.crummy.com/software/BeautifulSoup/. Accessed 1 Mar 2018
9. Coroutines with async and await syntax. https://www.python.org/dev/peps/pep-0492/. Accessed 1 Mar 2018

Design and Research on B2B Trading Platform Based on Consortium Blockchains

Xiaolan Xie[1,2], Qiangqing Zheng[1(✉)], Zhihong Guo[3], Qi Wang[1],
and Xinrong Li[1]

[1] College of Information Science and Engineering, Guilin University
of Technology, Guilin, Guangxi Zhuang Autonomous Region, China
zhengqiangqing@glut.edu.cn
[2] Guangxi Universities Key Laboratory of Embedded Technology and
Intelligent System, Guilin University of Technology, Guilin, China
[3] College of Mechanical and Control Engineering, Guilin University
of Technology, Guilin, Guangxi Zhuang Autonomous Region, China

Abstract. With the development of economy and technology, blockchains has become the preferred technology to solve the credit problems of both parties. Taking the sensitivity of transaction data into account, the use of blockchains technology in the B2B trading system is very appropriate. The credit problem of the B2B trading platform are solved in the article by introducing consortium blockchains technology, and a container-based cloud platform based on docker and kubernetes is built to improve the performance in the application of the consortium blockchains. First, it solves the problem of node performance bottleneck caused by the sudden increase of nodes, high-frequency transactions, and overclocking transactions. Second, it solves the problem of rapid iterative upgrade of node system versions with the rapid development of consortium blockchains technology, and securely stores consortium blockchains data and enterprise's own sensitive data. The platform, to a certain extent, solved the credit problems of the transactions between enterprises, and at the same time reduced the time cost and the economic cost of the company.

Keywords: Consortium blockchains · Docker · Kubernetes · Fabric
B2B

1 Research Background and Significance

With the rapid development of the Internet economy, the business model of enterprises has been constantly changing, the complexity of cooperation and transaction between enterprises has gradually increased, and credit issues have become increasingly important in cooperation and transactions [1]. The current common trading method is to ensure the safe execution of transactions through a trusted third-party platform.B2B (Business-to-Business) is a service platform for establishing purchasing relationships between companies and enterprises through the Internet [2]. Make sure to evaluate the degree of trust of participating companies accurately, on which base both parties to a transaction can fairly trade [3]. This is the basis for the B2B platform to operate.

© Springer Nature Switzerland AG 2018
X. Sun et al. (Eds.): ICCCS 2018, LNCS 11063, pp. 436–447, 2018.
https://doi.org/10.1007/978-3-030-00006-6_40

However, the evaluation standards of enterprise trust have not yet formed a set of recognized and authoritative systems. Most of the common evaluation indicators refer to feedback evaluation of the company, risk assessment status, and ability ranking in the field, but these indicators can only roughly measure the company's trust. In order to completely eliminate the concerns of both sides of the transaction, the judgment of some indicators alone is almost impossible to achieve. Unless the company has disclosed all its own data and health indicators to prove its degree of trust to a large extent. However, in this situation, the security of the company's index data will be in danger.

The development of blockchains technology has solved the trust problem to a certain extent [4]. Blockchains is essentially a large-scale Internet of value transmission. It builds a trust mechanism at the lowest cost, and that is also the most intuitive commercial value of blockchains. Therefore, for industries that require credit rating in terms of security and privacy, blockchains have a broader and rapid development space. According to the 2017 China Developer Survey released by Yunxi Community, blockchains are widely used in the supply chain and Internet of Things (IOT) and finance areas. details are shown in Fig. 1.

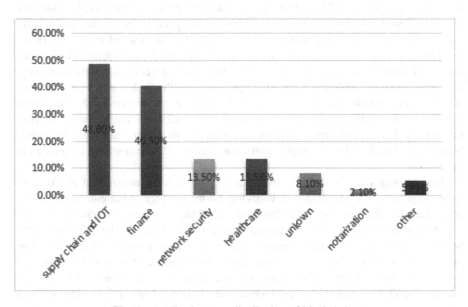

Fig. 1. Application area distribution of blockchains

2 Related Key Technology Research and Model Design

2.1 Analysis of Key Technologies

Blockchains can be divided into three types, namely public blockchains, private blockchains and consortium blockchains. The public blockchains uses Bitcoin as an application representative [5]. Beside the basic characteristics of blockchains technology, it has the characteristics of information disclosure, no access authority verification, and no difference storage of information data on all nodes. It is usually considered as "fully decentralized". The private blockchains manage and limit permissions, and write permissions to a specific organization [6]. The level of trust degree depends on the unilateral assessment of the management organizer. The read and write permissions and participation accounting rights in the consortium blockchains features can be managed by pre-set rules, while ensuring the confidentiality of the company's own data, and achieving decentralization between companies and solving their trust problems [7].

Advantages and Difficulties of Consortium Blockchains Technology
Advantages of Consortium Blockchains. The development of the consortium blockchains is getting more and more rapid. There are three main reasons for supporting its rapid development. First, the public blockchain synchronizes all data at regular intervals, which, to a certain extent, reveals the sensitive data of both parties. Compared with the public blockchain, the consortium blockchains can encrypt the sensitive information data of both parties of the transaction through the encrypted partition method to further protect the privacy of the enterprise. Compared with privacy blockchains, consortium blockchains has a nature of partial decentralized. Under the premise of ensuring security, one organization or enterprise in the alliance community can be prevented from dominating and preventing the interests of other enterprises from being harmed. Second, according to the set strategy, the consortium blockchains can select nodes in the consensus layer that satisfy the requirements in the community, then execute smart contracts, a set of script codes, on the nodes, and sign the transaction results, which increases transaction throughput and improves the efficiency. Thirdly, on the regulatory level, the consortium blockchains is autonomous and controllable, and the government certifies its development. Comparing with the public blockchains based on bitcoin applications, consortium blockchains have its own great advantage.

Disadvantages of Consortium Blockchains. Although the consortium blockchains technology has great advantages in verifying the trust degree of the enterprises in the B2B platform. But with the rapid development of the consortium blockchains, some outstanding problems need to be solved, which mainly includes the following three points: First of all, the node's performance requirements continue to increase. The number of enterprise nodes in the consortium blockchains continues to increase, and transactions between enterprise nodes become more frequent. Under this case, to increase the TPS (system throughput) while controlling the delay of the system within a certain range, means to increase the computing power of the node, that is, to strengthen the hardware configuration of the computer. For example, when the TPS is 1000/s and the system delay is required less than 300 ms, then the configuration of the computer needs to reach hexadeca-core and 32G memory. With the expansion of the size of the alliance, the configuration requirements will increase at the same time, which will undoubtedly cause a considerable economic burden on SMEs. Secondly, how to ensure rapid and iterative upgrade of the version of the node system to ensure its high availability is also a problem that needs to be solved urgently. The consortium blockchains are currently in a period of vigorous development. The technology is not yet mature and stable. When a more functional and service-friendly version emerges in the future, how to achieve iterative updating of the version in a node system that has already been established quickly and at a low cost becomes the currently primary problem that needs to be solved. Finally, we need to consider the problem of local data storage security of nodes on the consortium blockchains. In the alliance community, one of the common needs of enterprises is to ensure that their own sensitive data will not leak, but how to ensure the safe storage of these data in the event of a network outage or node downtime is also an urgent problem to be solved.

Container-Based Cloud Platform Cluster Technology Analysis Based on Docker and Kubernetes and its Support for Consortium Blockchains Technology
The container-based cloud platform integrates development and operation maintenance by abstracting the operating environment that the actual application needs to run. In addition, container technology also has many other powerful features and advantages. Here are three of the advantages. First, by deploying a container-based cloud platform that uses kubernetes as a cluster management tool [8], the resources of most of the lower-performing machines can be integrated. Through the preparation of a good scripting program and the use of remote control, one-click deployment of the confederation chain node system can be realized, thus enterprises who joining the consortium blockchains can reduce both time and cost of deploying the node. Second, Docker platform supports applications' rolling upgrades, which means iteratively upgrading system versions without affecting node system transactions, avoiding situations in which companies cannot trade due to system updates for periods of time. Third, GlusterFS is used in the cluster as a distributed storage solution for enterprise node blockchain data [9]. A multi-replica strategy is used to write data to different storage nodes at the same time, avoiding the loss of consortium blockchains data and sensitive data that are stored locally on the node due to a single machine crash. Thus, the data availability is guaranteed.

2.2 Model Design

The design of this platform refers to the alliance community that is based on the transaction requirements between SMEs. It combines the consortium blockchains technology with container-based cloud platform technology to design an alliance-based infrastructure model on the basis of the blockchain model. As shown in Fig. 4, the model consists of a data layer, a network layer, a consensus layer, a contract layer, and an application layer. The data layer structure of the blockchain is used in the data layer, and the storage method on it is optimized, and the distributed volume method of ClusterFS is used to store the data of the blockchain information of the alliance. A DHT-based structured P2P network is used to build a network layer that is used to complete transaction requests and data dissemination functions [10]. The consensus layer uses PBFT (Practical Byzantine Fault Tolerance) as a consensus algorithm to achieve consensus among the bookkeeper nodes, thus authenticating transaction records, and preventing tampering [11]. The contract layer uses a piece of script code that all participants to perform and compare and verify their results as a contract [12]. The application layer deploys a B2B trading platform based on consortium blockchains and container-based cloud platform details are shown in Fig. 2.

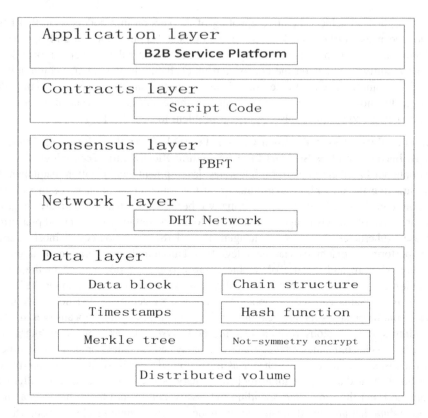

Fig. 2. B2B service platform model design based on consortium blockchains and container-based cloud platform

3 System Architecture Design

3.1 Network Structure Design of Consortium Blockchain

According to the purpose of the companies participating in the B2B platform, the participating companies are identified as producers or sellers and a supply chain is established. Each manufacturer or distributor represents a node and deploys a B2B trading platform system based on consortium blockchains and container-based cloud platform on the node. Peer-to-peer network concepts are used to link enterprise node systems. Each node needs to fulfill the responsibilities of the bookkeeper. In the event of a transaction, it also acts as a transaction cloud. The network structure is shown in Fig. 3:

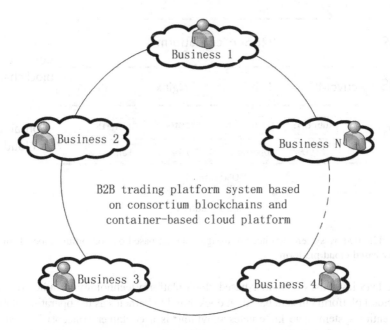

Fig. 3. Network structure design of consortium blockchains

3.2   Node System Architecture Design in the Network

With the continuous development of container technology, it has become a widely recognized way of sharing server resources. Container applications have become more and more widespread. Containerization of enterprise projects has become a new trend. Container-based cloud platform also has an irresistible attraction for traditional enterprises. It integrates the development and operation of the project. It makes the application platform-independent, requires no additional configuration environment, supports one-click deployment, and quickly updates the application version of the project. It lowered the company's production costs, and accelerated the application of the promotion and on-line. On this condition, whenever a new company joins the B2B platform and becomes a member of the alliance community, a new node will be formed in the consortium blockchains. The platform will deploy the B2B trading system based on the consortium blockchains and the container-based cloud platform in a one-click manner through the automation script. The architecture design of the system is shown in Fig. 4.

The node system integrates multiple low-performance computer resources by building a container-based cluster cloud platform, breaking the node's machine performance bottleneck caused by node increase or high-frequency transactions, and achieving a stable and iterative upgrade of the node chain deployment consortium blockchains solution. The distributed block storage function is realized locally for the alliance blockchain data, which improves the security of enterprise sensitive data. Node systems are divided into three layers according to the concept of cloud computing: IaaS: Infrastructure-as-a-Service, PaaS: Platform-as-a-Service [13], and SaaS: Software-as-a-Service.

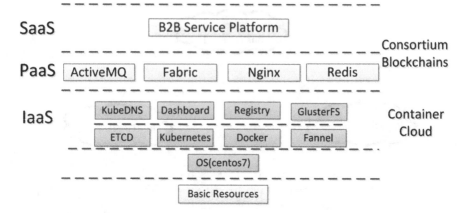

Fig. 4. B2B trading system architecture design diagram based on consortium blockchains and container-based cloud platform

The IaaS layer uses container-based cloud platform technology to build container-based cloud platform clusters based on docker and kubernetes as the operating platform of the entire system. The kubernetes (anything is a container concept) is used as a management tool for clusters, and etcd and flannel components are installed to realize real-time monitoring of service discovery and cluster network management [14], and to deploy DNS services and Dashboard services as cluster visualization interface management tools. GlusterFS open source project is used as a distributed storage solution for consortium blockchains data. GlusterFS is an open source distributed file system that uses tcp protocol and infiniband rdma protocol for data transmission. In order to save storage space, reduce data redundancy, and speed up operational efficiency, distributed block storage is used to distribute aggregate consortium blockchains data.

The ActiveMQ, Fabric, and Nginx services are deployed at the Paas layer. ActiveMQ middleware messaging components are used to build Docker-based ActiveMQ high-availability clusters for information collection [15]. It is stable, distributed and it has other characteristics. When the node surges and overclocks, it will eliminate peaks, stabilize the number of requests within a certain range, and increase the TPS and stability of the system. The flow of information between the parties to the transaction is monitored and the data are backup to prevent loss of messages due to a machine crash. Fabric is a platform for providing distributed ledger solutions to solve business credit problems and also to process information data collected by ActiveMQ master. According to the "endorsement strategy", select the satisfaction of the peer and the Orderer, using the consensus algorithm FBFT and the contract to achieve the signature authentication. The Orderer generates a new block and concurrent to all peers, and all peer verification and comparison. If the match is written to the local account book, complete the transaction. It is the cornerstone of the consortium blockchains. A docker-based Nginx cluster service is built, and the redis service is used to process requests from internal operations of the enterprise to access the B2B platform so as to implement load balancing.

The SaaS layer deploys the B2B service platform to implement functions such as initiation, subscription, and viewing of transactions.

4 Experimental Design and Results Analysis

Design a B2B trading platform based on consortium blockchains and container-based cloud platform based on equipment resources and system architecture design, simulating transactions between enterprises and analyzing the experimental results.

4.1 View Container Cloud Platform and Related Service Deployment List

The equipment resources used by the platform are shown in Table 1:

Table 1. Basic equipment resources

System	hostname	virtual/physical machine	GPU/CPU	Identity
Centos7	node1	Physical	CPU (quad)	Master/slave
Centos7	node2	Physical	CPU (dual)	Slave
Centos7	node3	Virtual	CPU (quad)	Slave
Centos7	node4	Virtual	CPU (quad)	Slave

According to the system architecture design diagram (Fig. 4), build a container cloud platform and deploy related services, use the dashboard-UI to view the docker-based container-based cloud platform with kubernetes as the cluster management tool and the related cluster services deployed, as shown in Fig. 5:

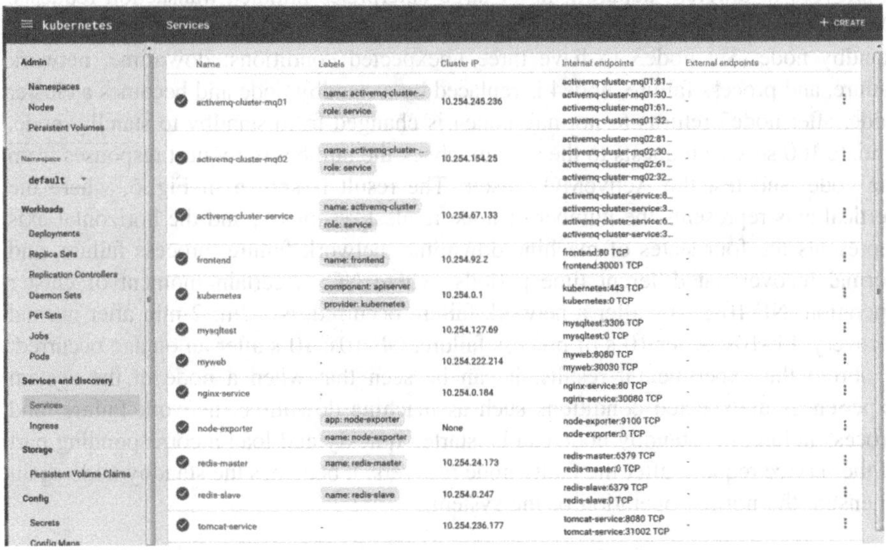

Fig. 5. Container-based cloud platform and list of deployed cluster services

From Fig. 5, it can be seen that ActiveMQ high-availability clusters are deployed in the platform. The cluster achieves high availability through the master-slaver model, deploys on three nodes, and spares one node as a spare node. At the same time, Nginx services and redis services are also deployed to achieve load balancing of access platform requests and increase the robustness of the system platform.

4.2   Test ActiveMQ High Availability Clusters and Results Analysis

Since the system is owned by the enterprise and exists as an accounting node in the affiliate blockchain network, the function of Pub/Sub to the transaction message is an important function of the platform. When the company is large, different employees of different departments will initiate different transaction requests, this requires the platform to have the function of publishing news messages, similarly, the platform also needs to have a transaction message subscription function. When the alliance chain is large, transaction requests are getting higher and higher, even at a certain stage, there will be data flood peak problems. How to reduce data flood peak and ensure the stable operation of systems and platforms has become a key issue. Configuring ActiveMQ High Availability Clustering combines low-latency, high-availability, and high-reliability solutions with distributed persistent storage such as levelDB, kahaDB, and other relational databases. By restricting the flow, setting priorities, and configuring the weights and other solutions, the core business of the enterprise can be ensured to operate normally; through the multi-copy mechanism, unexpected conditions such as machine downtime, network failure, and process failure can be ensured, and the master-slave device can be switched to ensure the stability of the platform.

The experiment conducted simulation tests for business scenarios in which different employees in different departments of large enterprises initiated transaction requests. Deploy the ActiveMQ cluster as a container on three machines with node4 as the standby node. Set node3 to have three unexpected conditions: downtime, network failure, and process failure, node4 is replaced by a standby node and becomes a cluster node, after node3 returns to normal, node4 is changed from standby to standby node. Initiate 100 service requests to the system, check the number of request responses from the node, and test the ActiveMQ cluster. The result is shown in Fig. 6, where the vertical axis represents the number of node request responses, and the horizontal axis represents the four states of machine downtime, network failure, process failure, and normal recovery at different time periods, where NC: a certain moment of cluster operation, NF-10s: 10 s after a network failure occurred, NC-2m: 2 min after normal recovery, PF-10s: After 10 s of process failure, OF-10s: 10 s after an outage occurred.

From the experimental results, it can be seen that when a node in the system experiences unexpected conditions such as machine downtime, network failure, and process failure, the standby node can be started quickly and load a corresponding part of the service request, after the faulty node recovers, it becomes the standby node again to ensure the normal operation of the system.

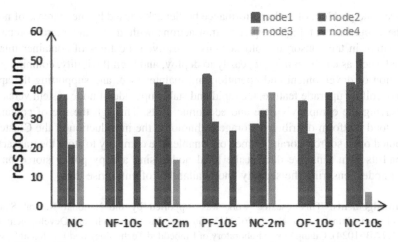

Fig. 6. The number of response requests from nodes in an ActiveMQ cluster

4.3   Test Platform Transfer Transaction

Due to the limited experimental environment, fabrics are used here to simulate transactions between companies. The results are shown in Fig. 7:

Fig. 7. Using fabric to simulate transaction transactions between enterprises

5   Summary

The idea of decentralization of the consortium blockchains is introduced to solve the credit problem of the enterprise transaction platform. The container-based cloud platform based on docker and kubernetes is used to make up for the defects of the consortium blockchains in practice. Through the integration of low-performance device resources, the problem of node performance bottleneck caused by the increase of nodes and the occurrence of high-frequency transactions with more and more companies participating in the consortium blockchains is resolved. Features of container mirrors are used, such as easily to migrate, easily to deploy, and high flexibility, combining the integration of development and operation and maintenance, and supporting the application of rolling upgrade feature, the rapid and stable upgrade of node system version is built, saving the company's time and economic costs. Through the use of container-based cloud platform distributed storage technology, the introduction of the ClusterFS distributed open source storage framework enables the company to store the transaction data and its own sensitive data in the local node using a copy policy stored on the unused nodes, ensuring the security and availability of enterprise data.

Acknowledgements. This research work was supported by the National Natural Science Foundation of China (Grant No. 61762031), Guangxi Key Research and Development Plan (No. 2017AB51024), GuangXi key Laboratory of Embedded Technology and Intelligent System.

References

1. Chen, K., Cheng, C., Yang, S.: Are China's sovereign credit ratings underestimated? J. Econ. Policy Reform **14**(4), 313–320 (2011)
2. Qu, W.G., Pinsonneault, A., Tomiuk, D., et al.: The impacts of social trust on open and closed B2B e-commerce: a Europe-based study. Inf. Manag. **52**(2), 151–159 (2015)
3. Li, Z., Penard, T.: The role of quantitative and qualitative network effects in B2B platform competition. Soc. Sci. Electron. Publ. **35**(1), 1–19 (2014)
4. Kraft, D.: Difficulty control for blockchain-based consensus systems. Peer-to-Peer Netw. Appl. **9**(2), 397–413 (2016)
5. Zhang, Y., Wen, J.: The IoT electric business model: using blockchain technology for the internet of things. Peer-to-Peer Netw. Appl. **10**(4), 983–994 (2017)
6. Schwarz, T., Schneider, A., Rogoza, R., et al.: P1084 long-term public health effects of vaccination against cervical cancer in Germany: results from a Markov model. Int. J. Antimicrob. Agents **29**(6), S292 (2007)
7. Kang, J., Yu, R., Huang, X., et al.: Enabling localized peer-to-peer electricity trading among plug-in hybrid electric vehicles using consortium blockchains. IEEE Trans. Ind. Inform. **PP**(99), 1 (2017)
8. Netto, H.V., Lung, L.C., Correia, M., et al.: State machine replication in containers managed by Kubernetes. J. Syst. Archit. **73**(C), 53–59 (2017)
9. Ren, Z., Shi, W., Wan, J., et al.: Realistic and scalable benchmarking cloud file systems: practices and lessons from AliCloud. IEEE Trans. Parallel Distrib. Syst. **PP**(99), 1 (2017)
10. Quanqing, X., Xiaoxiao, H., Bin, C., et al.: Facilitating effective resource publishing and searching in DHT networks. Hkie Trans. **16**(3), 32–41 (2009)
11. Anh, D.T.T., Zhang, M., Ooi, B.C., et al.: Untangling blockchain: a data processing view of blockchain systems. IEEE Trans. Knowl. Data Eng. **PP**(99), 1 (2017)
12. Hensher, D.A., Stanley, J.: Transacting under a performance-based contract: the role of negotiation and competitive tendering. Transp. Res. Part A Policy Pract. **42**(9), 1143–1151 (2008)
13. Xie, H.H., Gao, J.: Research and implementation of PaaS platform based on norm-governed and policy-driven autonomic model. Appl. Res. Comput. **28**(5), 1839–1842 (2011)

14. Negus, C.: Docker containers from start to enterprise (includes content update program): build and deploy with Kubernetes, Flannel. Cockpit Atomic. Vaccine **19**(Suppl. 1), S87–S95 (2016)
15. Jayalath, C., Stephen, J., Eugster, P.: Universal cross-cloud communication. IEEE Trans. Cloud Comput. **2**(2), 103–116 (2014)

Design and Simulation of a New Stacked Printed Antenna

Zhiwei Gao$^{(\boxtimes)}$, Weidong Liu, Qingyuan Fang, and Shugang Jiang

School of Information Science and Technology, Shijiazhuang Tiedao University,
Shijiazhuang, China
gao_zhiwei@163.com, liuwd_83@163.com,
617140612@qq.com, 499283062@qq.com

Abstract. The key component of the fully polarized electronic system is dual polarized antenna, which can sense the polarization information of the electromagnetic wave. In the thesis a design of dual polarized antenna is proposed, which combines the electronic radiation resource and magnetic radiation resource. The feeding ports of the antenna are mounted at the bottom of the antenna which is helpful for the array application. A metal reflector ground was introduced to achieve the unidirectional pattern. The radiation fields emitted by the electronic current resource and magnetic current resource are approximately orthogonal to each other among large space range, which is suitable for application case. The full wave electromagnetic simulation and optimization design of the proposed antenna were carried out and the designed antenna was fabricated. The measured port isolation of the designed antenna is above 20 dB. The design effectiveness is validated through the experiments.

Keywords: Dual-polarized antenna · Dipole · Microstrip patch antenna
Radiation pattern

1 Introduction

The design and implementation of dual-polarized antenna has become a hotspot in the field of antenna technology [1, 2]. The dual-polarized antenna devices capable of sensing electromagnetic polarization information have better performance than traditional single polarized electronic devices. Dual polarized antenna is the key components in communication system, and its function is to realize the full polarization signal processing algorithm through radiation or receiving two orthogonal polarization components of electromagnetic wave. The dual-polarized antennas includes dual-polarized dipole antennas, dual-polarized microstrip antennas, dual-polarized mouth antennas, etc. [3–5]. From the radiation mechanism, the dual-polarization antenna can be divided into the electric current source and magnetic current source with orthogonal placement. In the application of dual-polarized antenna, the main forms are the phased array and MIMO array. Compared with traditional literal antenna, dual polarized antenna also needs to consider the port isolation of polarization and cross polarization level of radiation field, the purpose of which is to achieve two better orthogonal polarization channel [6]; In the application of full polarization phased array antenna, the

© Springer Nature Switzerland AG 2018
X. Sun et al. (Eds.): ICCCS 2018, LNCS 11063, pp. 448–455, 2018.
https://doi.org/10.1007/978-3-030-00006-6_41

dual-polarized antennas needs to have the radiation and polarization patterns with sufficient width to achieve the expected beam scanning range. As for engineering applications, the installation of the antenna array space is usually limited, therefore the structure of dual polarized antenna units need to adapt to the antenna array structure, and the antenna unit is miniaturization. Generally feeding is introduced from the bottom of the antenna platform, connector size is small enough, and installation is firm and reliable. Therefore, the design and implementation of dual-polarization array antenna is an important and challenging task.

Considering the design difficulty, electrical performance and tooling cost of dual-polarized antenna unit, an optional implementation scheme is dual-polarized printed antenna. Dual-polarized microstrip antenna is the most common type of dual-polarized printed antenna [8, 9] and is widely used. Dual-polarization microstrip antenna using printed circuit technology processing, has the advantages of low profile, small size, light weight and low cost. In regard to the electric properties, double polarization structure has more implementation type and flexible feeding, such as microstrip line edge feed, feed microstrip line angle feed and electromagnetic coupling feeding [10, 11]. However, the working bandwidth of the microstrip antenna is narrow, and the polarization port isolation and radiation field of the dual-polarized antenna is higher. Although the improvement measures can extend the impedance bandwidth and the polarization performance of the microstrip antenna, the structure of the dual-polarized antenna is complex and the implementation of the project is more difficult. Both the printed dipole and the printed slot antenna are the common forms of microwave radiators, which also has the advantages of microstrip antenna in structure and processing, and their impedance bandwidth is wider. Printed dipole antenna which processes the dipole is in printing medium substrate, has the feeding with coaxial line and coplanar waveguide (CPW), and flexible design with rectangular, butterfly, round, oval, and many other shapes, even can realize the performance of ultra-wideband (UWB) [12–15]. Slot antenna usually can be the equivalent magnetic current source and is a kind of microwave radiator coupling with dipole antenna. Printing slot antenna structure is simple, and the aperture shape can be rectangular, index gradually deformation, annular, etc. According to the demand, it can be designed into narrowband, broadband, and ultra-broadband types. In the field of feeding, the printed slot antenna can use various forms [16–19], such as electromagnetic coupling feed, coplanar waveguide feed, etc. Therefore, the printed slot antenna is also a microwave antenna.

2 The Design of the Antenna

The design of the dual-polarized antenna structure is shown in Fig. 1, the dual-polarized antenna is composed of the electric vibrator and slot ring: the upper layer is for the electric vibrator, which is fed directly by the coaxial line at one end of the vibrator; the lower layer is slot ring, in which the one end of the coaxial line is connected to the open road microstrip line to conduct the coupled feeding. Because both the electric vibrator and the slit ring have the characteristics of bidirectional radiation, the metal plate part of the slit ring can also be used as the reflector of the vibrator at the same time, and a piece of metal reflector can be arranged at a distance of about $\lambda/4$ below the slit ring.

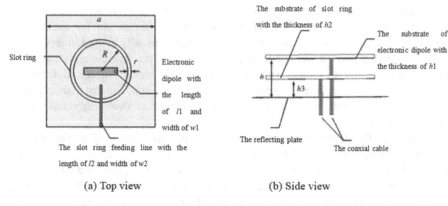

(a) Top view   (b) Side view

Fig. 1. Antenna schematic

When designing the dual-polarized antenna, firstly, the Rogers 5880 sheet with the dielectric constant $\varepsilon_r = 2.2$ of Rogers Co., Ltd. should be selected as the dielectric substrate. The size of the dielectric sheet is 32 mm × 32 mm × 1 mm and the basic structure and feeding form of the antenna were determined. As for the radius R of the ring, we can estimate the size of the ring by the empirical formula based on the previous theoretical analysis. For the width r of the slot and the width $w2$ of the feeding line, we consider optimizing the influence of the mutual coupling between the feeding line and the electric vibrator on the gain and cross-polarization of the pattern. Table 1 is the change of the parameter values when the gap width is changed within the slit ring vibration of 5 GHz. It can be seen that the smaller the slit width is, the smaller the inner diameter R of the slit ring is, and meantime cross polarization of the slit ring and the isolation between the two ports will be better.

Table 1. Rule of the parameters of the aperture circle vary with the width of the aperture

Aperture width/mm	Inner diameter/mm	Isolation/dB	Cross polarization/dB
0.5	9	−23	−21
0.8	11.2	−19	−16.5
1	12	−18	−16

The open microstrip line of the slot ring exerts a certain impact on the return loss, as shown in Fig. 2 is the changing curve of the slot ring port return loss with the open microstrip line. From the figure, we can see the thinner the open microstrip line, the smaller the return loss of the slit ring is, but in order to meet the processing precision and the convenience of welding, the feeder line cannot be too thin. For the electric vibrator part, the width and length are the most influential. Since we use the vibrator length is about $\lambda_g/4$. We can fine tune the height between the two dielectric plates and the ground on the basis of initially determination of $\lambda/4$.

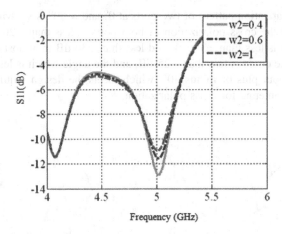

Fig. 2. Curve of return loss of aperture circle vary with open loop feed wire width

3   Simulation Results and Analysis

To optimize the antenna performance and structure, we adopt the full wave electro-magnetic simulation, and obtain a set of parameters: $a = 32$ mm, $R = 9.1$ mm, $r = 0.5$ mm, $l1 = 7.3$ mm, $w1 = 1.5$ mm, $l2 = 14$ mm, $w2 = 0.4$ mm, $h = 11.3$ mm, $h1 = h2 = 1$ mm, $h3 = 5.3$ mm. The simulation results of the antenna and the S parameter curve of the antenna is shown in Fig. 3.

From Fig. 3 we can see when the return loss of antenna is less than 10 dB, the working frequency of stacked dipole port is from 4.75 GHz to 5.25 GHz, aperture circle port 4.9 GHz to 5.1 GHz, whole antenna bandwidth 4.9 GHz to 5.1 GHz, and the isolation of two ports within the bandwidth are under −23 dB.

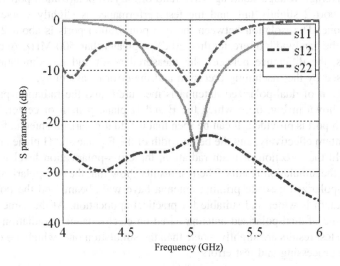

Fig. 3. S parameter curve of the antenna

The cross polarization pattern of two ports at 0° and = 90° is shown in Fig. 4. The figures show that the cross polarization of both ports is less than −20 dB, where the cross polarization is less than −35 dB, and less than −30 dB in almost all angles. The one of the aperture circle is less than −25 dB, and the angle which is less than −20 dB has a range of about plus or minus 40°, which meets the design requirements of the dual polarization antenna for cross-polarization.

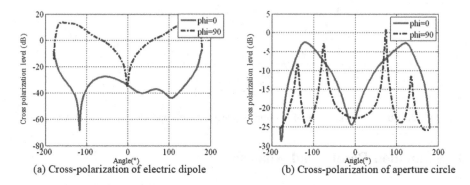

(a) Cross-polarization of electric dipole   (b) Cross-polarization of aperture circle

Fig. 4. Cross-polarization simulation results of dual polarization antenna

4   Processing and Testing

According to the structure and size of the designed cascade printing dual-polarized antenna, the prototype is assembled and the physical image of the antenna sample is shown in Fig. 5(a). The two polarization ports voltage standing wave ratio and isolation test results are shown in Fig. 5(b), (c) and (d) respectively. Between the bandwidth, the average voltage standing wave ratio of the two polarization port is about 2, the one of port 2 slightly tall, and the test performance is slightly worse than the simulation one. The isolation between the two polarization ports is about 24.7 dB at 5 GHz and the bandwidth of greater than 20 dB is greater than 500 MHz. According to the analysis, the difference between the measured result and the simulation one is mainly caused by the machining precision and the error of assembly.

The pattern of dual-polarized antenna is measured, and the radiation pattern test results are shown in Fig. 6, in which the E and H plane pattern of center frequency point of each port is provided. It can be seen that the dual-polarized antenna formed the radiation pattern effectively, and the beam width of the E plane and H plane are similar, about 95°. In the direction of main radiation, the cross-polarization level is −15 dB, higher than the simulation results. The test results show that the two polarization ports of the dual-polarized cascade printing antenna have wide beam, and the polarization direction pattern is wider and suitable for practical application. At the same time, the design scheme of dual-polarized antenna based on electromagnetic radiation source is correct. The test results are slightly worse than the simulation one, which are caused by the antenna processing and test errors.

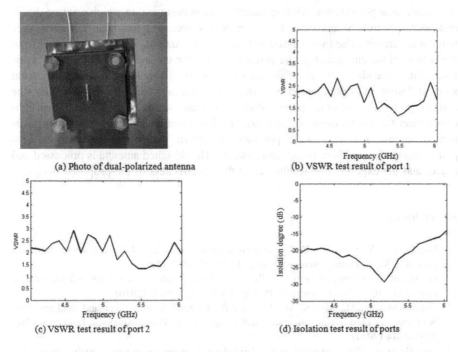

(a) Photo of dual-polarized antenna

(b) VSWR test result of port 1

(c) VSWR test result of port 2

(d) Isolation test result of ports

Fig. 5. Photo of dual-polarized antenna and test results of electronic principle

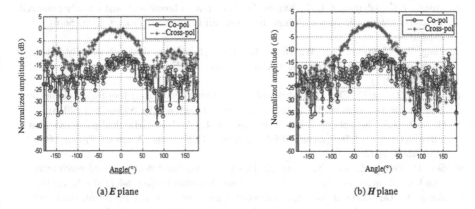

(a) E plane

(b) H plane

Fig. 6. Test patterns of printing dipole ports

5 Conclusions

Based on the radiation principle of dual polarization antenna units, a design scheme was proposed in this paper, which provides a new technical way for dual polarization antenna design. According to the equivalent principle of electromagnetic field, a kind of cascade dual polarization printing antenna unit is designed, in which printing dipole and aperture circle is used as electric current source and magnetic current source radiator separately. The two polarization ports of the antenna unit are introduced from the bottom of the antenna structure and are suitable for the application of phased array. Using full-wave electromagnetic simulation software to simulate the dual polarization antenna design and optimization with the bandwidth between 4.9 GHz–5.1 GHz, the antenna port isolation, cross polarization level, beam width and other technical indicators meet the requirements of dual polarization antenna, especially, the dual polarization antenna has very wide polarization pattern, which can be used in dual polarization radar and communication systems. The designed antenna is processed and tested, and the experimental results verify the effectiveness of the proposed design.

References

1. Liu, H., Liu, Y., Gong, S.: Design of a compact dual-polarised slot antenna with enhanced gain. IET Microwaves Antennas Propag. **11**(6), 892–897 (2017)
2. Li, M., et al.: Eight-port orthogonally dual-polarized antenna Array for 5G smartphone aplications. IEEE Trans. Antennas Propag. **64**(9), 3820–3830 (2016)
3. Esquius-Morote, M., Mattes, M., Mosig, J.R.: Orthomode transducer and dual-polarized horn antenna in substrate integrated technology. IEEE Trans. Antennas Propag. **62**(10), 4935–4944 (2014)
4. Zhu, G., et al.: Ultra-wideband dual-polarized patch antenna with four capacitively coupled feeds. IEEE Trans. Antennas Propag. **62**(5), 2440–2449 (2014)
5. Chaloun, T., Ziegler, V., Menzel, W.: Design of a dual-polarized stacked patch antenna for wide-angle scanning reflectarrays. IEEE Trans. Antennas Propag. **64**(8), 3380–3390 (2016)
6. Mishra, P.K., Jahagirdar, D.R., Kumar, G.: A review of broadband dual linearly polarized microstrip antenna designs with high Isolation. IEEE Antennas Propag. Mag. **56**(6), 238–251 (2014)
7. Yang, W., Chen, D., Che, W.: High-efficiency high-isolation dual-orthogonally polarized patch antennas using nonperiodic RAMC structure. IEEE Trans. Antennas Propag. **65**(2), 887–892 (2017)
8. Wen, D., Zheng, D., Chu, Q.: A dual-polarized planar antenna using four folded dipoles and its array for base stations. IEEE Trans. Antennas Propag. **64**(12), 5536–5542 (2016)
9. Holland, S.S., Schaubert, D.H., Vouvakis, M.N.: A 7–21 GHz dual-polarized planar ultrawideband modular antenna (PUMA) array. IEEE Trans. Antennas Propag. **60**(10), 4589–4600 (2012)
10. Sun, D., Zhang, Z., Yan, X., Jiang, X.: Design of broadband dual-polarized patch antenna with backed square annular cavity. IEEE Trans. Antennas Propag. **64**(1), 43–52 (2016)
11. Wang, Y., Du, Z.: Dual-polarized slot-coupled microstrip antenna array with stable active element pattern. IEEE Trans. Antennas Propag. **63**(9), 4239–4244 (2015)
12. Dastranj, A.: Very small planar broadband monopole antenna with hybrid trapezoidal–elliptical radiator. IET Microwaves Antennas Propag. **11**(4), 542–547 (2017)
13. Wu, W.: Zhang, Y.P: Analysis of ultra-wideband printed planar quasi-monopole antennas using the theory of characteristic modes. IEEE Antennas Propag. Mag. **52**(6), 67–77 (2010)
14. Lin, C.I., Wong, K.L.: Printed monopole slot antenna for internal multiband mobile phone antenna. IEEE Trans. Antennas Propag. **55**(12), 3690–3697 (2007)

15. Oh, J., Sarabandi, K.: Low profile, miniaturized, inductively coupled capacitively loaded monopole antenna. IEEE Trans. Antennas Propag. **60**(3), 1206–1213 (2012)
16. Ahdi Rezaeieh, S., Antoniades, M.A., Abbosh, A.M.: Gain enhancement of wideband metamaterial-loaded loop antenna with tightly coupled arc-shaped directors. IEEE Trans. Antennas Propag. **65**(4), 2090–2095 (2017)
17. Qing, X., Chen, Z.: Characteristics of a metal-backed loop antenna and its application to a high-frequency RFID smart shelf. IEEE Antennas Propag. Mag. **51**(2), 26–38 (2009)
18. Chi, Y., Wong, K.: Internal compact dual-band printed loop antenna for mobile phone application. IEEE Trans. Antennas Propag. **55**(5), 1457–1462 (2007)
19. Im, Y.T., Kim, J.H., Park, W.S.: Matching techniques for miniaturized UHF RFID loop antennas. IEEE Antennas Wirel. Propag. Lett. **8**, 266–270 (2009)

Digital Continuity Guarantee of Electronic Record Based on Data Usability in Big Data Environment

Jiang Xu[1,2], Jian Zhang[1,2], Yongjun Ren[1,2(✉)], and Hye-Jin Kim[3]

[1] Jiangsu Engineering Center of Network Monitoring,
Nanjing University of Information Science and Technology, Nanjing, China
renyi100@126.com
[2] School of Computer and Software, Nanjing University of Information Science
and Technology, Nanjing, China
[3] Business Administration Research Institute,
Sungshin W. University, Seoul, Korea

Abstract. At present some developed countries have put forward their digital continuity action plans. And the digital continuity has also become a hot spot in the research of electronic records. However, the technology and measures for the protection of the digital continuity are still lack.

In this paper, we first point out the necessity of ensuring the availability and completeness of the electronic record. Moreover, the technology framework of availability and completeness for electronic record are firstly proposed. Secondly, we make use of the coding theory to ensure the availability of electronic record. In addition, the technology of ensuring completeness for electronic record is constructed based on functional dependency theory, and the method of evaluating completeness of electronic record is present using the functional dependency theory.

Keywords: Electronic record · Digital continuity · Data completeness
Data availability

1 Introduction

With the development of e-commerce, e-government and smart city technologies, more and more electronic records are generated and stored in digital form, and the formats and types of the electronic records are diverse. But the electronic records can't be managed effectively, and traditional record storage strategy is no longer suitable for the storage of electronic records [1].

2 Problem Description

2.1 From Digital Continuity to Data Usability

Digital continuity is a way to ensure the long-term availability of information, what it specifically refers to is maintain and manage digital information to ensure that it can be

© Springer Nature Switzerland AG 2018
X. Sun et al. (Eds.): ICCCS 2018, LNCS 11063, pp. 456–466, 2018.
https://doi.org/10.1007/978-3-030-00006-6_42

used now and in the future when needed. We can ensure that information is complete, accessible and available by digital continuity.

2.2 Data Availability

In his award-winning speech, Gray, winner of the Turing Award, pointed out: Due to the development of the Internet, the amount of data newly generated every 18 months in the future will be the sum of the data amount ever [2]. In the past ten years, this prediction has been constantly confirmed. According to the "Digital Universe 2020" report jointly released by IDC and EMC, the global digital universe will expand to 40,000 EB by 2020. How to store and manage these data has become an urgent problem to be solved.

In the traditional storage mode, users need to buy their own storage devices to build storage systems, but also need their own monitoring system, maintenance, updates and other operations. Hasan et al. point out that the cost of managing and maintaining storage data is 5–7 times the storage hardware cost and about 74% of the total storage cost [3]. Therefore, users use traditional storage methods to store data, which not only requires a huge expense to purchase storage devices, but also needs to pay more expensive system maintenance and management costs. In addition, the traditional storage methods still have disadvantages such as not easy to expand, complex management and maintenance, and low resource utilization. Therefore, the traditional storage methods have been unable to deal with such a huge data size, find a new mass data storage methods become the trend [4].

Driven by the demand for mass storage, cloud storage emerges as the times require. It can solve the predicament faced by traditional storage methods, and once it comes out, it has received unprecedented attention from industry and academia. So, it has been rapidly developed [5, 6]. Cloud storage has great advantages over traditional storage both in terms of practicality and economy. It is bound to become the mainstream storage method [7, 8].

As cloud storage brings convenience and economic benefits to users, it also poses a serious threat to users' data security. In particular, it brings many new challenges in ensuring the integrity and correctness of user data. If there is data security problem, the data on CSP will not be usability. To solve the problem, redundant data needs to be taken to ensure data availability. At present, the main data redundancy mechanism has two complete copies and erasure codes.

2.3 Data Completeness

Usually, data completeness refers to the processing of the excess or deficiency of character, characteristic attribute and characteristic relationship in the data set. It assesses that the degree of data completeness, data specification, appropriate amount of data, concise and data coverage. According to the common problems [9], the data completeness issues specifically are divided into the following five kinds (see Table 1). If any kind of data completeness is violated in Table 1, it will violate the requirements of data completeness. In the table, the relationship completeness, content completeness and data accuracy have certain relevance.

Table 1. Category of data completeness

Category	Function Description
Size completeness	The size of the completeness of data set
Attribution completeness	The coverage degree of the required minimum attributes for each record in data table
Content completeness	The missing degree of table, records, data items, symbols in data set
Relationship completeness	The existence degree of feature, feature and feature in data set
Data completeness	The completeness degree of each property in data set

Definition 1. The violation of completeness pattern: there is a specific relations pattern $R(A_1 : d_1, \cdots A_n : d_n)$. And it exists n attributes $A_i(i = 1, \cdots n)$ in $R(A_1 : d_1, \cdots A_n : d_n)$, the corresponding domain is d_i and D is an instance of R. If any of the following conditions is satisfied, the violation of data completeness occurs.

(1) $\exists t_i \in R$, The values of t_i are in all attributes $A = \{A_1, \cdots, A_n\}$: if $V_{t_i[A_j]}$ is null then $v_{t_i[A_j]} = 0$, otherwise $v_{t_i[A_j]} = 1$; and $\wedge v_{t_i[A_j]} = 0$.

(2) $A = \{A_1, \cdots, A_n\}$, $A^s = \{A_{s_1}, \cdots, A_{s_m}\}$, $A \cap A^s \neq A^s$.

(3) $t_i \in R$, the total tuple of R is N_{t_i}, the number of tuple in R_{std} is N^s, $N_{t_i} < N^s$.

The conditions (1) and (2) are satisfied, it is called the violation of content completeness, if (3) is met, then called violation of scale completeness. All t_i, which satisfies the above conditions, will be added into the set of violating data completeness; that is $t_i \in \sum Vio(D_{com})$ in the pattern R. The above definition is idealized. When there exists a missing of field values in one relationship pattern, it is determined to the violation of data completeness. Such decision is too stringent in the actual information system. Attribute set contained in a relational schema is not always a subset of the standard attributes set, while it is usually the intersection of the standard attributes set and other relevant sets. It does not fully cover all the standard attributes, but records some related properties. Similarly, the decision of an amount of data also exists the problem. Thus, the extended violation of data completeness is further defined.

Definition 2. The extended completeness violation: In the information system, there is a specific relations pattern $R(A_1 : d_1, \cdots A_n : d_n)$. And it exists n attributes $A_i(i = 1, \cdots n)$ in $R(A_1 : d_1, \cdots A_n : d_n)$, the corresponding domain is d_i and D is an instance of R. If any of the following conditions is satisfied, the violation of data completeness occurs.

(1) $\forall t_i \in R$, The values of t_i are in some important attributes $A = \{A_1, \cdots, A_n\}$: if $V_{t_i[A_j]}$ is null then $v_{t_i[A_j]} = 0$, otherwise $v_{t_i[A_j]} = 1$; and $\wedge v_{t_i[A_j]} = 0. \forall t_i \in R$, n_{t_i} is the attribute number of t_i, $n_{t_{i-null}}$ is the attribute number of full records on t_i. Now $Q_{com1} = F(\sum((n_{t_i} - n_{t_{i-null}})/n_{t_i})) < q_{com1}$, where Q_{com1} represents the result 1 of data completeness assessment, q_{com1} is the standard coefficient 1 of the data completeness requirements, according to digital business continuity.

(2) $A = \{A_1, \cdots, A_n\}$, $A^s = \{A_{s_1}, \cdots, A_{s_m}\}$, $Q_{com2} = F(mat(A, A^s)) < q_{com2}$, where Q_{com2} represents the result 2 of data completeness assessment, q_{com2} is the standard coefficient 2 of the data completeness requirements, according to digital business continuity.

(3) $t_i \in R$, the total tuple of R is N_{t_i}, the number of tuple in R_{std} is N^s, $Q_{com3} = F(\sum ((N^s - N_{t_i})/N^s)) < q_{com3}$, where Q_{com3} represents the result 3 of data completeness assessment, q_{com3} is the standard coefficient 3 of the data completeness requirements, according to digital business continuity.

Where (1) and (2) are satisfied, it is called the violation of content completeness, if (3) is met, then called violation of scale completeness. When $Q_{comi} < q_{comi}$, it means the data completeness of R is low, and the degree of its completeness violation is $Vio(R, R_{std}).t_i$, which violates data completeness, will be added into the set of violating data completeness; that is $t_i \in \sum Vio(D_{com})$ in the pattern R.

3 Digital Continuity of Electronic Record Based on Data Usability

Data availability and data Completeness are two important factors of electronic record availability. In the following two sub-sections, the coding theory and the function dependency theory are respectively utilized to guarantee them.

3.1 Availability of Electronic Record Based on Coding Theory

In order to protect the data usability, this paper uses coding theory to encode electronic record, stores the corresponding hash value of each record block, locates the location of tampering record to reduce decoding complexity and supports dynamic update of electronic record. The method proposed in this paper can verify the record stored in the cloud servers.

The system consists of users of electronic record and cloud servers. The process is divided into three phases: record encoding, record verification and record recovery.

3.1.1 Coding of Electronic Record

The electronic record F is first segmented into data blocks $D_1, D_2, \cdots D_k$ and then the original record is encoded using the encoding matrix G, where G is the $k \times n$ matrix and $n > k$. And it is constructed by $G_1, G_2, \cdots G_n$. The code element $C_i(C_i = D_i G)$ is obtained after the original record is encoded. At the time of decoding, k code elements are randomly selected from C and combined into a decoding element Q, and the corresponding coding matrix is selected from G to form a decoding matrix P in order, and the original information is obtained by $D = QP^{-1}$.

Fountain Coding and Decoding of Electronic Record

If $D_{m \times k} G_{k \times k} = C_{m \times k}$, and G is invertible, $D = CG^{-1}$. When G is a matrix of $k \times n$ $(n > k)$, $D_{m \times k} G_{k \times n} = C_{m \times n}$, $D = (D_1, D_2, \ldots, D_k)$, $D_i = (d_{i1}, d_{i2}, \ldots, d_{im})^T$, $G = (G_1, G_2, \ldots, G_n)$, $G_i = (g_{1i}, g_{2i}, \ldots, g_{ki})^T$, $C = (C_1, C_2, \ldots, C_n)$, $C_i = (c_{11}, c_{2i}, \ldots, c_{mi})^T$.

Since $c_{ij} = \sum_{h=1,u=1}^{h=k,u=n} d_{hi}g_{uj}$, we take k columns in C to form the decoding unit Q, and take the corresponding k columns in G to form the decoding matrix $P_{k \times k}$. Therefore, as long as P is invertible, $D = QP^{-1}$.

How to make the decoding matrix P reversible, which are the k columns, and it is selected from of the coding matrix G. When any α_i is not equal and is not zero, the Vandermonde Matrix meets the requirement; That is, the square matrix, which composed of arbitrary k columns, is reversibility. Let $V = (\alpha_1, \alpha_2, \ldots, \alpha_n)$, when $\alpha_i \neq 0 (i \in (1, 2, \ldots, n))$, and $\alpha_i \neq \alpha_j (i \neq j)$, so let

$$G = \begin{bmatrix} \alpha_1^0 & \alpha_2^0 & \cdots & \alpha_n^0 \\ \alpha_1^1 & \alpha_2^1 & \cdots & \alpha_n^1 \\ \cdots & \cdots & & \cdots \\ \alpha_1^{k-1} & \alpha_2^{k-1} & \cdots & \alpha_n^{k-1} \end{bmatrix}$$

Therefore, a square matrix consisting of any arbitrary k columns is reversible. In theory, as long as k is large enough, any record can be encoded. However, the value of α_i^k increases exponentially with k increases. We can choose arbitrary k-th order invertible from G with high probability. According to random linear fountain coding, the probability of reversal for a k-th order square matrix, which is extracted from $k \times (k + \varepsilon)$ binary matrix, is 1-σ, where $\sigma = 2^{-\varepsilon}$. Thus, the binary matrix is adopted as the encoding matrix.

Hash Calculation

If there is data tampering in the data block, the server only needs to recalculate the Hash value of the data and compare it with the Hash value of the stored data block to distinguish the tampering data.

If the server itself cannot identify the tampering data, then the server should be less likely to successfully respond to the user's challenge to the server!

3.1.2   Verification of Electronic Record

The verification process of the electronic record is as follows

Build Block Tag of Electronic Record

Firstly, the electronic record is divided into n blocks by fountain coding, and then three master keys Key_1, Key_2 and Key_3 are calculated. The number of "challenge-response" is t and the number of blocks per challenge is s. Let $s = k + \varepsilon$ and $\varepsilon = -\ln \sigma$, σ is the probability of decoding failure. Finally, the tag of verification is calculated for each response, and the encoded record block, hash value and encryption verification tag are stored in the cloud server. The i-th verification tag is calculated as follows:

(1) Use the function f to calculate the i-th pre-processing key PK_i, and use the function h to calculate the index pre-processing key CK_i, where f and h both use the AES encryption function:

$$\begin{cases} Pk_i = f_{key_1}(i) \\ Ck_i = h_{key_2}(i) \end{cases}$$

(2) Use index preprocessing key CK_i and pseudo-random function g to calculate record block index I_j: $I_j = g_{Ck_i}(j)$, $I_j \in [1, 2, \ldots, t]$; $1 \subseteq j \leq n$

(3) Calculate i-th tag to be encrypted Tag_i and encrypt it using the function AES:

$$Tag_i = Hash(PK_i, Block(I_1), Hash(Block(I_1)), \ldots, Block(I_s), Hash(Block(I_s))$$

$$Tag'_i = AES_{key_3}(i, Tag_i)$$

Verification

In the i-th challenge process, the user firstly sends two preprocessing keys PK_i and CK_i calculated in the establishment phase to the server; the server calculates the tag Tag_i to be encrypted by using PK_i and CK_i and stores the encrypted verification label Tag'_i sent to the user, the user uses the server to return the label decoding, if the decryption is successful, then the verification is successful, otherwise the verification fails.

In the testing process, because the correct testing has no influence on the system, this article only analyzes the probability of misdetection. Suppose the user part of the data has been tampered with and the probability of verification is P_{esc}, so there is

$$P_{esc} = \left(1 - \frac{t}{n}\right)^s \tag{1}$$

Where t is the number of deleted or tampered data blocks, n is the total number of data blocks, and s is the number of blocks of authentication data. When the deleted ratio is $t/n = 1\%$ or the tampered ratio is $s = 512$, $P_{esc} \leq 0.6$. From (1) we can see that the larger s, the smaller the probability of false detection. In this paper, the amount of verification data $s = k + \varepsilon$ in the system ensures that the original data can be recovered with a high probability while ensuring the verification efficiency. However, the system in this paper also needs to consider the data verification failure. When the data verification fails, the server restores the data.

3.1.3 Recovery of Electronic Record

When user authentication fails, the server is provided with error feedback information k (k indicates the original data block size, i.e., the data block required for restoration or decoding). The server immediately uses the stored hash value to verify with the data block. If the verification succeeds, It is considered that the code block has not been tampered with, otherwise it is considered that the code block has been tampered with. Server statistics verify the number of code blocks passed v, if $v < k$ then that data recovery cannot be considered, or use the complete code block again tamper detection.

Tamper Detection

Assuming that the data information D before encoding is intact, the corresponding symbol C is also correct. Therefore, only the corresponding data information after coding is tampered with, and both the encoding matrix G and the symbol C may be tamper.

If some symbols C are tampered with, ΔC is a tampered part, the new symbol C^* can be expressed as $C^* = C + \Delta C$; correspondingly, the i-th row in Q may also be tampered with. If ΔQ is the tampering information contained in Q, that is, $Q^* = Q + \Delta Q$, then the corresponding decoding process $D^* = Q * P^{-1} = (Q + \Delta Q)\, P^{-1} = D + \Delta D$ (where ΔD is the tampering information included in the decoding process). Therefore, the k blocks included in the decoded information D^* when there is data tampering in G, $P^* = P + \Delta P$, ΔP is the tampering information contained in P, corresponding to $D^* = Q(P^*)^{-1} = Q(P + \Delta P)^{-1} = D + \Delta D$, that is, the decoding result is D^*, so tampering detection is necessary. The detection principle is as follows: Since DG = C randomly selects the correct check code block different from the decoding element Q from the data $Block_{k+1}$, it compares DG_{k+1} and C_{k+1} However, when $DG_{k+1} = C_{k+1}$, there is no tampering in the decoded data, otherwise, tampering is considered.

The server accepts the feedback parameter k from the user and calculates the hash value of the data block to obtain the correct code block set S, then selects k + 1 data blocks from the set S for self-verification. If Tamper detection is successful, the hash value of the indexed k + 1 data block is calculated and then the hash value is calculated and then the index order and the hash value are transmitted to the user. The user calculates and verifies the hash value according to the server index sequence and U leaf.

If the verification succeeds, the user sends the new coding matrix G_{n+1} to the server, and the server uses the decoding result in combination with G_{n+1} for coding and calculates the hash value of the finally coded symbol to send it. To the user, the user to verify the final result. If the verification fails and the server is required to verify again, the server sends the order of the code blocks in the set S and the hash value to the user. The user compares the hash value of the corresponding symbol, and if the verified number is greater than k, compares the result with G_{n+1} to the server, otherwise the report fails. The user calculates the hash value by himself and compares the result of the server calculation. If the result is consistent, it considers that the decoding is successful and instructs the server to recover the tampered data or the decoding fails. The following will analyze the accuracy of tampering detection.

Error Location and Recovery of Electronic Record
If the server tampering detection and verification is correct, then the server will be verified by the data block combination and calculate $VerS_1$:

$$VerS_1 = \text{Hash}(Sleaf_{I_1}, Sleaf_{I_2}, \ldots, Sleaf_{I_k});$$
$$I_i \in (1, 2, \ldots, n), i \in (1, 2, \ldots, k)$$

Where $Sleaf_i$ is the hash value corresponding to the i-th code block in the server. The server returns the sequence of $VerS_1$ and index to the user, which is calculated by the user according to the ordered index set Sub and its own stored hash value $Uleaf_i = \text{Hash}(Block_i)$. $VerU_1 = \text{Hash}(Uleaf_i)(i \in \text{Sub})$; when the authentication is successful, the user sends an instruction to request the server to recover the damaged data block.

When the user fails the verification again, the server sends the hash value $Sleaf_i$ corresponding to the block number i of the locally verified data block to the user, and the user verifies again to respond. In the verification process, the user XORs or statistically verifies the data obtained from the server with the corresponding hash value, and if the correct number is less than k, the data can not be recovered; otherwise, the index number and the encoding matrix are sent to Server; the server uses the index data block received from the user to decode and encode again, and sends the calculated hash value of the encoded symbol to the user, if the verification is correct, the data is updated; otherwise, the data recovery fails.

In the process of data restoration, the server randomly generates a new random matrix G and codes $C_{n+i} = DG_{n+i}$ (where $1 \leq i \leq$ n), and composes G_j and C_j into a new data $Block_j = \{G_j, C_j\}$ (where j > n + 1) instead of being tampered with and updating the corresponding Sleaf (i) by recalculating the hash value of the data block. After the server repairs the entire data, the server sends the Hash value of the updated data block to the user, and the user also updates the Hash value.

3.2 Completeness of Electronic Record

In classical relational data systems, functional dependency theory defines the semantics of the relationship between attributes, the theory is the abstract reflection of the built-in link of real-world data and plays an important role in designing data normalization, integrating schema, optimizing query, updating data and etc. In recent years, researchers have begun to use it to data cleaning, assign the relationship of semantic between the data, and detect incomplete data.

3.2.1 Completeness of Electronic Record Based on Functional Dependency Theory

In the section, the function dependency is used to detect the data completeness. A detecting example of attribute completeness is following, and other detections of the completeness are similar. Firstly, the specific measurement of the relational data completeness is defined. Let F be a relational functional dependency set. And measure functions of attribute completeness based on functional dependency is present as following.

Definition 3. True Complete Attribute Value.

Let t be any tuple of the relation $R(U,F)$, A is any attribute of R, X is a group of attribute of R. If $t[A]$ meets any one of the following 2 conditions, so $t[A]$ is a complete attribute value:

(1) $t[A]$ is not null;
(2) $t[A]$ is null, but F contains a functional dependency $X \rightarrow A$, which satisfied that $t[Y]$ is not null, for any $Y \in X$.

When the relation $R(U,F)$ is input, where $U = \{A_1, \cdots, A_m\}$ is an attribute set of R, F is a set of functional dependencies, R contains N tuples. The detection will output the completeness of R, i.e., $C(R)$.

Definition 4. Dominating Attribute Set

Let R be a relation, A is one attribute of R, X is a group of attributes of R, $A \notin X$. If there is a functional dependency $X \rightarrow A$, X is called a candidate dominating attribute set of attribute A. A candidate dominating attribute set is choosed as the dominating attribute set of attribute A, recorded as $Dom(A)$. For the value of attribute $t[A]$, its corresponding value of the dominating attribute set can be expressed as $t[Dom(A)]$. If attribute B has not dominating attribute set, then $t[Dom(B)] = t[B]$. In order to express the completeness of dominating attribute set, the functional dependency $\varphi : X \rightarrow A$, implied by F, is defined as a completeness function as following.

$$\rho(\varphi, t) = \begin{cases} 1 \ \forall Y \in X, t[Y] \neq \phi \\ 0 \end{cases}$$

The completeness $C(R)$ can be understood: when there is a functional dependency $\varphi : X \rightarrow A$, judging if the value of attribute $t[B]$ of one tuple t is really null. if we can find the same value of attribute $s[B]$ of the tuple s, and current data set contains a tuple s, in which a $s[B]$ is not null, the value of attribute B, which corresponds to all the tuples that contains value of attribute $t[A]$, is not null, even if value of attribute B of one tuple is null. We can simplify this problem by the following definition:

Defining the inverse mapping of φ is $\varphi^- : B \rightarrow A$, A is a dominating attribute set of B;mapping $\tau : t[A] \rightarrow l$, where $t[A]$ is a value of attribute set A of a tuple t among R, l is an unique identifier that can be distinguished ;mapping $\omega : (l, B) \rightarrow c$, where l is a identifier, B is a attribute, satisfying $\tau(t[\varphi^-(B)]) = l$, c is 0 or 1, thus has:

$c = 1 \Leftrightarrow \exists s \in R, s[B]$ is complete $\wedge \tau(s[\varphi^-(B)]) = l \wedge \rho(\varphi, s) = 1$

when $c = 1$, we call l is complete to B。

When there are two functional dependencies $\varphi_1 : A \rightarrow B$ and $\varphi_2 : A \rightarrow C$, the mapping ω is used to distinguish the completeness, which have the same value of dominating attribute. Therefore, Assessment the completeness of the value of attribute $t[B]$ is to search all the tuples of the value of attribute $t[\varphi^-(B)]$ which has a identifier $\tau(t[\varphi^-(B)])$. All the tuples, which have this identifier, are complete, if and only if the attribute value $s[B]$ of a tuple s, which has the same identifier, is complete. So the value of the real complete attribute can be formalized as:

$\forall t \in R, t[B]$ is complete. $\Leftrightarrow (\omega(l, B) = 1 \wedge \tau(t[\varphi^-(B)]) = l) \vee t[B]$ is not null.

So the completeness of the an attribute value can be transformed into the completeness of tuple with the same identifier. Therefore, solving $C(R)$ is transformed to solve the complete identifier $D(R)$.

Definition 5. Valid Identifier

l is a valid identifier, if l meet:there is $t \in R$, attribute A, and $\tau(t[A]) = l$.

Valid identifier set

For a identifier set L, A valid attribute set $set(L)$ can be defined: $set(L) = \{l \in L | l$ is a valid identifier$\}$. When the valid identifier is the given function τ, which has the corresponding identifier of the attribute value in the data set R, and only the collections of valid identifier are the valid identifier set.

$D(R)$:input relationship $R(U, F)$, where $U = \{A_1, L, A_m\}$ is an attribute set of R, F is the functional dependency set of R, R contains N tuples, three functions φ^-, τ and ω, identifier set L. The complete identifier set will be output by completeness detection, i.e., $D(R) = \{l | \omega(l, B) = 1 \wedge l \in set(L) \wedge \exists \varphi \in F : A \to B\}$.

Known complete identifier set $D(R)$, we can get $C(R)$ by the following algorithms:

$Num_{cpl} \leftarrow 0$ // the number of values of complete attribute

$Num_{tot} \leftarrow m \times N$ // the number of all values of the attribute

for $i = 1$ to m do

for $j = 1$ to N do

if $\tau(t_j[\varphi^-(A_i)]) \in D(R)$ then $Num_{cpl} = Num_{cpl} + 1$

$C(R) = Num_{cpl}/Num_{tot}$

When judgement whether a identifier belong to complete identifier set, if there is sufficient space to store the values of the valid identifier, we can get it by directly calculating the function τ and comparing them. So we can finish it within $O(1)$ time, here the time complexity of this algorithm is $O(N)$. If the limited space, the process is similar to the binary search, so this judgment is finished within $O(\lg|D(R)|)$. Because $\lg|D(R)|$ is sufficient small, the time complexity is $O(mN \lg|D(R)|) = O(N)$; Otherwise, it is $O(N \lg N)$. If the ordinal relationship of identifier is not defined, only sequential searching is done, thus, the judgement is finished within $O(|D(R)|)$. Because $|D(R)|$ is relatively small, the time complexity is $O(mN|D(R)|) = O(N)$; otherwise it is $O(N^2)$.

Now, the algorithm of calculation $D(R)$ is present: the completeness of each identifier is judged by the completeness of other same identifies, so we need a structure to record the completeness of an identifier. The completeness record unit of the identifier is $Rlu : (l, c)$, l is an identifier, which distinguishes Rlu, and $c = 0$ is incomplete while $c = 1$ is complete. The structure DP is the set of Rlu, which includes the completeness information of all the identifiers.

Initialize a map DP

for $i = 1$ to m do

for $j = 1$ to N do

$pos = DP.find(\tau(t_j[\varphi^-(A_i)]))$

if $t_j[A_i]$ is complete then $DP.add(\tau(t_j[\varphi^-(A_i)], 1)$ else $DP.add(\tau(t_j[\varphi^-(A_i)], 0)$

else if $t_j[A_i]$ is complete then $DP[pos].c = 1$

for $i = 1$ to $|DP|$ do

If $DP[i].c = 1$ then $D(R).add(DP[i], l)$

Because each identifier is unique and distinct, and each identifier needs to move to corresponding location to change the information of the completeness, we match the identifiers with real numbers by defining a mapping, which results in the digital ordering problem reduce into the problem of calculating $D(R)$, therefore the low bound can be gotten by the digital ordering problems.

4 Conclusion

This paper firstly analyzes the relation between the digital continuity and data usability of the electronic record, and points out the necessity of ensuring the availability and completeness of the electronic record. Moreover, the technology framework of data availability for electronic record is firstly proposed. Secondly, based on functional dependency theory, the technology of ensuring data completeness for electronic record is constructed, and the method of evaluating completeness of electronic record is present using the functional dependency theory.

Acknowledgments. This work is supported by the NSFC (NO. 61772280, 61702236), Jiangsu Province Natural Science Research Program (NO. BK20130809, BK2012461) and the PAPD fund from NUIST.

This work is funded by Natural Science Foundation of Jiangsu Province under Grant BK20160955, a project funded by the Priority Academic Program Development of Jiangsu Higher Education Institutions and Science Research Foundation of Nanjing University of Information Science and Technology under Grant20110430.

References

1. UK National Archives: Digital continuity marketing brochure: if you don't protect your digital assets, they can't protect you. Accessed 25 Feb 2018. http://www.Nationalarchives. gov.uk/documents/tna-digital-continuity.pdf. Hong, K.D., Son, Y..: A Study on the Smart Virtual Machine for Executing Virtual Machine Codes on Smart Platforms, pp. 93–106. Oxford University Press, Oxford (2015)
2. Gray, J.: What next? A few remaining problems in information technology, Manhattan (1999)
3. Hasan, R., Yurcik, W., Myagmar, S.: The evolution of storage service providers: techniques and challenges to outsourcing storage, ACM SSS 2005, pp. 1–8 (2005)
4. Ren, Y., Shen, J., Wang, J., Han, J., Lee, S.: Mutual verifiable provable data auditing in public cloud storage. J. Internet Technol. **16**(2), 317–323 (2015)
5. Zhangjie, F., Xinle, W., Guan, C., Sun, X., Ren, K.: Toward efficient multi-keyword fuzzy search over encrypted outsourced data with accuracy improvement. IEEE Trans. Inf. Forensics Secur. **11**(12), 2706–2716 (2016)
6. Zhangjie, F., Huang, F., Ren, K., Weng, J., Wang, C.: Privacy-preserving smart semantic search based on conceptual graphs over encrypted outsourced data. IEEE Trans. Inf. Forensics Secur. **12**(8), 1874–1884 (2017)
7. Gargn, N., Bawa, S.: Comparative analysis of cloud data integrity auditing protocols. J. Netw. Comput. Appl. **66**, 17–32 (2016)
8. Zhangjie, F., Xinle, W., Wang, Q., Ren, K.: Enabling central keyword-based semantic extension search over encrypted outsourced data. IEEE Trans. Inf. Forensics Secur. **12**(12), 2986–2997 (2017)
9. Ding, X., Wang, H., Zhang, X., Li, J., Gao, H.: Association relationships study of multi-dimensional data quality. J. Softw. **27**(7), 1626–1644 (2016)

Distributed Monitoring System for Microservices-Based IoT Middleware System

Rui Kang[✉], Zhenyu Zhou, Jiahua Liu, Zhongran Zhou,
and Shunwang Xu

Nari Group Corporation, State Grid Electric Power Research Institute,
Beijing, China
kangrui@sgepri.sgcc.com.cn

Abstract. Microservices based architecture is a promising middleware architecture of Internet of things for its advantages of agility and scalability. However, comparing to the native Service oriented Architecture (SOA), the widespread nature, no matter logically or physically, of this lightweight middleware system has made its organization, tracing and monitoring much harder, which could further compromise the effectiveness and performance. To this end, we design, implement and evaluate a new distributed monitoring system for microservices-based middleware of Internet of Things, which is designed as a cloud native system. This system is featured with supporting Kubernetes orchestration, instrument Java and Spring Cloud framework and owing the ability to obtain the performance metrics from all host and containers in an efficient way. Furthermore, it could collect the trace generated by a call from application frontend to each layered microservices, even fetching logging, and finally store them in a big data system for stream processing or map/reduce. The real implementation based evaluation has demonstrated the effectiveness of this system design.

Keywords: Middleware · Internet of Things · Microservice
Monitoring system

1 Introduction

1.1 Background

The Internet of Things (IoT) is being adopted in different application domains and is recognized as one of the key enablers of the future vision. Despite the standardization efforts and wide adoption of Web standards and cloud-computing technologies, however, building large-scale IoT middleware platforms in practice remains challenging.

One of the many challenges imposed by the Internet of Things (IoT) is building software systems and platforms that enable the cross-domain applications, such as smart grid/smart city platforms. Many research and standardization efforts has been put into dealing with the heterogeneity of IoT devices and communication protocols [37, 38], as well as service interoperability layers and frameworks [39, 40].

© Springer Nature Switzerland AG 2018
X. Sun et al. (Eds.): ICCCS 2018, LNCS 11063, pp. 467–477, 2018.
https://doi.org/10.1007/978-3-030-00006-6_43

The prevailing IoT middleware system are mostly developed with SOA architecture using microservices [1] and Docker [2] container to delivery into cloud computing infrastructure. SOA and microservices are two major architectures that are being used for decomposing systems into services. Both SOA and microservices suggest decomposition of systems into services available over a network and integratable across heterogeneous platforms. In both approaches, services co-operate to provide functionality for the overall system and thus share the same goal; however, the path to achieving the goal is different. SOA focuses on design of system decomposition into simple services, emphasizing service integration with smart routing mechanisms for the entire company's IT. Owning largest global system successfully, Google in 2010 published paper to explain his distributed tracing technology called Dapper [3], Some organization follow this concept of design and establish open source projects for example OpenZipkin [4] (Twitter contributed), Jaeger [5] (Uber contributed). Now Jaeger becomes incubating project of Cloud Native Computing Foundation under Linux Foundation, it coordinated with another incubating project called OpenTracing [6] providing distributed tracing infrastructure for microservices. In the side of computing resource management, Google also published a paper describing the Borgmon [7], and it leads one of engineers later establishing open source project Prometheus [8].

1.2   Motivations and Challenges

The monitoring system has large impact on the control and adjustment for the middleware system. It plays a very important role that all of machines and software are controlled under a monitoring system. It must has capable of metering distributed computing environments, watching Docker networking and microservices architecture, finding out resource usage, trace and log.

However, the large scale middleware systems have risen up many problems that existing maintaining tools may not work well to watch performance and manage trouble. Specifically, (1) microservices are resilience instance, so that the cloud platform allocates load balancer for them, control to scale up during runtime, the web frontend, middleware and database server were deployed in many work node. (2) Besides, when a request is arrived, the HTTP or TCP/UDP handle will be called from node to node through many virtual networks. (3) Furthermore, once a certain node becomes failure, it could affect application to damage infrastructure such as process out-of-memory and networking exhaustion. However, the distributed logging system have been a matured technology aggregating logs from cluster to perform centralized analysis, but it has limited function that it could not resolve causal relation of events as lacking request context.

1.3   Contributions

Considering aforementioned challenges, we propose a new distributed monitoring system design with real implementation and evaluation. Our work could serve as the new reference paradigm to design the middleware monitoring system. In summary, we mainly make following contributions:

- We propose an efficient and lightweight monitoring framework for microservices-based IoT middleware system, which could tackle the challenge of distributed data source and provide real time tracing.
- We implement our design into a real system and provide a real experiment based evaluation.
- The system could collect the trace generated by a call from application frontend to each layered microservices, even fetching logging, and finally store them in a big data system for stream processing or map/reduce.

2 Related Works

SOA and microservice based middleware system are correlated reference model for implementation. One of the main issues in SOA is system versioning since we do not know the service users. There are even cases when a company maintains over 20 different versions of the same service with a slightly modified interface to accept different data [33]. Microservices, on the contrary, suggest decomposition preferring smart services while considering simple routing mechanisms [27], without the global governance notable in SOA. Microservice followers often cite Conway's law [36], stating that "Organizations, which design systems are constrained to produce designs which are copies of the communication structures of these organizations.". It is fairly easy to selectively deploy overloaded microservice in order to scale it; however, it is not easy in SOA [29]. Self-contained microservices are more efficient when it comes to elasticity, scalability, automated, and continuous deploy with fast demand response. The above characteristics make microservices more cloud-friendly [30].

Industry seems to be in the shift towards microservices, leaving SOA behind. However, microservices are not a superset of SOA and many of its challenges do not exist in SOA. Various interpretations of these architectures [31] put part of the community on the side considering microservices to be a subset of SOA, although many others [32] see them as distinct architectures. According to Red Hat [34], SOA community considers the transition to microservices because the common SOA practice ties services to complex protocols stacks, such as SOAP, a protocol for web service communication, and WSDL, to describe a service [35].

In the recent years, a number of standards for the physical, network, and transport layers, as well as security mechanisms tailored to resource-constrained IoT devices have been introduced. The recently standardized CoAP [37] and MQTT [38] protocols together with HTTP finalize the protocol stack by building an application layer. The efforts focusing on interoperability across different application domains include IoT-A [40], OneM2 M [39], and FI-WARE [41]. IoT-A is a research project developing an Architectural Reference Model for IoT solutions. OneM2 M [39] is a global telecom initiative for interoperability of M2 M (Machine-to-Machine) and IoT devices and applications. Its main goal is to develop a common specification of a Service Layer Platform that builds on the existing IoT and Web standards, defining specifications of protocols and service APIs. Providing high-level APIs of services, OneM2 M defines a specification for interoperability of IoT platforms at the service layer. FI-WARE [41] is a research project aiming at building a platform for the Future Internet that would provide a novel service infrastructure built of reusable components (Generic Enablers). Several systems for specific use cases have been developed by the partners of the FI-WARE project so far [40, 42], and it remains to be seen whether it will receive adoption in the wider community. In [43], authors show that the level of generalization provided by the FI-WARE platform may lead to overly complex architecture in simple applications. The experience of the Web and the success of distributed systems built using its basic principles [45] encourages simple standards and flexibility in their implementation. Using Web standards and experience is recognized as a common approach to building IoT platforms. E.g., the urban IoT system described in [46] is built using RESTful Web services approach to design the service platform part of the system. The Web-based approach is also recommended by the IoT-A and has been successfully adopted in other projects to build Smart City platforms, e.g., SmartSantander [47] and ALMANAC [48].

3   System Design

3.1   Architecture

It is designed running with Docker and Kubernetes [10] orchestration as shown in Fig. 1. The components include data sample services, data collector services, big data sub-system, and monitoring dashboard. Data is processed from metrics, traces and logs into watching and alarm result. Metrics is metered by Google's cAdvisor [11], which can direct manage data from Docker host and it's containers, we developed an agent to polling data from cAdvisor, or from Heapster [12] that resided at Kubernetes. The agent service is responsible of sampling data and push to collector, another service receive and aggregate data from agents, transform them into structural and store as big data. We also developed trace sampling agent, implemented an OpenTracing API client as instrumentation of application language. The instrumentation create trace and spread it over request chains. This distributed information shall be sent to agent, and then another collecting service. All metering, tracing, logging data are analyzed in a big data system, to input alarm information and performance charts and trends.

3.2   Metrics Measurement

The measurement data indicate standard machine resource and their usage, networking throughput. We use Docker Compose [13] deploy both cAdvisor and our metering agent in each machine, but metering agent must be deployed alone for Kubernetes environment. Time series data modal is adopted.

Time Series Data Modal
Time series can represent streams of value which include timestamp. It is widely used in sensor, Internet of Thing, even in finance. We use following data modal mainly matching Map/Reduce processing.

Metric name: Every time series must be specified its general features, for example CPU_usage, the name must match such regular expression: [a-zA-Z_:][a-zA-Z0-9:]*.

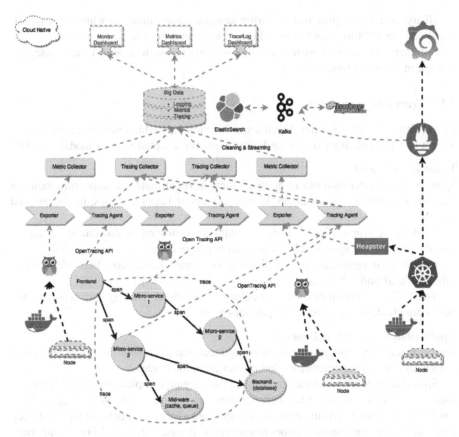

Fig. 1. Architecture of distributed metering and tracing

Labels: Every time series labeled a set of key/value pairs and uniquely identified in name and labels. Labels are for query and analysis dimensions, for example docker_image="foo", container_name="bar". The regular expression of label's key is [a-zA-Z_][a-zA-Z0-9_]*.

Samples: Sample are measured value from device at certain time. It is float64 data type.

Time series data structure can be encode into a particular notation for interchange among services. The notation is developed by OpenTSDB [14], it is like JOSN but has little difference and simpler, The format is defined as <metric name> {<labek name>=<label value>,...}.

Metric Data Type

Counter: A incremental numerical value, particularly used to count errors, request accumulation and so on.

Gauge: A arbitrary numerical value, typically used to meter for example CPU usage, memory allocating.

Histogram: A complex metric during samples observations in where it has additional counter field to record observations, a total sum field to count value.

Summary: A complex metric just like histogram, but it is used to calculate percentage in a sliding time window.

3.3 Traces Measurement

OpenTracing organization developed a specification [15] which became an incubating project of Cloud Native Computing Foundation. We adopted its data modal and API.

Trace Data Modal
Span: A logical operation object in which there have attributes of name, timestamp of creation, timestamp of termination, key/value pairs of labels and logs, its context and causality.

Context: A propagation data that is uniquely identified in distributed system, it include trace id and span id, also additional baggage items.

Causality: It represents the relationship of spans. There have two relationships called childOf and followFrom.

Trace: The collection of spans that belongs a call chain. The top span is parent, and others are child, or are follower of previous span.

Application Programing Interface
Tracer: It is an application instrument to produce span in edge of microservices, inject context in networking bandwidth and extract at another side.

Span data type: A data structure or object of language implementation. It include a context field that uniquely identified between services in a call chain. Tags field is consisting of some key/value pairs used query and analysis. Structured log field keep language, library and runtime errors or exception. Baggage items field is for important message that a call chain should take care.

Span context: An immutable functionality interface to access span.

3.4 Cloud Native

This monitoring system is designed to deploy into public or private cloud infrastructure, such as Aliyun, Baidu Cloud, Huawei Cloud, vSphere, OpenStack or Bare metal. The collector service must be configured with load balancer or provided scalability.

Our services expose a HTTP health check endpoint healthz, It is used for Docker and Kubernetes to test heartbeat its self. For example, It normally response HTTP status code 204 (no content). Also they are instrumented with Prometheus client for metrics scrapper (Figs 2 and 3).

3.5 Big Data Storage Component

We use open source projects ElasticSearch [16], Kafka [17], and Hadoop (HDFS, Map/Reduce and HBASE) to create Big Data system for data store of metrics, traces and logs stream, and generate information via ElasticSearch JSON Query. For detected events, we use Kafka message and stream to process alarm result on time. Here, Hadoop worked as archive backend.

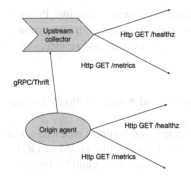

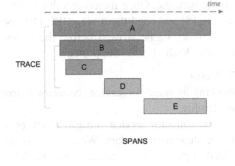

Fig. 2. Cloud native application   **Fig. 3.** Distribute tracing data modal

3.6 Kubernetes Orchestration

All monitoring components are delivered with Docker images and can be deployed via Kubernetes except of cAdvisor. Both agent and collector are managed as ReplicaSet, in contrast, ElasticSearch and Kafka are managed as StatefulSet.

Some open source can give each good features but not fit with a real enterprise completely, these inspired us to develop ourselves solution, it is designed of cloud native, firstly cloud monitor Docker and Kubernetes. The projects are open sourced at Github [9].

4 Implementation and Evaluation

4.1 Implementation Details

In this section, we mainly describe the implementation details of our system. Specifically, we specify the agent and the collectors, the distributed tracking and the other implementation details.

Metrics Measurement Agent and Collector

The measurement application is developed by Golang language, using Makefile to manage two services in one project, build both Agent and Collector Docker images with Dockerfile.

Golang's static link get us benefits of minimizing Docker image size. We use busybox as base image, thus our image only occupy ten and several Megabytes of all compute storage resources.

Agent

Generally agent service is working with cAdvisor together in each Docker compute node, while in Kubernetes, cAdvisor is not required. Instead, heapster must be deployed. The agent service default configured with a single processor core.

According 12-factors of microservices, agent is configured with command arguments or process environments for cAdvisor and Heapster service endpoint, and their polling periodic. Once metering value is fetched, agent transformed data into Protocol Buffer [18] and send them via gRPC [19] using goroutines for gain high concurrency.

Memory cache is used before the information is sent to collector service. Alternatively, Redis [20] is supported.

Collector

Working as stateless service, collector is load balanced and scaled by cloud for high availability.

The collector service is a gRPC server, it aggregates, and samples received value before store into big data. When event is arrived, even fatal log like OOM or OOM-Killed, it publish such message info Kafka where alarm generator should be triggered in time.

Protocol Buffer: It is developed by Google, and used to serialize structured data for RPC and HTTP/2. The payloads are very smaller compared with other technology, for example JSON. We defined Protocol Buffer of metering value exchanging between agent and collector, e.g. CPU and memory.

It worth to mention that the protocol buffer also worked for IDL(Interface Definition Language) of RPC framework, we use gRPC, a high performance client/server communication programming technology that can managing many transitions in one connection.

Distributed Tracing of Microservices

The tracing agent and collector are also Golang applications and Docker image delivery. Tracing agent has include an application instrumentation implemented OpenTracing API. Instrumentation is worked as client to instantiate tracer for manage span for agent, and inject and extract span context as carrier over distributed networking. Collector service received traces and span from agent, stored into big data after validation.

Instrumentation Library

Instrumentation is language and platform dependent OpenTracing API client, currently planned to support Golang and Java. The following demonstration combine instruments into Spring Boot [22] microservice developmet. Furthermore, Spring Framework [21] doesn't provide OpenTracing instrumentation API, there is an alternative way using low level library such as ApacheHttpClient to explicitly instrument tracing. Deeply, we can make a tracing extension for framework.

Traces Agent

Agent service deployed into each compute node, it is sampling traces and sending them to collector. Agent is worked at UDP transportation layer forwarding traces to collector. it is compatible with OpenZipkin using Apache Thrift [23] for data sterilization format and RPC communication.

Traces Collector

Collector service is also an Apache Thrift server, scaled in cloud to serve many agents. Collector is responsible of sample validation, indexing and time series transformation. If trace log include exception or error, it will produce triggered message to Kakfa to request alarm processing.

Apache Thrift

Apache Thrift is developed by Facebook and contributed to Apache Foundation. It is another popular RPC framework unifying interface definition, request arguments and returning data, its compiler support to generate client and service code for popular language like C, Go, Java, Python and so on.

PaaS integration

We have chosen Spring Cloud Netflix [24] as our Platform as a Service, and are using its circuit breaks component called Hystrix to develop and deploy microservices. We planned to extend tracing function into these components for example:

Big Data

The monitoring data can be directly queried from ElasticSearch according business logic. The alarm event are driven by Kafka pipe line to perform real time Map/Reduce. For history archiving, we are planning to use Hadoop for data mining.

Dashboard

The monitoring user interface is based on Java and HTML5, it is usually presenting monitoring information with tables and charts, with detailed analysis, and watching alarm event by consuming Kafka messages.

4.2   Evaluation Results

In this section, we provide the information regarding the performance. Specifically, we mainly provides the performance of response time for different type of transactions which is illustrated in Fig. 4.

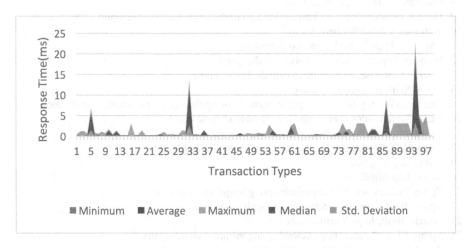

Fig. 4. Response time for different transactions

From this figure, we can easily tell that, for more than 98 types of query and search transactions over the distributed middleware system with 100 monitoring nodes, the maximum response delay is smaller than 25 miniseconds, while the average is smaller than 5 miniseconds. These results has illustrate the effectiveness of our system.

5 Conclusion

In this paper, we introduced a new distributed monitoring system for microservices based IoT monitoring System. It is based on industry standard monitoring data modal and architecture, resulting with big data processing. This structure is featured with compatible with Docker and kubernetes, which will be further benefit the cloud end data analysis and data mining. Both the structure design and implementation details are preseted. The real implementation based evaluation has demonstrate the advantage of this system.

References

1. Microservices. http://microservices.io
2. Docker. https://www.docker.com
3. Sigelman, B.H.: Dapper, a Large-Scale Distributed Systems Tracing Infrastructure. Google (2010). https://research.google.com/archieve/papers/dapper-2010-1.pdf
4. OpenZipkin. http://zipkin.io
5. Jaeger. http://jaeger.readthedocs.io/en/latest
6. OpenTracing. http://opentracing.io
7. Verma, A.: Large-scale cluster management at Google with Borg. Google (2015). https://research.google.com/pubs/archive/43438.pdf
8. Prometheus. https://prometheus.io
9. Github. https://github.com/tangfeixiong/go-to-docker/tree/master/metering
10. Kubernetes. https://kubernetes.io
11. cAdvisor. https://github.com/google/cadvisor
12. heapster. https://github.com/kubernetes/heapster
13. Docker Compose. https://github.com/dockre/compose
14. OpenTSDB. http://opentsdb.net
15. The OpenTracing Semantic Specification. https://github.com/opentracing/specification
16. ElasticSearch. https://www.elastic.co/products/elasticsearch
17. Kafka. https://kafka.apache.org
18. Protocol Buffer. https://developers.google.com/protocol-buffers
19. gRPC. https://grpc.io
20. Redis. https://redis.io
21. Spring Framework. https://projects.spring.io/spring-framework
22. Spring Boot. https://projects.spring.io/spring-boot
23. Apache thrift. https://thrift.apache.org
24. Spring Cloud Netflix. https://cloud.spring.io/spring-cloud-netflix
25. Apache spark. http://spark.apache.org
26. Murphy, N.: Site Reliability Engineering. O'Reilly Media, Sebastopol (2016). http://shop.oreilly.com/product/0636920041528.do

27. Balalaie, A., Heydarnoori, A., Jamshidi, P.: Migrating to cloud-native architectures using microservices: an experience report. In: Celesti, A., Leitner, P. (eds.) ESOCC Workshops 2015. CCIS, vol. 567, pp. 201–215. Springer, Cham (2016). https://doi.org/10. 1007/978-3-319-33313-7_15

28. Wolff, E.: Microservices: Flexible Software Architectures. CreateSpace Independent Publishing Platform (2016)

29. Xiao, Z., Wijegunaratne, I., Qiang, X.: Reflections on SOA and microservices. In: 4th International Conference on Enterprise Systems (ES), pp. 60–67 (2016)

30. Kratzke, N., Quint, P.-C.: Understanding cloud-native applications after 10 years of cloud computing - a systematic mapping study. J. Syst. Softw. **126**, 1–16 (2017)

31. Fowler, M.: Microservices resource guide (2016). http://martinfowler.com/microservices

32. Richards, M.: Microservices Vs Service-oriented Architecture. O'Reilly Media, Sebastopol (2015)

33. Cerny, T., Donahoo, Michael J.: Survey on concern separation in service integration. In: Freivalds, R.M., Engels, G., Catania, B. (eds.) SOFSEM 2016. LNCS, vol. 9587, pp. 518–531. Springer, Heidelberg (2016). https://doi.org/10.1007/978-3-662-49192-8_42

34. Cerny, M., Donahoo, J., Pechanec, J.: Disambiguation and comparison of soa, microservices and self-contained systems. In: Proceedings of the International Conference on Research in Adaptive and Convergent Systems, RACS 2017, pp. 228–235. ACM, New York (2017)

35. Josuttis, N.: Soa in Practice. O'Reilly Media, Sebastopol (2007)

36. Conway, M.E.: How do committees invent. Datamation **14**(4), 28–31 (1968)

37. Shelby, Z., Hartke, K., Bormann, C.: The Constrained Application Protocol (CoAP) (2014). http://coap.technology/

38. Message Queue Telemetry Transport (MQTT). http://mqtt.org

39. OneM2 M Alliance. http://onem2m.org

40. Zhao, Y., Wu, J., Li, W., Lu, S., Chen, B.: Navigation-driven handoff minimization in wireless networks. Wirel. Commun., Mob. Comput. (2017)

41. FI-WARE project. http://fi-ware.org

42. Havlik, D. et al.: Future Internet enablers for VGI applications (2013)

43. Chang, W., Jie, W.: Progressive or conservative: rationally allocate cooperative work in mobile social networks. IEEE Trans. Parallel Distrib. Syst. **26**(7), 2020–2035 (2015)

44. Chang, W., Jie, W., Tan, C.C.: Improving cooperative trajectory mapping applications with encounter-based error correction. Int. J. Parallel Emergent Distrib. Syst. **29**(1), 68–89 (2014)

45. Fielding, R.T.: Architectural styles and the design of network-based software architectures. Ph.D. dissertation, University of California, Irvine (2000)

46. Zhao, Y., Li, W., Wu, J., Lu, S.: Quantized conflict graphs for wireless network optimization. In: IEEE Conference on Computer Communications (INFOCOM 2015), Hong Kong, April 26–30, 2015

47. Theodoridis, E., Mylonas, G., Chatzigiannakis, I.: Developing aniot smart city framework. In: Fourth International Conference on Information, Intelligence, Systems and Applications (IISA) 2013, pp. 1–6, July 2013

48. ALMANAC project Web site. www.almanacproject.eu/

Efficient Processing of Top-K Dominating Queries on Incomplete Data Using MapReduce

Xiangwu Ding[1], Chao Yan[1(✉)], Yuan Zhao[2], and Zewei Yang[3]

[1] Donghua University, Songjiang 201620, Shanghai, China
yc.0616@qq.com
[2] New York University, New York City, NY 10003, USA
[3] Yangzhou University, Yangzhou 225000, Jiangsu, China

Abstract. Top-k dominating queries, which return the k best items with a comprehensive "goodness" criterion based on dominance, have attracted considerable attention recently due to its important role in many data mining applications including multi-criteria decision making. In the Big Data era, the modes of data storage and processing are becoming distributed, and data is incomplete commonly in some real applications. The related existing researches focus on centralized datasets, or on complete data in distributed environments, and do not involve incomplete data in distributed environments. In this work, we present the first study for processing top-k dominating queries on incomplete data in distributed environments. We show that, through detailed analysis, even though the dominance relation on incomplete data objects is non-transitive in general, the transitive dominance relation holds for some incomplete data objects with different bitmaps. We then propose an novel algorithm TKDI-MR based on MapReduce for processing TKD queries on incomplete data in distributed environments utilizing the aforementioned property. Extensive experiments with both real-world and large-scale synthetic datasets demonstrate that our approach is able to achieve good efficiency and stability.

Keywords: Incomplete data · Top-k dominating queries
Distributed environments · MapReduce

1 Introduction

Top-k queries [6] and skyline queries [1,7] are two types of preference-based queries which have been studied extensively in the past. The top-k dominating (TKD) queries [2,8,10,13] take advantage of both top-k and skyline queries,

This work is supported by the Jiangsu Natural Science Foundation (No. 202010006) and the Project of Shanghai Information Development Special Fund (No. XX-XXFZ-05-16-0139).

© Springer Nature Switzerland AG 2018
X. Sun et al. (Eds.): ICCCS 2018, LNCS 11063, pp. 478–489, 2018.
https://doi.org/10.1007/978-3-030-00006-6_44

and have received increasing attention in recent years since Papadias et al. [10] introduced the idea of TKD queries. A TKD query returns the k objects that dominate the maximum number of objects in a given dataset. Researchers have studied efficient algorithms for the processing of TKD queries [2,5,8–10,12–14], but most were focused either entirely on complete and incomplete data in centralized environments or entirely on complete data in distributed environments. In the era of Big Data, while more and more data brings new opportunities to TKD queries, it brings challenges as well: (i) The data quality problem is already a basic problem faced by data scientists, and incomplete data is common poor quality data [11]; (ii) The modes of storage and data processing are gradually shifting towards distributed [4].

In a real-time air quality acquisition system, it is difficult to collect complete data because of some objective factors. Table 1 shows the concentration data of air pollutants[1] from four stations at the same time in Beijing. The dash ("-") represents a missing data. The dominance relation on both complete and incomplete data is not of reflexivity or symmetry. The dominance relation is not of transitivity on incomplete data rather transitive on complete data. Taking data in Table 1 as an example, according to the definition of dominance on incomplete data, p_4 dominates p_3, p_3 dominates p_2. Since p_4 does not dominate p_2, the dominance relation is not of transitivity. If p_2 dominates p_4 (doesn't appear in Table 1), there would be a cyclical domination. Researches, processing TKD queries on incomplete data in centralized environments, are recently carried out. MIAO et al. [9] proposed a set of related algorithms in 2016.

Table 1. Air pollutant concentration data.

ID	Site	Air pollutants ($\mu g/m^3$)					
		SO_2	NO_2	$PM2.5$	O_3	$PM10$	CO
p_1	Longevity Nishinomiya	23	-	105	4	-	0.5
p_2	Dingling	64	64	84	40	-	5.2
p_3	Dongsi	62	-	67	24	90	1.9
p_4	Temple of Heaven	52	70	27	18	12	0.7
p_5	Dongdan	-	-	120	28	-	6

There is not much research work available for the processing of TKD queries on complete data in distributed environments. In literature [2], two effective algorithms are proposed based on dominance transitivity. However, for the TKD queries on incomplete data in distributed environments, to the best of our knowledge, there are no related researches yet. It will be more challenging since incomplete data does not have dominance transitivity in general. Therefore, an urgent problem has emerged as how to effectively perform TKD queries on incomplete data in distributed environments.

---

[1] https://data.epmap.org.

In this paper, we present the first systematic study for efficient processing of TKD queries on incomplete data in distributed environments. Through detailed analysis, it is found that, even dominance relation on incomplete data is not transitive in general, the dominance relation among some incomplete data objects with different bitmaps is of transitivity. For dealing with such queries on massive incomplete data, an efficient algorithm using MapReduce is proposed.

Contributions. In summary, the contributions of this paper are listed as follows:

- This paper studies the problems of TKD queries on incomplete data in distributed environments. According to the author's knowledge, this issue has not been resolved.
- Through detailed analysis, we find that, the dominance relation among some incomplete data objects with different bitmaps is of transitivity.
- Based on the nature above, a novel algorithm TKDI-MR using MapReduce is proposed. The efficiency and performance of TKDI-MR are verified through extensive experiments against diverse algorithms on synthetic and real datasets.

Roadmap. The rest of the article is organized as follows: Sect. 2 outlines related work in the area. Section 3 introduces some preliminary concepts regarding the topic of the research, and Sect. 4 describes the details of the TKDI-MR algorithm. Then, Sect. 5 offers performance evaluations based on diverse datasets and algorithms. Finally, Sect. 6 concludes the work and discusses future work in the area briefly.

2   Related Work

The processing of TKD queries is expensive as it requires exhaustive pairwise comparison operations to determine the dominance relation. The search space for TKD queries is the most important factor that influences the performance of the processing, and most researches concentrate on strategies deriving TKD objects by pruning search space as much as possible. Here, we present some related methods for processing TKD queries on complete and incomplete data in centralized environments, as well as complete data in distributed environments.

TKD queries take advantage of skyline queries and top-k queries. Papadias et al. [10] first put forward the idea of TKD query in 2005, and used K-dominating-BBS algorithm for TKD queries on complete data in centralized environments with R-tree. Then Yiu et al. [8,13] proposed two efficient algorithms taking advantage of aR-tree. In 2011, Tiaskas et al. [12] processed subspace TKD queries on vertically partitioned ordered files with a set of algorithms (BSA, UA, RA, DA). In 2017, based on efficient computation of domination scores and partitioned ordered files, Han et al. [5] proposed TDTS. However, it's impractical to establish an R-tree/aR-tree or ordered files directly on incomplete data due to the missing values.

In 2016, Miao et al. [9] proposed a set of algorithms (ESB, UBB, BIG, IBIG) for processing of TKD queries on incomplete data in centralized environments. ESB uses skyband to filter out objects falling out of the finals. UBB prunes search space based on upper-bound score, which is the minimum value on each dimension. In addition, combined with upper-bound scores and bitmaps, BIG and IBIG have better performances than ESB and UBB. As for in distributed environments, since each node can only get upper-bound scores from a local dataset rather than the whole one, UBB, BIG and IBIG are not suitable.

Daichi Amagata et al. [1] put forward two algorithms processing TKD queries on complete data in distributed environments in 2016. These algorithms both require two rounds of scan across the whole dataset, in the first of which the search space is pruned with dominance transitivity on complete data. Accordingly, these algorithms cannot be applied for processing of TKD queries on incomplete data in distributed environments.

3   Preliminaries

In this section, we present some basic concepts and definitions regarding the focus of our research. Table 2 depicts the basic notations that are frequently used in the upcoming sections.

Table 2. Overview of symbols.

Symbols	Descriptions
p	An incomplete data object
S	A d-dimensional incomplete dataset
M_p	The bitmap of p
$\prec$	Dominance
S_F	Top-k dominating objects with respect to S
S_C	The candidates with respect to S
BK_{M_p}	The bucket with bitmap M_p
dp	A domination point
MP_{dp}	The collection of strong-covering bitmaps with respect to dp

3.1   Basic Definitions

Let S be a d-dimensional dataset consisting of n incomplete data objects. $\forall p \in S$, $p(i)$ is the value on ith dimension. $\forall i : 1 \leq i \leq d$, if $p(i)$ is missing, $M_p[i] = 0$, otherwise $M_p[i] = 1$. For p and $q \in S$, $|M_p \& M_q| = |M_p \oplus M_q| = d$.

Definition 1 *(Comparable). For p and $q \in S$, if $M_p \& M_q \neq 00 \ldots 0$, p and q are comparable.*

Definition 2 *(Dominance).* *For p and $q \in S$, if: (1) $\forall i : 1 \leq i \leq d, M_p[i] \& M_q[i] = 1 \Rightarrow p(i) \leq q(i)$; (2) $\exists j : 1 \leq j \leq d, M_p[j] \& M_q[j] = 1 \wedge p(j) < q(j)$, it is said that p dominates q (denoted by $p \prec q$).*

Lemma 1. *For p and $q \in S$, if $p \prec q$, p and q are comparable.*

Proof. According to Definition 2, if $p \prec q$, $\exists j : 1 \leq j \leq d$, $M_p[j] \& M_q[j] = 1$. Then $M_p \& M_q \neq 00 \ldots 0$, p and q are comparable.

Definition 3 *(Domination Score).* *For $p \in S$, the number of objects dominated by p is the domination score of p (denoted by $p.score$), i.e., $p.score = |\{q | q \in S \wedge p \prec q\}|$.*

Definition 4 *(TKD Query).* *Given S, a top-k dominating (TKD) query returns k objects (denoted by S_F) with the highest dominance scores, i.e., $|S_F| = k$, and $\forall p \in S_F$, $\nexists q \in S - S_F$, $q.score > p.score$.*

Definition 5 *(Bucket).* *Given S and $p \in S$, let bucket BK_{M_p} represent the set of objects sharing the same bitmap M_p, i.e., $BK_{M_p} = \{q | q \in S \wedge M_p = M_p\}$.*

3.2 MapReduce

We implement a novel algorithm for processing of TKD queries based on Hadoop-MapReduce model. There are two procedures, each of which uses Common.map(id, p) (represented in Algorithm 1) to initialize p ($p \in S$) in the map phase, and only one reduce task is set due to the characteristics of TKD queries. In addition, we add a combiner [3] phase to perform early partial local aggregation at the end of the map phase to alleviate the computational burden during the reduce phase.

Algorithm 1. Common.map(id, p)

Input: An incomplete object p and its identifier id;
Output: A key-value pair, KV_{pair};
 1: $p.mid \leftarrow$ current map task identifier;
 2: $p.score \leftarrow 0$; $p.dscore \leftarrow 0$; $p.id \leftarrow id$;
 3: $KV_{pair} \leftarrow (p.mid, p)$;
 4: **return** KV_{pair};

---

4   Proposed Approach: TKDI-MR

The traditional skyband-based algorithms, under our detailed analysis, are capable of processing TKD queries on incomplete data in distributed environments. However, according to the nature of skyband, these algorithms would be limited by bucket. In order to break bucket constraints, a novel algorithm named TKDI-MR (processing of **TKD** queries on **I**ncomplete data using **MapR**educe) is proposed based on the fact that the dominance relation is transitive for some incomplete objects with different bitmaps.

This property, with good efficiency for pruning search space of incomplete data in distributed environments, is presented in Theorems 1 and 2. Before the proofs, domination point, covering and strong-covering are explained in Definitions 6, 7 and 8. The collection of strong-covering bitmaps and strong-covering bucket are given by Definition 9.

Definition 6 (Domination Point). *Given S, let Min_i ($1 \leq i \leq d$) be the minimum value on ith dimension. For $p \in S$, if $\exists i : 1 \leq i \leq d$, $p(i) = Min_i$, p is called a domination point.*

Example 1. For the objects in Table 1, the set of domination points is $\{p_1, p_2, p_4\}$.

Definition 7 (Covering). *For p and $q \in S$, if $M_p \& M_q = M_q$, p covers q.*

Definition 8 (Strong Covering). *For p and $q \in S$, p is a domination point and p covers q. Given $M = M_p \oplus M_q$, if*
$$M_p = M_q \vee (M_p \neq M_q \wedge (\forall i : 1 \leq i \leq d, (M[i] = 1 \wedge M_p[i] = 1) \Rightarrow p(i) = Min_i),$$
p is said to strongly cover q.

Example 2. For $p_1(23, -, 105, 4, -, 0.5)$ and $p_5(-, -, 120, 28, -, 6)$ in Table 1, p_1 is a domination point. $M_{p_1} \& M_{p_5} = 001101 = M_{p_5}$, $M = M_{p_1} \oplus M_{p_5} = 100000$, p_1 covers p_5; $M[1] = 1$, $p_1(1) = 23 = Min_1$, then p_1 strongly covers p_5.

Lemma 2. *If p strongly covers q and $p \prec q$, the objects dominated by q are all comparable with p.*

Proof. Considering p strongly covers q, according to Definitions 7 and 8, p covers q, i.e., $M_p \& M_q = M_q$. Assuming that $q \prec r$, from Lemma 1, $M_q \& M_r \neq 00 \ldots 0$. $M_p \& M_r = M_p \& M_q \& M_r = M_q \& M_r \neq 00 \ldots 0$, i.e., p and r are comparable.

Theorem 1. *If p strongly covers q and $p \prec q$, the objects dominated by q are dominated by p.*

Proof. Considering p strongly covers q, $M_p \& M_q = M_q$. Assuming that $q \prec r$, from Lemma 2, $M_p \& M_r \neq 00 \ldots 0$. Given $M = M_q \& M_r, \forall i : 1 \leq i \leq d$:

1. Assuming that $M[i] = 0$, there two cases: (1) If $M_q[i] = 1 \wedge M_r[i] = 0$, $M_p[i] \& M_r[i] = 0$; (2) Given $M_p[i] = 1$, if $M_q[i] = 0 \wedge M_r[i] = 1$, $M_p[i] \oplus M_q[i] = 0$. Since p strongly covers q, from Definition 8, $p(i) = Min_i \leq r(i)$ (ignoring the case: $M_p[i] = 0$).
2. Assuming that $M[i] = 1$, from $p \prec q$ and $q \prec r$, we know that $p(i) \leq q(i) \leq r(i) \wedge (\exists j : j = i, p(j) \leq q(j) < r(j))$.

Then in combination with Definition 2, we can get $p \prec r$.

From the Proof of Theorem 1 and p, q, r above, we know that if $p \prec q$ and $q \prec r$, $p \prec r$. In other words, there is dominance transitivity among them.

X. Ding et al.

Theorem 2. *For $p \in S$, if p is dominated and strongly covered by not less than k domination points, $p \notin S_F$.*

Proof. Assume that p is dominated and strongly covered by not less than k domination points $dp(dp \in S)$. From Theorem 1, we know the object dominated by q is also dominated by dp, i.e., $dp.score \geq p.score + 1 > p.score$. Therefore, p does not belong to the k objects with the highest domination scores, and $p \notin S_F$.

Definition 9 *(Collection Of Strong-covering Bitmaps and Strong-covering Bucket). For $dp \in S$, the collection of strong-covering bitmaps with respect to dp (denoted by MP_{dp}) consists of bitmaps of objects covered by dp, i.e., $BK_{M_p} = \{M_p | p \in S \wedge dp \text{ covers } p\}$. For bitmap $\in MP_{dp}$, BK_{bitmap} is a strong-covering bucket.*

The distributed TKDI-MR algorithm consists of two MapReduce procedures. In the first procedure, TKDI-MR scans S (consisting of several splits and stored on HDFS) thoroughly and prunes data space with Theorems 1 and 2. The set of candidates (denoted by S_C) is a superset of the final result. More specifically, in the map phase, objects in S are initialized by Algorithm 1. The objects with same mid are locally merged to form a local dataset S' ($S' \subseteq S$). The number of S' is equal to the number of map tasks. Then for each S', *combiner* calls TKDI-MR-step1.reduce(mid, S') represented by Algorithm 2 to partition all $p \in S'$ into corresponding bucket based on their bitmaps (M_p) and calculate dp for each bucket. Next, for each dp, Algorithm 2 determines the dominance relation between dp and the objects in BK_{bitmap} ($bitmap \in MP_{dp}$). The object dominated by k domination points (i.e. $p.dscore = k$) should be deleted based on Theorem 2. Then, for each S', the remaining objects form a (local) S'_C.

Finally, the output of all combiners (S'_C) are then shuffled to the reducer where Algorithm 2 is called again to process all S'_C to obtain (global) S_C of the entire dataset. S_C will be stored on HDFS.

For the second MapReduce procedure, TKDI-MR scans S again to compute domination scores of objects in S_C, and returns k objects with the highest scores. At first, the initializations of objects are same as the first procedure. After the map phase, for each S' ($S' \subseteq S$) consisting of objects with same mid, *combiner* calls CandComp.combiner(mid, S') (represented by the Algorithm 3). The algorithm obtains S_C by loading the candidate file stored on HDFS. Then, for $p \in S_C$, Algorithm 3 computes (local) $p.score$ with respect to S', and outputs ("global", p) when the calculation is over.

After the processing of *combiner*, all local domination scores of each object in S_C have been computed. Then for $p \in S_C$, reduce task obtains (global) $p.score$ by summing all (local) $p.score$ up. As the calculation is over, the k objects with the highest domination scores make up S_F. The pseudo code is shown as Algorithm 4.

Algorithm 2. TKDI-MR-step1.reduce(*symbol*, S)

Input: A *symbol* indicating different processes; An incomplete dataset S;

1: $S_c \leftarrow \emptyset$; $S_{dp} \leftarrow \emptyset$;
2: **FOR** each object p of S **DO**
3:    insert p into a bucket BK based on M_p (create BK_{M_p} if necessary)
4:    **IF** p is a domination point **THEN**
5:      $S_{dp} \leftarrow S_{dp} \cup \{p\}$
6: **FOR** each domination point dp of S_{dp} **DO**
7:    $MP_{dp} \leftarrow \{the\ strong\text{-}covering\ bitmaps\ of\ dp\}$;
8:    **FOR** each *bitmap* of MP_{dp} **DO**
9:      **FOR** each object p of BK_{bitmap} **DO**
10:       **IF** $dp \prec p$ **THEN** $p.dscore$ ++;
11:       **IF** $p.dscore \geq k$ **THEN** remove p from BK_{bitmap};
12: **FOR** each bucket BK **DO**
13:   $S_C \leftarrow S_C \cup \{remaining\ objects\ of\ BK\}$;
14: **IF** *symbol* is a *mid* **THEN**
15:   **FOR** each object p of S_C **DO**
16:     output("global", p); // the *symbol* is "global"
17: **IF** *symbol* equals "global" **THEN**
18:   **FOR** each object p of S_C **DO**
19:     output($p.id$, p) to the candidate file stored on HDFS ;

Algorithm 3. CandComp.combiner(*mid*, S)

Input: A map task identifier *mid*; An incomplete dataset S;

1: $S_C \leftarrow$ candidate file stored on the HDFS;
2: **FOR** each object p of S_c **DO**
3:    $p.score \leftarrow 0$;
4:    **IF** $p \prec q$ **THEN** $p.score$ + +;
5: **FOR** each object p of S_C **DO**
6:    output("global", p);

Algorithm 4. CandComp.reduce(symbol, S)

Input: a symbol indicating different processes, an incomplete dataset S;
Output: The k dominating objects with respect to S, S_F;

1: $S_c \leftarrow$ the candidate file stored on the HDFS; $S_F \leftarrow \emptyset$;
2: **FOR** each object p of S_C **DO**
3:    $p.score \leftarrow 0$;
4:    **FOR** each object q of S **DO**
5:      IF $p.id == q.id$ THEN $p.score$ + = $q.score$;
6: $S_F \leftarrow \{p \in S_C\ with\ k\ highest\ domination\ scores\}$;
7: **return** S_F;

---

5 Experiments

In this section, we evaluate the performance of our proposed TKDI-MR. We use Java to implement the algorithms proposed in this paper based on MapReduce. The version of jdk is 1.8. The version of Hadoop is 3.0.0-alpha4. Experiments are run on Hadoop clusters consisting of 4 LENOVO ThinkCentre M8400Ts (i7-3770CPU@3.40 GHz).

Because of some problems mentioned above, existing methods cannot directly solve the issues addressed in this article. In order to better evaluate TKDI-MR, we improve and implement another two applicable algorithms according to [1] as comparisons: (1) NAIVE-MR, scanning datasets once without pruning any data, is a basic distributed algorithm; (2) SKI-MR requires two rounds of scan based on skyband, and search space is pruned in the first round as well.

We use two real datasets AIR^2 and NBA^3: AIR contains more than 700,000 air pollutant data from 1,490 sites across the country, with six dimensions and missing rate of 32.7%; NBA records the statistical data of 441,232 NBA games between 1946 and 1985. Five dimensions are extracted from multiple statistics, with missing rate of 22.7%. We also generate two synthetic datasets AC and IND with six dimensions according to the methods in [2]. AC obeys anti-correlation distribution and IND obeys independent distribution.

The experimental part evaluates the algorithms from following aspects: size of dataset (denoted by c), size of the result (denoted by k) and missing rate (denoted by φ). For each dataset, parameter settings are shown in Table 3. The bold values indicate default settings.

Table 3. Parameter Settings

Dataset	Cardinality $c(10^5)$	Missing Rate φ(%)	Size of the result set(k)
AIR	7.1522	32.7	2, **4**, 8, 16, 32
NBA	4.41232	22.7	2, **4**, 8, 16, 32
IND	2, 4, **6**, 8, 10	15, 30, 45, **60**, 75, 90	4
AC	2, 4, **6**, 8, 10	15, 30, 45, **60**, 75, 90	4

5.1 The Effect of Dataset Size

Figure 1 shows the performances of three algorithms with varying c on IND and AC. As can be seen from the figure, NAIVE-MR has the worst performance overall. Since SKI-MR and TKDI-MR only calculate the domination scores of candidates, their execution times increase slightly. For TKDI-MR, the more c is, the more domination points are. Lots of domination points prunes objects across different buckets. As we can see from Fig. 1(c) and (d), TKDI-MR has a better filtering ability, and the pruning ratio is more than 90% on AC and IND.

---

[2] http://datacenter.mep.gov.cn.
[3] http://www.nbastats.net.

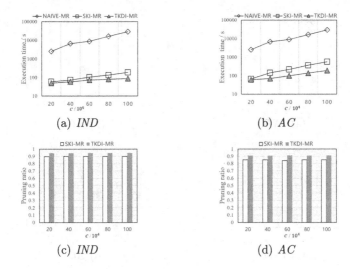

(a) *IND*   (b) *AC*

(c) *IND*   (d) *AC*

Fig. 1. The effect of c

5.2   The Effect of Missing Rate

Figure 2 evaluates the performances of these algorithms on synthetic datasets as φ varies. From Fig. 2(a) and (b), it can be seen that, when φ is low, the performance of SKI-MR is almost the same as the one of TKDI-MR. Once φ is over 45%., the execution time of SKI-MR increases more significantly than TKDI-MR. That is because SKI-MR is bound by buckets, and the most of objects with lower φ are relatively concentrated in several buckets. Then skyband can prune the search space effectively just by processing these bigger buckets. While φ is growing, objects are less complete and more scattered, leading to more even-sized buckets with limited pruning ability. However, TKDI-MR is not limited by buckets and has more stable performance according to theorem 1. Figure 2(c) and (d) well verify our explanations above. Thus, TKDI-MR is more stable and ensures efficiency.

5.3   Experiments on Real Datasets

The test for *AIR* and *NBA* focuses on the performances of these algorithms under different k values. From the results in Fig. 3, we can see that these algorithms have a significantly longer execution time on *AIR* due to the larger size. Under the variations of k, TKDI-MR has the best performance. For the pruning ability, TKDI-MR is stable at around 98.5% on *AIR* and 96% on *NBA*.

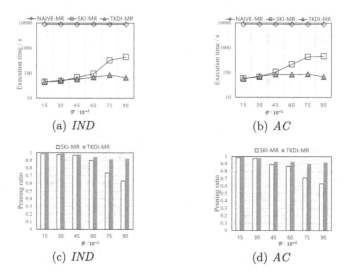

(a) *IND*   (b) *AC*

(c) *IND*   (d) *AC*

Fig. 2. The effect of φ

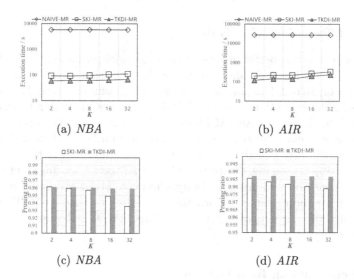

(a) *NBA*   (b) *AIR*

(c) *NBA*   (d) *AIR*

Fig. 3. The effect of k

6   Conclusion

In this paper, we first show that the transitive dominance relation holds for some incomplete objects with different bitmaps. We then presented a novel algorithm TKDI-MR that exploits this property based on MapReduce for processing TKD queries on incomplete data in distributed environments. To best of our knowledge, there has been no research on this topic. The theoretical advantages over other algorithms are reflected in experimental results on both real-world and large-scale synthetic datasets. We concluded by demonstrating TKDI-MR's effectiveness and stability when applied to large incomplete datasets in distributed environments.

An interesting direction for future work is the study of randomize techniques toward reducing computation time by sacrificing the accuracy of the answer. It is very interesting to provide analytical results for both the exact and the approximate solution.

References

1. Amagata, D., Sasaki, Y., Hara, T., Nishio, S.: Efficient processing of top-k dominating queries in distributed environments. World Wide Web-internet Web Inf. Syst. **19**(4), 545–577 (2016)
2. Borzonyi, S.: The skyline operator. In: Proceedings of the 17th International Conference on Data Engineering, pp. 421–430 (2001)
3. Dean, J., Ghemawat, S.: MapReduce: a flexible data processing tool. Commun. ACM **53**(1), 72–77 (2010)
4. Ghemawat, S., Gobioff, H., Leung, S.T.: The Google file system. ACM Sigops Oper. Syst. Rev. **37**(5), 29–43 (2003)
5. Han, X., Li, J., Gao, H.: Efficient Top-k Dominating Computation on Massive Data. IEEE Educational Activities Department (2017)
6. Ilyas, I.F., Beskales, G., Soliman, M.A.: A survey of top-k query processing techniques in relational database systems. ACM Comput. Surv. **40**(4), 1–58 (2008)
7. Khalefa, M.E., Mokbel, M.F., Levandoski, J.J.: Skyline query processing for incomplete data. In: IEEE International Conference on Data Engineering, pp. 556–565 (2008)
8. Man, L.Y., Mamoulis, N.: Efficient processing of top-k dominating queries on multidimensional data. In: International Conference on Very Large Data Bases, University of Vienna, Austria, pp. 483–494, September 2007
9. Miao, X., Gao, Y., Zheng, B., Chen, G., Cui, H.: Top-k dominating queries on incomplete data. In: IEEE International Conference on Data Engineering, pp. 1500–1501 (2016)
10. Papadias, D., Tao, Y., Fu, G., Seeger, B.: Progressive skyline computation in database systems. ACM Trans. Database Syst. **30**(1), 41–82 (2005)
11. Saha, B., Srivastava, D.: Data quality: The other face of big data. In: IEEE International Conference on Data Engineering, pp. 1294–1297 (2014)
12. Tiakas, E., Papadopoulos, A.N., Manolopoulos, Y.: Progressive processing of subspace dominating queries. VLDB J. **20**(6), 921–948 (2011)
13. Yiu, M.L., Mamoulis, N.: Multi-dimensional top-k dominating queries. VLDB J. **18**(3), 695–718 (2009)
14. Zhan, L., Zhang, Y., Zhang, W., Lin, X.: Identifying top k dominating objects over uncertain data. In: International Conference on Database Systems for Advanced Applications, pp. 388–405 (2014)

Energy-Efficient Cloud Task Scheduling Research Based on Immunity-Ant Colony Algorithm

Jianhong Zhai$^{(\boxtimes)}$, Xini Liu, and Hongli Zhang

School of Computer Science and Technology, Harbin Institute of Technology,
Harbin, China
zhaijh@hit.edu.cn

Abstract. The increasing power consumption in the date center has become a constraint to the development of the cloud computing. With the aid of traditional Immunity algorithm and ant colony algorithm, this paper present a new multi-object scheduling algorithm, which combined the immunity algorithm and ant colony algorithm. The new algorithm considers cloud environment dynamics and select energy-efficient and reduce execution time as the optimization target. This algorithm assigns the jobs to the resources according to the job length and resources capacities. Then, the paper compared this algorithm with other famous scheduling algorithm in a simulation tool–Clousim. The result of simulation proves the new algorithm has better performance.

Keywords: Cloud computing · Task scheduling · Energy-efficient
Immunity-ant colony algorithm · Cloudsim

1 Introduction

Cloud computing is a research result of the fusion of distributed computing, grid computing and autonomic computing [1]. Cloud computing providers offer infrastructure, platform and application in a "pay as needed" approach [2]. More and more universities, companies and individuals deploy scientific research, business applications, etc. to the cloud data center to reduce initial investment and post-maintenance costs [3].

In order to meet the needs of users, the number of data centers rapid increase. However, the increasing power and energy consumption of data centers has become a constraint on the development of cloud computing. It is estimated that in 2011, the date center consumed approximately 1.5% of all electricity worldwide [4], what's more, the date center energy consumption trend to doubling every five years. In stark contrast to high energy consumption, energy efficiency is generally low in the data center. According to Amazon's CEMS project [5], energy-related expenses accounted for 42% of the total budget, while the energy efficiency in the data center was only 50%. Energy consumption of data center is huge and low energy-efficiency, revealing the huge saving space in date center industry.

There are two main alternatives for making data center consume less energy: shutting server down or scaling down server's performance. In this paper, we proposes

© Springer Nature Switzerland AG 2018
X. Sun et al. (Eds.): ICCCS 2018, LNCS 11063, pp. 490–501, 2018.
https://doi.org/10.1007/978-3-030-00006-6_45

a task scheduling algorithm considering the relationship between server's performance and energy consumption and optimizing the energy consumption of the data center while ensuring the performance of the server. It can both greatly reduce the energy consumption and ensure QoS of cloud services at same time. At last, we compared this algorithm with other famous scheduling algorithm in a simulation tool–Clousim.

2 Related Work

Cloud task scheduling is the process of assigning user-submitted tasks to resources in resource pool according to a certain policy. WU et al. [6] proposed a QoS-driven cloud computing task scheduling algorithm, which divides the priority of task and dispatches the task to the server with the shortest waiting queue to ensure the completion time is small and load balancing. Li and Xu [7] proposed a load balancing task scheduling algorithm based on ant colony algorithm, which takes the task's maximum completion time and user's cost as the QoS expectation value and select the load balance of the virtual machine in the whole system as the standard to judge the scheduling result. Based on the traditional Min-Min algorithm, Chen et al. [8] introduced the improved load balancing algorithm to reduce the running time and improve the resource utilization. What's more, to meet the needs of different users, they divided the user cost into different intervals according to the quality of service.

Energy-efficient scheduling strategy must take the constraints of energy consumption and server performance into account. As most of the energy savings comes from DPM-like power management procedures, Quan et al. [9] took advantage of it, their strategy maximizing the load on the operational computer by migrating high-load applications to servers with high computing power, and shutting down as many low utilization servers as possible. Furthermore, there are many other different way to save the energy consumption. Duy et al. [10] proposed an energy-efficient scheduling algorithm which predict future requirements by historical records, thereby shutting down unused servers or starting servers to minimize the number of servers running. However, the system performance is not good enough. Liu et al. [11] mapped the cloud task scheduling problem to an integer programming problem, which minimizes the energy consumption of the data center by allocating tasks to the server assigned minimum tasks while maintaining the response time. The average energy consumption of the server is greatly reduced. Dzmitry et al. [12] focused on load balancing of traffic in the data center, their algorithm improve cloud task performance by satisfying the data communication requirements of the cloud task, minimizing congestion packet loss and communication latency in the network.

3 Model Establishment

Energy consumption model is mainly used to predict the power per unit of time of the system. CPU takes 40%–60% in servers' energy consumption, while other energy-consuming components' activity has strong link with CPU utilization. Some studies [13] show that the server's energy consumption and CPU utilization can be expressed as an approximate linear relationship. By analyzing the energy consumption of different servers under the energy efficiency test [14], the energy consumption model we used is as follows:

$$P_h = P_{base} + (P_{max} - P_{base}) * \left(1 + sin(1.5U + \pi) - e^{\frac{-sin(1.25U - \pi)}{2}}\right) \qquad (1)$$

Where P_{base} is the basic power consumption of the server, that is, to maintain the basic power consumption of the server boot work; U is the CPU usage current time. If the server load is too low, it will cause a waste of energy, but the high-load of server will make the server overheating, easily lead to damage and lead to lower quality of service users.

The most used energy-saving methods are Dynamic power management and dynamic voltage-frequency scaling. The server used in this experiment uses the DVFS technology to achieve energy-saving, then the power consumption of a server can be reduced proportionally to $V \wedge 2 * f$, where V is voltage of server and f is the chip frequency. Power consumption can be expressed as follows, where u is the CPU usage, c is a parameter:

$$P_h = P_{base} + (P_{max} - P_{base}) * \left(1 + sin\left(1.5cu^3 + \pi\right) - e^{\frac{-sin\left(1.25cu^3 - \pi\right)}{\sqrt{2}}}\right) \qquad (2)$$

In cloud computing, due to the uncertainty of service requests, that is, the number, size and arrival time of cloud tasks are uncertain. The task submission method used in this experiment is: there is a probability of $\mu(\mu \in [0, 1])$ that n tasks are submitted to the data center, while the number of tasks submitted to the data center n satisfies Poisson distribution:

$$P(N(t) = n) = \frac{\lambda^n}{n!} * e^{(-\lambda)} \qquad (3)$$

In order to meet the characteristics of the task submission in cloud, we set λ as an integer randomly selected in [100, 1000].

4   Ant Colony Algorithm

Ant colony algorithm [15] is a heuristic algorithm developed by ant foraging, it is an algorithm based on population evolution, which can effectively solve the NP problem. The basic idea of the ant colony algorithm is to simulate the ant pheromone left on the path in the foraging and to find the approximate global optimal solution of the combinatorial optimization problem according to the positive feedback effect of the pheromone. The key of ant colony algorithm is pheromone, which is the important factor in ant path selection and drives the whole algorithm forward. Task scheduling in the cloud environment is mainly for heterogeneous platforms, and in essence it belongs to the NP-optimization problem. What's more, the expansibility of the ant colony algorithm can also be fully expressed in the cloud environment: when the cloud computing system changes dynamically, the ant colony algorithm can continue to obtain the new optimal solution on the basis of the original optimal solution and can adapt to the cloud computing Of the dynamic characteristics [16].

In this section, we will elaborate the design of pheromone initialization, ant transfer probability calculation and update of pheromone in ant colony algorithm in cloud environment.

4.1 Pheromone Initialization

In this algorithm, we use the initial pheromone to represent the virtual machine's resources and load conditions current time. We select the computational power, bandwidth and load conditions of each virtual machine to characterize virtual machine's resources, so for each heterogeneous virtual machine, the initial pheromone is:

$$\tau_j(0) = w_1 * \frac{VMj\_mips}{toatal\_mips} + w_2 * \frac{VMj\_Bw}{toatal\_Bw} + w_3 * \left(1 - \frac{power_j}{toatal\_power}\right) \quad (4)$$

Where toatal_mips is the total computing power of all virtual machine, power$_j$ is the energy consumption of the server where virtual machine is located current time. w_1, w_2, w_3 are the proportion of computing capacity, the ratio of bandwidth and the proportion of energy consumption when the load is empty. In the real green computing, the resource's state of the server (which is embodied in computing power and bandwidth in this study) and the energy consumption of the server are important factors in the task scheduling process. In order to achieve a balance between server computing power, bandwidth, and server power consumption, w_1, w_2, and w_3 are set to 0.3, 0.3, and 0.4 respectively in this study.

4.2 Transfer Probability

For task i, the probability assigned to each virtual machine is related to the computing resource, load and energy consumption of virtual machine current time. In the algorithm, these factors are recorded as the expected value of task i assigned on virtual machine j. Then, the expected value is combined with the current corresponding pheromone to calculate the probability that virtual machines will be selected by ants. The transition probability of ants is calculated as follows:

$$P_{ij}^k(t) = \begin{cases} \dfrac{[\tau_{ij}(t)]^\alpha * [\eta_{ij}]^\beta}{\sum_{k \in h}[\tau_{ij}(t)]^\alpha * [\eta_{ij}]^\beta} \\ 0 \end{cases} \quad (5)$$

Where τ_{ij} is the current pheromone of the virtual machine j when task i is allocated in the current path k; α and β are the key parameter, their values will directly affect the convergence of the ant colony algorithm. According to some studies [17], in this experiment, the value of α is 3.0 and the value of β is 5.0. η_{ij} is the expected value that task i assigned to virtual machine, η_{ij} is calculated as follow:

$$\eta_{ij} = (1 - \frac{vmtime(t)_j}{totalvmtime}) * (\frac{1}{power_j} + \frac{VMj\_Bw}{toatalvm\_Bw}) \tag{6}$$

$vmtime(t)_j$ is the time the task cost from it is assigned to the virtual machine j to it is completed.

4.3 Pheromone Update

When the pheromone update, if all the pheromones on the path are updated accordingly, the result of the algorithm is not easy to be convergent; but if only updating the optimal result, the result may be the local optimal solution. Therefore, in this algorithm, we choose top 20% results to update the pheromone. The updating formula of the pheromone is as follows:

$$\tau_i(t+1) = (1 - \rho) * \tau_i(t) + \Delta\tau_i \tag{7}$$

Where ρ is the pheromone volatilization factor, which indicates the degree of volatilization of pheromone per unit time, $\rho \in [0, 1]$, and $\Delta\tau_i$ is the pheromone left by the previous ant in the path.

$$\Delta\tau_i^k = \begin{cases} \frac{2}{L_k} & i \in \text{path k} \\ 0 & others \end{cases} \tag{8}$$

Where L_k is the value of objecte function, it is the sum of the linear-normalized time of the virtual machine with the longest execution time and the linear-normalized total energy consumption in the Kth path (Kth allocation scheme), it can be computed as:

$$L_k = \frac{T - T_{Min}}{T_{Max} - T_{Min}} + \frac{E - E_{Min}}{E_{Max} - E_{Min}} \tag{9}$$

Where T and E represent the task completion time and energy consumption of the current distribution scheme respectively, T_{Min}, T_{Max}, E_{Min} and E_{Max} are calculated as follow, M in (10), (11) is the number of the tasks submitted:

$$T_{Min} = \frac{\sum filelength}{M * Mips\_max} + \frac{\sum Inputfilesize}{M * bw\_max} \tag{10}$$

$$T_{Max} = \frac{\sum filelength}{M * Mips\_min} + \frac{\sum Inputfilesize}{M * bw\_min} \tag{11}$$

$$E_{Min} = T_{Min} * P_{min} \tag{12}$$

$$E_{Max} = T_{Max} * P_{max} \tag{13}$$

5 Immunity-Ant Colony Algorithm

The ant colony algorithm uses the information of the early ant by the positive feedback that pheromone scattered on the path, and realize the exploration of the new path by using the negative feedback that pheromone reducing with time. However, the shortcomings of ant colony algorithm is also obvious: in the early period due to lack of pheromone, the implementation cycle is relatively long, the early accumulation of pheromone takes 60% of the time in ant colony algorithm. Immunity algorithm is a heuristic algorithm simulation of human immunity and evolutionary mechanism with the ability of fast global search; but with the lack of usage of feedback in system, Immunity algorithm is often used to do lots of redundant iterations after a certain degree. Through the combination of Immunity algorithm and ant colony algorithm, the initial pheromone distribution can be generated in the early stage by searching the feasible solution with the immunity algorithm, and finally the ant colony algorithm is used to improve the efficiency.

Immunity algorithm treats the objective function and constraint of the actual problem as antigens, and the feasible solution of the problem is regarded as an antibody, the value of the objective function represents the affinity between the antibody and the antigen. Immunity algorithm always chooses high affinity antibody with low concentration for replication cloning, which maintains the diversity of the antibody during evolution and accelerates the convergence rate of the algorithm [18].

5.1 Combination of Immunity Algorithm and Ant Colony Algorithm

For a hybrid heuristic algorithm, the traditional strategy is to set the former algorithm to run a fixed number of iterations, and then start the next algorithm. But the algorithm does not end in the right time will course an impact on the results. For this reason, a dynamic fusion strategy [19] is proposed to ensure that the immunity algorithm and ant colony algorithm converge at the best time. Details as follows:

(1) For the immunity algorithm, set the maximum and minimum number of iterations, iter_max and iter_min.
(2) In the iterative process of the immunity algorithm, the evolution rate of the progeny population is counted and set a minimum evolution rate. The evolution rate is the accepted subalgebra/generated subalgebra.
(3) When iter_min < iter < iter_max, in continuous g generation if the evolution rate is lower than the minimum evolution rate, it means that the current immunity algorithm is in low speed, should start the ant colony algorithm. Otherwise, continue the immunity iteration.

5.2 Vaccine Extraction

For the cloud task scheduling, the best allocation scheme and no obvious features. The feasible solution of the heuristic algorithm may contain the approximate solution of the global optimal solution. In our strategy, the ant colony algorithm is used to get some solution, then sort the solution according to the energy consumption and execution time. Some of the top 20% are selected as vaccines; the probability of individual selection is calculated as following, after that the roulette wheel selection is used to select vaccines randomly. Where L_i is calculated in (9):

$$P_i = \frac{L_i}{\sum L_j} \tag{14}$$

5.3 Mutation Operation

Mutation operations in immunity algorithms are similar to genetic algorithms. In order to prevent the phenomenon of degradation, this algorithm adopts the following method: randomly select two positions in the current solution, exchange the values of these two positions. In the algorithm, it means randomly exchange two tasks to other's virtual machine.

5.4 Authors and Affiliations

Vaccination is an operation that uses some of the obvious characteristics of the problem to contain the results with degeneration, in the premise of retaining the excellent characteristics of the antibody. We first select a vaccine H in the immunization library, for the antibody a_k, we randomly choose a start position $a_{k,i}$ and an end position $a_{k,j}$ in the sequence, the corresponding element fragment in H is replaced with fragment in antibody a_k.

Finally, the offspring are immunized to determine whether they have reached the standard of entry into the population. For the antibody group B, if the sub-antibody has more affinity than the parent antibody, the child antibody replaces the parent antibody. If the antibody's affinity is smaller than the parent's, the child antibody has a probability of replacing the parent antibody, the closer the degree of affinity to the offspring, the greater the probability of substitution:

$$P_i = \frac{aff_{bi}}{aff_{ai}} \tag{15}$$

Where aff_{bi} is the affinity of offspring and aff_{ai} is the affinity of parent.

$$aff = \frac{L_K}{density} \tag{16}$$

Where density is the concentration of the current individual, L_k is calculated in (9).

5.5 Pheromone Mapping

When the optimization speed of immunity algorithm is low or the maximum number of iterations is reached, the immunity algorithm stops and starts the ant colony algorithm. The result of the immunity algorithm needs to be converted to pheromone to generate the initial pheromone distribution. Each solution of the immunity algorithm is equivalent to an ant in Ant colony algorithm to obtain a path, the initial pheromone is calculated as follows:

$$\tau_0 = \tau_A(0) + \tau_I \tag{17}$$

Where $\tau_A(0)$ is the pheromone value set according to the state of the virtual machine, and it is calculated in (4) and τ_I is the pheromone distribution produced by the immunity algorithm, which is similar to the ant colony algorithm:

$$\tau_I^k = \begin{cases} \frac{4Q}{3L_k} & j \in k \\ 0 & others \end{cases} \tag{18}$$

The Immunity-ant colony algorithm can be defined with the following eight steps:

- **Step 1:** use the ant colony algorithm to form an ant antibody group B = [b$_1$, b$_2$...b$_m$], extract the vaccine
- **Step 2:** A new antibody group A$_i$ is obtained by selecting v antibodies with highest fitness from the group B, then the new generation of antibody group A$_{i+1}$ was obtained by mutating, vaccinating and immunizing the individual in A$_i$
- **Step 3:** Judge whether the result meet the condition starting the ant colony algorithm, if reached, go to step 4; otherwise go to 2
- **Step 4:** Apply the pheromone mapping update rule to generate the initial pheromone distribution
- **Step 5:** Place the ant on the virtual machine
- **Step 6:** Each ant chooses a virtual machine for the next task based on heuristic information, and the virtual machine's heuristics change as the workload of the virtual machine changes after the current task is allocated
- **Step 7:** After the completion of one iteration, the resulting paths are quickly sorted according to their merits, and the pheromones are updated based on the top 20% of the results.
- **Step 8:** Increase the number of generation, if the generation reach the standard, it stops. Otherwise, skip to 5 and continue.

6   Performance Evaluation

In order to evaluate the immunity-ant colony algorithm proposed in this paper, Cloudsim-4.0 is used as the simulator to simulate the execution environment and algorithm of resource scheduling strategy. In this study, Cloudsim is extended and rewritten, and the DatacenterBroker class in Cloudsim is modified to implement the immunity-ant colony scheduling algorithm and the dynamic submission of the simulation cloud task.

6.1   Experimental Evaluation

In order to ensure the authenticity of the experimental results, we use the real energy consumption provided by SPECpower [14] as severs' energy consumption in simulation. Table 1 shows the detailed configuration parameters of the lab environment.

Table 1. Parameters in Cloudsim

Type	Parameters	value
Datacenter	Amount	1
Server	Chips	44
	Bandwidth	1 Gbit/s
	Mips	1860–2660Mips
Virtual machine	Numbers	2000
	Mips	1000–2500 Mips
	Chips	1–2
	RAM	600–1700 MB
	Bandwidth	100 Mbit/s
	Supply strategy	Time sharing/space sharing
Tasks	Task number	100–500
	Total tasks	10k–55k
	Length of tasks	18000–180000MI

Among them, the task number refers to the number of tasks submitted to the cloud system every 0–30 s, total tasks means the total number of tasks successfully submitted to the cloud within one hour. According to the above, the immunity-ant colony algorithm in the parameters set in Table 2:

Table 2. Parameters in immunity-ant colony algorithm

Algorithm	Parameters	Value
Ant colony algorithm	Numbers of iterations	10
	Numbers of ant	20
	α	3.0
	β	5.0
	ρ	0.5
Immunity algorithm	iter_min	20
	iter_max	50
	g	5
	Mutation rate	0.2

6.2 Experimental Results and Analysis

In order to evaluate the performance of immunity ant colony algorithm, we use task complete time and energy consumption to evaluate.

Figure 1 is ten groups of experimental comparison results that the total number of them were 10000–55000. It can be seen from Fig. 1 that the sequential scheduling algorithm is obviously inferior to the other three scheduling methods; when the numbers of task is small, the results of the primitive ant colony algorithm and the immunity ant colony algorithm are not very different. As the task number increases, the advantage of immunity-ant colony algorithm is more and more obvious.

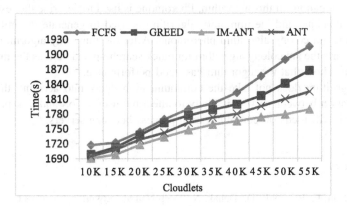

Fig. 1. Execution time comparison

Figure 2 shows the energy consumption of the data center under the sequential scheduling algorithm, greedy algorithm, primitive ant colony algorithm and immunity ant colony algorithm. From Fig. 2, it can be seen that the energy consumption of immunity ant colony algorithm is always the lowest, with the increase in the number of tasks, energy-saving advantages are becoming increasingly prominent.

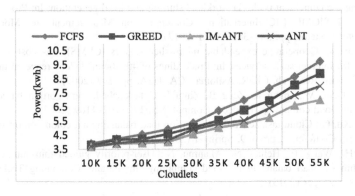

Fig. 2. Energy consumption comparison

Through the above experiments, in general, the immunity-ant colony algorithm scheduling strategy can make the task completion time, task energy consumption low, when the number of tasks is relatively large, the immunity ant colony algorithm can show superiority.

7 Conclusion and Future Work

This paper proposes an energy-saving scheduling algorithm based on immunity ant colony algorithm in dynamic cloud environment. The algorithm considers the dynamic characteristics of cloud task, takes task complete time and energy consumption of servers as evaluation. In this algorithm. Pheromone is used to describe the resources of the virtual machine and the immunity algorithm is used to generate the initial distribution of the ant colony algorithm pheromone. After the immunity algorithm evolves slowly, it starts the ant colony algorithm for quick searching and obtains the final result. Experiments show that the algorithm has good performance.

The algorithm does not take the communication delay into account, the cost of communication between servers is likely to affect the user's QoS and task processing. Future work will focus on communication process between servers.

References

1. Richardson, F., Reynolds, D., Dehak, N.: Deep Neural Network approaches to speaker and language recognition. IEEE Signal Process. Lett. **22**(10), 1671–1675 (2015)
2. Clerk Maxwell, J.: A Treatise on Electricity and Magnetism, 3rd edn., vol. 2, pp. 68–73. Clarendon, Oxford (1892)
3. Buyya, R., Yeo, C.S., Venugopal, S., Broberg, J., Brandic, I.: Cloud computing and emerging IT platforms: vision, hype, and reality for delivering computing as the 5th utility. Futur. Gener. Comput. Syst. **57**(3), 599–616 (2009)
4. Dastjerdi, A.V., Tabatabaei, S.G.H., Buyya, R.: A dependency-aware ontology-based approach for deploying service level agreement monitoring services in cloud. Softw. Pract. Exp. **42**(4), 501–518 (2012)
5. Liu, Z.H., Wierman, A., Chen, Y., Razon, B., Chen, N.J.: Data center demand response: avoiding the coincident peak via workload shifting and local generation. In: Proceedings of the ACM SIGMETRICS/International Conference on Measurement and Modeling of Computer Systems, pp. 341–342. ACM (2013)
6. Hamilton, J.: Cooperative expendable micro-slice servers (CEMS): low cost, low power servers for Internet-scale services. In: Proceedings of 4th Biennial Conference on Innovative Data Systems Research, CIDR, Asilomar, CA, USA, pp. 1–8 (2009)
7. Wu, X., Deng, M., Zhang, R., Zeng, B., Zhou, S.: A task scheduling algorithm based on QoS driven in cloud computing. Procedia Comput. Sci. **17**, 1162–1169 (2013)
8. Li, K., Xu, G.: Cloud task scheduling based on load balancing ant colony optimization. In: Chinagrid Conference, pp. 3–9. Springer (2011)
9. Chen, H., Wang, F., Helian, N., Akanmu, N.: User-priority guided min-min scheduling algorithm for load balancing in cloud computing. In: Parallel Computing Technologies, pp. 1–8. Springer (2013)

10. Quan, D.M., Mezza, F., Sannenli, D.: T-Alloc: a practical energy efficient resource allocation algorithm for traditional data centers. Futur. Gener. Comput. Syst. **28**(5), 791–800 (2012)

11. Duy, T.V.T., Sato, Y., Inoguchi, Y.: Performance evaluation of a green scheduling algorithm for energy savings in cloud computing. In: Parallel & Distributed Processing, Workshops and Phd Forum, pp. 1–8. IEEE (2010)

12. Liu, N., Dong, Z., Rojas-Cessa, R.: Task scheduling and server provisioning for energy-efficient cloud-computing data centers. In: IEEE 33rd International Conference on Distributed Computing Systems Workshops Task, pp. 226–231. IEEE (2013)

13. Kliazovichl, D., Arzo, S.T., Granelli, F., Bouvry, P., Khan, S.U.: e-STAB: energy-efficient scheduling for cloud computing applications with traffic load balancing. In: IEEE International Conference on Green Computing and Communications and IEEE Internet of Things and IEEE Cyber, Physical and Social Computing e-STAB, pp. 7–13. IEEE (2013)

14. Kusic, D., Kephart, J.O., Hanson, J.E., et al.: Power and performance management of virtualized computing environments via look ahead control. Clust. Comput. **12**(1), 1–15 (2009)

15. Server Power and Performance characteristics. http://www.spec.org/power_ssj2008/. Accessed 2 Nov 2017

16. Dorigo, M., Maniezzo, V., Colorni, A.: The ant system: optimization by a colony of cooperating agents. systems man and cybernetics, Part B. Cybernetics **26**(1), 29–41 (1996)

17. Calheiros, R.N., Ranjan, R., De Rose, C.A.F., Buyya, R.: CloudSim: a novel framework for modeling and simulation of cloud computing infrastructures and services. In: Software: Practice and Experience, vol. 41, pp. 23–50. Computer Science (2011)

18. Duan, H.: Ant Colony Algorithms: Theory and Applications. Science Press, Beijing (2005)

19. Ulutas, B.H., Kulturel-Konak, S.: An artificial immune system based algorithm to solve unequal area facility layout problem. Expert Syst. Appl. **39**(5), 5384–5395 (2012)

20. Xiong, Z., Li, S., Chen, J.: Hardware and software partitioning of dynamic fusion of genetic algorithm and ant algorithm. J. Softw. **16**(4), 503–511 (2005)

Enhancing Location Privacy
for Geolocation Service
Through Perturbation

Yuhang Wang[1], Hongli Zhang[1], and Shen Su[2]($\boxtimes$)

[1] Research Center of Computer Network and Information Security Technology,
Harbin Institute of Technology, Harbin 150001, China
[2] Cyberspace Institute of Advanced Technology, Guangzhou University,
Guangzhou 510006, China
sushen@gzhu.edu.cn

Abstract. Third party geolocation services have been widely used in various of location dependent scenarios, such like the searching of Internet of things (IoT) and the location-based services (LBSs). Despite the privacy preservation on using geolocation, which has been widely discussed in last decades, the equally severe issue of the privacy preservation on obtaining geolocation gained much fewer efforts from the researchers. In this paper, we propose a location perturbation scheme to protect location privacy in third party geolocation services. On the basis of the fundamental of positioning technologies, we design a perturbing method to blur the real location by adjusting the underlying signal space fingerprint information. Then a differential privacy mechanism is applied to the perturbation process to further strengthen the privacy level. Evaluation result are illustrated to show the practicality of our approach.

Keywords: Location privacy · Third party geolocation service
Location perturbation · Differential privacy · Location based services
Internet of Things

1 Introduction

The geolocation of people and device is significant for various of application scenarios. Geolocation is the crucial key for people to access information services, also it is a important property of the smart devices in the Internet of things. More and more frequent that people are required to send their geolocation to retrieve LBSs, and they also be more interesting to search the geolocation of devices and infrastructures. One of the result of this trend is the emerging of the third party geolocation services, which is carried out by a third party provider and focusing on offer the positioning service to people and device. Based on today's positioning technologies, the provider of the geolocation services can locate the people and device by estimate their fingerprint of wireless signal space information, and they will send the geolocation to the requesters. In other words,

© Springer Nature Switzerland AG 2018
X. Sun et al. (Eds.): ICCCS 2018, LNCS 11063, pp. 502–511, 2018.
https://doi.org/10.1007/978-3-030-00006-6_46

service providers will know the geolocation even before the requester. This causes a location privacy concerns in such services, and the user, in contrast, wish to avoid of being watched or even analysed by the services providers.

Although the privacy threat situation in this scenario is familiar to the situation of the third party LBS providers, and the latter has been widely discussed, however, the semantic information needs to protect in this two situation are totally different. In the LBS scenario, the information to be protect is the geolocation coordinates and the relevance side information (such as the identity and the LBS request), on the other hand, the information need to protect in geolocation service is the wireless signal space information, which is completely different to the geolocation in semantic. This difference will result that the location privacy preservation approach which focused on LBS scenario cannot function in geolocation services, which need to be solved by the special designed schemes.

In one of our earlier works, we for the first time proposed the computational approach to solve this problem. We explore the possibility of noise addition and perturbation method into the signal space information, and the relevant obfuscating algorithm was given to induce the service provider. However, the threat model we used to evaluate the threat was assumed to be naive. In this work, a robust threat model and fine grained privacy metric was adopted to enforce the privacy level our approach offered, and we provide a enhanced differentially private perturbation based scheme. Service provider will be induced in a more strict threat assumptions, and the validation carried out by real world evaluation proves the effectiveness of our approach.

We mainly make contributions as follows:

1. On the basis of today's positioning technologies, we propose a formal model to construct the wireless signal access points in order to describe their spatial topology.
2. We proposed a differentially private perturbation based scheme, which can induce service provider to generate the perturbed geolocation, which to a certain extend diverge from the real location, while at the same time remains the usability of the geolocation.
3. The customise based privacy requirement model as well as the differential privacy metric was involved together in order to measure the privacy level and to balance the usability and privacy.
4. The evaluation on real world third party geolocation service (Google location service) was carried out to verify the effectiveness of our work.

The remainder of the paper is organized as follows. Section 2 restate our previous work briefly to illustate the basic system model of this approach. We describe the design details of our approach in Sect. 3. Sections 4 provide the experimental evaluations. Section 5 briefly reviews the related work, and finally, Sect. 6 concludes the paper.

2   System Model

The fundamental of the mostly used positioning technologies are much the same, and has been well surveyed in [1,2]. Generally, the wireless signal space identifier and the signal strength are being used to estimate the geolocation through various kind of positioning algorithms. In those positioning technics, no matter what positioning algorithms the service provider adapted, the work from the user side is almost the same, it is, to first sense and collect his surrounding wireless infrastructure signal in proximity, and then send them to the service provider and wait for the service result. This fundamental leads to the diversity of geolocation service scenario to the other scenarios such like LBS scenario, on of the most significant difference is that user do not know their geolocation yet when they wish to perform the preservation. Those approaches which focus on protecting the geolocation information will be powerless in this scenario. In our previous work, we, for the first of time, make the progress on this front and proposed the basic fundamental to the location privacy preservation in this scenario.

The goal of location privacy in the geolocation service is to induce the service provider from knowing the accurate geolocation of the user. In order to achieve this basic intent, the protection from the user side should focus on the wireless signal information which send to the service provider, two limitations are exist in such kind of protection. On one hand, by applying the protect technics on the raw wireless signal information, its output must be remain "positionable" from the perspective of the service provider, both the technologies based on noise fabrication and the cloaking are not working in such scenario. On the other hand, the user side knowledge about the whole area wireless infrastructure is limit, and the business model of today's geolocation service decide that the service provider will keep secret of their whole area wireless infrastructure database, this makes the location privacy preservation more difficult.

To conquer these limitations, in our previous work, we first defined a formal model of the spatial topology of the wireless infrastructures, and with the help of this model, we can specify those "positionable" access points (APs) set which we wish to use as the candidate of our preservation technics. Figure 1 illustrate this graph-based model of the topology of wireless infrastructure. An undigraph G was used to formulate the APs (vetexes) identifier and their signal cover area overlapping relations (edges). Note that G do not contains the geolocation coordinates of APs, it only contains the topology information of them. Then, due to the real world sensing in proximity active, the "positionable" relation of APs can be transformed into a complete subgraph in G. Based on G, we can utilise the infrastructure's spatial distribution and perform the privacy preservation schemes, in addition, compare to the positioning database owned by service provider, G is fairly easy to obtain for the preservation broker.

We use the trusted third party (TTP) architecture to perform the preservation, the TTP contains the G of whole area, and perform the preservation between the user and the service provider as a broker. Based on the system model and the architecture mentioned above, in this paper, we design a differential

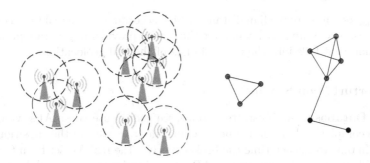

Fig. 1. Graph model of the wireless infrastructures.

perturbation method to protect location privacy in geolocation service, next section will introduce our method in detail.

3   Our Proposed Schemes

The basic idea of our approach is to induce the service provider to generate a perturbed geolocation which has a certain distance with the real geolocation, and at the same time remains the similarity with the real geolocation. The similarity is guaranteed by the enforcement of the differential privacy. On the other hand, the distance will be balanced with the privacy requirement customised by the user, the mutually exclusive requirement of privacy level and the geolocation distortion will be merged into one single metric to measure how much privacy the user actually need and how much we offered.

3.1   Privacy Level

We grade the privacy requirement and the accuracy requirement in to N level from insignificant to critical, which will be denote as P and A separately. Higher P indicates the higher privacy requirement, and higher A means higher accuracy requirement. Apparently, P and A are mutual exclusive, and it is only consistent if they meet the inequality of

$$N - 1 \leq P + A \leq N + 1$$

However, user may customize their requirement which is insufficient to this limit, in this situation, the preservation will satisfy the higher parameter of this two, and the merged privacy level metric can be defined as

$$PL = \frac{P^2 + (N - A)^2}{P + A}$$

We use PL to measure how much privacy our scheme should perform into the real location, and the distance D of perturbation are defined as a interval

$$D \in [\frac{L_{base}}{N} \times PL, \frac{L_{base}}{N} \times (PL + 1)]$$

Here L_{base} denotes are median distance which according to the real world density of active users. Our approach will force the service provider to generate perturbed geolocation that falls into the interval of D of the real geolocation.

3.2 Perturbation Scheme

Clique Database. As illustrated above, we should use those APs which can consist a complete subgraph (clique) in G in order to construct the "positionable" AP set. In our work, each time the broker receives the real AP set from the user, it will find an appropriate perturbed AP set in G and replace the real AP set with the perturbed one. However, it has been proved to be extremely time-consuming to find the clique in a undigraph, and the high demand of responding time of geolocation service cannot suffer from such delay. To conquer this limitation, we use a clique database to caching the cliques in G. The database could be built during the offline time of the broker, and will not influence the experience of service.

We perform the traversal of G to find all the cliques in it by using the brute-force algorithm, note that the broker only keep the clique with the maximum number of vertexes for each snippet of G. Based on the Clique Database, the broker performs the perturbation each time by choosing one of the clique in the database as the perturbed AP set and send it to retrieve the geolocation which we wish the service provider to generate.

Perturbation. In our approach, the real AP set will be replaced with the perturbed AP set to retrieve the geolocation from the service provider. We have ensured the perturbed AP set to be positionable by the graph model and the clique database. Further we wish the perturbed AP set can induce the service provider to generate the geolocation which meet the distance and differential privacy requirement. To realize this front, we estimate the distance between two overlapped APs by perform the signal strength distance conversion. In this paper, the pervasive function of this conversion was adopted, which can be formally described as:

$$d = 10 \times \frac{|rssi| - A}{10 \times n}$$

Here $rssi$ is the received signal strength of AP in some location of the overlap area, A is the 1 m rssi of general AP and n indicates the attenuation factor. Both the parameter here can be measured or inherit from the background knowledge. Then, the estimation of the distance between APs (denote as d_{AP}) can be calculated out by the trigonometric function calculation.

We consider d_{AP} as the weight of the edge in G, and then the weighted adjacent graph (WAG) with the corresponding clique database can be used to perturb the real AP set. Given the distance interval each time the preservation is needed, we can use d_{AP} to generate several perturbed AP sets that location into the ring of distance interval. The random method will be used if more than 1 perturbed AP set are exist in the distance interval.

Further, as the inference attacks could be used by the service provider, we will further ensure the perturbation satisfies the ϵ differential privacy. Due to the definition of differential privacy, we use l_p and l_r to represent the perturbed geolocation and the real geolocation separately, and we treat the geolocation as the binary turple of x and y, for any two geolocations l_i and l_j which generated from the perturbed AP sets, the ϵ indistinguishability would be met if the projection would satisfy:

$$P(x_i \to x_p) \leq e^\epsilon P(x_j \to x_p) \text{ and}$$
$$P(y_i \to y_p) \leq e^\epsilon P(y_j \to y_p)$$

where $\epsilon \geq 0$. We achieve this by performing the Laplace distribution with $\lambda > 0$ to perturb the to be located geolocations which will be located in the distance interval ring. In conclusion, Algorithm 1 illustrates our location privacy preservation scheme into steps.

Algorithm 1. Geolocation Perturbation Algorithm

Require:
    Real AP set AP_r;
    Customised privacy requirement and accuracy requirement P and A;
    $WAG(V, E, w)$ and the clique database;
Ensure:
    Perturbation AP set AP_p;
1: generate privacy level PL;
2: generate distance interval D;
3: **if** $AP_r \cap V \neq \emptyset$ **then**
4:     random choose vertex v_r in $AP_r \cap V$;
5:     locate vertexes $V_c$andiate in WAG with the distance to v_r satisfies the distance interval;
6:     **for** each vertex in $V_c$andiate **do**
7:         search clique database with the vertex, return the candidate perturbed AP sets;
8:     **end for**
9:     randomly choose 1 perturbed AP set from the candidates as AP_p;
10:    **return** AP_p;
11: **else**
12:    return $\emptyset$;
13: **end if**

---

4   Experimental Results

As the privacy was ensured by the differential privacy mechanism, the privacy evaluation we focused on is to valid the correctness of the geolocation returns from the service provider, in order to see whether the actually returned geolocation meet our expectation of the perturbations. Evaluations on the performance are also been carried out in our experiment.

Among these third party geolocation scenarios, without losing the universality, we choose the mobile Internet scenario as the experiment basis. We use the Google Location Service as the geolocation service, and performs our preservation on the Android based device which support this service. the broker was realised on the regular web server with 32 GB DDR4 RAM and the Intel 2.80 GHz 16 core CPU. We used the open public Wifi data from Locky of city Tokyo in Japan, Fig. 2 shows the spatial distribution of the APs we used to generate WAG and the clique database.

Fig. 2. Spatial distribution of public Wifi in urban area of Tokyo.

4.1   Correctness of Geolocation

We evaluate the deviation between the geolocation which we wish to induce the service provider from locate in (denote as $L_{perturb}$) and the actually returned geolocation (denote as L_real). The distance between two kind of geolocations are evaluated, we study the impact of the size of the clique database set on the deviate distance of our approach. Figure 3 shows the result.

Obviously, lower deviation indicates the higher consistency between $L_{perturb}$ and L_{real}, and obviously higher privacy our approach will offer during the geolication service. As shown in Fig. 3, in general, this deviation is fairly small even in the worst case, the meter level deviation is tolerable since it does not exceed the regular geolocation service error interval which is generally in 20 m level in the state of the art technologies. The deviation declines as the size of the clique database enlarges, this is caused by the more abundant of candidate as the vertexes in WAG become more. Overall, the result verifies the effectiveness of our basic idea and the perturbation schemes.

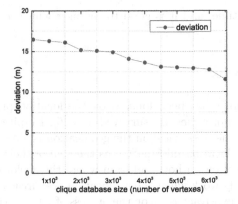

Fig. 3. Deviation between the returned geolocation and the expectation vs. size of the clique database.

Performance. Since the time delay is the most critical factor for the real-time geolocaiton service, in our experiment, we focus our attention on the impact of our preservation on the service delay. We evaluate the CPU time of our algorithm, and study the effect of the size of the clique database on the CPU time. We compared the result to the real-time brute-force clique finding algorithm on the WAG. Figure 4 show the experiment result.

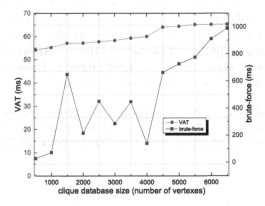

Fig. 4. CPU time of VAT and the brute-force algorithm with incremental size of the clique database.

The adoption of the clique database greatly decline the CPU time of our perturbation process, compared to the brute-force algorithm, more than a order of magnitude of time was saved and remains between 20 ms and 40 ms level as the clique database enlarges. This ms level delay are tolerable for the real-time geolocation service. On the other hand, the increase of the privacy level does not effect the CPU time, and it is good to the user which need a high privacy requirement.

5   Related Works

Large amount of efforts has been focused on the location privacy in the LBS scenario, and these approaches are surveyed in [3–6]. Despite the methodology of these approaches, the basic view on the geolocation is almost the same, most of them treat the geolocation information as the goal of their preservation, and they do not put attention on how and from where the geolocation comes from. These approaches only work when the geolocation are already be given.

On the contray, the privacy issue on the process of retrieve the geolocation are to some extent ignored, and much less works contribute to this front. [7] argued this severe privacy concerns in their literature at 2013. Meanwhile, researches like [8] which focus on the privacy in the WSN positioning, however, they do not take the third party service provider into consideration. The encryption-based method are proposed in [9] to resist the location privacy from geolocation service provider. In our previous work, we for the first time proposed a computational method to preserve location privacy in the geolocation scenario.

6   Conclusion

In this paper, we designed a perturbation-based approach to preserve the location privacy in the pervasive third party geolocation services. On the basis of the topology model of the wireless infrastructures, we designed the perturbation method by searching the proper replacement of the real AP set. Then, we further ensure the differential privacy of the perturbation result. Evaluation result shows the effectiveness and the practicality of our approach.

Acknowledgement. This work was supported by National Natural Science Foundation of China (Grant No. 61572153, 61723022, 61601146), and the National Key research and Development Plan (Grant No. 2018YFB0803504, 2017YFB0803300).

References

1. Liu, H., Darabi, H., Banerjee, P., et al.: Survey of wireless indoor positioning techniques and systems. IEEE Trans. Syst. Man Cybern. Part C (Appl. Rev.) **37**(6), 1067–1080 (2007)
2. Ahmadi, H., Bouallegue, R.: Exploiting machine learning strategies and RSSI for localization in wireless sensor networks: a survey. In: 2017 13th International Wireless Communications and Mobile Computing Conference (IWCMC), pp. 1150–1154. IEEE (2017)
3. Chi, C., Moh, M.: Trahectory priavcy in location-based services and data publication. ACM SIGKDD Explor. Newsl. **13**, 19–29 (2011)

4. Joh, K.: A survey of computational location privacy. Pers. Ubiquitous Comput. **13**, 391–399 (2009)
5. Mar, W.: A classification of location privacy attacks and approaches. Pers. Ubiquitous Comput. **18**, 163–175 (2014)
6. Yu, W., Hong, Z., Xiang, Y.: Research on location privacy on mobile internet. Commun. **36**, 230–243 (2015)
7. Mar, L.D., Cui, C.: Privacy challenges in third-party location services. In: 14th IEEE International Conference on Mobile Data Management, pp. 63–66. IEEE Press, Milan (2013)
8. Tip, N.O., Ras, K.B., Po, C.: Attacks on public WLAN-based positioning systems. In: 7th Proceedings of the International Conference on Mobile Systems, pp. 29–40. ACM, Wroclaw (2009)
9. Li, H., Lim, S., Hao, Z.: Achieving privacy preservation in WiFi fingerprint-based Localization. In: INFOCOM Proceedings IEEE, pp. 2337–2345. IEEE, Toroto (2014)

Facebook5k: A Novel Evaluation Resource Dataset for Cross-Media Search

Sadaqat ur Rehman[1], Yongfeng Huang[1], Shanshan Tu[2(✉)],
and Obaid ur Rehman[3]

[1] Tsinghua National Laboratory for Information Science and Technology,
Beijing, China
z-sun15@mails.tsinghua.edu.cn, yfhuang@tsinghua.edu.cn
[2] Beijing University of Technology, Beijing, China
sstu@bjut.edu.cn
[3] Sarhad University of Science and IT, Peshawar, Pakistan
obaid.ee@suit.edu.pk

Abstract. Semantic concepts selection for model construction and data collection is an open research question. It is highly demanding to choose good multimedia concepts with small semantic gaps to facilitate the work of cross-media system developers. Since, this work is very scarce therefore; this paper contributes a new real-world web image dataset created by NGN Tsinghua Laboratory students for cross media search. Unlike previous datasets, such as Flicker30k, Wikipedia and NUS have high semantic gap, results in leading to inconsistency with real time applications. To overcome these drawbacks, the proposed Facebook5k dataset includes: (1) 5130 images crawled from Facebook through users feelings; (2) Images are categorized according to users feelings; (3) Facebook5k is independent of tags and language, rather than uses feelings for search. Based on the proposed dataset, we point out key features of social website images and identify some research problems on image annotation and retrieval. The benchmark results show the effectiveness of the proposed dataset to simplify and improve general image retrieval.

Keywords: Cross-media retrieval · Facebook5k dataset
Semantic concepts

1 Introduction

Current era has observed a rapid growth of Multimedia Information Retrieval (MIR). Regardless of constant hard work in the development and construction of new MIR techniques and dataset respectively, the semantic gap is high between images and high-level concepts. In order to reduce the semantic gap, we need a promising paradigm to focus on modeling high-level semantic concepts, either by object recognition or image annotation. This kind of concept-based multimedia search system has been presented into numerous real-world search systems [17–19]. Among various approaches, the first step is dataset selection with high-level

© Springer Nature Switzerland AG 2018
X. Sun et al. (Eds.): ICCCS 2018, LNCS 11063, pp. 512–524, 2018.
https://doi.org/10.1007/978-3-030-00006-6_47

Fig. 1. Concept taxonomy of Facebook5K

concepts and small semantic gaps that is relatively easy for machines under-standing and training.

However, existing cross-media datasets totally ignored these issues. For exam-ple, firstly, they have shortcoming in media types and categories. Such as, Wiki dataset [2] contains only two types of media (image and text). Similarly, the Pascal VOC 2012 dataset [1] has only 20 different classes. However, cross-media retrieval implicates numerous domains under real-world Internet conditions. Cross-media retrieval systems trained on scanty domain datasets have compli-cations in handling queries from anonymous domain. Second, they lack context information such as link relations. Such context information is quite accurate, and provides significant evidences to improve cross-media retrieval system accu-racy. Third, popular cross-media datasets have small sizes, such as Xmedia, IAPR TC-12 dataset [3] (20,000 samples) and the Wiki dataset [2] (2,866 sam-ples). The lack of appropriate data makes difficulties for retrieval systems learn-ing to evaluate the robustness in real-world galleries. Fourth, datasets i.e. ALIPR [4], SML [5], either just used all the image annotation keywords associated with training images, or unenforced any constraint to the annotation vocabulary for example ESP [6], LabelMe [7], and AnnoSearch [8]. Therefore, these datasets essentially disregard the alterations among keywords in terms of semantic gap. A brief summary of some cross-media datasets is provided in Table 1.

Although, there is no doubt these efforts provide significant contribution to cross-media research community in terms of standardization of concept corpus

514   S. Rehman et al.

thus open the gateway for researchers to focus ongoing work on a well-defined set of semantics. Nevertheless, we suggest that semantic gap is non-uniform in a low-level feature space realistically and neglecting semantic gap differences is inappropriate. For example, it is well known that modeling broad theme i.e. "Asia" is more challenging than modeling specific theme i.e. "sky" due to absence of significant visual feature that can represent the concept of "Asia". In addition, researchers typically choose local features and color features to model concepts like "sky", and "sunset" respectively.

Motivated by this, this paper focus on the below key issues: Are tags cover the whole scenario in an image? How can cross-media search benefit from users uploading images online? How the contents of image varies according to different users feelings? In other words, how to choose semantic concepts that can be better modeled and simply annotated? To address these problems, this paper makes two major contributions. First, collection of a new large-scale cross-media dataset, named Facebook5k. It contains 5130 image-feelings pairs collected from Facebook[1]. It differentiate itself from the current datasets in two aspects: varied domains and rich context information. Eventually, it provides a more realistic benchmark for cross-media study. Therefore, we construct a standard dataset keeping in mind the research issues to focus research efforts on cross-media retrieval algorithm development rather than the laborious compared methods and results. Second, to the best of our knowledge, it is the first effort to collect a huge dataset of high-level concepts with small semantic gaps on user's semantic descriptions.

Social networking websites i.e. Facebook, Instagram[2], Flicker[3] etc. provides images with rich textual features [9]. Usually these textual features are very close to the semantics of the images i.e. objects name, locations, landmarks, or people present, which helps the users to retrieve relevant images within photo sharing websites using a simple text-based search. According to recent survey [10,20], in every minute more than 2,000 images are uploaded to Flickr, which rises to 12,000 images per second during peak hours. When users upload images to different social websites, they usually categorized the contents of various images through semantic descriptions.

The rest of the paper is organized as follows: Sect. 2 describes the proposed dataset characteristics, collection, potential application and some example images from the proposed dataset. The diversity of the proposed dataset is presented in Sect. 3. Ground truth selection and training set construction are described in Sects. 4 and 5 respectively. Noise level estimation of Facebook5k and its pre-processing, including expert annotations are described in Sect. 6. Section 7 describe some opens discussion. Finally, we conclude the paper and provide some useful future direction in Sect. 8.

---

[1] facebook.com.
[2] instagram.com.
[3] flickr.com.

2   Proposed Dataset

This section describe a new dataset called Facebook5k, which is comprised of 5130 images collected from Facebook. The complete Facebook5k dataset will be available on NGN[4] soon.

2.1   Dataset Collection

Each step in the dataset collection is briefly explained below.

Seed User Gathering. In order to obtain the real emotion of user associated with the image rather than image contents, we obtain seed users by sending queries to Facebook with various key words, i.e. happy hungry, love, etc.

User Candidate Generation. For this purpose, we develop a web spider to crawl the accounts of the users who are following the seed users. This step repeats a number of times until we get a long list of user candidates.

Feelings Collection. Another web spider collects feelings as a text associated with the corresponding images by visiting the homepages of different users present in the candidate list. We find that about 80% of the users feelings companied images.

Data Pruning. We pruned the data that justify any of the following situations, and is called garbage data.

- Feelings without images;
- Tweets not associated with images or feelings;
- Repeated images with same ID;
- Error images.

In result, we obtain 5130 image-feelings pairs in total. An image and feeling text appearing in one piece of tweet are considered as a pair. Some examples in this new dataset are presented in Fig. 3, 4, 5, 6, 7, 8, 9 and 10.

2.2   Dataset Characteristics

Dataset play a key role in the evaluation of cross-media retrieval methods. The proposed dataset includes a set of images highly associated with users feelings. These images are crawled from Facebook, along with users associated feelings. The Facebook5k dataset is highlighted as: First, since it is collected from social media website, hence it covers a broad range of domains under a single roof of feelings, such as love, hungry, thankful etc.

---

[4] http://ngn.ee.tsinghua.edu.cn/.

Second, the relationship between the image and user feeling is often very strong. In the example, first row of Fig. 3, image has a strong knot with the associated feeling. Such is the case in realistic scenario.

Third, Facebook5k is a large-scale dataset, containing 5130 image-feelings pairs, which helps to evade overfitting in system training. Furthermore, it helps the system to test the robustness of cross-media retrieval techniques under a wealth of data.

Fourth, it helps to reduce the semantic gap by providing more accessible visual content descriptors using high-level semantic concepts.

To our knowledge, this is the first dataset collected from Facebook of high-level concepts with small semantic gaps on user's semantic descriptions, and ground-truth of 24 concepts for the whole dataset. Also we believe that this is the only cross-media dataset comprising the above mentioned characteristics.

Table 1. Multimodel datsets summarization

Dataset	Modality	No. of samples	Image features	Text feature	Categories
Wiki	Image-text	2, 866	SIFT+BOW	LDA	10
NUS-WIDE	Image/tags	186,577	6 types	Tag occurrence feature	81
Pascal-VOC	Image/tags	9,963	3 types	Tag occurrence feature	20
Flickr30K	Image/sentences	31,783	-	-	-
Twitter-100K [12]	Image-text	100,000	-	-	-
INRIA-Websearch	Image-text	71,478	-	-	353

2.3   Potential Application Scenario

The proposed dataset provides more practical standard for cross-media retrieval. The potential application scenarios are detailed below.

– Social media website such as Facebook provide predefined emoticons for users to choose when posting a tweet. These emoticons are highly correlated with the posted image and user interpretation of the image. Hence, it is more useful and interesting to link the range of emoticons with users images and recommend suitable image for users according to his/her feelings about the contents of the posts.
– Social network addiction produced huge amount of multimodal data in the internet, which is roughly organized and its annotations are time-consuming and expensive. Apparently, labeling such large-scale multimodal data is challenging. Adding users feeling to images can improve the learning rate of semantic correlations among multimodal data.

2.4   Example Images

The dataset include images of range of feelings i.e. happy (Fig. 3), sad (Fig. 4), wonderful (Fig. 5), cold (Fig. 6), hungry (Fig. 7), love (Fig. 8), excited (Fig. 9) and thankful (Fig. 10).

3   Diversity of the Image Collection

The Facebook5k comprises numerous images of like pose but varying illumination, viewing angle and background. The reason is, most of the images uploaded on social websites with same feeling have similar visual content. For example, "smile" must be common among different people having the feeling of happiness as shown in Fig. 3. However, the viewing angle (Fig. 13), background (Fig. 14) and time schedule (Fig. 15) varies. Therefore, this makes the standard Facebook5k compatible for content-based retrieval tasks as it permits a variety of exemplary quests to explore the efficiency of retrieval systems with these fluctuating settings.

4   Ground Truth for 8 Feelings

In order to analyze the usefulness of research work conducted on Facebook5k, we manually annotate the ground-truth for eight different categories, as described in Fig. 1. Regarding annotations, we have undertaken several rounds of proof analysis by co-authors and external colleagues. Hence, we carefully selected the 8 different feelings in such a way that: (a) they are not inconsistent with the concepts defined in [13–16]. (b) They mainly correspond to the common feelings in Facebook. (c) They give clear evidence of users general perception regarding input image. (d) They belong to different classes comprising happy, sad, excited, wonderful etc.

Since, annotation is challenging task, keeping in mind the following guidelines. If a desire concept exist in the image, label it as positive; if the concept does not exist in the image, or if the annotator is ambiguous regarding the concept, then label it as negative. The number of relevent images for individual users feeling is shown in Fig. 2.

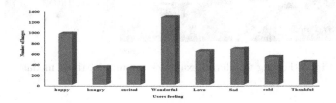

Fig. 2. Facebook5K dataset total images for different users feeling

The key feature about the proposed dataset is that we manually annotate all the images therefore, the chances of error is very less. To ease researchers in system development, we divided the proposed dataset into two parts i.e. testing and training. 4000 images to be used for training and the remaining 1130 images for testing.

5   Training Set Construction

This is the most important phase of dataset construction as the efficiency of the learning system totally depend on it. In other words, we need to construct an effective training set for each concept that we want to learn. Training set of each associated target concept must meet the fundamental two properties. (1) The label must be reliable for individual concept of each image. (2) The training samples must possess the properties to cover the entire feature space of the original dataset [11].

Fig. 3. Feeling happy examples (smiling, laughing)

Fig. 4. Feeling sad examples (crying, serious, loose)

Fig. 5. Feeling wonderful examples (mountain, river, medal)

6   Noise in the Dataset

The key questions arise here are; is the concept of feelings set by the users for associated image possess appropriate features to train intelligent systems for concept detection/classification? What is the quality of associated concept set by the users? Which type of concept can be chosen for accurate detection? To address these questions, we calculate the noise-level of Facebook5k. We simply calculate the precision and recall of the associated feelings in light of ground-truth for 24 different concepts as shown in Fig. 11. It is clear from Fig. 11 that

Fig. 6. Feeling cold examples (cap, shivering, jacket, snow)

Fig. 7. Feeling hungry examples (food, person)

Fig. 8. Feeling love examples (kissing, hugging)

Fig. 9. Feeling exited examples (traveling, luggage, vehicle, road)

Fig. 10. Feeling thankful examples (wedding, birthday, cake, dancing)

both the average precision and average recall of the original feelings are about 0.75, explicitly, one quarter of the feelings are noisy. Here we define F score as a level of noise measurement:

$$Noise\ level = 1 - F \tag{1}$$

$$F = \frac{2 \times precision \times recall}{precision + recall} \tag{2}$$

An annotated keyword is considered correct subject to its appearance in the ground truth annotation of the target image. We define the Precision and Recall mathematically in Eqs. (3) and (4).

$$precision = \frac{TP}{TP + FP} \tag{3}$$

$$recall = \frac{TP}{TP + FN} \tag{4}$$

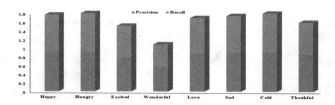

Fig. 11. Precision and recall for 8 different users feelings

where TP (True Positive) represent the total number of positive samples, FP (False Positive) represent the negative samples predictive to be positive, FN (False Negative) represents the number of positive samples predicted to be negative and TN (True Negative) represents the number of negative samples predicted to be negative. Noise of the original feelings for different concepts are shown in Fig. 12.

To improve calculation effects of the number of positive samples and noise level for each concept, we perform the annotation by getting help from expert image scientists as the benchmark for non-tagged image annotation. Hence, we can observe that both the number of positive samples in the dataset and the noise level of the target concept affect the annotation performance.

The number of positive samples influence the results positively. Average precision is directly proportional to the number of positive samples for a firm target concept, i.e. average precision for a target concept is increasing by increasing the positive samples and vice versa. Example of such concepts are "mountain", "grass", "car" and "road". However, the noise level has adverse effects on the outcomes. The noise level increases as the amount of semantic gap of the target concept increases [9].

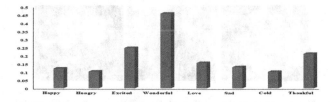

Fig. 12. The noise level for 8 different users feeling

7   Discussion

In this section we discuss that why the proposed dataset is important in cross-media retrieval? We constructed the Facebook5k dataset, keeping in mind the broad-spectrum cover in a single image. Since, a single image unveil thousand words therefore, we feel the need of such dataset, which has a strong knot with the users description. We introduced eight different feelings with 24 concepts, which cover many important aspects of daily life. We pick some key features from users feeling which are described below:

Fig. 13. Same users feeling from different viewing angles

Fig. 14. Same users feeling with different background

Feeling Happy: Users normally share posts with smiling faces with this status. However, there are many cases when the users upload images with a diverse effect.

Feeling Cold: Shivering, warm hat, jacket are the common tags associated with this kind of posts.

Feeling Hungry: Normally, users post this kind of tweets from a restaurant or hotel while taking dinner, breakfast or lunch.

Fig. 15. Users feelings captured in different time span i.e. in the morning, during the day and at night

Feeling Excited: This is a broad feeling however, the data we pruned for this kind of feeling shows users excitement about traveling from one place to another, first time experience and getting into a new place/job. However, many other images have different scenario with the same feeling.

Feeling Love: This is very special type of feeling as it come with users hugging or kissing. People link this feeling with images when they kiss or hug their love one or pets.

Feeling Wonderful: This kind of feeling engulf a large spectrum due to its generalization. Therefore, we capture more than 1250 picture only for this feeling inorder to make it easy for machine understanding.

Feeling Thankful: Feeling thankful is gratitude. Users can feel grateful for everything and anything. Therefore, normally posts associated with this kind of feeling have marriages, birthday, festivals etc.

Feeling Sad: As the name suggests, images associated with this kind of feelings have crying or serious poses.

8   Conclusion and Future Work

We tried to construct a dataset having high-level concepts with small semantic gap. Among many other multimedia datasets constructed, it is the first efforts, which concentrate on semantic concepts for data collection. The ground-truth annotation of 24 different concepts have many potential applications in concept detection, query optimization and multimedia information retrieval. This dataset can be used for the assessment of users image relationship and multi-label image classification, particularly with the use of visual and text features. Furthermore, we discussed some open research questions and delivered the standard solution.

However, much effort need to be done in future since there is no perfect system ever evolved yet. In the future, we plan to increase the number of images and users feeling for Facebook5k. Also, we plan to design an effective learning method for this dataset.

Acknowledgments. This work is supported in part by the National Natural Science Foundation of China (No. U1405254, U1536115, U1536207).

References

1. Hwang, S.J., Grauman, K.: Reading between the lines: object localization using implicit cues from image tags. IEEE Trans. Pattern Anal. Mach. Intell. **34**, 1145–1158 (2012)
2. Rasiwasia, N., Costa Pereira, J., Coviello, E., Doyle, G., Lanckriet, G.R., Levy, R., Vasconcelos, N.: A new approach to cross-modal multimedia retrieva. In: Proceedings of the 18th ACM International Conference on Multimedia, pp. 251–260 (2010)
3. Grubinger, M., Clough, P., Müller, H., Deselaers, T: The IAPR TC-12 benchmark: a new evaluation resource for visual information systems. In: International Workshop Ontoimage, vol. 5 (2006)
4. Li, J., Wang, J.Z.: Real-time computerized annotation of pictures. IEEE Trans. Pattern Anal. Mach. Intell. **30**, 985–1002 (2008)
5. Carneiro, G., Chan, A.B., Moreno, P.J., Vasconcelos, N.: Supervised learning of semantic classes for image annotation and retrieval. IEEE Trans. Pattern Anal. Mach. Intell. **29**, 394–410 (2007)
6. Von Ahn, L., Dabbish, L: Labeling images with a computer game. In: Proceedings of the SIGCHI Conference on Human Factors in Computing Systems, pp. 319–326. ACM (2004)
7. Russell, B.C., Torralba, A., Murphy, K.P., Freeman, W.T.: LabelMe: a database and web-based tool for image annotation. Int. J. Comput. Vis. **77**, 157–173 (2008)
8. Wang, X.-J., Zhang, L., Jing, F., Ma, W.-Y.: Annosearch: image auto-annotation by search. In: IEEE computer Society Conference on Computer Vision and Pattern Recognition, vol. 2, pp. 1483–1490. IEEE Press, New York (2006)
9. Lu, Y., Zhang, L., Tian, Q., Ma, W.-Y.: What are the high-level concepts with small semantic gaps? In: IEEE Conference on Computer Vision and Pattern Recognition (CVPR). IEEE Press, New York (2008)
10. Peng, Y., Huang, X., Zhao, Y.: An overview of cross-media retrieval: Concepts, methodologies, benchmarks and challenges. IEEE Trans. Circuits Syst. Video Technol. **28**(9), 2372–2385 (2018)
11. Tang, J., Song, Y., Hua, X.-S., Mei, T., Wu, X.: To construct optimal training set for video annotation. In: Proceedings of the 14th ACM International Conference on Multimedia, pp. 89–92. ACM (2006)
12. Hu, Y., Zheng, L., Yang, Y., Huang, Y.: Twitter100k: a real-world dataset for weakly supervised cross-media retrieval. IEEE Trans. Multimed. **20**, 927–938 (2017)
13. Barnard, K., Duygulu, P., Forsyth, D., de Freitas, N., Blei, D.M., Jordan, M.I.: Matching words and pictures. J. Mach. Learn. Res. **3**, 1107–1135 (2003)
14. Fei-Fei, L., Fergus, R., Perona, P.: Learning generative visual models from few training examples: an incremental bayesian approach tested on 101 object categories. Comput. Vis. Image Underst. **106**, 59–70 (2007)
15. Naphade, M., et al.: Large-scale concept ontology for multimedia. IEEE Multimed. **13**, 86–91 (2006)
16. Snoek, C.G.M., Worring, M., Van Gemert, J.C., Geusebroek, J.-M., Smeulders, A.W.M.: The challenge problem for automated detection of 101 semantic concepts in multimedia. In: Proceedings of the 14th ACM International Conference on Multimedia, pp. 421–430. ACM Press (2006)

17. Lu, Y.-J., Nguyen, P.A., Zhang, H., Ngo, C.-W.: Concept-based interactive search system. In: Amsaleg, L., Guðmundsson, G.Þ., Gurrin, C., Jónsson, B.Þ., Satoh, S. (eds.) MMM 2017. LNCS, vol. 10133, pp. 463–468. Springer, Cham (2017). https://doi.org/10.1007/978-3-319-51814-5_42
18. Kambau, R.A., Hasibuan, Z.A.: Concept-based multimedia information retrieval system using ontology search in cultural heritage. In: Second International Conference on Informatics and Computing (ICIC), pp. 1–6. IEEE Press, New York (2017)
19. Kambau, R.A., Hasibuan, Z.A.: Evolution of information retrieval system: critical review of multimedia information retrieval system based on content, context, and concept. In: 11th International Conference on Information & Communication Technology and System (ICTS), pp. 91–98. IEEE Press, New York (2017)
20. Li, X., Uricchio, T., Ballan, L., Bertini, M., Snoek, C.G.M., Bimbo, A.D.: Socializing the semantic gap: a comparative survey on image tag assignment, refinement, and retrieval. ACM Comput. Surv. (CSUR) **49** (2016)

Greedy Embedding Strategy for Dynamic Graphs Based on Spanning Tree

Yanbin Sun, Mohan Li, Le Wang$^{(\boxtimes)}$, and Hui Lu

Cyberspace Institute of Advanced Technology, Guangzhou University,
Guangzhou 510006, China
yanbin_hit@foxmail.com, limohan.hit@gmail.com, {wangle,luhui}@gzhu.edu.cn

Abstract. In dynamic graphs, node additions and node/link failures cause coordinate updates and routing failures for greedy geometric routing. To avoid the packet local minima, the whole topology should be re-embedded, which causes high overhead. In this paper, a sufficient condition that a spanning tree can be greedily embedded into a metric space is found, which can help us avoid re-embedding. Based on the sufficient condition, a dimensional expanding strategy (DES) for online greedy embedding in high dimensional metric spaces is proposed, which can avoid re-embedding, as well as reducing the overhead.

Keywords: Greedy embedding · Geometric routing · Dynamic graph

1 Introduction

With the constant growth of the network size, scalable routing becomes a major concern for network communications. Two key measures for scalable routing are the size of the routing table and the path stretch. The routing table contains multiple routing entries and it should scale sub-linearly with the network size. The path stretch is the radio of the length of routing path and the shortest path, which should be as low as possible. However, the lower the path stretch is, the more routing entries are needed. A good trade-off between the routing table and the path stretch is demanded. Recently, geometric routing is proposed as an effective solution and provide both scalable routing tables and low path stretches.

For geometric routing schemes, each node in the network is assigned a physical or virtual coordinate. Instead of maintaining large routing tables, each node only stores the coordinates of its neighbors and uses greedy forwarding for routing. Nodes always forward the packet to the neighbor which is the closest to the destination. The early geometric routing schemes [2,8,12] cannot guarantee point-to-point connectivity, since the packet may be trapped into local minima, i.e., there is no next hop for greedy forwarding. Greedy embedding [11], which greedily embeds the network topology into a metric space, guarantees that the

---

The first two authors have the same contributions to this paper.

© Springer Nature Switzerland AG 2018
X. Sun et al. (Eds.): ICCCS 2018, LNCS 11063, pp. 525–530, 2018.
https://doi.org/10.1007/978-3-030-00006-6_48

distance-decreasing next-hop to the destination can always be found. The geometric routing using greedy embedding is called *greedy geometric routing*.

Kleinberg proved in [9] that: For an arbitrary connected finite graph G and its spanning tree T, the greedy embedding of T is also a greedy embedding of G. Base on Kleinberg's work, the greedy embedding of spanning tree is adopted as a universal greedy embedding for arbitrary graphs, such as [1,6,7,14]. The greedy embedding of a spanning tree is to assign each node a coordinate by traversing the tree from the root node to leaves. Each node obtains its coordinate from its parent. The greedy geometric routing works well in static graphs, it is easy to implement in a distributed fashion and guarantees 100% routing success.

However, in dynamic graphs, node additions and node/link failures cause coordinate updates and routing failures for greedy geometric routing. In general, the node coordinate is produced by its parent according to the parent coordinate and the number of siblings. When a new node joins, the sibling number is changed. Some siblings should be re-embedded, as well as all nodes on the subtrees rooted at these siblings. The node/link failure make the embedded spanning tree unconnected, which invalidate the greedy property of greedy embedding. To avoid the packet local minima, the whole topology should be re-embedded, which cause high overhead.

In this paper, we propose a dimensional expanding strategy (DES) for online greedy embedding in high dimensional metric spaces. The strategy can avoid re-embedding the topology, and thereby reducing the overhead.

The rest of this paper is organized as follows. Section 2 discusses the related work. Section 3 designs and analyzes the dimensional expanding strategy. Section 4 concludes the paper.

2   Related Work

For most greedy embedding algorithms, they concern with three properties:

- Description complexity [10]: Description complexity is the maximum number of bits to describe a coordinate $f(\cdot)$ in an embedding algorithm, and it is determined by two aspects: the dimensionality of the metric space and the coordinate of each dimension, i.e., the coordinate value.
- Path stretch: Greedy embedding provides a greedy routing path between any pairs of nodes by greedy forwarding. Path stretch of greedy embedding is the ratio of the routing path length to the shortest path length in G.
- mobile property [3]: The online embedding algorithm enables an incremental embedding for new joining nodes without disturbing the global embedding, i.e., coordinate updates.

According to the dimension number of the metric space, the greedy embedding scheme can be divided into two parts: schemes for the low dimensional metric space and schemes for the high dimensional metric space.

Greedy embeddings of the low dimensional metric space focus primarily on the Euclidean space and the hyperbolic space. Papadimitriou and Patajczak [11] conjectured that any 3-connected planar graph can be greedily embedded into 3-dimensional Euclidean space.

Eppstein [4] proposes a greedy embedding scheme for 2-dimensional hyperbolic space with description complexity $O(\log n)$ bits. Goodrich [5] proposes a greedy embedding scheme for 3-connected planer graphs in 2-dimensional euclidean space description complexity $O(\log n)$ bits.

Kleinberg [9] proposed general greedy embedding approach and achieved a greedy embedding in 2-dimensional hyperbolic space.

Sahhaf [13] experimentally studies the overhead. Though the overhead is lower than BGP protocol, most of the failures are temporary.

3   Dimensional Expanding Strategy

Instead of concerning with detailed embedding algorithms, we summarize common properties of different algorithms. Based on these properties, we analyze the conditions for online embedding and propose the dimensional expanding strategy from a new perspective.

Lemma 1 ([3]). *For any two unequal nodes s, u of G in a metric space, let l be a bisector (line, plane or hyperplane) which bisects the segment $[f(s), f(u)]$ and divides the metric space into two regions. If there is a node t, then $d(f(u), f(t)) < d(f(s), f(t))$ if and only if $f(t)$ is in the same region with $f(u)$.*

Theorem 1. *A spanning tree T can be greedily embedded into a metric space if: for any non-leaf node $f(s)$ in T, an embedded sub-tree T_u which is rooted at a child $f(u)$ of $f(s)$ is in the same region with $f(u)$ according to the bisector of $[f(s), f(u)]$, and the region does not overlap with regions of other children.*

Proof. Any edge (s, u) divides the spanning tree T into two parts: T_u and T/T_u. The two parts are embedded into two regions respect with the bisector of $[f(s), f(u)]$. According to Lemma 1, for each node u_i $(u_i \neq u)$ in T_u, $d(f(u), f(u_i)) < d(f(s), f(u_i))$. Similarly, for each node s_i $(s_i \neq s)$ in T/T_u, $d(f(s), f(s_i)) < d(f(u), f(s_i))$. Thus, for any node z, its parent node is the next hop to any nodes of T/T_z, and its children are the next hop to any nodes of T_z.

The greedy embedding of a spanning tree is from top to down. Each embedded non-leaf node greedily embeds its children into a metric space. From the perspective of regions, each embedded node has its own region in the metric space, it divides the region into multiple regions for its children according to Lemma 1. If the region of a child is determined, then its coordinate is obtained according to the coordinate of parent and the edge weight. Let C_s denote the coordinate of a non-leaf node s in a metric space, u is a child of s. R_u denotes the region of node u assigned by s, w_s^u denotes the weight of edge (s, u), then the greedy embedding of u is expressed as $f(C_s, R_u, w_s^u) \to C_u$.

The static greedy embedding adopts a fixed division strategy in a metric space. An non-leaf node s divides its region into $k + 1$ (k is the children number)

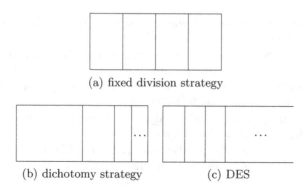

(a) fixed division strategy

(b) dichotomy strategy   (c) DES

Fig. 1. Strategies of greedy embedding

regions and assigns each child a region. For the convenience of analysis, we adopt a rectangle to denote a region of a node regardless the dimensionality and the type of metric space, as shown in Fig. 1(a). Each child obtains its coordinate in its assigned region and recursively embeds its children in the region. However, when a new child joins, the value of k changes. To embeds the new child, s needs to re-divide one or some regions of its children. Thus, all coordinates of these children are changed. More important, the sub-trees rooted at these children should be re-embedded.

Online greedy embedding guarantees the coordinates of existing nodes do not need to be updated when new nodes join. To satisfy the online property of greedy embedding, there should be an unassigned region left for the new joining node so that the assigned regions of existing nodes are stable.

An existing strategy for online greedy embedding is dichotomy (Fig. 1(b)) in the low-dimensional metric space, e.g., 2-dimensional hyperbolic space [3]. Since the dimensionality of the low-dimensional metric space is determined, the region of parent node is fixed. The parent does not assign the whole region for its children. Instead, it divides the region into two parts: the assigned region and the unassigned region. For each time, the parent divides half of the unassigned region for a child. Thus, there will always be $(1/2)^k$ of the region of s left for the new joining node, and the unassigned region can be sustained divided if the coordinate precision is high enough.

Dimensional expanding strategy (DES) is an online embedding strategy from another perspective. It is suitable for the high-dimensional metric space. As shown in Fig. 1(c), since the dimensionality of high-dimensional metric space is variable, the parent node can extend its region by increasing the dimensionality of the metric space. The region of the parent node is considered as infinite. For any new joining node, there will always be a new region divided for the node. However, the dimensionality cannot be extended unlimited, it should be sub-linear to the size of network.

4 Conclusions

This paper proves a sufficient condition that a spanning tree T can be greedily embedded into a metric space. Based on the sufficient condition, a dimensional expanding strategy (DES) for online greedy embedding in high dimensional metric spaces is proposed, which can avoid re-embedding the topology, and thereby reducing the overhead.

Acknowledgments. This work is supported by the National Natural Science Foundation of China (No. 61572153, No. 61702220, No. 61702223).

References

1. Camelo, M., Papadimitriou, D., Fabrega, L., Vila, P.: Geometric routing with word-metric spaces. IEEE Commun. Lett. **18**(12), 2125–2128 (2014)
2. Caruso, A., Chessa, S., De, S., Urpi, A.: GPS free coordinate assignment and routing in wireless sensor networks. In: Proceedings of the 24th IEEE International Conference on Computer Communications (INFOCOM), pp. 150–160. IEEE (2005)
3. Cvetkovski, A., Crovella, M.: Hyperbolic embedding and routing for dynamic graphs. In: Proceeding of the 28th IEEE International Conference on Computer Communications (INFOCOM), pp. 1647–1655. IEEE (2009)
4. Eppstein, D., Goodrich, M.T.: Succinct greedy graph drawing in the hyperbolic plane. In: Tollis, I.G., Patrignani, M. (eds.) GD 2008. LNCS, vol. 5417, pp. 14–25. Springer, Heidelberg (2009). https://doi.org/10.1007/978-3-642-00219-9_3
5. Goodrich, M.T., Strash, D.: Succinct greedy geometric routing in the Euclidean plane. In: Dong, Y., Du, D.-Z., Ibarra, O. (eds.) ISAAC 2009. LNCS, vol. 5878, pp. 781–791. Springer, Heidelberg (2009). https://doi.org/10.1007/978-3-642-10631-6_79
6. Herzen, J., Westphal, C., Thiran, P.: Scalable routing easy as PIE: a practical isometric embedding protocol. In: Proceeding of the 19th IEEE International Conference on Network Protocols (ICNP), pp. 49–58. IEEE (2011)
7. Hofer, A., Roos, S., Strufe, T.: Greedy embedding, routing and content addressing for darknets. In: Proceedings of 2013 Conference on Networked Systems (NetSys), pp. 43–50. IEEE (2013)
8. Karp, B., Kung, H.T.: GPSR: greedy perimeter stateless routing for wireless networks. In: Proceedings of the 6th Annual International Conference on Mobile Computing and Networking, pp. 243–254. ACM (2000)
9. Kleinberg, R.: Geographic routing using hyperbolic space. In: Proceeding of the 26th IEEE International Conference on Computer Communications (INFOCOM), pp. 1902–1909. IEEE (2007)
10. Maymounkov, P.: Greedy embeddings, trees, and euclidean vs. lobachevsky geometry. Technical report (2006)
11. Papadimitriou, C.H., Ratajczak, D.: On a conjecture related to geometric routing. In: Nikoletseas, S.E., Rolim, J.D.P. (eds.) ALGOSENSORS 2004. LNCS, vol. 3121, pp. 9–17. Springer, Heidelberg (2004). https://doi.org/10.1007/978-3-540-27820-7_3
12. Rao, A., Ratnasamy, S., Papadimitriou, C., Shenker, S., Stoica, I.: Geographic routing without location information. In: Proceedings of the 9th Annual International Conference on Mobile Computing and Networking, pp. 96–108. ACM (2003)

13. Sahhaf, S., Tavernier, W., Colle, D., Pickavet, M., Demeester, P.: Experimental validation of resilient tree-based greedy geometric routing. Comput. Netw. **82**, 156–171 (2015)

14. Westphal, C., Pei, G.: Scalable routing via greedy embedding. In: Proceeding of the 28th IEEE International Conference on Computer Communications (INFOCOM), pp. 2826–2830. IEEE (2009)

Heterogeneous Cloud Resources Management: Truthful Mechanism Design in Shared Multi-minded Users

Xi Liu, Jing Zhang, Xiaolu Zhang, and Xuejie Zhang$^{(\boxtimes)}$

School of Information Science and Engineering, Yunnan University,
Kunming, People's Republic of China
xjzhang@ynu.edu.cn

Abstract. We address the problem of dynamic virtual machine provisioning and allocation of heterogeneous cloud resources. Existing works consider each user requests single bundle (single-minded), but a user may request multiple bundles (multi-minded). Thus, our object is to provide and allocate efficiently multiple VMs considering multi-minded setting to maximize social welfare. We formulate this problem in an auction-based setting and design optimal and approximation mechanisms. In addition, we show the approximation is $\frac{a_{max}}{a_{min}}\sqrt{R\frac{c_{max}}{c_{min}}} + 2$, where c_{max}/c_{min} is the maximum/minimum available resources, and a_{max}/a_{min} is the maximum/minimum requested resources. Furthermore, we show our proposed mechanisms are truthful, that is, they drive the system into an equilibrium where any user does not have incentives to maximize her own profit by untruthful value. Experimental results demonstrate that our proposed approximation mechanism gets the near-optimal allocation within a reasonable time whiling to giving the users incentives to report their true declarations.

Keywords: Truthful mechanism design
Virtual machine provisioning · Multi-minded · Single-parameter

1 Introduction

Cloud providers provider their resources into virtual machine (VM) instances based on the pay-as-you-go model for users for specific periods of time in Infrastructure as a Service. For example, Amazon EC2 [1] offer multiple types of VMs to users. Since the fixed pricing and spot market pricing [1] model create difficulties for cloud providers when deciding the prices of VMs. To over this drawback, we consider the auction-based pricing to provisioning and allocation VMs in this paper. In addition, we not only consider the revenue of cloud providers, but also consider the utility of users. Thus, the aim of this paper is to design an efficient allocation mechanism to maximize social welfare [2] that is the sum of the revenue and utility.

© Springer Nature Switzerland AG 2018
X. Sun et al. (Eds.): ICCCS 2018, LNCS 11063, pp. 531–542, 2018.
https://doi.org/10.1007/978-3-030-00006-6_49

Existing works consider a user requests a bundle of VMs and bids for this bundle (single-minded user [3]). However, a user may request multiple bundles, where she becomes a winner if she is assigned exactly one of her requested bundles (multi-minded [4]). Thus, we consider the single-parameter domains of multi-minded, that is a user requests some bundles, but her bid for every bundle must be the same [5]. In addition, the value for each user (requested VMs and bid) is private. That is only she knows her true value, and this information are private and neither the cloud providers nor the other users have access to it. However, a user is self-interested and may declares untruthful value to maximize her utility. This strategic operations may reduce social welfare and inflict losses on other users. Therefor, one of the goals in this paper is to design truthful mechanism to incentive users to declare truthful values.

By considering the truthful property, the VM provisioning and allocation problem is moved from the area of algorithm design to that of mechanism design. Incentive compatibility, however, puts additional constraints on the design of mechanisms. Unfortunately, the simple greedy algorithm that satisfies monotone property can guarantee truthful [3], but it is only applied to single-minded. The main challenge of our work is to design a truthful mechanism considering multi-minded in the single-parameter domains. Additionally, we interest in mechanism that consists of a social efficiency allocation algorithm to get the approximate allocation for large-scale instances. One of the key properties of our proposed mechanism is truthful that encourages users prefer to declare true values in order to improve the social welfare and increase the utility.

We address the problem of VM provisioning and allocation of heterogeneous cloud resources in shared multi-minded users in the single-parameter domains (VMPAHM). First, we formulate the VMPAHM problem in an accurate mathematical model. Second, we design an optimal mechanism for solving VMPAHM problem. Unfortunately, the VMPAHM problem is strongly NP-hard. Thus, we design an approximation mechanism consists of an allocation algorithm and a payment algorithm. In addition, we show the approximation is $\frac{a_{max}}{a_{min}}\sqrt{R\frac{c_{max}}{c_{min}}}+2$, where c_{max}/c_{min} is the maximum/minimum available resources, and a_{max}/a_{min} is the maximum/minimum requested resources. Furthermore, we show our proposed approximation mechanism is truthful. This makes it drives the system into an equilibrium where any user does not have incentives to maximize her own utility by untruthfully reporting her declaration. The experiment results show that the performance of our proposed approximation mechanism performs very well and achieves a good balance of performance and time.

1.1   Related Work

Mechanism design [2] is a sub-field of game theory aiming at reaching systems equilibria while maintaining desired properties. The Vickrey-Clarke-Groves (VCG) mechanism [6–8] is known to be truthful for optimizing social welfare. If the allocation algorithm satisfies monotone property and the payment algorithm realizes critical payment, the mechanism is truthful for single-minded [3].

However, this approach cannot be used for the multi-minded setting. However, Sandholm [9] proved that solving the allocation determination problem is computationally hard. In addition, the VMPAHM problem is strongly NP-hard, and there is no fully polynomial time approximation scheme for solving it, unless $P = NP$ [10]. Thus, designing truthful mechanism for VMPAHM is difficult.

Researchers have investigated the problem of the truthful auction mechanism for resource allocation [11,12]. Lehmann et al. [13] studied the combinatorial auctions and proposed scheme that guarantee truthfulness for the greedy mechanism. In addition, they proposed a greedy truthful allocation. Zaman et al. [14] proposed an auction-based mechanism for VM allocation, and showed it is truthful. Bonacquisto et al. [15] proposed a procurement market based on auction-based for resource allocation. Zhou et al. [16] proposed an efficient truthful mechanism with soft deadlines for the resource provisioning. Fu et al. [17] proposed the core-selecting VM mechanism based on the combinatorial auctions, and showed it is truthful. Zhang et al. [18] studied a framework for truthful resource allocation, and proposed an truthful online mechanism. Shi et al. [19] also studied the online auction, and proposed the truthful mechanism based on randomized auction. However, none of these works considered multi-minded.

Our work is different from all previous works. The closest work to ours was by Mashayekhy et al. [20] and Nejad et al. [21]. Mashayekhy et al. [20] studied the VM provisioning and allocation, and proposed an optimal mechanism and a polynomial time approximation scheme mechanism. Nejad et al. [21] proposed a greedy truthful mechanism. However, they all assumed the user submits the single request. Thus, in this paper, we not only consider the multi-minded setting, but also design the optimal and approximation truthful mechanism.

1.2 Organization

The remainder of this paper is organized as follows. The next section proposes the accurate mathematical model. Section 3 presents a truthful optimal mechanism. Section 4 describes a truthful greedy mechanism. Section 5 evaluates the performance of our proposed mechanisms. Section 6 summarizes the results and lists ideas for future work.

2 Preliminary

We focus on the multi-minded combinatorial auctions with a single seller and multiple users, where the cloud providers are considered the single seller. Let $\mathcal{R} = \{1, ..., R\}$ be a set of R types of resources such as core, ram and disk sizes. Let $\mathcal{VM}$ be the set of of M types of VMs such that m, $m \in \mathcal{VM}$, offers a resources vector $w_{m1}, ..., w_{mR}$, where w_{mr} means that one VM instance of type $m \in \mathcal{VM}$ offers the amount of resources of type $r \in \mathcal{R}$. Table 1 presents the four types of general purpose (M3) VM instances offered by Amazon EC2 [1]. The cloud providers have restricted capacity, c_r, on each resource $r \in \mathcal{R}$, available for allocation.

Table 1. General Purpose (M3) VM Instance Types Offered by Amazon EC2 [1]

Instance Type	m3.medium	m3.large	m3.xlarge	m3.2xlarge
	1	2	3	4
Cores	1	2	4	8
Ram(GB)	3.75	7.5	15	30
Disk sizes(GB)	4	32	80	160

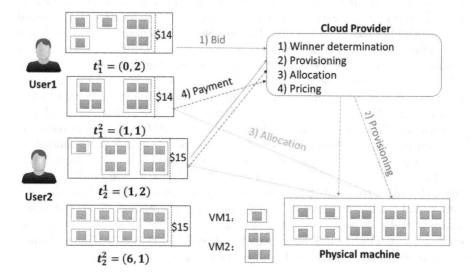

Fig. 1. A high-level view of VMPAHM.

There is a finite set of users $\mathcal{U}$ ($|\mathcal{U}| = N$), where each user submits a set θ that has the K different bundles $\theta_i^1(\mathbf{t}_i^1, b_i), ..., \theta_i^K(\mathbf{t}_i^K, b_i)$, where $\mathbf{t}_i^k = (t_{i1}^k, ..., t_{iM}^k)$ is the vector of requested VMs. Let $\mathbf{d}_i = (\mathbf{d}_i^1, ..., \mathbf{d}_i^K)$ be the allocation vector of user i, and $\mathbf{a}_i^k = (a_{i1}^k, ..., a_{iR}^k)$ be the vector of user i' kth requested resources, where $a_{ir}^k = \sum_{m \in \mathcal{VM}} t_{im}^k w_{mr}$ for $\forall r \in \mathcal{R}$. For example, user i requests two bundles $\theta_i^1((2, 1, 0, 1), \$25)$ and $\theta_i^2((2, 2, 1, 2), \$25)$, where θ_i^1 means user i requests 2 m3.medium VM instances, 1 m3.large VM instance, 0 m3.xlarge VM instance and 1 m3.2xlarge VM instance, and she is willing to pay \$25 for this VMs. Without loss of generality, we assume $a_{ir}^k > 0$ and $c_r \geq a_{ir}^k$ for $\forall r \in \mathcal{R}$, $\forall i \in \mathcal{U}$ and $k = 1, ..., K$.

To simply understand how the multiple VMs are allocated to multiple users in the VMPAHM problem, see Fig. 1. In this scenario, we consider only one type of resource and two types of VMs: VM_1, consisting of one resource; and VM_2, consisting of four resources. The resource pool offers 16 resources ($c_{11} = 16$). We assume that each user submits two different bundles. User 1 bids \$14 and requests three VM_1 ($t_{11}^1 = 3$) and one VM_2 ($t_{12}^1 = 1$) in the first bundle, and zero VM_1 ($t_{11}^2 = 0$) and two VM_2 ($t_{12}^2 = 2$) in the second bundle. User 2 bids $15 and requests one VM_1 ($t_{21}^1 = 1$) and two VM_2 ($t_{22}^1 = 2$) in the first bundle, and six VM_1 ($t_{21}^2 = 6$) and one VM_2 ($t_{22}^2 = 1$) in the second bundle. The mechanism employed by the cloud providers satisfies the first bundle of user 1 and the first bundle of user 2, Then, the resource pool providers four VM_1 and three VM_2, and allocates three VM_1 and one VM_2 to user 1, and one VM_1 and two VM_2 to user 2. Thus, two users as winners and the social welfare is $b_1 + b_2 = \$29$. Note that, in our model, each user can submit multiple bundles, while each user can submit only one bundle in the existing works. Compared with previous works, our model can be conforming to the actual needs and obtain greater social welfare.

For every user i, we define her valuation function as follows:

$$v_i(\mathbf{d}) = \begin{cases} b_i, \mathbf{d}_i^k \le \mathbf{a}_i^k, \exists k \le K \\ 0, \text{ otherwise,} \end{cases} \tag{1}$$

Every user $i \in \mathcal{U}$ is individual rationality and bids so as to maximize her quasi-linear utility, defined as:

$$u_i(\mathbf{d}) = \tilde{b}_i - pay_i, \tag{2}$$

where $\tilde{b}_i$ is the true bid of user i, and pay_i is her payment.

Definition 1 (Truthful mechanism). *A mechanism is called truthful (or incentive compatible) if $\forall i \in \mathcal{U}$ with a true valuation θ_i and any other valuation $\hat{\theta}_i$, we have that $u_i(\theta_i, \theta_{-i}) \ge u_i(\hat{\theta}_i, \theta_{-i})$.*

The integer programming formulation of the VMPAHM problem (called IP-VMPAHM) can be formulated as:

$$\text{Maximize} \sum_{i \in \mathcal{U}} v_i(\mathbf{d}_i) \tag{3}$$

$$\sum_{i \in \mathcal{U}} d_{ir} \le c_r, \forall r \in \mathcal{R} \tag{4}$$

The objective (3) is to find an allocation $\mathbf{d} = \{\mathbf{d}_1, ..., \mathbf{d}_N\}$ to maximize social welfare. Constraints (4) guarantee that the allocation capacity of each resource type is less than or equal to that available in the resource pool.

3 Truthful Optimal Mechanism for VMPAHM

In this section, we design an optimal mechanism that solves VMPAHM problem. The VCG [6–8] is the only auction mechanism that is both truthful and efficient. Thus, we propose a VCG-based optimal mechanism for VMPAHM, called VCG-VMPAHM. We define the VCG-VMPAHM mechanism as follows

Definition 2 (VCG-VMPAHM mechanism). *The VCG-VMPAHM mechanism consists of an allocation algorithm A and a payment algorithm P*

(i) A is an optimal allocation function maximizing the optimal social welfare,
(ii) $p_i(\mathbf{d}^*) = \sum_{j \in U, i \neq j} v_j(\mathbf{d}_j') - \sum_{j \in U \setminus \{i\}} v_j(\mathbf{d}_j^*)$, where $\mathbf{d}^*$ is the optimal allocation for $\mathcal{U}$, and $\mathbf{d}'$ is the optimal allocation for $\mathcal{U} \setminus \{i\}$, so $\sum_{j \in U, i \neq j} v_j(\mathbf{d}_j')$ is the optimal welfare without user i's participation, and $\sum_{j \in U \setminus \{i\}} v_j(\mathbf{d}_j^*)$ is the optimal welfare except user i's value.

VCG-VMPAHM mechanism is truthful, because it obtains the optimal allocation and implements VCG-based payments. However, the execution time of VMPAHM problem becomes prohibitive for high demand. Therefor, we design a truthful approximation mechanism for VMPAHM in the next section.

4 Truthful Approximation Mechanism for VMPAHM

In this section, we design an approximation mechanism for VMPAHM, G-VMPAHM.

Definition 3 (G-VMPAHM mechanism). *The G-VMPAHM mechanism consists of an allocation algorithm G-ALLOC and a payment algorithm G-PAY.*

G-VMPAHM mechanism is summarized in the Algorithm 1. It first collects requests from users, and calls G-ALLOC to obtain an allocation (line 3). Then, it calls the G-PAY to calculate payment for each user (line 5). Finally, the winners charge their payments and receive their requested VM instances from cloud providers.

Algorithm 1. G-VMPAHM()

1: /*Wait users and collect requests*/
2: /*Provisions and allocates VM instances*/
3: $(\mathbf{d}, V)$ =G-ALLOC(θ,$\mathbf{c}$);
4: /*Payment*/
5: **pay**=G-PAY(θ,$\mathbf{d}$);
6: /*Recovery the resources from users*/

The G-ALLOC is summarized in the Algorithm 2. This is a modification to the greedy algorithm of [22] for multi-minded single-parameter setting. G-ALLOC first calculates the bid density for each user and sorts all users' requested bundles in non-increasing order of bid density. The bid density is defined as follows:

$$f_i^k = \frac{v_i(\mathbf{a}_i^k)}{\sqrt{\sum_{r \in \mathcal{R}} \frac{a_{ir}^k}{c_r}}}, k = 1, ..., K, \forall i \in \mathcal{U} \tag{5}$$

Algorithm 2. G-ALLOC(θ,c)

1: **for each** $i \in \mathcal{U}$
2:    $f_i^k = \dfrac{v_i(\mathbf{a}_i^k)}{\sqrt{\sum_{r \in \mathcal{R}} \frac{a_{ir}^k}{c_r}}}$ for each $k = 1, ..., K$;
3: **sort** the bid densities in non-increasing order of f into *list*;
4: $\mathbf{d} = \mathbf{0}$;
5: **while** $\sum_{j \in \mathcal{U}} d_{jr} \leq c_r$ for each $r \in \mathcal{R}$ **and** *list* $\neq \varnothing$
6:    pick the highest bid density f_i^k from the *list*;
7:    **if** $v_i(\mathbf{d}_i) = 0$ **and** $\sum_{j \in \mathcal{U}} d_{jr} + a_i^k \leq c_r$ for each $r \in \mathcal{R}$
8:      $\mathbf{d}_i^k = \mathbf{a}_i^k$;
9:    remove the bid densities f_i^k from the *list*;
10: **return** $\mathbf{d}, \sum_{i \in \mathcal{U}} v_i(\mathbf{d}_i)$;

Algorithm 3. G-PAY(θ,d)

1: **pay** $= \mathbf{0}$;
2: **for each** $i \in \mathcal{U}$
3:    **if** $v_i(\mathbf{d}) = b_i$
4:      $j \leftarrow$ if user $j(v_j(\mathbf{d}) = 0)$ wins with $\theta_j^{k'}$, user i loses;
5:      $pay_i = min_{k \leq K} b_j \sqrt{\sum_{r \in \mathcal{R}} a_{ir}^k / c_r} / \sqrt{\sum_{r \in \mathcal{R}} a_{jr}^{k'} / c_r}$;
6: **return pay**;

Then, algorithm picks priority the user who has the highest bid density to allocate resources until the resources constraint is violated or no more users require resources. Finally, it returns the resulting allocation vector and the welfare.

The G-PAY is summarized in the Algorithm 3. The idea of G-PAY is based on the critical payment. First, the payments are set to zero, that is, the losers pay nothing. Then, for each winner $i \in \mathcal{U}$, algorithm finds the user j: if user j wins and obtains the resources, user i will lose because the resource pool does not have available resources to fulfill her requested resources. After that, the payment is set to the minimum value that make the bid density be no less than that of user j. Finally, the algorithm returns the payment vector of all users.

4.1 Properties

Theorem 1. *G-VMPAHM mechanism is truthful.*

Proof. If user i ($i \in \mathcal{U}$) wins in the G-VMPAHM and submits a different $\hat{\theta}_i$, where θ_{-i} is fixed. Let u_i, $\hat{u}_i$ be the utility of user i gains, pay_i^c, $p\hat{a}y_i^c$ the minimum payment that she must bid to win, pay_i, $p\hat{a}y_i$ the payment based on the G-PAY, and $\mathbf{d}_i$, $\hat{\mathbf{d}}_i$ the allocation for the θ_i and $\hat{\theta}_i$, respectively.

If user i wins, G-PAY finds the user j ($j \in \mathcal{U}$) who has the smallest index such that if user j wins, user i loses. G-PAY then computes the minimum valuation pay_i that user i must bid to obtain one of her required bundles. In other words, if user i bids less than the value pay_i and is considered after user j by G-ALLOC, the requested resources of user i are against the available resources and thus user i loses. If user i bids more than the value pay_i and is allocated resources before user j, user i wins. Thus, we have $pay_i = pay_i^c, p\hat{a}y_i = p\hat{a}y_i^c$.

In the following, we consider three cases to analyse the performance of G-VMPAHM.

- User i loses with $\hat{\theta}_i$. We have $\hat{u}_i = 0 \leq u_i$.
- User i wins with $\hat{\theta}_i$ and $v_i(\hat{\mathbf{d}}_i) = 0$. We have $\hat{u}_i = b_i - p\hat{a}y_i^c \leq 0 \leq u_i$.
- User i wins with $\hat{\theta}_i$ and $v_i(\hat{\mathbf{d}}) > 0$. We assume user i wins with the bundle $\hat{a}_i^{\hat{k}}$ and G-PAY finds the user j (line 8). Obviously, we have $\mathbf{a}_i^k \leq \hat{\mathbf{a}}_i^{\hat{k}}$, and $pay_i^c \leq$

$$b_j \sqrt{\sum_{r\in\mathcal{R}} a_{ir}^k / c_r} / \sqrt{\sum_{r\in\mathcal{R}} a_{jr} / c_r} \leq b_j \sqrt{\sum_{r\in\mathcal{R}} \hat{a}_{ir}^{\hat{k}} / c_r} / \sqrt{\sum_{r\in\mathcal{R}} a_{jr} / c_r} =$$

$p\hat{a}y_i^c$. If user i with θ_i wins, we have $\hat{u}_i = b_i - p\hat{a}y_i \leq b_i - pay_i = u_i$. Otherwise, we have $b_i < pay_i^c \leq p\hat{a}y_i^c$, and thus $\hat{u} = b_i - p\hat{a}y_i < 0 = u_i$.

Theorem 2. *The approximation of G-ALLOC is* $\frac{a_{max}}{a_{min}} \sqrt{R \frac{c_{max}}{c_{min}}} + 2$, *where* $c_{min} \leq c_r \leq c_{max}$ *for each* $r \in \mathcal{R}$ *and* $a_{min} \leq a_{ir}^k \leq a_{max}$ *for each* $i \in \mathcal{U}, r \in \mathcal{R}$ *and* $k = 1, ..., K$.

Proof. The approximation of G-ALLOC is $\frac{a_{max}}{a_{min}} \sqrt{R \frac{c_{max}}{c_{min}}} + 1$ in the case of single-minded [22]. Let $\gamma = \frac{a_{max}}{a_{min}} \sqrt{R \frac{c_{max}}{c_{min}}} + 1$. The idea of proof is inspired from [5].

Let $\mathcal{W}, \mathcal{O}$ be the set of winners, $\mathbf{d}, \mathbf{o}$ the allocation, and V, OPT the welfare in the greedy and the optimal allocations, respectively. Let $\mathcal{O}_1 = \mathcal{O} \cap \mathcal{W}$ and $\mathcal{O}_2 = \mathcal{O}\backslash\mathcal{W}$. If we transform all users in $\mathcal{O}_2$ to be the single-minded users that only requests the bundle that is in the optimal allocation, the optimal allocation and the greedy allocation will not change. Let V_2 be the welfare obtained by greedy algorithm with resource $c_r - \sum_{i\in\mathcal{O}_1} o_{ir}$ for each $r \in \mathcal{R}$. We get that $\sum_{i\in\mathcal{O}_2} v_i(\mathbf{o}_i) \leq \gamma \cdot V_2 \leq \gamma \cdot V$.

Clearly, then, $OPT = \sum_{i\in\mathcal{O}_1} v_i(\mathbf{o}_i) + \sum_{i\in\mathcal{O}_2} v_i(\mathbf{o}_i) = \leq V + \gamma \cdot V = (1+\gamma)V$.

Theorem 3. *The time complexity of the G-ALLOC is* $O(KN\log(KN) + NKR)$.

5   Experimental Results

In this section, we evaluate the performance of G-VMPAHM mechanism. The optimal results in VCG-VMPAHM are obtained by CPLEX [23]. We perform the experiments on a machine with 4 core 2.8 GHz Intel Core i5 processors with 4 GB ram. The experimental platform environment uses $C\#$ in Visual Studio 2013.

5.1 Experiment Setup

We evaluate four types of VMs (Table 1), assemble from 2 types of resources (core and memory). The configurations of resource pool are based on the Titan system [24] at Oak Ridge National Laboratory [25]. We investigate a resource pool with 51200 cores and 124900 GB memory. Each user requests a set of bundles and the maximum number of each VM of Amazon EC2 type is 5 in each bundle. In this experiments, we use $k = 3, ..., 7$. We generate a random bid for each user between 1.00 and 10.00.

5.2 Analysis of Results

In this experiment, we compare the performance of G-VMPAHM and VCG-VMPAHM for different number of choices. For each simulation, we average over 50 times to obtain data points to eliminate randomness. Since VCG-VMPAHM could not find the optimal solutions even after 10 hours or thrown out of memory ranging from 6-minded to 7-minded, and thus, there are no bars in the plots for those cases. In addition, the computation ratio of VCG-PMRM is 20% for 5-minded, and thus, the bars in figure are only the average of valid values.

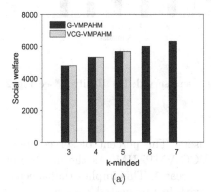
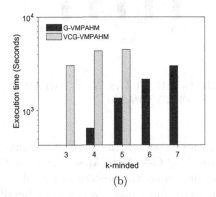

| (a) | (b) |

Fig. 2. G-VMPAHM vs. VCG-VMPAHM: (a) Social welfare; (b) Execution time. (*VCG-VMPAHM was not able to determine the allocation ranging from 6-minded to 7-minded in a feasible time or thrown out of memory, and computation ratio was 20% for 5-minded.)

Figure 2a shows social welfare obtained by VCG-VMPAHM and G-VMAPHM. Results show that the social welfare obtained by mechanisms increase with the increase of the number of minds. In addition, G-VMPAHM obtains the near-optimal social welfare from 3-minded to 5-minded. However, VCG-VMPAHM cannot find the optimal welfare in a feasible time, while G-VMPAHM obtains the social welfare from 6-minded to 7-minded. The gap in social welfare between G-VMPAHM and VCG-VMPAHM is amazed, and G-VMPAHM can obtain social welfare for larger instances given the fact that G-VMPAHM performs very well.

Figure 2b shows the execution times on a logarithmic scale. Results show that the execution time increases with the increase of number of mindes. Note that VCG-VMPAHM cannot find the optimal social welfare ranging from 6-minded to 7-minded. In particular, it is obvious that G-VMPAHM is significantly faster than VCG-VMPAHM. As shown in the Fig. 2a and 2b, G-VMPAHM not only obtains the near-optimal social welfare, but also it finds the resulting allocation in a reasonable time. This is due to the fact that G-VMPAHM is more appropriate for larger instances setting.

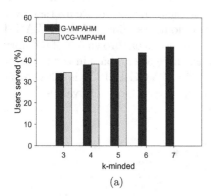

(a)

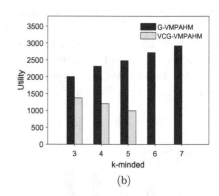

(b)

Fig. 3. G-VMPAHM vs. VCG-VMPAHM: (a) Users served; (b) Utility. (*see Fig. 2 note on VCG-VMPAHM)

Figure 3a shows the percent of served users. The percent of served users obtained by G-VMPAHM is very close to VCG-VMPAHM. As the number of minds increases, the percent of served users increases. This implies that mechanism serves more users by selecting bundles with few requested resources.

Figure 3b shows the utility obtained by both mechanisms. As the number of minds increases, the utility obtained by G-VMPAHM are all increase. This can be explained that users can declare better bid densities as the number of minds increases, and their prices employed by G-VMPAHM decrease. According to the figure, G-VMPAHM obtains more utility. This is due to the fact that G-VMPAHM is beneficial for the uses to use this mechanism.

Figure 4a and b show the percentage of resource utilization for both mechanisms. Results show that the memory is the scarce resource and the percentage of memory approaches one hundred percent. The percentage of resource utilization for both mechanisms increase with the increase in the number of minds. This is due to the fact that with more minds, our proposed mechanisms can better utilize heterogeneous resources to obtain more social welfare.

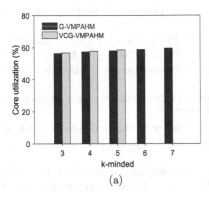
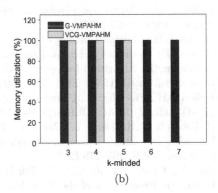

(a)   (b)

Fig. 4. G-VMPAHM vs. VCG-VMPAHM: (a) Core utilization; (b) Memory utilization. (*see Fig. 2 note on VCG-VMPAHM)

6 Conclusion and Future Work

We addressed the problem of VM provisioning and allocation of heterogeneous cloud resources in shared multi-minded in the single-parameter domains. We proposed an optimal and an approximation mechanism for solving VMPAHM. In addition, we showed our proposed approximation mechanism is truthful. Experimental results demonstrated that our proposed mechanism obtained near-optimal social welfare in reasonable amount of time and better utilized heterogeneous resources. As a result, our proposed approximation mechanism was the best choice for both cloud providers and users. For future work, we will plan to extend the proposed mechanisms for cloud resource provisioning with time-varying workloads.

Acknowledgement. The work was supported in part by the National Natural Science Foundation of China [Nos. 61662088,11301466,11361048], the Natural Science Foundation of Yunnan Province of China [No. 2014FB114], and Program for Excellent Young Talents, Yunnan University.

References

1. Amazon EC2 Instances. http://aws.amazon.com/cn/ec2
2. Nisan, N., Ronen, A.: Algorithmic mechanism design. Games Econ. Behav. **35**, 166–196 (2001)
3. Mu'Alem, A., Nisanb, N.: Truthful approximation mechanisms for restricted combinatorial auctions. Games Econ. Behav. **64**(2), 612–631 (2008)
4. Dobzinski, S., Nisan, N.: Mechanisms for multi-unit auctions. J. Artif. Intell. Res. **37**, 85–95 (2010)
5. Babaioff, M., Lavi, R., Pavlov, E.: Mechanism design for single-value domains. In: Proceedings of the 20th National Conference on Artificial Intelligence, vol. 1, pp. 241–247 (2005)

6. Vickrey, W.: Counterspeculation, auctions, and competitive sealed tenders. J. Finance **16**(1), 8–37 (1961)
7. Clarke, E.H.: Multipart pricing of public goods. Public Choice **11**(1), 17–33 (1971)
8. Groves, T.: Incentives in teams. Econometrica **41**(4), 617–631 (1973)
9. Sandholm, T.: Algorithm for optimal winner determination in combinatorial auctions. Artif. Intell. **135**(1–2), 1–54 (2002)
10. Kellerer, H., Pferschy, U., Pisinger, D.: Knapsack Problems. Springer, Heidelberg (2004). https://doi.org/10.1007/978-3-540-24777-7
11. Hajiesmaili, M.H., Deng, L., Chen, M., Li, Z.: Incentivizing device-to-device load balancing for cellular networks: an online auction design. IEEE J. Selected Areas Commun. **35**(2), 265–279 (2017)
12. Zhu, Y., Fu, S., Liu, J., Cui, Y.: Truthful online auction for cloud instance subletting. In: Proceedings of the IEEE 37th International Conference on Distributed Computing Systems (2017)
13. Lehmann, D., Ita O'Callaghan, L., Shoham, Y.: Truth revelation in approximately efficient combinatorial auctions. J. ACM **49**(5), 577–602 (2002)
14. Zaman, S., Grosu, D.: A combinatorial auction-based mechanism for dynamic VM provisioning and allocation in clouds. IEEE Trans. Cloud Comput. **1**(2), 129–141 (2013)
15. Bonacquisto, P., Di, G., Modica, G.P., Tomarchio, O.: A procurement auction market to trade residual cloud computing capacity. IEEE Trans. Cloud Comput. **3**(3), 345–357 (2015)
16. Zhou, R., Li, Z., Wu, C., Huang, Z.: An efficient cloud market mechanism for computing jobs with soft deadlines. IEEE/ACM Trans. Network. **25**(2), 793–805 (2016)
17. Fu, H., Li, Z., Wu, C., Chu, X.: Core-selecting auctions for dynamically allocating heterogeneous VMs in cloud computing. In: Proceedings of the 2014 IEEE International Conference on Cloud Computing, pp. 152–159 (2014)
18. Zhang, H., Li, B., Jiang, H., Liu, F., Vasilakos, A.V., Liu, J.: A framework for truthful online auctions in cloud computing with heterogeneous user demands. IEEE Trans. Cloud Comput. **65**(3), 805–818 (2016)
19. Shi, W., Zhang, L., Wu, C., Li, Z., Lau, F.C.M.: An online auction framework for dynamic resource provisioning in cloud computing. IEEE/ACM Trans. Network. **24**(4), 2060–2073 (2016)
20. Mashayekhy, L., Nejad, M.M., Grosu, D.: A PTAS mechanism for provisioning and allocation of heterogeneous cloud resources. IEEE Trans. Parallel Distrib. Syst. **26**, 2386–2399 (2015)
21. Nejad, M.M., Mashayekhy, L., Grosu, D.: Truthful greedy mechanisms for dynamic virtual machine provisioning and allocation in clouds. IEEE Trans. Parallel Distrib. Syst. **26**(2), 594–603 (2015)
22. Krysta, P.: Greedy approximation via duality for packing, combinatorial auctions and routing. In: Jędrzejowicz, J., Szepietowski, A. (eds.) MFCS 2005. LNCS, vol. 3618, pp. 615–627. Springer, Heidelberg (2005). https://doi.org/10.1007/11549345_53
23. Ibm, ILOG CPLEX Optimizer. http://www-01.ibm.com/software/commerce/optimization/cplex-optimizer/
24. Titan. http://www.olcf.ornl.gov/titan/
25. Top 500 Supercomputers. http://www.top500.org

Hyper-graph Regularized Multi-view Matrix Factorization for Vehicle Identification

Bin Qian[1]([✉]), Xiaobo Shen[2], Zhenqiu Shu[3], Xiguang Gu[1], Jin Huang[1], and Jiabin Hu[1]

[1] Traffic Management Research Institute of the Ministry of Public Security, Wuxi 214151, China
qianbin_nust@126.com
[2] School of Computer Science and Engineering, Nanjing University of Science and Technology, Nanjing 210094, China
[3] School of Computer Engineering, Jiangsu University of Technology, Changzhou 213001, China

Abstract. Recent vehicle identification systems based on radio frequency identification (RFID) often suffer from the challenges including long distance limitation and risk of malevolent tampering. A natural idea is to integrate multiple visual features with RFID information to improve the identification performance. In this paper, we propose an improved visual feature representation method, called hyper-graph regularized multi-view matrix factorization (HMMF), for vehicle identification. The proposed HMMF pushes cross-view clusters towards a common embedding, and maintains the high-order within-view structure simultaneously. We further propose semi-supervised HMMF (SemiHMMF) to incorporate the labels to utilize the partial labels of RFID data. An iterative optimization algorithm is developed based on multiplicative rules. Experiments on two real-world datasets demonstrate the effectiveness of the proposed methods on vehicle identification.

Keywords: Matrix factorization · Multi-view · Vehicle identification
RFID · Hyper-graph · Multiplicative rules

1 Introduction

Vehicle identification, as a significant component of urban surveillance, attracts massive focuses in computer vision field [1,2]. Recently, there is growing interest in passive UHF RFID technology for automatic vehicle identification (AVI) in electronic toll collection (ETC) [3,4]. RFID based vehicle identification systems have well reading reliability, especially when facing inclement weather, rate can be as high as 95%. However, they suffer from the challenges including long distance limitation and risk of malevolent tampering. Therefore, it is natural to integrate other information, e.g., visual information that is easily obtained

© Springer Nature Switzerland AG 2018
X. Sun et al. (Eds.): ICCCS 2018, LNCS 11063, pp. 543–554, 2018.
https://doi.org/10.1007/978-3-030-00006-6_50

544   B. Qian et al.

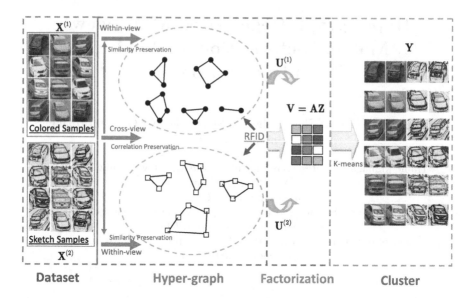

Fig. 1. The flowchart of the proposed HMMF. First, multiple visual features are extracted from original images. Then the features are further factorized by the proposed multi-view learning model, and hyper-graph structure and partial labels of RFID data are incorporated. Finally, the shared embedding is used for the vehicle identification.

through widely distributed urban cameras, to enhance the identification performance [5] (Fig. 1).

In recent decades, vision based multi-view learning has attracted a lot of attention due to its significance for feature extraction and information mining [6,7]. Multi-view features, i.e., color, shape and texture features from the same vehicle image, can provide consistent and complementary information, and integrating these multi-view features appropriately has been shown superior to using single-view feature [8]. Until now many multi-view clustering methods have been proposed, including two main categories: spectral based and subspace based methods. Spectral based methods are extended from single-view clustering methods with extra similarity constraint, e.g., minimizing disagreement constraint [9], co-training constraint [10] and co-regularized constraint [11]. Subspace based multi-view clustering methods first project multi-view data into a common low-dimensional subspace and then apply any clustering algorithms such as K-means to learn the partition [12]. A typical subspace based method is Canonical Correlation Analysis (CCA) [13], which analyzes linear correlations among multiple feature sets. Nonnegative matrix factorization (NMF) [14], which obtains interpretable representations with the nonnegative constraint, is a classical subspace representation method for clustering. However, NMF fails to perform on negative data owing to the nonnegative constraint. Moreover, most existing NMFs are designed only for single view. The above drawbacks limit its use in many real-world applications.

Recently, several NMF variants have been applied to multi-view clustering, and achieve promising results. In [15], collective NMF (ColNMF) is proposed for relational learning. ColNMF treats multi-view clustering as a latent space searching problem, and decomposes each view into two matrices, i.e., projection matrix and shared coefficient matrix. Liu *et al.* [16] propose a multi-view clustering method based on nonnegative matrix factorization (MNMF), which tries to seek a factorization that gives compatible clustering solutions across multiple views and achieves promising results. However, compared with ColNMF, the derivation of MultiNMF is complicated and the model is hard to extend. To adapt to the semi-supervised scenario, Wang *et al.* [17] propose a semi-supervised multi-view NMF (SMNMF) method, which takes the label information as additional hard constraints. NMF assumes that data points are sampled from euclidean space, thus it fails to exploit the geometric structure of the data. In order to consider the manifold information, graph regularized multi-view NMF (GMNMF) [18] is proposed to preserve the local affinity structure within each view, which shows its brilliant performance on multi-view clustering task. GMNMF constructs a k-nearest neighbor within each view based simple graph to consider the local invariance. However, the high-order relationship among samples is neglected in graph-based learning methods, which only consider the pairwise relationship between two samples. To consider the high-order relationship of complex data, some researchers have tried to apply hyper-graph to matrix factorization and achieved satisfying results in some fields [19–21]. Nevertheless, these methods are not designed for multi-view learning and they do not fully consider the cross-view correlation among multi-view data. On the other hand, in practical vehicle identification applications, partial reliable RFID labels can be obtained and these methods do not consider such semi-supervised information.

Inspired by the hyper-graph assumption [19–21], we propose a novel multi-view matrix factorization method, called hyper-graph regularized multi-view matrix Factorization (HMMF), for vehicle identification. The basic idea of HMMF is to push cross-view clusters towards a common embedding, and to maintain the high-order within-view structure simultaneously. Furthermore, we further propose semi-supervised HMMF, by extending HMMF to semi-supervised scenario. Our experimental evaluations on two real data sets show that our proposed methods outperform state-of-the-art multi-view matrix factorization methods for vehicle identification.

In the following, we first briefly review some related works. Then, we present our proposed methods and report the experimental results. Finally, we conclude the paper.

2   Related Works

This section briefly introduces a basic multi-view NMF clustering method, which is also named collective matrix factorization (ColNMF) [15]. Some mathematical symbols and definitions are first given.

Given a data set $\mathbf{X} = \{(\mathbf{x}_i^{(1)}, \mathbf{x}_i^{(2)}, \cdots, \mathbf{x}_i^{(m)}, y_i), i = 1, \cdots, n\}$, where $\mathbf{x}_i = (\mathbf{x}_i^{(1)}, \mathbf{x}_i^{(2)}, \cdots, \mathbf{x}_i^{(m)})$ is the ith example, $\mathbf{x}_i^{(q)} \in \mathbb{R}^{p_q}$ is the instance of the ith example in the qth view, m is the number of views, and y_i is its cluster label. ColNMF aims at clustering $\mathbf{x}_i$ into it's corresponding cluster label y_i through each single view's factorization with the shared coefficient matrix. The objective can be formulated as

$$\min_{\mathbf{U}^{(q)}, \mathbf{V}} F(\mathbf{U}^{(q)}, \mathbf{V}) = \sum_{q=1}^{m} \|\mathbf{X}^{(q)} - \mathbf{U}^{(q)}\mathbf{V}^{\mathrm{T}}\|^2 = \sum_{q=1}^{m} \sum_{i=1}^{p_q} \sum_{j=1}^{n} (x_{ij}^{(q)} - \sum_{l=1}^{r} u_{il}^{(q)} v_{jl})^2,$$

$$s.t. \ \mathbf{U}^{(q)} \geq 0, \mathbf{V} \geq 0,$$

$$(1)$$

where $\mathbf{X}^{(q)}$ represents all the samples of the qth view, $\mathbf{U}^{(q)}$ represents the projection matrix of the qth view, and $\mathbf{V}$ is the shared coefficient matrix. According to the multiplicative rules of [14], the updating rules of ColNMF in Eq. (1) can be introduced as follows:

$$(u_{il}^{(q)})^{t+1} \leftarrow (u_{il}^{(q)})^t \frac{\mathbf{X}^{(q)}\mathbf{V}}{\mathbf{U}^{(q)}\mathbf{V}^{\mathrm{T}}\mathbf{V}}, \qquad v_{jl}^{t+1} \leftarrow v_{jl}^t \frac{\sum_{q=1}^{m}(\mathbf{X}^{(q)})^{\mathrm{T}}\mathbf{U}^{(q)}}{\sum_{q=1}^{m}\mathbf{V}(\mathbf{U}^{(q)})^{\mathrm{T}}\mathbf{U}^{(q)}}. \qquad (2)$$

3 Approach

This section introduces the proposed hyper-graph regularized multi-view matrix factorization (HMMF) and its semi-supervised extension model (SemiHMMF).

3.1 Formulation

The original NMF fails to perform on negative data owing to the nonnegative constraint. However, in many real-world applications, negative feature data widely exists. Thus, in order to incorporate negative data information in multi-view applications, we first relax the constraint in Eq. (1) and propose a multi-view matrix factorization framework that is formulated as:

$$\min_{\mathbf{U}^{(q)}, \mathbf{V}} J_1(\mathbf{U}^{(q)}, \mathbf{V}) = \sum_{q=1}^{m} \|\mathbf{X}^{(q)} - \mathbf{U}^{(q)}\mathbf{V}^{\mathrm{T}}\|^2, \quad s.t. \ \mathbf{V} \geq 0. \qquad (3)$$

Note that Eq. (3) is more closely connected to the K-means clustering method [22].

Multi-view NMF fails to discover the geometrical structure of inner-view space. In real world, geometrical information of each view can improve learning performance. Thus, we further consider the graph structure information. Especially, we use hyper-graph [19–21] to capture the high-order within-view structure, which shows excellent performance in single-view clustering.

The hyper-graph can be modeled as $G^H = (V^H, E^H, \mathbf{W})$ where the vertex set, V^H, corresponds to the data points; E^H is the hyperedge set where each hyperedge, e, is a subset of the vertex set V^H. Denote the weight corresponding to the hyperedge e as $w(e)$. Denote the incidence matrix $\mathbf{H}$ as $\mathbf{H}(v, e) = 1$ if $v \in e$; otherwise $\mathbf{H}(v, e) = 0$. Based on the above definitions, the vertex degree of each vertex can be given as $d(v) = \sum_{e \in E} w(e) \mathbf{H}(v, e)$. The edge degree of a hyperedge, e, is defined as $\delta(e) = \sum_{e \in E} \mathbf{H}(v, e)$. The weight matrix, $\mathbf{W}$, where $W_{ij} = \sum_{e \in E(i,j)} \frac{w(e)}{\delta(e)}$ is the weight between any two vertices in the hypergraph. Let $\mathbf{D}_v^H$, $\mathbf{D}_e^H$ and $\mathbf{W}_e$ denote the diagonal matrices of vertex degrees, hyperedge degrees and the edge weight, respectively. Then the unnormalized hypergraph laplacian matrix is formulated as $\mathbf{L} = \mathbf{D} - \mathbf{S}$, where $\mathbf{S} = \mathbf{H}\mathbf{W}_e\mathbf{D}_e^{-1}\mathbf{H}^{\mathrm{T}}$. Finally, the hyper-graph regularization can be derived as

$$
J_H = \frac{1}{2} \sum_{i,j=1}^{n} \|\mathbf{v}_i - \mathbf{v}_j\|^2 S_{ij} = \sum_{i=1}^{n} \mathbf{v}_i^{\mathrm{T}} \mathbf{v}_i \mathbf{D}_{ii} - \sum_{i,j=1}^{n} \mathbf{v}_i^{\mathrm{T}} \mathbf{v}_j S_{ij}
$$

$$
= \mathrm{Tr}(\mathbf{V}^{\mathrm{T}}\mathbf{D}\mathbf{V}) - \mathrm{Tr}(\mathbf{V}^{\mathrm{T}}\mathbf{S}\mathbf{V}) = \mathrm{Tr}(\mathbf{V}^{\mathrm{T}}\mathbf{L}\mathbf{V}).
$$

(4)

By incorporating the hyper-graph regularization term, hyper-graph regularized multi-view matrix factorization (HMMF) is formulated as

$$
\min_{\mathbf{U}^{(q)},\mathbf{V}} J_1(\mathbf{U}^{(q)}, \mathbf{V}) = \sum_{q=1}^{m} \|\mathbf{X}^{(q)} - \mathbf{U}^{(q)}\mathbf{V}^{\mathrm{T}}\|^2 + \lambda \mathrm{Tr}(\mathbf{V}^{\mathrm{T}}\mathbf{L}^{(q)}\mathbf{V}),
$$

$$
s.t. \ \mathbf{V} \geq 0,
$$

(5)

where λ is the regularization parameter and $\mathbf{L}^{(q)}$ denotes the hyper-graph laplacian matrix of the qth view.

Recently, RFID based vehicle identification technology has shown its unique advantage for its high recognition rate and low cost. However, long distance constraint limits its performance and only partial stable identity labels can be provided. In order to utilize these label information, we further extend our model by incorporating the partial label of RFID.

Assume that the label information of the first g vehicles $\mathbf{X}_g = [\mathbf{x}_1, \mathbf{x}_2, \cdots, \mathbf{x}_g] \in \mathbb{R}^{p \times g}$ is provided by RFID device and the rest vehicles $\mathbf{X}_u = [\mathbf{x}_{g+1}, \mathbf{x}_{g+2}, \cdots, \mathbf{x}_n] \in \mathbb{R}^{p \times (n-g)}$ are missed. We use c to denote the number of vehicles. Let $\mathbf{B}$ denote the indicator matrix, i.e., $b_{ij} = 1$ if and only if image $\mathbf{x}_i$ is from the j-th car; $b_{ij} = 0$ otherwise. Thus the label constraint matrix $\mathbf{A}$ can be defined as follows:

$$
\mathbf{A} = \begin{pmatrix} \mathbf{B}_{g \times c} & \mathbf{0} \\ \mathbf{0} & \mathbf{I}_{n-g} \end{pmatrix},
$$

(6)

where $\mathbf{I}_{n-q}$ denotes an identity matrix. By incorporating the label into HMMF, it can be imposed by an auxiliary matrix $\mathbf{Z} \in \mathbb{R}^{(c+n-g) \times p}$

$$
\mathbf{V} = \mathbf{A}\mathbf{Z}.
$$

(7)

From Eq. (7), the images from the same vehicle can be merged together in the new subspace. Thus, the obtained multi-view representation has the consistent label with the original data, and can have higher discrimination. The final objective function of the proposed SemiHMMF can be expressed as follows:

$$\min_{\mathbf{U}^{(q)}, \mathbf{V}} J(\mathbf{U}^{(q)}, \mathbf{V}) = \sum_{q=1}^{m} \|\mathbf{X}^{(q)} - \mathbf{U}^{(q)} \mathbf{Z}^T \mathbf{A}^T\|^2 + \lambda \mathrm{Tr}(\mathbf{Z}^T \mathbf{A}^T \mathbf{L}^{(q)} \mathbf{A} \mathbf{Z}), \tag{8}$$

$$s.t.\ \mathbf{Z} \geq 0.$$

3.2   Optimization

In essence, the objective in Eq. (8) is a multivariable optimization problem. We develop an efficient optimization algorithm based on multiplicative rules to update the variables alternately.

The objective in Eq. (8) can be reformulated by using matrix property:

$$
\begin{aligned}
J &= \sum_{q=1}^{m} \|\mathbf{X}^{(q)} - \mathbf{U}^{(q)} \mathbf{Z}^T \mathbf{A}^T\|^2 + \lambda \mathrm{Tr}(\mathbf{Z}^T \mathbf{A}^T \mathbf{L}^{(q)} \mathbf{A} \mathbf{Z}) \\
&= \sum_{q=1}^{m} (\mathbf{X}^{(q)} - \mathbf{U}^{(q)} \mathbf{Z}^T \mathbf{A}^T)^T (\mathbf{X}^{(q)} - \mathbf{U}^{(q)} \mathbf{Z}^T \mathbf{A}^T) + \lambda \mathrm{Tr}(\mathbf{Z}^T \mathbf{A}^T \mathbf{L}^{(q)} \mathbf{A} \mathbf{Z}) \\
&= \sum_{q=1}^{m} (\mathbf{X}^{(q)})^T (\mathbf{X}^{(q)}) - 2(\mathbf{X}^{(q)})^T \mathbf{U}^{(q)} \mathbf{Z}^T \mathbf{A}^T + \mathbf{A} \mathbf{Z} (\mathbf{U}^{(q)})^T (\mathbf{U}^q) \mathbf{Z}^T \mathbf{A}^T \\
&\quad + \lambda \mathrm{Tr}(\mathbf{Z}^T \mathbf{A}^T \mathbf{L}^{(q)} \mathbf{A} \mathbf{Z}).
\end{aligned}
\tag{9}
$$

Denote H is the Lagrange function corresponding to Eq. (9) and Let Φ be the Lagrange multiplier for constraint $\mathbf{Z} \geq 0$. Taking the partial derivative of H with respect to $\mathbf{Z}$, then we have

$$\frac{\partial H}{\partial \mathbf{Z}} = \sum_{q=1}^{m} -2\mathbf{A}^T (\mathbf{X}^{(q)})^T (\mathbf{U}^{(q)}) + 2\mathbf{A}^T \mathbf{A} \mathbf{Z} (\mathbf{U}^{(q)})^T (\mathbf{U}^{(q)}) + 2\lambda \mathbf{A}^T \mathbf{L} \mathbf{A} \mathbf{Z} + \Phi. \tag{10}$$

Using KKT conditions $\Phi_{ij} Z_{ij} = 0$, we derive the following update rules:

$$(\mathbf{U})^{(q)} \leftarrow (\mathbf{X}^{(q)})(\mathbf{Z}^T \mathbf{A}^T)^\dagger, \tag{11}$$

$$\mathbf{Z} \leftarrow \mathbf{Z}.* \frac{\sum_{q=1}^{m}(\mathbf{A}^T(\mathbf{X}^{(q)})^T(\mathbf{U}^{(q)}))^+ + (\mathbf{A}^T \mathbf{A} \mathbf{Z}(\mathbf{U}^{(q)})^T(\mathbf{U}^{(q)}))^- + \lambda \mathbf{A}^T(\mathbf{S})^{(q)} \mathbf{A} \mathbf{Z}}{\sum_{q=1}^{m}(\mathbf{A}^T(\mathbf{X}^{(q)})^T(\mathbf{U}^{(q)}))^- + (\mathbf{A}^T \mathbf{A} \mathbf{Z}(\mathbf{U}^{(q)})^T(\mathbf{U}^{(q)}))^+ + \lambda \mathbf{A}^T(\mathbf{D})^{(q)} \mathbf{A} \mathbf{Z}},$$
$$\tag{12}$$

where $(\mathbf{Z}^T \mathbf{A}^T)^\dagger$ is the Moore-Penrose pseudo-inverse of $(\mathbf{Z}^T \mathbf{A}^T)$ and $\mathbf{M}^+ = \frac{|\mathbf{M}|+\mathbf{M}}{2}$, $\mathbf{M}^- = \frac{|\mathbf{M}|-\mathbf{M}}{2}$.

The flowchart of the proposed method is shown in Algorithm 1. After we obtain the shared latent matrix $\mathbf{V}$, the cluster label is obtained by K-means.

Algorithm 1. SemiHMMF

Data: Vehicle multi-view visual feature dataset $\mathbf{X}^{(q)}, q = 1 \cdots m$, regularization
parameter λ, nearest neighbor parameter k.
1. Initialize matrices $\mathbf{U}^{(q)}$ and $\mathbf{Z}$ randomly;
2. Construct label constraint matrix $\mathbf{A}$ by Eq. (6);
3. Construct hyper-graph regularization $(\mathbf{Z}^{\mathrm{T}}\mathbf{A}^{\mathrm{T}}\mathbf{L}\mathbf{A}\mathbf{Z})$ by Eq. (4);
while *not converge* **do**
　　4. Update $\mathbf{U}^{(q)}$ by Eq. (11).
　　5. Update $\mathbf{Z}$ by Eq. (12).
end
6. Compute $\mathbf{V}$ by Eq. (7);
Output: V

(a)   (b)

Fig. 2. Some sample images from two databases. (a) VehicleID database. (b) VeRi database.

4   Experiment

4.1   Experimental Settings

This section evaluates the proposed methods by performing vehicle clustering on two public image databases: VehicleID database [23] and VeRi database [24]. Some sample images are shown in Fig. 2. For simplicity, 76 Fourier coefficients feature and 314-dimensional color histogram feature are extracted for further multi-view data fusion. To evaluate the effectiveness and efficiency, we present quantitative evaluations of our proposed HMMF and SemiHMMF, and compare them with some related methods: ColNMF [15], MNMF [16], SMNMF [17], and GMNMF [18]. Additionally, NMFs with single view (SV1, SV2) are also adopted as two baselines for comparison. We utilize K-means to cluster the low-dimensional shared representation and set the number of clusters as the number of vehicles. The clustering performance is evaluated by clustering Accuracy (AC) and Normalized Mutual Information (NMI) measures, which have been widely used for clustering. For the RFID embedding scene, we randomly choose 20% images from each vehicle as the available label information, and use them to construct the label constraint matrix. Finally, we mix the labeled images and unlabeled images as a whole for vehicle clustering tasks.

4.2 Experimental Results and Analysis

Tables 1 and 2 report the clustering results on VehicleID and VeRi databases, respectively. From the experimental results, we have the following conclusions:

Table 1. Clustering performance on VehicleID database

(a) AC(%)

c	SV1	SV2	ColNMF	MNMF	SMNMF	GMNMF	HMMF	SemiHMMF
5	72.00	69.00	72.00	78.50	83.70	80.21	84.28	**87.45**
10	65.01	60.77	66.45	69.76	77.89	70.33	74.87	**80.98**
15	61.86	59.12	65.87	65.88	72.33	66.54	67.45	**74.30**
20	60.51	59.33	59.65	64.34	70.60	67.83	69.54	**75.09**
25	55.90	58.49	58.10	60.30	67.09	63.67	68.90	**73.80**
30	52.77	55.80	54.97	55.31	62.45	58.74	59.85	**69.04**
35	46.30	51.85	52.90	54.39	60.71	57.21	60.53	**67.98**
40	44.40	48.33	51.30	52.45	57.53	57.11	57.65	**64.33**
Avg	57.34	57.84	60.16	62.62	69.29	67.21	67.88	**74.12**

(b) NMI(%)

c	SV1	SV2	ColNMF	MNMF	SMNMF	GMNMF	HMMF	SemiHMMF
5	53.18	49.45	54.89	60.43	67.92	65.41	65.56	**69.85**
10	43.21	40.11	48.87	52.15	60.99	54.32	59.98	**65.30**
15	43.92	41.88	50.32	55.31	61.50	56.75	58.23	**64.90**
20	42.85	42.64	48.98	53.27	62.31	56.87	58.00	**63.86**
25	39.40	41.98	46.43	47.50	58.95	52.43	54.89	**58.31**
30	36.11	38.91	37.99	40.71	50.76	43.90	48.96	**53.42**
35	31.52	35.00	35.78	36.90	40.65	37.77	41.44	**48.09**
40	29.17	33.34	32.46	34.57	40.11	36.01	39.90	**46.38**
Avg	39.92	40.41	44.47	47.61	55.40	50.43	53.37	**58.76**

(1) We observe that HMMF outperforms GMNMF on both databases. This is mainly attributed to the fact that the hyper-graph technique is applied. It shows that hyper-graph Laplacian regularizer can better reveal the intrinsic geometrical structure.

(2) SemiHMMF is superior to HMMF. SemiHMMF considers the RFID label as additional information, while HMMF is unsupervised. It implies that RFID information plays an important role for vehicle identification. It also verifies the importance of RFID information.

Table 2. Clustering performance on VeRi database

(a) AC(%)

c	SV1	SV2	ColNMF	MNMF	SMNMF	GMNMF	HMMF	SemiHMMF
5	55.35	62.87	66.56	68.90	74.39	74.80	77.08	**79.90**
10	52.77	58.43	60.10	62.95	68.99	70.31	71.39	**76.24**
15	45.88	51.79	51.00	54.80	60.38	65.93	68.34	**72.09**
20	41.67	50.78	43.90	54.99	59.94	55.79	58.90	**63.42**
25	38.41	45.91	37.90	45.88	52.92	54.38	56.79	**60.11**
30	34.39	42.10	39.76	44.07	49.30	45.44	49.76	**54.31**
35	34.21	43.80	38.77	45.91	50.21	47.98	53.16	**58.77**
40	31.06	37.71	32.56	39.10	43.87	40.38	45.97	**51.60**
Avg	41.72	49.17	46.32	52.08	57.50	56.88	60.17	**64.56**

(b) NMI(%)

c	SV1	SV2	ColNMF	MNMF	SMNMF	GMNMF	HMMF	SemiHMMF
5	38.67	43.12	45.80	48.77	51.34	52.83	53.90	**57.08**
10	35.21	40.36	37.89	41.88	47.59	48.91	50.21	**54.65**
15	29.20	32.76	31.84	34.91	39.67	40.58	43.34	**45.10**
20	25.51	29.01	29.87	29.80	33.90	36.81	38.90	**41.09**
25	21.22	27.90	28.07	30.12	33.10	34.89	34.92	**38.41**
30	17.20	22.38	24.89	25.11	29.34	26.70	27.38	**30.92**
35	20.45	26.90	26.90	28.09	32.65	30.18	33.71	**35.90**
40	16.12	23.56	21.77	23.90	28.88	26.45	29.07	**33.11**
Avg	25.45	30.75	30.88	32.82	37.06	37.17	38.93	**42.03**

(3) HMMF always outperforms two single-view NMFs, which validates that HMMF can explicitly integrate the visual information among different views and improve the vehicle identification.

Figure 3 shows the AC performance of HMMF with the varying parameters λ and k. As we can see from Fig. 3, the AC of HMMF is relatively stable when λ varies from 0.1 to 1. For parameter k, which controls the neighbor number of hyper-graph, plays a crucial role in the proposed algorithm. It needs to be chosen carefully.

In order to verify the convergence of the proposed methods, we plot the convergence curves of HMMF and SemiHMMF on two datasets. From Fig. 4, we observe that both the two methods can converge within 250 iterations, which shows the well convergence ability of our proposed methods.

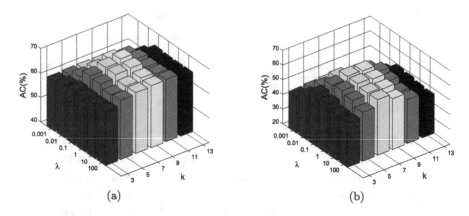

Fig. 3. Parameters analysis. (a) VehicleID database. (b) VeRi database.

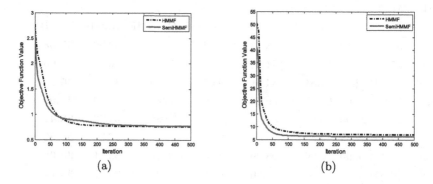

Fig. 4. Convergence curves of HMMF and SemiHMMF methods. (a) VehicleID database. (b) VeRi database.

5   Conclusions

In this paper, we present a novel matrix factorization method, called hyper-graph regularized multi-view matrix factorization (HMMF), for multiple visual features representation and vehicle identification. Both within-view and cross-view structures are considered in HMMF. A semi-supervised HMMF (SemiHMMF) considers the limited labels of RFID data in a parameter-free way. Experimental results on VehicleID and VeRi databases demonstrate the superiority of our methods.

Acknowledgments. This paper is supported by national key research and development program of China (Grant No. 2017YFC0804806), national natural science foundation of China (Grant No. 61603159) and natural science foundation of Jiangsu province (Grant No. BK20160293).

References

1. Huang, C.L., Liao, W.C.: A vision-based vehicle identification system. In: International Conference on Pattern Recognition, Cambridge, UK, pp. 364–367 (2004)
2. Wang, Z., et al.: Orientation invariant feature embedding and spatial temporal regularization for vehicle re-identification. In: IEEE Conference on Computer Vision and Pattern Recognition, Venice, Italy, pp. 379–387 (2017)
3. Hoffman, A.J., Pretorius, A., Wang, Y.: Geometry based analysis of an alternative RFID interrogator placement for electronic vehicle identification. In: International Conference on Intelligent Transportation Systems, Las Palmas, Spain, pp. 2390–2397 (2015)
4. Wang, Y., Bialkowski, K.S., Pretorius, A.J., Plooy, A.G.W.D., Abbosh, A.M.: In-road microwave sensor for electronic vehicle identification and tracking: link budget analysis and antenna prototype. IEEE Trans. Intell. Transp. Syst. **19**, 123–128 (2018)
5. Berz, E.L., Tesch, D.A., Hessel, F.P.: A hybrid RFID and CV system for item-level localization of stationary objects. In: International Symposium on Quality Electronic Design, Santa Clara, USA, pp. 331–336 (2017)
6. Shen, X.B., Shen, F.M., Sun, Q.S., Yang, Y., Yuan, Y.H., Shen, H.T.: Semi-paired discrete hashing: learning latent hash codes for semi-paired cross-view retrieval. IEEE Trans. Cybern. **47**, 4275–4288 (2017)
7. Shen, X.B., Sun, Q.S., Yuan, Y.H.: A unified multiset canonical correlation analysis framework based on graph embedding for multiple feature extraction. Neurocomputing **148**, 397–408 (2015)
8. Yao, X., Han, J., Zhang, D., Nie, F.: Revisiting co-saliency detection: a novel approach based on two-stage multi-view spectral rotation co-clustering. IEEE Trans. Image Process. **26**, 3196–3209 (2017)
9. Sa, V.R.D.: Spectral clustering with two views. In: ICML Workshop on Learning with Multiple Views, Bonn, Germany, pp. 20–27 (2005)
10. Kumar, A., Iii, H.D.: A co-training approach for multi-view spectral clustering. In: International Conference on Machine Learning, Bellevue, USA, pp. 393–400 (2011)
11. Kumar, A., Rai, P.: Co-regularized multi-view spectral clustering. In: International Conference on Neural Information Processing Systems, Granada, Spain, pp. 1413–1421 (2011)
12. Wang, X., Guo, X., Lei, Z., Zhang, C., Li, S. Z.: Exclusivity-consistency regularized multi-view subspace clustering. In: IEEE Conference on Computer Vision and Pattern Recognition, Honolulu, USA, pp. 923–931 (2017)
13. Shen, X.B., Sun, Q.S.: A novel semi-supervised canonical correlation analysis and extensions for multi-view dimensionality reduction. J. Visual Commun. Image Represent. **25**, 1894–1904 (2014)
14. Lee, D.D., Seung, H.S.: Learning the parts of objects by non-negative matrix factorization. Nature **401**, 788–791 (1999)
15. Singh, A.P., Gordon, G.J.: Relational learning via collective matrix factorization. In: Proceedings of the 14th ACM SIGKDD International Conference on Knowledge Discovery and Data Mining, pp. 650–658. ACM (2008)
16. Liu, J., Wang, C., Gao, J., Han, J.: Multi-view clustering via joint nonnegative matrix factorization. In: Proceedings of the 2013 SIAM International Conference on Data Mining, pp. 252–260. Society for Industrial and Applied Mathematics (2013)

17. Wang, J., Wang, X., Tian, F., Liu, C.H., Yu, H., Liu, Y.: Adaptive multi-view semi-supervised nonnegative matrix factorization. In: Hirose, A., Ozawa, S., Doya, K., Ikeda, K., Lee, M., Liu, D. (eds.) ICONIP 2016. LNCS, vol. 9948, pp. 435–444. Springer, Cham (2016). https://doi.org/10.1007/978-3-319-46672-9_49

18. Zhang, X., Gao, H., Li, G., Zhao, J., Huo, J., Yin, J.: Multi-view clustering based on graph-regularized nonnegative matrix factorization for object recognition. Inf. Sci. **432**, 463–478 (2018)

19. Zeng, K., Yu, J., Li, C., You, J., Jin, T.: Image clustering by hyper-graph regularized non-negative matrix factorization. Neurocomputing **138**, 209–217 (2014)

20. Wang, W., Qian, Y., Tang, Y.Y.: Hypergraph-regularized sparse NMF for hyperspectral unmixing. IEEE J. Selected Top. Appl. Earth Observations Remote Sens. **9**, 681–694 (2016)

21. Huang, S., Wang, H., Ge, Y., Huangfu, L., Zhang, X., Yang, D.: Improved hypergraph regularized nonnegative matrix factorization with sparse representation. Pattern Recognit. Lett. **102**, 8–14 (2018)

22. Ding, C., Li, T., Jordan, M.I.: Convex and semi-nonnegative matrix factorizations. IEEE Trans. Pattern Anal. Mach. Intell. **32**, 45–55 (2010)

23. Liu, X., Liu, W., Ma, H., Fu, H.: Large-scale vehicle re-identification in urban surveillance videos. In: IEEE International Conference on Multimedia and Expo, pp. 1–6. IEEE (2016)

24. Liu, H., Tian, Y., Yang, Y., Pang, L., Huang, T.: Deep relative distance learning: tell the difference between similar vehicles. In: IEEE Conference on Computer Vision and Pattern Recognition, pp. 2167–2175. IEEE (2016)

Inconsistent Selection of Optimal Frame Length in WMSN

Yanli Wang[1]([✉]), Yuanyuan Hong[1], Ziyi Qiao[1], and Baili Zhang[1,2]

[1] School of Computer Science and Engineering, Southeast University, Nanjing 211189, China
Wyl15295640505@126.com
[2] Research Center for Judicial Big Data, Supreme Count of China, Nanjing 211189, China

Abstract. In traditional wire networks and wireless networks (e.g. WLAN, Cellular mobile network), optimal frame length is calculated according to the maximum data throughput, and adopted by every nodes in the network. But it is not suitable for Wireless Multimedia Sensor Network (WMSN), which mostly concerns effective utilization of limited energy instead of data throughput, and the nodes in the WMSN may have a very different channel environment. By adopting new benefit model in this paper the issue of optimal frame length is explored and an algorithm named OFLA is presented to achieve approximate optimal value. The one contributions of this article is a new benefit model of frame length in WSMN has been proposed. Another is with the new model and the algorithm, each node in WMSN can bring out the optimal frame length independently to compose the packets for the longest life-span of WMSN.

Keywords: WMSN · Optimal frame length

1 Introduction

Compared with the traditional Wireless Sensor Network (WSN), Wireless Multimedia Sensor Network (WMSN) needs to transmit large amount of multimedia data, which focus more on the optimal of energy consumption to extend the life-span of network as much as possible. As the basic unit of WMSN, energy consumption of Sensor node can hence be divided into three domains: sensor data acquisition, microprocessor data storage and processing, data transmission and reception by wireless module, in which the module of data transmission and reception by wireless is the most principal part of all energy consumption. In order to estimate the transmission energy consumption of WMSN nodes, the previous literature [4] adopts a computational model, $e = \sigma_s + \delta_s x$, x is the bytes sent, δ_s is the sensor energy consumption per bytes, and σ_s is the start sending consumption. For instance in the Mica2 node, the typical value is $\sigma_s = 0.645\,\mathrm{mJ}$, $\delta_s = 0.0144\,\mathrm{mJ}$, each transmission requires a large start-up power consumption, which is equivalent to sending nearly 45 bytes of energy. In view of this, due to start-up power consumption, the shorter the sending packets, the greater the average of the unit information energy consumption after the allocation, and the longer the sending packets, the lower the average of the information energy consumption after

X. Sun et al. (Eds.): ICCCS 2018, LNCS 11063, pp. 555–566, 2018.
https://doi.org/10.1007/978-3-030-00006-6_51

the allocation. Therefore, in addition to reducing the transmission of redundant information, the opportunity of sending packets can be fully used for data transmission in WMSN. For instance, in order to reducing energy consumption per unit of information transmission, the data can be grouped together as much as possible to increase the frame length of the transmitted message and reduce the number of transmissions, under the premise of satisfying the freshness of data. However, due to the existence of transmission collisions and channel errors, messages may fail to be sent and may need to be retransmitted. Once retransmitted, energy consumption per unit of information will increase exponentially. The longer the message, the higher the bit error rate and the greater the retransmission probability. Therefore, from the perspective of energy consumption, there is an optimal value for the length of the packet sent by the node, i.e. the length of the network packet. Because of the diversity and dynamic of the channel environment of each node, the optimal value of the packet length of each node is inconsistent and dynamic.

The selection of the optimal frame length for network grouping is not a new problem. Many researchers have conducted substantial research work in this field [6–15]. For wired networks, the packet frame length has long been viewed as a parameter that needs to be determined during the network design phase in the early stages. The previous research mainly focus on the relationship between optimal frame length with various factors such as the channel error, route hops, buffer size, and channel attenuation. Once the frame length is determined, the whole network is consistent and rarely adjusted [6, 7]. With the rapid development of WLAN, the instability of the wireless channel makes the adaptive adjustment of the packet frame length a hot issue of research. Many solutions have been proposed [6–14] to keep the network throughput at a maximum, including dynamic adjustment strategy for frame length [9], channel state dependent protocol [10, 11], adaptive channel error control technique [13–15]. Furthermore, the relevant literature [16, 17] has conducted similar studies on the optimal frame length and channel adaptation strategy in the wireless cellular network environment. Some Chinese researches also conducted some relative research on this issue. Xi et al. provide a detailed analysis on the relationship between throughput and frame length in the error channel, and obtains the optimal frame length at a specific error rate by numerical simulation method. Cheng et al. derive a closed-form solution of the optimal frame length to maximizes the throughput, according to the features of throughput variation with packet length.

Different from other types of wireless networks (e.g. WLAN, Cellular mobile network), the WMSN generally does not require high data throughput while WMSN requires much lower power consumption. In many application scenarios, energy cannot be supplemented. In the case of intelligent transportation, WMSN has been wide used in big city and expressway to monitor the traffic flow and guide the vehicles to select a reasonable route avoid traffic congestion. If there are situations violating the traffic rules, intelligent transportation should be able to automatically identify and store them. In view of the extensive use of WMSN, It is necessary to reduce the energy consumption and increase its life-span of equipment. Therefore, the allocation and usage of the limited energy are first to consider when designing WMSN. Even to a certain extent, other performance such as channel utilization, data update frequency, and query response speed can be tradeoff to reduce energy consumption, instead of pursuing maximum data throughput and channel utilization of network transmissions. Therefore, the optimal frame length problem in WMSN needs special research, while the previous technologies are not often applicable. From the available literature, there are inadequate studies in this area. Thus, this paper aims to conduct a detailed research on this issue, and establish the best frame length computational model which takes the unit information energy consumption as the minimum goal. Furthermore, the paper proposes a simple and practical optimal frame length approximate solution algorithm OFLA, suitable for WMSN nodes with limited computing capabilities. It is hope to realize independent and dynamic adjustment of each node's own packet frame length and maximize node lifetime.

The one contributions of this article is a frame length optimization model with the lowest energy consumption per data unit is established in light of WMSN with nodes sending and receiving data. Another is a cross-layer optimization plan for the network is proposed that each node independently calculates its own optimal frame length and directly implements it at the application layer according to its own channel conditions and data transmission requirements. Its innovation is mainly reflected in the fact that the selection and optimization of the packet frame length is not limited to the network design stage, but can be dynamically adjusted according to the network conditions, and also reflected in the fact that the packet frame length is no longer globally consistent. Because of the wide distribution of WMSN, each node channel environment can be very different, each node in the WMSN can determine the optimal packet frame length of the node according to its own situation instead of using the same data frame length of the entire network. This is unsuitable for previous networks that require the highest data throughput, because these networks aim at transmitting data, a inconsistent frame will result in constantly reassemble messages during the message transmission process, thus causing significant delay and process. But WMSN does not require high throughput and high response speed generally. Moreover, due to the need of data fusion and data compression, the message reassembly becomes necessary means to reduce the data transmission volume in the WMSN. Therefore, it creates no extra cost for recombination due to the different frame length.

2   The Model of Energy Consumption

If we let L be the length of information that needs to be transmitted which is called payload in the message, and H be bytes of message header (including the end of check bit), σ_s be the energy consumption of starting transmitting, δ_s be the energy of transmission consume per byte, then we obtain e_{L+H}, the energy consumption of every transmission is:

$$e_{L+H} = \sigma_s + \delta_s(L+H) = \sigma_s + \delta_s L + \delta_s H = e_0 + \delta_s L \tag{1}$$

where $e_0 = \sigma_s + \delta_s H$ is the fixed energy consumption of starting radio frequency and transmitting H bytes, which can be a determined value according to every node in WMSN. In order to simplify the discussion, this value is used as a fundamental unit to normalize energy consumption, so the (1) becomes:

$$e = eL + H/e0 = 1 + (\delta s/e0)L = 1 + \delta L \tag{2}$$

Where $\delta = \delta_s/e_0$ is the energy consumption of transmitting per byte after normalization.

Because of channel bit error and the collision due to competition between channels, every transmission of network message may fail, p is used to signify the probability of failure in every transmission (assume that this statistic is stable and can be constant within a period of time), then a conclusion can be reached:

With just one time of transmission, the probability of success is $1 - p$, while the probability of failure is p, and the total normalized energy consumption is e (without considering the energy consumption of reception[1] and Ack).

With two times of transmissions, the probability of success is $p(1 - p)$ while the probability of failure is p^2, and the total normalized energy consumption is $2e$;

With three times of transmissions, the probability of success is $p^2(1 - p)$ while the probability of failure is p^3, and the energy consumption is $3e$;

Assuming the maximum times of retransmission after packet sending is R, the probability of success is $p^R(1 - p)$ while the probability of failure is p^{R+1} and the energy consumption is $(R + 1)e$ after $R + 1$ times of transmissions. Thus, after transmitting $L + H$ bytes message, the actual energy consumption is (the message may be successfully transmitted or be discarded after failing in R times of retransmissions):

$$
\begin{aligned}
e_p &= (1 - p)e + p(1 - p)2e + p^2(1 - p)3e + \ldots + p^R(1 - p)(R+1)e + p^{R+1}(R+1)e \\
&= (1 - p)(1 + 2p + 3p^2 + \ldots + (R+1)p^R)e + p^{R+1}(R+1)e \\
&= \frac{1 - p^{R+1}}{1 - p}e \qquad // \, solving \, by \, geometric \, progression \\
&\approx \frac{e}{1 - p} \qquad\qquad // \, p^{R+1} << 1
\end{aligned}
$$

Therefore, the energy consumption of transmitting unit message is (There are only L bytes payload information in the $L + H$ bytes message):

$$e_u = \frac{e_p}{L} = \frac{1 + \delta L}{(1 - p)L} = \frac{1}{(1 - p)L} + \frac{\delta}{1 - p} \tag{3}$$

If no regard is given to p, it's not difficult to find that when L gets larger, the frame length of packet gets larger and the energy consumption of transmitting unit information gets lower from (3). However, as the length of message increases, the probability of failing in transmission will get higher because of p, which means that the changes in L have an impact on the value of p.

---

[1] The receive energy consumption and receive bytes, and the numbers of nodes participate in receive are in the approximately linear relationship, so it can be discussed like transmission energy consumption, it will be studied in another paper because of the limited space.

For wireless network, transmission error and collision conflict are causes for the failure of message transmission. Because the general network communication including WMSN adopts a system without correcting coding, like channel attenuation or noise interference resulting in any bit error in the message when transmitting packet data or grouped confirmation message, in that way the transmission of all packet data is seen as failure after which packet data needs to be retransmitted. If Pb signifies error rate, the length of effective information in packet message as 8L bit, the length of packet message header as 8H bit, the length of grouped confirmation message as 8HACK (is 8H generally), the probability of error in packet transmission pf is [19]:

$$p_f = 1 - \left(1 - P_b\right)^{8L + 8H + 8H_{ACK}} = 1 - \left(1 - P_b\right)^{8L + 16H}$$

Except transmission error, another reason of packet transmission failure is packet collision due to the competition between wireless channels. If P_c signifies the probability of packet collision, it is connected with the implementation of physical layer and the degree of network business but it has little to do with packet frame length. Therefore, p, the probability of packet message transmission failure is:

$$p = p_f + P_c - p_f P_c = 1 - \left(1 - P_b\right)^{8L + 16H} + P_c\left(1 - P_b\right)^{8L + 16H} \tag{4}$$

Substitution (4) into (3) gives:

$$e_u = \frac{1 + \delta L}{(1 - P_C)(1 - P_b)^{8L + 16H}L} = \frac{1 + \delta L}{(1 - P_C)(1 - P_b)^{16H}(1 - P_b)^{8L}L}$$
$$\text{let } a = \left(1 - P_C\right)\left(1 - P_b\right)^{16H}, d = \left(1 - p_b\right)^8 \tag{5}$$
$$\text{gets } e_u = \frac{1 + \delta L}{ad^L L}$$

Then the minimum value of e_u can be obtained by using the method of taking the derivative, that is finding the partial derivation of L refer to (5):

$$e'_u = \frac{-ad^L\left(\delta lndL^3 + lndL^2 + l\right)}{\left(ad^L L\right)^2} = \frac{\delta lndL^3 + lndL^2 + l}{ad^L L^2}$$

Let $e'_u = 0$, gets $\delta \ln dL^3 + \ln dL^2 + l = 0$, get the extreme value of e_u, that is

$$L^3 + \frac{l}{\delta}L^2 + \frac{l}{\delta lnd} = 0 \tag{6}$$

(6) is a cubic equation in one unknown quantity, needs to solve by inductive method instead of deductive method.

Let $L = y - \frac{1}{3\delta}$ substitute into (6) and formulate, gets

$$y^3 = py + q = 0 \tag{7}$$

where $p = -\frac{1}{3\delta^2}, q = \frac{2}{27\delta^3} + \frac{1}{\delta lnd}$.

Taking Cartan formula, we can get solution of Eq. (7):

$$L_1 = u + v \quad L_2 = ue + ve^2 \quad L_3 = ve + ue^2$$

in which:

$$e = cos\left(\frac{2\pi}{3}\right) + isin\left(\frac{2\pi}{3}\right)$$

$$u = \left(-\frac{q}{2} + \sqrt{\left(\frac{q}{2}\right)^2 + \left(\frac{p}{3}\right)^3}\right)^{\frac{1}{3}} \quad v\left(-\frac{q}{2} - \sqrt{\left(\frac{q}{2}\right)^2 + \left(\frac{p^3}{3}\right)}\right)^{\frac{1}{3}}.$$

Considering L is a real number in $(0, L_{max}]$, it is not difficult to find the optimum frame length is L_1 when e_u is minimum (The proof of the value of e_u which corresponding with L_1 is the only minimum, it can be done by taking the second derivative, specific steps are omitted).

3 The Implementation of Algorithm

Through the derivation of the theoretical model, the formula for calculating the optimal frame length can be obtained. However, there are certain difficulties in the implementation of the specific algorithm. On the one hand, the calculation process is cumbersome, and it is not suitable for WMSN nodes with weak computing power. On the other hand, The value of Pc and Pb cannot be directly obtained by the calculation of this node. First of all, in many cases it cannot be distinguished whether the transmission failure is the cause of the collision or the cause of the transmission error. Therefore, Pc is difficult to estimate. Secondly, it is also difficult to obtain Pb directly. Although it can be used to replace the bit error rate by the node itself, in many cases it cannot accurately reflect the actual error conditions of the transmission channel. Strictly speaking, the Pb value should be sent to the local node by the receiving end node statistics, but this will lead to a certain amount of communication overhead and increase the complexity of management. For this reason, a simple optimization algorithm is proposed to obtain an approximate solution with the best frame length. The starting point is relatively difficult to conduct direct statistics of Pc and Pb, somewhat easy to send the statistics of the failure probability p. As long as the failure record and the total number of transmissions are used to estimate, then (3) is used to perform the optimal frame length approximation through simple feedback iterations. The specific algorithm is as follows:

```
Algorithm 1: Optimal Frame Length Approximation Algorithm OFLA
Begin :

    L=L_max;  ΔL= L_max/2^n ;    // L_max generally equal to MTU

    first_time=TRUE ; Direct=1;

    benifit=0;  e_cur=0;

    While (;;)

    {

        Sleep(20);

        If snd_pkt_sum % Times!= 0 then continue;

        //Calculate once every certain sending cycle

    p=fail_times/ Times;

        /* Calculate the average transmission failure probability during this peri-
        od*/

    fail_times=0;        // Clear

    e_cur=(1+δL)/(1-p)L;       // Current energy consumption

    If first_time=FALSE then

    {

            benefit= e_last - e_cur;    // Revenue calculation

            if  |benefit| >= B_0  then ΔL= Lmax/2^n ;

            /* The difference in the return value is too large, and the search for
            the maximum step size is resumed to avoid ΔL is too small to have
            fast convergence after p jump.*/

            if benefit > 0

            // Approximate in the original direction

            {

                L=L- direct*ΔL ;

                e_last =e_cur ;

            }

            Else

            // Approximate in the opposite direction, with a smaller step

            {

                Direct=- Direct;

                If (ΔL/2>=min) ΔL=ΔL/2;

                L=L-direct*ΔL

                e_last =e_cur ;

            }

        }

        else {    // first_time=TURE

            e_last = e_cur;

            L=L-ΔL* Direct ;

            first_time=FALSE;

        }

        frame_len=L;

    }

End
```

After dynamically obtaining the optimal frame length, the length of the network message can be adjusted in several ways to achieve the lowest energy consumption per unit of information. One of the most direct methods is to adjust the frame length as the maximum transmission unit length (MTU) of the MAC layer, but it involves the modification of the MAC layer; Another method is to use the optimal frame length as the application message organization basis, that is, to determine the quantity of information in the current packet according to the length, the modification of the underlying protocol may not be involved, and at the same time, it avoids the sub-packeting operation of the MAC layer and improves the efficiency of data transmission and protocol analysis. This is a cross-layer optimization idea and it is also the method used in this paper. For each node in the WMSN, the message organization should be differentiated due to the nature of the data transmitted and the geographical location in the network. For those end nodes, it is relatively simple, mainly relying on the node's cache, and buffering those data with low real-time requirements. When these data are accumulated to a certain extent, they are sent at the optimal or near-optimal length to avoid using short-messages. Based on data fusion and data compression, those intermediate cluster nodes or routing nodes, especially sink nodes close to sinks, perform data classification at the application layer and strive to strive to send the data with the lowest energy consumption per unit each time according to the node's own optimal frame length, but for those packets that exist condition of transmission delay, such as an emergency, packets can be prioritized or packaged immediately, regardless of whether the packet length is optimal or not.

4   Experiment

A series of contrast experiments will be done to verify the effectiveness of analysis and algorithm above, especially to research on how unit information energy consumption and data throughput change along with frame length under different channel conditions and the validity of OFLA.

4.1   A Subsection Sample

In order to reduce the impact of other factors, only two Mica2 nodes A, B are selected in this experiment, connecting with two computers (PC_a and PC_b) separately by USB wire. On the one hand, it can supply power to nodes and avoid the situation of battery voltage drops too fast to ensure the continuity and veracity of experiment when taking intensive experiment with battery powered nodes. On the other hand, those lots of statistic can be transferred to PC for different kinds of process because of saving in the limited storage space of nodes. An electromagnetic shielding laboratory is need to be used as experiment environment, is an ideal environment under conditions that bit error rate is controllable, where some research is done. In this research stage, only one-way data transmission test is done, it allows A to send and B to accept and response, in this situation the probability of collision can be ignored, and the relationship between energy consumption and the length of message can be researched dedicatedly.

The main function of program running in node A is to allocate 2M random data into packet according to the setting frame length, and send them to node B once in 2 s. In this process, the next packet can be transmitted only after receiving ACK from node B, otherwise, the message will be retransmitted until it has been confirmed or reach the upper limit of retransmission times R (take 5 in this experiment), and at the same time, the length of frame and times of failures in each transmission should be sent to PC_a periodically by USB wire to calculate the total times of transmissions and failures, as well as the probability of failure. In addition, the another important task of PC_a is to calculate and save the energy consumption per transmission of A according to formula $e = \sigma s + \delta sx$, which is use for calculating unit information energy consumption of node A. There is also a program in node B, which is mainly responsible for receiving message from node A and checking them by CRC, replying ACK message if the message has been passed or not respond for not. It also record the times of bit errors and the frame length and the times of message that are received correctly, which are sent to PC_b periodically for calculating and saving bit error rate and calculating data throughput with the total times of transmission in PC_a.

4.2   Experiment Procedure and Result Analysis

Through adjusting the distances between nodes, setting obstacles and using signal interference source properly, channel environment in 4 kinds of bit error rate can be obtained. According to different error rate, the experiment is divided into four stages, and 7 to 9 groups tests are done according to transmission frame length in each stage. In every test, the 2M random data will be sent from node A to node B in stable channel environment and fixed frame length conditions, then calculate normalized unit information energy consumption and data throughput in PC. At the end of each stage, with snd_ pkt_sum = 2000 as a statistical period, calculating the approximation of optimal frame length under this channel conditions by running OFLA and comparing with previous experimental values. The specific experimental results are as follows:

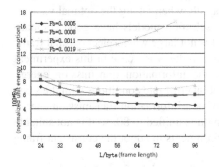

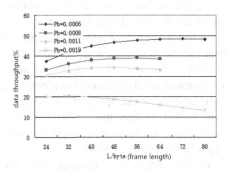

Fig. 1. The unit information energy consumption changes with frame length

Fig. 2. The data throughput changes with frame length

In Fig. 1, the concave curve group shows that unit energy consumption will achieve the minimum value when frame length is taken to the certain value under different channel conditions. The convex curve in Fig. 2 shows that when frame length is taken to the certain value, network data throughput achieves the values of two optimal frame length are not much different when they obtain extremum separately, it can be further verified from Table 1 below.

Table 1. The energy consumption, throughput in different selection models.

Pb		Optimal frame length	The unit energy consumption	Throughput
0.0005	The model of throughput	72	4.61	48.26
	The model of energy consumption	96	4.5	47.14
	Difference	Δ24	▽2.4%	▽2.3%
0.0008	The model of throughput	52	6.05	38.95
	The model of energy consumption	72	5.88	38.6
	Difference	Δ12	▽2.8%	▽0.8%
0.0011	The model of throughput	48	6.95	34.38
	The model of energy consumption	64	6.81	33.31
	Difference	Δ16	▽2%	▽3.1%
0.0019	The model of throughput	32	12.61	20.4
	The model of energy consumption	40	12.48	19.8
	Difference	Δ8	▽1%	▽2.9%

It is not difficult to see that the optimal frame length between two models has a gap but not very large, and the difference between them get smaller when channel bit error rate increases. The performance will not drop rapidly when taking the optimal value in one of models which shows that two different selection models have good compatibility, that is the loss of network data throughput is not large when select optimal frame length in the model of energy consumption, even in the worst case in this experiment the loss is not more than 3.1%. In addition, the information transmission energy consumption is very different in different channel bit error rate conditions with the same frame length, for example, the max difference of unit information transmission energy consumption get three times when the frame length is unified to 80, so it is not suitable for WMSN with nodes in different channel environments to adopt the consistent frame length in the whole network.

Finally, determining optimal frame length in the model of energy consumption under different channel conditions in group test, and comparing with the convergency value obtained by OFLA, the result is shown in Table 2 below.

Table 2. The comparison of two kinds of optimal frame length.

P_b	0.0005	0.0008	0.0011	0.0019
Group test	96	72	64	40
OFLA algorithm	92	70	66	42

There is a certain error between these two kinds of values shown in Table 2, because the change of frame length in group test is 8 Bytes as an unit, which is at a coarse-grained level. But, OFLA, which is dynamic and adjustable with 2 Bytes as an unit, is effective and superior to calculate the optimal frame length.

5 Conclusion

Aiming at the energy limitation of WMSN in wireless signal transmission, an optimal frame length optimization model with the lowest energy consumption per unit of information is established, and a simple algorithm suitable for WMSN node execution with limited computing power is proposed. This algorithm is used to calculate the optimal frame length, and it can dynamically realize the independent selection and adjustment of the frame length of each WMSN node. The experimental results show that using the model and algorithm of this paper, the dynamic adjustment of the frame length can obtain the optimal transmission energy consumption, and it does not cause a great loss of data throughput.

References

1. Akyildiz, I.F., Su, W., Sankarasubramaniam, Y.: Wireless sensor networks: a survey. Comput. Netw. **38**(4), 393–422 (2002)
2. Khan, J.A., Qureshi, H.K., Iqbal, A.: Energy management in wireless sensor networks: a survey. Comput. Electr. Eng. **41**(C), 159–186 (2015)
3. Li, J., Li, J., Shi, S.: The concept problem and research progress of sensor network and perception data management. J. Softw. **14**(10), 1818–1827 (2003)
4. Adam, S., Rebecca, B., Jun, Y.: Constraint-chaining: on energy-efficient continuous monitoring in sensor networks. In: Proceedings of the 2006 ACM SIGMOD International Conference on Management of Data, pp. 157–168. ACM press (2006)
5. Hadzi-Velkov, Z., Spasenovski, B.: Saturation throughput-delay analysis of IEEE 802.11 DCF in fading channel. In: IEEE International Conference on Communications, vol. 1, pp. 121–126. IEEE (2010)
6. Spragins, J.D., Hammond, J.L., Pawlikowski, K.: Telecommunications: Protocols and Design. Addison Wesley Publishing Company Inc., Boston (1991)
7. Hamid, A., Fikri, A.H.: Wireless multimedia sensor network. In: Proceedings of the 2009 IEEE International Conference on Communications, pp. 1–5. IEEE Press (2011)
8. Sarraf, M.: Optimum Packet Length in a Fadin Channel Environment Along with Random Bit Errors an Finite Buffer Size, AT&T Technical Memorandum, No. 140360000 (1991)
9. Lettieri, P., Srivastava, M.B.: Adaptive frame length control for improving wireless link throughput, range, and energy efficiency. In: IEEE INFOCOM, pp. 564–571 (1998)
10. Khelil, A.A.: Comparative effectiveness evaluation of map construction protocols in wireless sensor networks. IEEE Syst. J. **8**(3), 708–716 (2014)
11. Bakshi, B.S., Krishna, P., Vaidya, N.H.: Improving performance of TCP over wireless networks. In: Proceedings of the 18th International Conference on Distributed Computing Systems, pp. 365–373 (1997)
12. Hadzi, V.Z., Spase, N.B.: Saturation throughput-delay analysis of IEEE 802.11 DCF in fading channel. In: IEEE ICC 2003, pp. 121–126 (2003)

13. Lettieri, P., Fragouli, C., Srivastava, M.: Low power error control for wireless links. In: Proceedings of the Third ACM/IEEE International Conference on Mobile Computing and Networking (1997)

14. Singh, J., Pesch, D.: Smart error-control strategy for low-power communication in wireless networked control system. Telecommun. Syst. **55**(2), 253–269 (2014)

15. Dong, X.J., Varaiya, P.: Saturation throughput analysis of IEEE 802.11 wireless LAN for a lossy channel. IEEE Commun. Lett. **9**(2), 100–102 (2005)

16. Chien, C., Jain, R., Lettieri, P.: Adaptive radio for multimedia wireless links. IEEE J. Sel. Areas Commun. **18**(5), 793–813 (1999)

17. Phan, V., Glisic, S.: MAC Layer packet-length adaptive CLSP/DS-CDMA radio networks: performance in flat rayleigh fading channel. In: IEEE ISCC 2002, Taormina, Italy, pp. 161–166 (2002)

18. Xi, Y., Wei, J.: The optimal frame length analysis and channel adaptive strategy for error channel. J. Commun. **27**(5), 84–89 (2006)

19. Cheng, Y., Zhang, Y., Gao, X.: the probabilistic analysis of packet loss of wireless LAN in error channel. J. Commun. **28**(5), 126–131 (2007)

20. Liu, Y., Seet, B.C.: Optimal network structuring for large-scale WMSN with virtual broker based publish/subscribe. In: Recent Trends in Telecommunications Research, pp. 1–5. IEEE (2018)

21. Poojary, S., Pai, M.M.M: Multipath data transfer in wireless multimedia sensor. In: Network International Conference on Broadband, Wireless Computing, Communication and Applications, pp. 379–383. IEEE Computer Society (2010)

22. Mohajerzadeh, A.H., Yaghmaee, M.H., Toroghi, N.N.: Routing protocols for wireless multimedia sensor network: a survey. J. Sens. **2013**(1), 1–11 (2013)

23. Zuo, Z., Lu, Q., Luo, W.: A two-hop clustered image transmission scheme for maximizing network lifetime in wireless multimedia sensor networks. Comput. Commun. **35**(1), 100–108 (2012)

Influence Maximization Algorithm in Social Networks Based on Three Degrees of Influence Rule

Hongbin Wang[1] , Guisheng Yin[1] , Lianke Zhou[1(✉)] ,
Xiaolong Chen[1] , and Dongjia Zhang[2]

[1] College of Computer Science and Technology, Harbin Engineering University,
Harbin 150001, China
zhoulianke@hrbeu.edu.cn
[2] Aerospace Science and Industry Corp, Beijing 1100048, China

Abstract. Influence maximization algorithms in social networks are aimed at mining the most influential TOP-K nodes in the current social network, through which we will get the fastest spreading speed of information and the widest scope of influence by putting those nodes as initial active nodes and spreading them in a specific diffusion model. Nowadays, influence maximization algorithms in large-scale social networks are required to be of low time complexity and high accuracy, which are very hard to meet at the same time. The traditional Degree Centrality algorithm, despite of its simple structure and less complexity, has less satisfactory accuracy. The Closeness Centrality algorithm and the Betweenness Centrality algorithm are comparatively highly accurate having taken global metrics into consideration. However, their time complexity is also higher. Hence, a new algorithm based on Three Degrees of Influence Rule, namely, Linear-Decrescence Degree Centrality Algorithm, is proposed in this paper in order to meet the above two requirements for influence maximization algorithms in large-scale social networks. This algorithm, as a tradeoff between the low accuracy degree algorithm and other high time complexity algorithms, can meet the requirements of high accuracy and low time complexity at the same time.

Keywords: Social networks · Influence maximization
Three degrees of influence rule · Linear-Decrescence Degree Centrality

1 Research Background

The concept of "social network" [1] was first proposed by the British anthropologist Radcliffe Brown when he studied the social structure in the 1930s, which was used to describe all kinds of social relations among the organizations, individuals and between the organization and individuals. The main purpose of maximizing the influence of social network is to dig out the TOP-K nodes set with the greatest influence in the network through the existing social network relationship. And it has been widely applied in important fields such as marketing, disease prevention and rumor control.

© Springer Nature Switzerland AG 2018
X. Sun et al. (Eds.): ICCCS 2018, LNCS 11063, pp. 567–578, 2018.
https://doi.org/10.1007/978-3-030-00006-6_52

For example, in the field of marketing, "viral marketing" [2–4] and "word of mouth effect" [5, 6] are the best applications for maximizing social network influence and social network communication models. Business companies always want to promote the newly developed products to the market at the lowest cost and to be accepted by the majority of the population. For this end, they will target a small number of "influential" users and present them the new product's samples for its free trial first.

In the field of rumor control [8, 9], where people can freely talk and discuss about the national political and social hot events through various domestic social networks such as WeChat, Zhihu, microblogging and so on. However, while it allows people to express themselves freely, some unscrupulous criminals are trying to propagate rumors that violate the facts through these platforms, attempting to use these rumors to deceive and incite the masses to do something that endangers the country and society. Therefore, how to limit and control rumors into a small range in the early stages becomes also a major issue in social network analysis.

2 Research Status Quo

In recent years, the social network influence maximization algorithm has been widely focused and studied by researchers. In 2003, Kempe et al. [7] First demonstrated that the problem of maximizing influence was the NP-hard problem. Therefore, the heuristic algorithm and the greedy algorithm have become two major directions in solving the problem of influence maximization.

2.1 Heuristic Algorithms

The heuristic algorithm mainly considers the static structure characteristics of the social network such as the degree of nodes, the shortest path between nodes, network density, aggregation coefficients and betweeness.

Degree Centrality(DC) is the most direct and primitive measure of the centrality of nodes. It believes that there is a positive correlation between the degree and the influence of the node. It is shown is in formula (1).

$$DC(u) = d(u) \tag{1}$$

Where $DC(n)$ represents the degree centrality of node u, and $d(u)$ represents its degree.

Betweeness Centrality (BC), is the betweeness of nodes. This algorithm believes that the larger the betweeness of nodes, that is, the larger of the number of nodes that are in the critical path (shortest path) between nodes in the social network, the greater its control over the communication between all nodes. It is shown in formula (2).

$$BC(u) = \sum_{i \in V} \sum_{j \neq i \in V} \frac{\delta_{ij}(u)}{\delta_{ij}} \tag{2}$$

Where δ (u) represents the betweeness of node u, δ_{ij} represents the number of shortest paths between nodes i and j, and $\delta_{ij}(u)$ indicates that there are $\delta_{ij}(u)$ shortest paths between the two nodes that passes node u.

Closeness Centrality (CC), which reflects the distance of nodes from the other nodes in the social network. The basic idea of this algorithm is that the smaller the cost of the node to communicate with the rest of the nodes, and the more important the node's position is in the network, that is, the greater the influence and is shown in formula (3).

$$CC(u) = \frac{n-1}{\sum\limits_{v \neq u, v \in V} dis(u, v)} \tag{3}$$

Where $CC(u)$ represents the Closeness Centrality of the node, n represents the number of nodes in the network, and dis(u,v) represents the shortest path from node u to node v.

Since the DC algorithm is low in complexity but also low in accuracy and the BC and CC algorithms are of high precision but are highly complex, Professor Chen et al. [8] have put forward the Local Centrality algorithm (LC) as a compromise solution. The algorithm not only considers the nearest neighbor nodes of a node, but also takes the neighbor nodes of its neighbor nodes into account. It is shown in formula (4) and formula (5).

$$LC(u) = \sum_{v \in \Gamma(u)} Q(v) \tag{4}$$

$$Q(v) = \sum_{w \in \Gamma(v)} N(w) \tag{5}$$

Where $\Gamma(u)$ represents the nearest neighbor nodes set of node u, and $N(w)$ represents the number of its neighbor nodes and the number of neighbor nodes of its neighbor nodes. Thus, by definition, the LC algorithm, when estimating the influence, assumes that the influence can be propagated by the original activated node u through node v, node w, and node x to node z after four degrees, as shown in Fig. 1.

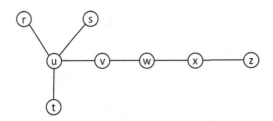

Fig. 1. Range of influence of LC algorithm

2.2   Greedy Algorithm

The basic research of the greedy algorithm is focused on the hill-climbing greedy algorithm, which selects the node with the greatest influence each time to calculate the local optimal solution. After several iterations, the global optimal solution is obtained. The biggest advantage of this algorithm is that it has high accuracy and can achieve the optimal approximation of 1-1 / e-ε. However, the disadvantage is that the algorithm is highly complex, needing long running time, which cannot meet the fast-computation requirement of large-scale social network.

Three Degrees of Influence Rule. Nicolas Kristakis, Harvard University Sociology Professor and James Fuller, the philosophy doctor of University of California, San Diego, have put forward three degrees of influence rule [9] in their work on the social network- "Large Connection: How social networks are formed and the impact on the behavior of the human reality" for the first time. Dr. James Fuller pointed out that our behaviors, attitudes and so on follow the so-called "three degrees of influence rule" in terms of its spread in the real life: these acts, attitudes will not only cause influence in the circle of our friends (first degree), but also in the second degree distance (friends of friends) and in the third degree distance (friends of friends' friends).

The algorithm Ideas of Linear-Decrescence Degree Centrality. As stated by three degrees of influence rule above, the spread of influence in the social network is not boundless, but limited to within three degrees, and the influence is almost zero beyond the degree. In addition, even if the influence can spread within three degrees, the size is not fixed, but gradually decay. It is based on the above two theories that this paper proposes a new algorithm to maximize the influence of social network, that is, Linear-Decrescence Degree Centrality algorithm. The formula for Linear-Decrescence Degree Centrality algorithm is shown in formula (6) and formula (7).

$$LDDC(n) = |F(n)| + \alpha(|S(n)| + \beta|T(n)|) \tag{6}$$

$$F(n) \cap S(n) \cap T(n) = \varnothing \tag{7}$$

where α denotes the decrescence coefficient when the influence of node n propagates from the nodes within the first degree to the second degree (i.e., the neighbor node of n's neighbor nodes), and β means the decrescence coefficient when the influence of node n propagates from the nodes within the second degree to the third degree (i.e., the neighbor node of the neighbor node of n's neighbor nodes), and $0 \leq \alpha, \beta \leq 1$. The pseudo-code description of Linear-Decrescence Degree Centrality algorithm is shown in Algorithm 1.

The pseudo-code description of LDDC algorithm

Algorithm 1: LDDC Algorithm

Input(G(V, E))
Output (the LDDC(i) value of each node I in the network)
1: for i = 1 to n
2:    F(i) = {the neighbor nodes of i }
3: end for
4: for i = 1 to n do
5:    for j in F(i)
6:       k = j's neighbor nodes
7:       if k ∉ F(i) && k ≠ i
8:          S(i) = S(i) ∪ {j}
9:    end for
10:end for
11: for i = 1 to n do
12:    for j in S(i)
13:       k = j's neighbor nodes
14:       if k ∉ F(i) && k ∉ S(i) && k ≠ i
15:          T(i) = T(i) ∪ {j}
16:    end for
17: end for
18: for i = 1 to n do
19:    LDDC(i) = |F(i)| +α(|S(i)| + β|T(i)|)
20: end for

For example, in Fig. 2, if we are going to solve the LDDC of node 10 and let's assume that $\alpha = 0.7$ and $\beta = 0.4$. in The neighbor node of node 10 the first degree are 6, 11, 23, namely, F (n) = {6,11,23}, | F (n) | = 3; the neighbor nodes of node 10 the second degree are1, 12, 14, 20, 21, 22, that is, S (n) = {1, 12, 14, 20, 21, 22}, | S (n) | = 6; the neighbor nodes of node 10 the third degree are 2, 3, 4, 5, 7, 8, 9, 13, 15, 16, 17, 18, 19, i.e., T (n) = {2,3,4,5,7,8,9,13,15,16,17,18, 19, | T (n) | = 13. Although node 23 belongs to both the first degree node set and the second degree node set of node 10, it belongs to F (n) only after processing.

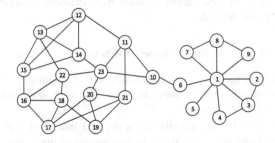

Fig. 2. Example graph of a social network

3   Experimental Results and Analysis

In this section, the true influence of the nodes in each data set is simulated and used as the standard set, the approximant influence estimated through the LDDC algorithm is used as the experimental set, and the approximation of influence through DC algorithm, BC algorithm, CC algorithm, LC algorithm is used as the contrast set. It should be noted that, in calculating the influence value through LDDC algorithm, it is found that when $\alpha = 0.7 \pm 0.05$ and $\beta = 0.4 \pm 0.05$, through a large number of experimental calculations and summary, there is less variation in the experimental results, and the experiment achieves its best effect. Therefore, in this paper, all calculation of influence involved in the LDDC algorithm, the unified value has been taken, that is, $\alpha = 0.7$, $\beta = 0.4$.

3.1   Selection of Data Sets

The three data sets are either non-directional networks or have been processed as non-directional networks. The static structural features of each data set are shown in Table 1.

Table 1. The static structural features of experimental data sets

Statistics items	Dolphin	Email	Blog
Number of nodes (n)	62	1133	3982
Number of edges (m)	159	5451	6803
Average degree (<k>)	5.129	9.622	3.417
Maximum degree (kmax)	12	71	189
Average path length	3.111	3.606	6.252
Network density	0.084	0.009	0.001
Focusing factor	0.290	0.254	0.493

The dolphin dataset is a social network dataset that records the daily contact between a group of dolphins living in a community in Doubtful Sound, New Zealand. The email dataset is a social network dataset that records email communications between members of University of Rocía de Villegill, Spain. The blog dataset is a social network dataset of community relationships between bloggers on the MSN (Windows Live) Spaces website.

3.2   Simulation of True Value of Nodes' Influence

In this paper, the SIR epidemic model is used to conduct the influence spread. The true value of influence of the node is simulated and used as a standard to measure the effectiveness of the LDDC algorithm.

In the SIR model [10], the population is divided into three categories: the susceptible, the infected and the immunized. In the process of obtaining the true value of influence of the node, only one node is set as the initial infected node. $F(t)$ is the total number of infected nodes and immune nodes at time t, and $F(t)$ is used to evaluate influence of the initial infected node at time t. Obviously, $F(t)$ increases as time t grows, and finally stabilizes, that is, there is no infected node in the final network, then $F(t)$ is expressed as $F(tc)$. Therefore, $F(tc)$, as a single initial infection node influence, the greater it is, the greater the impact of the node. Finally, we can use the $F(tc)$ value of the node to simulate the approximant true influence of the node. Considering that in practical applications, the propagation of influence is more important in the early stages, $F(t)$ at $t = 10$ is used instead of $F(tc)$ in the final steady state. If there is no special explanation, $F(t)$ refers to the total number of infected nodes and immuned nodes at t = 10.

3.3   Results and Analysis

Position Offset Method. The so-called position offset method refers to the method that first sorts $F(tc)$ value obtained by propagating the single node through the SIR model in descending order, using it as the measure standard, namely, the true value influence of the node, and the sorted results of $F(tc)$ represent the rank of true infleuence), then calculates position offset between the sorting positions derived from the algorithm proposed in this paper as well as other centrality algorithms and the measure standard. The smaller the position offset, the closer to the true sorting results, which means the more accurate the algorithm.

Table 2. The TOP-10 sorting centrality value of the centrality algorithms in the dolphin data set

TOP-K	DC	CC	BC	LC	LDDC	F(t)
1	12	26.77	422.88	2232	34.62	39.83
2	11	26.02	404.50	2100	33.4	39.64
3	11	25.49	218.46	2052	32.76	39.51
4	10	25.49	208.36	1847	32.64	39.18
5	9	24.97	184.90	1706	31.64	38.74
6	9	24.32	173.69	1675	30.84	38.72
7	9	23.85	171.24	1582	30.62	38.26
8	9	23.70	164.65	1541	28.98	38.06
9	9	23.55	159.71	1538	28.18	37.91
10	9	23.40	141.52	1521	27.94	37.67

Taking the dolphin data set as an example, the $F(t)$ value of the TOP-10 nodes and the corresponding node names sorted by the $F(t)$ value at t = 10 are shown in Tables 2 and 3 respectively. For example, the $F(t)$ value of the node 33 is the largest, ranking the first in the LDDC algorithm, and the offset position is OP33 = $|1 - 1| = 0$; in the LC algorithm it ranks the 4th, and the position offset is OP33 = $|1 - 4| = 3$. Then it can be concluded that the LDDC algorithm is more accurate for node 33. Furthermore, let's

Table 3. The TOP-10 nodes ranking of the centrality algorithms in the dolphin data set

TOP-K	DC	CC	BC	LC	LDDC	F(t)
1	14	33	33	37	33	33
2	37	37	13	45	37	37
3	45	40	36	14	36	40
4	51	36	1	33	40	36
5	13	50	17	50	50	14
6	17	20	40	40	20	20
7	20	43	37	16	14	50
8	29	14	14	21	43	45
9	33	13	51	18	13	16
10	57	21	43	20	45	38

Table 4. The calculation of position offset in the dolphin dataset

	TOP-10	TOP-20	TOP-30	TOP-40	TOP-50
DC	70	145	228	329	394
CC	16	45	84	102	147
BC	75	156	246	341	405
LC	37	101	167	210	244
LDDC	14	47	81	95	124

take a look at node 36, whose $F(t)$ value ranks the 4th. It ranks the 3rd in the LDDC algorithm, and the position offset is $OP36 = |4 - 3| = 1$; it ranks the 4th in CC algorithm, and its position offset is $OP36 = |4 - 4| = 0$, so the CC algorithm is more accurate for node 36. Then, for each centrality algorithm, the position offset is obtained for each node, and the total position offset of the algorithm is obtained. The offset position of the TOP-10 nodes is compared with the $F(t)$ result, shown in formula (8).

$$PO_{TOP-K} = \sum_{u \in TOP-K} PO_u \qquad (8)$$

Table 4 is the calculated value of the position offset of the node set of the centrality algorithm TOP-10 $\sim$ TOP50, using the ranking of results, $F(t)$, in the SIR propagation model in the dolphin social network as the measure standard. Figure 3 is the corresponding line graph.

The line graphs of position offset in the email data set, and blog data set are shown in Figs. 4 and 5.

An observation of Figs. 3, 4 and 5 shows that position offset values of LDDC algorithm and CC algorithm are smaller and closer, indicating that the influence ranking of LDDC algorithm and CC algorithm are closer to the real influence ranking; and position offset values of LC Algorithm, BC algorithm and DC algorithm are larger, indicating that there is a larger difference in the estimated influence rank and the rank of

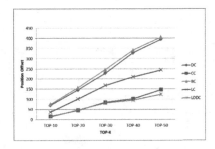

Fig. 3. The line graph of position offset in the dolphin dataset

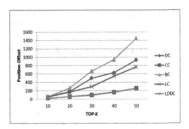

Fig. 4. The line graph of position offset in the email data set

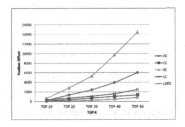

Fig. 5. The line graph of position offset in the blog data set

true influence. Therefore, according to the position offset method, the accuracy of these centrality algorithms can be ranked from high to low as: LDDC algorithm> = CC algorithm> LC algorithm> DC algorithm ≈ BC algorithm (Fig. 6).

It is shown that the $F(t)$ of the node increases gradually with the increase of the estimated influence of the LDDC algorithm and the CC algorithm, displaying a strong positive correlation in the dolphin data set. DC algorithm and LC algorithm also show a certain positive correlation, but it is slightly weaker; and BC algorithm's correlation is the weakest.

An observation of Fig. 7: the scatterplot of correlation for the email dataset, shows that the LC algorithm has the strongest positive correlation, followed by the LDDC algorithm and the CC algorithm, and the positive correlation of the DC algorithm and the BC algorithm is relatively weak.

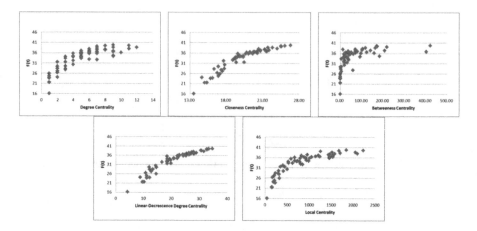

Fig. 6. The scatterplot of correlation for the dolphin dataset

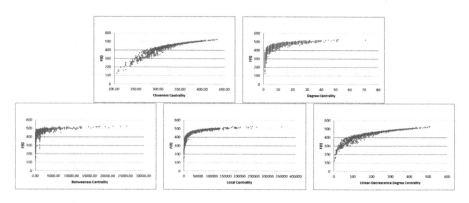

Fig. 7. The scatterplot of correlation for the email dataset

An observation of Fig. 8: the scatterplot of correlation for the blog dataset, shows that the positive correlation of the LDDC algorithm and the CC algorithm is strong, and that of the DC algorithm, LC algorithm and BC algorithm between F(t) is weak.

TOP-K Difference Method. Taking the LDDC algorithm and the LC algorithm of the dolphin dataset as an example, the difference between the TOP-10 nodes is shown in Table 5, where nodes of the LC algorithm which are not included in TOP-10 nodes of the LDDC algorithm are 16, 21, 18, so we use them as the initial set of activated nodes, propagating through the SIR propagation model, and observe the final influence range F (t). Similarly, the LDDC algorithm uses 36, 43, and 13 as the initial set of active nodes. Then the propagation results of LC algorithm and the LDDC algorithm in the dolphin data set within t = 10 are shown in Fig. 9.

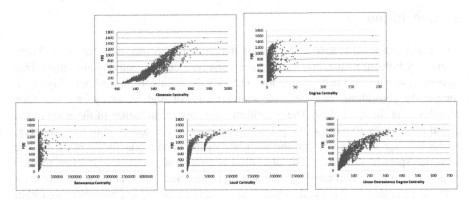

Fig. 8. The scatterplot of correlation for the blog dataset

Table 5. TOP-10 differences between the LDDC algorithm and LC algorithm in the dolphin data set

Algorithm name	LC	LDDC
TOP-10 node name	37	33
	45	37
	14	36
	33	40
	50	50
	40	20
	16	14
	21	43
	18	13
	20	45
The name of different nodes in TOP-10	16,21,18	36,43,13

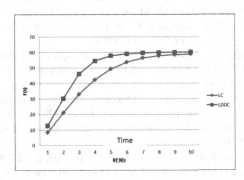

Fig. 9. TOP-10 differences between the LDDC algorithm and LC algorithm in the dolphin data set

4 Conclusion

This paper proposes a new algorithm of maximizing the influence based on Three Degrees of Influence Rule, that is, the linear-crescence degree centrality algorithm. This algorithm, as a tradeoff between the low accuracy degree algorithm and other high time complexity algorithms, can meet the requirements of high accuracy and low time complexity at the same time. The algorithm estimates the influence of the node in the global network by looking at the potential influence of the node within three degrees, taking into account the law that the influence of the node gradually decays when the influence spreads outwardly. The algorithm is simple in calculation and low in time complexity, with a short running time and high precision. It has good scalability even in the large-scale social network. Lastly, the validity of the linear attenuation algorithm is verified by the method of position offset method, correlation method and TOP-K difference method.

Acknowledgments. This work was funded by the National Natural Science Foundation of China under Grant (No. 61772152 and No. 61502037), the Basic Research Project (No. JCKY2016206B001, JCKY2014206C002 and JCKY2017604C010), and the Technical Foundation Project (No. JSQB2017206C002).

References

1. Guo, K.H.: Application of reliability assessment methods of small sample based on Bayes theory. Sci. Tech. Innov. Prod. (2014)
2. Liu, Q.: Study on the influence of prior reliability for bayesian estimation. In: International Conference on Reliability, Maintainability and Safety, pp. 407–410 (1999)
3. Maeda, T., Kimura, M.: A Study on Linearized Growth Curve Models for Software Reliability Data Analysis. Ieice Technical Report 106, pp. 21–26 (2006)
4. Yang, R., Tang, J., Sun, D.: Association rule data mining applications for Atlantic tropical cyclone intensity changes. Weather Forecast. **26**, 337–353 (2010)
5. Norman, A.T., Russell, C.A.: The pass-along effect: investigating word-of-mouth effects on online survey procedures. J. Comput. Mediat. Commun. **11**, 1085–1103 (2006)
6. File, K.M., Cermak, D.S.P., Prince, R.A.: Word-of-mouth effects in professional services buyer behaviour. Serv. Ind. J. **14**, 301–314 (1994)
7. Kempe, D., Kleinberg, J., Tardos, É.: Maximizing the spread of influence through a social network. In: ACM SIGKDD International Conference on Knowledge Discovery and Data Mining, pp. 137–146 (2003)
8. Chen, D., Shang, M., Lv, Z., Fu, Y.: Detecting overlapping communities of weighted networks via a local algorithm. Phys. A **389**, 4177–4187 (2010)
9. Vanderweele, T.J.: Inference for influence over multiple degrees of separation on a social network. Stat. Med. **32**, 591 (2013)
10. Balkew, T., Model, S., Rate, R.R., Analysis, P.P.: The SIR Model When S(t) is a Multi-Exponential Function. Dissertations & Theses - Gradworks 14, 50-50 (2010)

Influencing Factors Analysis of Desert Precipitation Based on Big Data

Xue Wang, Pingzeng Liu[✉], and Xueru Yu

Shandong Agricultural University, Tai'an 271000, China
lpz8565@126.com

Abstract. To analyse the long-term effects and disturbances of other meteorological factors on precipitation, the historical information of the Ewenki Banner from 1991 to 2010 for a total of 20 years is taken as an example to construct the dynamic relationship between precipitation and temperature, humidity, wind speed and sunshine hours. The results show that each variable has a first-order single integer sequence at the 1% level of significance and has a stable long-term equilibrium relationship at the 5% level of significance. The vector autoregressive model (VAR) also passes the stability test to satisfy the preconditions for running. According to the analysis of impulse response and variance decomposition, the influence of humidity is greatest except for 43.29% of precipitation subject to its influence. The contribution of humidity reaches 43.85%, exceeding the impact of precipitation itself. The impact of sunshine hours on precipitation has a certain lag period and the fluctuations in the later period are relatively large. The impact of wind speed and temperature on the precipitation is not obvious. The model better simulates the impact of various influencing factors on precipitation and proves its feasibility in the analysis of the influencing factors of desert precipitation, which has certain practical significance.

Keywords: VAR model · Impulse response · Variance decomposition

1 Introduction

China is one of the countries most affected by desertification in the world. According to the results and analysis of the fifth national monitoring report on desertification and desertification released by the State Forestry Administration, as of 2014, the total area of desertified land nationwide was 261.1593 million hectares. Desertification area accounted for 78.45% of desertification monitoring area, accounting for 27.2% of the total land area [1]. Soil moisture status is an important ecological factor in desert ecosystems [2], and it is also a key factor that restricts plant growth [3, 4]. It determines the occurrence or reversal of land desertification and is the main regulator of land desertification. However, the lack of precipitation in the sand area, strong evaporation, low soil moisture content [5], poor soil water retention, large losses and low effective utilisation rate make water resources extremely scarce. Precipitation, as an important source of moisture in sandy and desert areas [6, 7], has an impact on the movement of

© Springer Nature Switzerland AG 2018
X. Sun et al. (Eds.): ICCCS 2018, LNCS 11063, pp. 579–588, 2018.
https://doi.org/10.1007/978-3-030-00006-6_53

dunes and the distribution of vegetation. At the same time, it is also very important to respond to the desert ecological environment and global climate change [8, 9].

In many studies on precipitation, the construction of the model has become an irreplaceable method [10]. Hu used the artificial neural network to establish a short-term climate prediction model for precipitation and provided a prediction method with obvious statistical forecasting skills for the short-term climate prediction of precipitation [11]. Jin et al. adopted a neural network based on genetic algorithm for short-term climate prediction modelling research [12]. Chen et al. introduced the SVM method into weather forecasting experiments for the first time [13]. Huang et al. proposed the empirical mode decomposition. At present, the algorithm has obtained good application effects in many aspects. Bi Shuoben applied the short-term climate prediction method that combines EMD and SVM to the Guangxi seasonal precipitation forecast [14]. Kong Demeng proposed an extreme learning machine model based on the co-integration theory for the deficiency of the traditional precipitation forecasting model and applied this model to the prediction of seasonal average precipitation in the Wannan region [15]. However, the overall trend of precipitation data is not stable. In the aspect of studying the influence of other factors on the disturbance of precipitation, there are still some limitations [16–18].

Based on the "Elion Ecological Desert Big Data Platform" project, VAR model, pulse test and variance decomposition methods are combined to quantitatively analyse the impact of precipitation on other meteorological factors and the impact of other meteorological factors on precipitation. It is intended to explore the impact relationship between precipitation and other meteorological factors and hope to provide more accurate data support for desert macro planning and ecological precision management from the perspective of statistical analysis and big data. At the same time, it provides a scientific theoretical basis for the production management and decision making of the government, enterprises, and farmers, and serves to promote the healthy development of the desert greening project.

2   Experimental Materials

2.1   Data Sources and Process

This study selects a total of 20 years of historical information from 1991-2010 in desert sand meteorological data in Inner Mongolia. The data comes from China Meteorological Data Network. The Ewenki flag (area code: 50525) is selected as the sampling point, and the collects information included five kinds of information: temperature, humidity, precipitation, wind speed, and sunshine hours. Data is collected hourly, with good integrity and continuity. The software used for data processing is Eviews6.0.

2.2   Method

Vector Autoregressive Model. Vector autoregressive model is based on the statistical properties of data to establish a model, which is often used to predict interrelated time series systems and to analyse the dynamic effects of random disturbances on variable systems. The VAR model constructs a model by taking each endogenous variable in the system as a function of the lag value of all endogenous variables in the system. It extends the univariate autoregressive model to the "vector" autoregressive model consisting of multiple time series variables, thus avoiding the requirements of structured models.

Pulse Response Function. Impulse response function can be used to describe the response of an endogenous variable to the impact caused by the error term. That is the degree of influence on the current value and future value of the endogenous variable after applying a standard deviation magnitude impact on the random error term. In practical applications, since the VAR model is a non-theoretical model, it does not require any priori constraints on the variables. Therefore, in analysing VAR models, it is often not to analyse how one variable affects another but to analyse the dynamic impact on the system when an error term changes or the model is impacted [19, 20].

Variance Decomposition. Variance decomposition is to analyse the impact of each structural shock on changes in endogenous variables and further evaluate the importance of different structural shocks. Therefore, the variance decomposition gives relatively important information for each random disturbance that affects the variables in the VAR model [21].

3   Model Construction

Whether the selected variables of the model are reasonable, whether each variable is a stationary sequence, whether there is a long-term stable equilibrium relationship between the sequences, and whether the overall model of each variable can run smoothly is a prerequisite for using the VAR model for analysis. Therefore, before using the model for correlation analysis, it should first test the feasibility of the model.

3.1   Stability Test

The unit root test is the stationarity test of the sequence. Only a stable time series, that is, no random trend or trend, can be used for econometric analysis. Otherwise, there will be a pseudo regression. Because there are unit roots in the precipitation series in the actual data, it is a non-stationary sequence. Therefore, it is necessary to perform differential processing before the estimation process. The D operator is used for differentials. When setting the first-order difference, just add the sequence name after D. For example, D (PRECIPITATION) sets the first-order differential sequence of precipitation. Subsequently, the unit root test of the first-order differential sequence of each variable is continued.

Compare the ADF statistics of the first-order differential sequences in Table 1 with the critical values at the 1% (-2.575144), 5% (-1.942224), and 10% (-1.615772) significance test levels. The statistics of the first-order differences of all sequences are less than the value at the 1% significant level. From this, it can be judged that each first-order difference sequence is a first-order single integer sequence at the 1% level of significance. Therefore, in the following analysis, the paper uses the differential sequence of the above variables to study.

Table 1. ADF test results of the first-order difference of each variable.

Sequence	Unit root test statistics	P
D(PRECIPICATION)	−16.70731	0.0000
D(AIR_TEMPERATURE)	−15.96254	0.0000
D(AIR_HUMIDITY)	−16.06606	0.0000
D(SUNSHINE_DURATION)	−13.89242	0.0000
D(WIND_SPEED)	−12.74020	0.0000

3.2   Lag Test

In the time series analysis, since the real-time time series is usually non-stationary, it can be differentiated to make it smooth (as in the previous first-order differential processing of each data). However, this will lose the total amount of long-term information that is necessary to analyse the problem. So we can use co-integration to solve the problem, and finally achieve the purpose of determining the long-term and stable equilibrium relationship among various variables. The Johansen co-integration test is based on the regression coefficient test, and its premise is to establish a VAR model. Since VAR is unconstrained and co-integration is constrained, it is necessary to pay attention to the choice of the lag period when doing co-integration tests. The optimal lag of the co-integration test is the optimal lag of VAR minus 1. Therefore, the first step is to determine the maximum lag order of the VAR model.

In Table 2, five statistical evaluation indicators of 0–7 VAR model are given: LR, FPE, AIC, SC and HQ values, and the minimum lag period given by each evaluation index is marked with "*". Some scholars believe that comparing AIC and SC to make them take the minimum p-value is the request. Some people think that when the minimum value of AIC and SC corresponds to different p-values, only LR test can be used. Other scholars believe that if there are inconsistencies in the test results, the lag order of VARs will be determined based on most of the principles. It can be seen that

Table 2. Lag results.

Lag	LogL	LR	FPE	AIC	SC	HQ
0	−4099.681	NA	1.38e+09	35.23331	35.30737	35.26317
1	−3751.500	678.4299	86003234	32.45922	32.90356	32.63840
2	−3535.752	411.1233	16732696	30.82191	31.63653	31.15040
3	−3442.134	174.3791	9291482.	30.23291	31.41782*	30.71072
4	−3379.783	113.4638	6752100.	29.91230	31.46749	30.53942
5	−3330.225	88.05549	5480910.	29.70150	31.62697	30.47794*
6	−3302.073	48.81286	5352073.	29.67444	31.97020	30.60020
7	−3273.398	48.48835*	5209488.*	29.64290*	32.30894	30.71797

no matter which method chooses, the lag order is 7. Therefore, the lag model of the VAR model is defined as seventh order and the VAR (7) model is established. Therefore, the optimal lag order of the co-integration test is 6.

3.3   Co-integration Test

To check whether there is a long-term stable equilibrium relationship between D (PRECIPITATION), D(AIR_TEMPERATURE), D(AIR_HUMIDITY), D(SUN-SHINE_DURATION) and D(WIND_SPEED), the Johansen co-integration test is used.

There are five deterministic trends in the Johansen co-integration test. This experiment has co-integration equations in various situations as shown in Table 3. With a test level of 0.05, the Trace Statistic results are all greater than the critical value of 0.05, and the probability P values are all less than 0.05. Therefore, at the 5% level of significance, there is a long-term stable equilibrium relationship between D(PRE-CIPITATION), D(AIR_TEMPERATURE), D(AIR_HUMIDITY), D(SUN-SHINE_DURATION), and D(WIND_SPEED). That is, there is a co-integration relationship.

Table 3. Johansen co-integration test results.

Data Trend	None	None	Linear	Linear	Quadratic
Test Type	No Intercept	Intercept	Intercept	Intercept	Intercept
	No Trend	No Trend	No Trend	Trend	Trend
Trace	4	5	5	5	5
Max-Eig	4	3	5	5	5

3.4   Granger Causality Test

Granger causality is a method that can measure the inter-relationship between time series and has been favoured for the past ten years. Both economics [22], meteorology, and neuroscience [23] have a wide range of applications. The Granger causality test makes sense only if there is a co-integration between the sequences. The selection of the lag order here has been obtained in the previous paragraph, with a value of 7. The results of the certification show that there is a "cause and effect" relationship between the sequences (Table 4). That is, a change in one variable can effectively explain the change in another variable.

3.5   VAR Model

The establishment of a VAR model is a prerequisite for variance decomposition and impulse response analysis. If a VAR model would be created, the original sequence needs to be stationary or smooth after all the first-order differences of all variables. If the sequence is not stable, that is, the order is different; the original sequence needs to be co-integrated. If there is a co-integration relationship, a VAR model can be done. Since the data satisfies the above conditions, it is possible to establish and run a VAR model.

Table 4. Causality statistics of each sequence.

Null Hypothesis:	Obs	F-Statistic	Prob.
PRECIPITATION does not Granger Cause AIR_TEMPERATURE	233	9.32048	4.E-10
AIR_TEMPERATURE does not Granger Cause PRECIPITATION		12.2493	3.E-13
AIR_HUMIDITY does not Granger Cause AIR_TEMPERATURE	233	10.3580	3.E-11
AIR_TEMPERATURE does not Granger Cause AIR_HUMIDITY		15.4803	2.E-16
SUNSHINE_DURATION does not Granger Cause AIR_TEMPERATURE		3.07907	0.0041
AIR_TEMPERATURE does not Granger Cause SUNSHINE_DURATION	233	9.51101	3.E-10
WIND_SPEED does not Granger Cause AIR_TEMPERATURE	233	5.97227	2.E-06
AIR_TEMPERATURE does not Granger Cause WIND_SPEED		16.2273	4.E-17
AIR_HUMIDITY does not Granger Cause PRECIPITATION	233	15.1461	4.E-16
PRECIPITATION does not Granger Cause AIR_HUMIDITY		11.1097	5.E-12
SUNSHINE_DURATION does not Granger Cause PRECIPITATION	233	9.57325	2.E-10
PRECIPITATION does not Granger Cause SUNSHINE_DURATION		8.89593	1.E-09
WIND_SPEED does not Granger Cause PRECIPITATION	233	14.4006	2.E-15
PRECIPITATION does not Granger Cause WIND_SPEED		15.2254	4.E-16
SUNSHINE_DURATION does not Granger Cause AIR_HUMIDITY	233	12.9990	6.E-14
AIR_HUMIDITY does not Granger Cause SUNSHINE_DURATION		5.73034	4.E-06
WIND_SPEED does not Granger Cause AIR_HUMIDITY		7.87160	2.E-08
AIR_HUMIDITY does not Granger Cause WIND_SPEED	233	6.82923	2.E-07
WIND_SPEED does not Granger Cause SUNSHINE_DURATION		4.84705	4.E-05
SUNSHINE_DURATION does not Granger Cause WIND_SPEED	233	15.2254	4.E-16

3.6   Stationarity Test

To achieve the purpose of analysing the relationship between variables, it is also necessary to first test the stability of the entire model. Experiments prove that all the characteristic roots of the VAR model are less than 1, that is, the whole tribe in the unit circle (Fig. 1). It shows that the VAR model is in a stable state as a whole, and the preconditions for the analysis of related problems using the VAR model are satisfied. Subsequent analysis can be performed, and subsequent analysis results are reasonable.

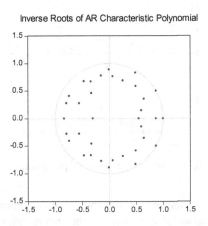

Fig. 1. Analysis of unit root test results.

4 Results and Analysis

After the model tests, the preconditions for the analysis using the VAR model are satisfied. However, whether it can simulate the dynamic impact and duration of the selected variable on precipitation well, it is also necessary to perform impulse response and variance decomposition analysis to verify whether it has certain practical significance.

4.1 Impulse Response

Impulse response analysis is an important aspect of the VAR model to describe the dynamic characteristics of the system. It describes the trajectory of each variable's change or impact on itself and all other variables and shows the influence process of each influencing factor and the positive and negative influence through the impulse response graph. According to the sample data capacity, the experiment sets the shock response period to 7 periods. The impulse response curve of precipitation is plotted (Fig. 2), and the trajectory of precipitation changes is analysed to determine the influence of different influencing factors on precipitation.

The curve PRECIPITATION is the impulse response track where precipitation is affected by its factors. When a positive standard deviation impact is applied to the precipitation, there is a more obvious negative response after the current precipitation period, and in the next few periods, the fluctuations centred around zero. It shows that the sudden increase in precipitation will not have much impact on the precipitation in the coming years. In the long run, the change in precipitation is stable. The curve

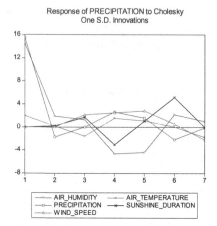

Fig. 2. Impulse response of precipitation.

AIR_HUMIDITY indicates the pulsation response of the precipitation to humidity. It can be seen that the impact of humidity on the precipitation within three years is positive. It is consistent with common sense that the higher the air humidity is, the easier it is to produce precipitation. The curve AIR_TEMPERATURE is the temperature-dependent pulse response trace of precipitation. It can be seen that the impact of temperature on precipitation is fluctuating. The curve WIND_SPEED indicates that the wind speed has a positive effect on the first few periods of precipitation and has a hysteresis effect. The curve SUNSHINE_DURATION shows that the effect of sunshine hours on precipitation increases year by year.

4.2 Variance Decomposition

From the perspective of the impulse response function, the impact of various factors on the impact of precipitation is positive and negative. However, on the whole, the curve of precipitation after impact is relatively flat. It also shows that there is a certain degree of adjustment between meteorological factors. To further analyse the extent of the contribution of various influencing factors in the course of long-term precipitation changes, the variance of the precipitation is also decomposed.

Precipitation is gradually reduced by own impact, decreasing from the initial 53.05% to 43.29%. The effect of humidity on precipitation is relatively high and stable and has remained at about 45%. In addition to humidity, the impact of other factors on precipitation from the initial period to the seventh period although there is a slight fluctuation, overall shows an increasing trend (Table 5). In the long run, except for 43.29% of the change in precipitation, it is determined by itself. The degree of influence from high to low is: 43.85% is affected by humidity, 6.68% is affected by light, 3.99% is affected by wind speed, and 2.18% is affected by temperature.

Table 5. Variance decomposition results of precipitation.

Period	S.E.	AIR_HUMIDITY	AIR_TEMPERATURE	PRECIPITATION	SUNSHINE_DURATION	WIND_SPEED
1	6.5251	46.09010	0.862532	53.04737	0.000000	0.000000
2	7.2213	46.21298	0.856642	52.91872	0.010939	0.000714
3	7.4711	45.43428	1.350775	51.61816	0.644275	0.952504
4	7.7919	45.52605	1.688908	48.34783	2.371386	2.065829
5	8.1402	46.39427	1.805351	45.98412	2.428684	3.387573
6	8.4854	44.34536	1.694677	43.94682	6.783495	3.229643
7	8.6103	43.85465	2.182192	43.29362	6.682418	3.987120

5 Conclusion

To analyse the influence relationship between various meteorological factors and precipitation in desert areas, and to understand the influence of other meteorological factors on precipitation disturbance and other meteorological factors when the precipitation is impacted, an analytical model is established.

(1) Innovatively apply VAR, which is mainly used in the economics, to the analysis of precipitation in a special desert area. Through the analysis of impulse response and variance decomposition, the impact relationship between meteorological factors such as precipitation is analysed, which is of great significance for macroscopically grasping the overall state of desert precipitation.

(2) The experimental results show that from the perspective of the 7th period, the precipitation is most affected by the humidity, followed by itself, which is 43.85% and 43.29%, respectively. Because of the high degree of correlation between the two, it is possible to increase the amount of precipitation in desert areas from the perspective of increasing air humidity. The model provides a good theoretical basis for the analysis of the influencing factors of precipitation in the Elion Ecological Desert Big Data Platform.

(3) The data selected for the experiment are all meteorological data and have certain limitations. In the following studies, more practical factors such as human activity area and vegetation coverage should be added to the model to improve the practical significance of the analysis further.

Acknowledgements. The project is funded by Elion Resources Group.

References

1. Tu, Z., Li, M., Sun, T.: Results and analysis of the fifth national desertification and desertification monitoring. Forestry Resour. Manag. **01**, 1–5 (2016)
2. Xu, L., Zhou, H., Li, Y., Li, H., Tang, Y.: Analysis of the precipitation stability and variety trend in desert region of northern China. Adv. Water Sci. **19**(06), 792–799 (2008)
3. Lu, R., Tang, Q., Wei, D., Zhang, C.: Study on rainfall infiltration of different dunes in Dongsha Lake of Qinghai Lake. Chin. Desert Sci. **33**(03), 797–803 (2013)

4. Yao, S., Zhang, T., Zhao, C.: Multi-time-scale analysis on precipitation in Naiman Banner of Horqin Sandy Land in 1970–2010. J. Desert Res. **34**(02), 542–549 (2014)

5. Feng, W., Yang, W., Li, W., Dang, H., Liang, H.: Response of soil moisture to precipitation in fixed dunes of Salix in Maowusu Sandy Land. J. Soil Water Conserv. **28**(05), 95–99 (2014)

6. Feng, W., et al.: Response of soil moisture to rainfall in a mobile dune in the Mu Us Sandy Land. J. Desert Res. **35**(02), 400–406 (2015)

7. Wei, Y., Guo, K., Chen, J.: Supplementary effects of rainfall patterns on soil moisture in the Kubuqi Desert. Chin. J. Plant Ecol. **32**(06), 1346–1355 (2008)

8. Wang, N., Ma, N., Chen, H., Chen, X., Dong, C., Zhang, Z.: Preliminary analysis of precipitation characteristics in the hinterland of Badain Jaran Desert. Adv. Water Sci. **24**(02), 153–160 (2013)

9. Wu, L., Su, Y., Zhang, Y.: Effects of simulated precipitation on apparent carbon flux of biologically crusted soils in the Gurbantunggut Desert in xinjiang. Acta Ecol. Sin. **32**(13), 4103–4113 (2012)

10. Monteleoni, C., Schmidt, G.A., Saroha, S., et al.: Tracking climate models. Stat. Anal. Data Min. ASA Data Sci. J. **4**(4), 372–392 (2011)

11. Hu, J., Zhang, L., Yu, R.: Application of neural network model to forecast precipitation in flood season in Hubei Province. Meteorol. J. **59**(06), 776–783 (2001)

12. Jin, L., Wu, J., Lin, K., et al.: Short-term climate prediction model of neural network based on genetic algorithms. Plateau Meteorol. **24**(6), 981–987 (2005)

13. Feng, H., Chen, Y.: A new method for non-linear classify and non-linear regression problems II: application of support vector machine to weather forecast. Q. J. Appl. Meteorol. **15**(03), 355–365 (2004)

14. Bi, S., Xu, W., Zhai, Z., Chen, Y., Wang, B.: Application of EMD to seasonal precipitation in Guangxi. J. Appl. Meteorol. Sci. **21**(03), 366–371 (2010)

15. Kong, D.M., Li, W.-D., Wu, J.-R.: Application of extreme learning machine model in precipitation prediction based on cointegration theory. Water Resour. Power **35**(09), 1–3 (2017)

16. Nugroho A., Subanar, Hartati S., et al.: Vector autoregressive model for rainfall forecast and isohyet mapping in Semarang – Central Java – Indonesia. Int. J. Adv. Comput. Sci. Appl. **5** (11) (2014)

17. Saputro, D.R.S, Wigena, A.H., Djuraidah, A.: Model Vector Autoregressive, Untuk Peramalan curah hujan di Indramayu, (vector autoregressive model for forecast rainfall in Indramayu). Forum Statistika Dan Komputasi (2011)

18. Liu, Y.Y., Tseng, F.M., Tseng, Y.H.: Big Data analytics for forecasting tourism destination arrivals with the applied vector autoregressive model. Technol. Forecast. Soc. Change **130**, 123–134 (2018)

19. Lütkepohl, H.: Asymptotic distributions of impulse response functions and forecast error variance decompositions of vector autoregressive models. Rev. Econ. Stat. **72**(1), 116–125 (1990)

20. Lütkepohl, H., Saikkonen, P.: Impulse response analysis in infinite order co-integrated vector autoregressive processes. J. Econ. **81**(1), 127–157 (1995)

21. Bleach, I.T., Beckmann, C., Both, C., et al.: A principal-components variance decomposition of monthly and quarterly vector autoregressive models of the U.S. Economy. Comput. Econ. Financ. **69**(4), 675–683 (2002)

22. Silvapulle, P.: Testing for linear and nonlinear Granger causality in the stock price-volume relation: Korean evidence. Q. Rev. Econ. Financ. **39**(1), 59–76 (1997)

23. Roebroeck, A., Formisano, E., Goebel, R.: Mapping directed influence over the brain using Granger causality and fMRI. Neuroimage **25**(1), 230–242 (2005)

Interactive Construction of Criterion Relations for Multi-criteria Decision Making

Le Sun[1(✉)] and Jinyuan He[2]

[1] College of Computer and Software, Nanjing University of Information Science and Technology, Nanjing, China
sunle2009@gmail.com
[2] Center for Applied Informatics, Victoria University, Melbourne, Australia
jinyuan.he@live.vu.edu.au

Abstract. Multi-criteria decision making (MCDM) is a category of techniques for solving decision making problems based on the performance of multiple criteria. One shortcoming of the existing MCDM techniques is that they rarely consider the relations among decision criteria. Nevertheless, different types of criterion relations significantly impact the results of the decision making problem. In this paper, we solve this problem by establishing and measuring different types of relations among decision criteria. We propose a MCDM framework, named InterDM, to rank a set of alternatives based on the utilities of both singleton criteria and criterion coalitions, in which we design an Interactive Interpretive Structural Modeling technique to construct consistent criterion relations. We use a case study of ranking cloud services to demonstrate the efficiency of InterDM.

Keywords: Multi-criteria decision making · Cloud service selection
Criterion interdependence

1 Introduction

Researchers have developed and applied multi-criteria decision making (MCDM) techniques to various areas such as decision support systems, objective optimization, and performance simulation [15]. In this paper, we focus on problems with finite decision alternatives and criteria. Solutions of these problems are a ranking of alternatives. One key task for solving these problems is to identify relations among criteria and to aggregate criteria utilities based on their relations to obtain an overall evaluation of alternatives. However, most MCDM techniques assume the selection criteria are independent [5, 21]. This assumption does not take into account the fact that there are different types of relations among criteria, and both the singleton criteria and the criterion coalitions can influence the ranking results of the alternatives and the final decisions of the MDCM problems. In

© Springer Nature Switzerland AG 2018
X. Sun et al. (Eds.): ICCCS 2018, LNCS 11063, pp. 589–600, 2018.
https://doi.org/10.1007/978-3-030-00006-6_54

reality, components in a complex system are interdependent with each other in different forms. Different types of interrelations influence the performance of the overall system in different ways [9].

There are three forms of inter-relationship among criteria: supportive, conflicting, and independent [10]. Supportive criteria are similar with each other in terms of functions, so that they influence each other's utility positively, while their coalition influence the system utility negatively. Conflicting criteria have opposite impacts with each other. The increase of a criterion utility causes the decrease of the utilities of its conflicting criteria. There is no relation among independent criteria.

We use a motivating scenario to present the significance of modeling criterion relations in cloud service selection. Assume a service user prefers low cost to good service performance and his actual preference on three purchasing criteria (cost, availability, uptime) is $(0.7, 0.1, 0.2)$. If he rates a service1 and a service2 in terms of the same criteria as $(8, 6, 7)$ and $(5, 10, 16)$ respectively, simple weighted additive approach will recommend service2 based on $utility(service2) = 5*0.7 + 10*0.1 + 16*0.2 > utility(service1) = 8*0.7 + 6*0.1 + 7*0.2$. Obviously, the result is inaccurate and conflicts with the service user's preference. The reason for such a recommendation is mainly because of the ignorance of a fact that high availability always comes with high uptime. Therefore, the redundant consideration of these two criteria results in over-estimation of service2. This scenario well explains how a lack of consideration of criterion interactions over-estimates an alternative. In fact, it is also important to consider criterion interactions in various real decision area.

Interpretive structural modeling (ISM) [12] is a classical technique that measures and constructs interactive relations of elements. ISM is a technique of constructing element relations in a decision system. These relations represent organized knowledge that explains the decision system in a simple way. One disadvantage of ISM is that it can only model the single-type element relations, e.g., i is *preferred* to j; or i supports j, in a system, which can cause inaccurate problem solving due to the lack of the complete relation modeling.

Based on the above discussion, this study aims to solve two research issues: issue (1) - identify different relation types among criteria, and issue (2) - measure the influence of the singleton criteria and the criterion coalitions on decision results. We propose a MCDM framework that helps decision makers build the criterion relations and rank alternatives. We mainly describe the interactive framework of building criterion relational networks based on decision makers' preference, namely I-ISM, which allows the decision maker adjust the relations interactively during the relation identification process, until a consistent relation network is built. The proposed MCDM framework is named as *Interactive Criterion Relation Construction and Decision Making* (InterDM). We use a running example of ranking cloud storage services to show the practical applications of InterDM.

This paper is organized as: Sect. 2 discusses related work of Cloud service selection; Sect. 3 introduces the basic definitions and properties of the proposed

MCDM framework; and presents a running example of applying the MDCM framework to the cloud service selection; Sect. 4 concludes this paper.

2   Related Work

Multi-criteria decision-making (MCDM) [16] generally refers to a multi-attribute decision making problem with discrete solution spaces. Assume there are m alternatives to be evaluated, and each alternative is evaluated by n criteria, an MCDM problem is in the form of Eq. 1, where v_{ij} represents the value of criterion j of alternative i. The solution is to find the alternative with the optimal utility.

$$
A = \begin{bmatrix}
v_{11} & v_{12} & v_{13} & \cdots & v_{1n} \\
v_{21} & v_{22} & v_{23} & \cdots & v_{2n} \\
\vdots & \vdots & \vdots & \ddots & \vdots \\
v_{m1} & v_{m2} & v_{m3} & \cdots & v_{mn}
\end{bmatrix}
\tag{1}
$$

Simple weighted addition (SWA) [1] is the most simple and popular method. If each criterion has a weight, e.g. w_j, $j \in [1, n]$, the overall SWA value of alternative i is $U_i^{swa} = \sum_{j=1}^{n} w_j * v_{ij}$. AHP [2] is a hierarchic decision Modeling that includes several consistent pair-wise comparison matrices. It has been applied to solve various MDCM problems, such as solar farm site selection [19], cloud service allocation [6], and power substation location selection [8]. TOPSIS [7] ranks the alternatives based on the distances from the current criterion values to the ideal and negative solutions. Balcerzak et al. [3] applied TOPSIS to analyse the European sustainable development.

However, one of the disadvantages of the above discussed methods is they do not consider the influence of the types and degrees of the interactive relations among criteria on the decision making solutions. The fuzzy integral methods [4] and the Interpretive Structural Modeling (ISM) [13] were proposed to address this problem. A fuzzy integral is a utility aggregating operator that can measure the influence of the performance of a criterion and the criterion interactions on the overall system performance. Liou et al. [11] proposed a fuzzy integral-based model for supplier evaluation. Zhang et al. [22] discussed the application of fuzzy integral on the city sustainability evaluation. Shen et al. [17] applied the fuzzy integral approach for solving financial planning problems in insurance businesses. Interpretive Structural Modeling (ISM) [13] is capable of finding the importance degree of each alternatives, and their direct and transitive relations. It has been widely applied in decision making area, for example, the supply chain risk analysis [20], education quality analysis [14], and waste management analysis [18].

3   Interactive Criterion Relation Construction and Decision Making

This section introduces the framework of *Interactive Criterion Relation Construction and Decision Making* (InterDM), which builds an Interactive Interpretive Structural Modeling (I-ISM) model to identify relations among decision criteria. The identified relations and weights can be aggregated by using k-order additive choquet integral to obtain utilities of alternatives. We assume that the resulting criterion relational structure is symmetric. Moreover, we propose to integrate supportive and conflicting characteristics of relations into the ISM in order to present a clear picture of the types of criterion relations, and to facilitate the identification of fuzzy measures.

3.1   Interpretive Structural Modeling

We introduce some basic definitions and operations of I-ISM. Let $C = \{c_1, c_2, ..., c_n\}$ be a set of criteria, $F = \{f_1, f_2, ..., fn\}$ be the performance values of the criteria, and $SC \subset C$ be a subset of C. Given $\forall c_i, c_j \in C$:

Definition 1. *An interactive relation from c_i to c_j is defined as a value pair $r_{ij} = (s_{ij}, x_{ij})$, where $s_{ij} \in \{-1, 0, 1\}$ indicates the type of the relation, i.e., how c_i influences c_j; and $x_{ij} \in [0, 1]$ is the interactive degree of the relation, i.e., how the relation will influence the system performance. Details are specified as below:*

- $r_{ij} = (s_{ij} = -1, x_{ij} \neq 0)$: c_i *negatively influences* c_j, *i.e.,* $f_i \downarrow$ (*resp.* $\uparrow$) $\Rightarrow$ $f_j \uparrow$ (*resp.* $\downarrow$), *namely* c_i **conflicts to** c_j, *represented as* r_{ij}^c;
- $r_{ij} = (-1, x_{ij} \neq 0) \& r_{ji} = (-1, x_{ji} \neq 0)$: c_i *and* c_j *negatively influence each other, i.e.,* $f_i \downarrow$ (*resp.* $\uparrow$) $\Leftrightarrow$ $f_j \uparrow$ (*resp.* $\downarrow$), *namely* c_i *is* **conflicting with** c_j, *represented as* r_{ij}^{cc};
- $r_{ij} = (s_{ij} = 1, x_{ij} \neq 0)$: c_i *positively influences* c_j, *i.e.,* $f_i \uparrow$ (*resp.* $\downarrow$) $\Rightarrow$ $f_j \uparrow$ (*resp.* $\downarrow$), *namely* c_i **supports** c_j, *represented as* r_{ij}^s;
- $r_{ij} = (1, x_{ij} \neq 0) \& r_{ji} = (1, x_{ji} \neq 0)$: c_i *and* c_j *positively influence each other, namely* c_i *is* **supportive with** c_j, *represented as* r_{ij}^{ss};
- $r_{ij} = (0, 0)$: c_i *is* **independent with** c_j, *represented as* r_{ij}^u.

Property 1. (1) $r_{ij} = r_{pq} \Leftrightarrow x_{ij} = x_{pq} \& s_{ij} = s_{pq}$; (2) $r_{ij} = -r_{pq} \Leftrightarrow x_{ij} = x_{pq} \& s_{ij} = -s_{pq}$;

Definition 2. *Given a relation r_{ij}, if $r_{ij} = r_{ji}$, then r_{ij} is a symmetric relation, represented as* $c_i \overleftrightarrow{r_{ij}} c_j$.

The relations *support* and *conflict to* are asymmetric relations; *supportive with*, *conflicting with*, and *independent with* are symmetric relations.

Property 2. $r_{ii} = r_{ii}^{ss} = (1, 1)$, i.e., a relation is supportive with itself with the interactive degree of 1.

Property 3. $\forall c_i, c_j$, if r_{ij}^{ss}, $f_{ij} < f_i + f_j$; if r_{ij}^{cc}, $f_{ij} = f_i + f_j$, where f_{ij} refers to the importance degree of the interaction between c_i and c_j to the system.

Property 4. Given any two relations r_{ij} and r_{pq}, if $x_{ij} > x_{pq}$, for $\forall s_{ij} \& s_{pq}$, the importance of the interaction between criteria c_i and c_j towards the system is higher than the importance of the interaction between criteria c_p and c_q.

The concept of *path* and the *length* of path in I-ISM are similar to the concepts in ISM.

Definition 3. *A path from c_i to c_j, written as p_{ij}, indicates a relation between them (i.e., r_{ij}), containing a series of linked elements between c_i and c_j. The length of r_{ij}, represented as l_{ij}, is the number of arcs between c_i and c_j. If $l_{ij} = 1$, r_{ij} is a direct relation, represented as $c_i r_\phi c_j$; if $l_{ij} > 1 \& l_{ij} < +\infty$, r_{ij} is a transitive relation, represented as $c_i r_{\{k,c_1...c_k\}} c_j$, where $c_1, ..., c_k$ are elements on the path p_{ij}, k is the number of elements; if $l_{ij} = +\infty$, r_{ij} is r_{ij}^u (represented as $c_i r_\infty c_j$).*

In the sequel sections, we will only concern about the type and direction of a relation between two criteria. We use $c_i s c_j$ to represent $c_i r c_j$, e.g., if $r_{ij}^s = \{1, \forall x_{ij}\}$, then $c_i r_{ij}^s c_j = c_i \{1, \forall x_{ij}\} c_j = c_i \overrightarrow{1} c_j$.

Property 5. Let m be the number of paths between element c_i and c_j, all the paths between c_i and c_j are represented as: $P_{ij} = \{p_{ij}^1 \cup p_{ij}^2 \cup ... \cup p_{ij}^m\}$. If $m = 0$, $r_{ij} = r_{ij}^u$.

Inconsistency is incident to a manually assigned relation matrix. Establishing consistent relations is essential for building a consistent and stable reachability matrix. To efficiently build consistent criterion relations, we define two context-aware logical operators *logic addition*($\triangledown$) and *logic multiplication*($\overline{\wedge}$), and relational operators *relation addition*($\vee$) and *relation multiplication*($\wedge$). These logical operators are used to operate the Characteristic matrix of an SSIM to determine the types of relations. $\triangledown$ and $\vee$ aggregate two relational paths between two vertices to determine a unique relation between the two criteria. $\overline{\wedge}$ and $\wedge$ aggregate a set of relations on a path to find a transitive relation between the two vertices. They are defined as: Given a set of variables $s_1, s_2, ..., s_n \in \{-1, 0, 1\}$,

Definition 4. *Logic addition ($\triangledown$) has properties:*

- $s_i \triangledown 0 = s_i$;
- $1 \triangledown 1 = 1$, $-1 \triangledown - 1 = -1$, $1 \triangledown - 1 = \infty$;
- $\triangledown$ satisfies left associativity: $s_i \triangledown s_j \triangledown s_k = (s_i \triangledown s_j) \triangledown s_k, i, j, k \in \{1, ..., n\}$.

Definition 5. *Relational addition ($\vee$) has properties:* $r_{ij}^1 \vee r_{ij}^2 \vee ... \vee r_{ij}^m = ((s_{ij}^1 \triangledown s_{ij}^2 \triangledown ... \triangledown s_{ij}^m), max\{x_{ij}^1, x_{ij}^2, ..., x_{ij}^m\})$.

From Definition 5, if there are m relational paths between vertices c_i and c_j, then their interaction degree $x_{ij} \geq \forall x_{ij}^k, k \in \{1, ..., m\}$.

Definition 6. *Logic multiplication ($\overline{\wedge}$) satisfies:*

- $s_i \overline{\wedge} 0 = 0$;
- $1 \overline{\wedge} 1 = 1$, $-1 \overline{\wedge} - 1 = 1$, $1 \overline{\wedge} - 1 = -1$;
- $\overline{\wedge}$ satisfies left associativity: $s_i \overline{\wedge} s_j \overline{\wedge} s_k = (s_i \overline{\wedge} s_j) \overline{\wedge} s_k, i, j, k \in \{1, ..., n\}$.

Definition 7. *Relational multiplication ($\wedge$) satisfies: for the kth path between c_i and c_i, $r^k_{i,i+1} \wedge r^k_{i+1,i+2} \wedge \dots \wedge r^k_{j-1,j} = ((s^k_{i,i+1}\overline{\wedge}s^k_{i+1,i+2}\overline{\wedge}\dots\overline{\wedge}s^k_{j-1,j}), min\{x^k_{i,i+1}\overline{\wedge}x^k_{i+1,i+2}\})$.*

Definition 7 indicates that if a relation r_{ij} is a transitive relation, then $x_{ij} \leq x_{pq}$, where $x_{pq} \in \{x_{i,i+1}, x_{i+1,i+2}, \dots, x_{j-1,j}\}$.

Definition 8. *A $SSIM$ of I-ISM is defined as $SSIM = (ChM, InD)$;*

$$ChM = \begin{pmatrix} s_{11} & \cdots & s_{1n} \\ \vdots & \ddots & \vdots \\ s_{n1} & \cdots & s_{nn} \end{pmatrix}$$ *is the Characteristic Matrix of $SSIM$; and $InD =$*

$$\begin{pmatrix} x_{11} & \cdots & x_{1n} \\ \vdots & \ddots & \vdots \\ x_{n1} & \cdots & x_{nn} \end{pmatrix}$$ *is the interactive matrix of $SSIM$.*

Property 6. $SSIM * SSIM = (ChM * ChM, InD * InD)$.

Property 7. A $SSIM$ is consistent, and an RM is stable (i.e. $RM = RM^k = RM^{k+1}$), consistent, and symmetric (i.e., $\forall c_i, c_j, r_{ij} = r_{ji}$).

Property 8. For a set of relations $R = \{r_{ij}\}$, if one of the following two cases exists, there is inconsistency in R: (1)$\exists r_{ij} = -r_{ij}$; (2)if there are m paths between c_i and c_j, $\exists r^a_{ij} \neq r^b_{ij}$, $a, b \in \{m\}$, then the corresponding $SSIM$ is inconsistent.

Figure 1 shows an example (Example 1) of using logic operations ($\overline{\vee}, \overline{\wedge}, \vee$ and $\wedge$) to interactively check inconsistencies and build consistent criterion relations.

Example 1. Give criteria $\{c_1, c_2, c_3, c_4\}$, Fig. 1(a) shows an initial $SSIM$ built by a decision maker, indicating the initial relations among criteria:

(1) $c_1 \overleftrightarrow{1} c_4$: c_1 and c_4 are directly supportive with each other;
(2) $c_1 \overrightarrow{-1} c_3$: c_1 directly conflict to c_3;
(3) $c_1 \overleftrightarrow{1} c_4 \overleftrightarrow{1} c_3 \Rightarrow c_1 1\overline{\wedge}1 c_3$: c_1 and c_3 are transitively supportive with each other via c_4;
(4) Inconsistencies:
  - based on (2) and (3), $c_1 \overrightarrow{-1 \cup 1^2_{c_4}} c_3 \Rightarrow c_1 \overrightarrow{-1\overline{\vee}1} c_3 \Rightarrow c_1 \overrightarrow{\infty} c_3$: the relation from c_1 to c_3 cannot be determined due to the conflicting relation between their direct relation $\overrightarrow{-1}$ and their transitive relation via c_4.
  - $c_1 \overrightarrow{-1_{\{1,c_3\}}} c_2$ & $c_2 \overrightarrow{1_{\{2,c_3c_4\}}} c_1 \Rightarrow c_1(-1\overline{\vee}1)c_2 \Rightarrow c_1(\infty)c_2$: the relation between c_1 and c_2 are not symmetric.

We then raise the power of the initial $SSIM$ to identify the transitive relations, until the matrix reaches its stable state.

(1) Check the direct inconsistent relations in $SSIM$. If there are direct inconsistencies, return the position of the inconsistent relations, and then decision makers revise the $SSIM$, e.g., if the initial $SSIM$ is:$ChM_0 =$

$$
\begin{array}{cccc}
 & c_1 & c_2 & c_3 & c_4 \\
\end{array}
$$

$$
\begin{array}{c}
c_1 \\ c_2 \\ c_3 \\ c_4
\end{array}
\begin{pmatrix}
1 & 0 & -1 & 1 \\
0 & 1 & 1 & 0 \\
0 & 1 & 1 & 1 \\
1 & 0 & 1 & 1
\end{pmatrix}, \text{ the revised consistent matrix is } ChM_1 =
$$

$$
\begin{array}{cccc}
 & c_1 & c_2 & c_3 & c_4 \\
\end{array}
$$

$$
\begin{array}{c}
c_1 \\ c_2 \\ c_3 \\ c_4
\end{array}
\begin{pmatrix}
1 & 0 & -1 & 1 \\
0 & 1 & 1 & 0 \\
-1 & 1 & 1 & 1 \\
1 & 0 & 1 & 1
\end{pmatrix}, \text{ which corresponds to Fig. 1a;}
$$

(2) Or else, raise the power of ChM, and record the additive vectors and the median matrix in each power-raised step, i.e., $ChM^k, k = \{2, 3, ...\}$.

(3) If there are inconsistencies in the vectors or in the median matrix, the raising process will be terminated, and the conflicting elements will be detected and be returned to decision makers as feedbacks, e.g., $ChM^0 =$

$$
\begin{array}{cccc}
 & c_1 & c_2 & c_3 & c_4 \\
\end{array}
$$

$$
\begin{array}{c}
c_1 \\ c_2 \\ c_3 \\ c_4
\end{array}
\begin{pmatrix}
1 & -1 & \infty & \infty \\
-1 & 1 & 1 & 1 \\
\infty & 1 & 1 & \infty \\
\infty & 1 & \infty & 1
\end{pmatrix}.
$$

It shows that the relations among c_1, c_3, c_4 are inconsistent. Therefore, the additive vectors for the two positions are returned to the decision makers, e.g., the additive vector for position (c_3, c_1) in ChM_2 is calculated as: $c_3?c_1 \Leftarrow (-1, 1, 1, 1)\overline{\wedge}(1, 0, -1, 1)^T = ((-1\overline{\wedge}1)\overline{\vee}(1\overline{\wedge}0)\overline{\vee}(1\overline{\wedge}-1)\overline{\vee}(1\overline{\wedge}1)) = (-1\overline{\vee}0\overline{\vee}-1\overline{\vee}1) \Rightarrow c_3 r_\infty c_1$. The meaning of the additive vector $(-1\overline{\vee}0\overline{\vee}-1\overline{\vee}1)$ is: $c_3 \overrightarrow{-1} c_1$, $c_3 \overrightarrow{0_{\{1,c_2\}}} c_1$, $c_3 \overrightarrow{-1} c_1$, $c_3 \overrightarrow{1_{\{1,c_4\}}} c_1$. ChM_1 shows that the transitive relation from c_3 to c_1 through c_4 is conflict with the direct relation from c_3 to c_1.

For positions (c_1, c_3), (c_1, c_4), (c_3, c_4), (c_4, c_1), and (c_4, c_3), the additive vectors are $c_1 r_\infty c_3 \Leftarrow (-1\overline{\vee}0\overline{\vee}-1\overline{\vee}1)$; $c_1 r_\infty c_4 \Leftarrow (1\overline{\vee}0\overline{\vee}-1\overline{\vee}1)$; $c_3 r_\infty c_4 \Leftarrow (-1\overline{\vee}0\overline{\vee}1\overline{\vee}1)$; $c_4 r_\infty c_1 \Leftarrow (1\overline{\vee}0\overline{\vee}-1\overline{\vee}1)$; $c_4 r_\infty c_3 \Leftarrow (-1\overline{\vee}0\overline{\vee}1\overline{\vee}1)$.

(4) The experts adjust the relation matrix based on the returned additive vectors and the powered matrix, e.g., the six additive vectors in last step shows that the inconsistencies are: $c_1 \overleftrightarrow{r}_{\{1,c_4\}} c_3$, $c_1 \overleftrightarrow{r}_{\{1,c_3\}} c_4$, $c_3 \overleftrightarrow{r}_{\{1,c_1\}} c_4$. Thus, the relations among c_1, c_3, and c_4 need to be reviewed and adjusted by decision makers, e.g., suppose after reviewing, the relation is changed to $c_3 \overleftrightarrow{-1} c_4$ (see Fig. 1b).

(5) Restart the powering process based on the new matrix ChM^1, until the stable matrix is achieved and there is no feedback in the process. The reachability matrix is obtained, e.g., the final stable and symmetric reachability matrix is $RM * ChM = ChM^3 = ChM^4 = ... = ChM^\infty =$

$$\begin{array}{c}\\c_1\\c_2\\c_3\\c_4\end{array}\begin{array}{cccc}c_1 & c_2 & c_3 & c_4\end{array}\left(\begin{array}{cccc}1 & & & \\-1 & 1 & & \\-1 & 1 & 1 & \\1 & -1 & -1 & 1\end{array}\right)$$. The reachability diagram is shown in Fig. 1c. We

can see that the relation $c_4 \overleftarrow{-1}_{\{1, c_1 \text{ or } c_3\}} \overrightarrow{} c_2$ is an identified transitive relation, and $c_1 \overleftrightarrow{-1} c_2$ is an identified direct relation.

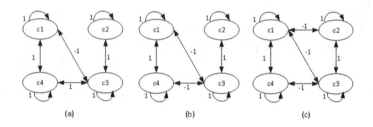

Fig. 1. Interactive relations among criteria c_1, c_2, c_3, c_4

3.2 Supportive and Conflict Power for Criterion Ranking

After establishing relations among criteria, we introduce definitions of *driver power*, *dependence power*, *supportive power* and *conflict power* as below.

Let N be a set of criteria for a decision system, $i, j \in N, i \neq j$:

Definition 9. $\forall i, j$ *that* i *supports or is supportive with* j, *the* **driver power** *of* i *is* $Dr(i) = \Sigma_{j \in N}(s_{ij})$; *and the* **dependence power** *of* j *is defined as* $Dp(j) = \Sigma_{i \in N}(s_{ij})$.

Definition 10. $\forall i, j$ *that* i *is supportive with* j, *the* **supportive power** *of* i *is defined as* $S(i) = \Sigma_{j \in N}(s_{ij} x_{ij})$. *For* $\forall i, j$ *that* i *is conflict with* j, *the* **conflict power** *of* i *is defined as* $Cf(i) = \Sigma_{j \in N}(s_{ij} x_{ij})$.

Theorem 1. $Cf(i) - S(i) \geq Cf(j) - S(j) \Rightarrow i$ *is more important than* j *(i.e.* $i \succeq j$); *and* $Cf(i) + S(i) \geq Cf(j) + S(j) \Rightarrow i \succeq j$.

Proof. Based on definitions of *supportive with* and *conflicting with*, the more a criterion being conflicting with the other criteria, the more important the criterion is to the system; while the more a criterion being supportive with the other criteria, the less important the criterion is to the system. Therefore, the higher the value of $Cf(i) - S(i)$, the higher importance degree (or satisfaction degree) the criterion i has.

Based on definitions of *driver power* and *dependence*, the more a criterion being connective with other criteria (i.e., having higher driver power and dependence), the more important the criterion is. Therefore, the higher the value of $Cf + S$, the higher importance degree (or satisfaction degree) the criterion has.   □

Table 1. SSIM of nine criteria of a Cloud service

SSIM	0	1	2	3	4	5	6	7	8
0	1	1	1	-1	0	0	0	0	0
1	1	1	0	0	0	0	0	0	0
2	0	0	1	-1	0	0	0	0	0
3	-1	0	-1	1	0	0	0	0	1
4	0	0	0	0	1	1	0	0	1
5	0	0	0	0	1	1	0	0	0
6	0	0	0	0	0	0	1	1	0
7	0	0	0	0	0	0	1	1	0
8	0	0	0	1	1	0	0	0	1

Table 2. RM and ranking of nine criteria

RM	0	1	2	3	4	5	6	7	8	$Cf - S$	$Cf + S$	Rank
0	1	1	1	-1	-1	-1	0	0	-1	1	7	I
1	1	1	1	-1	-1	-1	0	0	-1	1	7	I
2	1	1	1	-1	-1	-1	0	0	-1	1	7	I
3	-1	-1	-1	1	1	1	0	0	1	-1	7	II
4	-1	-1	-1	1	1	1	0	0	1	-1	7	II
5	-1	-1	-1	1	1	1	0	0	1	-1	7	II
6	0	0	0	0	0	0	1	1	0	-2	2	III
7	0	0	0	0	0	0	1	1	0	-2	2	III
8	-1	-1	-1	1	1	1	0	0	1	-1	7	II

We use an example of ranking the importance of nine QoS criteria of a cloud storage service based on the SSIM and the supportive&conflict powers. Assume for any criteria i and j, $x_{ij} = 1$, the SSIM of nine QoS criteria is shown in Table 1, and Table 3 gives the definition of the nine QoSs. We raise the power of SSIM to get a stable Reachability Matrix (RM in Table 2). Based on the stable RM matrix, we first rank criteria in terms of $Cf - S$ values, and then the criteria with similar $Cf - S$ will be ranked in terms of $Cf + S$ values. The ranking result of the nine criteria is shown in Table 2. We can see that the first three criteria are the most important for the system.

3.3 Criterion Partition Based on Stable Reachability Matrix

In this section, we introduce Hierarchic and Block partition procedures to help easily inspect and construct criterion relations.

Block Partition: $\Pi_B = (B_1, ..., B_h)$, where $B_l = \{i \in A - B_0 - B_1 - ... - B_{l-1} | r_{ij}^{ss}, \forall j \in B_l$, and $r_{ik}^{cc} || r_{ik}^u, \forall k \notin B_l\}$.

For example, the relation partition induced by the reachability matrix RM in Table 2 is $\Pi_R = \{\{0, 1, 2\}, \{3, 4, 5, 8\}, \{6, 7\}\}$, where 1 represent a supportive relation, and -1 represent a conflict relation.

Given the block partition of a set of criteria, and the assumption that $x_{ij}^{cc||ss} = 1$ and $x_{ij}^u = 0$, we define a hierarchic partition to rank the importance degree of criteria for the decision system.

Hierarchic Partition: $\Pi_H = (H_1, ..., H_h)$, where $H_l \in \{i \in A - H_0 - H_1 - \cdots - H_{l-1} | Cf(i) = Cf(j)\&S(i) = S(j), \forall j \in H_l; Cf(i) < Cf(k)\&S(i) > S(k), \forall k \in H_g, g < l\}$.

The values of $Cf - S$ and $Cf + S$ of criteria are used to rank the criteria respectively. Table 2 column *Rank* shows the ranking of nine criteria for Cloud

Table 3. Definitions of nine criteria for evaluating Cloud services

ID	Type	Criteria	Metric
1	B	Availability (av)	av = uptime/(uptime+downtime)
2	B	Reliability (re)	if $av^0 \geq av^1, re = 1$; else $re = 1 - (av^1 - av^0)/av^1$, where av^0: real availability and av^1: availability in SLA
3	B	Scalability (sc)	If service upgrade requires file re-uploading, sc = 0; else sc = 1
4	B	Storage capacity (stc)	Maximum storage capacity
5	C	Latency (la)	Average time (s) of uploading a file (1MB)
6	B	Data transfer speed (dts)	Maximum throughput (MB/s)
7	B	Type of customer services (tcs)	Number of customer services matching user requests * 0.8 + number of the other provided customer services * 0.2
8	C	Response speed of customer service (rscs)	Time (mins) a service provider answers support requirements
9	C	Price of the storage service (cost)	$/month/50GB$

service evaluation based on the values of $Cf - S$ or $Cf + S$. The tab *Rank* indicates that criteria av, re and sc are the most important. The criterion ranking hierarchies can be established based on *Rank*, which is shown in Fig. 2. In Fig. 2, the arcs are all bi-direction, representing the symmetric relation between criteria. The arcs with dotted lines represent the supportive relations between criteria, while the arcs with solid lines represent the conflicting relations.

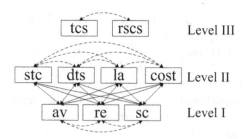

Fig. 2. Hierarchic Partition of Criteria

4   Conclusion

In this paper, we proposed an Interactive MCDM framework: InterDM, to rank alternatives based on the influence of both singleton criteria and criterion coalitions. We described a case study of cloud service selection to demonstrate the efficiency of InterDM. In the future, we are going to compare the proposed InterDM with more traditional MCDM methods to validate the stability, accuracy and time efficiency of InterDM.

Acknowledgments. This work is partially supported by the National Natural Science Foundation of China (Grants No 61702274) and the Natural Science Foundation of Jiangsu Province (Grants No BK20170958).

References

1. Abdullah, L., Adawiyah, C.R.: Simple additive weighting methods of multi criteria decision making and applications: a decade review. Int. J. Inf. Process. Manage. **5**(1), 39 (2014)
2. Badri, M., et al.: An analytic hierarchy process for school quality and inspection: model development and application. Int. J. Educ. Manage. **30**(3), 437–459 (2016)
3. Balcerzak, A.P., Pietrzak, M.B.: Application of topsis method for analysis of sustainable development in european union countries. Chapters **1**, 82–92 (2016)
4. Dursun, M.: A fuzzy mcdm framework based on fuzzy measure and fuzzy integral for agile supplier evaluation. In: AIP Conference Proceedings. AIP Publishing (2017)
5. Dweiri, F., Kumar, S., Khan, S.A., Jain, V.: Designing an integrated ahp based decision support system for supplier selection in automotive industry. Exp. Syst. Appl. **62**, 273–283 (2016)
6. Ergu, D., Kou, G., Peng, Y., Shi, Y., Shi, Y.: The analytic hierarchy process: task scheduling and resource allocation in cloud computing environment. J. Supercomput., 1–14 (2013)
7. Gupta, N., Singh, Y.: Optimal selection of wind power plant components using technique for order preference by similarity to ideal solution (topsis). In: International Conference on Electrical Power and Energy Systems (ICEPES), pp. 310–315. IEEE (2016)
8. Kabir, G., Sumi, R.S.: Power substation location selection using fuzzy analytic hierarchy process and promethee: a case study from bangladesh. Energy **72**, 717–730 (2014)
9. Saaty, T.L.: The analytic network process. Iranian J. Oper. Res. **1**(1), 1–27 (2008)
10. Le, S., Dong, H., Hussain, F.K., Hussain, O.K., Ma, J., Zhang, Y.: Multicriteria decision making with fuzziness and criteria interdependence in cloud service selection. In: 2014 IEEE International Conference on Fuzzy Systems (FUZZ-IEEE), pp. 1929–1936. IEEE (2014)
11. Liou, J.J., Chuang, Y.C., Tzeng, G.H.: A fuzzy integral-based model for supplier evaluation and improvement. Inf. Sci. **266**, 199–217 (2014)
12. Mandal, A., Deshmukh, S.: Vendor selection using interpretive structural modelling (ISM). Int. J. Oper. Prod. Manage. **14**(6), 52–59 (1994)

13. Mathiyazhagan, K., Govindan, K., NoorulHaq, A., Geng, Y.: An ism approach for the barrier analysis in implementing green supply chain management. J. Cleaner Prod. **47**, 283–297 (2013)
14. Mehta, N., Verma, P., Seth, N.: Total quality management implementation in engineering education in India: an interpretive structural modelling approach. Total Qual. Manage. Bus. Excellence **25**(1–2), 124–140 (2014)
15. Mosavi, A.: A multicriteria decision making environment for engineering design and production decision-making. Int. J. Comput. Appl. **69**(1) (2013)
16. Rezaei, J.: Best-worst multi-criteria decision-making method. Omega **53**, 49–57 (2015)
17. Shen, K.Y., Hu, S.K., Tzeng, G.H.: Financial modeling and improvement planning for the life insurance industry by using a rough knowledge based hybrid mcdm model. Inf. Sci. **375**, 296–313 (2017)
18. Trivedi, A., Singh, A., Chauhan, A.: Analysis of key factors for waste management in humanitarian response: an interpretive structural modelling approach. Int. J. Disaster Risk Reduction **14**, 527–535 (2015)
19. Uyan, M.: Gis-based solar farms site selection using analytic hierarchy process (AHP) in karapinar region, Konya/Turkey. Renew. Sustain. Energy Rev. **28**, 11–17 (2013)
20. Venkatesh, V., Rathi, S., Patwa, S.: Analysis on supply chain risks in indian apparel retail chains and proposal of risk prioritization model using interpretive structural modeling. J. Retail. Consum. Serv. **26**, 153–167 (2015)
21. Xu, X., Liu, Z., Wang, Z., Sheng, Q.Z., Yu, J., Wang, X.: S-ABC: a paradigm of service domain-oriented artificial bee colony algorithms for service selection and composition. Future Gener. Comput. Syst. **68**, 304–319 (2017). https://doi.org/10.1016/j.future.2016.09.008, http://www.sciencedirect.com/science/article/pii/S0167739X16303053
22. Zhang, L., Xu, Y., Yeh, C.H., Liu, Y., Zhou, D.: City sustainability evaluation using multi-criteria decision making with objective weights of interdependent criteria. J. Cleaner Prod. **131**, 491–499 (2016)

Iteratively Modeling Based Cleansing Interactively Samples of Big Data

Xiangwu Ding and Shengnan Qin[✉]

School of Computer Science and Technology, Donghua University,
Shanghai, China
1780598498@qq.com

Abstract. Taking advantage of big data means analyzing it and building prediction model on it. However, the data obtained in reality often contains dirty data due to various factors. One method of using big data is to clean the whole data at first, and then train predictive model on cleaned data, but existing cleaning approaches often need lots of completely clean data as guide to fix errors, that is impractical to obtain many clean data. Another method is to train predictive model on raw data directly, which causes the model is not accurate. Therefore, we explore the iterative updating model process and propose an updating algorithm combining data cleaning and conjugate gradient. In this paper, we incrementally update initial model trained on raw data towards the optimum by cleaning samples instead of whole data at each iteration. And the updating direction is established according to gradient of data. After multiple iterations, we can obtain the optimal model that still works well without cleaning data when new data comes in. We also present cluster descent sampling algorithm to accelerate model convergence. Our evaluation on real datasets shows that the approach significantly improves model accuracy compared with training model directly on raw data.

Keywords: Statistical model · Interactive data cleaning
Conjugate gradient optimization algorithm · Cluster descent sampling

1 Introduction

With the rapid development of information technology, especially data acquisition technology and storage technology, many countries have accumulated petabytes(PB) scale data in multiple areas [1]. Statistical models trained on large data contribute to some important predictive applications such as fraud detection, automatic content classification and recommendation system. However, "large" doesn't mean "good", there are often serious quality problems in data. To obtain more accurate and useful information, it's important to clean

This work is supported by the Project of Shanghai Information Development Special Fund (No. XX-XXFZ-05-16-0139).

data including imputing the missing value and processing the inconsistent data before training model [2]. If the step is ignored, the statistical model may seriously deviate from true result. We take the simplest linear model as an example, as it shown in Fig. 1, the red dotted line represents the model trained on dirty data, while the black solid line is the model fitted with clean data. To avoid expensive cleaning cost, lots of research works clean subsets of data, which sample part of samples and clean them, then train model on the cleaned samples. Clearly, the result is suspect, as shown in Fig. 2, the model with partial data can't reflect the data distribution.

Survey [3] shows, many studies don't approach cleaning as one-off preprocessing step, but rather analyze and clean iteratively. The specific operation flow diagram is shown in Fig. 3. For statistical models, iteratively cleaning some data and re-training on partial clean dataset can lead to misleading results even in the simplest models due to Simpson paradox [4], which two sets of data under certain conditions will satisfy a certain nature when discussed separately while may lead to opposite conclusion when combined. When we train model on mixed dirty data and clean data, the model obtained may deviate from true result. As shown in Fig. 4, the model fitted on mixed data seriously deviates from the correct model.

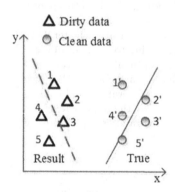

Fig. 1. Linear regression model. (Color figure online)

Fig. 2. Fitting model on partially clean data.

Instead of proposing new cleaning algorithm, this paper proposes a model updating algorithm combining data cleaning and conjugate gradient algorithms. First, We select samples to clean and calculate the gradient of data to establish the updating direction. Then according to updating algorithm, we update model incrementally instead of retraining model. With constantly cleaning data, the model is better and better, and converges to optimum eventually. In order to accelerate the model convergence speed, we also propose cluster descent sampling algorithm to select the records with high influence on result at each iteration. With the increasing popularity of the statistical modeling, many researches focus on how to improve data quality through machine learning, while our work is to study how to improve model through data cleaning.

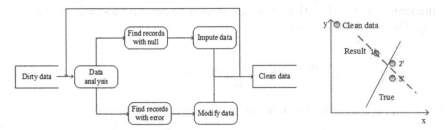

Fig. 3. Data cleaning flow diagram.

Fig. 4. Fitting model on mixed data.

The rest of the paper is organized as follows: We introduce some preliminary concepts regarding the topic of the research in Sect. 2 and present our solutions, including model updating algorithm and sampling algorithm in Sect. 3. Then, We demonstrate the validity of our approach in Sect. 4. Finally Sect. 5 concludes the work and discusses future work.

2   Preliminaries

In this section, we present some basic concepts regarding the focus of our research. Table 1 shows the symbols used in this paper.

Table 1. Symbol table.

Symbol	Description
R	Raw data
b	The size of samples
T	The number of iteration
$\theta^{(d)}$	Initial model trained on raw data
S	A batch sample select from R_{dirty}
$C(\cdot)$	Clean function, can be clean tools or exist clean algorithm
R_{dirty}	A collection of dirty data, subset of R, that is $R_{dirty} \to \{\}$
R_{clean}	A collection of clean data, the complement of R_{dirty} w.r.t.R
$\theta^{(c)}$	The optimal model, that is, training on completely clean data
$\theta^{(t)}$	The current optimal model at each iteration,$t \in \{1, 2, \cdots T\}$ $\theta^{(0)} = \theta^{(d)}$

2.1   Loss Function

Assuming that x is feature vector, y is label, $\{(x_i, y_i)\}_{i=1}^{N}$ is already labeled train examples. Searching the optimal model is to find a vector of model parameter θ by minimizing the loss function φ, which is used to measure loss and degree of error [5]. The formula is as follows:

$$\theta^* = \arg\min_{\theta} \sum_{i=1}^{N} \varphi(x_i, y_i, \theta) \tag{1}$$

For example, the loss function of linear regression model is as follows:

$$\varphi(x_i, y_i, \theta) = \left\| \theta^T x_i - y_i \right\|^2 \tag{2}$$

2.2   Conjugate Gradient Algorithm

The conjugate gradient algorithm only needs to calculate the first derivative, and its convergence rate is better than the gradient descent algorithm. It is a fast and accurate algorithm which has quadratic cut-off property and can find the minimum by doing n-searches, especially suitable for solving large-scale optimization problem [6].

In the n-dimensional space, we find the minimum value of the function according to Eq. 3 [7,8].

$$x_{t+1} = x_t + \alpha_t d_t, \qquad t = 1, 2, ..n \tag{3}$$

where x_1 is selected randomly, α_t is the step factor, d_t is searching direction composed of $-g_t$ and $-d_{t-1}$.

$$d_t = \begin{cases} -g_t & t=1 \\ -g_t + \beta_t d_{t-1} & t \geq 2 \end{cases} \tag{4}$$

where $g_t = \nabla\varphi(x_t)$ is the gradient of the function $\varphi(x_t)$ at point x_t, β_t is parameter, it influences the speed and memory space of algorithm, d_t varies with β_t [9–11]. Grippo and Lucidi [12] designed Armijo Linear Search, and proved the global convergence of PRP method under this search for general non-convex function. In this paper, we use PRP parameter, that is:

$$\beta_k^{PRP} = g_k^T (g_k - g_{k-1}) / \|g_{k-1}\|^2 \tag{5}$$

3   Iteratively Modeling Based Cleansing Interactively Samples

The main idea of iteratively modeling is to combine data cleaning and conjugate gradient algorithm. As in Sect. 2.1, conjugate gradient algorithm is suitable for solving large-scale optimization problems, and it can converge to the optimal point from any initial point. Similarly, we treat the model trained on the raw data as the starting point, clean iteratively samples and incrementally update

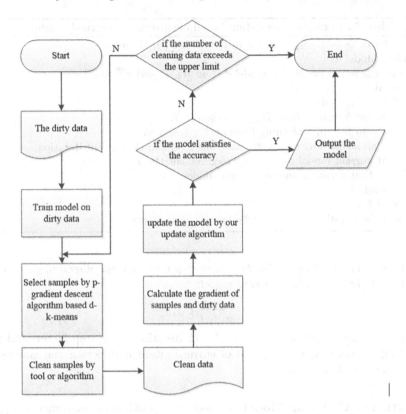

Fig. 5. Iteratively modeling based cleansing interactively samples of big data.

the model. Finally the model can converge to optimum. The specific algorithm flow is shown in Fig. 5.

First, the raw data R as input data, that is $R_{dirty} = R, R_{clean} = \emptyset$, and we train initial model $\theta^{(d)}$ on R_{dirty}. Because of the good convergence of conjugate gradient algorithm, the initial model $\theta^{(d)}$ needs not be very precise. For the missing values in the data, we fill them in arbitrary placeholder. Then we select samples S from R_{dirty} and clean these, the cleaned records are recorded as S'. Finally, the searching direction, which is composed of the gradient of data, serves as updating direction to update model towards $\theta^{(c)}$. If the number of iteration reaches the upper limit or the precision of model is within range, we stop iterating. Otherwise, we repeat above process from the sampling operation.(Represented in the Algorithm 1)

3.1 Updating Model

The conjugate gradient algorithm uses conjugate direction generated by the gradient direction of the current point as the search direction at each iteration and converges from any point to the optimum.

Algorithm 1. Iteratively modeling based cleansing interactively samples.

Input: Dirty Data $R_{dirty} = R$, Clean Function $C(\cdot)$, Model M
Output: Model $\theta^{(c)}$
1: Train the initial prediction model $\theta^{(d)}$ on R_{dirty} and $\theta^{(0)} = \theta^{(d)}$;
2: **repeat**
3:    **for** $i \in [1, T]$ **do**
4:        Select b records from R_{dirty} as sample S;
5:        Clean S with a cleaning function $C(\cdot)$, and as S';
6:        Call algorithm2 to get $\theta^{(t)}$, that the model in the current iteration;
7:        **if** current model meets users requirement **then**
8:            End iterating and output the model;
9:        **end if**
10:    **end for**
11: **until** the iteration limit is reached or R_{dirty} is empty

---

Definition 1. *updating model: For given step factor α_t and direction d_t, according to formula 6 to update current model:*

$$\theta^t \leftarrow \theta^{t-1} + \alpha_t d_t \tag{6}$$

Where θ^t is the output model in the $t - th$ iteration, α_t is step factor, and the updating direction d_t is composed of current gradient direction and conjugate direction of the last iteration.

Direction of Updating Model. Consider the problem in one dimension (i.e., the parameter is a scalar value) and take square loss function as an example, our goal is to find the point θ that minimizes curve $l(\theta)$. The consequence of dirty data is that the wrong loss function is optimized. As shown in Fig. 6, the blue dotted line is loss function on dirty data. Optimizing the loss function finds minimum point $\theta^{(d)}$ (blue star). However, the true loss function on clean data is in red, thus the optimal value on the dirty data is in fact a suboptimal point on clean curve (red circle). Return to this paper, the model obtained at each iteration is only current optimal model based dirty data, and is not true optimal model. As shown in Fig. 7, the red star can be considered as the model $\theta^{(c)}$, and the red circle can be regarded as $\theta^{(t)}$. Our work is to incrementally update $\theta^{(t)}$ towards $\theta^{(c)}$.

Since records are independent of each other, we calculate the batch gradient of data according to formula 7:

$$g^*(\theta) = \nabla\varphi(\theta) = \frac{1}{|N|}\nabla\varphi\left(x_i^{(c)}, y_i^{(c)}, \theta\right) \tag{7}$$

where $g^*(\theta)$ represents the gradient calculated on clean data, $\nabla\varphi\left(x_i^{(c)}, y_i^{(c)}, \theta\right)$ is the gradient of $(x_i^{(c)}, y_i^{(c)})$, $|N|$ is the size of the dataset.

Calculating $g^*(\theta)$ requires whole data to be clean, however, our job is to get optimal model through cleaning data, there is contradiction between them.

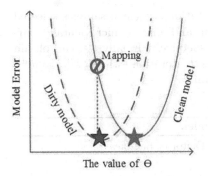

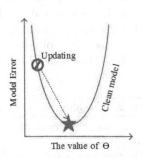

Fig. 6. The optimal point on dirty data mapping to clean data is sub-optimal point. (Color figure online)

Fig. 7. Moving sub-optimal towards true optimal. (Color figure online)

Definition 2. *Approximating gradient $g^*(\theta)$: For $g^*(\theta)$, we approximately calculate it from two aspects:*

$$g^*(\theta) = \frac{|R_{clean}|}{|N|} \cdot g_C(\theta) + \frac{|R_{dirty}|}{|N|} \cdot g_S(\theta) \qquad (8)$$

Where $g_C(\theta)$ is the gradient computed on already cleaned data R_{clean} and $g_S(\theta)$ is estimated according to samples from dirty data R_{dirty}, $|R_{clean}|$ and $|R_{dirty}|$ represent the number of R_{clean} and R_{dirty} respectively.

Assuming that time-consuming step is data cleaning and not the numerical operations, we calculate g_C using the whole clean data.

Definition 3. *Calculating g_C: We calculate the batch gradient of clean data, that is, averaging the gradient of whole data in R_{clean}:*

$$g_C(\theta) = \frac{1}{|R_{clean}|} \sum_{i \in R_{clean}} \nabla\varphi\left(x_i^c, y_i^c, \theta\right) \qquad (9)$$

To avoid cleaning whole data, we take advantage of the gradient of S sampled from R_{dirty} to estimate g_S. It should be noted that cleaning S before calculating.

Definition 4. *Approximating gradient g_S: We calculate the gradient of samples S selected from R_{dirty}, and re-weight the average by their respective sampling probability and the size of class which record is located.*

$$g_S(\theta) = \frac{1}{|S|} \sum_{i \in S} \frac{|R_{dirty}|}{p(i) * |N_i|} \nabla\varphi\left(x_i^c, y_i^c, \theta\right) \qquad (10)$$

Where $p(i)$ represents the probability of $i \in S$ being sampled, $|N_i|$ is the size of class that i located, this is introduced in Sect. 3.2. $|R_{dirty}|$ is the size of dirty data R_{dirty}.

The Algorithm of Updating. At each iteration, we clean samples selected from S at first, then calculate the gradient and update incrementally current model according to formula 8 and 6 respectively. Finally, we can obtain model $\theta^{(t+1)}$ based $\theta^{(t)}$ obtained in the $t-th$ iteration, where $\theta^{(0)} = \theta^{(d)}$, $t = \{0, 1, \cdots T\}$. (Represented in the Algorithm 2)

Algorithm 2. The algorithm of updating model.

Input: R_{dirty}, R_{clean}, Current Model $\theta^{(t)}$, Step Factor α, Samples S
Output: Model $\theta^{(t+1)}$

1: Using cleaning function $C(\cdot)$ to clean S as S';
2: According to formula 10 to calculate the gradient on the sample of newly clean S' and denoted as $g_S(\theta^{(t)})$;
3: According to formula 9 to calculate the gradient of R_{clean} and denoted as $g_C(\theta^{(t)})$;

4: Determine the direction of the model updating according to the gradient $g(\theta^{(t)})$ and d_{t-1}, and update the model using formula(5), denotes as $\theta^{(t+1)}$:
$$\theta^{t+1} \leftarrow \theta^t - \partial \left(\frac{|R_{dirty}|}{|N|} * g_S\left(\theta^{(t)}\right) + \frac{|R_{clean}|}{|N|} * g_C\left(\theta^{(t)}\right) - \beta_k * d_{k-1} \right)$$
5: Update the data set, remove records from R_{dirty}, and add into R_{clean}:
$R_{dirty} = R_{dirty} - S$, $R_{clean} = R_{clean} \cup S'$;

Example 1. *Recall that we use SVM to train initial model on the raw data R_{dirty} and clean 500 records in batches of 10. The whole data is treated as dirty with $R_{dirty} = R$ and $R_{clean} = \emptyset$. The gradient of SVM is given by the following function:*

$$\nabla\varphi(x, y, \theta) = \begin{cases} -y \cdot x & if \ yx \cdot \theta < 1 \\ 0 & if \ yx \cdot \theta \geq 1 \end{cases} \tag{11}$$

For each iteration t, a sample of 50 records S is selected from R_{dirty}, and we apply clean function $C(\cdot)$ to clean S. We estimate the gradient on the newly cleaned data and calculate the gradient on the already clean data(initially non-existent); Then we update current model according to above formulas; Finally, $R_{dirty} = R_{dirty} - S$, $R_{clean} = R_{clean} \cup S$ and continue to the next iteration.

3.2 P-Gradient Descent Sampling Algorithm Based d-k-Means

Obviously, with the number of cleaning records increases, the model's error decreases monotonously. The worst case is to clean all dirty records, which will spend lots of time and cost. It can accelerate the convergence rate of model by choosing records that contribute a lot to the improvement of the model at each iteration.

Reference [13] has shown that sampling probability of the record is related to its gradient:$p_i \propto \left\| \nabla\varphi\left(x_i^{(c)}, y_i^{(c)}, \theta^{(t)}\right) \right\|$. Intuitively, a record with high gradient is preferred. But finding the optimal sampling distribution needs to know

---

Algorithm 3. P-Gradient descent sampling algorithm based d-k-means.

Input: R_{dirty}, R_{clean}, Threshold Parameter d, Sample Parameter p

Output: Sample Set S

1: Set the clustering center set $U = \{\}$ and the sample set $S = \{\}$;

2: Select record from R_{dirty} as initial clustering center and join U;

3: **repeat**

4:    Calculate the distance that record in the R_{dirty} to each point in the clustering center U;

5:    **if** distance exceeds threshold d **then**

6:        Select the sample i as new clustering center and join U, namely $U \leftarrow U \cup i$;

7:    **else**

8:        Select the nearest cluster center for sample i, and add i to the class the cluster center is located;

9:    **end if**

10: **until** All records have a corresponding class

11: R_{dirty} is divided into multiple sets N_i, respectively ,the size of each set is $|N_i|, i \in \{1, 2, \cdots t\}$.

12: **for all** N_i **do**

13:    Set the collection of storing gradients $G_i = \{\}$, and sample set selected from the dirty set $S_i = \{\}$;

14:    Select the sample from set N_i, the size is $p*b*|N_i|/|R_{dirty}|$, calculate the gradient of samples and storage in G_i;

15:    Arrange G_i in descending order, and choose the first $b*|N_i|/|R_{dirty}|$ samples to storage in S_i;

16:    Merge S_i into S, namely, $S \leftarrow S_i \cup S$.

17: **end for**

---

clean value of records. We use the gradient of dirty data to approximate: $p_i \propto \left\| \nabla \varphi \left(x_i^{(d)}, y_i^{(d)}, \theta^{(t)} \right) \right\|$.

The diversity and difference of samples are ignored if samples are selected only according to gradient, samples should contain as many types as possible. We use clustering method $k-$means [14] to divide the dirty data into multiple classes, ensuring that any type of data can be sampled. K-means needs to choose k samples beforehand as initial points, while we don't know the number of types in the data.

We introduce distance threshold parameter d based K-means. First, we select a record as initial cluster center and calculate the distance from other records to cluster center. If the distance less than the d, we add the record into this class. Otherwise, the first record that exceeds the threshold is added cluster center set. Then we calculate the distance from rest samples to the clustering center, select the nearest clustering center within threshold range and add the record into the located class. We repeat above until all records can find their own class. Owing to the heavy workload and high cost of calculating all gradient, we introduce sample parameter p to reduce the computational cost. Through samples to approximate all, we select $p*b$ samples from R_{dirty}, calculate their gradient and rank. Finally, We select the first b samples as S. (Represented in Algorithm 3)

When $p = 1$, the sample algorithm degenerates to randomly select b samples from R_{dirty}. When p is too large, the cost of algorithm will become high. The size of p need to weigh the cost and validity. The experiment shows that the changed trend of model is stable when p increases to a certain range.

4   Experiment

4.1   Experimental Environment

Our experiments run on PC with 8GB RAM, i5 CPU, 64 bit window10 system and 2 processors each with 3 GHz speed. And the development tool is Anaconda3, we use Python to implement the experiments.

4.2   Experimental Data

We use two real datasets: (i) Dataset 1 is a real-medical dataset of thyroid patients provided by a large tertiary hospital in China, with serious quality problems in data. There are 407000 medical records, and 149000 of them have empty value. The data includes patient information, thyroid ultrasonography information, puncture blood test result and other attributes. (ii) Dataset 2 is US Census 1990 dataset, which is extracted by 1% of the proportion from the whole sample data, the total number of transactions is 2458285, including 68 attributes such as ancestors, ethnic group and birthplace. We randomly inject 25% errors in the data, that is, randomly select records from data, and randomly select the attributes of this record to add error. The dataset is divided into training dataset and test dataset by the ratio of 8:2.

4.3   Experimental Results and Analysis

To demonstrate the validity of this method, the model trained based on raw dataset as a benchmark. Similarly, we also implement updating model by randomly sampling data as a comparison, to prove the efficiency of sampling algorithm proposed in this paper.

US Census 1990 Dataset. We use SVM model to train data, and default sample 5000 records at each iteration, the model is measured with accuracy. Accuracy is defined as the radio of the number of correct records to the number of records predicted. We backup the data before injecting error to clean data. The result of experiment is shown in Fig. 8.

As shown in Fig. 8, the model obtained by our updating algorithm works better in contrast to the model trained directly on raw data. With the increase of cleaning records, the accuracy of model increases monotonously and eventually tends to be gentle, i.e. the model converges to optimum. Compared with the update algorithm by randomly sampling, our sampling algorithm is faster to converge, the model is stable when cleaning 20000 records. However, the model

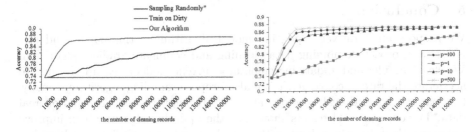

Fig. 8. Experimental comparison diagram.

Fig. 9. Experimental comparison based different value of the parameter p.

using randomly sampling is not convergent when cleaning up 150000 records. It is not difficult to explain, our sampling method is to choose records with high value cleaning at each iteration, which can improve the model better and faster.

Thyroid Medical Dataset. We predict the benign and malignant thyroid nodules by using logical regression model (LR), and we use precision and recall to evaluate model. The precision is defined as the ratio of the number of values that have been correctly updated to the total number of values that were updated, while the recall is defined as the ratio of the number of values that have been correctly updated to the number of incorrect values in the entire database. To ensure the correctness of imputing missing value, we use medical professional to fill empty value. The result is shown in Table 2.

Table 2. Comparison of thyroid nodule prediction experiment.

Algorithm	Precision (%)	Recall (%)
LR	68.22	61.57
LR^+	88.42	87.63

LR is the model directly building on the raw data. LR^+ is the final convergent model by updating iteratively based our approach. As shown in Table 2, LR^+ has better performance than LR, the precision and recall rate improves significantly.

The Influence of Parameter. We introduce parameter p in the sampling algorithm, so we observe the model by changing value of p. The experiment is completed on US Census 1990 dataset.

When $p = 1$, the algorithm degenerates into randomly sampling to update model, as show in Fig. 9, with the increase of p, the convergence speed of model will accelerate. However, the numerical computation and run time will also increase. It can be seen that the convergence rate of the model is almost the same when $p = 100$ and $p = 500$. We choose the appropriate value, which can reduce numerical computation and keep converging rate.

5 Conclusion

We propose an iteratively updating model algorithm in this paper, and this is a new approach combining data cleaning and conjugate gradient algorithm. We clean samples and update incrementally current model at each iteration. To accelerate the rate of convergence, we also propose sampling algorithm. Finally, this paper tests and evaluates our approach through two experiments on real data. The experimental results show that the updating algorithm can improve the model than directly trained on the raw data and our sampling algorithm has better convergence than randomly sampling.

The next step of the research work is that (i) introduce detector to detect the error in the data, ensuring the samples must be wrong, which can reduce the cost and speed up the convergence rate. (ii) we dont propose new cleaning algorithm in this paper, our next work is to study new cleaning method.

References

1. Li, J.Z.: State-of-the-art of research on big data usability. Ruan Jian Xue Bao/J. Softw. **27**(7), 1605–1625 (2016)
2. Fan, W.F.: Relative information completeness. In: Proceedings of the Twenty-Eighth ACM SIGMOD-SIGACT- SIGART Symposium on Principles of Database Systems, vol. 35(4), pp. 97–106. ACM, New York (2009)
3. Krishnan, S., et al.: Towards reliable interactive data cleaning: a user survey and recommendations. In: HILDA, pp. 1–4 (2016)
4. Simpson, E.H.: The interpretation of interaction in contingency tables. J. Roy. Stat. Soc. F. Ser. B (Methodol.), S. JSTOR **1951**, 56–60 (1951)
5. Fan, W.F., Geerts, F.S.: Conditional functional dependencies for capturing data inconsistencies. ACM Trans. Database Syst. (TODS) **33**(2), 6–18 (2008)
6. Chen, K.Z.: Optimization Calculation Method. Xi'an Electronic Science and Technology University Press, Xi'an (1985)
7. Miao, D.J.: Approximate functional dependency mining algorithm in probability database. J. Comput. Res. Dev. **52**(12), 2857–2865 (2015)
8. Xie, J.Y., Yang, J.S.: A sampling-based approach to information recovery. In: Iscataway, S. (ed.) Proceedings of the ICDE, pp. 476–485. IEEE Computer Society (2008). https://doi.org/10.1109/ICDE.2008.4497456
9. Fan, W.: Discovering conditional functional dependencies. IEEE Trans. Knowl. Data Eng. **23**(5), 683–698 (2011)
10. Chen, H.Q., Ku, W.S.: Leveraging spatio-temporal redundancy for RFID data cleansing. In: Proceedings of the SIGMOD, pp. 51–62. ACM Press, New York (2010). https://doi.org/10.1145/1807167.1807176
11. Diallo, T.: Discovering (frequent) constant conditional functional dependencies. Int. J. Data Mining Model. Manage. **4**(3), 205–223 (2012)
12. Grippo, L.: Convergence conditions, line search algorithms and trust region implementations for the polak-ribiere conjugate gradient method. Optim. Metiiods Softw. **20**, 71–98 (2005)
13. Zhao, P., Zhang, T.: Stochastic optimization with importance sampling for regularized loss minimization. In: ICML, pp. 12–22 (2015)
14. Yakout, M., Berti-Equille, L.: Don't be SCAREd: Use SCalable automatic REpairing with maximal likelihood andbounded changes. In: Proceedings of the SIGMOD, pp. 553–564 (2013)

Label Noise Detection Based on Tri-training

Hongbin Zhu[1(✉)], Jiahua Liu[1,2,3], and Ming Wan[1,2,3]

[1] State Grid Corporation of China, Beijing, China
hbzhu@sgcc.com.cn, {liujiahua,
wanming}@sgepri.sgcc.com.cn
[2] Nari Group Corporation, Nanjing, China
[3] Nanjing Nari Information and Communication Technology Co. Ltd,
Nanjing, China

Abstract. In machine learning, noise contained in the training dataset can be divided into attribute noise and label noise. Many works prove that label noise is more harmful compared to attribute noise. A set of noise filtering algorithms have been proposed to identify and remove noise prior to learning. However, almost all existing works solve this problem in a pure supervised way. It means noise identification is only based on the information of labeled data. In fact, unlabeled data are available in many applications, and the amount of unlabeled data is usually much bigger than labeled data. Therefore, in this paper, we consider to make use of unlabeled data to improve the performance of noise filtering. Tri-training is a powerful semi-supervised learning algorithm. It is adopted in this work because it is independent in the view of data. Finally, a set of experiments are conducted to prove the effectiveness of the proposed method.

Keywords: Label noise · Unlabeled data · Tri-training

1 Introduction

Constructing a generalization model needs a learning algorithm and a training dataset. In general, a suitable learning algorithm and a sufficient amount of training data are required to build a good model. Obviously if the quality of the training data is not good, the quality of the model will be influenced. Usually the low quality of training data is due to the existing of noises in the training dataset. Thus, noise handling is crucial for model construction.

Many types of noises exist in the training dataset. Among them, the literatures in machine learning mainly focus on two types: feature noise and label noise [1]. Feature noise means the feature values of a training instance are incorrect. While label noise means a training instance is mislabeled. Although both feature noises and label noises are harmful for data analysis. Their extents of harm and handling ways are different. Removing feature noises is not always helpful especially when the noises are also present in the future. However, removing label noises are consistently helpful to improve the classification accuracy [2]. In this work, we focus on label noise to study.

Label noises exist in many real applications due to various reasons. First, it is generated because human's input mistakes. For example, it belongs to class 1, but input as class 2 by input mistake. Second, it is generated by the knowledge shortage. For

© Springer Nature Switzerland AG 2018
X. Sun et al. (Eds.): ICCCS 2018, LNCS 11063, pp. 613–622, 2018.
https://doi.org/10.1007/978-3-030-00006-6_56

example, when a new disease occurs, maybe the medical doctors cannot recognize it. This will result in the incorrect labeling. Third, the label noise is generated because some information is missing for labeling. For example, if some medical tests are missing, a medical doctor might make a mistake in diagnosing.

The hazards of label noises have been comprehensively studied [3–10]. To handle label noises, there are two main approaches: algorithm level approaches and data level approaches. The former either adopts robust algorithms or modify existing algorithms in order to remove or reduce the effect of label noises. The latter explicitly processes the training dataset prior to learning. Algorithm level approaches suffer from two limitations. First, although the algorithms are modified to be robust, the label noises still exist. This is an implicit way to handle noises. Usually the performance is not very good. Second, this type of approaches is not ubiquitous. For example, designing a robust decision tree is totally different with a support vector machine. By contrast, the data level approaches are independent of the classification algorithms. Once processed, any classification algorithms can be used. So in many applications, it is more preferred. In data level approaches, a straightforward and effective method is noise filtering which removes noises prior to training. There are several benefits with noise filtering, such as reduced training time, reduced model complexity, and improved classification accuracy.

Label noise filtering is challenging in most cases. In the literature, many different methods have been proposed and used for different purposes. Because k-nearest neighbor is sensitive to label noises, many approaches have been proposed to utilize its property. The key idea is check whether a sample's label is consistent with its neighbors. If it is consistent, then the label of this sample is reliable. Otherwise, it might be mislabeled. In addition to kNN, ensemble learning has also been used for label noise filtering. The key idea is to make use of the strengths of multiple classifiers to make a more accurate identification of noises. Diversity is a key issue in ensemble learning which can be generated by employing either different algorithms or different training datasets.

Existing works on ensemble learning based noise filtering are different either on the step of classifiers construction and/or decision fusion [11–13]. However, almost all of them are supervised. A common way is to build an ensemble of classifiers based on some training instances. Then noise filtering is conducted on the remaining training instances. The limitation for this supervised solution is two-fold. First, the training set is mislabeled. When its subset is used for learning, the noise filter tends to unreliable. Second, it neglects the value of unlabeled data. In fact, unlabeled data has been proved to be helpful for supervised learning. This learning method is called semi-supervised learning. Semi-supervised learning can overcome the limitations of supervised learning. Therefore, in this work, we propose to use the idea of semi-supervised learning for label noise filtering.

Tri-training is a popular semi-supervised learning algorithm. It is superior to the well-known co-training algorithm because it neither requires the instance space to be described with two sufficient and redundant views nor does it put any constraints on the supervised learning algorithm. Its applicability is better than co-training style algorithms. Tri-training needs some labeled data as seeds. In our work, the initial labeled data are mislabeled, thus, we need to develop a method to select the clean labeled data as seeds. To this end, we propose to use the concept of multiple voting. Finally the performance improvement of the proposed method is demonstrated with extensive experiments on the benchmark datasets.

The rest of this paper is organized as follows. Section 2 is the related works. Section 3 introduces the details the proposed method. In Sect. 4, the experiments are conducted and the experimental results are analyzed. In Sect. 5, this paper is concluded.

2   Related Works

In data analysis, label noises exist with different ratios in many applications, such as medical applications and industrial applications [14, 15]. They are harmful for learning in many aspects. It can increase the training time, make the model more complex, and also decrease the classification accuracy [16–18].

Increasing the model complexity means the size of model becomes bigger and the interpretability becomes worse. For example, the model of decision tree and support vector machine can be more complex because of unlabeled data. The classification accuracy is heavily dependent on the quality of training data. Therefore, if mislabeled training data exist, the classification accuracy will be decreased. This is more evident for nearest neighbor classifiers.

Constructing a generalization model needs a learning algorithm and a training dataset. To reduce the effect of label noises, we can find the solution either from the learning algorithm or the training dataset. The former is called algorithm level approach. It focuses on improving the robustness of the learning algorithm, so that bad effect of label noises can be alleviated. On the other hand, the latter is called data level approach which focuses on improving the quality of the training data. It is usually believed data level approaches are more preferred than algorithm level approaches in most cases because data level approach is more straightforward. And the applicability of data level approaches is broader. Our work is included in data level approaches. Specially, we focus on label noise filtering.

Label noise filtering is to employ some classifiers to identify and eliminate the label noises before learning. Based on the number of involved classifiers, it can be divided into single classifier based and multiple classifiers based approaches. Most single classifier based approaches are based on k nearest neighbors because kNN is very sensitive to label noises. Multiple classifiers based approach usually performs better than single classifier based. The reason is because an ensemble classifiers has better performance if two conditions hold: (1) the probability of a correct classification by each individual classifiers is greater than 0.5 and (2) the errors in the predictions by each individual classifiers are independent. We will employ multiple classifiers based method in this work. As the necessary background knowledge, the representative algorithm in this category will be presented in this section.

In ensemble learning based approaches, a set of base level classifiers will be constructed and their classification results on the training instances will be used for label noise identification. In detail, an instance is treated as mislabeled if x of m classifiers misclassify it. Obviously, x is equal or less than m. The minimal and maximal value of x is 1 and m respectively. If x is smaller, the condition for noise identification is looser. Meanwhile, we have more chances to remove noise-free instances. On the other hand, if x is bigger, we have more chances to retain noisy instances. Majority filter (MF) and consensus filter (MF) are the popular algorithms in this group [3]. MF identifies a label noise if more than half of the m classifiers do not agree with this label. CF identifies a label noise only if all the m classifiers do not agree with this label. CF is more conservative than MF.

The algorithm of the majority filter is shown in Fig. 1. In step 1, the training dataset will be separated into n subsets. In step 2, the noisy subset is initialized as empty. In steps 3–18, each subset will be checked iteratively. In detail, when checking a subset E_i, the remaining data will be used to train y classifiers based on a number of learning algorithms. Because each algorithm is different, the diversity will be generated between each classifier. The variable ErrorCounter is used to determine whether a sample is mislabeled. Initially ErrorCounter is 0. Once a classifier does not agree with its label, then ErrorCounter = ErrorCounter + 1. As shown at Step 15, for MF, if more than half of the classifiers do not agree with the label, then this sample will be treated as mislabeled. The algorithm of CF is similar to MF. The difference is at step 15. In CF, a sample is identified as mislabeled only if all the classifiers do not agree with its label.

3   Our Approach

In Sect. 2, we have introduced the classical majority filtering (MF) and consensus filtering (CF) algorithms. In MF/CF, firstly the training dataset is divided into two parts. One part is used to train multiple classifiers. Then these classifiers will be used to identify the mislabeled instances in the other part. This belongs to supervised learning. Similar to MF/CF, most of existing works for label noise filtering follow this supervised learning framework. Supervised learning faces difficulties when the amount of training data is insufficient. In fact, in many machine learning tasks, the number of labeled data is limited. On the other hand, usually a large amount of unlabeled data is available. In the scenario where both labeled and unlabeled data exist, semi-supervised learning is a good choice. Semi-supervised learning is between supervised and unsupervised learning. In semi-supervised learning, when unlabeled data are used together with a small amount of labeled data, the learning performance can be improved.

In this work, we propose to use the idea of semi-supervised learning to solve the problem of label noise filtering. In this framework, we are given a set of samples $x_1, \ldots, x_l \in X$ with corresponding labels $y_1, \ldots, y_l \in Y$. Additionally some unlabeled examples $x_{l+1}, \ldots, x_{l+u} \in X$ are given. Some labels in $y_1, \ldots, y_l$ are incorrect. Our idea is to use these unlabeled data to improve the label noise identification accuracy.

In Fig. 2, the hollow circles represent the unlabeled data. The solid circles represent the labeled data. The blue solid circle is the labeled data with correct label. And the red solid circle is the labeled data with incorrect label. Usually the number of unlabeled data is much larger than labeled data. The number of correct labels is larger than unlabeled data.

As shown in Fig. 3, in the literature, there are many types of semi-supervised learning algorithms, such as self training, generative models, graph based algorithms,

---

Algorithm 1 Majority Filter (MF)

Input: E (training set)
Parameters: n (number of subsets), y (number of learning algorithms), $A_1, A_2, \ldots, A_y$ (y learning algorithms)
Output: A (detected noisy subset of E)

1: form n disjoint almost equally sized subsets of E_i, where
    $\bigcup_i E_i = E$
2: $A \leftarrow \emptyset$
3: **for** $i = 1 \ldots n$ **do**
4:      form $E_t \leftarrow E \backslash E_i$
5:      **for** $j = 1, \ldots y$ **do**
6:          induce H_j based on examples in E_t and A_j
7:      **end for**
8:      **for** every $e \in E_i$ **do**
9:          $ErrorCounter \leftarrow 0$
10:         **for** j=1,$\ldots$,y **do**
11:             **if** H_j incorrectly classifies e **then**
12:                 $ErrorCounter \leftarrow ErrorCounter + 1$
13:             **end if**
14:         **end for**
15:         **if** $ErrorCounter > \frac{y}{2}$, **then**
16:             $A \leftarrow A \cup \{e\}$
17:         **end if**
18:     **end for**
19: **end for**

Fig. 1. Majority filtering algorithm

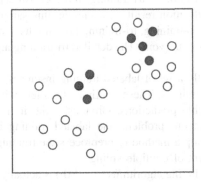

Fig. 2. Noise filtering scenario

and multiview algorithms. Self training and expectation maximization are the popular semi-supervised algorithms. They are based on single view and single classifier. Single view means that only one feature set is required. Single view learning has several limitations. Especially it is difficult to select unlabeled instances with predictions.

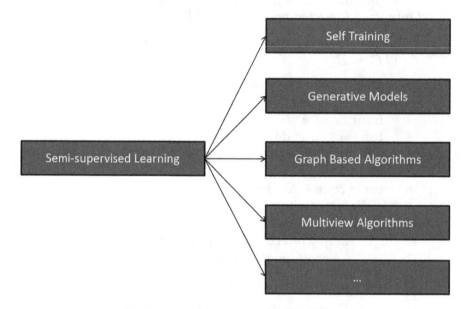

Fig. 3. Taxonomy of semi-supervised learning

Multiview learning tends to be more robust. Co-training is a well-known multiview semi-supervised learning algorithm. It requires two views which are complement to each other. For example, when classifying a webpage, the text in this webpage is one view. And the other webpages which link to this webpage is the other view.

Tri-training is a form of co-training. It is a kind of ensemble learning based semi-supervised learning algorithm. In tri-training, three classifiers are employed. If two classifiers give the classification result on a sample, this sample will be added to the labeled data. Superior to co-training, tri-training does not have any requirements on the data. Thus, it is selected in our work. The detailed tri-training algorithm can be referred to [19].

In Tri-training, initially a set of labeled training instances are required as seeds to construct the multiple classifiers. These multiple classifiers will classify the unlabeled data and select the reliable predictions. Obviously, the initial labeled instances are crucial. Unfortunately, in our problem, the labeled training instances include label noises. We have to develop a method to preprocess the training data. To this end, we propose to use the concept of multiple voting.

Most existing noise filtering algorithms (like MF) is actually single voting based. In their algorithms, the training data will be divided into different subsets. One subset is taken out for checking, and the other subsets are used to train the multiple classifiers.

This follows an iterative manner so that all the subsets will be checked. Since the checking is only based on one-time voting of the classifiers, they are called single voting based. Single voting based algorithm suffers from the instability. Each time the partition of training data is random. Therefore, the performance of single voting is dependent on the partitioning.

To reduce the effect of single voting, a multiple voting idea is used in this work (Fig. 4). In multiple voting, instead of one-time partitioning, the training instances will be partitioned for several times. Finally the decision fusion is used to combine the results.

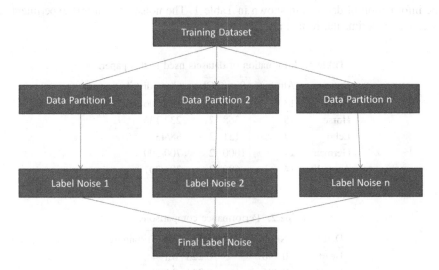

Fig. 4. Concept of multiple voting

In essence, multiple voting is a combination of several single voting detectors. Each sing voting detector will output a label noise set. Finally a fusion policy is needed. Fusion policy can be defined in many ways. If it is loose, some label noises will be retained. Our motivation here is to maintain the integrity of labeled data. Therefore, we would like to define a strict rule for fusion. If any single voting detector identifies an instance as noise, then finally the instance will be treated as label noise.

4 Experiments

In this experiment, we will verify whether our approach is valid. The experimental setup will be presented firstly. Then the experimental results will be analyzed. We will compare our approach with majority filtering (MF) based on the benchmark datasets from UCI data repository. Each dataset is divided into training set and test set. A noise filtering algorithm works on the training data and removes the label noises. Note that the original dataset is noise-free. We have to manually make some noises.

For each dataset D, the detailed experiment procedures include: (1) D is randomly divided into a labeled set L and unlabeled set U. (2) Ten cross-validations on L will be used to evaluate the performance of a noise filter. (3) The average classification error rates with different noise filtering methods are obtained by averaging different cross-validation results. Classification error rate is the measure to evaluate the performance of our approach.

In Tri-training and majority voting, three algorithms are employed, including 1-NN, Naïve bayes, and Decision Tree. Finally 1-NN is used for calculating the classification accuracy.

Five datasets are used in this experiment: heart, horse, echo, german, and austrilian. The information of datasets in shown in Table 1. The noise ratio in this experiment is 10%. The experimental results are shown in Table 2.

Table 1. Information of datasets used in this paper.

Dataset	Attribute	Size	Class	Class distribution
Heart	13	294	2	188/106
Horse	15	368	2	232/136
Echo	7	131	2	88/43
German	24	1000	2	700/300
Australian	14	690	2	383/307

Table 2. Performance comparisons.

Datasets	No noise filter	MF	MF-Tritraining
Heart	0.290	0.223	0.194
Horse	0.326	0.224	0.200
Echo	0.417	0.319	0.244
German	0.329	0.288	0.256
Australian	0.270	0.176	0.153

Several observations can be obtained from Table 2.

(1) When the training dataset includes mislabeled data, noise filtering is necessary. For example, for the dataset Heart, if the mislabeled ratio is 10%, then the classification accuracy is 0.290 without noise filter. When using MF, the accuracy is improved to 0.223. When using MF-Tritraining, the accuracy is further improved to 0.194.

(2) MF-Tritraining is superior to MF. For all the five benchmark datasets, the classification accuracy is improved when unlabeled data is used based on tri-training algorithm.

5 Conclusions

Label noises are harmful for data analysis tasks. Noise filtering has been widely used to handle them to reduce their negative effect. Most existing methods are supervised, which only consider the information of labeled data. However, in addition to labeled data, usually a large amount of unlabeled data is also available in many real applications.

The success of semi-supervised learning inspires us to consider the possibility to use unlabeled data to improve the performance of noise filter. Specially, we use tri-training algorithm to implement our idea. Tri-training is a kind of co-training, but it does not require two views representation of the training data. A set of experimental result show that our idea is effective.

References

1. Zhu, X., Wu, X.: Class noise vs. attribute noise: a quantitative study. Artif. Intell. Rev. **22**(3), 177–210 (2004)
2. Quinlan, J.R.: Induction of decision trees. Mach. Learn. **1**(1), 81–106 (1986)
3. Brodley, C.E., Friedl, M.A.: Identifying mislabeled training data. J. Artif. Intell. Res. **11**, 131–167 (1999)
4. Gamberger, D., Lavrač, N., Džeroski, S.: Noise elimination in inductive concept learning: a case study in medical diagnosis. In: Arikawa, S., Sharma, A.K. (eds.) ALT 1996. LNCS, vol. 1160, pp. 199–212. Springer, Heidelberg (1996). https://doi.org/10.1007/3-540-61863-5_47
5. Gamberger, D., Lavrac, N., Dzeroski, S.: Noise detection and elimination in data preprocessing: experiments in medical domains. Appl. Artif. Intell. **14**(2), 205–223 (2000)
6. Rico-Juan, J.R., Inesta, J.M.: Adaptive training set reduction for nearest neighbor classification. Neurocomputing **138**, 316–324 (2014)
7. Calvo-Zaragoza, J., Valero-Mas, J.J., Rico-Juan, J.R.: Improving kNN multi-label classification in Prototype Selection scenarios using class proposals. Pattern Recogn. **48**(5), 1608–1622 (2015)
8. Kanj, S., Abdallah, F., Denoeux, T., Tout, K.: Editing training data for multi-label classification with the k-nearest neighbor rule. Pattern Anal. Appl. **19**(1), 145–161 (2015)
9. Roli, F.: Multiple classifier systems. In: Li, S.Z., Jain, A.K. (eds.) Encyclopedia of Biometrics, pp. 1142–1147. Springer, New York (2015). https://doi.org/10.1007/978-1-4899-7488-4
10. Wozniak, M., Grana, M., Corchado, E.: A survey of multiple classifier systems as hybrid systems. Inf. Fusion **16**, 3–17 (2014)
11. Kuncheva, L.I., Rodriguez, J.J.: A weighted voting framework for classifiers ensembles. Knowl. Inf. Syst. **38**(2), 259–275 (2014)
12. Sun, S.: Local within-class accuracies for weighting individual outputs in multiple classifier systems. Pattern Recogn. Lett. **31**(2), 119–124 (2010)
13. Saez, J.A., Galar, M., Luengo, J., Herrera, F.: Tackling the problem of classification with noisy data using Multiple Classifier Systems: analysis of the performance and robustness. Inf. Sci. **247**, 1–20 (2013)
14. Zhao, Y.C., Li, W.Z., Wu, J., Lu, S.L.: In: 2015 IEEE Conference on Computer Communications, pp. 26–30. IEEE, Hong Kong (2015)
15. Zhao, Y.C., Li, W.Z., Lu, S.L.: J. Netw. Comput. Appl. **74**, 11–20 (2016)

16. Saez, J.A., Galar, M., Luengo, J., Herrera, F.: Analyzing the presence of noise in multi-class problems: alleviating its influence with the one-vs-one decomposition. Knowl. Inf. Syst. **38** (1), 179–206 (2014)
17. Barandela, R., Valdovinos, R.M., Sanchez, J.S.: New applications of ensembles of classifiers. Pattern Anal. Appl. **6**(3), 245–256 (2003)
18. Sanchez, J.S., Kuncheva, L.I.: Data reduction using classifier ensembles. In: ESANN, pp. 379–384 (2007)
19. Zhou, Z.H., Li, M.: Tri-training: exploiting unlabeled data using three classifiers. IEEE Trans. Knowl. Data Eng. **17**(11), 1529–1541 (2005)

Long Short Term Memory Model for Analysis and Forecast of PM2.5

Leiming Yan[✉], Min Zhou, Yaowen Wu, and Luqi Yan

Jiangsu Engineering Center of Network Monitoring, School of Computer and Software, Nanjing University of Information Science and Technology, Nanjing, China
lmyan@nuist.edu.cn, wakaka4639@163.com, Lucyqi_Yan@163.com, wuyaowen1997@gmail.com

Abstract. Atmospheric PM2.5 is a pollutant that has a major impact on the atmospheric environment and human health. Based on LSTM, we construct two prediction models, Stack LSTM and Encoder-Decoder, and evaluate the prediction performance of the model through four years of meteorological data training and testing models in Nanjing, Beijing, and Sanya. In the experiment, using the meteorological factors, contaminant factors, seasonal factors, and the normalized results of PM2.5 as input, the daily average PM2.5 concentration is predicted from 1 to 3 days. Experimental results show that the LSTM model has better performance than Random Forest and Encoder-Decoder. Using Nanjing as an example, comparing the forecast results of Nanjing PM2.5 with the data released by the environmental authorities, it is found that the value of the PM2.5 concentration predicted by the LSTM model is very close to the value of PM2.5 monitored by Nanjing's environmental authorities. In prediction of PM2.5 for three consecutive days, the Root Mean Square Error (RMSE) of the LSTM model is only 18.96. Under the LSTM model, the prediction result of the three cities are better than other prediction models, which shows that the LSTM model has a good adaptability in predicting the PM2.5 concentration.

Keywords: PM2.5 · Forecasting · LSTM model · Air pollution Deep learning

1 Introduction

With the development of global industrialization and urbanization, the problem of air pollution has become more and more serious [1]. In recent years, PM2.5 has become the principal air pollutant. PM2.5 refers to particulate matter whose diameter is less than 2.5 micron in ambient aerodynamics [2]. Although PM2.5 is only a component of the Earth's atmospheric composition, it has an impact on air quality and visibility, along with traffic. Due to which, the incidence of accident in areas with severe PM2.5 concentration is higher than in other regions [3]. Compared with coarser atmospheric particles, PM2.5 is small and rich in a lot of toxic and harmful substances which have long residence time and long distance in atmosphere. PM2.5 can penetrate into the sensitive area of human respiratory system, hence inhalation of PM2.5 will increase

© Springer Nature Switzerland AG 2018
X. Sun et al. (Eds.): ICCCS 2018, LNCS 11063, pp. 623–634, 2018.
https://doi.org/10.1007/978-3-030-00006-6_57

respiratory disease and cause cardiovascular disease [4]. Long-term exposure to high levels of PM2.5 is an important risk factor for heart and lung cancer mortality [5], which causes a great impact on both atmospheric environmental quality and human health. Therefore, the prediction of PM2.5 becomes crucial at this time.

Studies have shown that changes in concentration of atmospheric pollutants mainly depend on the condition of weather [6]. In addition, other air pollutants (such as SO2, CO, CO2, etc.) also affect the concentration of PM2.5 [7]. Due to the wide range of sources of PM2.5 (including industrial process, energy production at power station, vehicular traffic, residential heating, transportation, natural disaster, and complex physical and chemical process), the forecasting of PM2.5 has become a daunting task. The traditional PM2.5 prediction methods include numerical model prediction methods and statistical prediction methods. In 2014, Chen [8] used the Gaussian diffusion model to predict the concentration of PM2.5 in Wuhan City, which improved the accuracy of PM2.5 prediction to some extent. However, their model's requirements for weather data are extremely demanding. Qiang [9] established a forecast model of PM2.5 in the case of low rainfall in Baoji City, which achieved good results in both autumn and winter. However, only meteorological factors are analyzed in his discussion. The lack of consideration of contaminant factors causes an incomplete result in his research. At present, a relatively complete PM2.5 prediction system named Model-3 community multi-scale air quality system (CMAQ), which was developed by the Environmental Protection Agency, is capable of providing 24–48 h of air quality prediction. However, this system can make short-term predictions only, whose accuracy is not satisfying.

Based on LSTM (Long Short-Term Memory), this paper adds meteorological factors and pollutants as input parameters, constructs Stack LSTM and Encoder-Decoder models to predict the PM2.5 concentration in multiple cities. Also, using Random Forest as a basic method, the prediction performance of these three prediction models for PM2.5 concentration is compared, and the validity of LSTM model and Encoder-Decoder model is further verified.

2   Related Works

At the present stage, the prediction model of PM2.5 includes regression model (linear and non-linear regression model), artificial neural network, support vector model, fuzzy logic model, and Hidden Markov model [10].

In recent years, the regression model has been widely used in the prediction field of PM2.5. For example, Cobourn [11] proposed a prediction model based on non-linear regression and back-draft airflow trajectory concentration to predict the average daily maximum concentration of PM2.5. Also, Wang Si and Wang Zhe et al. [12] used the multiple linear regression model to predict the concentration of PM2.5 in Beijing and achieved good results. However, the model is not persuasive enough for lack of sample.

Artificial Neural Network (ANN) which has good adaptability in dealing with non-linear problems (such as environmental pollution) is also applied to the prediction of PM2.5. Besides, Back Propagation Neural Network (BPNN) and Radial Basis Function Neural Network (RBFNN) are commonly used. For example, Sun et al. [13]

successfully realized the prediction of PM2.5 by combining the principal component analysis with early termination training to improve the Back Propagation (BP) neural network. Some researchers combine ANN with other smart technologies for concentration prediction of PM2.5. For instance, Zhang et al. [14] established a mixed prediction model based on average empirical model decomposition and regression neural network, which aimed at the prediction of the average daily PM2.5 concentration in Xi'an City in the future.

At this stage, the SVM model is gradually increasing its proportion in the prediction field of PM2.5. For example, Xie et al. [15] established a PM2.5 concentration prediction model based on LIBSVM, which predicted the average concentration of PM2.5 at 5 monitoring points in Hefei with a good result. Liu et al. [16] proposed a method combining support vector machine with fuzzy granulation time series to predict the future change trend and scope of the mass concentration of PM2.5, whose result indicated that it can predict the concentration of PM2.5 with a good performance.

Besides regression models, artificial neural network models and (SVM) models, other models such as support vectors, fuzzy logic, and hidden Markov models are also involved in the prediction field of PM2.5. Sosowski et al. [17] used wavelet and vector machine model to predict daily climate pollution. TE Alhanafy et al. [18] deployed a combination of fuzzy logic and neural network to predict the pattern of changes in nitrogen dioxide or sulfur dioxide in urban areas. Sun et al. [19] whose focus was on the period of high concentration of PM2.5 proposed an improved Hidden Markov Model to predict the daily average concentration of PM2.5.

In summary, this paper establishes the LSTM model to predict the concentration of PM2.5 based on the neural network topological structure of RNN (Recurrent Neural Network). We compare it with the traditional Random Forest and Encoder-Decoder models with respect to PM2.5 prediction.

3 Model

3.1 Analysis and Selection of Eigenvalues

Generally, we are faced with the choice of input vector in the process of using artificial neural network to predict the PM2.5 concentration. The sources of PM2.5 are complex and there are many influencing factors, which are mainly divided into pollutant factors and meteorological factors. At the same time, there are obvious correlations with seasonal change. At this point, the determination of the input features of the predictive model becomes a complex and arduous task. In order to comprehensively consider the influence of various factors, a feature value with a large correlation with PM2.5 concentration is extracted. Then, we analyze the influencing factors of PM2.5 through the correlation coefficient method.

Data Analysis in Sanya
According to the data of the whole year, the correlation coefficient between pollutants is shown in Table 1:

Figure 1 shows the correlation coefficient between PM10 and PM2.5:

Table 1. Correlation coefficient of PM2.5 and various pollutants in Sanya

	PM10	SO2	CO	NO2	O3_8 h
PM2.5	0.958	0.371	0.464	0.362	0.772

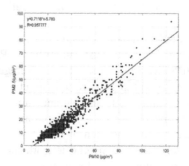

Fig. 1. Correlation coefficient between PM10 and PM2.5 in Sanya

Combing Table 1 and Fig. 1, we conclude that the concentration of each factor is linearly related. The distribution of PM2.5 and PM10 points is very concentrated and the correlation coefficient reaches 0.958. Therefore, the correlation between PM2.5 and PM10 concentration is the greatest. Similarly, the correlation between PM2.5 and NO2 concentration is the smallest.

The correlation coefficient between meteorological factors is shown in Table 2:

Table 2. Correlation coefficient between meteorological factors in Sanya

	Temperature	humidity	Pressure	Wind	Precipitation
PM2.5	−0.421	−0.471	0.422	0.132	−0.132

As can be seen from Table 2, the relative humidity in the meteorological factors has a relatively large correlation with the influence of PM2.5, and a small correlation with the wind speed.

In summary, we find that the concentration of PM2.5 in Sanya is relevant to six factors, which are PM10, CO, O3, temperature, humidity and air pressure. Therefore, we use these six factors as input variable values for the PM2.5 prediction model.

Data Analysis in Beijing

Based on Tables 3 and 4 (rainfall data is deleted due to lacking), we select PM10, CO, NO2, temperature, humidity and wind speed as input variables for the PM2.5 prediction model.

Table 3. Correlation coefficient between meteorological factors in Sanya

	PM10	SO2	CO	NO2	O3_8 h
PM2.5	0.849	0.529	0.830	0.779	−0.135

Table 4. Correlation coefficient between meteorological factors in Beijing

	Temperature	Humidity	Pressure	Wind	Precipitation
PM2.5	−0.162	0.404	0.061	−0.429	\

Table 5. Correlation coefficient of PM2.5 and various pollutants in Nanjing

	PM10	SO2	CO	NO2	O3_8 h
PM2.5	0.917	0.608	0.665	0.617	−0.056

Table 6. Correlation coefficient between meteorological factors in Nanjing

	Temperature	Humidity	Pressure	Wind	Precipitation
PM2.5	−0.313	−0.119	0.250	−0.255	−0.172

Data Analysis in Nanjing

Based on the correlation coefficient in Tables 5 and 6, we select PM10, CO, NO2, temperature, air pressure and wind speed as input variables for the PM2.5 prediction model.

The PM2.5 concentration value fluctuates with seasonal factors. Therefore, in order to reflect the quarterly changes of PM2.5 in each month more clearly. In addition to the six factors we selected, we also add the monthly average PM2.5 value this month to reflect its monthly changes.

3.2 Randomforest

The random forest model is a model based on many decision tree classifiers. A decision tree classifier refers to a classifier that uses a tree structure to classify samples when classified. When training, multiple trees perform prediction on training data to obtain the best training results. In this paper, we train the model using 1000 decision tree. Which is used as a baseline method for comparison with the LSTM model.

3.3 Encoder-Decoder Model

Encoder-Decoder is not actually a concrete model, but a type of framework, which is mainly divided into two parts: encoding and decoding. The encoding is to transform the input sequence into a fixed-length vector, while decoding is to convert the previously generated fixed vector into an output sequence [20]. Figure 2 is a simple Encoder-Decoder structure.

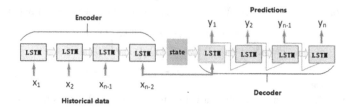

Fig. 2. Encoder and decoder neural network structure

3.4   Stack LSTM Sequential Model

The single neuron LSTM model is actually a special RNN (Recurrent Neural Network) neural network model. RNN refers to an artificial neural network in which nodes are oriented and connected into a loop. The difference between LSTM and RNN is that it adds a "processor" to determine whether the information is useful or not. The structure of this processor is called cell.

We define LSTM with 50 neurons and 1 neuron in the output layer for predicting contamination in the first hidden layer. In fact, this hidden layer also contains the compression information of the factors affecting the PM2.5 concentration in the previous time step. In the experiment, we use the PM2.5 concentration and other factors in Nanjing from 2014 to 2016 as input variables to train the network. At the same time, we used the mean absolute error (MAE) loss function and the stochastic gradient descent algorithm in training the network structure to minimize the error function value. Also in each training step, the error function is calculated as the root mean square error between the observed and predicted PM2.5 concentrations. In terms of the choice of optimizer, we conduct a large number of experimental tests and choose the *Nadam* optimizer in the end. In our implementation, the number of neurons in the first layer is determined based on the number of input variables and the number of neurons in the second layer. The last layer contains a single neuron that represents the network output, the predicted PM2.5 concentration. To better predict PM2.5, we have stacked two layers of LSTM neural network structures.

4   Experiments

4.1   Data Sources

This experiment uses air quality index data for three consecutive years in Nanjing, Beijing, and Sanya from 2014 to 2016, which is downloaded from the PM2.5 historical data monitoring website https://www.aqistudy.cn/historydata/weather.php, including PM2.5 concentration, PM10 concentration, SO2 concentration, CO concentration, NO2 concentration, O3 concentration. Meteorological data for these three cities are downloaded from the https://www.wunderground.com website and included average temperature, relative humidity, pressure, wind speed, and precipitation.

4.2   Evaluate Metric

Root mean square error (RMSE), also known as standard error, is the square root of the ratio of the square of the observed value to the true deviation and the number of observations n. The standard error is very sensitive to very large or very small errors in a set of measurements, so the standard error can well reflect the degree of dispersion of a data set. Therefore, we use the root mean squared error (RMSE) indicator to evaluate the performance of the model in this experiment.

4.3   Features Selection

In the experiment, for the choice of parameters, we choose the RMSE of the one-day data forecast in Nanjing as the basis. We use the control variable method to find the best loss function and optimizer for the LSTM model. The control loss function is equal to *mse*, batch size 50 and the number of epochs is 200. The optimizer parameters are changed to obtain the corresponding standard error as shown in Table 7.

Table 7. RMSE of different loss factions

Loss	mse	mse	mse	mse	mse	mse	mse
Optimtizer	sgd	rmsprop	adagrad	adadelta	adam	Adamax	nadam
RMSE	29.782	27.991	27.989	27.887	28.401	28.095	27.508

According to Table 7, we choose the *Nadam* function to optimize the network, keep the batch size 50, the epochs 200 unchanged, and select different loss functions to obtain the corresponding RMSE, as shown in Table 8.

Table 8. RMSE of different optimizer factions

Loss	mae	mape	squqred-hinge	binary-crossentropy	Logcosh
Optimtizer	nadam	nadam	nadam	Nadam	Nadam
RMSE	27.200	27.229	27.593	28.089	27.487

The batch size is 50, optimizer is *Nadam* and loss function is *Mae*, we change the epochs to obtain the corresponding RMSE, as shown in Fig. 3. Also, we control the *Nadam* parameters of the optimizer, the epochs and the *Mae* of the loss function unchanged, and change the batch size to get the corresponding standard error, as shown in Fig. 4.

From the above tables, we conclude that in the LSTM model, when the parameters mae loss function and the nadam optimizer are selected and the batch size is 50 and the epochs is 200, the RMSE reaches the minimum, which means the PM2.5 forecast performance is the best at this time.

630   L. Yan et al.

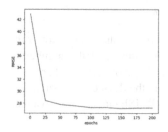 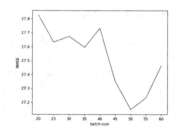

Fig. 3. RMSE of different epochs   **Fig. 4.** RMSE of different batch-size

4.4   Forecasting Result

In this experiment, we select the same data set and divided the same training samples and test samples. We use Random Forest, Encoder-Decoder, and LSTM models to predict PM2.5 concentrations in Beijing, Nanjing, and Sanya in two modes, Short-term prediction and longer-term prediction: PM2.5 concentration 1 day before input and its influencing factors PM2.5 concentration after one day of prediction (96 days of test sample), and after 7-day PM2.5 concentration prediction 3 days of PM2.5 concentration (test sample 288 days). Figures 5, 6 and 7 are the experimental results of the three models in Nanjing in the first prediction mode.

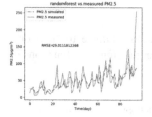 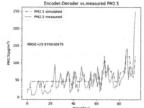 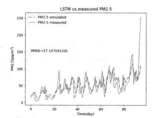

Fig. 5. Prediction result of random forest model in Nanjing

Fig. 6. Prediction result of encoder-decoder model in Nanjing

Fig. 7. Prediction result of LSTM model in Nanjing

Through the analysis of the above pictures, we find that when using all the factors of the day to predict the PM2.5 concentration of the following day (taking Nanjing as an example), the random forest model and the Encoder-Decoder model have the same predict ability, where the RMSE value is about 29 or so. The random forest predictions are more accurate and more stable in a slight degree, while the predict ability of LSTM is relatively outstanding, with RMSE reaching up to 27.

In order to further study the prediction problem of PM2.5, we also use the second model where we predict PM2.5 concentration for 3 days based on the data of the previous 7 days in Sanya. Figures 8, 9 and 10 are the experimental results for the three models in this mode.

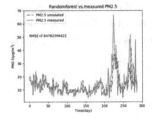 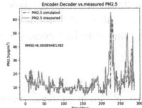 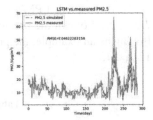

Fig. 8. Prediction result of random forest model in Sanya

Fig. 9. Prediction result of encoder-decoder model in Sanya

Fig. 10. Prediction result of LSTM model in Sanya

Experiments show that under the second model, the predicted values of the three models are close to the data released by the Sanya City Environmental Protection Department. However, there are still some distinctions between these models. When we increase the number of forecast days and appropriately expand the test data, the LSTM model has more obvious advantages in long-term prediction because of its cell processor compared to the random forest model and the Encoder-Decoder model.

4.5 Comparison and Analysis of Experimental Results

Based on the above experimental results, we can know the error values of the PM2.5 concentration under the random forest, Encoder-Decoder, and LSTM models in Beijing, Nanjing, and Sanya. In order to further compare the PM2.5 prediction capabilities of these three models, we use three models to conduct experimental simulations for Beijing, Nanjing, and Sanya, and organize all experimental results into a tabular form, as shown in Table 9.

Table 9. Result of prediction mode 1

Model city	Randomforest	LSTM	Encoder-Decoder
Nanjing	29.01118123	27.14704133	29.97993098
Sanya	8.682448419	8.659808257	12.92999755
Beijing	38.54999093	34.189678	38.69563179

Based on the data in the above table, we find that the RMSE values of Sanya in the three cities are relatively small, and the three models have a better accuracy in Sanya than in other cities. This is because the concentration of PM2.5 throughout the year in Sanya is at a low value and does not fluctuate, which is easier to learn and predict for prediction models. Combining the forecasting results of the three models for each city, the predict ability of LSTM is clearly ahead of the random forest model and the Encoder-Decoder model. We conclude that LSTM is the best predictor of the three models under this mode.

Next, we predict PM2.5 concentration for 3 days based on the data of the previous 7 days, and obtain the predicting result of each model, as shown in Table 10. Taking Beijing as an example, the prediction of PM2.5 concentration is as shown in Figs. 11, 12 and 13.

Table 10. Result of prediction mode 2

Model city	Randomforest	LSTM	Encoder-Decoder
Nanjing	19.5697977	18.95503221	20.97271375
Sanya	7.647623964	7.046222832	8.000894614
Beijing	40.4472888	39.97889965	36.39467828

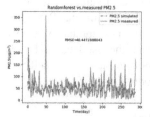 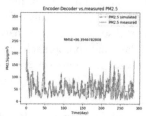 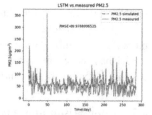

Fig. 11. Prediction result of random forest model in Beijing

Fig. 12. Prediction result of encoder-decoder model in Beijing

Fig. 13. Prediction result of LSTM model in Beijing

The experimental data show that the RMSE values of the three models in Beijing are relatively large than in other cities, which is because the annual PM2.5 concentration values in Beijing are relatively higher, and the influencing factors are more complex, with seasonal fluctuations. This bouncing irregularity is very detrimental to machine learning and prediction. Based on the RMSE value of each city, we find that the predicted value of the LSTM model is close to the predicted value of the random forest, but the prediction effect of LSTM is still the best, and the prediction effect of the Encoder-Decoder model is the worst of the three models.

In summary, under the two prediction modes, the prediction ability of LSTM model is more prominent. The predictive levels of the three models from high to low are: LSTM, Random Forest, and Encoder-Decoder. Among them, the random forest model is good at learning and predicting a group of data with little fluctuation and relatively stable, and the prediction effect is good, which is close to the prediction result of the LSTM model. However, when dealing with data such as Beijing and Nanjing, where PM2.5 fluctuates with seasons, it will be at a disadvantage. The Encoder-Decoder model was originally applied in the field of language translation. Compared with the other two models, the learning ability of the prediction needs to be improved. However, due to the principle of encoding and decoding, it is extremely sensitive to peaks in data, especially for cities with large data bounce in Beijing, enabling it to predict peaks precisely while the LSTM model and the Random Forest cannot. The LSTM model neutralizes the superiority of the random forest model in prediction of flat-state data and the sensitivity of the Encoder-Decoder model to the peak point. For the prediction of PM2.5 concentration in each city, the trend of LSTM model prediction and the coincidence of peak point are the most consistent among the three models, and therefore it is the best model among the three models.

5 Conclusion

In this paper, we use Random Forest, Encoder-Decoder, and LSTM models to predict the PM2.5 concentration in Beijing, Nanjing, and Sanya in two modes, first is to predict PM2.5 concentration based on the data of the previous day, and second is to predict PM2.5 concentration for 3 days based on the data of the previous 7 days. Through the analysis and comparison of these experimental results, we reach the following conclusions: for forecasting the PM2.5 concentration in cities like Sanya, where the annual concentration of PM2.5 is at low value with small fluctuation, these three model have the same performance and are similar to the data released by local environmental authorities. However, the LSTM model shows better prediction ability than the Random Forest and Encoder-Decoder model when applied to cities like Beijing and Nanjing, where the concentration of PM2.5 is fluctuant. Under the second mode where we predict PM2.5 concentration for 3 days based on the data of the previous 7 days, the LSTM model is superior to the Random Forest and Encoder models in predicting PM2.5 in Beijing and Nanjing. However, while predicting PM2.5 concentration in Sanya, the distinction between the prediction ability of the three models is not very clear. Comparing with the first prediction mode, in the second prediction model, the three models have significantly enhanced the prediction performance in Nanjing, while the growth rate in Sanya is not very clear, however, the prediction ability in Beijing decreases. At the same time, the LSTM model also showed the best performance in the second prediction mode, but compared to the first prediction mode, the advantage of the LSTM model over the random forest and the Encoder-Decoder model are not so obvious.

Acknowledgements. This work is supported by the NSFC [grant numbers 61772281, 61703212, 61602254]; Jiangsu Province Natural Science Foundation [grant number BK2160968]; the Priority Academic Program Development of Jiangsu Higher Education Institutions (PAPD) and Jiangsu Collaborative Innovation Center on Atmospheric Environment and Equipment Technology (CICAEET).

References

1. Wang, Z.: Air pollution and exercise: a perspective from China. Res. Q. Exerc. Sport. **87**(3), 242–244 (2016)
2. Qiu, X., et al.: Chemical composition and source apportionment of PM10 and PM2.5 in different functional areas of Lanzhou, China. J. Environ. Sci. **40**, 75–83 (2016)

3. Yang, J.: Study on the impact of PM2.5 on China's traffic environment. Guide Sci. Educ. (4), 156 (2016). (in Chinese)
4. Weber, S.A., Insaf, T.Z., Hall, E.S., Talbot, T.O., Huff, A.K.: Assessing the impact of fine particulate matter (PM2.5) on respiratory-cardiovascular chronic diseases in the New York city metropolitan area using hierarchical bayesian model estimates. Environ. Res. **151**, 399–409 (2016)
5. Pope III, C.A., et al.: Lung cancer, cardiopulmonary mortality, and long-term exposure to fine particulate air pollution. JAMA **287**(9), 1132–1141 (2002)
6. Li, J., et al.: Non-parameter statistical analysis of impacts of meteorological conditions on PM concentration in Beijing. Res. Environ. Sci. **22**(6), 663–669 (2009)
7. Zhang, Y., Hu, J., Wang R.: PM_(2.5) Prediction Model Based on Neural Network. J. Jiangsu Norm. Univ. (Nat. Sci. Ed.) **33**(1), 63–65 (2015). (in Chinese)
8. Chen, J., Gao, Y., Zhang, Y., Yang, Y., Liu, B.: Study on PM2.5 diffusion model and prediction. J. Math. Pract. Theory **44**(15), 16–27 (2014). (in Chinese)
9. Qiang, L., Liu, K., Zhang, Y., Xue, P.: Establishment of Urban Air PM2.5 forecasting model by linear regression method–a case study of Baoji City. Energy Conserv. (2), 125–127 (2014). (in Chinese)
10. Feng, X., Li, Q., Zhu, Y., Hou, J., Jin, L., Wang, J.: Artificial neural networks forecasting of PM2.5 pollution using air mass trajectory based geographic model and wavelet transformation. Atmos. Environ. **107**, 118–128 (2015)
11. Cobourn, W.G.: An enhanced PM2.5 air quality forecast model based on nonlinear regression and back-trajectory concentrations. Atmos. Environ. **44**(25), 3015–3023 (2010)
12. Dimitriou, K., Kassomenos, P.: A study on the reconstitution of daily PM10 and PM2.5 levels in Paris with a multivariate linear regression model. Atmos. Environ. **98**, 648–654 (2014)
13. Sun, R., Zhao, S., Zhang, X., Li, H., Sheng, L., Feng, Y.: A PM2.5 prediction method based on improved BP neural network algorithm (in Chinese). Sichuan. Environment **34**(4), 85–90 (2015)
14. Zhang, P., et al.: Study on prediction and spatial variation of PM2.5 pollution by using improved BP artificial neural network model of computer technology and GIS. Comput. Model. New Technol. **18**(12), 107–115 (2014)
15. Xie, S., Qian, B., Yang, B.: Prediction model of PM2.5 concentration based on LIBSVM. J. Luoyang Inst. Sci. Technol. (Nat. Sci. Ed.) **27**(2), 9–12 (2017). (in Chinese)
16. Guyon, I., Weston, J., Barnhill, S., Vapnik, V.: Gene selection for can- cer classification using support vector machines. Mach. Learn. **46**(1–3), 389–422 (2002)
17. Osowski, S., Garanty, K.: Forecasting of the daily meteorological pollution using wavelets and support vector machine. Eng. Appl. Artif. Intell. **20**(6), 745–755 (2007)
18. Alhanafy, T.E., Zaghlool, F., Moustafa, A.S.E.D.: Neuro fuzzy modeling scheme for the prediction of air pollution. J. Am. Sci. **6**(12), 605–616 (2010)
19. Sun, W., Zhang, H., Palazoglu, A., Singh, A., Zhang, W., Liu, S.: Pre- diction of 24-hour-average PM2.5 concentrations using a hidden markov model with different emission distributions in northern california. Sci. Total Environ. **443**, 93–103 (2013)
20. Bahdanau, D., Cho, K., Bengio, Y.: Neural machine translation by jointly learning to align and translate. arXiv preprint arXiv:1409.0473 (2014)

Matching Algorithm of Composite Service Based on Indexing Mechanism in BPM

Qiubo Huang[1]([✉]), Yuxiao Qian[1], Guohua Liu[1], and Keyuan Jiang[2]

[1] Donghua University, Shanghai 201620, China
huangturbo@dhu.edu.cn
[2] Purdue University Northwest, Hammond, IN 46323, USA

Abstract. Service matching technology has promoted the development of Business Process Management (BPM). It's significant for us to know how to retrieve a qualified service from a large number of candidate services in the library, and how to match and compose the services more appropriately. For the first part, this paper introduces the definition of the service model and rules of service matching. Next, in order to accelerate retrieval speed of services, we propose an indexing mechanism for the parameters of the service. Then, we would introduce the matching algorithm of composite services based on indexing mechanism. At the same time, this paper also analyzes the time complexity and space complexity of the algorithm. Through several simulation experiments, we verify the feasibility of the algorithm. After comparing the Back-Front algorithm, Front-Back algorithm, Service Composition Algorithm Based on AND/OR Graph with our algorithm, we find out the comparison results about the matching time and the retrieved number of composite services. The experiment results show that the matching algorithm based on indexing mechanism can greatly improve the matching speed and get more composite services without compromising the quality of service combination.

Keywords: BPM · Service matching · Service model · Indexing mechanism
Composite services

1 Introduction

The current intelligent manufacturing relies more on Business Process Management (BPM). The business processes management is an organized management method that aims at improving the quality and services' development through identifying, designing, modeling, documenting, controlling and improving the business processes to achieve integrated operational results that can link the resources and guide them towards achieving the organization's strategic goals [1]. In BPM, current research is focused on the research of service model. There are some similarities and differences between the service model used in this article and Web services [2]. The service model can usually run simultaneously. Secondly, the successor service can partly accept the output of the predecessor service or combine multiple services as its predecessor services. Finally, because the service model is the abstraction of realistic production, the data delivered between services can be first processed and then used.

© Springer Nature Switzerland AG 2018
X. Sun et al. (Eds.): ICCCS 2018, LNCS 11063, pp. 635–647, 2018.
https://doi.org/10.1007/978-3-030-00006-6_58

There are few researches on the matching of composite service model which is data-centric in BPM. Various methods [3–6] have been suggested for dynamic web service composition. But, most of them have some disadvantages like high complexity, high computational cost. Approaches of considering the problem of service composition as a graph search problem result in data redundancy and complicate the search process. Literature [7] proposed AO* algorithm for AND/OR graph. It is based on representing the web services semantic relationship using an AND/OR directed graph built at the design time. It applies different optimization techniques based on the redundancy analysis and service dominance to group and reduce the number of services and relations, and finally run a search algorithm over the reduced graph to generate all paths between every pair of node of this graph. However, the algorithm does not consider the complexity of the input and output parameters of the services and the rules of users. Literature [8] proposed two matching algorithm of composite service: Front-Back(F-B) and Back-Front(B-F). The Front-Back algorithm matches the output of the predecessor service as the input of the successor service. Back-Front algorithm searches for the output of the predecessor service according to the known input of the successor service. The time complexity of Front-back is $O(n^2)$, which is very inefficient when the candidate sets are very large. Back-Front algorithm would find fewer results when matching services.

2   The Definitions of Related Conception

2.1   Service Model

A service model is usually a complex composite service which is made up of multiple candidate services [9]. The following is a formal definition of the service model:

Definition 1. Input and Output parameters: An input or output parameter is a multi-tuples (cat, name, $P_1, P_2, \ldots, Pn$), where:

- "cat" is the ID of the category of the products [10]. For example, in the product category, ID of the first-level catalog of Textile Products is 17 and its corresponding secondary catalogs include:
  - ID:1701–Cotton, Chemical Fiber Textile and Dyeing Products
  - ID:1702–Wool Textile, Dyeing and Finishing Products
  - ID:1703–Hemp Textiles
  - ......

  If we have a product of cotton cloth, its corresponding "cat" (ID) is 17010501.

- "Name" is the name of the parameter, such as "cotton cloth".
- $P1, P2, \ldots, Pn$ are the other properties of the parameter. Such as size, color, etc. Their attributes include name, type and value range. For example, the name of a size attribute is "size", the type is "enumeration of size", and the value range is "extra small, small, medium large and extra large". An example of the input and output parameters is as follows:

```
<p cat="17010501" name= "cotton cloth">
  <attr name="size">
    <type>enum</type>
    <range>small,middle,large</range>
  </attr>
  <attr name="color">
    <type>enum</type>
    <range>white,blue,black, purple</range>
  </attr>
</p>
```

Definition 2. Service Model: The service model is a tri-tuples (name, in, out). Where:

- "Name" is the name of the service model.
- "In" is the set of input parameters for a service, containing various types of parameters required by the service, which can be considered as raw materials of factories in reality.
- "Out" is a set of output parameters of a service, containing various types of parameters of the service output, which could be considered as factory-produced products in reality. An example of a Service Model is as follows:

```
<ServiceModel>
  <name>sportswear </name>
  <in>
    <p cat="17010501" name=" cotton
cloth">
    <!--can refer to definition 1 and be omit-
ted here -->
      < attr/>
      < attr/>
    </p>
    < p cat =" 4211060101" name=" metal
zipper">
      < attr/>
      < attr/>
    </p>
  </in>
```

```
<out>
  <p cat=" 18121501" name=" Sportswear">
    < attr name="size">
      <type>enum</type>
      <range>small, medium , large</range>
    < attr>
    < attr name="color">
      <type>enum</type>
      <range> white,blue,black,...... </range>
    </ attr>
    < attr name=" materials">
      <type>enum</type>
      <range>cotton,......</range>
    </ attr>
  </p>
</out>
</ ServiceModel >
```

The above service model is a model whose inputs are cotton cloth and metal zipper, output is sportswear.

Definition 3. Service: A service is a four-tuples (ID, C, in, out). ID is the unique identification of the service.

2.2   Rules of Service Matching

The user provides a service model (denoted as r) and we need to check the service library to find out if there are candidate services (denoted as s) that could meet the requirements of inputs and outputs of service model r.

The service model and the candidate service are matched only when the set of input and output parameters of the service model and candidate service are matched with each other. There are two kinds of service matching: one is the matching of the service model and the candidate service; the other is the matching of the successor service and the predecessor service.

(1) Matching of a service model and a candidate service

This Can be divided into two categories:

1>Matching of a single service model and a single candidate service. In this case, the set of input and output parameters of the service model matches the set of input and output parameters of a single candidate service. As shown in Fig. 1, the set of input parameters for the service model (r) is $r_{in} = \{a, b, c\}$ and the set of output parameters is $r_{out} = \{x, y, z\}$. $s_{in} = \{a, b\}$ is the set of input parameters for candidate service s, which is the subset of r_{in} (i.e. $s_{in} \subseteq r_{in}$). Since the provided input of the service model r can satisfy the input of the service s, their input parameters are matched. If s_{in} contains parameters that are not in r_{in}, i.e. $s_{in} - r_{in} \neq \varnothing$ which means the service mode r can't provide some of the parameters required by service s, e.g. $s_{in} = \{a, b, d\}$, then their input parameters do not match.

In addition, output parameter of the candidate service s_{out} contains r_{out} (i.e. $r_{out} \subseteq s_{out}$), e.g. $s_{out} = \{m, n, x, y, z\}$. Since the required output of the service model r can be satisfied by the input of the service s, their output parameters are matched. If $r_{out} - s_{out} \neq \varnothing$, e.g. $s_{out} = \{m, n, y, z\}$, the set of output parameters are not matched (Fig. 1).

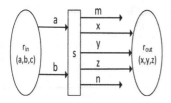

Fig. 1. Matching of a single service model and a single candidate service

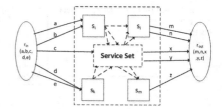

Fig. 2. Single service model and composite services

2>Matching of a single service model and composite services. For some complex service models, it is necessary to combine multiple candidate services to meet the requirements of the service model (see Fig. 2). The set of input parameters for the service model (r) is $r_{in} = \{a, b, c, d, e\}$ and the set of output parameters is $r_{out} = \{m, n, x, y, z\}$. For such a service model, it may be impossible to find a single candidate service to meet the requirements. A combination of candidate services is needed at this time. Figure 2 is an example of combination of several candidate services that matches the requirements of r. The dotted box in the middle represents a combination of not-specifically-specified services which may be included in the composite service.

(2) **Matching of services**

The matching between services is matched by the input of the successor service s_i^{in} and the output of the predecessor service s_{i-1}^{out} (see Fig. 3).

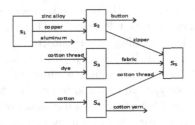

Fig. 3. Matching of successor and predecessor Services

The matching can also be divided into two categories:
1> Matching of a single predecessor service and a successor service. In this case, the output of the predecessor service s_{i-1}^{out} contains the input of the successor service s_i^{in}, i.e. $s_i^{in} \subseteq s_{i-1}^{out}$. e.g. $s_1^{out} = \{$zinc alloy, copper, aluminum$\}$, $s_2^{in} = \{$zinc alloy, copper$\}$. The output of service s_1 contains the input of service s_2, so s_1 and s_2 are matched.

In real production, this means the predecessor manufacturer can provide the successor manufacturer all of the raw materials which he needs.

2> Matching of multiple predecessor services combination and a successor service. For the input parameters of the successor service s_i^{in}, there is no single predecessor service s_{i-1}^{out} can meet the condition $s_i^{in} \subseteq s_{i-1}^{out}$. This requires a combination of predecessor services (see Fig. 3). e.g. $s_5^{in} = \{$zipper, fabric, cotton thread$\}$, and we can't find a single service in the service library whose output parameters can contain s_5^{in}. However, since $s_2^{out} = \{$button, zipper$\}$, $s_3^{out} = \{$fabric$\}$ and $s_4^{out} = \{$cotton thread, cotton yarn$\}$. then $s_2^{out} \cup s_3^{out} \cup s_4^{out} = \{$button, zipper, fabric, cotton thread, cotton yarn$\}$, so $s_5^{in} \cup s_2^{out} \cup s_3^{out} \cup s_4^{out}$. We can say that the combination of s_2, s_3 and s_4 can be a precursor of s_5.

In real production, it means the successor manufacturer needs to find more than one manufacturer and buy raw materials from them.

3   Service Indexing Mechanism

3.1   Create Index Table of Service

The matching process described above needs to repeatedly search for the library for services that meets the requirements. Because of the large number of services in the library, it takes a long time to find the appropriate services. Indexing service parameters can speed up the process. It is an innovation of this paper to accelerate the matching speed of composite service model in BPM by using indexing mechanism. The structure of indexing can be implemented using a hash table. When design the indexing mechanism, it is important to specify the "key" value. We can simply concatenate the names of the parameters, and then different order can get different keys.

Creating an index table of services is based on input (or output) parameters. Input parameter set of service s is $r_{in} = \{i_1, i_2, \ldots, i_n\}$, where i_i is the ith parameter. According to the algorithm of Subset Partitioning [11], we can get all non-empty subsets $r_{s\_i}(1 \leq i \leq 2^n - 1)$, including $2^n - 1$ subsets: $r_{s\_1} = \{i_1, i_2, \ldots, i_n\}$(which contains all the n elements), $r_{s\_2} = \{i_1, i_2, \ldots, i_{n-1}\}$, ..., (which contain n−1 elements), ..., $r_{s\_}2^n - 1 = \{i_n\}$. The process of subset partitioning can be implemented by function **Subset** (whose prototype can be found in Fig. 4). The input parameter index table of service s will contain $2^n - 1$ entries: each use names of parameters in r_{s_i} as the key and service s as the value (or one of an array of values). Following the above method, we can create the input parameters index table of s_2, s_3 and s_4 (see Fig. 5).

List<ParameterSet> **Subset**(ParameterSet r_{c_i});
   Input: A parameter set with n parameters.
   Return value: A list of length 2^n-1. Each element is a subset of r_{c_i}, and their parameters are all different.

Fig. 4.   Prototype of function Subset

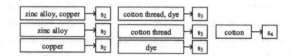

Fig. 5.   Service index table based on input parameters

According to the above method, we can also create an index table of output parameters of s_2, s_3 and s_4 (see Fig. 6).

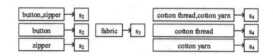

Fig. 6.   Service index table based on output parameters

3.2   Indexing Based on Product Categories

The parameters in this paper are all industrial products or raw materials. Each product (or material) belongs to a category. We can divide all parameters of a service into subsets according to the secondary level of their categories, which can reduce the number of subsets. For input and output parameters set $r = \{r_1, r_2, \ldots, r_n\}$, r_i is the ith parameter of r.

For example, in Fig. 3, service s_5 has 3 input parameters. According to the subset partition algorithm, we will get $2^3 - 1 = 7$ subsets. And we observed that the product secondary category of 2 parameters, fabric and cotton thread, is 1701, and the product secondary category of the other parameter zipper is 4211, so we can divide these 3 parameters into 2 subsets (cotton thread, fabric) and (zipper) and create index entries separately, then we can significantly reduce the number of the subsets (index entries). The number of subsets will be $(2^2 - 1) + 1 = 4$. The subset partitioning according to the product's secondary category can be implemented by a function DivideByCategory (see Fig. 7 for the prototype).

List<ParameterSet> **DivideByCategory**(ParameterSet r);
   Input: a parameter set with n parameters.
   Return value: a list of parameter set and parameters in each set have the same product secondary category.

Fig. 7. Prototype of function DivideByCategory

For the input parameter set of service s_5 (see Fig. 8(1)), two parameter sets r_{c_1}, r_{c_2} (see Fig. 8(2)) can be obtained according to the function of DivideByCategory. Call function Subset for r_{c_1}, r_{c_2} respectively and we can get the key for index (Fig. 8(3)).

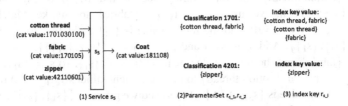

Fig. 8. Indexing based on parameter classification

3.3   Service Matching Based on Index Table

First, we introduce the function Index.

We can use a key r_{s_i} which is generated from the parameters by function **Subset** (see Fig. 8) to get the value which is an array of services $(s_1, s_2, \ldots, s_i, \ldots)$ by using function **Index** to search the index table.

For example, $r_{s\_i} = \{fabric\}$, we can find service s_3 by using function **Index**, whose prototype can refer to Fig. 9.

> List<Service> **Index**(ParameterSet r_{s_i});
> Input: A parameter set with n parameters.
> Return value: an list of services and output parameters of each service match r_{s_i}.

Fig. 9. Prototype of function Index

Then we introduce the algorithm MatchOnIndex.

For parameter set r_{c_i} whose elements all have the same secondary level product category (see Fig. 8(2)), algorithm MatchOnIndex can get all services which match r_{c_i}.

Algorithm 1: MatchOnIndex(r_{c_i})
Input: a parameter set
Return value: A list of services which match r_{c_i}
1: if(r_{c_i} == null) return null;
2: initialize s_{m_i}
3: r_s = Subset(r_{c_i});
4: foreach(Parameter r_{s_i} in r_s) {
5:   var s_p = Index(r_{s_i});
6:   if(s_p != null) s_p.Add(MatchOnIndex($r_{c\_i} - r_{s\_i}$));
7:   if(!s_{m_i}.Contains(s_p)) s_{m_i}.Add(s_p); }
8:   return s_{m_i} ;

For example, $r_{c\_1} = \{$cotton thread, fabric$\}$. The process of executing the algorithm MatchOnIndex(r_{c_1}) is as follows: call the function of Subset(r_{c_1}) and get $r_s = \{\{$cotton thread, fabric$\}, \{$cotton thread$\}, \{$fabric$\}\}$. Then we traverse rs:

- $r_{s\_1} = \{\{$cotton thread, fabric$\}\}$ and the return value of Index(r_{s_1}) is null.
- $r_{s\_2} = \{$cotton thread$\}$ and the return value of Index(r_{s_2}) is $\{s_3\}$, so we get $s_p = \{\{s_3\}\}$. Then, we use $r_{c\_1} - r_{s\_2} = \{$fabric$\}$ to invoke MatchOnIndex ($r_{c\_1} - r_{s\_2}$) recursively and the return value is $\{s_1\}$. Add $\{s_1\}$ to s_p and we get $s_p = \{\{s_3\}, \{s_1\}\}$. Add s_p to s_{m_1} and get $s_{m\_1} = \{\{\{s_3\}, \{s_1\}\}\}$.
- $r_{s\_3} = \{$fabric$\}$ and the return value of Index(r_{s_3}) is $\{s_1\}$, so $s_p = \{s_1\}$. Then, we use $r_{c\_1} - r_{s\_3} = \{$cotton thread$\}$ to invoke MatchOnIndex($r_{c\_1} - r_{s\_3}$) recursively and the return value is $\{s_3\}$. Add $\{s_3\}$ to s_p and we get $s_p = \{\{s_1\}, \{s_3\}\}$. Since s_p is already contained in s_{m_1}, s_p will not be added to s_{m_1} again.

Finally, the return value of MatchOnIndex(r_{c_1}) is $\{\{s_3\}, \{s_1\}\}$.

If the number of parameters in r_{c_i} is m, the time complexity of the MatchOnIndex is $O((2^m - 1) * m)$.

For parameter set r which can be an input parameter set for a single service, an input parameter set for multiple services combination, or an output parameter set for a user-supplied service model, algorithm of SearchOnIndex(r) can retrieve all services which match r.

Algorithm 2: SearchOnIndex(r)

Input: a parameter set

Return value: services which match r

1: r_c = DivideByCategory(r);

2: foreach(Parameter r_{c_i} in r_c) {

3:   s_{m_i} = MatchOnIndex(r_{c_i});

4:   for each s_{m_i}, take a set of services and add it to s_m ;

5: }

6: return s_m;

For example, $r = \{\text{cotton thread}, \text{fabric}, \text{zipper}\}$. The process of executing the algorithm SearchOnIndex(r) is as follows: call function DivideByCategory(r) and get $r_c = \{\{\text{cotton thread}, \text{fabric}\}, \{\text{zipper}\}\}$. $r_{c\_1} = \{\text{cotton thread}, \text{fabric}\}$ and return value of MatchOnIndex(r_{c_1}) is $s_{m\_1} = \{\{s_3\}, \{s_1\}\}$, which is added to s_m. So, returned services of SearchOnIndex(r) are $\{\{\{s_3\}, \{s_1\}\}, \{\{s_2\}\}\}$.

If the number of parameter sets in r_c is k, the time complexity of the SearchOnIndex is $O(k * ((2^m - 1) * m))$.

4 Matching Algorithm SMOS and Analysis of Time Complexity

We introduce the algorithm ServiceMatchOnSubset(SMOS).

For output parameters r_{out} given by the user, the algorithm ServiceMatchOnSubset (r_{out}) can construct a service combination graph for the user.

Algorithm 3: ServiceMatchOnSubset(r_{out})

Input: output parameters of the service model

Output: a service combination graph

1: s_m = SearchOnIndex(r_{out});

2: if(s_m != null) {

3:   foreach(service s_{m_i} in s_m) {

4:     s.AddChild(s_{m_i});

5:     get input parameters r_{m_i} of s_{m_i} ;

6:     ServiceMatchOnSubset(r_{m_i});

    }

  }

7: return s ;

The implementation of algorithm ServiceMatchOnSubset is as follows: Firstly, initialize s as an empty service set. Secondly, the algorithm SearchOnIndex is called and the service set s_m is returned. For example, we can get $\{\{s_{11}\}, \{s_{12}, s_{13}\}, \{s_{14}, s_{15}, s_{16}\}\}$ which is shown in Fig. 10. Thirdly, traverse s_m and add s_{m_i} as a child node to s. For input parameters(r_{m_i}) of s_{m_i}, call algorithm ServiceMatchOnSubset recursively. In Fig. 10, the child node of s_{11} is $\{\{s_{111}\}, \{s_{112}, s_{113}\}\}$.

The graph of composite services can be constructed in Fig. 10. This figure is just an example of composite services graph.

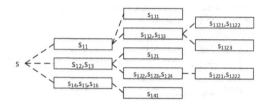

Fig. 10. composite service graph

If there are i composite services in s_m and the recursive depth is j, the time complexity of the ServiceMatchOnSubset is $O(j_*i_*(k_*((2^{m}-1)_*m)))$. In our experiment, when the number of services n > 10000, the average of i is around n/100, then we can consider the time complexity of the ServiceMatchOnSubset is $O(j_*n_*(k_*((2^{m}-1)_*m)))$.

5 Experimental Analysis

5.1 Space Complexity and Time Complexity Analysis of Algorithm ServiceMatchOnSubset

For n services, there are an average of c input parameters and d output parameters for each service (c, d $\ll$ n). The space complexity is $O(2^{c}{\cdot}n)$ when establishing a service indexing based on input parameters. The space complexity is $O(2^{d}{\cdot}n)$ when establishing a service indexing based on output parameters. Because c, d $\ll$ n, we can consider that the space complexity of algorithm SMOS is O(n).

From Chap. 4, we know that the time complexity of the algorithm SMOS is $O(j_*n_*(k_*((2^{m}-1)_*m)))$. And the time complexity of the algorithm Front-Back(F-B) is $O(n^2)$. The time complexity of AO* algorithm is $O(n_*\log_2^n)$. In our research, when the number of services is more than 5000, algorithm SMOS shows great advantages in time complexity.

5.2 The Feasibility of Algorithm ServiceMatchOnSubset and Comparison with Existing Algorithms

In order to verify the feasibility of the algorithm and the differences with the existed algorithms, we compared the service matching time and the number of service combinations by simulation experiment.

We randomly generated a total of 20,000 services in the process of "spinning", "weaving", "dyeing", "rinsing", "tailoring" and "printing" in the textile industry whose input and output parameters contains name, type, range. The number of input and output parameters for each service ranges from 1 to 5. The number of input parameters for composite service ranges from 1 to 20. For each input parameters of composite service, generating 1 to 10 different parameter sets by dividing secondary level product category. The number of parameters in each parameter set ranges from 1 to 10.

The output of the service model for the experiment is a coat with a metal zipper, white cotton, sleeve lace, and blue neckline and inputs are aluminum, cotton, dyes, nylon.

Since the research on Matching Algorithm of Composite Service in BPM is still in the developing stage, we first verify the feasibility of the algorithm. Because of the large number of services in the service library, we randomly take out different amounts of data and compare them. For each amount of data, we randomly take 10 groups to carry on the experiment and obtains its average value as the experiment result. The number of service combinations is accurate to single digit and matching time is accurate to one decimal place (see Fig. 11).

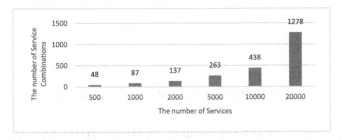

Fig. 11. The number of Service combinations

As the amount of data increases, the number of matched services gradually increases. For all service combinations, we verified its correctness. On this basis, we use the same dataset to carry out the same experiment on the other three algorithms. Comparison of service matching time for these four algorithms (see Fig. 12).

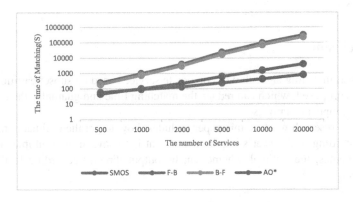

Fig. 12. The comparison of Matching Time

Experimental results show that the matching time of F-B algorithm and B-F algorithm are much higher than the other two algorithms in the same data volume. As the data volume increases, both AO* and SMOS grow linearly, but SMOS grows more slowly.. Therefore, SMOS algorithm is more suitable for large data volume service matching. In addition, we also compare the number of effective service combinations for the four algorithms (see Fig. 13).

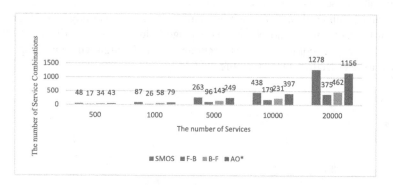

Fig. 13. The comparison of service combinations

We respectively analyzed data for 5000, 10,000 and 20,000. When the amount of data is 5,000, the number of service combinations matched SMOS is 2.7 times than F-B and 1.8 times than B-F and 1.05 times than AO*. When the amount of data is 10,000, the number of service combinations matched by SMOS is 2.4 times than F-B and 1.9 times than B-F and 1.1 times than AO*. When the amount of data is 20,000, the number of service combinations matched by SMOS is 3.4 times than F-B and 2.7 times than B-F and 1.1 times than AO*. As the amount of data increases, the number of service combinations matched by SMOS and AO* increases and the increasing speed is faster than F-B and B-F, so SMOS and AO* have more advantages in the number of matching service.

6   Conclusion

In this paper, matching algorithm of composite service based on subset partitioning and indexing is proposed, which can reduce the matching time and guarantee the number of matching composite services.

The next research work of this paper includes: how to get the optimal combination service according to the user's requirements, that is to say, in the multiple composite service schemes, the optimal scheme can be output directly according to the user's requirements.

References

1. Alzoubi, M., Khafajy, A.: The impact of business process management on business performance superiority. Int. J. Bus. Manag. Rev. **3**(2), 17–34 (2015)
2. Zhang, D.: Design and Implementation of ArtiFlow Manager. Yanshan University (2010)
3. Hussain, M., Paul, A.: A survey on graph based web service discovery and composition techniques. Int. J. Eng. Adv. Technol. **3**(5), 142–146 (2014)
4. Wu, N.: Dynamic composition of web service based on cloud computing. Int. J. Hybrid Inf. Technol. **6**(6), 389–398 (2013)
5. Moo, F., Hernández, R., Madera, F.: Web service composition using the bidirectional dijkstra algorithm. IEEE Latin Am. Trans. **14**(5), 2522–2528 (2016)
6. Yang, Z., Shang, C., Liu, Q., Zhao, C.: A dynamic web services composition algorithm based on the combination of ant colony algorithm and genetic algorithm. J. Comput. Inf. Syst. **6**(8), 2617–2622 (2010)
7. Elmaghraoui, H., Benhlima, L., Chiadmi, D.: Dynamic web service composition using AND/OR directed graph. In: International Conference of Cloud Computing Technologies and Applications, pp. 1–8. IEEE Computer Society (2017)
8. Liu, Z., Zhang, J., Guo, H.: Web service discovery and composition based-on syntactical matching algorithm. Comput. Eng. Appl. **42**(20), 190–192 (2006)
9. Rao, J., Su, X.: A survey of automated web service composition methods. In: Cardoso, J., Sheth, A. (eds.) SWSWPC 2004. LNCS, vol. 3387, pp. 43–54. Springer, Heidelberg (2005). https://doi.org/10.1007/978-3-540-30581-1_5
10. NBSPRC Homepage, http://www.stats.gov.cn/tjsj/tjbz/tjypflml/. Accessed 25 Mar 2018
11. Zhai, J., Gao, Y., Wang, X.: An attribute reduction algorithm based on a partition subset. J. Shandong Univ. **41**(4), 24–28 (2011)

MFI-5 Based Similarity Measurement of Business Process Models

Zhao Li[1], Jun Wu[1], Shuangmei Peng[1], Peng Chen[1(✉)], Jingsha He[1], Yiwang Huang[2], and Keqing He[3]

[1] College of Computer and Information Technology,
China Three Gorges University, Yichang, China
chenpeng@ctgu.edu.cn
[2] School of Data Science, Tongren University, Tongren, China
[3] Computer School, Wuhan University, Wuhan, China

Abstract. With the increasing use of business process model management techniques, a large number of business process models are being developed in the industry, so the corresponding enterprises and organizations usually need to maintain a large business process set. An approach is presented based on the Meta-model for process model registration (MFI-5) to accurately measure the similarity of process models. First, based on MFI-5, the Process Model Description Framework (PMDF) is constructed. According to PMDF, a similarity feature set of the process model (*SFS*) is defined. Second, the Business Process Modeling Notation (BPMN) is utilized to describe corresponding business process, and the BPMN models are obtained. Further the BPMN models are identified and quantified by using *SFS*, so the model vectors are obtained. At last, the Tanimoto Coefficient-based algorithm is utilized to calculate the similarity between any two vectors, the similarity measure matrix of the BPMN models can be extracted. We illustrate the approach in the context of measuring the similarity of the online sales service processes, the result of which shows that the proposed approach can facilitate business process recommendation.

Keywords: Business Process Model · MFI-5 · PMDF · Similarity measure

1 Introduction

The last decade has witnessed the dramatic progress and popularity of business process management techniques, those business processes of organizations and enterprises are becoming increasingly complex, which in particular presents a series of challenges to flexible modeling, efficient scheduling, intelligent analysis and compliance control of processes [1]. Business Process Management (BPM) is committed to providing support for process analysis, definition, execution, monitoring and management, which aims at improving product quality and service levels. BPM is the common basic technology of modern information systems, which achieves rapid development in academic and industrial fields. For example, SAP possesses over 600 business process models and collects many Dutch government process models [2] which are generally used to

© Springer Nature Switzerland AG 2018
X. Sun et al. (Eds.): ICCCS 2018, LNCS 11063, pp. 648–661, 2018.
https://doi.org/10.1007/978-3-030-00006-6_59

describe the internal processes of certain services. With the growing amount of the business process models in enterprises, the specific methods and tools for business process management are increasingly needed.

This paper focuses on the approach for measuring the similarity of process models, which is based on the Meta-model for process model registration (MFI-5, see Fig. 1) [3]. MFI-5 ignores the definitions of sequence characteristics of business processes, so it lacks of characteristics for describing the sequence of execution between different process elements. In order to solve this problem and effectively achieve the goal of process modeling in practical application, we appropriately clip the elements in the abstract meta-class layer in MFI-5 and remove the elements which are not directly involved in process construction in the practical application, then add the directed association feature (Association) that describes the sequence in which the processes are executed, thus the Process Model Description Framework (PMDF, see Fig. 2) is built. The similarity feature set of process model (*SFS*) is defined according to PMDF while the Business Process Modeling Notation (BPMN) [4] widely used in industry is utilized to model the actual process, then the BPMN models are obtained. According to *SFS*, we can identify and quantify those BPMN models and also extract the vectors of each model in multiple features. So the similarity of the vectors in each feature is calculated according to the Tanimoto Coefficient-based similarity algorithm, then the similarity of any two process models is obtained by taking into account all these similarities of two models in 7 features.

In this paper, an approach for measuring similarity of process models is proposed based on MFI-5, which includes the following 5 stages:

- *Stage1*-construct PMDF and define *SFS*: we construct PMDF and define *SFS*.
- *Stage2*-identify and quantify the BPMN models: we quantify each BPMN model according to the seven feature dimensions of PMDF and obtain seven vectors of the process model in seven features.
- *Stage3*-select any two models and calculate the similarity of two vectors in each feature respectively: we employ the Tanimoto Coefficient-based algorithm to respectively calculate the seven similarities of vectors in all the features.
- *Stage4*-measure the similarity of process models: we equally weigh the similarities of vectors in all the features and obtain the similarity of any two models.
- *Stage5*-extract the similarity matrix of process models: to intuitively illustrate the measurement results, we extract the similarity matrix according to the similarity between any two process models.

The rest of this paper is organized as follows. Section 2 discuss related work about similarity measure of process models. In Sect. 3, we illustrate the construction of PMDF and *SFS*. Section 4 presents the approach of process models similarity measurement. We conclude our work and discuss the future work in Sect. 5.

2 Related Work

The researches on the similarity measurement of process models have attracted increasing attention from academic and industrial community. Obtaining a similar process model from the process model library has been extensively studied. The similarity measurement between two process models generally involves three aspects: (1) text similarity; (2) structure similarity; (3) behavior similarity [5].

Text similarity. Akkiraju et al. [6] evaluated similarity from the perspective of process texts. Dijkman et al. [7] synthetically measured the similarity of the text concepts at each node of the process and referred it as an important measure of the similarity of two process models. Ehrig et al. [8] evaluated the semantic similarity between two process elements by measuring grammatical, semantic and structural similarities, then integrated these metrics into an overall similarity measurement of process models.

Structure similarity. Yan et al. [9] selected specific features to describe the process models and evaluated the similarity according to the number of similar features between two process models. Cao et al. [10] indicated that the graph edit distance can be replaced with the maximum common graph to achieve better performance in query. Huang et al. [11] proposed an improved graph-based process model search method. Lu et al. [12] explored the structure-based similarity measurement of processes.

Behavior similarity. In addition to text similarity and structure similarity, the process models query based on behavior similarity has caught the attention of academic community. Zha et al. [13] provided a process similarity measurement based on the Transformation Adjacency Set (TAR). Jin et al. [14] extracted four behavior features from process models: existence, causality, conflict and concurrency, then based on which calculated the behavior similarity between two process models. Jin et al. [15] also measured the similarity of process models based on behavior and adopt the specific indexes to search similar models. Grigori et al. [16] employed the idea of process models similarity to discover services that match users' requirements.

Furthermore, there are also other work on modeling languages, query methods, clustering, etc. The standard process modeling notation is of great importance for the description of processes, which provides a wide range of modeling options. Cheikh-rouhou et al. [17] described the limitations of BPMN under time constraints. In [18], Geiger et al. analyzed BPMN2.0-based approach and implementation. Li et al. [19] conducted a formal study of BPMN based on extended Petri net. Syukriilah et al. [20] analyzed the structure similarities of Petri net-based process models. BPMN can allocates the corresponding process resources according to the role played by participants in the process, and this allocation is consistent and structured [21]. Xue et al. [22] proposed an adaptive approach for BPMN-based workflow implementation. To explore the impact of individuals and related factors on the comprehensibility of process models, Qiao et al. [23] proposed a method for clustering and retrieving business processes based on modeling techniques and structure matching investigated.

This paper not only focuses on the structure similarity and behavior similarity of process models simultaneously, but also proposes a method for similarity measurement of process model based on MFI-5, further provides decision support for process recommendations.

3 Construction of Similarity Feature Set

3.1 Meta-model for Process Model Registration

The approach proposed in this paper is based on MFI-5 (Meta-model for process model registration, see Fig. 1), which is developed by the authors. We can utilize a specific modeling language to describe a certain kind of process model and then select the related metadata from this model, thus further leverage MFI-5 to register and manage the selected metadata. This is the main function of MFI-5.

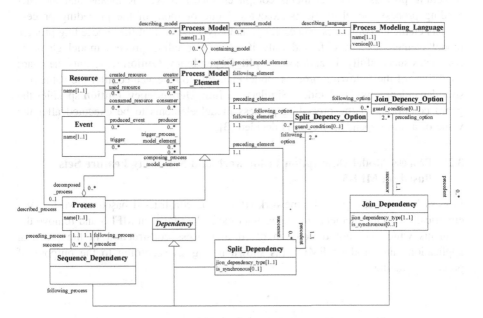

Fig. 1. Meta-model for process model registration

A **Process_Model** is used as a representation of a process, and it describes the contained process model elements using a specified **Process_Modelling_Language**. The **Process_Model_Elements** include **Processes** and *Dependencies* between processes and/or other process model elements. For each process model element, there are some **Events** that can be used to trigger a process model element or to be produced by a process model element. To achieve a particular goal, some **Resources** are used, created or consumed by a process model element [3].

Dependencies represent the control constrains among processes represented by a process model. A dependency can be specialized as a **Sequence_Dependency**, a **Split_Dependency**, or a **Join_Dependency**. A sequence dependency specifies that the processes are executed in order. A split dependency specifies that when the preceding process model element is completed, one or more of the following process model elements will execute in parallel. A join dependency specifies that the following process model element will start when the selected preceding process model elements are completed. In a split dependency, a split dependency type is used to specify a logical gate for the following processes. In a join dependency, similarly, a join dependency type is used to specify a logical gate for the preceding processes. The values of both a split dependency type and a join dependency type can be XOR, OR and AND. For a split dependency type, XOR means that one and only one of the succeeding process model elements is allowed to execute, OR means that one or more of the succeeding process model elements are allowed to execute, and AND Means that all of the succeeding process model elements must execute. For a join dependency type, XOR means that the succeeding process model element executes if one and only one of the preceding process model elements completes successfully, OR means that the succeeding process model elements executes if one or more of the preceding process models elements completes successfully, and AND means that the succeeding process model element executes if, and only if, all of preceding process model elements completes successfully. In addition, a **Split_Dependency_Option** represents the guard conditions of the following process model elements to be executed after the value of a split dependency type is decided. Similarly, a **Join_Dependency_Option** specifies the guard conditions of the preceding process model elements to be executed after the value of a join dependency type is decided [3].

3.2   Process Model Description Framework and Similarity Feature Sets Based on MFI-5

Process Model Description Framework (PMDF) is constructed based on MFI-5. We empirically clip the elements in the abstract meta-class layer in MFI-5 and remove the elements which are not directly involved in process construction in the practical application, and produce PMDF (as shown in Fig. 2) according to the purpose of process modeling.

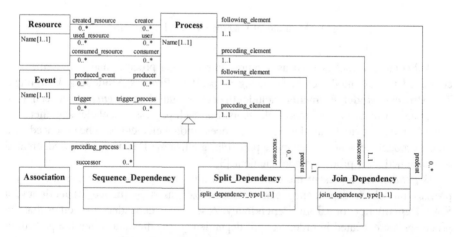

Fig. 2. Process Model Description Framework

PMDF consists of 6 Class features (**Process, Resource, Event, Sequence_ Dependency, Split_Dependency, Join_Dependency**) and 1 **Association** feature (the arrow starts from a Class feature and ends with the other Class feature). These 6 Class features are respectively used to indicate corresponding process model elements involved in the execution of the process. The Association features describe the association between any two Class features, and further indicate the execution order of process model elements. The above 7 similarity features must be equally weighed in the similarity measurement of process models. Table 1 illustrates the scope of each feature.

Table 1. The scope of similarity features

No	Feature	Scope
1	Process	collection of related, structured activities or tasks that achieve a particular goal
2	Resource	asset that is utilized, created or consumed by a process model element
3	Event	occurrence of a particular set of circumstances
4	Sequence_Dependency	kind of control constraint between process, specifying that the processes are executed in order
5	Split_Dependency	kind of control constraint between process model elements, specifying that if the preceding process model element is completed, one or more of the following process model elements will execute in parallel
6	Join_Dependency	kind of a dependency, specifying that the following process model element will start when the selected preceding process model elements are completed
7	Association	directed relations between processes

In the following sections of this paper, these 7 similarity features specified in Table 1 must be employed to accurately describe the process model and obtain the vector of the model in each feature. In this paper, these similarity features constitute SFS, see formula (1):

$$SFS = \left\{ \begin{array}{cc} \text{Process} & \text{Sequence\_Dependency} \\ \text{Resource} & \text{Split\_Dependency} \\ \text{Event} & \text{Join\_Dependency} \\ & \text{Association} \end{array} \right\} \tag{1}$$

The successful definition of SFS provides metadata support for the description of the process model, which is the basis of Tanimoto Coefficient-based vectors similarity calculation.

4 Similarity Measurement of Process Model

4.1 Description of Process Model

In the field of process similarity measurement and process mining, BPMN has become a universal graphical description language and has been widely used in process modeling [21]. BPMN is suitable for process description because of its graphical features, appropriate level of abstraction which is located between the process instances and MFI-5, and adaptability to complex application scenarios. In this section, we adopt BPMN to describe the actual business processes of 3 online sales services and obtain the corresponding BPMN models, which provide support for the vectorization of the BPMN model. These 3 online sales services are offered from three different E-commerce companies which are used to process online shopping requests. The corresponding BPMN model of each company is shown in Fig. 3.

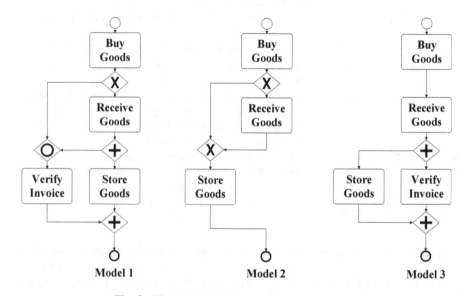

Fig. 3. The BPMN models of online sales services

In Model 1 (*M1*), the user executes the process of "**Buy Goods (BG)**" first, then executes the exclusive logical gate "XOR" which belongs to a split dependency type, then one and only one of the succeeding process is allowed to execute according to the specific context. That is to say if "**Receive Goods (RG)**" is chosen to execute, the parallel logical gate "AND" which belongs to a split dependency type, the compatible logical gate "OR" which belongs to a join dependency type, "**Verify Invoice (VI)**", "**Store Goods (SG)**", the parallel logical gate "AND" which belongs to a join dependency type, and "**End**" (the bold circle) will be allowed to execute. Similarly, the means for analyzing *M1* can be also applied to Model 2 (*M2*) and Model 3 (*M3*). Furthermore, the feature of "Resource" is additionally considered in BPMN model to further reflect the direct participants and enhance the comprehensibility of BPMN model. The "Resource" of *M1*, *M2*, and *M3* are described in Table 2.

Table 2. The scope of "Resource"

Model Id	Resource
M1	Jack, Brook, Lily
M2	Jack, Brook
M3	Jack

In Table 2, the direct participants of *M1* are Jack, Brook, and Lily, so the "Resource" of *M1* is Jack, Brook, and Lily. Similarly, we can see that the "Resource" of *M2* is Jack and Brook, the "Resource" of *M3* is Jack.

4.2   Identification and Quantification of BPMN Models

To calculate the similarity between process models effectively, the *SFS* is utilized to identify and quantify the BPMN models, and the 7 vectors of each process model in 7 features are obtained, which provide support for the Tanimoto Coefficient-based similarity calculation of vectors. In this section, we take these three online sales services BPMN models as an example (see Fig. 3) to identify and quantify the BPMN models.

Similarity Feature 1 (Process)

The BPMN models in Fig. 3 contain four distinct types of process (rectangular boxes): BG, RG, VI and SG. Each BPMN model will be translated into a vector of four feature values, one for each distinct type of process. These features values measure the number of times a specific type of process is repeated in the model. They are defined as follows:

ModelId	BG	RG	VI	SG
M1	1	1	1	1
M2	1	1	0	1
M3	1	1	1	1

Similarity Feature 2 (Resource)

The BPMN models in Fig. 3 contain three distinct types of resource: Jack, Brook and Lily. Each BPMN model will be translated into a vector of three feature values, one for each distinct type of resource. These features values measure the number of times a specific resource participate in the event of the model. They are defined as follows:

ModelId	Jack	Brook	Lily
M1	1	1	1
M2	1	1	0
M3	1	0	0

Similarity Feature 3 (Event)

The BPMN models in Fig. 3 contain two distinct types of event (circles): Start and End. Each BPMN model will be translated into a vector of two feature values, one for each distinct type of event. These features values measure the number of times a specific type of event is repeated in the model. They are defined as follows:

ModelId	Start	End
M1	1	1
M2	1	1
M3	1	1

Similarity Feature 4 (Sequence_Dependency)

The BPMN models in Fig. 3 contain one type of sequence dependency. Each BPMN model will be translated into a vector of one feature value. This feature value measures the number of times a specific type of sequence dependency is executed in the model. It is defined as follows:

ModelId	Sequence_Dependency
M1	0
M2	0
M3	1

Similarity Feature 5 (Split_Dependency)

The BPMN models in Fig. 3 contain one type of split dependency. Each BPMN model will be translated into a vector of one feature value. This feature value measures the number of times a specific type of split dependency is executed in the model. It is defined as follows:

ModelId	Split_Dependency
M1	2
M2	1
M3	1

Similarity Feature 6 (Join_Dependency)

The BPMN models in Fig. 3 contain one type of join dependency. Each BPMN model will be translated into a vector of one feature value. This feature value measures the number of times a specific type of join dependency is executed in the model. It is defined as follows:

ModelId	Join_Dependency
M1	2
M2	1
M3	1

Similarity Feature 7 (Association)

The BPMN models in Fig. 3 contain five distinct association relations: Buy Goods → Receive Goods (BG → RG), Buy Goods → Verify Invoice (BG → VI), Receive Goods → Store Goods (RG → SG), Buy Goods → Store Goods (BG → SG) and Receive Goods → Verify Invoice (RG → VI). Each BPMN model will be translated into a vector of five feature values, one for each distinct association relation. These feature values measure the number of times a specific association occurs in the model. They are defined as follows:

ModelId	BG → RG	BG → VI	RG → SG	BG → SG	RG → VI
M1	1	1	1	0	1
M2	1	0	1	1	0
M3	1	0	1	0	1

4.3 Tanimoto Coefficient-Based Similarity Calculation of Vector

The similarity between two BPMN models can be represented by the similarity computed between the two vectors of each feature, then these seven similarities will be obtained and given equal importance [24], that is to say we will equally weigh the importance of all the features. So the similarity between two BPMN models will be calculated according to these seven similarities of all the features.

In calculating the similarity between two vectors of each feature, we employ the Tanimoto Coefficient algorithm [25]. According to these BPMN models of online sales services illustrated in Fig. 3, we can see that the BPMN model set (*MS*) contains three models, which is defined in Formula (2):

$$MS = \{M1, M2, M3\} \qquad (2)$$

In referring to the Tanimoto Coefficient algorithm and the *SFS* shown in Formula (1), we define Formula (3) to calculate the similarity between corresponding two vectors of each feature for any two models in *MS*.

$$Sim(MA_i, MB_i) = Tanimoto(MA_i, MB_i)$$
$$= \frac{MA_i \times MB_i}{|MA_i| \times |MA_i| + |MB_i| \times |MB_i| - MA_i \times MB_i},$$
$$MA, MB \in MS, i = 1, 2, \ldots, 7 \qquad (3)$$

It is noteworthy that, in Formula (3), *MA* and *MB* respectively denote any two models in *MS*, MA_i and MB_i respectively represent the two vectors of any two models in the *i*-th feature, and *i* is an integer between 1 and 7 (including integers 1 and 7). *Sim* (MA_i, MB_i) denotes the similarity between MA_i and MB_i, and $Sim(MA_i, MB_i) = Tanimoto(MA_i, MB_i)$. The similarity is computed in the range [0, 1]. According to Formula (1), (2) and (3), the seven similarities of any two models in each feature are obtained, which are shown in Table 3.

Table 3. Similarity of Vectors in 7 Features of BPMN Models

i	1			2			3			4			5			6			7		
	Process			Resource			Event			Sequence_ Dependency			Split_ Dependency			Join_ Dependency			Association		
	M1	M2	M3	M1	M2	M3	M1	M2	M3	M1	M2	M3	M1	M2	M3	M1	M2	M3	M1	M2	M3
M1	1	0.75	1	1	0.67	0.33	1	1	1	1	1	0	1	0.67	0.67	1	0.67	0.67	1	0.40	0.75
M2	0.75	1	0.75	0.67	1	0.50	1	1	1	1	1	0	0.67	1	1	0.67	1	1	0.40	1	050
M3	1	0.75	1	0.33	0.50	1	1	1	1	0	0	1	0.67	1	1	0.67	1	1	0.75	0.50	1

In Table 3, the vector similarity of $M1$ and $M2$ is 0.75 in Feature Process, is 0.67 in Feature Resource, is 1 in Feature Event, is 1 in Feature Sequence_Dependency, is 0.67 in Feature Split_Dependency, is 0.67 in Feature Join_Dependency, and is 0.40 in Feature Association. Similarly, the vector similarities of other models in each feature can be obtained.

According to Table 3, the similarity of two models are produced by averaging out the vector similarities in all the features. Formula (4) is defined to calculate the similarity of any two models in MS.

$$Sim(MA, MB) = \frac{\sum_{i=1}^{7} Sim(MA_i, MB_i)}{7}, MA, MB \in MS \qquad (4)$$

In Formula (4), $Sim(MA, MB)$ denotes the similarity between MA and MB.

The similarity matrix (SM) of the three BPMN models illustrated in Fig. 3 is constructed according to the outcome of similarity measurement:

$$SM = \begin{bmatrix} & M1 & M2 & M3 \\ M1 & 1 & 0.73 & 0.63 \\ M2 & 0.73 & 1 & 0.68 \\ M3 & 0.63 & 0.68 & 1 \end{bmatrix}$$

In referring to the SM, it is obvious that the SM is symmetric. The similarity between $M1$ and $M2$ is 0.73, the similarity between $M1$ and $M3$ is 0.63, and the similarity between $M2$ and $M3$ is 0.68.

4.4   Steps for Similarity Measurement

The metadata-based similarity measurement of process models in this paper can be illustrated in the following three steps:

- *Step1*: *describe the process models*. We employ BPMN to describe actual business processes to obtain corresponding MS.
- *Step2*: *identify and quantify the BPMN models*. According to the SFS and MS, we identify and quantify the vectors of any two models in each feature, further respectively extract the two vectors MA_i and MB_i.

- *Step3: calculate the similarity between vectors based on the Tanimoto Coefficient algorithm.* We input MA_i and MB_i into Formula (3), and output the corresponding $Sim(MA_i, MB_i)$, then input the $Sim(MA_i, MB_i)$ into Formula (4), further output the $Sim(MA, MB)$ and SM.

5 Conclusion

Many challenges and difficulties in exploring business process similarity are still exist. In this paper, we proposes an approach based on MFI-5 for measuring similarity of process models, which consists of three steps: describe the process models; identify and quantify the BPMN models; and calculate the similarity between vectors based on the Tanimoto Coefficient distance algorithm. The major contributions of this work are:

- Using the seven features of PMDF cropped from MFI-5 as the foundation to enhance the practicability of similarity measurement between business process models.
- Vectorizing the actual BPMN models, which improving the accuracy of similarity calculation.

Acknowledgment. This work was supported by the National Key Research and Development Program of China (2016YFC0802500, 2016YFB0800403); the National Natural Science Foundation of China (61562073); the Humanities and Social Sciences Planning Fund of Ministry of Education (20171304); the Hubei Provincial Natural Science Foundation of China (2018CFC852); and the Natural Science Foundation of Hubei Provincial Department of Education (B2015240).

References

1. Wang, J., Yin, J., Dou, W.: Business process management technology preface. J. Softw. **26**(3), 447–448 (2015)
2. Yan, Z., Dijkman, R.: Paul Grefen.: Fast business process similarity search. Distrib. Parallel Databases **30**(2), 105–144 (2012)
3. ISO/IEC-19763-5. Metamodel framework for interoperability (MFI)-part 5: metamodel for process model registration. https://www.iso.org/standard/53761.html. Accessed 15 May 2018
4. Comax, M., Chessa, S., Rieu, D., et al.: Evaluating the appropriateness of the BPMN 2.0 standard for modeling service choreographies: using an extended quality framework. Softw. Syst. Model. **15**(1), 1–37 (2016)
5. Cao, B., Wang, J., Fan, J., et al.: Mapping elements with the hungarian algorithm: an efficient method for querying business process models. In: International Conference on Web Services (ICWS), pp. 129–136. IEEE, New York (2015)
6. Akkiraju, R., Ivan, A.: Discovering business process similarities: an empirical study with SAP best practice business processes. In: Maglio, P.P., Weske, M., Yang, J., Fantinato, M. (eds.) ICSOC 2010. LNCS, vol. 6470, pp. 515–526. Springer, Heidelberg (2010). https://doi.org/10.1007/978-3-642-17358-5_35

7. Dijkman, R., Dumas, M., Van Dongen, B., et al.: Similarity of business process models: metrics and evaluation. Inf. Syst. **36**(2), 498–516 (2011)

8. Ehrig, M., Koschmider, A., Oberweis, A.: Measuring similarity between semantic business process models. In: International Conference on Conceptual Modeling, pp. 71–80. Springer, Heidelberg (2007)

9. Yan, Z., Dijkman, R., Grefen, P.: Fast business process similarity search with feature-based similarity estimation. In: Meersman, R., Dillon, T., Herrero, P. (eds.) OTM 2010. LNCS, vol. 6426, pp. 60–77. Springer, Heidelberg (2010). https://doi.org/10.1007/978-3-642-16934-2_8

10. Cao, B., Yin, J., Li, Y., et al.: A maximal common subgraph-based method for process retrieval. In: IEEE 20th International Conference on Web Services (ICWS), pp. 316–323. IEEE, New York (2013)

11. Huang, H., Peng, R., Feng, Z.: Efficient and exact query of large process model repositories in cloud workflow systems. IEEE Trans. Serv. Comput. (2015). https://doi.org/10.1109/tsc.2015.2481409, https://ieeexplore.ieee.org/document/7274764/

12. Lu, Y., Yu, H., Ming, Z., Wang, H.: A similarity measurement based on structure of business process. In: IEEE 20th International Conference on Computer Supported Cooperative Work in Design (CSCWD), pp. 498–503. IEEE, New York (2016)

13. Zha, H., Wang, J., Wen, L., et al.: A workflow net similarity measure based on transition adjacency relations. Comput. Ind. **61**(5), 463–471 (2010)

14. Jin, T., Wang, J., Wen, L.: Querying business process models based on semantics. In: Yu, J. X., Kim, M.H., Unland, R. (eds.) DASFAA 2011. LNCS, vol. 6588, pp. 164–178. Springer, Heidelberg (2011). https://doi.org/10.1007/978-3-642-20152-3_13

15. Jin, T., Wang, J., Wen, L.: Efficient retrieval of similar workflow models based on behavior. In: Sheng, Quan Z., Wang, G., Jensen, Christian S., Xu, G. (eds.) APWeb 2012. LNCS, vol. 7235, pp. 677–684. Springer, Heidelberg (2012). https://doi.org/10.1007/978-3-642-29253-8_64

16. Grigori, D., Corrales, C., Bouzeghoub, M., et al.: Ranking BPEL processes for service discovery. IEEE Trans. Serv. Comput. **3**(3), 178–192 (2010)

17. Cheikhrouhou, S., Kallel, S., Jmaiel, M.: Toward a time-centric modeling of business processes models. In: IEEE 23rd International WETICE Conference, pp. 326–331. IEEE, New York (2014)

18. Geiger, M., Harrera, S., Lenhard, J., et al.: BPMN 2.0: the state of support and implementation. Future Gener. Comput. Syst. **80**(3), 250–262 (2017)

19. Li, Z., Zhou, X., Keli, W., et al.: BPMN formalization based on extended petri nets model. Comput. Sci. **43**(11), 40–48 (2016)

20. Syukriilah, N., Kusumo, D., Widowati, S.: Structural similarity analysis of business process model using selective reduce based on Petri Net. In: 3rd International Conference on Information and Communication Technology (ICoICT), pp. 1–5. IEEE, New York (2015)

21. Brocke, J., Rosemann, M.: Handbook on Business Process Management 1. 1st edn. Springer, Heidelberg (2010)

22. Xue, Z., Man, J., Zhang, C., et al.: Research on adaptability of BPMN based workflow execution process. Inf. Secur. Technol. **7**(5), 56–58 (2016)

23. Qiao, M., Akkiraju, R., Rembert, A.J.: Towards efficient business process clustering and retrieval: combining language modeling and structure matching. In: Rinderle-Ma, S., Toumani, F., Wolf, K. (eds.) BPM 2011. LNCS, vol. 6896, pp. 199–214. Springer, Heidelberg (2011). https://doi.org/10.1007/978-3-642-23059-2_17

24. Appice, A., Malerba, D.: A co-training strategy for multiple view clustering in process mining. IEEE Trans. Serv. Comput. **9**(6), 832–845 (2016)
25. Kumar, A., Gupta, S., Singh, K., et al.: Comparison of various metrics used in collaborative filtering for recommendation system. In: 8th International Conference on Contemporary Computing (IC3), pp. 150–154. IEEE, New York (2015)

MLS-Join: An Efficient MapReduce-Based Algorithm for String Similarity Self-joins with Edit Distance Constraint

Decai Sun[1,2]([✉]) and Xiaoxia Wang[3]

[1] College of Information Science and Technology, Bohai University,
Jinzhou 121007, China
sdecai@163.com
[2] Key Laboratory of Big Data in Digital Publishing, SAPPRFT, Beijing, China
[3] Research and Teaching Institute of College Basics, Bohai University,
Jinzhou 121007, China
wxxsdc@163.com

Abstract. String similarity joins is an essential operation in data integration. The era of big data calls for scalable algorithms to support large-scale string similarity joins. In this paper, we study scalable string similarity self-joins with edit distance constraint, and a MapReduce based algorithm, called MLS-Join, is proposed to supports similarity self-joins. The proposed self-join algorithm is a filter-verify based method. In filter stage, the existing multi-match-aware select substring scheme is improved to decrease the amount of generated signatures and to eliminate redundant string pairs including self-to-self pairs and duplicate pairs. In verify stage, the dataset is read only once by use of the techniques of positive/reversed pairs and combined key. Experimental results on real-world datasets show that our algorithm significantly outperformed state-of-the-art approaches.

Keywords: Similarity joins · Self-joins · MapReduce · Big data
Data integration

1 Introduction

Data integration and cleaning has received significant attention in the last three decades, because it is an essential operation in big data processing. The string similarity joins [1–3] is widely used in many applications, such as data integration and cleaning, near duplicate detection, entity resolution, document clustering, cloud data searching [4, 5], and so on [6]. It can find all similar string pairs from collections of strings. The degree of similarity can be computed by various measurements, including Jaccard distance, cosine similarity, edit distance [7, 8], hamming distance, etc.

In this paper, we study string similarity joins with edit distance constraint, which find all similar string pairs, such that the edit distance of each string pair is not larger than a given threshold. Edit distance [8] has two distinctive advantages over alternative distance or similarity measurements. On one hand, it reflects the ordering of characters

© Springer Nature Switzerland AG 2018
X. Sun et al. (Eds.): ICCCS 2018, LNCS 11063, pp. 662–674, 2018.
https://doi.org/10.1007/978-3-030-00006-6_60

in the string. On the other hand, it is more robust to noisy data for the tolerance of trivial displacement.

Existing methods to address similarity joins can be broadly classified into two categories [9]. The first one is in-memory algorithms. It means that the algorithm is run on one computer and the important data, such as index, can be shared in memory. Most of existing in-memory algorithms employ a filter-verify framework, such as AllPair [6], PPJoin [10], EDJoin [11], VChunkJoin [12], PartEnum [13] and PassJoin [14]. In filter stage, the signatures are generated for each string and then candidate pairs are found in the same signatures. In verify stage, candidate pairs are verified and the final true pairs are found. AllPair [6] is a q-gram-based method. It first generates q-grams for each string and then selects the first $q\tau + 1$ grams as a gram prefix based on a pre-defined order. It prunes the string pairs with no common grams and verifies the survived string pairs. EDJoin [11] improves AllPair using location-based and content-based mismatch filter by decreasing the number of grams. PartEnum [13] partitions strings into pieces and enumerates deletion neighborhoods on the pieces as signature to do similarity joins. VChunkJoin [12] uses qchunks with different lengths as signatures and employs the prefix-filter framework to do similarity joins. PassJoin [14] is a similarity joins algorithm for edit distance. It won the champion in the similarity joins competition organized by EDBT 2013. One big challenge in PassJoin is to generate high-quality signatures for two strings.

The second method is parallel algorithms. A parallel algorithm runs on a computer cluster, and it is difficult to share data among these computer nodes. There are a lot of works on similarity joins using Map-Reduce framework [8, 9, 15–19]. Vernica et al. [15] utilizes the prefix filtering to support set-based similarity functions. They used each token in its prefix as a key and the string as a value to generate the key-value pairs. However, a single token will generate many false positives and thus lead to poor pruning power. V-SMART-Join [16] is a 2-stage algorithm for similarity joins on sets. They also used a single token as a key. Afrati et al. [17] proposed multiple algorithms to perform similarity joins in a single MapReduce stage. However, it is expensive to transfer the strings using a single MapReduce stage for long strings. Lin et al. [8] extended PassJoin algorithm for large-scale data using MapReduce framework, and proposed two algorithms to do similarity joins, i.e. PassJoinKMR and PassJoinKMRS. However, the verification in reduce is very time-consuming because the string set will be scanned repeatedly in getting candidate string pairs' contents. Deng et al. [9] also extended PassJoin and proposed a new MapReduce based algorithm, called MassJoin, to support both set-based and character-based similarity functions. They devised a merge-based algorithm to significantly reduce the number of key-value pairs without sacrificing the pruning power. They also developed a light-weight filter unit based method to prune large numbers of dissimilar pairs while not significantly increasing the transmission cost. Ma et al. [18] proposed a parallel similarity joins on massive high-dimensional data using MapReduce. Chen et al. [19] present two sampling based partition methods using MapReduce to support scalable metric similarity joins.

In this paper, we focus on how to support large-scale similarity self-joins using MapReduce. MapReduce [9, 19] is a famous framework proposed by Google to facilitate processing large-scale data in parallel. In literature, PassJoin [14] is a self-join algorithm but an in-memory algorithm. PassJoinKMR [8] is a self-join algorithm based on MapReduce framework, but the verify efficiency is low. MassJoin [9] supports self-joins although it is designed for two sets. However, MassJoin can't eliminate some redundant string pairs, such as self-to-self pair $<R_i, S_i>$, $R = S$ and duplicate pair $<R_i, S_j>$, $<R_j, S_i>$, $R = S$. To improve MassJoin's performance on self-joins, we develop effective techniques to eliminate the redundant pairs and devise a novel self-join algorithm using MapReduce framework. To summarize, we make the following contributions.

(1) We devise a filter-verify based similarity self-join algorithm, called MLS-Join, which is an improved method based on Merge+Light of MassJoin, and the self-join speed is increased.
(2) In filter stage, we adopt the improved multi-match-aware select substring scheme to decrease the amount of generated signatures and eliminate the redundant pairs including self-to-self pairs and duplicate pairs.
(3) In verify stage, we generate positive pairs and reversed pairs to make the two strings' contents and IDs in each candidate pair completely, and the string set is scanned only once in verify.
(4) In verify stage, we adopt the technique of combined key to eliminate the redundant pairs deeply.

The rest of this paper is organized as follows. We formalize our problem in Sect. 2. Section 3 introduces our algorithm's framework. Experimental results are provided in Sect. 4 and the conclusion is made in Sect. 5.

2   Problem Formulation

We focus on self-joins with edit distance [7] constraint. The problem to be solved is formalized as follows.

Definition 1 (String Similarity Self-Joins with Edit Distance Constraint). *Given a set of strings S and an edit distance threshold τ, a similarity self-join finds all similar string pairs $<s_i, s_j>$, $i < j$, $s_i \in S$, $s_j \in S$ such that $ed(s_i, s_j) \le \tau$.*

For the example string set S below, the number before flag # is string ID and the others are contents of strings. Suppose threshold $\tau = 1$, then string pair <1, 3> is a similar pair as their edit distance is not larger than 1.

Example string set S:

1#TAATGA
2#TAATTGTGT
3#TAAGTGA
4#TAACGTTACT

3   The MLS-Join Framework

To avoid enumerating all string pairs from the given string set, we adopt a filter-verify framework. Our MLS-Join contains four MapReduce stage totally, i.e., count, filter, verify1 and verify2. Count stage counts the characters' frequencies for count filter. Filter stage generates index signatures and match signatures and emits candidate pairs with partition-based filter. Verify1 stage gets strings' contents to be used with positive/reversed pairs and eliminates the duplicated IDs by using a non-repeated hash set. Verify2 stage makes the two contents in each candidate pair completely with combined key, and then the final true pairs are found by length-aware verification method. The framework of MLS-Join is shown in Fig. 1.

MLS-Join Framework

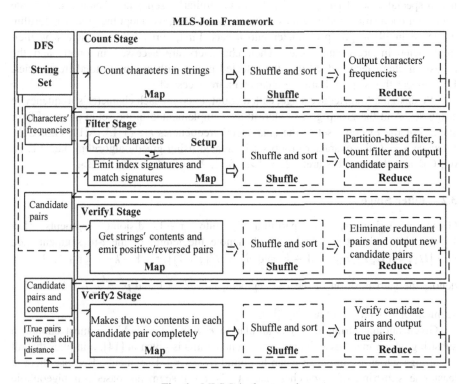

Fig. 1. MLS-Join framework

3.1   Count Stage

Given a string, we can split it into characters. The occurrences of each character are counted and a new vector is formed by their frequencies according to a fix character order. For the example set S, string 1's vector is <3, 0, 1, 2> with the character order {A, C, G, T}. In a word, the vector is a representative of string's statistical feature. The length of vector for a string is not the same in different dataset. Long vector implicates more statistical feature but it also involves large transmission cost. To reduce the size, we group the characters into n sets and keep the vector with length of n.

The similarity between two strings can be scaled by the total difference of their vectors, such as the vector similarity between string 1 and 3 is $|3 - 3| + |0 - 0| + |1 - 2| + |2 - 2| = 1$. On the contrary, two strings must not be a similar pair if their vector similarity is larger than a certain threshold.

Lemma 1. *Given two strings* r, s *with vectors* $<g_1^r, g_2^r, \cdots, g_n^r, >$, $<g_1^s, g_2^s, \cdots, g_n^s, >$ *and an edit distance threshold* τ, *if* $\sum_{i=1}^{n} |g_i^r - g_i^s| > 2\tau$, r *and* s *cannot be a similar pair, i.e.,* $ed(r, s) > \tau$.

The lemma details the relationship between vector similarity and edit distance, and it is a special case of lemma 8 in [9]. In our similarity self-join scheme, we generate vector for each string and take it as a filter feature. Here, we adopt the greedy algorithm proposed in [9] to group character into n sets. First, sort all the characters by their frequencies in decreasing order. Then characters are accessed in order, and the accessing character is added into the selected group with minimum total frequencies. Last, repeat this step until all the characters are accessed.

We design a MapReduce stage, called count, to count each character's frequency in string set. And the group greedy algorithm is implemented in the setup phase of filter stage. For the example set S, the characters' frequencies are (T:13, A:11, G:6, C:2). Suppose $n = 3$, the character group set is created using greedy algorithm, i.e., {T, A, (G, C)} and their vectors are: <2, 3, 1>, <5, 2, 2>, <2, 3, 2>, <4, 3, 3>.

3.2 Filter Stage

Given a string r, we partition it into $\tau + 1$ disjoint segments. Let $k = l - \lfloor l/(\tau+1) \rfloor \times (\tau+1), l = |r|$, l_i denote the length of the i-th segment, i.e., $l_i^l = \lfloor l/(\tau+1) \rfloor, 1 \le i \le \tau + 1 - k$ and $l_i^l = \lceil l/(\tau+1) \rceil, \tau + 1 - k < i \le \tau + 1$. Let p_i^l denote the start position of the i-th segment, i.e., $p_1^l = 1$ and $p_i^l = \sum_{j=1}^{j<i} l_j^l + 1$. The i-th segment of r is represent as $r[p_i^l, l_i^l]$.

Given another string s, if s is similar to r within threshold τ s must contain a substring which matches a signature of r. The lemma is given in [14], it implies that all the strings which is similar to r can be found by r's $\tau + 1$ segments. Because there at least one substring of s matches one of r's $\tau + 1$ segments based on pigeonhole principle.

Similarity joins finds similar pairs between two string sets, whereas self-join in one set. MassJoin is designed for two sets joins. It can also perform self-join with $R = S$ but a lot of invalid similar pairs including self-to-self pairs slow down the join speed sharply. Here, we improve the partition-based filter to decrease the redundant pairs in self-joins. We design a MapReduce stage, called filter, to generate strings' signatures and eliminate the string pairs which is found but they are not similar pairs according to the filter criterion.

In map phase, we generate index signatures and match signatures for a given string.

We introduce how to generate index signatures first. The input split of each map is a string which denote as r. We partitioned r into $\tau + 1$ disjoint segments, and emit each segment as an index substring. The key-value pair is $<r[p_i^l, l_i^l], (I, i, |r|, rid, g_r)>$. I is the flag of index signature, rid is r's string ID in set, g_r is r's vector. For the example set S, suppose $\tau=1$, the index signatures are shown in Table 1.

Table 1. Index signatures

String ID	Index signatures, <Key,value> pair
1	<TAA,(I,1,6,1,<2,3,1>)> <TGA,(I,2,6,1,<2,3,1>)>
2	<TAAT,(I,1,9,2,<5,2,2>)> <TGTGT,(I,2,9,2,<5,2,2>)>
3	<TAA,(I,1,7,3,<2,3,2>)> <GTGA,(I,2,7,3,<2,3,2>)>
4	<TAACG,(I,1,10,4,<4,3,3>)> <TTACT,(I,2,10,4,<4,3,3>)>

Now, we discuss how to generate match signatures. If a given string s is similar to r, it requires to have a signature matching one of index signatures of r. Intuitively, the start position of i-th substring of s, e.g., x_i^l, can be any integer in $[1, |s| - l_i^l + 1]$. The length of string r is uncertain then it will generate all substring in $[1, |s|]$ to match string r in different length. However this method will generate large numbers of signatures. To simplify, Massjoin's Merge+Light algorithm [9] emits all substring with l_i^l in $[\lfloor(|s| - \tau)/(\tau+1)\rfloor, \lceil(|s|+\tau)/(\tau+1)\rceil]$ and start position x_i^l in $[1, |s| - l_i^l + 1]$, i.e., $<s[x_i^l, l_i^l], (|s|, x_i^l, sid, g)>$. But it generates excess match signatures although the generate time and the transmission cost are decreased.

We adopt the multi-match-aware select substring scheme [9] to emit match signatures, but some important parameters are changed to eliminate the redundant pairs for self-joins. We emit signatures for i-th segment of s where $1 \leq i \leq \tau+1$, l in $[|s| - \tau, |s|]$ and x_i^l in $[\perp_i^l, \top_i^l]$, $\perp_i^l = \max(1, \max(p_i^l - i + 1, p_i^l + |s| - l - (\tau+1-i)))$, $\top_i^l = \min(|s| - l_i^l + 1, \min(p_i^l + i - 1, p_i^l + |s| - l + (\tau+1-i)))$, i.e., $<s[x_i^l, l_i^l], (|s|, x_i^l, sid, g_s)>$. In our scheme, the range of l is differ from MassJoin's $[|s| - \tau, |s| + \tau]$. This is because MassJoin generates match signatures for string with all possible length in set R. While our self-joins only match the strings in self-set, it does not need to generate match signatures for strings which are longer than s. If a longer string w is similar to s it will be found by w's match signatures. For the example set S, string 1 does not emit match signatures for length 7 but for 5 and 6, and string 3 emits match signatures for length 6 and 7. The candidate pair <1, 3> can be found by the matches between index signatures of 1 and match signatures of 3.

In our algorithm, the same signatures are emitted once although they are generated by different segments. We eliminate redundant signatures by using a hash set. Initially the hash set is an empty set. The generated signature is will be discarded if the hash set contain it. Otherwise, it will be emitted and added into the hash set. The match signatures of example set S are shown in Table 2.

In shuffle phase, the key-value pairs are shuffled and pairs with same signature are transferred to the same reduce node. The input of a reducer is a key-value pair <signature, list(*value*)>. First the values are extracted and processed to be an index value or

Table 2. Match signatures

String ID	Match signatures, <Key,value> pair
1	<TA,(6,1,1,<2,3,1>)> <TAA,(6,1,1,<2,3,1>)> <TGA,(6,4,1,<2,3,1>)>
2	<TAAT,(9,1,2,<5,2,2>)> <GTGT,(9,6,2,<5,2,2>)> <TGTGT,(9,5,2,<5,2,2>)>
3	<TAA,(7,1,3,<2,3,2>)> <TGA,(7,5,3,<2,3,2>)> <GTGA,(7,4,3,<2,3,2>)>
4	<TAAC,(10,1,4,<4,3,3>)> <TAACG,(10,1,4,<4,3,3>)> <TTACT,(10,6,4,<4,3,3>)>

a match value by the flag of I. Then the values are added into two different lists separately, e.g., Ilist and Slist. There are no candidate pairs for this signature if Ilist is null or Slist is null, because there are no matches between match signatures and index signatures. Suppose $Ilist[i]$ is the i-th item in Ilist and $Slist[j]$ is the j-th item in Slist, and the pair $< Ilist[i], Slist[j] >$, $Ilist[i] = (i, |r|, rid, g_r), Slist[j] = (|s|, x_i^j, sid, g_s)$, is a candidate pair. We adopt the multi-match-aware filter criterion again to eliminate some false positives. The filter criterion includes (1) $rid \neq sid$, (2) $|s| - \tau \leq |r| \leq |s|$, (3) $\perp_i^l \leq x_i^l \leq T_i^l$ and (4) $sim(g_r, g_s) \leq 2\tau$. The first condition eliminates the self-to-self pairs, and the second discards the pairs which strings' lengths do not meet the requirements. The third checks the start position of signature in s whether it is legal or not, and the last one eliminates the pairs which vector similarity below the standard. At last, the reduce result is emitted, i.e., $< sid, list(rid) >$.

For the example above, the other signatures are invalid except TAA and TGA. The reduce result is: signature TAA emits <3, (1)> and TGA emits <3, (1)>.

3.3 Verify1 Stage

At end of filter stage, all candidate pairs are drawn out. Then some problems can be discovered from the filter result. (1) There exist some redundant pairs. (2) We cannot verify the candidate pairs because there are only strings' IDs but contents.

We discuss the second problem first. PassJoinKMR [8] did not address the method how to read the strings' contents in verify stage but a line in pseudo-code. A simple way is to read directly before verification. But it is very time-consuming because the string set will be scanned one time for each candidate pair. MassJoin [9] proposed a smart method that read each set only once for two sets joins, while the set is scanned twice for self-joins. Here a new content acquire method is proposed to avoid scanning dataset more than once.

We design a MapReduce stage, called verify1, to acquire string content. The input of map phase includes string set S and the output of filter stage. In map phase, the source type of input is judged first. For a string s of set S, we emit a key-value pair with string ID as key, flag # and string's content as value, i.e., $< sid, \#s >$. For a key-value pair of filter result denoted as, we emit the positive pairs and the reversed pairs. For example, let $< sid, list(rid) >$ be a key-value pair of filter result. The positive pairs of $< sid, list(rid) >$ is itself, and the reversed pairs are formed with rid as key and sid as value, i.e., we emit key-value pair $< rid, sid >$ for each rid in $list(rid)$. For the example set S, the map result is shown as follows.

$<1, \#\text{TAATGA}>$ $<2, \#\text{TAATTGTGT}>$ $<3, \#\text{TAAGTGA}>$
$<4, \#\text{TAACGTTACT}>$ $<3, 1>$ $<1, 3>$ $<3, 1>$ $<1, 3>$

The key-value pairs are shuffled and the shuffle result $<rsid, list(id/\#s)>$ of example set S is shown as follows.

$<1, (\#\text{TAATGA}, 3, 3)>$ $<2, (\#\text{TAATTGTGT})>$
$<3, (\#\text{TAAGTGA}, 1, 1)>$ $<4, (\#\text{TAACGTTACT})>$

Now we discuss the first problem which is can also be seen from shuffle result above. In reduce phase, we eliminate the duplicated IDs for each key-value pair. First we create a non-repeated hash set to store IDs. The $list(id/\#s)$ is split into values, and each value is processed to be an ID or string's content by flag #. The IDs are added into the hash set. At last we traverse the whole hash set and form a $list(id)$ with all IDs in hash set. The content $\#s$ will be discarded if its $list(id)$ is null because there is no string match it. Otherwise, we emit $<rsid\#s, list(id)>$. The reduce result of example above is shown as follows.

$<1\#\text{TAATGA}, 3>$ $<3\#\text{TAAGTGA}, 1>$

In verify1 stage, the dataset is scanned only once. However the reversed pairs generated are duplicated one, it will take some time to transmit and process. But compare with whole dataset, it is worth it because the size of dataset is very large.

3.4 Verify2 Stage

At the end of verify1 stage, the strings' contents to be used are extracted and the others are discarded. Until now we still cannot verify the candidate pairs because two strings' contents in each pair are incomplete. Superficially, there still exist some duplicated pairs in the result of verify1 stage.

Here we design a MapReduce stage, called verify2, to make two contents in each candidate pair completely. The input of map phase is the result of verify1 stage. For the key-value pair $<rsid\#s, list(id)>$, we extract $rsid$ from $rsid\#s$ first. Then we form a new combined key with $rsid$ and an ID in $list(id)$, and let the bigger one behind of the smaller one, i.e., $[id1, id2], id1 = \min(rsid, id), id2 = \max(rsid, id)$. For each ID in $list(id)$, we emit $<[id1, id2], rsid\#s>$. For the example set S, the map result is:

$<[1, 3], 1\#\text{TAATGA}>$ $<[1, 3], 3\#\text{TAAGTGA}>$

The shuffle result $<[id1, id2], rsid\#s>$ is:

$<[1, 3], (1\#\text{TAATGA}, 3\#\text{TAAGTGA})>$

As shown in shuffle result, we get two contents for each candidate pair and there are no duplicated pairs actually. In reduce phase, the input of reduce phase is a key-value pair $<[id1, id2], list(rsid\#s)>$ and two strings' contents are extracted from it. Let $s1$

denote the string $id1$'s content and $s2$ denote $id2$'s content, and a candidate pair is presented as $<id1\#s1, id2\#s2>$. At last, the length-aware verification method proposed in [14], is used to verify the candidate pairs. A candidate pair is a true pair if $ed(s1, s2) \leq \tau$, and the final result key-value pair is emitted, i.e., $<ed(s1, s2), (id1\#s1, id2\#s2)>$. The final result of the example set S is:

$$< 1, (1\#TAATGA, 3\#TAAGTGA) >$$

The main purpose of verify2 stage is to make the two strings' contents in each candidate pair completely and to verify each candidate pair. We implement it by use of combined key and the candidate pairs are verified with length-aware verification method which will be detailed below.

3.5   Length-Aware Verification

To verify a given candidate pair $<r, s>$, the straightforward method is dynamic-programming algorithm [14]. Dynamic-programming use a matrix M with $|r| + 1$ rows and $|s| + 1$ columns to compute their edit distance. Actually, it is needn't to compute all elements of the edit matrix. We only need to check whether their edit distance is not larger than τ. An improvement based on length-aware verification method [14] only computes $M(i, j)$ for $i - \lfloor (\tau - \Delta)/2 \rfloor \leq j \leq i + \lfloor (\tau + \Delta)/2 \rfloor$ where $\Delta = |s| - |r| \leq \tau$ and let $|s| \geq |r|$. The method also employed an early termination technique, i.e., once each value in $M(i, *)$ is larger than τ then the computation will be early terminated. This is because the values in the following rows $M(k > i, *)$ must be larger than τ based on the dynamic-programming algorithm. In our verify2 stage, we employ the length-aware verification method to verify the candidate pairs.

4   Experiment

4.1   Experiment Environment

We implement our algorithm with Java under Hadoop 1.2.1, we also implement PassJoinKMR [8] and MassJoin's Merge+Light (we called MassjoinML) [9] with the same tool. The two real datasets to be used are DBLP (http://dblp.uni-trier.de/xml/) and GBEST (http://www.ncbi.nlm.nih.gov/). DBLP is an academic bibliography data set commonly used in database community, only author and title are reserved here. GBEST is an Expressed Sequence Tags database of NCBI GenBank, and other information are deleted except the gene sequence. The information of datasets is shown in Table 3.

Table 3. Datasets

Dataset	Size (MB)	Number of strings	Average length	Alphabet size
DBLP	301	3,203,996	89.1	96
GBEST	351	1,020,109	352.7	5

All experiments were performed on Hadoop and run on a 4-node cluster. Each node had Intel i5 4590 3.7 GHz processor with 4 cores, 16 GB RAM, and 1 TB disk. Each node is installed 64-bit Ubuntu 15.10, Java 1.7, and Hadoop 1.2.1. We run MassjoinML for self-joins with two same sets, i.e., R and S and set $R = S$. The group number of DBLP is set to 30 in both MassjoinML and MLS-Join, and 5 for GBEST.

4.2 Performance

The most important evaluation criterion for similarity joins is time consumption. CPU time is the amount of time for which a central processing unit (CPU) was used for processing instructions of all tasks in a hadoop job. The CPU is time a good criterion to evaluate similarity join algorithms. In a filter-verify based algorithm, the time consumption include two parts, i.e., filter time and verify time.

The performance of an algorithm varies from its parameters (edit distance) and input dataset. We perform the MassJoinML and MLS-Join on DBLP with edit distances 0, 2, 4, 6, 8, on GBEST with 0, 4, 8, 12, 16. We also perform PassJoinKMR on DBLP with edit distances 0 and 2 but they aren't successful within six hours, so we will not discuss anymore. Both MassJoinML and MLS-Join include four stages, i.e., count, filter, verify1, verify2. Count stage is a part of filter stage because it counts characters' frequencies for the count filter of filter stage. So CPU time of filter includes count stage and filter stage, and CPU time of verify includes verify1 stage and verify2 stage. The experimental result is calculated and shown in Fig. 2.

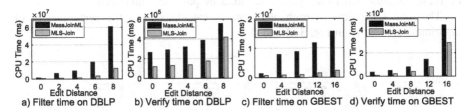

Fig. 2. Filter time and verify time on DBLP and GBEST

Figure 2(a) illustrates the CPU time of filter on DBLP, and Fig. 2(c) on GBEST. Figure 2(b) illustrates the CPU time of verify on DBLP, and Fig. 2(d) on GBEST. As shown in Fig. 2 both filter time and verify time of MLS-Join are all shorter than those of MassJoinML. The reasons are presented as follows. (1) In MLS-Join, the dataset is read only once in count stage, whereas MassJoinML read twice for the input is both R and S, $R = S$. (2) The amount of signatures is decreased with the improved multi-match-aware select substring scheme, and then all self-to-self pairs and more redundant pairs are eliminated in filter stage. (3) In MLS-Join, the dataset is also read only once in verify1 stage, whereas MassJoinML read twice in both verify1 and verify2. (4) In MLS-Join, the redundant candidate pairs are eliminated immediately by the technique of combined key in verify2 stage.

Filter stage is the most important stage in both MLS-Join and MassJoinML because good filter scheme will eliminate more invalid string pairs. In filter stage, the amount of input data (File Input Format Counters) determines the time of reading files from DFS. The amount of map output (Map output materialized bytes) determines the time for shuffle. The amount of reduce output (File Output Format Counters) is total bytes of candidate pairs, and it is a representative of filter ability. These values are recorded in Table 4.

Table 4. Data processed in filter stage

Data Set	Algorithm	File Input Format Counters (Bytes Read)	Map output materialized bytes (Reduce shuffle bytes)	File Output Format Counters (Bytes Written)
DBLP	MassJoinML	633,067,300	87,007,249,489	783,546,531
($\tau = 8$)	MLS-Join	316,533,650	22,014,234,632	223,021,045
GBEST	MassJoinML	737,887,636	73,724,168,738	2,778,487,603
($\tau = 16$)	MLS-Join	368,943,818	14,581,323,067	666,264,028

As shown in Table 4, the MLS-Join's input data is the half of that of MassJoinML because the dataset is read only once. The data of map output is decreased by use of improved multi-match-aware select substring scheme. The data of reduce output is also decreased because self-to-self pairs and duplicate pairs are eliminated.

The total CPU time of each algorithm is calculated, and the performances of algorithms are shown in Fig. 3(a) and (b).

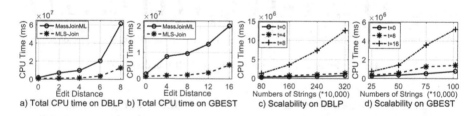

a) Total CPU time on DBLP   b) Total CPU time on GBEST   c) Scalability on DBLP   d) Scalability on GBEST

Fig. 3. Total CPU time and scalability

Figure 3(a) illustrates the comparison of total CPU time between MLS-Join and MassJoinML on DBLP, and Fig. 3(b) on GBEST. As shown in Fig. 3(a) and (b), the total CPU time of MLS-Join is always shorter than that of MassJoinML because both filter time and verify time are decreased.

Now we test the scalability of our algorithm. We vary the number of strings in the dataset and calculate the CPU time, Fig. 3(c) and (d) shows the results. We can see that our algorithm achieves nearly linear scalability.

5 Conclusion

In this paper, we research on the problem of string similarity self-joins with edit distance constraints. We proposed a MapReduce-based framework to do efficient similarity self-joins. In filter stage, we improved existing multi-match-aware select substring scheme to eliminate self-to-self pairs and duplicate pairs. In verify stage, our algorithm read dataset only once by using the techniques of positive/reserved pairs and combined key. Experimental results on real-world datasets show that our method outperforms state-of-the-art approaches.

Acknowledgements. This work is supported by the Humanity and Social Science Youth foundation of Ministry of Education of China (15YJC870021, 15YJC870028), Scientific Research Foundation of the Education Department of Liaoning Province of China (L2015010), NSFC (61602056), Doctoral Scientific Research Foundation of Liaoning province (20141138), Natural Science Foundation of Liaoning Province of China (0517271803, 2015020009).

References

1. Yu, M., Li, G., Deng, D., Feng, J.: String similarity search and join: a survey. Front. Comput. Sci. **10**, 399–417 (2016)
2. Pagh, R.: Large-scale similarity joins with guarantees. In: 18th International Conference on Database Theory, ICDT 2015, pp. 15–24. Dagstuhl, Brussels (2015)
3. Silva, Y.N., Pearson, S.S., Chon, J., et al.: Similarity joins: their implementation and interactions with other database operators. Inf. Syst. **52**(8–9), 149–162 (2015)
4. Fu, Z., Wu, X., Guan, C., et al.: Toward efficient multi-keyword fuzzy search over encrypted outsourced data with accuracy improvement. IEEE Trans. Inf. Forensics Secur. **11**(12), 2706–2716 (2016)
5. Fu, Z., Ren, K., Shu, J., et al.: Enabling personalized search over encrypted outsourced data with efficiency improvement. IEEE Trans. Parallel Distrib. Syst. **27**(9), 2546–2559 (2016)
6. Chen, X., Chen, S., Wu, Y.: Coverless information hiding method based on the Chinese character encoding. J. Internet Technol. **18**(2), 313–320 (2017)
7. Levenshtein, V.: Binary codes capable of correcting deletions, insertions, and reversals. Sov. Phys. Dokl. **10**(8), 707–710 (1966)
8. Lin, C., Yu, H., Weng, W., He, X.: Large-scale similarity join with edit-distance constraints. In: Bhowmick, S.S., Dyreson, C.E., Jensen, C.S., Lee, M.L., Muliantara, A., Thalheim, B. (eds.) DASFAA 2014. LNCS, vol. 8422, pp. 328–342. Springer, Cham (2014). https://doi.org/10.1007/978-3-319-05813-9_22
9. Deng, D., Li, G.L., Hao, S., et al.: MassJoin: a MapReduce-based method for scalable string similarity joins. In: IEEE 30th International Conference on Data Engineering, ICDE 2014, pp. 340–351. IEEE, New York (2014)
10. Xiao, C., Wang, W., Lin, X., et al.: Efficient similarity joins for near-duplicate detection. ACM Trans. Database Syst. **36**(3), 1–41 (2011)
11. Xiao, C., Wang, W., Lin, X.: Ed-join: an efficient algorithm for similarity joins with edit distance constraints. Proc. VLDB Endowment **1**(1), 933–944 (2008)
12. Wang, W., Qin, J., Xiao, C., et al.: Vchunkjoin: an efficient algorithm for edit similarity joins. IEEE Trans. Knowl. Data Eng. **25**(8), 1916–1929 (2013)

13. Arasu, A., Ganti, V., Kaushik, R.: Efficient exact set-similarity joins. In: 32nd International Conference on Very Large Data Bases, pp. 918–929. VLDB Endowment, Seoul (2006)
14. Li, G., Dong, D., Wang, J., et al.: PASS-JOIN: a partition-based method for similarity joins. Proc. VLDB Endowment **5**(3), 253–264 (2011)
15. Vernica, R., Carey, M.J., Li, C.: Efficient parallel set-similarity joins using MapReduce. In: 2010 ACM SIGMOD International Conference on Management of data, pp. 495–506. ACM, Indianapolis (2010)
16. Metwally, A., Faloutsos, C.: V-SMART-join: a scalable MapReduce framework for all-pair similarity joins of multisets and vectors. Proc. VLDB Endowment **5**(8), 704–715 (2012)
17. Afrati, F.N., Sarma, A.D., Menestrina, D., et al.: Fuzzy joins using MapReduce. In: IEEE 28th International Conference on Data Engineering, pp. 498–509. IEEE, Washington, DC (2012)
18. Ma, Y., Meng, X., Wang, S.: Parallel similarity joins on massive high-dimensional data using MapReduce. Concurrency Comput. Pract. Experience **28**(1), 166–183 (2016)
19. Chen, G., Yang, K., Chen, L., et al.: Metric similarity joins using MapReduce. IEEE Trans. Knowl. Data Eng. **29**, 656–669 (2017)

Multi-dimensional Regression for Colour Prediction in Pad Dyeing

Zhao Chen[1], Chengzhi Zhou[2], Yijun Zhou[1], Lingyun Zhu[2], Ting Lu[1],
and Guohua Liu[1(✉)]

[1] School of Computer Science and Technology, Donghua University,
Shanghai 201620, China
{chenzhao,ghliu}@dhu.edu.cn
[2] School of Information Science and Technology, Donghua University,
Shanghai 201620, China

Abstract. This paper aims to predict fabric colours by analyzing the relationship between multiple process parameters and colours of dyed fabrics in pad dyeing. The task is approached as a multi-dimensional regression problem. Within the framework of machine learning designed for colour prediction, two models, back-propagation neural network (BPNN) and multi-dimensional support vector regressor (M-SVR) are implemented. The process parameters are fed to these multi-dimensional regression models to predict the fabric colours measured in CIELAB values. The raw data used in our study are directly provided by a dyeing and printing manufacturer. As our experiments show, BPNN outperforms M-SVR with a relatively large data set while M-SVR is more accurate than BPNN is with a relatively small data set.

Keywords: Colour prediction · Machine learning
Multi-dimensional regression · Back-propagation neural network (BPNN)
Multi-dimensional support vector regressor (M-SVR) · CIELAB

1 Introduction

Colour is one of the most important quality parameters for clothes. In conventional manufacturers, colour recipe designing is a subjective and time-consuming process. The environment of production lines can be very different than that of colour-matching laboratories, where the recipes are designed and tested. Therefore, the colour of a dyeing product might be deviated from what being expected. If that happens, the dyeing recipe needs to be modified and the product must be degraded, reworked or dumped, depending on the level of colour deviation. For the sake of cutting expenses

This research has been financially supported by grants from the Young Scientists' Sailing Project of Science and Technology Commission of Shanghai Municipal (No. 17YF1427400), the National Natural Science Foundation of China (No. 61702094), the Fundamental Research Funds for the Central Universities (No. 17D111206), the National Key R&D Program of China (No. 2017YFB0309800) and the Shanghai Municipal Natural Science Foundation (No. 18ZR1401200).

© Springer Nature Switzerland AG 2018
X. Sun et al. (Eds.): ICCCS 2018, LNCS 11063, pp. 675–687, 2018.
https://doi.org/10.1007/978-3-030-00006-6_61

and reducing pollutions, it is imminent to search for methods that can increase the first time pass rate of dyeing products.

In the literature, generative models in machine learning are applied to data prediction. For example, artificial neural network (ANN) is used for the prediction of the duration of dyeing [1] and the prediction of CIELAB values [2]. Genetic algorithm is also adopted for colour recipe prediction [3]. However, most existing methods focus on the effects of recipes while neglecting fabric parameters. Although reference [4] considers numerous factors in prediction of colour changes, it does not see the potential of non-linear determinant models in colour prediction.

Provided adequate first-hand records in the colour matching lab of Huafang Limited Company, Shandong Province, China, this work aims to model the relationship between eight factors (including fabric parameters and dyeing recipes) and CIELAB values of dyed fabrics by a multi-dimensional regression problem. These factors are selected because they are considered very closely related to dyeing quality from an empirical perspective. To reach the goal, this paper proposes a scheme based on one generative model and one determinant model, which are back-propagation neural network (BPNN) and multi-dimensional support vector regressor (M-SVR), respectively. The reasons for the selection of BPNN and M-SVR are threefold. First, these models are fit for modelling the data used in colour prediction. They can handle multi-dimensional data samples and depict non-linearity in the relationship between the process parameters and the outcome colours. Second, these models each have their own strengths. M-SVR is advantageous in dealing with samples of a small amount while BPNN is capable of learning inherent features in large data sets. Third, as BPNN and M-SVR belong to different categories of machine learning models, their performances can indicate the potential of their own category in colour prediction and provide references for users to choose between the two types of models. In our experiments, the parameters of BPNN and M-SVR are delicately tailored to real data. Their performances are evaluated by two criteria, sample-wise error (SE) and root-mean-square error (RMSE).

The contributions of this paper are summarized as follows.

(1) Raw data from Huafang Limited Company are analyzed within the framework of machine learning for the first time. The study can be of some practical values when our findings are applied to the real colour matching procedure in the dyeing and printing manufacturer.

(2) Colour prediction in pad dyeing is explicitly expressed as a multi-dimensional regression estimation problem, approached by two types of models, BPNN and M-SVR. To the best of our knowledge, M-SVR has not been adapted for colour prediction yet.

(3) Experimental results validate the effectiveness of the multi-dimensional regression approach in colour prediction. Moreover, they prove that M-SVR is indeed better than BPNN with a small data set while BPNN outperforms M-SVR as the data set gets larger.

The rest of this paper is organized as follows. Section 2 provides the background knowledge of multi-dimensional regression models and the CIELAB colour space. Section 3 presents our method of adapting the multi-dimensional regression models for colour prediction. Section 4 gives empirical validation of our method and further discusses about the results. Finally, Sect. 5 concludes the paper.

2 Preliminaries

2.1 Multi-dimensional Regression

The multi-dimensional regression estimation problem, given two variables $\mathbf{x} \in R^n$ and $\mathbf{y} \in R^m$, can be described by the empirical function as follows,

$$\min_{\mathbf{w}} \sum_{i=1}^{I} \|\mathbf{y}_i - r(\mathbf{x}_i, \mathbf{w})\|^2, \tag{1}$$

where $\mathbf{x}_i \in R^n$ and $\mathbf{y}_i \in R^m (i = 1, 2, \cdots, I)$ are i.i.d. samples observed from $\mathbf{x}$ and $\mathbf{y}$, respectively. $\mathbf{w} \in R^m$ is the weight vector and $r(\bullet)$ is the multi-dimensional regression function. The outcome of $r(\bullet)$ is the predicted value, or say, estimated regression value, which can be denoted as $\hat{\mathbf{y}}_i$. When $m = 1$, the optimization problem defined by function (1) boils down to a single-dimensional regression problem.

2.2 BPNN

Artificial neural networks (ANN) are information processing methods inspired by the biological nervous system. They can be used as regression tools. First being proposed by Rumelhart et al. [5], BPNN is a typical ANN, involving back propagation of errors and forward propagation of information, as presented in Fig. 1(a).

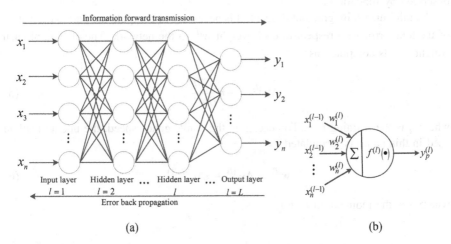

(a)   (b)

Fig. 1. Illustration of BPNN with its (a) structure and (b) an exemplary neuron [6].

Given a BPNN of $L - 2$ hidden layers, one input layer and one output layer, let l denote the index of each layer, where $l = 1, 2, \cdots, L$. For the input layer in Fig. 1(a), $\mathbf{x}^{(1)} = \mathbf{x}_i \in R^n$, where $\mathbf{x}_i$ is defined in function (1). As illustrated by Fig. 1(b), the output $y_p^{(l)}$ of the pth neuron ($p = 1, 2, \cdots, P^{(l)}$, where $P^{(l)}$ is the total number of neurons in layer l) in the lth layer is generated by mapping the linear combination of the all neuron outputs $\mathbf{x}^{(l-1)} \in R^K$ from the $l - 1$th to a new feature subspace, as follows,

$$y_p^{(l)} = f^{(l)}((\mathbf{w}^{(l)})^T \cdot \mathbf{x}^{(l-1)} + \theta_p^{(l)}), \tag{2}$$

where $\mathbf{w}^{(l)} \in R^K$ and $\theta_p^{(l)} \in R$ are the weight and the bias on the connection between the $(l - 1)$th layer and the pth neuron in the lth layer, respectively. $f^{(l)}(\bullet)$ is an activation function, which plays the role of non-linear mapping. In our study, it is defined as the following Sigmoid function,

$$f^{(l)}(a) = \frac{1 - e^{-(\lambda a)}}{1 + e^{-(\lambda a)}}, \ a \in R, \tag{3}$$

Where λ is the gain factor and $f^{(l)}(\bullet)$ is within the range of $(-1, 1)$.

Let $\hat{\mathbf{y}}_i = [y_1^{(L)}, y_2^{(L)}, \cdots, y_p^{(L)}, \cdots, y_m^{(L)}]^T$, i.e., the final output of the BP neural network. The total error between the predicted outcomes $\hat{\mathbf{y}}_i$ and the actual values $\mathbf{y}_i$ is denoted by E, which is minimized, as follows, so as to optimize the network,

$$\min_{\mathbf{w}^{(l)}, \theta_p^{(l)}} E\left(\mathbf{x}_i, \mathbf{y}_i, \mathbf{w}^{(l)}, \theta_p^{(l)}\right) = \frac{1}{2} \sum_{i=1}^{l} \|\mathbf{y}_i - \hat{\mathbf{y}}_i\|^2. \tag{4}$$

It can be seen that function (4) defines a multi-dimensional regression problem as described by function (1).

To minimize E by gradient descent, it is necessary to compute the partial derivative of the total error with respect to each weight $\mathbf{w}^{(l)}$ in the network. The change of each weight $\mathbf{w}^{(l)}$ is computed as

$$\Delta \mathbf{w}^{(l)} = -\eta \frac{\partial E}{\partial \mathbf{w}^{(l-1)}}, \tag{5}$$

where η is the learning rate. To accelerate the convergence speed, the update method used in this paper is formulated as

$$\mathbf{w}^{(l)} = \Delta \mathbf{w}^{(l)} + \alpha \Delta \mathbf{w}^{(l-1)}, \tag{6}$$

where α is the momentum factor.

2.3 M-SVR

The regular support vector regression (SVR) algorithm is single objective. Perez-Cruz *et al.* [7] designed the M-SVR algorithm for multiple-output regression problems, which employs the kernel trick and finds a hyper-spherical insensitive zone to make sure that every sample is penalized equally by solving the optimization problem as follows,

$$\min_{\mathbf{w}^j, b^j, \xi_i} \sum_{j=1}^{m} \|\mathbf{w}^j\|^2 + C \sum_{i=1}^{l} \xi_i, \tag{7}$$

$$s.t. \quad \|\mathbf{y}_i - \mathbf{W}\varphi(\mathbf{x}_i) - \mathbf{b}\|^2 \le \varepsilon + \xi_i, \ \xi_i \ge 0, \ \forall i = 1, 2, \cdots, I$$

where ξi is the slack variable, ε is the tolerance value and C is the penalty factor. $\varphi(\bullet)$ is a nonlinear transformation function that maps the training data $\mathbf{x}_i$ to a higher dimensional space, i.e., $R^n \rightarrow R^H$ and $n \le H$. $\mathbf{W} = [\mathbf{w}^1, \cdots, \mathbf{w}^m]^T$ and $\mathbf{b} = [b^1, \cdots, b^m]^T$ define a k-dimensional linear regressor in the H-dimensional feature space. It can be inferred that

$$\hat{\mathbf{y}}_i = \mathbf{W}\varphi(\mathbf{x}_i) + \mathbf{b}, \tag{8}$$

whereas $\hat{\mathbf{y}}_i$ is the estimated value of $\mathbf{y}_i$ as defined in model (1). As can be seen, the nonlinear problem in the original data subspace becomes linear in the high-dimensional subspace spanned by $\varphi(\bullet)$, which defines the kernel function $\mathbf{H}$ as $\mathbf{H} = \boldsymbol{\varphi}\boldsymbol{\varphi}^T$. Given the Karsh-Kuhn-Tucker Theorem, function (7) is rewritten as follows,

$$\min_{\mathbf{w}^j, b^j, \xi_i} \max_{\alpha_i, \mu_i} \ell(\mathbf{x}_i, \mathbf{y}_i, \mathbf{W}, \mathbf{b}, \xi_i, \alpha_i, \mu_i) = [\sum_{j=1}^{m} \|\mathbf{w}^j\|^2 + C \sum_{i=1}^{l} \xi_i$$

$$- \sum_{i=1}^{l} \alpha_i(\varepsilon + \xi_i - \|\mathbf{y}_i - \mathbf{W}\varphi(\mathbf{x}_i) - \mathbf{b}\|^2) - \sum_{i=1}^{l} \mu_i \xi_i], \tag{9}$$

where α_i and μ_i Lagrange multipliers. Function (9) can be solved by the iterative reweight least square (IRWLS) method [8]. Meanwhile, the Representor Theorem [9] is applied, which states that the best solution can be expressed as the linear combination of the training samples in the Hilbert feature space,

$$\mathbf{w}^j = \sum_{i=1}^{l} \beta_i^j \varphi(\mathbf{x}_i) = \boldsymbol{\varphi}^T \boldsymbol{\beta}^j, \tag{10}$$

where $\boldsymbol{\varphi} = [\varphi(\mathbf{x}_i), \cdots, \varphi(\mathbf{x}_n)]^T$ and $\boldsymbol{\beta}^j$ holds the linear combination coefficients. With Eq. (10), the solution to function (9) can be derived as follows

$$\begin{bmatrix} \mathbf{H} + \mathbf{D}_\alpha^{-1} & 1 \\ \alpha^T \mathbf{H} & \alpha^T 1 \end{bmatrix} \begin{bmatrix} \beta^j \\ b^j \end{bmatrix} = \begin{bmatrix} \mathbf{y} \\ \alpha^T \mathbf{y}^j \end{bmatrix}, \tag{11}$$

where $\boldsymbol{\alpha} = [\alpha_1, \alpha_2, \cdots, \alpha_n]^T$ and $\mathbf{y}^j = [y_{1j}, y_{2j}, \cdots, y_{lj}]^T$. $\mathbf{D}_\alpha$ is the diagonal matrix obtained from $\boldsymbol{\alpha}$.

2.4   CIELAB

CIELAB is an absolute colour space, which comprises three dimensions, L^*, a^* and b^*. L^* represents the difference between light (where $L^* = 100$) and dark (where $L^* = 0$), a^* represents the difference between green $(-a^*)$ and red $(+a^*)$ and b^* represents the difference between yellow $(+b^*)$ and blue $(-b^*)$ [2].

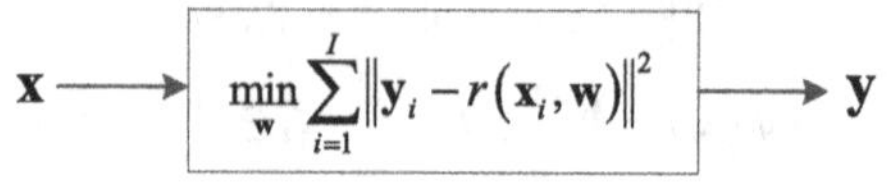

$$\mathbf{x} \longrightarrow \boxed{\min_{\mathbf{w}} \sum_{i=1}^{l} \left\| \mathbf{y}_i - r(\mathbf{x}_i, \mathbf{w}) \right\|^2} \longrightarrow \mathbf{y}$$

Fig. 2. Multi-dimensional regression model for color prediction.

3   Methodology

3.1   Model

For colour prediction [10], we model the relationship between process parameters and CIELAB values of dyed fabric as a multi-dimensional regression problem defined by function (1) and illustrated by Fig. 2. There are eight process parameters considered in an unknown input sample $\mathbf{x} = \{x_j\}_{j=1}^{n} \in R^n$, where $n = 8$. x_1 is the whiteness index of the fabric to be dyed and x_2 stands for the type of the fabric. $\{x_3, x_4, x_5\}$ and $\{x_6, x_7, x_8\}$ represent the name and the concentration of each type of dye chemical, respectively. The output, denoted by $\mathbf{y} = [L^*, a^*, b^*]^T \in R^m$, where $m = 3$, holds the CIELAB values being predicted. Two machine learning models, BPNN and M-SVR,

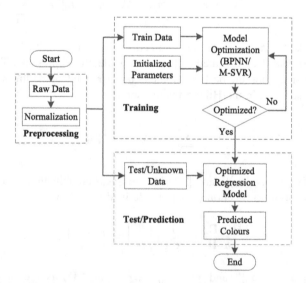

Fig. 3. Implementation of multi-dimensional regression for colour prediction.

are adopted due to their potential in non-linear mapping and multi-dimensional regression. It should be noted that the M-SVR model is used as the solution of the colour prediction problem for the first time, to the best of our knowledge. Our experiments will demonstrate the applicability of M-SVR and BPNN to data sets of different sizes.

3.2 Implementation

The process of color prediction by multi-dimensional regression within the framework of machine learning is illustrated by Fig. 3. The algorithm of the framework with BPNN or M-SVR implemented is provided by Algorithm 1.

Algorithm 1 Multi-dimensional regression for colour prediction

Input: $\mathbf{x}_i \in R^n$, $\mathbf{x}_{i_{pred}} \in R^n$ and $\mathbf{y}_i = [L_i^*, a_i^*, b_i^*]^T \in R^m$, where $n \in N^*$, $m \in N^*$, $i = 1, 2, \cdots, I$ and $i_{pred} = 1, 2, \cdots, I_{pred}$.

Step 1. Preprocessing

1: Let $\mathbf{X} = \{\mathbf{x}_i\}_{i=1}^{I}$, $\mathbf{X}_{pred} = \{\mathbf{x}_{i_{pred}}\}_{i_{pred}=1}^{I_{pred}}$ and $\mathbf{Y} = \{\mathbf{y}_i\}_{i=1}^{I}$.

2: $\bar{\mathbf{X}} \leftarrow$ normalized $\mathbf{X}$; $\bar{\mathbf{X}}_{pred} \leftarrow$ normalized $\mathbf{X}_{pred}$; $\bar{\mathbf{Y}} \leftarrow$ normalized $\mathbf{Y}$.

Step 2. Training

3: If BPNN is selected

4:   Initialize L, $P^{(l)}$, $\mathbf{w}^{(l)}$, $\theta_p^{(l)}$, η and α in formulations (2)-(6), where

5:   $l = 1, 2, \cdots, L$ and $p = 1, 2, \cdots, P^{(l)}$; let $\mathbf{w}^{0(l)} \leftarrow \mathbf{w}^{(l)}$ and $\theta_p^{0(l)} \leftarrow \theta_p^{(l)}$.

6:   Optimize by function (4), i.e., $\{\mathbf{w}^{(l)}, \theta_p^{(l)}\} \leftarrow \arg \min_{\mathbf{w}^{(l)}, \theta_p^{(l)}} E\left(\bar{\mathbf{X}}, \bar{\mathbf{Y}}, \mathbf{w}^{0(l)}, \theta_p^{0(l)}\right)$.

7:   Apply function (2) and obtain $model \leftarrow \{f^{(l)}(\bullet), \mathbf{w}^{(l)}, \theta_p^{(l)}\}$.

8: Else if M-SVR is selected

9:   Initialize $\mathbf{W}$, $\mathbf{b}$, C, ε, ξ_i, α_i, μ_i, $\boldsymbol{\beta}^j$ and $\mathbf{H}$ in functions (7)-(11), where

10:   $j = 1, 2, \cdots, m$; let $\mathbf{W}^0 \leftarrow \mathbf{W}$, $\mathbf{b}^0 \leftarrow \mathbf{b}$, $\xi_i^0 \leftarrow \xi_i$, $\alpha_i^0 \leftarrow \alpha_i$ and $\mu_i^0 \leftarrow \mu_i$.

11:   Optimize by function (9), i.e.,

12:   $\{\mathbf{W}, \mathbf{b}\} \leftarrow \arg \min_{\mathbf{w}^j, b^j, \xi_i} \max_{\alpha_i, \mu_i} \ell\left(\bar{\mathbf{X}}, \bar{\mathbf{Y}}, \mathbf{W}^0, \mathbf{b}^0, \xi_i^0, \alpha_i^0, \mu_i^0\right)$.

13:   Apply function (8) and obtain $model \leftarrow \{\varphi(\bullet), \mathbf{W}, \mathbf{b}\}$.

14: End

Step 3. Test/ Prediction

15: $\hat{\mathbf{Y}} \leftarrow model\left(\bar{\mathbf{X}}_{pred}\right)$, where $\hat{\mathbf{Y}} = \{\hat{\mathbf{y}}_{i_{pred}}\}_{i_{pred}=1}^{I_{pred}}$ and $\hat{\mathbf{y}}_{i_{pred}} = [\hat{L}_{i_{pred}}^*, \hat{a}_{i_{pred}}^*, \hat{b}_{i_{pred}}^*]^T$.

Output: $\hat{\mathbf{y}}_{i_{pred}} \in R^m$.

4 Experiments

4.1 Raw Data

The first-hand data gathered by Huafang Limited Company are used in our experiments. After being preprocessed, two data sets are acquired. One consists of 200 samples (denoted by data set 1) while the other contains 505 (denoted by data set 2). Each sample is denoted by $\{\mathbf{x}_i, \mathbf{y}_i\}$ ($i = 1, 2, \cdots, I$, $I = 200$ or 505), where $\mathbf{x}_i \in R^n$ ($n = 8$) holds the values of eight major process parameters involved in dyeing a piece of fabric and $\mathbf{y}_i \in R^m$ ($m = 3$) contains the CIELAB values of the dyed fabric, as explained in Subsect. 3.1. Given that there are 2 whiteness indexes, 12 types of fabric of different components and 22 types of dyes, $x_{i1} \in (0, 1)$, $x_{i2} = 1, 2, \cdots, 12$ and $x_{i3,4,5} = 0, 2, \cdots, 21$. It should be noted that each colour is acquired by a combination of 3 types of dyes with different concentrations. For example, a colour recipe consists of "SNE Orange", "SNE Blue" and "SHE Red", which are quantified by $[x_{i3}, x_{i6}] = [5, 1.52], [x_{i4}, x_{i7}] = [16, 3.75]$ and $[x_{i5}, x_{i8}] = [20, 1.58]$, respectively. Each $\mathbf{y}_i = [L_i^*, a_i^*, b_i^*]^T$ is measured by Datacolour 650 from a piece of dyed fabric under illuminant D65.

4.2 Setup

Multi-dimensional regression between $\mathbf{x}_i$ and $\mathbf{y}_i$ is carried out by Algorithm 1. To evaluate the performance, the raw data described in the previous subsection are divided into two parts, the training set and the test set, denoted by $\{\mathbf{x}_{i_{train}}, \mathbf{y}_{i_{train}}\}$ ($i_{train} = 1, 2, \cdots, I_{train}$) and $\{\mathbf{x}_{i_{pred}}, \mathbf{y}_{i_{pred}}\}$ ($i_{pred} = 1, 2, \cdots, I_{pred}$), respectively. The training samples are randomly selected while the ratio between the number of the training samples and that of all the available samples (referred to as train-to-total ratio, TTR) is fixed. For the input of Algorithm 1, $\{\mathbf{x}_i, \mathbf{y}_i\}$ is replaced with $\{\mathbf{x}_{i_{train}}, \mathbf{y}_{i_{train}}\}$. Meanwhile, $\mathbf{y}_{i_{pred}}$ is only used for the evaluation. Two types of regression errors, SE and RMSE defined as follows are used for performance evaluation.

$$SE = \sqrt{\left(\hat{\mathbf{y}}_{i_{pred}} - \mathbf{y}_{i_{pred}}\right)^T \left(\hat{\mathbf{y}}_{i_{pred}} - \mathbf{y}_{i_{pred}}\right)}, \tag{12}$$

$$RMSE = \sqrt{\frac{1}{I_{pred} m} \sum_{i_{pred}=1}^{I_{pred}} \left(\hat{\mathbf{y}}_{i_{pred}} - \mathbf{y}_{i_{pred}}\right)^T \left(\hat{\mathbf{y}}_{i_{pred}} - \mathbf{y}_{i_{pred}}\right)}. \tag{13}$$

Major parameters of BPNN and M-SVR in Algorithm 1 are fine-tuned in each case, with their values listed in Tables 1 and 2. For BPNN, training epochs, performance goal, learning rate and minimum performance gradient are set as 10000, 1E−3, 0.05 and 1E−6, respectively. For M-SVR, radial basis function (RBF) is selected and the performance goal of M-SVR is 1E-4. Since the training data are selected randomly, every experiment with its unique settings is repeated for ten times. Hence, every numerical result presented in this section is the average of all the results yielded by the

Table 1. Optimal parameter values for BPNN and M-SVR when data set 1 is processed.

TTR	The best structure of BPNN $(P^{(1)}/P^{(2)}/P^{(3)}/P^{(4)})$	M-SVR	
		The best C	The best g
50%	8/9/5/3	25	0.02
60%	8/10/6/3	2	32
70%	8/10/5/3	2	32
80%	8/10/4/3	0.125	0.5

Table 2. Optimal parameter values for BPNN and M-SVR when data set 2 is processed.

TTR	The best structure of BPNN $(P^{(1)}/P^{(2)}/P^{(3)}/P^{(4)})$	M-SVR	
		The best C	The best g
20%	8/8/5/3	0.25	0.8
30%	8/11/3/3	0.75	0.3
40%	8/7/7/3	0.25	0.35
50%	8/11/8/3	0.125	0.8
60%	8/10/8/3	0.2	0.3
70%	8/11/8/3	0.3	0.3
80%	8/11/7/3	0.25	0.35
90%	8/11/8/3	0.0625	0.5

ten repetitions in each scenario. All the algorithms are implemented by MATLAB R2015a installed on a PC with Intel i5-3210 M CPU @2.50 GHz.

4.3   Results

Tables 3, 4 and Fig. 4 demonstrate the effectiveness of Algorithm 1. It can be seen that both methods are capable of performing colour prediction.

Table 3. SE of colour prediction by BPNN and M-SVR for data set 1.

TTR	BPNN			M-SVR		
	min SE	max SE	mean SE	min SE	max SE	mean SE
50%	**0.047**	2.20	0.61	0.138	**1.56**	**0.59**
60%	0.097	3.15	0.72	**0.060**	1.35	**0.54**
70%	0.151	2.83	0.70	**0.112**	1.61	**0.57**
80%	0.364	1.90	0.81	**0.083**	1.37	**0.71**

M-SVR outperforms BPNN in most cases as data set 1 is used. Meanwhile, BPNN outperforms M-SVR in most cases as data set 2 is used. Since data set 2 contains twice as many samples as data set 1 does, it could be inferred that BPNN is more powerful

Table 4. SE of colour prediction by BPNN and M-SVR for data set 2.

TTR	BPNN			M-SVR		
	min SE	max SE	mean SE	min SE	max SE	mean SE
20%	**0.04**	2.00	0.65	0.16	**1.25**	**0.61**
30%	0.11	2.12	0.62	**0.10**	**1.47**	**0.60**
40%	**0.03**	2.36	**0.56**	0.04	**1.39**	0.61
50%	**0.04**	2.49	**0.49**	0.10	**1.56**	0.57
60%	**0.02**	1.47	**0.47**	0.11	**1.43**	0.61
70%	**0.07**	**1.50**	**0.50**	0.08	1.62	0.59
80%	**0.11**	1.31	**0.46**	0.17	**1.25**	0.63
90%	**0.03**	1.43	**0.53**	0.17	**1.21**	0.74

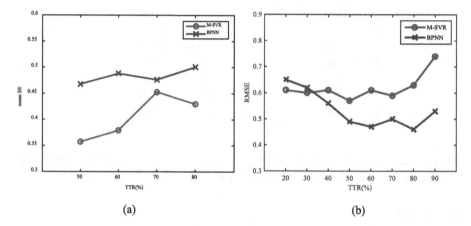

(a)   (b)

Fig. 4. Mean SE of colour prediction by BPNN and M-SVR for (a) data set 1 and (b) data set 2.

dealing with large data sets than M-SVR is. In fact, support-vector-based methods are widely accepted as being especially good with data sets of small sizes, since only a small number of informative samples, i.e., support vectors, are needed to construct their decision hyperplanes. Compared to M-SVR, BPNN enjoys flexibility in structure, which can be designed and tailored to specific data. With multiple layers, BPNN realizes complex non-linear mapping that can accurately model the relationship between multiple on-line processing parameters and product colours.

The time costs in Table 5 indicate that M-SVR is more efficient than BPNN with data set 1. As Table 6 shows, BPNN is slightly less time-consuming than M-SVR with data set 2. Being a determinant model, M-SVR involves multi-dimensional matrix calculation to optimize its goal function, which can be computational expensive with large data sets.

The effects of changes in major parameters of BPNN and M-SVR on the prediction error measured by RMSE are analyzed in Figs. 5 and 6, respectively. TTR is fixed at

Table 5. Time cost (seconds) of BPNN and M-SVR for colour prediction with data set 1.

TTR	50%	60%	70%	80%	mean
BPNN	47.00	48.00	48.50	49.50	48.25
M-SVR	**11.83**	**15.62**	**21.61**	**28.52**	**19.40**

Table 6. Time cost (seconds) of BPNN and M-SVR for colour prediction with data set 2.

TTR	20%	30%	40%	50%	60%	70%	80%	90%	mean
BPNN	48.7	47.7	49.0	**51.3**	**53.7**	**56.0**	**57.0**	**58.7**	52.8
M-SVR	**11.8**	**24.8**	**44.0**	79.3	120.0	160.0	220.0	292.8	119.1

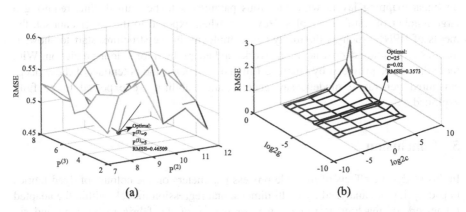

Fig. 5. Parameter analysis of (a) BPNN and (b) M-SVR for data set 1 while TTR = 50%.

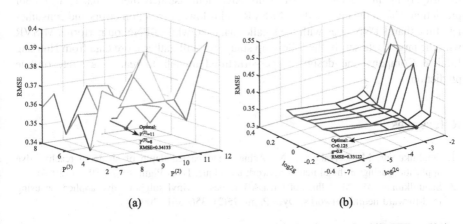

Fig. 6. Parameter analysis of (a) BPNN and (b) M-SVR for data set 2 while TTR = 50%.

50% for both models. The number of neurons for the input and the output layer of BPNN is 8 and 3, respectively. For data set 1, BPNN performs the best with an 8-9-5-3 structure while M-SVR yields the best results with the penalty factor equal to 25 and the RBF kernel width equal to 0.02. For data set 2, the optimal structure of BPNN is 8-11-8-3 while the optimal { penalty factor, kernel width} of M-SVR is {0.123,0.8}.

4.4   Discussion

From the analysis in the previous subsection, it can be seen that M-SVR outperforms BPNN on the smaller data set and BPNN outperforms M-SVR on the larger data set in both effectiveness and efficiency. The reason behind this lies in the nature of the two models. The determinant models such as M-SVR only require a few good training samples for estimation of an accurate hyperplane or hypersphere for decision. Meanwhile, the generative models such as BPNN must learn features through multiple nonlinear-mapping layers with numerous parameters to be trained, thus requiring a large number of training samples. However, when exposed to the larger data set, the merits of BPNN, such as flexibility and complexity in the structure, start to show. It inspires us to study deeper neural networks and adapt them for colour prediction. With more data to be provided by Huafang Limited Company, the potentials of those deep-structured generative models, say generalization ability, are expected to be fully exploited.

5   Conclusion

In this study, the effects of multiple process parameters on the colours of dyed fabrics in pad dyeing are analyzed by multi-dimensional regression models within the adapted framework of machine learning. Two parameters of the fabric to be dyed and six parameters of the dyeing recipes are considered, since they are empirically regarded as closely related to dyeing quality. Two models, BPNN and M-SVR, are employed because both of them can handle multi-dimensional samples and depict the non-linearity lying in the data. Experiments have demonstrated their capacity in colour prediction. Given the current data, M-SVR yields lower prediction errors and consumes less time than BPNN does with the smaller data set, while BPNN outperforms M-SVR with the larger data set. In the follow-up study, we will gather more data from Huafang Limited Company and design deeper-structured models to realize accurate on-line prediction.

References

1. Senthilkumar, M., Selvakumar, N.: Achieving expected depth of shade in reactive dye application using artificial neural network technique. Dyes Pigm. **68**(2), 89–94 (2006)
2. Senthilkumar, M.: Modelling of CIELAB values in vinyl sulphone dye application using feed-forward neural networks. Dyes Pigm. **75**(2), 356–361 (2007)

3. Gorji Kandi, S., Amani Tehran, M.: Color recipe prediction by genetic algorithm. Dyes Pigm. **74**(3), 677–683 (2007)
4. Balci, O., Tuğrul Oğulata, R.: Prediction of the changes on the CIELAB values of fabric after chemical finishing using artificial neural network and linear regression models. Fibers Polym. **10**(3), 384–393 (2009)
5. Rumelhart, D., Hinton, G., Williams, R.: Learning representations by back-propagating errors. Nature **323**, 533–536 (1986)
6. Liu, J., Chen X., Lin Z., Diao S.: Multiobjective optimization of injection molding process parameters for the precision manufacturing of plastic optical lens. In: Mathematical Problems in Engineering, pp. 1–13 (2017)
7. Pérez-Cruz, F., Camps-Valls, G., Soria-Olivas, E., Pérez-Ruixo, J.J., Figueiras-Vidal, Aníbal R., Artés-Rodríguez, A.: Multi-dimensional function approximation and regression estimation. In: Dorronsoro, José R. (ed.) ICANN 2002. LNCS, vol. 2415, pp. 757–762. Springer, Heidelberg (2002). https://doi.org/10.1007/3-540-46084-5_123
8. Perez-Cruz, F., Navia-Vazquez, A., Alarcon-Diana, P., Rodríguez, A.: An IRWLS procedure for SVR. In: Signal Processing Conference 2000, European, pp. 1–4. IEEE (2000)
9. Schoelkopf, B., Smola, A.: Learning with kernels. Nature **323**(9), 533–536 (1986). IEEE Transactions on Signal Processing 52 (8), 2165–2176 (2004)
10. Iqbal, M., Khatri, Z., Ahmed, A., Mughal, J., Ahmed, K.: Prediction of low-sensitivity reactive dye recipe in exhaust dyeing influenced by material to liquor ratio and nature of salt. J. Saudi Chem. Soc. **1**(16), 1–6 (2012)

Multi-situation Analytic Hierarchy Process Based on Bayesian for Mobile Service Recommendation

Weihong Wang$^{(\boxtimes)}$, Fuxiang Zhou, Yuhui Cao, Dawei Zhang, and Jieli Sun

Heber University of Economics and Business,
Shijiazhuang 050061, Hebei, China
wangwhs@163.com

Abstract. Aiming at that the mobile service recommendation results are inaccurate when the preparatory recommendation schemes are similar, this paper proposes a multi-situation Analytic Hierarchy Process based on Bayesian (MSAHPB). Firstly, the three-layer model of AHP was constructed. Then, introducing the multiple situation elements into the standard layer of the MSAHPB model. In order to determine the mutual influence between scenarios, different situations are used as criteria to estimate the impact of each situation on the recommended target. After that, establishing the relational judgment matrix for the adjacent two layers, in which the Bayesian is used instead of the method of assigning matrix by artificial experience. Deducing the weighted values of each situation by Bayesian formula, taking the prior probability of events as a benchmark. Then, to ensure that each matrix satisfies the consistency criterion, this paper tests the consistency of each judgment matrix according to the 1–9 scale, and calculates the matching degree between each scheme and target. Finally, using food service recommendation as an example, the experimental results showed that the method we proposed is effective.

Keywords: Multi-situation AHP · Mobile service recommendation
Judgment matrix

1 Introduction

The number and type of mobile services are increasing rapidly with the popularity of mobile Internet, which has caused the research on mobile service recommendation technology to become the focus of academia. Although many scholars have a lot of research on mobile service recommendation methods, the research is still in its infancy. Such as the context-aware recommendation method [1–3], the recommendation method based on location information [4–7] and user situation similarity analysis service recommendation [8–10]. Almost all of these methods recommend similar services to users with similar characteristics by sensing the similarity between users or services. But these methods only consider the influence of several factors on the results, not take into account the influence of multi-situation interaction on the service recommendation results. Therefore the MSAHPB is proposed for mobile service recommendation in this

© Springer Nature Switzerland AG 2018
X. Sun et al. (Eds.): ICCCS 2018, LNCS 11063, pp. 688–698, 2018.
https://doi.org/10.1007/978-3-030-00006-6_62

paper. The method still follows the three-level analytic model of AHP. AHP, as a data analysis method, has the function of assessing the degree of mutual influence between multiple-situation. We consider the current state of user, features of the target and demand of the service object as the service situations, from which extracts the key words as situation elements to compose the set S, the elements of the set S as the criterion to form the second layer of the model, that is, the situation layer; Because the value of the matrix elements in the AHP is assigned by expert experience, this has a certain influence on the accuracy of the results. Bayesian can use the prior probability of the event, combined with the subsequent posterior probability to infer the probable value of the event, and the deduced results become more and more accurate over time. Therefore, this article defines the use of Bayesian to improve AHP, to deduce the ratio of the importance between every two schemes in the same situation. This method not only takes into account the effect of the interaction between the situation, but also reduces the influence degree of subjective factors in the construction of judgment matrix. It will improve the accuracy of the analysis results when the preparatory recommendation schemes are similar, and then can be better applied to the mobile service recommendation.

The paper is organized as follows: The Sect. 2 as the basis of the study, including application of Bayesian principle in mobile service recommendation, and related research on AHP; In the Sect. 3, we describe we describe the idea of MSAHPB and the construction process of the MSAHPB method; The instance analysis of MSAHPB is given in Sect. 4; Finally, the article gives the conclusion and outlook.

2 Related Research

At present, Bayesian is currently applied in many service recommendation fields, for example, Xu [11] propound the personalized recommendation of travel route under the condition of satisfying the characteristic items specified by the user. In the literature [12], recommendation in digital library is proposed, the Bayesian is used to express the knowledge of the information user's query behavior. The literature [13] proposes a recommendation model, in which the Bayesian network model is used to calculate the user-product match probability. These methods only consider service recommendations in a single situation, but in reality, the recommendation results are influenced by the interaction of user, environment, and demand target features. When all the recommended schemes are similar to the situation selected by the system, the recommendation results are no longer significant. At the same time, AHP is often used to handle decision problems. Bian [14] used the AHP to identify influential node in the network. Singh [15] also proposed using AHP to elaborate recommendations for the most appropriate scale of hydropower development for Nepal. However, we find that the analysis result of AHP is still influenced by some of subjective factors. This problem is also put forward by Deng [16], Chatterjee et al. [17] and Liu [18] in their respective literature.

In summary, it can be found that in the existing mobile service recommendation, the impact of the multi-situation interaction on the recommendation result is still insufficient. Moreover, most of the recommended methods are based on the results of similarity matching speculation. When the similarity between the preparatory schemes is similar, the optimal recommendation result is no longer obvious. So this paper decided to combine the Bayesian principle with the analysis of the hierarchy to propose the MSAHPB to further improve the quality of service recommendations.

3 Description of MSAHPB

3.1 The Idea of MSAHPB

AHP is a multi-element decision analysis method proposed by Saaty [19], which combined with qualitative and quantitative analysis. But, the construction conditions of the decision matrix are mainly based on subjective analysis of empirical data of AHP, which leads to inaccurate analysis results. For this reason, the study decided to adopt Bayesian to improve the analytic hierarchy process. Using the improved method to construct the decision matrix, we first need to obtain the prior probability of each situation under each situation element from the existing data. Then, the Bayesian is used to infer the importance ratio between each two situations in the same situation and assign it to the matrix. In the definition of MSAHPB, Pm_{uv} $(u, v \in \{1, 2, ..., n\})$ is used to represents the matching degree between the u scheme and the situation S_m in comparison with the v scheme. Using the parameter Pm_n denotes the probability of application scheme n under situation S_m, which is the prior probability extracted, and will bused to the Bayesian formula [20]:

$$P_m(u) = \frac{P_m(u|v)P_m(v)}{P_m(v|u)} \Rightarrow \frac{P_m(u|v)}{P_m(v|u)} = \frac{P_m(u)}{P_m(v)} = p_{m_{uv}} \quad (1)$$

Finally, the result calculated by Eq. (1) is added to decision matrix S_m.

3.2 Construction of MSAHPB

According to the content description in the previous section, the method construction needs to first obtain the prior probability that each restaurant is selected under each feature value. Next, to determine the recommended content to meet the conditions of building a three-tier model analysis of the conditions, namely the target layer T, the situation layer $S = \{s_1, s_2, ..., s_m\}$, the plan layer $P = \{P_1, P_2, ..., P_n\}$. The three-tier model as follows (Fig. 1).

Then according to the user's demand information and the current situation to construct the judgment matrix O, and each user should have a unique judgment matrix.

$$O = \begin{bmatrix} S_{11} & S_{12} & \cdots & S_{1m} \\ S_{21} & S_{22} & \cdots & S_{2m} \\ \vdots & \vdots & \cdots & \vdots \\ S_{m1} & S_{m2} & \cdots & S_{mm} \end{bmatrix}, m \in \{1, 2, \cdots, m\} \quad (2)$$

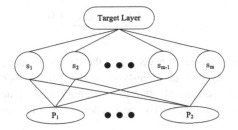

Fig. 1. The three-tier model of AHP.

In the matrix, S_{ij}, $(i, j \in \{1, 2, ..., m\})$ represents the athirst degree achieved by the i-situation compared with the j-situation to the target T, which is obtained through analyzing the user requirement information and the current situation analysis. Data analysis process strictly abide by the 1–9 scale requirements and probability statistics:

$$S_{ij} = \frac{P(i - \text{situation happening when the restaurant is selected})}{P(j - \text{situation happening when the restaurant is selected})} \tag{3}$$

If $i = j$, then $S_{ij} = 1$, After the establishment of the matrix O is successful, the maximum eigenvalue and eigenvector of the judgment evidence are calculated.

Then, we lead Bayesian into the method. According to the formula (1) combined with the 1–9 scale, the corresponding judgment matrix is established for the relationship between each situation element and the preparation scheme:

$$S_m = \begin{bmatrix} P_{m_{11}} & P_{m_{12}} & \cdots & P_{m_{1n}} \\ P_{m_{21}} & P_{m_{22}} & \cdots & P_{m_{2n}} \\ \vdots & \vdots & \cdots & \vdots \\ P_{m_{n1}} & P_{m_{n2}} & \cdots & P_{m_{nn}} \end{bmatrix}, (m, n) \in \{1, 2, \cdots, m\} \tag{4}$$

Then the maximum eigenvalue λ_{max} and eigenvector W_m of each decision matrix are calculated. After all the largest eigenvalues λ_{max} have been obtained, the next step is to calculate the consistency index of each matrix to test the consistency of the judgment matrix. Before calculating, it is first determined whether the values of the eigenvectors corresponding to the largest eigenvalue are all positive real numbers. If there is a negative real number, the matrix must not pass the consistency check, and the matrix needs to be corrected until it meets the standard. When the eigenvector of the matrix satisfies the condition, the value of the consistency indicator CI_m is calculated. Next, find the corresponding average random consistency index RI according to the order n of the matrix, and calculate the consistency ratio CR according to formula (4). When $CR < 0.10$, the matrix passes the consistency check, otherwise the matrix needs to be appropriately modified. When all matrices are tested with consistency, the overall consistency of the structural model is also examined:

$$CR' = \frac{(CI_1, CI_2, \cdots, CI_m) * W_0}{RI} \tag{5}$$

W_0 in formula (4) is the feature vector of the decision matrix between the target layer and the situation layer in the three-layer model. Finally, based on all the eigenvector values obtained, we can calculate the matching ratio value of each scheme to achieve the goal O by formula (5). The best scheme is the best one.

$$H = \begin{bmatrix} W_1, W_{2,...,} W_m \end{bmatrix}^* W_0 \tag{6}$$

Through the above description, the final MSAHPB method model is shown below (Fig. 2).

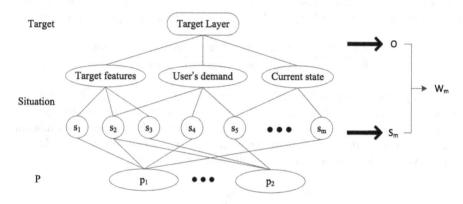

Fig. 2. The three-tier model of AHP.

4   Instance Evolution and Analysis

4.1   Procedure of Experiment

In order to verify the validity and accuracy of the method proposed, experiments were conducted using city restaurant recommendation session data collected from the Entree system. The data is divided into two parts, including 167 restaurants, 256 feature values, and 7.68 M of recommended restaurant session data for three consecutive years. First, we used the cloud platform to screen out more than 6,000 valid data from the original data and analyzed the similarity of each restaurant's features. The selected data content attributes are shown in Table 1 below. The purpose was to filter out better restaurants with similar features (Table 2).

Table 1. Table data content attributes.

Name	Ranges	Instructions
No. of restaurants	1–167	Each number represents a restaurant
No. of feature	1–257	Each restaurant has multiple features
Preference	L–S	L = Browse, M = Cheaper, N = Nicer, O = Closer, P = More traditional, Q = More creative, R = More lively, S = Quieter
Recommendation	1–167	Restaurant which was recommended for practical use

Table 2. Table data feature attributes of the different restaurants

Case number	Target restaurant	Situations	The number of the restaurants in the schemes
1	Don Roth's	L, M, N, P, Q, R, S	39, 57, 71, 147, 175, 240, 458, 260, 365, 414, 508, 585
2	Jilly's Cafe	L, M, N, P, Q, R, S	3, 17, 41, 45, 53,62, 120, 122, 134, 138, 175, 192, 274, 333, 343, 394, 517, 543, 546, 553, 614, 650, 653, 654
3	Sage's	L, M, N, P, Q, R	22, 31, 41, 122, 163, 199, 200, 207, 308, 333, 350, 459, 501, 546, 621, 627, 645, 654
4	Como Inn	L, M, N, O, Q, R	71, 147, 207, 214, 240, 306, 409, 458
5	Retreat	L, N, P, Q, R, S	41, 61, 134, 138, 149, 207, 214, 240, 303, 306, 333, 409, 451, 458, 546
7	Joe-n-Giuseppe	L, M, N, P, Q, R, S	11, 149, 163, 245, 295, 333, 525, 564, 596, 604, 627, 662
8	Athenian Room	L, M, N, P, Q, R, S	69, 107, 132, 167, 217, 370, 381, 542, 566, 591, 653, 672
9	Saloon	L, M, N, Q, R, S	47, 57, 132, 167, 260, 289, 334, 337, 370, 381, 542, 651, 653
10	TRIO	L, M, N, P, Q, R, S	122, 175, 200, 226, 242, 246, 260, 349, 438, 585, 627, 650, 660, 662

Then according to the session data, we calculate the value of the influence of the restaurant's characteristics on each restaurant's recommendation result, and calculate the value in the judgment matrix O to fill in. Because of various data, this paper takes a group of samples as examples, the sample data (The probability of the occurrence of the situation under the specified target and the probability of the selection of the scheme in the situation. Follow the order of L-S) is shown in the following Table 3.

694   W. Wang et al.

Table 3. Data of the sample.

Name	L	M	N	O	P	Q	R	S	Actual results
Target	0.2698	0.3016	4.3333	0.0000	0.0794	0.1588	0.0794	0.0476	Option 1 was
Scheme 1 (C$_1$)	0.3438	0.0313	0.5000	0.0000	0.0000	0.0313	0.0938	0.0000	selected
Scheme 2 (C$_2$)	0.4667	0.0000	0.5333	0.0000	0.0000	0.0000	0.0000	0.0000	
Scheme 3 (C$_3$)	0.6667	0.0000	0.3333	0.0000	0.0000	0.0000	0.0000	0.0000	
Scheme 4 (C$_4$)	0.4545	0.0455	0.2273	0.0000	0.1818	0.0455	0.0455	0.0000	

Then, the first line of data is brought into Eq. 2, and matrix O is calculated.

$$O = \begin{bmatrix} 1.0000 & 0.8947 & 1.3077 & 3.4000 & 9.0000 & 3.4000 & 5.6667 \\ 1.1176 & 1.0000 & 1.4615 & 3.8000 & 9.0000 & 3.8000 & 6.3333 \\ 0.7647 & 0.6842 & 1.0000 & 2.6000 & 9.0000 & 2.6000 & 4.3333 \\ 0.2941 & 0.2632 & 0.3846 & 1.0000 & 5.0000 & 1.0000 & 1.6667 \\ 0.1111 & 0.1111 & 0.1111 & 0.2000 & 1.0000 & 0.2000 & 0.3333 \\ 0.2941 & 0.2632 & 0.3846 & 1.0000 & 5.0000 & 1.0000 & 1.6667 \\ 0.1765 & 0.1579 & 0.2308 & 0.6000 & 3.0000 & 0.6000 & 1.0000 \end{bmatrix} \quad (7)$$

Secondly, a restaurants is selected as the starting point, and restaurants with similar characteristics are selected as recommendation schemes, and then each parameter value in the determination matrix S_m is calculated according to formula (1). Take one of the data sets as an example.

$$p_{1_{12}} = \frac{P_i(C_1|C_2)}{P_i(C_2|C_1)} = \frac{P_i(C_1)}{P_i(C_2)} \approx \frac{0.3438}{0.4667} \approx 0.7366 \quad (8)$$

$$S_1 = \begin{bmatrix} 1.0000 & 0.7366 & 0.5156 & 0.7563 \\ 1.3576 & 1.0000 & 0.7000 & 1.0267 \\ 1.9394 & 1.4286 & 1.0000 & 1.4667 \\ 1.3223 & 0.9740 & 0.6818 & 1.0000 \end{bmatrix} \quad (9)$$

Again, the maximum eigenvalues and eigenvectors are determined for all the judgment matrices, and consistency checks are performed for each matrix. If some matrices that do not meet the consistency requirements will be given appropriate corrections. Each eigenvalues that satisfies the conditions is calculated in the following Table 4.

Finally, all the result sets meeting the requirements are calculated, the matching degree of each target relative to the target is calculated.

$$H = [W_1, W_2, \cdots, W_7] * W_0 = [0.430426, 0.132522, 0.133675, 0.303377]^T \quad (10)$$

Table 4. Eigenvalues.

W_0	W_1	W_2	W_3	W_4	W_5	W_6	W_7
0.261922	0.178959	0.407407	0.313688	1.000000	0.407407	0.673469	1.000000
0.289411	0.241592	0.000000	0.334601	0.000000	0.000000	0.000000	0.000000
0.206945	0.345132	0.000000	0.209125	0.000000	0.000000	0.000000	0.000000
0.084426	0.235317	0.592593	0.142586	0.000000	0.592593	0.326531	0.000000
0.022215							
0.084426							
0.050656							

And then, It can be seen from the H value that the recommended scheme of the MSAHPB method is scheme 1. This is the same as the actual result.

4.2 Analysis of Results

In order to verify the usability of the method, we first conducted comparative experiments on different restaurants with multiple similarities by different methods. Ten restaurants were selected as references for the experiment, each with different feature. We used NBC as the control method. NBC is a method of recommendation based on Naive Bayes Classifier.

In the experiment, we selected the top five similarity degrees for grouping experiment. Under different similarities, the actual recommendation results are different. We recorded the results of the recommendations for each set of experiments and finally compiled the accuracy of the recommendations. Simultaneously, we conducted experiments on the data on a quarterly basis to demonstrate Bayesian reliability. The experimental results are shown in Figs. 3 and 4 below:

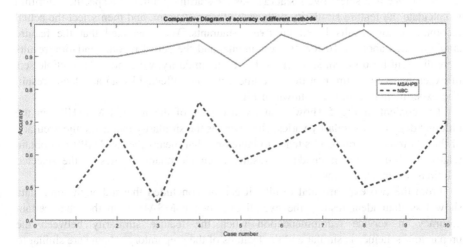

Fig. 3. Under the same conditions, the average accuracy of different recommended methods is compared.

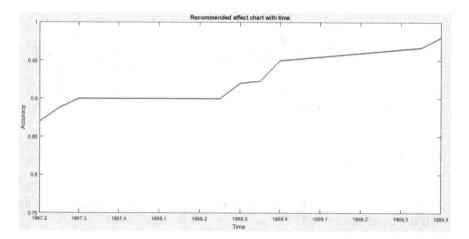

Fig. 4. The average accuracy of the recommended results of the MSAHP method increases with time.

As can be seen from the Figs. 3 and 4, in the case where the features of the plan restaurants are similar to the features of the reference restaurants, the accuracy of the recommended results based on each restaurant is relatively accurate. Besides, with the increase of data volume, the accuracy of the recommended results is improved. Inferred from this, our method is feasible in service recommendation. And through repeated experiments, when the situations of the preparatory programs are very similar, the accuracy of the recommended method can reach 0.93.

Then, In order to verify that MSAHPB can obtain relatively accurate recommendation results when the characteristics of the selected solutions are similar, we performed experiments on accuracy rate for different feature similarities in the same restaurant. We first select five restaurants-as the starting point, use a specific algorithm to calculate the feature similarity with each other restaurant, and then select the actual recommendation results based on five restaurants. We calculated that the feature similarity was about 6–10 for five restaurants, and the actual recommendation results were different for different similarities. For each similarity, we conducted multiple sets of experiments to ensure that the experiment was not affected by an accidental result. The experimental results are shown in Fig. 5:

The content in Fig. 5 shows that the accuracy of the method MSAHPB in the different degrees of similarity varies. However, as the similarity increases, the accuracy of the recommendation results tends to increase. That means the MSAHPB can obtain relatively accurate recommendation results when the characteristics of the selected solutions are much similar.

From the two experimental results, it can be concluded that although some data show less than ideal results, the overall display the MSAHPB method has certain accuracy in service recommendation when the feature similarity between the preparatory schemes is similar and the features of the preparatory scheme are similar to those of the reference sample.

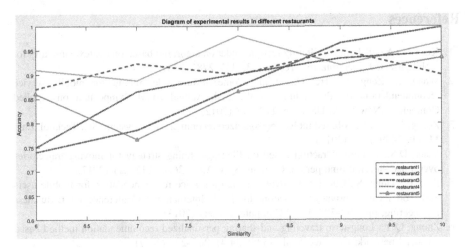

Fig. 5. Under the condition of certain similarity, the recommended result diagram of MSAHP method for different scene targets.

5 Conclusions

With the development of the mobile Internet service, users will expect the accuracy of mobile service recommendation increasingly, which requires technicians to continuously update the key methods to meet the needs of society. The Multi-situation Analytic Hierarchy Process based on Bayesian proposed in this paper, which reduces the interference of subjective factors to data analysis to a certain extent, and takes into account the influence of interactions between various situations on the recommendation results. Through the comparative experiments on different restaurants with multiple similarities, and the experiments on accuracy rate for different feature similarities in the same restaurant, we verify that when the user's situation is similar, the method can achieve relatively an accurate service recommendation result that is satisfactory to users. Besides, we consider the consistency test range and accuracy is limited, which may lead to a slight bias in the final recommendation results. In the ensuing work, we will continually explore and attempt to apply other test scales to the method, so as to achieve more efficient service recommendation.

Acknowledgements. This work is supported in part by the Ministry of Education's Funding for Returning Students Studying Abroad Projects of China (No. C2015003042), the Key Teaching Research project of Hebei University of Economics and Business (No. 2018JYZ06) and the Education technology research Foundation of the Ministry of Education (No. 2017A01020).

References

1. Xu, F.L.: A collaborative filtering recommendation algorithm based on context similarity for mobile users. J. Electron. Inf. Technol. **33**(11), 2785–2789 (2011)
2. Wang, J., Zeng, C., He, C., et al.: Context-aware role mining for mobile service recommendation. In: Proceedings of the 27th Annual ACM Symposium on Applied Computing. New York, USA, pp. 173–178 (2012)
3. Zhang, C.Y.: A LBS-based mobile personalized recommendation system. Sci. Technol. Eng. **11**(30), 7439–7442 (2011)
4. Yang, D.S.: Feature extraction based on filtering-refining strategy for moving trajectories over a user-specific time period. Comput. Syst. Appl. **26**(1), 217–221 (2017)
5. Piao, C., Dong, S., Cui, L.: A novel scheme on service recommendation for mobile users based on location privacy protection. In: IEEE International Conference on E-Business Engineering, pp. 300–305. IEEE Computer Society (2013)
6. Zhong, Q.Y.: Long-term traveling and sharing personalized recommendation method based on social network. Comput. Appl. Softw. **34**(4), 265–271 (2017)
7. Liu, S.D.: Approach to network services recommendation based on mobile users' location. J. Softw. **11**, 2556–2574 (2014)
8. Zhao, X.M.: A new fusion scene food recommendation algorithm. Comput. Modernization **7**, 20–24 (2015)
9. Shen, Y.G.: A context-aware collaborative filtering algorithm on mobile recommendation. Sci. Technol. Eng. **14**(8), 4–52 (2014)
10. Cimino, M.G.C.A., Lazzerini, B., Marcelloni, F., et al.: A collaborative situation-aware scheme for mobile service recommendation. In: International Conference on Intelligent Systems Design and Applications, pp. 130–135. IEEE (2012)
11. Xu, P.: Personalized travel route recommendation system based on naive bayesian method. Softw. Herald **14**(12), 152–154 (2015)
12. Ma, J.: Research on personalized document recommendation system of digital library based on bayesian network. Sci. Technol. Vis. **26**, 38–39 (2012)
13. Jiao, M.H.: Collaborative filtering recommendation based on bayesian network cognitive feedback. Control Eng. **24**(7), 1310–13179 (2017)
14. Bian, T.: Identifying influential nodes in complex networks based on AHP. Physica A Stat. Mech. Appl. **479**(4), 422–436 (2017)
15. Singh, R.P.: Analytical hierarchy process (AHP) application for reinforcement of hydropower strategy in Nepal. Renew. Sustain. Energy Rev. **55**, 43–58 (2016)
16. Deng, X.: Supplier selection using AHP methodology extended by D numbers. Expert Syst. Appl. **41**(1), 156–167 (2014)
17. Chatterjee, K.: Unified Granular-number-based AHP-VIKOR multi-criteria decision framework. Granular Comput. **2**(4), 1–23 (2017)
18. Liu, P.: Probabilistic linguistic TODIM approach for multiple attribute decision-making. Granular Comput. **12**, 1–10 (2017)
19. Zhang, J.J.: Fuzzy analytic hierarchy process. Fuzzy Syst. Math. **14**(2), 80–88 (2000)
20. Reinhardt, H.E.: Statistical decision theory and bayesian analysis. In: Berger, J.O. Statistical Decision Theory and Bayesian Analysis, pp. 85–93. Springer, New York (1985). https://doi.org/10.1007/978-1-4757-4286-2

Multi-source Enterprise Innovation Data Fusion Method Based on Hierarchy

Jinying Xu[1(✉)], Yuehua Lv[1], and Jieren Cheng[2]

[1] Zhejiang Science and Technology Information Institute,
Hangzhou 310006, China
793032295@qq.com
[2] Hainan University, Haikou 570228, China

Abstract. As a main body of innovation behavior, enterprise involves a lot of application systems, which accumulate a large amount of data resources. It is necessary to integrate enterprise innovation behavior data set to provide users with unified data view. This paper proposes a multi-source data fusion method based on multi-level. It describes the information fusion model from 3 levels: data level, feature level and decision level. The experimental results show that the fusion method can meet the needs of enterprise's innovation behavior in data fusion and decision analysis.

Keywords: Enterprise innovation behavior · Data fusion · Data layer
Feature layer · Decision layer

1 Introduction

As the main body of innovation behavior, enterprise involves many application systems in the process of production, R & D and service, and accumulates lots of innovative behavior data resources. The data has the following features, such as volume is large, the level of variables is large, and the unit composition is quite different. However, the data in a single application system is incomplete, integrated data which are formed by multiple system datas, can fully reflect the innovation capability of enterprises, and meet the integrated and intelligent application needs of enterprise innovation behavior. At present, different system data have different data patterns. Data integration needs to build a global and unified data mode to achieve multi-source data fusion.

Traditional relational database lacks performance, function and cost advantages when storing large data sets. It is more difficult to process and query large data sets. Therefore, it is urgent to design and optimize data storage models for big data.

Data fusion is a technology that aims at a certain decision task, uses various technologies to effectively synthesize and optimize multiple model data, obtains the consistency judgment of the data, and obtains more accurate and more stable decision results. The existing classical data fusion methods are mainly two types: reasoning based method, such as Bayesian inference [1], evidential reasoning [2], fuzzy reasoning neural [3], neural network reasoning [4], etc.; estimation based method, such as Maximum likelihood estimation [5], least square method [6], Calman filtering [7], particle filter [8], etc. Literature [9] has discussed the classic information fusion

© Springer Nature Switzerland AG 2018
X. Sun et al. (Eds.): ICCCS 2018, LNCS 11063, pp. 699–708, 2018.
https://doi.org/10.1007/978-3-030-00006-6_63

methods, algorithms, architectures and models. Thomopoulos has proposed 3 levels of fusion modeling based on signal level, evidence level and dynamic level, which can be sequentially completed and cross implemented. Pau has proposed a model of information fusion based on behavior knowledge, which fuses the original information attribute level after extracting, calibrating and associating the original data, the model. Zhong [10] has proposed a deep and shallow 2 layers feature fusion method to achieve complementarity between different levels of features. Xin [11] has used hesitant fuzzy sets correlation coefficient method to identify and identify multi-source heterogeneous data fusion in hesitant fuzzy framework. SUN [12] has proposed multi-attribute decision making, which is implemented in an interval framework by fusion data.

Based on the field research and detailed demand analysis of enterprise innovation behavior information, this paper integrates multi-source data distributed in different systems, and studies a method of multi-source data fusion based on hierarchical structure. The data fusion technology of enterprise innovation behavior filters and analyzes the data of service data, innovation features and enterprise information, and makes intelligent analysis of the comprehensive situation of enterprise innovation through a certain number of algorithms and rules.

This paper applies data fusion technology from 3 levels: data layer, feature layer and decision level to achieve data fusion. As shown in Fig. 1.

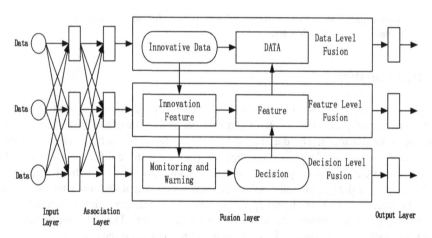

Fig. 1. Multi-source information fusion model for enterprise innovation behavior.

The information fusion of data layer collects enterprise innovation data, establishes the data information model, and eliminates redundant data and interfering noise, which makes model accurate and minimization of response to physical signs in order to enhance system preprocessing performance and ensure data quality. The information fusion of the feature layer extracts the feature information of the data to reflect the data attributes, and uses the association and fusion processing of the feature information to greatly reduce the storage of multidimensional information, which reduces the processing burden of the system and ensures the correctness of the results. Information fusion at the decision-making level is the fusion method that can directly reflect the change of target attributes in the fusion model. Based on the status information of multiple innovative feature parameters, it makes decisions on the enterprise's innovation behavior.

2   Information Fusion Model Based on Data Layer

The multi-source information for corporate innovation has the characteristics of multiple sources, heterogeneous, and time-varying. The research and construction of multi-source data fusion model realizes the joint perception of enterprise innovation behavior through the interconnection of data. The data level fusion constructs the information fusion model from 2 levels, which are atomic semantic model and compound information description model to realize the modeling of metadata and the storage of data Ontology, to describe the relationship between data and data and realize the unification of multi-source data.

2.1   Data Collection

Data sources are the basis of data fusion. The distributed data of corporate innovation behavior mainly comes from various types of structured, semi-structured and unstructured data generated during the production process of the enterprise, such as innovation service innovation project, technical data, data market data, enterprise data. Innovative service data includes service provider, service content, service contract, service amount and so on. Innovation project data includes data reporting, progress, acceptance, performance and so on. Technical market data includes technical achievements, technical requirements, contract registration and other information. Enterprise data includes enterprise type, R & D investment, scientific and technological achievements, enterprise sales revenue and other data.

The data acquisition is realized by combining the application system data extraction technology and the real-time data acquisition technology of Web data. The Segmentation Technology, ETL, XML and SQL Server transaction processing technology are used to extract application system's data of and web resource data to realize the synchronization of innovative data. The transformation of storing data to XML Schema documents, generation and uploading of XML files, mapping of XML files to corresponding tables of server data base are utilized, to realize the synchronous download and upload of data to achieve data integrity and consistency.

2.2   Data Information Model

The data information model is formed by atomic data model and composite information model from bottom to top. The atomic data model describes and represents the basic data concept of enterprise innovation behavior. The composite information model defines the relationship between atomic information models from system perspective. As shown in Fig. 2.

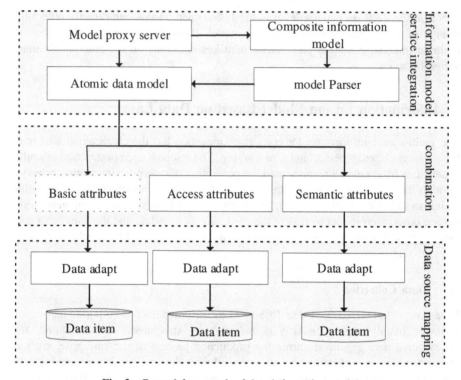

Fig. 2. General framework of data information model.

In this paper, we define atomic data model from 3 attributes, which are basic attributes, access attributes and semantic attributes. It corresponds to data item of database, and can be accessed individually as smallest data unit. Basic attributes refer to the most basic features of data,such as name, type, size, and so on. For example, the basic properties of patent are the patent's type, patent's number, patentee, date of authorization, and so on. These data represent the characteristics of the patent. Access attribute is the access rights of data, such as read-only, written, readable, and so on. Any data has access properties, such as the patent holder has the ownership. Semantic attributes refer to the descriptive semantics of data. For example, a patent belongs to an industrial field, and a paper contains research topics. By different adapter connections, the distributed heterogeneous data sources are mapped to persistent access objects, and encapsulated into atomic semantic models and stored in the semantic service library.

The composite information model is composed of multiple atomic data models to reflect the characteristic semantic information. There are basic and extended relationships. The basic relationship describes the qualitative relationship between data, such as "has role in" representing the role of data concept in another data concepts. For instance, the relationship between project leader and project indicates that the project leader plays some roles in the project. Extended relation describes the abstract relationship between data in the real process, such as "co-ordination" representing the coordination relationship between data concept and another data concept. For example, an innovative behavior needs the coordination of innovation and service resources between enterprises and enterprises achieves. We describe the big data of innovation behavior of small and medium-sized enterprises through composite information combination as information fusion model.

3 Information Fusion Model Based on Feature Layer Fusion

Feature level fusion is the subsequent fusion processing for feature information of enterprise innovation data. According to information characteristic index, it puts forward characteristic attribute and clustering data. Based on the analysis of the index of enterprise innovation capability in the existing research results [13–17], according to the characteristics of enterprises in the actual research process, this paper puts forward the index of enterprise innovation capability, which are combined with the availability of research purpose and data, as shown in Table 1.

Table 1. Index of enterprise innovation capability.

No	Field name	Type
1	Patent ownership for every 100 R & D personnel	Decimal
2	Number of papers published for every 100 R & D personnel	Decimal
3	Number of items for every 100 R & D personnel	Decimal
4	Proportion of funds for transformation activities in the funding of scientific and technological activities	Decimal
5	Proportion of technology absorption and expenditure in the introduction of Technology	Decimal
6	Proportion of the cost of technology introduction in scientific and technological activities	Decimal
7	Proportion of scientists in scientific and technological personnel	Decimal
8	Proportion of funds for the development of new products in scientific and technological activities	Decimal
9	Proportion of new products' Sales income in total sales income	Decimal

According to the indexes, we can process the original data of enterprises, extract the attributes that have important influence on the innovation ability of enterprises and reflect the characteristics of innovation, and take these attributes as the attribute sets of innovation characteristics. Based on the characteristic attribute sets of innovation, the clustering of enterprises is achieved by clustering the local distribution of enterprises samples, and enterprises with different characteristics are clustered.

In this paper, the K-means algorithm is used to divide the enterprise samples according to the enterprise innovation behavior. K-means algorithm is an automatic classification method, which is used to realize that difference between groups and groups is the biggest and the similarity between groups is the most.

The algorithm input values are the sample number of enterprise innovation behavior denoted by n, cluster number denoted by m, and sample data which are

704   J. Xu et al.

denoted by $c_1, c_2, c_3,..., c_n$ and used as cluster centers. These input value are finished preprocessing in data layer fusion. The output value is m classification model with n samples each of which is classified into a type of m arbitrary group. The algorithm performs the following instructions. First, calculate Euclidean distance between the remaining samples x and the cluster center. If

$$d(x,c_j) = \min\{d(x,c_i)\}i = \{1,2,..n\} \quad (1)$$

then $x \in X_j$ is divided into cluster X_j which is the nearest corresponding sample center c_j. Second, calculate the new cluster center for each sample cluster, using calculation formula:

$$c_j = \frac{1}{m}\sum_{x \in X_j} x\, j = \{1,2,..n\} \quad (2)$$

Where m is the number of samples in the class X_j. If the absolute value of the difference between the calculated value and the last calculated value is more than a given threshold:

$$|c_j - c_{j-1}| > \lambda j = \{1,2,..n\} \quad (3)$$

then repeats this instructions, else end.

4   Information Fusion Model Based on Decision Layer Fusion

Based on the combination of fuzzy information granulation technology and SVM modeling technology, this paper establishes an information fusion model based on decision level fusion, which uses the regression fitting ability of the model to restore database defect data and uses predict ability of the model to evaluate the innovation ability of enterprise comprehensively

4.1   Fuzzy Information Granulation

In order to improve the decision-making generalization ability of the information fusion model, the information granulation algorithm is used to preprocess the original data. The core idea of information granulation is to split the whole to the subpart, and define the similar and indistinguishable set of elements as information particles. At present, there are mainly 3 kinds of information granulation model based on Set Theory which are the model based on the theory of coarse sugar set, the model based on quotient space theory, and the model based on fuzzy set theory [18]. The uncertainty and incompleteness of the data for enterprise innovation behavior conforms to the characteristics of fuzzy set theory which conforms to the characteristics of fuzzy sets theory to effectively deal with knowledge and ability with uncertainty and incompleteness. So this paper selects information granulation method based on fuzzy set theory to preprocess data.

Fuzzy information granulation algorithm uses fuzzy set to represent information granules, and decomposes whole into several subset. Each information particle is a subset containing max, mid and min 3 parameters.

$$A(x, min, mid, max) = \begin{cases} 0 & x < min \\ \frac{x-min}{mid-min} & min \leq x \leq mid \\ 0 & x < a \\ \frac{max-x}{max-mid} & mid < x \leq max \\ 0 & x > max \end{cases} \qquad (4)$$

where min represents the minimum change of the information particle data, mid represents the average level of the data in the information particles, max represents the maximum value of the change of the data in the information particles.

4.2 Support Vector Machine Prediction Model

Support vector machine (SVM) is a classical classification algorithm, which is based on statistical machine learning theory and structural risk minimization principle on the basis of learning methods. Its core idea is to set high feature space by mapping inseparable data and realize correct and reasonable partition of the sample in the high latitude space.

This paper assumes that linear separable samples is (x_i, y_i), where $x_i \in R^d$, $x_i \in \{-1, +1\}$ and $i \in \{1, 2, \ldots m\}$. In order to solve the nonlinear problem, radial basis function is selected as the kernel function which is

$$K(t, t_a) = \exp\left(-\gamma |t - t_a|^2\right) \qquad (5)$$

where t_a represents the center of the kernel function, and the width parameter of the function is expressed by γ which controls the radial action range of the function. In order to obtain the objective function and constraint condition of the regression problem, according to the maxmil-margin principle and derivation of Vapnik et al., we get:

$$\begin{cases} \min \frac{1}{2} \|\omega\|^2 + C \sum_i (\varepsilon_i + \varepsilon_i^*) \\ |y_i - \omega \cdot x_i - b| \leq \varepsilon_i \end{cases} \qquad (6)$$

where ω is the weight vector, b is biased, C is fault-tolerant penalty factor, ε_i is relaxation factor and $\varepsilon_i \geq 0$. We supposes ε_i is 2 in the article. According to the Lagrange theorem, the dual description of the optimization problem is obtained:

$$\begin{cases} \max \sum_{i=0}^m b_i - \frac{1}{2} \sum_{i=1}^m \sum_{j=1}^m b_i b_j y_i y_i (x_i . x_j) \\ \text{s.t.} \sum_{j=1}^m b_{ji} y_j = 0 (0 \leq b_j \leq C) \end{cases} \qquad (7)$$

where b_i is not 0 and b_i's corresponding sample is called the support vector. It reveals that part of training samples which are at the edge of distribution play a key role in classifying. If the sample set (x_i, y_i) is linear inseparable where $x_i \in R^{d\Xi}$ and $x_i \in \{-1, +1\}$, $i \in \{1, 2, \ldots m\}$, the optimal classification surface is constructed by using nonlinear mapping to divide the high dimensional linear separable of the input space. According to relationship

$$K(x_i, y_i) = \;<\Phi(x_i)\Phi(x_j)> \tag{8}$$

where $K(x_i, y_i)$ satisfied the Mercer condition, we infer linear nonseparable sample optimal classification function:

$$f(x) = sgn\left\{\sum\nolimits_{i=1}^{1} a_i y_i K(x_i, x_j) + b\right\} \tag{9}$$

5 Analysis of Experimental Results

In order to verify the performance of the multi-layer structure model in the realization of large data fusion, simulation experiment is carried out on the enterprise innovation behavior data. Business application system data and web data are collected,which are in the innovation fields for 4 thousand small and medium sized enterprises of science and technology in Zhejiang, and describe innovative behavior information such as research projects, patents, new products, papers, technical services, etc. According to Table 1 and formula (1)–(9), multi level enterprise multi-source data model is applied to enterprise innovation behavior dataset. Compared with other classical fusion algorithm, the average response time is taken as the test index. Fusion method is better than the other two algorithms in the response time of large data fusion to some degree, and support the application requirements of enterprise innovation behavior in data fusion and decision analysis, as shown in Figs. 3 and 4.

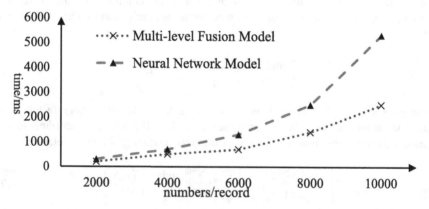

Fig. 3. Average response time test result of multi-level fusion model and neural network model.

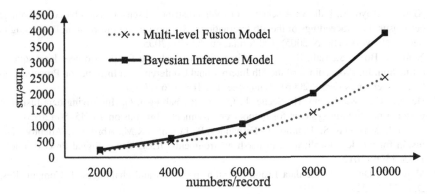

Fig. 4. Average response time test result of multi-level fusion model and Bayesian inference model.

6 Conclusion

In this paper, the data of enterprise innovation behavior has the characteristics of large amount of data, multiple levels of variable and large difference in element, and the problem of incomplete data in a single application system. In order to form a data set of enterprise innovation behavior and provide a unified data view for users, this paper proposes a multi-level enterprise data fusion model based on data layer, feature layer and decision layer. The experimental result shows that the multi-level information fusion model can support the needs of enterprise innovation behavior in data integration analysis, which can help the enterprise innovation behavior monitoring and improve the efficiency of distributed data integration.

Acknowledgment. This work is partially supported by Social Development Project of Public Welfare Technology Application of Zhejiang Province [LGF18F020019], the National Natural Science Foundation of China [61762033, 61702539], Major science and technology special projects of Zhejiang Province [2015C01040], Soft Science Project of Zhejiang Province [2017C25027, 2016C35069].

References

1. Guerriero, M., Svensson, L., Willett, P.: Bayesian data fusion for distributed target detection in sensor networks. IEEE Trans. Signal Process. **58**(6), 3417–3421 (2010)
2. Garvey, T.D., Lowrance, J.D., Fischler, M.A.: An inference technique for integrating knowledge from disparate sources. In: Proceedings of the 7th International Joint Conference on Artificial Intelligence (IJCAI 1981), Columbia, pp. 319–325 (1981)
3. Gupta, I., Riordan, D., Sampalli, S.: Cluster-head election using fuzzy logic for wireless sensor networks. In: Proceedings of the 3rd Annual Communication Networks and Services Research Conference (CNSR 2005), Halifax, pp. 255–260 (2015)
4. Filippidis, A., Jain, L.C., Martin, N.: Fusion of intelligent agents for the detection of aircraft in SAR images. IEEE Trans. Pattern Anal. Mach. Intell. **22**(4), 378–384 (2000)

5. Xiao, L., Boyd, S., Lall, S.: A scheme for robust distributed sensor fusion based on average consensus. In: Proceedings of the 4th International Symposium on Information Processing in Sensor Networks (IPSN 2005), California, pp. 63–70 (2005)

6. Xiao, L., Boyd, S., Lall, S.: A space-time diffusion scheme for peer-to-peer least-squares estimation. In: Proceedings of the 5th International Conference on Information Processing in Sensor Networks (IPSN 2006), Tennessee, pp. 168–176 (2006)

7. Herrera, E.P., Kaufmann, H., Secue, J., Quirós, R., Fabregat, G.: Improving data fusion in personal positioning systems for outdoor environments. Inf. Fusion 14, 45–56 (2013)

8. Prieto, J., Mazuelas, S., Bahillo, A., Fernandez, P., Lorenzo, R.M., Abril, E.J.: Adaptive data fusion for wireless localization in harsh environments. IEEE Trans. Signal Process. 60(4), 1585–1596 (2012)

9. Meng, X., Du, Z.: Large data fusion research: problems and challenges. J. Comput. Res. Dev. 53(2), 229–246 (2016)

10. Zhong, W., Fang, X., Hang, H.: The features of the deep layer and the model fusion of speaker recognition. Acoust. J. 43(2), 263–272 (2018)

11. Xin, G., Sun, G., Xiao, Y.: Multi source heterogeneous data fusion and recognition based on statistical correlation coefficient of hesitant fuzzy sets. Syst. Eng. Electron Technol. 40(3), 509–517 (2018)

12. Sun, G., Guan, X.: Research on hybrid multi-attribute decision-making. In: International Conference on Cyber-Enabled Distributed Computing and Knowledge Discovery 2016, Henan, pp. 272–277 (2016)

13. Xu, L., Jiang, X., Chong, Y.: Enterprise innovation ability evaluation index system of scientific research management. Sci. Res. Manage. (S1), 126–122 (2015)

14. Danli, D., Zeng, X.: The research on comprehensive evaluation of high-tech enterprise innovation ability of China's scientific research management. Dyn. Veloc. Featur. Perspect. 38(07), 44–53 (2017)

15. Zhou, J., Jun, T.: Investigation and analysis of innovative behavior of high tech enterprises and high tech enterprises. Shanghai Econ. Res. (1), 68–76 (2017)

16. Li, C., Ping, L.: Evaluation of technological innovation capability of electric power enterprises based on cloud model. Res. Sci. Technol. Manag. 2, 68–72 (2017)

17. Yang, S., Luo, W.: Research on the evaluation of independent innovation ability of industrial enterprises. Jiangsu Sci. Technol. Inf. 2, 23–26 (2017)

18. Zhang, S., Zhu, J., Liu, X.: Asymmetric fuzzy language consensus model based on information granulation. Syst. Eng. Electron Technol. 37(10), 2304–2317 (2015)

Network Public Opinion Emotion Classification Based on Joint Deep Neural Network

Xiaoling Xia[✉], Wenjie Wang[✉], and Guohua Yang[✉]

Donghua University, Shanghai, China
sherlysha@dhu.edu.cn, wwjlea@163.com,
yangguohua@beyondbit.com

Abstract. The analysis of the emotional tendency of public opinion data in the network can help to grasp the dynamics of public opinion in a timely and accurate way, and extract the trend of public opinions. At present, the neural network model has been proved to have a good performance in sentiment classification. Therefore, according to the characteristics of public opinion information, this paper proposes a joint deep neural network to extract high-dimensional features of word-level convolutional neural network (CNN), and then input it into the long short term memory network (LSTM) to learning sequence characteristics. This model was used to emotionally categorize the Weibo commentary data of "Yulin Maternal Jumping Event" and obtained high classification accuracy.

Keywords: Emotional classification · Convolutional neural network
Long short term memory network · Public opinion analysis

1 Introduction

With the rapid development of Internet communication technology, the number of Chinese Internet users has reached 772 million. Web applications such as Weibo, blogs, forums, and news have undoubtedly become the largest public opinion sites in social life. For example, as of September 2017, Weibo monthly active users totaled 376 billion, a year-on-year increase of 27% compared to 2016. With the explosive development of traditional portal websites and new media platforms, the enthusiasm and participation of the public in participating in online interactions has been skyrocketing. As a result, a large amount of valuable public information with subjective opinions has been generated by users. Through the analysis of these information, we can understand the attitudes and opinions of public opinion on a certain policy, event, or product, extract the trend of public opinion, accurately collect the opinions of the people, grasp the trend, and help the government and enterprises make timely and effective decisions.

There are a lot of satire, metaphor, and non-mainstream ideas in public sentiment information, and the syntactic structure is not standardized. However, the feature extraction method based on text statistics [1] and knowledge dictionary [2] in traditional sentiment analysis technology only considers the morphological contact between

© Springer Nature Switzerland AG 2018
X. Sun et al. (Eds.): ICCCS 2018, LNCS 11063, pp. 709–718, 2018.
https://doi.org/10.1007/978-3-030-00006-6_64

characters or words, often ignores much connotation information. It is difficult to make emotional judgements for public opinion information that needs to consider deep meanings. Deep learning can learn complex functions by construction a nonlinear multilayer network structure. [3] confirmed the effectiveness of deep learning in natural language processing and verified the ability to learn deep-seated structured semantic information.

In the mainstream deep learning emotion classification neural network model, the classification method based on CNN (convolutional neural network) or RNN (Recurrent neural network) performs better [4, 5]. CNN can extract high-dimensional features from different parts of the sentence through a convolution filter, but lacks the ability to learn the sequence correlation of sentences. RNN has good continuous modeling capabilities but cannot extract features in parallel. Therefore, this paper combines the advantages of two kinds of neural network structures and adopts a joint deep learning model to conduct sentiment analysis on the public opinion information in the network.

2   Related Work

2.1   Sentiment Classification Research

Sentiment classification is to determine the positive and negative sentiment of document-level, sentence-level or element-level comment texts. According to the classification of learning methods, sentiment classification can be divided into supervised, semi-supervised or unsupervised research methods. This paper studies supervised sentiment analysis. In 2002, Pang et al. [6] proposed the concept of text classification for the first time. Supervised machine learning methods (Bayes, maximum entropy, and support vector machines, etc.) were used to classify the impact assessment data and achieved good results. The semi-supervised classification method is suitable for classification with only a few marked data, and has less dependence on the test set's domain, topic, and time limit. Self-learning was used to expand the scale of positive and negative sentiment annotation, and iterative learning was used to improve the accuracy of SVM sentiment classification. Li et al. [7] proposed a semi-supervised machine leaning algorithm to dynamically generate new corpus in different stochastic subspaces to solve the problem of unbalanced corpus. The unsupervised leaning method is applicable to datasets without emotional tagging information, and emotion classification should be performed through prior knowledge. Zagibalov et al. [8] achieved unsupervised sentiment classification methods for Chinese product data by automatically selecting seed words.

2.2   Research on Sentiment Classification Based on Deep Learning

Deep learning simulates the human brain for analysis and learning. The data is transformed into a high-level, abstract feature expression through a superimposed model of multilayer nonlinear network. It has been successfully applied in image processing and speech recognition, so it also provides a new idea for emotional classification. Glorot et al. [9] applied deep learning methods to the sentiment analysis of large-scale online reviews. By extracting deeper text expression features, the accuracy was greatly improved. Mikolov et al. [10] optimized the neural network model and proposed RNN. By using the hidden layer repeatedly, a new hidden layer is calculated jointly with the newly added timing information. Therefore, the hidden layer contains all the context semantic information, which reduces the parameters and reduced complexity. In 2012, Sundermeyer et al. [11] explained how to use the LSTM (Long Short Term Memory Recurrent Neural Network) to construct a language model, which can solve the problem of long-distance dependence of text content. In 2015, Liu et al. [12] used LSTM with different length and time steps to perform emotion classification. In 2014 Kim [13] used CNN to classify preprocessed word vectors and achieved high classification accuracy. Lee [14] used CNN and RNN to texts and sent them to ANN for classification.

At present, most of the Chinese text sentiment classification still stays in the shallow machine learning stage. In view of the urgent need for performance improvement of sentiment classification in online public opinion analysis, this paper proposes a joint deep learning model for sentence-level sentiment analysis of traditional shallow sentiment classification models, combining the advantages of CNN which the multi-layer convolution structure can extract high-level abstract features and the advantages of LSTM for training sequence texts, put CNN and LSTM in a unified architecture for semantic modeling.

3   Joint Deep Neural Network

3.1   Fundamental

This paper applies CNN to text data and extracts high-dimensional features through convolution operations. In order not to disturb the original sequence of data, this experiment does not perform pooling operation. Finally, the extracted continuous features are sent to the LSTM network. This structure enables remote dependencies to be learned from higher-order sequence features. Therefore, in theory, compared with the traditional CNN and LSTM networks, this network can combine the advantages of both, learn long-term dependencies from the characteristics of high-dimensional sequence to classify. Therefore, the network may have a good applicability to comment data classification. The final output of the model is the last hidden layer unit of the LSTM. Since the final sentiment analysis result is positive and negative, we finally choose sigmoid as the classification function to obtain the final sentiment classification results. The model structure is shown in Fig. 1.

3.2   Feature Extraction Based on Convolution

The convolutional neural network consists of a convolutional layer and a pooling layer. The neurons in the convolutional layer share the convolutional kernel to obtain the feature map through the convolution operation. Next, the pooling layer further generalizes the features, such as calculating the maximum or average values of the feature values of the subdomains. The convolution operation for the text is a one-dimensional

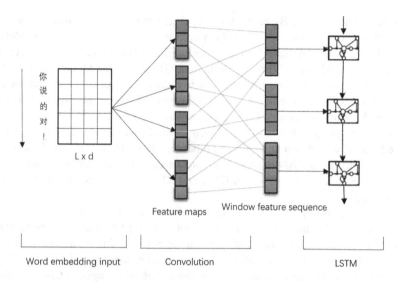

Fig. 1. Joint deep learning sentiment classification model

convolution operation. A filter slides over the text sequence and extracts features at different location in the text. If $x_i \in R^{L \times d}$ represents the i-th d-dimensional word vector in a sentence of length L and the vector $m \in R^{k \times d}$ is a filter for the convolution operation, which k is the length of the filter. Then for any position j in a sentence, a window vector w_j with k consecutive word vectors obtained by convolution can be denoted as:

$$w_j = [x_j, x_{j+1}, \cdots, x_{j+k-1}] \tag{1}$$

The convolution kernel m performs a convolution operation on the input vector to generate the feature map $c \in R_{L-k+1}$. Each element c_j of the feature map for the window vector w_j is produced as follows, where $b \in R$ is a bias term and f is the activation function:

$$cj = f(wj \circ m + b) \tag{2}$$

The nonlinear transformation function chosen in this paper is ReLU, and uses different length filters to generate multiple feature maps, thereby extracting different feature vectors in the sentence. Usually in CNN pooling will continue after convolution, but pooling will disrupt the original order of the data. The LSTM depends on the sequence characteristics of the original word sequence. Therefore, this model will not apply pooling after the convolution operation.

3.3   LSTM

The judgment of one sentence emotion is not relying on a word in isolation, but connecting each word in a sentence to understand the emotion of the sentence, and the more backward a word is, the more it can represent the commenter's emotions. However, the traditional neural network cannot process continuous data input, while the RNN can save information in the network, and has the features of post-iterators are more important, therefore is widely used in natural language processing. However, RNN has the problem of gradient extinction when dealing with long distance dependencies. LSTM improves the traditional RNN, remember the information of the previous nodes through the 'gate mechanism', and the hidden layer nodes are replaced by the short-term memory storage grid to save important information for a long time, which solves the long-distance dependence problem and is suitable for the processing of sequence data. LSTM networks has a series of duplicate modules at each step for the traditional RNN. Assume that the current time is t, x_t is the input word vector at time t, the oblivion gate is f_t, the input gare is i_t, and the output gate is o_t. These gates together determine how to update the current memory cell c_t and the current hidden neuron stare h_t. Using d to represent the dimensions of all vectors in the LSTM architecture, the transfer function of the LSTM is defined as follows:

$$i_t = \sigma(W_i \cdot [h_{t-1}, x_t] + b_i) \tag{3}$$

$$f_t = \sigma\left(W_f \cdot [h_{t-1}, x_t] + b_f\right) \tag{4}$$

$$q_t = tanh\left(W_q \cdot [h_{t-1}, x_t] + b_q\right) \tag{5}$$

$$c_t = f_t \odot c_{t-1} + i_t \odot q_t \tag{6}$$

$$h_t = o_t \odot tanh\left(c_t\right) \tag{7}$$

Here $\odot$ denotes vector multiplication by elements, f_t is used to control how much information is to be discarded from old memory cells, i_t determines how much information to store in the current memory cell, o_t determines what to output from the current memory cell. From the above formula, we can see that LSTM can solve the problem of long-term dependence of sequence data. Therefore, we choose to input the high-dimensional sequence features extracted from convolution into LSTM to learn the long-term dependence relationships exiting in the sentences.

3.4   Word Vector Training

In NLP, the most commonly used word vector representation methods is one-hot representation and distributed representation. The former is simple to represent, but the similarities between words cannot be characterized, and it is easy to cause dimensional disasters and it is difficult to apply them to deep learning algorithms. Word2vec is a shallow neural network model that Mikolov [15] introduced in his research that converts words into word vectors. After the conversion, semantically similar word vectors have similar distances in space. Therefore, the word2vec is used to training word vector in this paper.

First remove duplicates and remove comments less than 5 words for all acquired corpus. There is a problem of word segmentation and removal of stop words in the Chinese text analysis. Because it is impossible to determine whether removal of the stop word can improve the final classification result, the results of the word2vec training under different stop words are compared below. After the segmentation of the text, two different stop word lists are used to remove the stop words. The stop word list 1 contains Chinese punctuation and commonly used helper words, a total of 782 stop words. Stop word list 2 only includes commonly used punctuation. After removing the stop words, word2vec is used to conduct word vector training. Through modeling, semantically similar words are grouped together in the word vector space. The following results can be obtained by word vector training (Tables 1 and 2).

Table 1. word2vec training results (remove stop words based on stop word list 1).

Five words related to "酒店"		Five words related to "医院"	
Name	Degree of association	Name	Degree of association
店	0.7042416334152222	家属	0.9720237355096436
宾馆	0.6871802210807800	医生	0.9699680805206299
饭店	0.6824790239334106	产妇	0.9555250406265259
如家	0.6337162852287292	谁	0.9371803998947144
想订	0.6082584857940674	孩子	0.9200285673141480

Table 2. word2vec training results (remove stop words based on stop word list 2).

Five words related to "酒店"		Five words related to "医院"	
Name	Degree of association	Name	Degree of association
如家	0.8586675214767456	医生	0.9900782108306885
大酒店	0.8341443729400635	家属	0.9718022346496582
首都	0.8079073524475098	孩子	0.9485532641410828
一家	0.7938951253890991	产妇	0.9483207464218145
优质	0.7839782238006592	风险	0.9141252040863037

Based on the training results above, it can be seen that the results of removing the stop words according to the stop word 2 are better. And the above results are input into the joint neural network for training, the word vector trained with the stop word list 1 generates a severe overfitting phenomenon. It can be seen that removing a large number of stop words does not necessarily improve the experimental results, but will result in an overfitting phenomenon. Therefore, the following experiments in this paper use the stop word list 2 to remove the stop words and only remove the common punctuation marks.

4 Experimental Results and Analysis

4.1 Experimental Dataset

The dataset for emotional classification in this experiment is mainly originates from Weibo's commentary on "Yulin Maternal Jumping Event" obtained through crawlers, and after removing the empty comments and short comments with less than 5 words, 90580 pieces of data remain. Due to the lack of annotated data, 10000 records of Tansongbo Hotel's comments, and 10000 pieces of annotation data in the evaluation task of NLPCC2014 (the 3rd Natural Language Processing and Chinese Computing Conference) and 4000 pieces of annotation data in the evaluation task of COAE2016 (the 7th Chinese Orientation Analysis and Evaluation) were added to the training data, as shown in the table below. All data are ultimately divided into positive and negative emotions (Table 3).

Table 3. Experimental dataset distribution.

Data sources	Number of comments	Data usage
1 Crawled comments	10000 (3147 positive review)	Training, test model
2 hotel reviews	10000 (7000 positive review)	
3 NLPCC 2014	10000 (5000 positive review)	
4 COAE 2016	4000 (2000 positive review)	
5 Crawled comments	80580	Emotional classification with model

In all reviews used for neural network training, 80% is used for neural network modeling and 20% is used for testing of model effects. The neural network modeling process uses random cross-validation method in which 80% is used for training and 20% is used to evaluate the convergence effect of each iteration.

4.2 Model Parameter Settings

This experiment was divided into two groups. The first group of experiments compared the classification accuracy of joint neural network under different parameter settings. The second set of experiments compares the accuracy of the neural network model of this paper with the accuracy of other neural network models. the ReLU function was used as an activation function throughout the experiment and drop out were used to prevent over-fitting. Table 4 shows the parameter settings in the CNN and LSTM.

4.3 Experimental Results

The experimental method of the first group is the single factor variable method. The joint deep neural network is adjusted by different factors. The number of filters n and the filter window size is m. The comparison experiment results are show in Table 5.

The experimental results show that the use of different filter sizes and numbers will have an impact on the experimental results. The accuracy increases with the number of

Table 4. Model parameter settings.

Parameter/Function name	Parameter/Function settings
Activation function	ReLU
Drop out probability	0.25
L2 regularization	0.001
Word vector dimension	100
Length of filters	3
Number of filters	64
Batch-size	32
Number of iterations	50

Table 5. Sorting results for different filter numbers n and filter window size m.

n	m = 3	m = 4	m = 4, 5	m = 3, 4, 5
20	89.0%	88.1%	88.0%	89.1%
50	91.5%	89.4%	89.9%	90.8%
100	91.9%	91.5%	91.1%	90.2%
200	91.6%	91.0%	90.5%	89.9%
300	90.8%	91.1%	90.4%	88.8%

filters increases, but when the number exceeds 100, the accuracy starts to fluctuate, and the improvement effect began to be less obvious. Different from the expected result, comparing the accuracy of experiments using filters of the same size and multiple filters of different sizes, using a single convolution layer of the same size yields better results and when the convolution kernel size is 3, the classification result is best. Therefore, for the experimental data, convolution kernel size 3 is used for single layer convolution operation.

The second group compares the classification accuracy of the joint deep neural network with other machine learning models. The models being compared are as follows:

Model 1: SVM model,
Model2: Logistic Regression model,
Model3: CNN model with four convolutional layers,
Model4: Single-layer LSTM model,
Model5: This paper's CNN and LSTM joint model.

Five tests were performed for each model. Each time, 20% of the public opinion were randomly selected as the test. The remaining data sets were used for training. The final average classification accuracy of the five tests was shown in Table 6.

According to the experimental results, it can be seen that the joint deep neural networks in this paper has the highest accuracy of sentiment classification compared with other single neural networks. The accuracy of the deep learning model is more than 10% higher than that of the shallow learning model. This is because the shallow

Table 6. Comparison of model accuracy

Model for emotional classification	Accuracy
SVM	76.60%
Logistic regression	75.10%
CNN	86.73%
LSTM	85.80%
CNN+LSTM	91.86%

machine learning method fails to fully consider the semantics of the corpus and the word order information, while the CNN can extract the higher-level features through the convolution operation and therefore has better classification performance. Due to the large proportion of short commentaries in the corpora of the public opinion message, most of the comments are within 40 words. Therefore, the single LSTM in model 4 does not perform well and its accuracy is not high.

5 Summary and Outlook

This paper combining CNN with LSTM and verified it on the internet public opinion emotion classification of a topic. The convolutional neural network is equivalent to a feature extractor. It learns the high-dimensional features of the phrase level through a convolution layer, and passes the extracted high-dimensional sequence features into the LSTM to learn long-term dependency features in sequence data. Experiments have verified the effectiveness of the joint neural network for short public opinion text sentiment classification and achieved good accuracy. The next research focuses on the optimization of the joint deep neural network model in this paper, and uses this model in conjunction with the theme of public opinion for more detailed emotional classification.

References

1. Liu, B., Huang, T., Cheng, J.: The automatic text classification method based on statistics. J. Chin. Inf. Process. **16**(6), 18–24 (2002)
2. Qin, X., Yuan, C.A., Peng, Y.: Based on the dictionary method and genetic algorithm for text feature extraction. Comput. Eng. Des. **29**(21), 5651–5654 (2008)
3. Zheng, W.L., Zhu, J.Y., Peng, Y.: EEG-based emotion classification using deep belief networks. In: IEEE International Conference on Multimedia and Expo, pp. 1–6. IEEE Press, Chengdu (2014)
4. Zhai, S., Zhang, Z.: Semisupervised autoencoder for sentiment analysis. In: Proceedings of the Thirtieth AAAI Conference on Artificial Intelligence, pp. 1394–1400. AAAI Press, Phoenix (2016)
5. Socher, R., Huval, B., Manning, D.: Semantic compositionality through recursive matrix-vector spaces. In: Proceedings of the Conference on Empirical Methods in Natural Language Processing, pp. 1201–1211. ACL, Jeju Island (2012)

6. Pang, B., Lee, L.: A sentimental education: sentiment analysis using subjectivity summarization based on minimum cuts. In: The Association for Computational Linguistics, pp. 271–278. ACL, Bulgaria (2004)

7. Li, S., Wang, Z., Zhou, G., Lee, S.Y.M.: Semi-supervised learning for Imbalanced Sentiment Classification. In: Proceeding of International Joint Conference on Artificial Intelligence, pp. 1826–1831. IJCAI/AAAI, Barcelona (2011)

8. Zagibalov, T., Carroll, J.: Automatic seed word selection for unsupervised sentiment classification of Chinese text. In: Proceedings of the 22nd International Conference on Computational Linguistics, pp. 1073–1080. Coling 2008 Organizing Committee, Manchester (2008)

9. Glorot, X., Bordes, A., Bengio, Y.: Domain adaptation for large scale sentiment classification: a deep learning approach. In: Proceedings of the 28th International Conference on Machine Learning, pp. 513–520. Omnipress, Bellevue (2011)

10. Mikolov, T., Zweig, G.: Context dependent recurrent neural network language model. In: IEEE Spoken Language Technology Workshop, pp. 234–239. IEEE, Miami (2012)

11. Sundermeyer, M., Schluter, R., Ney, H.: LSTM neural networks for language modeling. In: 13th Annual Conference of the International Speech Communication Association, pp. 194–197. ISCA, Portland (2012)

12. Liu, P.F., Qiu, X.P., Chen X.CH.: Multi timescale long short-term memory neural network for modelling sentences and documents. In: Proceedings of the 2015 Conference on Empirical Methods in Natural Language Processing, pp. 2326–2335. ACL, Lisbon, Portugal (2015)

13. Kim, Y.: Convolutional neural networks for sentence classification. In: Proceedings of the 2014 Conference on Empirical Methods in Natural Language Processing, pp. 1746–1751. ACL, Doha (2014)

14. Lee, J.Y., Dernoncourt, F.: Sequential short-text classification with recurrent and convolutional neural networks. In: The 2016 Conference of the North American Chapter of the Association for Computational Linguistics, pp. 515–520. ACL, San Diego (2016)

15. Milkolov, T., Kombrink, S., Burget, L.: Extensions of recurrent neural network language model. In: IEEE International Conference on Acoustics, Speech & Signal Processing, pp. 5528–5531. IEEE, Prague Congress Center, Prague (2011)

Optimizing Cuckoo Feature Selection Algorithm with the New Initialization Strategy and Fitness Function

Yingying Wang, Zhanshan Li$^{(\boxtimes)}$, Haihong Yu, and Lei Deng

College of Computer Science and Technology, Jilin University, Changchun, China
zslizsli@163.com
http://ccst.jlu.edu.cn/index.htm

Abstract. In machine learning and data mining tasks, feature selection is an important process of data preprocessing. Recent studies have shown that Binary Cuckoo Search Algorithm for Feature Selection (BCS [1]) has the better ability to classification and dimension reduction. However, by analyzing BCS algorithm, we notice that the randomness of initialization and the defects of fitness function severely weaken the classification performance and dimension reduction. Therefore, we propose a new feature selection algorithm FS_CSO, which adopts the chaotic properties of the Chebyshev as a new initialization strategy to get the better original populations (solutions), and combines the information gain and the L1-norm as a new fitness function to accelerate the convergence of the algorithm. We validate FS_CSO with various experimental data on small, medium and large datasets on the UCI dataset. In the experiment, FS_CSO uses the KNN, J48 and SVM classifiers to guide the learning process. The experimental results show that FS_CSO has a significant improvement in classification performance and dimension reduction. Comparing the FS_CSO algorithm with the more efficient feature selection algorithms proposed in recent years, FS_CSO is highly competitive in terms of accuracy and dimension reduction.

Keywords: FS_CSO · Fitness function · Initialization strategy
Feature selection

1 Introduction

Feature selection can remove the irrelevant and redundant features so that it can avoid the disaster of dimension, reduce the difficulty of classifier learning, and improve classification performance [2]. The reason why feature selection is a difficult problem is that the search space increases exponentially with the number of features [3]. In the case of a large amount of data, the exhaustive

---

Supported by National Natural Science Foundation of China (No. 61672261); Jilin province natural science foundation (No. 20180101043JC).

© Springer Nature Switzerland AG 2018
X. Sun et al. (Eds.): ICCCS 2018, LNCS 11063, pp. 719–730, 2018.
https://doi.org/10.1007/978-3-030-00006-6_65

method is not feasible, and most algorithms are subject to locally optimal or computationally expensive problems.

In recent years, many scholars have applied evolutionary algorithms such as Genetic Algorithms (GA), Particle Swarm Optimization (PSO) and Ant Colony Algorithm (ACO) to feature selection and obtained good results in terms of time efficiency. For example, Zhu et al. [4] proposed a feature selection algorithm combining genetic algorithm and local search method. Tabacchi et al. [5] proposed an unsupervised feature selection algorithm for ant colony optimization (UFSACO). Rodrigues and Yang et al. [1] converted the cuckoo algorithm into a binary form, which was then applied to the feature selection algorithm.

Yang [9] proposed the cuckoo search algorithm (CS) which is a new metaheuristic search algorithm. Then Rodrigues and Yang et al. [1] proposed a feature selection algorithm based on the binary cuckoo algorithm (BCS). Compared with other evolutionary algorithms, BCS generally has higher classification accuracy and better generalization performance. However, we find some drawbacks of BCS algorithm. On the one hand, when BCS algorithm initializes nests, it only uses a random method (that is, randomly selects some features from the n-dimensional features into the feature subset) to complete the initialization process, which is too blind and arbitrary to get the better original populations, and usually obtains the worse populations. The random initialization process may result in an inability to obtain the optimal feature subset in subsequent iterations. On the other hand, the fitness function that measures the pros and cons of nests in the BCS algorithm is too simple to take into account the relevance of feature, category and dimension reduction. Therefore, it is not guaranteed that the subset of features with high accuracy and low dimension can be obtained. Obviously, a suitable fitness function is particularly important.

Tan [6] research shows that the Chaos phenomenon lies between certainty and randomness, has exquisite internal structure, and has the gradual phenomenon of ergodicity, regularity and randomness. It can not only overcome premature convergence by ensuring that the global optimum solutions being found, but also guarantee the search speed by making the algorithm have good performance. The research by Lai [7] and Liu [8] shows that the information gain can measure the correlation between features and categories and L1-norm can measure the sparsity of the matrix respectively.

Based on the above analysis, we propose two key improvements to the BCS algorithm. First, using the Chebyshev chaotic phenomenon to initialize nests can make the internal structure of nests more refined and avoid the blindness caused by excessive randomness. At the same time, we need a more appropriate fitness function to search for a better nest. Information gain measures the relevance of feature and category; The L1-norm measures the sparsity of the matrix, and the L1-norm can be used to measure the degree of dimension reduction. Therefore, we use the information gain and L1-norm to rebuild the fitness function. In this paper, we redefine the method of nests initialization, and rebuild the fitness function. We try to select the feature subset with smaller dimension on the basis of improving the classification performance of the algorithm. For simplicity, the improved BCS is abbreviated as FS_CSO (Optimizing Cuckoo Feature Selection

Algorithm). At last, we compare FS_CSO with state of the art feature selection algorithms including BCS proposed in recent years. The experimental results on small, medium and large UCI dataset, show that the FS_CSO generally has better classification performance and dimension reduction. Table 1 is the details of the algorithms.

The organization of this paper is as follows. Section 2 introduces CS algorithm and feature selection. Section 3 describes the BCS algorithm. Section 4 proposes the FS_CSO algorithm. Section 5 describes the results of the experiment. Section 6 draws a conclusion of this paper.

Table 1. Information of related algorithm

Algorithm	Description/Published year
UFSACO	Unsupervised algorithm of ACO [5]/2014
UPFS	Unsupervised probabilistic algorithm of ACO [10]/2016
FS-NEIR	Neighborhood effective information ratio [4]/2013
PSO(4-2)	Particle swarm optimization algorithm [11]/2014
NSM	Neighborhood soft margin algorithm [12]/2010
RRFS	Filter techniques for feature selection [13]/2012
FSFOA	Random forest algorithm [14]/2016
TRACK	Tracking ratio assignment and K means clustering algorithm [15]/2014
HGAFS	Hybrid genetic algorithm [16]/2007
BCS	Cuckoo search algorithm [1]/2013
SVM-FuzCoc	Support vector machine [17]/2010
SFS, SBS, SFFS	Greedy hill-climbing algorithm [17]/2010
TV, LS	Laplasse feature selection algorithm [18]/2006

2   Related Work

2.1   L1-Norm

The L1-norm is the sum of the absolute values of each element in a vector, also known as the "Lasso regularization". Both the L1-norm and the L2-norm reduce the risk of over-fitting, but the former has the added advantage of being more accessible to the "sparser" solution than the latter. Briefly, the former has solutions of fewer non-zero components. This property of L1-norm becomes a good feature selection method. In feature selection, L1-norm can be used to measure the extent of the dimension reduction. We can also measure the dimension reduction by finding the number of features in the feature subset. However, if you use this method as a model of the evaluation function, it will be easy to over-fitting.

2.2   Information Gain

Information entropy is the most commonly used measure of the sample set purity. Assuming that the proportion of the k-th sample in the current sample set D is pk (k = 1, 2, ..., d), the information entropy of D is defined as:

$$Ent(D) = -\sum_{k=1}^{d} p_k log_2^{p_k} \qquad (1)$$

If the value of Ent (D) is smaller, the purity of D will be higher.

Assuming that the attribute a has V possible values a^1, a^2, ..., a^V, if a is used to divide the sample set D, then there will be V branch nodes, of which the r-th branch node contains all samples in the attribute a with the value of av are denoted as D^v. We calculate the entropy of D^v according to Eq. (1), and then consider the different number of samples contained in the branch nodes, and give the branch nodes weights $|D^v|/|D|$. That is, the influence of the branch nodes will be greater if it has more samples. The information gain is obtained by dividing the sample set D with the attribute a can be calculated.

$$Gain(D, a) = Ent(D) - \sum_{v=1}^{V} \frac{|D^v|}{|D|} Ent(D^v) \qquad (2)$$

In general, the greater information gain means the greater "purity boost" achieved using the attribute a to divide. In other words, the greater information gain is, the stronger the association of attribute and category is.

2.3   Chebyshev Chaotic Sequence

The theory of chaos, proposed by Poincare in the late 19th century, is a combination of qualitative thinking and quantitative analysis. According to chaos theory, very small changes in initial conditions will make a huge difference to their future status after continuous amplification. Chebyshev chaos sequence has a delicate inner structure. It can overcome premature convergence and ensure search speed. Chebyshev chaotic sequence is a kind of one-dimensional chaotic map whose iterative equation is simple and easy to implement. The definition formula is as follows:

$$x_{i+1}^{j} = cos(\omega * \arccos(x_i^j)) \quad (-1 \leqslant x_i^j \leqslant 1) \qquad (3)$$

x_{i+1}^{j} represents the j-th eigenvalue of the (i + 1)-th nest generated by the j-th feature of the i-th nest.

3   BCS Algorithm

The CS algorithm generally solves the continuous optimization problem. And if we want to apply the CS algorithm to the feature selection, we need to make the CS algorithm discrete. The BCS [1] algorithm transforms the CS algorithm into a binary algorithm that can deal with discrete problems. The BCS algorithm treats the nest as a 0–1 sequence or as a binary sequence. "0" indicates that the corresponding feature is removed during the learning process or the corresponding feature is not selected into the feature subset. And "1" indicates that the corresponding feature is selected to participate in the learning process. Firstly, the BCS algorithm is initialized to the nest. Then it determines whether exotic eggs are found by iterative recording the nest fitness and it updates the nests by Lévy flight. Finally, it gets the optimal iterative solution. In the nest initialization phase, each nest is randomly selected some features. This initialization method has some uncertainties, and the following steps of the algorithm depend on the initialization. Therefore, the BCS algorithm may not obtain the optimal feature subset due to the randomness of initialization. In the recording of the nest adaptation value phase, calculate the fitness value of each nest according to the fitness function, and get the optimal nest position at the same time. Only good fitness function can get a good solution. The fitness function used in the BCS algorithm is too simple to measure the pros and cons of a nest.

When BCS determines whether exotic eggs can be found, it sets a probability that is represented by Pa in advance. And after testing, the value is generally set to 0.25. r is a random probability by randomly generating. When r>Pa, a new bird nest is created to replace the original bird nest. On the contrary, the original nest remains unchanged. This process needs to ensure that the best nest in the original nests is not replaced.

In the Lévy flight phase, the updating method of Lévy flight's step size needs to be different from CS algorithm. BCS algorithm gets Lévy flight transformation formula according to the method proposed by Kennedy et al.:

$$S(x_i^j(t)) = \frac{1}{1 + e^{-x_i^j(t)}} \tag{4}$$

$$x_i^j(t+1) = \begin{cases} 1, & \text{if } S(x_i^j(t)) > \sigma \\ 0, & \text{otherwise} \end{cases} \tag{5}$$

Here $\sigma \backsim U(0, 1)$, $x_i^j(t)$ represents the j-th eigenvalue of the i-th nest at the t-th iteration.

In the initialization phase of BCS algorithm, each bird nest is initialized in a random way, which is blind and arbitrary. If features of the feature subset are similar to each other when the nest is initialized, some other high-quality features will be omitted, and the optimal solution will not be obtained. In the process of updating the nest, the fitness function is too simple to measure the advantages and disadvantages of the feature subset. If there is not a good subset evaluation, it is obvious that you will not get a good nest or optimal solution.

4 FS_CSO Algorithm

As mentioned above, the BCS algorithm has good results, but there are still some shortcomings. In this section, two improvements are proposed for the shortcomings. At the same time, experiments show that the improved FS_CSO algorithm has better performance.

4.1 Initialization Strategy

The new initialization strategy comes from the chaotic sequence or the chaotic property of Chebyshev mapping [19]. We use the chaotic properties of the Chebyshev mapping to initialize nests. The definition of the Chebyshev mapping is given in Eq. (3). After testing, the sequence is optimal when ω is 4. Figure 1 is a Chebyshev mapped image:

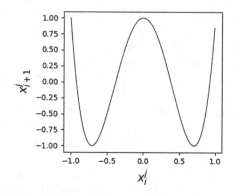

Fig. 1. Chebyshev-mapping

According to Eq. (3) and Fig. 1, we can see that the value of chaos sequence generated by Chebyshev mapping is different from the 0–1 sequence we want, so we need to do further processing. First, we generate the first nest, which randomly generates d numbers within $[-1, 1]$ (d is the number of features of the corresponding dataset) and then generates the next nest sequence according to Eq. (3). In this way, the next nest is generated according to the previous nest. Finally, we get the specified number of nest sequences, but these sequences are not a 0–1 sequence. So we need to do a quantification process. When the value in the sequence is greater than 0, the value is set to "1". And when the value in the sequence is less than or equal to 0, the value is set to "0". So the quantification process can be used to obtain a 0–1 sequence, and the initialization of the nest is completed.

4.2 Fitness Function

In the CS algorithm, the fitness function [20] that is defined as fitness is only suitable for the search algorithm. In the BCS algorithm, the fitness function is too simple. Feature selection that is a data pre-processing process has two main requirements. First, the classification accuracy of the feature subset is high or the features that the feature subset needs to be obtained is strongly related to the category. Second, the feature subset has as few features as possible so as to avoid dimension disaster. According to the first requirement, we introduce the information gain. If the information gain of a subset is high, the "purity improvement" obtained by dividing the subset of features will be better. According to the second requirement, we introduce the L1-norm [8] that measures the sparsity of a matrix. The smaller L1-norm is, the sparser the matrix will be, that is, the number of features of feature subset will be less. By making efforts to improve the fitness function as described above, we obtain a new fitness function:

$$fitness = -(1 - \mu) * L1 + \mu * Gain \qquad (6)$$

In the formula, Gain represents the information gain, L1 is the L1-norm, and μ is a weight which can be adjusted according to the different requirements of accuracy and dimension reduction.

Algorithm1 gives the pseudo code of the FS_CSO algorithm, and indicates the improvement in bold.

Algorithm 1

Input:
   probability of being discovered pa, number of nests n, number of iterations m, dimension of dataset d, wights μ
Output:
   The best feature set best_nest
1: begin
2: **Initialize nests with the Chebyshev chaotic map**
3: **For i = 1 d do**
4: **   first_nest[i] ← random(-1, 1)**
5: **end for**
6: **nest = Chebyshev(first_nest, n)**
7: Initialize the fitness function
8: For j = 1 n do
9:     fitness[j] ← -∞
10: end for
11: best_nest ← -∞
12: For i=1 m do
13: **   For j =1 n do**
14: **   fit(nest[j]) = -(1 - μ) * L1(nest[j]) + μ * Gain(nest[j])**
15: **   if fit(nest[j])>fitness[j]**
16: **   fitness[j] = fit(nest[j])**
17: **   end for**
18:     best_nest ← get_best_nest(nest, nest)
19:     Update nests by Lévy flights (Equation 1)
20:     best_nest ← get_best_nest(nest, new_nest)
21:     For i n do
22:         r ← random(0, 1)
23:         if r>pa
24:             replace nest[j] for new solution
25:     end for
26:     best_nest ← get_best_nest(nest, new_nest)
27: end for
28: return the best_nest which shows selected feature subset

Lines 1–6 represent the process of initializing nests, first_nest represents the first nest generated by a random function and nest represents the array of all initialized nest sequences by Chebyshev mapping and first_nest as the initial sequence. Lines 7–11 represent initialized fitness values, fitness is an array of all nests' fitness values that are initialized to $-\infty$, and the fitness value of the optimal nest is also initialized to $-\infty$, where n is numbers of nests.

Lines 12–27 represent the process of nest update and iteration. m represents the number of iterations, and get_best_nest () represents the optimal nest function based on the original nest and the updated nest. First, we calculate and update the fitness function value of each nest, and then update the nest by Lévy flight. Afterwards, we remove the poor nest by comparing r that is generated randomly with Pa. Finally, we get the current optimal nest. Line 28, the global optimal bird nest is obtained by iterative updating and initialization, that is to say, the optimal feature subset is obtained.

In terms of time complexity, the FS_CSO is consistent with BCS, and the time overhead is slightly higher than that of BCS. The reason for this is that chaos sequences are generated by the Chebyshev mapping. The BCS algorithm only generates initialized nests randomly, and FS_CSO needs to calculate the next generation nest sequence. But the calculation is very small and negligible. In space, it also did not produce additional storage.

5   Experimental Results and Analysis

In the experiment, we used the open machine learning toolkit scikit-learn. The programming language is python. All experiments are performed on a DELL with Intel Core i5 CPU (3.30 GHz), 4G memory.

5.1   Datasets

We test the performance of the FS_CSO algorithm on UCI datasets of different sizes, including three small-scale datasets, two medium-scale datasets and three large-scale datasets. Wine, Glass, Heart are small-scale datasets. Ionosphere, Derma-tology are medium-scale datasets. Sonar, SpamBase, Arrhythmia are large-scale datasets. Table 2 gives specific information of datasets. According to contrast algorithms, we use 10-fold cross validation, 2- fold cross validation, and use 70% as training set 30% as testing set. And CA (Classification Accuracy) and DR (dimension Reduction) are used as evaluation criteria.

5.2   Parameter Setting

We have tried to vary the number of host nests (or the population size n)and the probability Pa, So we have used n = 5, 10, 15, 20, 50, 100, 150, 250, 500, Pa = 0, 0.01, 0.05, 0.1, 0.15, 0.2, 0.25, 0.4, 0.5 and α = 0.01, 0.05, 0.1, 0.15, 0.2, 0.3, 0.5. In FS_CSO algorithm and BCS algorithm, we found that n = 30, Pa = 0.25 and α = 0.1 are highly sufficient for most datasets or optimization problems. μ is the weight of the information gain in the fitness function. We have tried to vary the number of μ and we have used μ = 1, 0.9, 0.8, 0.7, 0.6, 0.5. We ran ten times on the different datasets and found that μ taking value 0.7 is the best. ω is the parameter the parameter that generates a chaotic sequence by Chebyshev mapping. Only when $\omega = 4$, we can guarantee that the range of value is $[-1, 1]$ and evenly distributed.

Table 2. Specific information of the selected datasets

DataSet	Feature	Class	Instance
Wine	13	3	178
Glass	19	6	214
Heart	13	2	270
Ionosphere	34	2	351
Dermatology	34	6	366
Sonar	60	2	208
SpamBase	57	2	4601
Arrhythmia	279	16	452

Table 3. Test results on Ionosphere

Ionosphere	Accuracy(%)	DR(%)	Classifier
FS_CSO	**97.22(10-fold)**	88.24	5NN
BCS	85.71(10-fold)	76.47	5NN
FSFOA	89.43 (10-fold)	54.28	5NN
PSO(4-2)	87.27(10-fold)	**90.41**	5NN
FS_CSO	**97.36(10-fold)**	**91.18**	3NN
BCS	85.71(10-fold)	76.47	3NN
FSFOA	92.3(10-fold)	61.76	3NN
NSM	92(10-fold)	88.23	3NN
FS_CSO	**96.19(70 % ⌣ 30 %)**	88.23	1NN
BCS	88.57(70% ⌣ 30%)	47.06	1NN
FSFOA	89.52(70% ⌣ 30%)	54.28	1NN
SVM-FuzCoc	89.46(70% ⌣ 30%)	88.23	1NN
SFS	87.75(70% ⌣ 30%)	65.88	1NN
SBS	84.61(70% ⌣ 30%)	77.64	1NN
SFFS	88.32(70% ⌣ 30%)	75.29	1NN
FS_CSO	**97.14(2-fold)**	78.23	Rbf-svm
BCS	94.28 (2-fold)	52.94	Rbf-svm
FSFOA	94.58 (2-fold)	57.14	Rbf-svm
HGAFS	92.76 (2-fold)	**82.35**	Rbf-svm
FS_CSO	**95.23 (70 % ⌣ 30 %)**	70.59	J48
BCS	91.43 (70% ⌣ 30%)	35.29	J48
FSFOA	95.12 (70% ⌣ 30%)	47.05	J48
UFSACO	88.61(70% ⌣ 30%)	11.17	J48
FS_CSO	**99.22(10-fold)**	**85.29**	J48
BCS	89.52(10-fold)	82.35	J48
FSFOA	93.16(10-fold)	68.57	J48
FS-NEIR	92.59(10-fold)	82.35	J48

Table 4. Test results on Wine

Wine	Accuracy(%)	DR(%)	Classifier
FS_CSO	**99.99(10-fold)**	**84.62**	3NN
BCS	88.89(10-fold)	15.38	3NN
FSFOA	98.87(10-fold)	42.58	3NN
NSM	98(10-fold)	53.84	3NN
FS_CSO	**98.88(2-fold)**	**61.54**	Rbf-svm
BCS	93.26(2-fold)	53.85	Rbf-svm
FSFOA	96.06(2-fold)	37.17	Rbf-svm
HGAFS	98.31(2-fold)	53.85	Rbf-svm
FS_CSO	**99.32(10-fold)**	**84.62**	J48
BCS	88.89(10-fold)	15.38	J48
FSFOA	96.06(10-fold)	21.42	J48
FS-NEIR	95.04(10-fold)	61.53	J48

Table 5. Test results on Glass

Glass	Accuracy(%)	DR(%)	Classifier
FS_CSO	**80.95(70% ⌣ 30%)**	**44.44**	1NN
BCS	68.25(70% ⌣ 30%)	33.33	1NN
FSFOA	71.88(70% ⌣ 30%)	40	1NN
SFS	72.24(70% ⌣ 30%)	26.66	1NN
SFFS	71.77(70% ⌣ 30%)	37.77	1NN
FS_CSO	**72.73(2-fold)**	**66.67**	Rbf-svm
BCS	61.68(2-fold)	11.11	Rbf-svm
FSFOA	68.22(2-fold)	60	Rbf-svm
HGAFS	65.51(2-fold)	44.44	Rbf-svm
FS_CSO	**90.91(10-fold)**	**55.56**	J48
BCS	68.18(10-fold)	11.11	J48
FSFOA	75.7(10-fold)	50	J48
FS-NEIR	68.53(10-fold)	22.22	J48

Table 6. Test results on Heart

Heart	Accuracy(%)	DR(%)	Classifier
FS_CSO	**88.89(10-fold)**	**76.92**	3NN
BCS	62.96(10-fold)	53.85	3NN
FSFOA	85.18(10-fold)	35.71	3NN
NSM	84(10-fold)	69.23	3NN
FS_CSO	**85.19(2-fold)**	69.23	Rbf-svm
BCS	72.59(2-fold)	53.85	Rbf-svm
FSFOA	84.07(2-fold)	50	Rbf-svm
HGAFS	82.59(2-fold)	**76.92**	Rbf-svm
FS_CSO	**88.89(10-fold)**	61.53	J48
BCS	74.07(10-fold)	46.15	J48
FSFOA	85.15(10-fold)	48.07	J48
FS-NEIR	79.86(10-fold)	46.15	J48

5.3   Comparison of Experimental Results

We compare the FS_CSO algorithm with other classical algorithms, and Table 2, 3, 4, 5, 6, 7, 8 and 9 shows the experimental results. And the best classification accuracy and dimension reduction of each classifier are shown in bold.

Table 7. Test results on Dermatology

Dermatology	Accuracy(%)	DR(%)	Classifier
FS_CSO	**99.07(70 % ⌣ 30 %)**	61.76	1NN
BCS	94.11 (70% ⌣ 30%)	41.18	1NN
FSFOA	97.27(70% ⌣ 30%)	45.71	1NN
SVM-FuzCoc	94.11 (70% ⌣ 30%)	64.7	1NN
SFS	94.02(70% ⌣ 30%)	44.7	1NN
SBS	91.78(70% ⌣ 30%)	58.23	1NN
SFFS	93.7 (70% ⌣ 30%)	**62.35**	1NN
FS_CSO	**98.15(10-fold)**	47.06	J48
BCS	94.59(10-fold)	21.42	J48
FSFOA	96.99 (10-fold)	21.42	J48
FS-NEIR	93.95(10-fold)	**70.58**	J48
FS_CSO	**98.15(70% ⌣ 30%)**	70.59	J48
BCS	95.37(70% ⌣ 30%)	50	J48
FSFOA	90.09(70% ⌣ 30%)	44.11	J48
UFSACO	95.28(70% ⌣ 30%)	26.47	J48

Table 9. Test results on Sonar

Sonar	Accuracy(%)	DR(%)	Classifier
FS_CSO	85.71(70% ⌣ 30%)	**88.33**	5NN
BCS	75.41(70% ⌣ 30%)	40	5NN
FSFOA	**86.98(70 % ⌣ 30 %)**	44.26	5NN
PSO(4-2)	78.16(70% ⌣ 30%)	81.26	5NN
FS_CSO	**95.24(70 % ⌣ 30 %)**	**75**	1NN
BCS	88.52(70% ⌣ 30%)	65	1NN
FSFOA	85.43(70% ⌣ 30%)	57.37	1NN
SVM-FuzCoc	73.17(70% ⌣ 30%)	68.33	1NN
SFS	66.43(70% ⌣ 30%)	61.33	1NN
SBS	62.2(70% ⌣ 30%)	45.33	1NN
SFFS	64.55(70% ⌣ 30%)	61.33	1NN
FS_CSO	**90.48(10-fold)**	83.33	J48
BCS	85.71(10-fold)	76.67	J48
FSFOA	82.69(10-fold)	52.45	J48
FS-NEIR	75.97(10-fold)	**91.66**	J48

Table 8. Test results on SpamBase

SpamBase	Accuracy(%)	DR(%)	Classifier
FS_CSO	**90.26(70 % ⌣ 30 %)**	45.61	Rbf-svm
BCS	81.88(70% ⌣ 30%)	12.5	Rbf-svm
UFSACO	87.78(70% ⌣ 30%)	29.82	Rbf-svm
RRFS	88.8(70% ⌣ 30%)	29.82	Rbf-svm
TV	87.74 (70% ⌣ 30%)	29.82	Rbf-svm
LS	87.58(70% ⌣ 30%)	29.82	Rbf-svm
FS_CSO	**95.59(70 % ⌣ 30 %)**	45.61	J48
BCS	91.69(70% ⌣ 30%)	19.30	J48
UFSACO	92.57(70% ⌣ 30%)	29.8	J48
RRFS	91.69(70% ⌣ 30%)	29.8	J48
TV	91.97 (70% ⌣ 30%)	29.8	J48
LS	91.99(70% ⌣ 30%)	29.8	J48

Table 10. Test results on Arrhythmia

Arrhythmia	Accuracy(%)	DR(%)	Classifier
FS_CSO	**69.57(10-fold)**	**89.96**	Rbf-svm
BCS	58.70(10-fold))	50.54	Rbf-svm
UPFS	63.70(10-fold)	85. 66	Rbf-svm
TRACK	59.29(10-fold)	85.66	Rbf-svm
UFSACO	58.86(10-fold)	85.66	Rbf-svm
TV	62.59(10-fold)	85.66	Rbf-svm
LS	61.50(10-fold)	85.66	Rbf-svm
FS_CSO	**67.39(10-fold)**	60.57	J48
BCS	50.89(10-fold)	50.54	J48
UPFS	55.56(10-fold)	**92.83**	J48
TRACK	57.30(10-fold)	**92.83**	J48
UFSACO	38.52(10-fold)	**92.83**	J48
TV	58.86(10-fold)	**92.83**	J48
LS	40.49(10-fold)	**92.83**	J48

On Wine, Glass, SpamBase, both the classification accuracy and dimension reduction of FS_CSO algorithm are the highest. On the Heart, the accuracy of classification is the highest; On the Ionosphere, the classification accuracy is also the highest, and FS_CSO is about 40% higher than BCS in the 1-NN classifier. On the Sonar, FS_CSO increases the classification accuracy and the dimension reduction by 30% compared with the SBS in the 1-NN classifier. On the Arrhythmia, the dimension reduction is a little lower than other algorithms, but the classification accuracy is increased by at least 10%.

It can be shown from Tables 2, 3, 4, 5, 6, 7, 8 and 9 that the BCS dimension reduction is not good. The improved FS_CSO algorithm has an obvious improvement on the dimension reduction, at least 10% and up about 60%. The reason why FS_CSO's dimension reduction is better than BCS is that the L1-norm is added to measure the pros and cons of the nest. From Tables 4, 5 and 6, we can see that the FS_CSO algorithm is the best on the classification accuracy and the dimension reduction in small scale datasets. It can be seen from Tables 3 and 7 that the classification accuracy of FS_CSO is the highest among the middle scale datasets, only the dimension reduction of the individual classifiers is slightly lower than the highest; From Tables 8, 9 and 10, we can see that the accuracy of classification is the highest in large-scale datasets. On Sonar and SpamBase, the dimension reduction of individual is slightly lower, but the classification accuracy of the corresponding algorithm is much lower than that of FS_CSO. On the Arrhythmia, except for the BCS algorithm, the other algorithms fix the number of features of feature subset. Their dimension reduction is high, but the classification accuracy is very low. Some are even lower than 50% on classification accuracy. The lower classification accuracy of feature selection has no meaning. But FS_CSO algorithm obviously improves the classification accuracy.

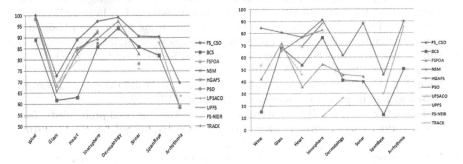

Fig. 2. Classification accuracy   **Fig. 3.** Dimension reduction

Figure 2 shows the classification accuracy of different algorithms and Fig. 3 shows the dimension reduction of different algorithms. We can clearly see, from Figs. 2 and 3, that the classification accuracy of FS_CSO is higher than that of other algorithms or basically the same and the dimension reduction is greatly improved. Only the individual dimension reduction of FS_CSO is slightly lower, but when the dimension reduction is low, the classification accuracy will be greatly improved.

6   Conclusions

In this paper, we propose two improvements to BCS algorithm. In the initialization phase of FS_CSO, we adopt a new initialization strategy, and use Chebyshev mapping to generate chaotic sequences. Therefore the initial nest can overcome premature convergence and other defects. In the update nest phase, the fitness function is rebuilt by considering the information gain and the L1-norm. FS_CSO algorithm is tested and compared with many different algorithms in a large number of datasets. The experimental results on classification accuracy and dimension reduction show that FS_CSO generally outperform the other comparison algorithms.

References

1. Rodrigues, D., Pereira, L.A., Yang, X.S.: BCS: a binary cuckoo search algorithm for feature selection. In: IEEE International Symposium on Circuits and Systems (ISCAS), pp. 465–468. IEEE (2013). https://doi.org/10.1109/iscas.2013.6571881

2. Hall, M.A.: Correlation-based feature selection for machine learning (1999)
3. Guyon, I., Elisseeff, A.: An introduction to variable and feature selection. J. Mach. Learn. Res., 1157–1182 (2003)
4. Zhu, W., Si, G., Zhang, Y., et al.: Neighborhood effective information ratio for hybrid feature subset evaluation and selection. Neurocomputing **99**, 25–37 (2013)
5. Tabakhi, S., Moradi, P., Akhlaghian, F.: An unsupervised feature selection algorithm based on ant colony optimization. Eng. Appl. Artif. Intell. **32**, 112–123 (2014). https://doi.org/10.1016/j.engappai.2014.03.007
6. Tan, Z.: A privacy-preserving multiserver authenticated keyagreement scheme based on Chebyshev chaotic maps. Secur. Commun. Netw. **9**(11), 1384–1397 (2016)
7. Lai, C.M., Yeh, W.C., Chang, C.Y.: Gene selection using Information Gain and Improved Simplified Swarm Optimization. Elsevier Science Publishers B. V. (2016)
8. Liu, Y., Gao, Q., Miao, S.: A non-greedy algorithm for L1-norm LDA. IEEE Trans Image Process. **26**(2), 684–695 (2016)
9. Yang, X.S., Deb, S.: Cuckoo search via Lévy flights. In: World Congress on Nature & Biologically Inspired Computing, pp. 210–214. IEEE (2009)
10. Dadaneh, B.Z., Markid, H.Y., Zakerolhosseini, A.: Unsupervised probabilistic feature selection using ant colony optimization. Expert. Syst. Appl. **53**, 27–42 (2016). https://doi.org/10.1016/j.eswa.2016.01.021
11. Xue, B., Zhang, M., Browne, W.N.: Particle swarm optimisation for feature selection in classification: novel initialisation and updating mechanisms. Appl. Soft Comput. **18**, 261–276 (2014). https://doi.org/10.1016/j.asoc.2013.09.018
12. Hu, Q., Che, X., Zhang, L., et al.: Feature evaluation and selection based on neighborhood soft margin. Neurocomputing **73**(10–12), 2114–2124 (2010)
13. Lazar, C., Taminau, J., Meganck, S., et al.: A survey on filter techniques for feature selection in gene expression microarray analysis. IEEE/ACM Trans. Comput. Biol. Bioinf. (TCBB) **9**(4), 1106–1119 (2012)
14. Ghaemi, M., Feizi-Derakhshi, M.R.: Feature selection using forest optimization algorithm. Pattern Recogn. **60**, 121–129 (2016)
15. Wang, D., Nie, F., Huang, H.: Unsupervised feature selection via unified trace ratio formulation and K-means clustering (TRACK). In: Calders, T., Esposito, F., Hüllermeier, E., Meo, R. (eds.) ECML PKDD 2014. LNCS (LNAI), vol. 8726, pp. 306–321. Springer, Heidelberg (2014). https://doi.org/10.1007/978-3-662-44845-8_20
16. Huang, J., Cai, Y., Xu, X.: A hybrid genetic algorithm for feature selection wrapper based on mutual information. Pattern Recognit. Lett. **28**(13), 1825–1844 (2007). https://doi.org/10.1016/j.patrec.2007.05.011
17. Moustakidis, S.P., Theocharis, J.B.: SVM-FuzCoC: a novel SVM-based feature selection method using a fuzzy complementary criterion. Pattern Recogn. **43**(11), 3712–3729 (2010). https://doi.org/10.1016/j.patcog.2010.05.007
18. He, X., Cai, D., Niyogi, P.: Laplacian score for feature selection. In: Advances in Neural Information Processing Systems, pp. 507–514 (2006)
19. Rajyaguru, J., Villanueva, M.E., Houska, B.: Chebyshev model arithmetic for factorable functions. J. Glob. Optim. **68**(2), 413–438 (2017)
20. Min, F., Xu, J.: Semi-greedy heuristics for feature selection with test cost constraints. Granul. Comput. **1**(3), 199–211 (2016)

Prediction of Garlic Price Based on ARIMA Model

Baojia Wang, Pingzeng Liu$^{(\boxtimes)}$, Chao Zhang, Junmei Wang,
and Liu Peng

Shandong Agricultural University, Tai'an 271018, China
lpz8565@126.com

Abstract. In recent years, garlic prices have fluctuate drastically, and garlic price prediction has always been the focus of attention. In order to study the price fluctuations of garlic and predict garlic prices, the most commonly used time series forecasting method autoregressive integrated moving average (ARIMA) model is used in this article to predict garlic prices. Combining the monthly average price data for 2010–2017 in Shandong, China, which is representative of the world. Using the powerful data analysis function of R language, forecast the monthly average price of garlic in the first half of 2018 in Shandong province. The results of experiment show that the ARIMA model has good effect in predicting the short-term garlic price fluctuation, and the garlic price fluctuation trend in the first half of 2018 is to rise first and then fall. Finally, according to several major factors which affecting the price fluctuation of garlic, some suggestions such as the establishment of garlic growth model, the improvement of forecast methods, and the strengthening of market supervision are proposed.

Keywords: Price prediction · ARIMA model · R language · Garlic

1 Introduction

China is the main producer and exporter of garlic in the world. Both the planting area and the total amount are the top of the world [1]. Although garlic as a small agricultural product is not as strategically important as bulk agricultural products, due to its rigid consumption and closely related to the daily life of residents, the accurate forecast of garlic price fluctuations is related to the formulation of relevant policies and the stability of the market economy [2]. Based on this, the Shandong provincial agriculture department combined with Shandong Agricultural University, Jin Xiang county government and surrounding enterprises to build garlic industry chain big data platform. One of the tasks of the platform is to study how to predict the trend and rule of garlic price fluctuation. According to the monthly price of pepper in Guizhou province from January 2007 to December 2010, Han [3] established a ARIMA (1, 1, 1) model to predict the price of pepper in the coming months by using seasonal decomposition method, and the relative error of the model was less than 9%; Liu et al. [4] take cabbage monthly price data as an example, build a non-stationary time series ARIMA (p, d, q) model and predict the future monthly price of cabbage. The results show that ARIMA

© Springer Nature Switzerland AG 2018
X. Sun et al. (Eds.): ICCCS 2018, LNCS 11063, pp. 731–739, 2018.
https://doi.org/10.1007/978-3-030-00006-6_66

(0, 1, 1) model can well simulate and predict the price trend of cabbage month; Liu et al. [5] used the ARIMA model to predict the price of edible fungi in Jiangsu Province, and proved the validity of the ARIMA model for edible mushroom price prediction; Shi [6] used the ARIMA model to analyze and forecast the garlic week price in Qingdao. Based on the above research, we can see that the ARIMA model has a significant effect in predicting the short-term fluctuation of agricultural product prices, and it is a mature and effective prediction method and is widely used. In view of this, this paper takes Shandong province garlic the average monthly price data base, relying on the powerful function of R language analysis on the data, the establishment of ARIMA model to predict the price of garlic in Shandong Province, in order to further verify the effectiveness of the ARIMA model in the price of garlic, and provide a reference for Agriculture Department of Shandong province to stabilize the price of garlic.

2　ARIMA Model Principle

ARIMA model (autoregressive integrated moving average), it is also called the differential autoregressive moving average model. It is a time series prediction method proposed by Boakes and Jenkins in 1970s [7]. The ARIMA model usually uses the past values of the time series to predict future data values. That is, starting from the observed time series data, first analyze the data characteristics and then select a black box, if the black box can convert the observed time series into a white noise sequence which is a series of random numbers that are not related to each other, then the black box is correct, and the black box is the ARIMA model to be selected. The ARIMA model fits the difference stationary sequence. In fact, it is the combination of the difference operation and the ARMA model. The ARIMA (p, d, q) model can be used for modeling the no seasonal time series. It can smooth the sequence by appropriate d-order (d is an integer) difference operation. After the time sequence data is stabilized, the ARIMA (p, d, q) model is transformed into a ARMA (p, q) model. For the time series with obvious seasonal factors, the ARIMA model takes full advantage of the seasonal information in the time series by making the difference operation of the cycle length, so that the time sequence becomes a stationary sequence, and its residual sequence is also a stationary sequence. The general representation of the ARIMA (p, d, q) model is:

$$\Phi(B)(1 - B)^d x_t = \theta(B)\varepsilon_t \tag{1}$$

In the formula, $\Phi(B)$ is a p-order AR (autoregressive) model, $\theta(B)$ is a q-order MA (moving average) model.

3   ARIMA Model Establishment

3.1   R Language Overview

R language is not only a computer high-level language, but also a practical tool for calculation, statistics, analysis and drawing. It is a free, free, open-source and excellent software. It is widely used in the field of statistics and big data [8, 9]. R language has a wealth of online resources, providing a lot of practical and high-quality packages, expansion packs and a variety of mathematical operations, statistical operations function, so that users can use the expression as a function input parameters or only a few parameters and specify the database to get on flexible and convenient data analysis and statistics. This function is very conducive to drawing and statistical simulation, and even allows users to customize a new statistical calculation method that meets the requirements [10]. Its main functions are: array operations; data storage and processing; complete and consistent statistical analysis and charting; as a programming language, simple and powerful manipulation of data input and branching, loop operations and support for user-defined functions. Based on this, this paper uses R language to construct ARIMA model to analyze and predict time series.

3.2   Model Establishment

The basic flow of the ARIMA model is established. The general steps are as follows:

(1)   The first step in establishing the ARIMA model is to determine whether the time series is stable. If the sequence is not stable, the data is processed smoothly. Judging whether it can be stable or not can be based on sequence timing diagram or ADF unit root test. Generally, the time series of garlic price is non-stationary, and it needs to be differentiated to make it a stable sequence.

(2)   After the series is stationary, the model can be ordered based on the ACF diagram and the PACF diagram of the differential back-off sequence. Generally, the order of the model is obtained by using the automatic ordering function of the R language.

(3)   After determining the order of the model, the residual white noise test should be performed, and the test can prove that the model is successfully fitted.

(4)   Finally, use the model that has passed the test for analysis and prediction.

4   Experiment Procedure

4.1   Data Sources

Shandong Province is the main producing area of garlic in China. It is the distribution center for garlic all over the country, and its price also the wind vane of garlic price. Its domestic market share of garlic produced by it is over 70% [11]. The Department of Agriculture of Shandong Province, in conjunction with Shandong Agricultural University, Jin Xiang County Government and neighboring companies, jointly established a big data platform for the garlic industry chain. The Department of Agriculture of Shandong Province provided data on the average monthly wholesale price of garlic in the province from 2010 to 2017 for analysis by the Key Lab of Smart Agriculture at Shandong Agricultural University. The data from the garlic industry chain big data platform.

4.2   Experimental Procedure

Seasonal Decomposition. In order to better predict the price of garlic, the seasonal decomposition of garlic price data is first used to understand the trend of the garlic price (Fig. 1).

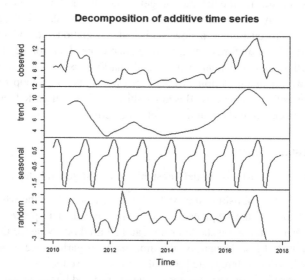

Fig. 1. Monthly mean price seasonal decomposition of garlic

We can obtain the seasonal term, trend term and random term of the garlic price time series by using decompose function of R. From trend and seasonal, it can be seen that garlic price in Shandong province showed a trend of rising first, then decreasing and then rising again, and the period is one year. The garlic price is the highest in February and March (the price rises before and after the Spring Festival), and the lowest in May and June (new garlic marketing and price drop). In the second half of 2010, the price of garlic continued to rise, and a large amount of hot money poured into the garlic market to stir up the price, while the price in the second half of 2011 dropped by the "cliff-break style" due to the high price of garlic in 2010 and the large-scale expansion of garlic farmers. As a result, the price of garlic dropped in 2011. In 2016, as the temperature continued to decline, garlic was on a large scale, and garlic price continued to rise. It can be seen that the price of garlic is greatly affected by factors such as planting area, climate, and market speculation.

ARIMA Model Establishment. The first step in establishing the ARIMA model is to test the stability of the time series data. The line graph of time series is obtained by using R, and then the stability of the sequence is judged. The no-stationary time series is processed by logarithmic or differential treatment, and then the stability of the post processing sequence is judged again. Repeat the above process until it becomes a stationary sequence. At this time the number of difference is d in the ARIMA (p, d, q) model. After the stabilization process, the ARIMA (p, d, q) model is transformed into a ARMA (p, q) model (Fig. 2).

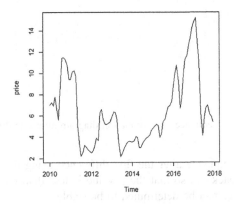

Fig. 2. The monthly average price of garlic

From the time series broken line graph, we can see that the garlic result is periodic monotonous trend, so the sequence is not stable. If we want to smooth the advanced processing, we need to make a difference for it (Fig. 3).

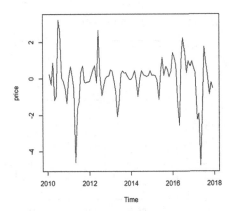

Fig. 3. Time series of monthly average price difference of garlic

The observations after the first-order difference of the original time series fluctuate around the zero-mean value, and it can be roughly estimated that the monthly average price time series of garlic after the first-order difference is stable. The ADF unit root test

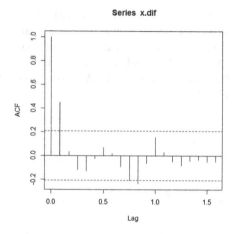

Fig. 4. The sequence autocorrelation diagram after one differential

is performed on the sequence after the first difference using the instruction in the R language expansion package, so that the p value is less than 0.05, and the sequence after the first difference can be determined to be stable.

After the sequence is stationary, it is necessary to determine which model the sequence fits to base on the autocorrelation coefficient and the partial correlation coefficient. If autocorrelation tails, partial correlation truncation, it is suitable for AR model; autocorrelation truncation, partial correlation tailing, is suitable for MA model; autocorrelation and partial correlation are trailing, it is suitable for ARMA model (Fig. 5).

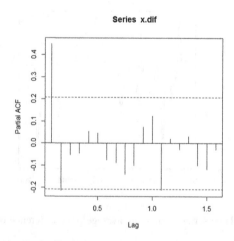

Fig. 5. Auto-correlation of partial autocorrelation after one differential

From Fig. 4, difference autocorrelation sequence and 5 differential backward autocorrelation map, we can see that the sequence after 1 order difference is suitable for ARMA model, that is, the original sequence is suitable for ARIMA model. Using the automatic order function auto.arima of R language for automatic model order ARIMA model, many are automatically determined in the original data, but the difference in the data after automatic order, calculated results of intermediate poor need to add previous order difference as the final model difference scores of variables. Finally, the ARIMA ((1, 1, 0) (1, 1, 0)) [12] model is fitted. After the white noise test, the forecast function is used to predict the price trend for the next 6 months (Fig. 6).

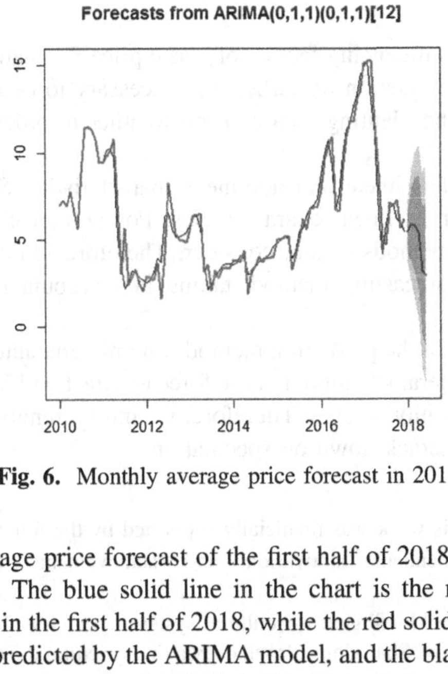

Forecasts from ARIMA(0,1,1)(0,1,1)[12]

Fig. 6. Monthly average price forecast in 2018

The monthly average price forecast of the first half of 2018 was obtained through the forecast function. The blue solid line in the chart is the monthly average price predicted by ARIMA in the first half of 2018, while the red solid line is the 2010–2017 month average price predicted by the ARIMA model, and the black solid line is the real data of the monthly average price in 2010–2017. The whole model fits well, and the trend is very obvious. It is an effective method for the short-term prediction of garlic price. According to the results of the forecast, the monthly average price of garlic in Shandong province will rise first and then decrease in the first half of 2018, as shown in Table 1.

Table 1. The ARIMA model predicts the price of garlic in the first half of 2018

	January 2018	February 2018	March 2018	April 2018	May 2018	June 2018
Predicted value	5.413766	5.831954	5.753360	5.346642	3.159430	2.887703

5   Conclusions and Suggestions

Garlic as a special small agricultural product, its price fluctuations are very intense, and vulnerable to a variety of factors. The ARIMA model of time series analysis has a good effect on the prediction of agricultural product prices and can well predict the trend of garlic price fluctuations. Therefore, based on the research of ARIMA model to predict the price of agricultural products, the ARIMA model is used to forecast the price of garlic. The experimental results show that the ARIMA model has a good effect in predicting the price of garlic and is an effective method to predict the price of garlic.

In order to better predict the garlic price and grasp its fluctuation trend and laws, the following suggestions based on several major factors affecting garlic prices are proposed in this article:

(1) Yield is the main influencing factors of garlic price fluctuations, in order to grasp the total annual production of garlic, it is necessary to establish a garlic growth model based on the planting area and the weather in order to better predict the price of garlic.

(2) Garlic price contains linear and nonlinear characteristics. Single ARIMA model can only consider its linear characteristics. For nonlinear characteristics, traditional prediction methods cannot consider. Therefore, it is necessary to improve the garlic price forecasting method, taking into account the non-linear part of garlic prices.

(3) The improvement of the prediction method can only guarantee the price prediction of garlic in the general situation, but the forecast effect will be discounted once the special human situation occurs. Therefore, we must strengthen supervision of the garlic market and crack down on speculation.

Acknowledgements. This work was financially supported by the following project:

(1) Shandong independent innovation and achievements transformation project (2014ZZCX07106).

(2) The research project "Intelligent agricultural system research and development of facility vegetable industry chain" of Shan-dong Province Major Agricultural Technological Innovation Project in 2017.

(3) Monitoring and statistics project of agricultural and rural resources of the Ministry of Agriculture.

References

1. Pan, Y.H.: Analysis and prospects of chinese garlic industry development. Food Nutr. China **18**(11), 22–26 (2012)
2. Yao, S., Zhou, Y.H.: An analysis on the supply response of garlic in China—an empirical investigation based on the micro panel data. Collected Essays Finance Econ. (2013)
3. Han, W.: The application of ARIMA model in the prediction of the price of agricultural products in guizhou. J. Anhui Agric. Sci. **123**(4), 65–84 (2011)
4. Liu, F., Wang, R.J., Chuan-Xi, L.I.: Application of ARIMA model in forecasting agricultural product price. Comput. Eng. Appl. **45**(25), 238–242 (2009)

5. Liu, X., Zhang, Y.: Edible fungus price forecast analysis based on the ARIMA model: to boris apricot mushroom in Jiangsu province as an example. Ecol. Econ. (2012)
6. Shi, G., Li, M.: Forecast and analysis of garlic price time series in Qingdao city based on ARIMA model. Shandong Agric. Sci. **49**(5), 168–172 (2017)
7. Chen, Q., Guan, T., Yun, L.: Online forecasting chlorophyll a, concentrations by an autoregressive integrated moving average model: feasibilities and potentials. Harmful Algae. **43**, 58–65 (2015)
8. Huang, Y., Wang, H., Wang, Y.: An empirical study of coal product sales forecast based on R language. Comput. Digital Eng. (2017)
9. Yang, X., Wu, D.W.: The application of R language in big data processing. Sci. Technol. Inf. **23**, 19–20 (2013)
10. Xiaolong, X.U.: Data privacy protection mechanism for cloud storage based on data partition and classification. Comput. Sci. **40**(2), 98–102 (2013)
11. Cai-Cai, L.I., Qin, N., Zhou, Y.: Characteristics of and factors affecting garlic price fluctuations in Shandong. Fujian J. Agric. Sci. **10**, 1150–1155 (2017)

Author Index

Printed in the United States
By Bookmasters